A Flight Dynamics and Automatic Flight Controls

Jan Roskam
Ackers Distinguished Professor of Aerospace Engineering
The University of Kansas, Lawrence

Part I

1995

DARcorporation

Design, Analysis and Research Corporation

120 East 9th Street, Suite 2 • Lawrence, Kansas 66044, U.S.A.

PUBLISHED BY

Design, Analysis and Research Corporation (*DARcorporation*)
120 East Ninth Street, Suite 2
Lawrence, KS 66044
U.S.A.
Phone: 913-832-0434
Fax: 913-832-0524

Library of Congress Catalog Card Number: 94-83444

ISBN 1-884885-17-9

In all countries, sold and distributed by
Design, Analysis and Research Corporation
120 East Ninth Street, Suite 2
Lawrence, KS 66044
U.S.A.

TABLE OF CONTENTS

PART I

Table of Contents

Symbol	Description	Unit(s)
Regular (Continued)		
dm	Airplane mass element	slugs
D_1	Coefficient in denominator of longitudinal transfer function	ft/sec^4
D_1	Inertia ratio defined by Eqn (5.180)	——
D_2	Coefficient in denominator of lateral–directional transfer function	ft/sec^4
D_α	Coefficient in numerator of angle–of–attack–to elevator transfer function	ft/sec^5
D_β	Coefficient in numerator of angle–of–sideslip to aileron or rudder transfer function	ft/sec^5
D_u	Coefficient in numerator of speed–to–elevator transfer function	ft^2/sec^6
D_ψ	Coefficient in numerator of heading–angle to aileron or rudder	ft^2/sec^6
D	Drag (airplane)	lbs
$\overline{D}_1$	Denominator of longitudinal transfer functions	ftrad^4/sec^5
$\overline{D}_2$	Denominator of lateral–directional transfer functions	ftrad^5/sec^6
D_p	Propeller diameter	ft
ds	Airplane surface area element	ft^2
d_T	Distance of a thrust line projection onto the XZ–plane to the c.g.	ft
dv	Airplane volume element	ft^3
$e = 2.7183$	Napierian logarithm constant	——
e	Oswald's efficiency factor	——
E_1	Coefficient in denominator of longitudinal transfer function	ft/sec^5
E_2	Coefficient in denominator of lateral–directional transfer function	ft/sec^5
f	Equivalent parasite area of the airplane	ft^2
f(t)	Function of time	lbs

Symbol	Description	Unit(s)
$C_{T_{z_\alpha}} = \partial C_{T_z}/\partial\alpha$	Variation of airplane thrust coefficient in the Z–axis direction with angle of attack	1/rad
$C_{T_{y_\beta}} = \partial C_{T_y}/\partial\beta$	Variation of airplane thrust coefficient in the Y–axis direction with sideslip angle	1/rad
C_x	Force coefficient along the stability X–axis	———
$C_{x_\alpha} = \partial C_x/\partial\alpha$	Variation of airplane X–axis force coefficient with angle of attack	1/rad
$C_{x_q} = \partial C_x/\partial(q\bar{c}/2U_1)$	Variation of airplane X–axis force coefficient with dimensionless pitch rate	1/rad
$C_{x_u} = \partial C_x/\partial(u/U_1)$	Variation of airplane X–axis force coefficient with dimensionless speed	———
C_y	Side force coefficient (airplane)	———
C_{y_0}	Side force coefficient for zero sideslip angle and zero control surface deflections	———
$C_{y_\beta} = \partial C_y/\partial\beta$	Variation of airplane side force coefficient with sideslip angle	1/rad
$C_{y_{\dot\beta}} = \partial C_y/\partial(\dot\beta b/2U_1)$	Variation of airplane side force coefficient with dimensionless rate of change of angle of sideslip	1/rad
$C_{y_{\delta_a}} = \partial C_y/\partial\delta_a$	Variation of airplane side force coefficient with aileron angle	1/rad
$C_{y_{\delta_r}} = \partial C_y/\partial\delta_r$	Variation of airplane side force coefficient with rudder angle	1/rad
$C_{y_p} = \partial C_y/\partial(pb/2U_1)$	Variation of airplane side force coefficient with dimensionless rate of change of roll rate	1/rad
$C_{y_r} = \partial C_y/\partial(rb/2U_1)$	Variation of airplane side force coefficient with dimensionless rate of change of yaw rate	1/rad
C_x	Force coefficient along the stability Z–axis	———
$C_{z_{\dot\alpha}} = \partial C_z/\partial(\dot\alpha\bar{c}/2U_1)$	Variation of airplane Z–axis force coefficient with dimensionless rate of change of angle of attack	1/rad
$C_{z_q} = \partial C_z/\partial(q\bar{c}/2U_1)$	Variation of airplane Z–axis force coefficient with dimensionless pitch rate	1/rad
$C_{z_u} = \partial C_z/\partial(u/U_1)$	Variation of airplane Z–axis force coefficient dimensionless speed	———

SYMBOLS AND ACRONYMS

Symbol	Description	Unit(s)
Regular		
a_{bw}	Moment arm of bobweight (see Figure 4.41)	ft
a_{ds}	Moment arm of downspring (see Figure 4.41)	ft
a_t	Tab spring moment arm	ft
A	Aspect ratio, also a combination function of hingemoment coefficients: see Eqn (4.160)	———
A, B, C, D	Coefficients for control surface hingemoment rates	———
A_i	Inlet area	ft^2
A_1	Coefficient in denominator of longitudinal transfer function	ft/sec
A_2	Coefficient in denominator of lateral–directional transfer function	ft/sec
A_α	Coefficient in numerator of angle–of–attack–to–elevator transfer function	ft/sec^2
A_β	Coefficient in numerator of angle–of–sideslip to aileron or rudder transfer function	ft/sec^2
A_u	Coefficient in numerator of speed–to–elevator transfer function	ft^2/sec^3
A_θ	Coefficient in numerator of pitch–attitude–to–elevator transfer function	ft/sec^3
A_ϕ	Coefficient in numerator of bank–angle to aileron or rudder transfer function	ft/sec^3
A_ψ	Coefficient in numerator of heading–angle to aileron or rudder transfer function	ft/sec^3
$[A]$	System matrix as defined in Eqn (4.228)	See Eqn (4.228)
$\{B\}$	Column matrix as defined in Eqn (4.228)	See Eqn (4.228)
b	Span	ft
B_1	Coefficient in denominator of longitudinal transfer function	ft/sec^2
B_2	Coefficient in denominator of lateral–directional transfer function	ft/sec^2

Symbol	Description	Unit(s)

Regular (Continued)

Symbol	Description	Unit(s)
B_α	Coefficient in numerator of angle–of–attack–to–elevator transfer function	ft/sec^3
B_β	Coefficient in numerator of angle–of–sideslip to aileron or rudder transfer function	ft/sec^3
B_u	Coefficient in numerator of speed–to–elevator transfer function	ft^2/sec^4
B_θ	Coefficient in numerator of pitch–attitude–to–elevator transfer function	ft/sec^4
B_ϕ	Coefficient in numerator of bank–angle to aileron or rudder	ft/sec^4
B_ψ	Coefficient in numerator of heading–angle to aileron or rudder	ft/sec^4
c	chord	ft
c	viscous damping constant	$lbs/ft/sec$
$\bar{c}$	Mean geometric chord	ft
c_d	Section drag coefficient	——
c_f	Flap or control surface chord	ft
C_1	Coefficient in denominator of longitudinal transfer function	ft/sec^3
C_1	Inertia ratio defined by Eqn (5.180)	
C_2	Coefficient in denominator of lateral–directional transfer function	ft/sec^3
C_α	Coefficient in numerator of angle–of–attack–to–elevator transfer function	ft/sec^4
C_β	Coefficient in numerator of angle–of–sideslip to aileron or rudder	ft/sec^4
C_u	Coefficient in numerator of speed–to–elevator transfer function	ft^2/sec^5
C_θ	Coefficient in numerator of pitch–attitude–to–elevator transfer function	ft/sec^5
C_ϕ	Coefficient in numerator of bank–angle to aileron or rudder	ft/sec^5
C_ψ	Coefficient in numerator of heading–angle to aileron or rudder	ft/sec^5
C_D	Drag coefficient (airplane)	——
C_{D_0}	Drag coefficient (airplane) for zero angle of attack	——

Symbol	Description	Unit(s)
$\overline{C}_{D_0}$	Drag coefficient (airplane) for zero lift coefficient	———
$C_{D_\alpha} = \partial C_D/\partial\alpha$	Variation of airplane drag coefficient with angle of attack	1/rad
$C_{D_{\dot\alpha}} = \partial C_D/\partial(\dot\alpha\overline{c}/2U_1)$	Variation of airplane drag coefficient with dimensionless rate of change of angle of attack	1/rad
$C_{D_{i_h}} = \partial C_D/\partial i_h$	Variation of airplane drag coefficient with stabilizer incidence angle	1/rad
$C_{D_{\delta_e}} = \partial C_D/\partial\delta_e$	Variation of airplane drag coefficient with elevator deflection angle	1/rad
$C_{D_q} = \partial C_D/\partial(q\overline{c}/2U_1)$	Variation of airplane drag coefficient with dimensionless pitch rate	1/rad
$C_{D_u} = \partial C_D/\partial(u/U_1)$	Variation of airplane drag coefficient with dimensionless speed	1/rad
C_f	Airplane equivalent skin friction coefficient	———
C_h	Control surface hingemoment coefficient	———
$C_{h_\alpha} = \partial C_h/\partial\alpha$	Variation of control surface hingemoment coefficient with angle of attack	1/rad
$C_{h_{\beta_v}} = \partial C_{h_r}/\partial\beta$	Variation of rudder hingemoment coefficient with angle of sideslip	1/rad
$C_{h_\delta} = \partial C_h/\partial\delta$	Variation of control surface hingemoment coefficient with control surface deflection	1/rad
$C_{h_{\delta_t}} = \partial C_h/\partial\delta_t$	Variation of control surface hingemoment coefficient with control surface tab deflection	1/rad
$C^t_{h_{\delta_t}} = \partial C_{h_t}/\partial\delta_t$	Variation of control surface tab hingemoment coef– cient about the tab hingeline with respect to tab deflection	1/rad
$C_{h_u} = \partial C_h/\partial(u/U_1)$	Variation of control surface hingemoment coefficient with respect to speed	———
$C_{h_q} = \partial C_h/\partial(q\overline{c}/2U_1)$	Variation of control surface hingemoment coefficient with respect to pitch rate	1/rad
$C_{h_{\dot\delta_e}} = \partial C_h/\partial(\dot\delta_e\overline{c}_e/2U_1)$	Variation of elevator hingemoment coefficient with respect to elevator rate	1/rad
$C_{h_{\dot\delta_r}} = \partial C_h/\partial(\dot\delta_r b_e/2U_1)$	Variation of rudder hingemoment coefficient with respect to rudder rate	1/rad
c_l	Section lift coefficient	———

Symbol	Description	Unit(s)
$c_{l_\alpha} = \partial c_l / \partial \alpha$	Variation of section lift coefficient with angle of attack	1/rad
$c_{l_\delta} = \partial c_l / \partial \delta$	Variation of section lift coefficient with control control surface deflection angle	1/rad
C_l	Rolling moment coefficient (airplane)	——
C_{l_0}	Rolling moment coefficient for zero sideslip angle and zero control surface deflections	——
$C_{l_\beta} = \partial C_l / \partial \beta$	Variation of airplane rolling moment coefficient with angle of sideslip	1/rad
$\overline{C}_{l_\beta} = \partial \overline{C}_l / \partial \beta$	Variation of airplane component rolling moment coefficient with sideslip angle, but based on component reference geometry	1/rad
$C_{l_{\dot\beta}} = \partial C_l / \partial(\dot\beta b / 2U_1)$	Variation of airplane rolling moment coefficient with dimensionless rate of change of angle of sideslip	——
$C_{l_{\delta_a}} = \partial C_l / \partial \delta_a$	Variation of airplane rolling moment coefficient with aileron deflection angle	1/rad
$C_{l_{\delta_r}} = \partial C_l / \partial \delta_r$	Variation of airplane rolling moment coefficient with rudder deflection angle	1/rad
$C_{l_{i_h}} = \partial C_l / \partial i_h$	Variation of airplane rolling moment coefficient with differential stabilizer angle	1/rad
$C_{l_p} = \partial C_l / \partial(pb/2U_1)$	Variation of airplane rolling moment coefficient with dimensionless rate of change of roll rate	1/rad
$C_{l_r} = \partial C_l / \partial(rb/2U_1)$	Variation of airplane rolling moment coefficient with dimensionless rate of change of yaw rate	1/rad
$C_{l_{T_\beta}} = \partial C_{l_T} / \partial \beta$	Variation of airplane rolling moment coefficient due to thrust with sideslip angle	1/rad
C_L	Lift coefficient (airplane)	——
C_{L_0}	Lift coefficient (airplane) for zero angle of attack	——
$C_{L_\alpha} = \partial C_L / \partial \alpha$	Variation of airplane lift coefficient with angle of attack	1/rad
$C_{L_{\dot\alpha}} = \partial C_L / \partial(\dot\alpha \overline{c}/2U_1)$	Variation of airplane lift coefficient with dimensionless rate of change of angle of attack	1/rad
$C_{L_{i_h}} = \partial C_L / \partial i_h$	Variation of airplane lift coefficient with stabilizer incidence angle	1/rad

Symbol	Description	Unit(s)

Regular (Continued)

Symbol	Description	Unit(s)
$C_{L_{\delta_e}} = \partial C_L/\partial \delta_e$	Variation of airplane lift coefficient with elevator deflection angle	1/rad
$C_{L_q} = \partial C_L/\partial(q\bar{c}/2U_1)$	Variation of airplane lift coefficient with dimensionless pitch rate	1/rad
$C_{L_u} = \partial C_L/\partial(u/U_1)$	Variation of airplane lift coefficient with dimensionless speed	——
c_m	Section pitching moment coefficient	——
$c_{m_{ac}}$	Section pitching moment coefficient about the a.c.	——
c_{m_0}	Section pitching moment coefficient at zero angle of attack	——
$\bar{c}_{m_0}$	Section pitching moment coefficient at zero lift	——
$c_{m_\alpha} = \partial c_m/\partial\alpha$	Variation of section pitching moment coefficient with angle of attack	1/rad
C_m	Pitching moment coefficient (airplane)	——
C_{m_0}	Pitching moment coefficient (airplane) for zero angle of attack	——
$\bar{C}_{m_0}$	Pitching moment coefficient (airplane) for zero lift	——
$C_{m_\alpha} = \partial C_m/\partial\alpha$	Variation of airplane pitching moment coefficient with angle of attack	1/rad
$C_{m_{\dot\alpha}} = \partial C_m/\partial(\dot\alpha\bar{c}/2U_1)$	Variation of airplane pitching moment coefficient with dimensionless rate of change of angle of attack	1/rad
$C_{m_{i_h}} = \partial C_m/\partial i_h$	Variation of airplane pitching moment coefficient with stabilizer incidence angle	1/rad
$C_{m_{\delta_e}} = \partial C_m/\partial \delta_e$	Variation of airplane pitching moment coefficient with elevator deflection angle	1/rad
C_{m_T}	Pitching moment coefficient due to thrust	——
$C_{m_{T_{N_p}}}$	Pitching moment coefficient due to propeller normal force coefficient	——
$C_{m_q} = \partial C_m/\partial(q\bar{c}/2U_1)$	Variation of airplane pitching moment coefficient with pitch rate	1/rad
$C_{m_u} = \partial C_m/\partial(u/U_1)$	Variation of airplane pitching moment coefficient with dimensionless speed	——
$C_{m_{T_\alpha}} = \partial C_{m_T}/\partial\alpha$	Variation of airplane pitching moment coefficient due to thrust with angle of attack	1/rad

Symbol	Description	Unit(s)
Regular (Continued)		
$C_{m_{T_u}} = \partial C_{m_T}/\partial(u/U_1)$	Variation of airplane pitching moment coefficient due to thrust with dimensionless speed	———
C_n	Yawing moment coefficient (airplane)	———
C_{n_0}	Yawing moment coefficient for zero sideslip angle and zero control surface deflections	1/rad
C_{N_p}	Propeller normal force coefficient	
$C_{n_\beta} = \partial C_n/\partial\beta$	Variation of airplane yawing moment coefficient with angle of sideslip	1/rad
$C_{n_{\dot\beta}} = \partial C_n/\partial(\dot\beta b/2U_1)$	Variation of airplane yawing moment coefficient with dimensionless rate of change of angle of sideslip	1/rad
$C_{n_{\delta_a}} = \partial C_n/\partial\delta_a$	Variation of airplane yawing moment coefficient with aileron deflection angle	1/rad
$C_{n_{\delta_{r_{drag}}}} = \partial C_n/\partial\delta_{r_{drag}}$	Variation of airplane yawing moment coefficient with drag rudder deflection angle	1/rad
$C_{n_{i_h}} = \partial C_n/\partial i_h$	Variation of airplane yawing moment coefficient with differential stabilizer angle	1/rad
$C_{n_{\delta_r}} = \partial C_n/\partial\delta_r$	Variation of airplane yawing moment coefficient with rudder deflection angle	1/rad
$C_{n_{\delta_s}} = \partial C_n/\partial\delta_s$	Variation of airplane yawing moment coefficient with spoiler deflection angle	1/rad
$C_{n_p} = \partial C_n/\partial(pb/2U_1)$	Variation of airplane yawing moment coefficient with dimensionless rate of change of roll rate	1/rad
$C_{n_r} = \partial C_n/\partial(rb/2U_1)$	Variation of airplane yawing moment coefficient with dimensionless rate of change of yaw rate	1/rad
$C_{n_{T_\beta}} = \partial C_{n_T}/\partial\beta$	Variation of airplane yawing moment coefficient due to thrust with sideslip angle	1/rad
C_T	Thrust coefficient	———
$C_{T_{x_u}} = \partial C_{T_x}/\partial(u/U_1)$	Variation of airplane thrust coefficient in the X–axis direction w.r.t. dimensionless speed	———
$C_{T_{x_\alpha}} = \partial C_{T_x}/\partial\alpha$	Variation of airplane thrust coefficient in the X–axis direction with angle of attack	1/rad
$C_{T_{x,y\ or\ z}}$	Thrust coefficient component in the X,Y or Z axis direction	
$C_{T_{z_u}} = \partial C_{T_z}/\partial(u/U_1)$	Variation of airplane thrust coefficient in the Z–axis direction w.r.t. dimensionless speed	———

Symbol	Description	Unit(s)
Regular (Continued)		
f_{pl}	Preload of downspring	lbs
$\vec{F}$	Force per unit area (aerodynamic and/or thrust)	lbs/ft^2
$\vec{F}_A$	Total aerodynamic force vector	lbs
f_{A_x} , f_{A_y} , f_{A_z}	Perturbed values of F_{A_x} , F_{A_y} and F_{A_z}	lbs
F_{A_x} , F_{A_y} , F_{A_z}	Aerodynamic force components along XYZ	lbs
F_{OEI}	Factor which accounts for drag induced yawing moment	_____
F_a	Aileron wheel or stick force	lbs
F_r	Rudder pedal force	lbs
F_s	Stick force (or wheel force)	lbs
f_{T_x} , f_{T_y} , f_{T_z}	Perturbed values of F_{T_x} , F_{T_y} and F_{T_z}	lbs
F_{T_x} , F_{T_y} , F_{T_z}	Thrust force components along XYZ	lbs
$\vec{F}_T$	Total thrust force vector	lbs
$\vec{g}$	Acceleration of gravity	ft/sec^2
g_x , g_y , g_z	Acceleration of gravity components along XYZ	ft/sec^2
G	Gearing ratio for a flight control surface	rad/ft
G(s)	Open loop transfer function	varies
$\vec{h}$	Angular momentum vector for spinning rotor(s)	slugft^2/sec
h_x , h_y , h_z	Components of $\vec{h}$ along XYZ	slugft^2/sec
HM	Hinge moment about control surface hingeline	ftlbs
i_c	Canard incidence angle	deg or rad
i_h	Horizontal tail (stabilizer) incidence angle	deg or rad
i_v	Vertical tail (stabilizer) incidence angle	deg or rad

Symbol	**Description**	**Unit(s)**
Regular (Continued)		
i , j , k	Unit vectors along XYZ	——
I_{xx} , I_{yy} , I_{zz}	Airplane moments of inertia about XYZ	slugsft^2
I_{xy} , I_{yz} , I_{xz}	Airplane products of inertia about XYZ	slugsft^2
I_R	Rotor moment of inertia about its spin axis	slugsft^2
$J = U/nD_p$	Propeller advance ratio	——
k	Spring constant	lbs/ft
k_α , k_q	Feedback gain constant w.r.t. angle–of–attack or pitch rate	deg/deg
$K_{1 \text{ through } 7}$	Constants used in Eqn (4.225) or (4.239) or (4.240)	see Eqns
$K_{sw \text{ or } sw}$	Gearing constant between cockpit control wheel or stick and aileron or spoiler deflection	rad/ft
K_{ds}	Downspring constant	lbs/ft
K_α	Angle–of–attack–to–elevator feedback gain	rad/rad
K_q	Pitch–rate–to–elevator feedback gain	rad/rad/sec
K_r	Yaw–rate–to–rudder feedback gain	rad/rad/sec
K_t	Tab spring constant	lbs/ft
$K_{\alpha_{\delta_e}}$	Zero frequency gain in the angle–of–attack–to elevator transfer function	——
$K_{u_{\delta_e}}$	Zero frequency gain in the speed–to–elevator transfer function	ft/sec
$K_{\theta_{\delta_e}}$	Zero frequency gain in the pitch–attitude–to–elevator transfer function	——
$K_{\beta_{\delta_{a \text{ or } r}}}$	Zero frequency gain in the angle–of–sideslip to aileron or rudder transfer function	——
$K_{\phi_{\delta_{a \text{ or } r}}}$	Zero frequency gain in the bank–angle to aileron or rudder transfer function	——
$K_{\psi_{\delta_{a \text{ or } r}}}$	Zero frequency gain in the heading–angle to aileron or rudder transfer function	——

Symbol	Description	Unit(s)

Regular (Continued)

Symbol	Description	Unit(s)
l	Characteristic length	ft
l_A , m_A , n_A	Perturbed values of L_A , M_A and N_A	ftlbs
l_c	Distance from the canard a.c. to the c.g.	ft
l_h	Distance from hor. tail a.c. to the c.g.	ft
l_s	Moment arm of stick (see Figure 4.41)	ft
L	Lift	lbs
L	also: overall airplane length	ft
L_A , M_A , N_A	Aerodynamic moment components about XYZ	ftlbs
$L_\beta = \dfrac{\overline{q}_1 S b C_{l_\beta}}{I_{xx}}$	Roll angular acceleration per unit sideslip angle	rad/sec^2/rad
$L_p = \dfrac{\overline{q}_1 S b^2 C_{l_p}}{2 I_{xx} U_1}$	Roll angular acceleration per unit roll rate	1/sec
$L_r = \dfrac{\overline{q}_1 S b^2 C_{l_r}}{2 I_{xx} U_1}$	Roll angular acceleration per unit yaw rate	1/sec
$L_{\delta_a} = \dfrac{\overline{q}_1 S b C_{l_{\delta_a}}}{I_{xx}}$	Roll angular acceleration per unit aileron angle	rad/sec^2/rad
$L_{\delta_r} = \dfrac{\overline{q}_1 S b C_{l_{\delta_r}}}{I_{xx}}$	Roll angular acceleration per unit rudder angle	rad/sec^2/rad
l_T , m_T , n_T	Perturbed values of L_T , M_T and N_T	ftlbs
L_T , M_T , N_T	Thrust moment components about XYZ	ftlbs

Symbol	Description	Unit(s)
m	Airplane mass (or just mass)	slugs
$\dot{m}'$	Mass flow rate through an engine	slugs/sec
M	Mach number	———
MM	Maneuver margin	fraction m.g.c.
MP	Maneuver point	fraction m.g.c.

Symbol	Description	Unit(s)

Regular (Continued)

$$M_\alpha = \frac{\overline{q}_1 S \overline{c} C_{m_\alpha}}{I_{yy}}$$ — Pitch angular acceleration per unit angle of attack — $1/sec^2$

$$M_{T_\alpha} = \frac{\overline{q}_1 S \overline{c} C_{m_{T_\alpha}}}{I_{yy}}$$ — Pitch angular acceleration per unit angle of attack (due to thrust) — $1/sec^2$

$$M_u = \frac{\overline{q}_1 S \overline{c} (C_{m_u} + 2C_{m_1})}{I_{yy} U_1}$$ — Pitch angular acceleration per unit change in speed — rad/sec/ft

$$M_{T_u} = \frac{\overline{q}_1 S \overline{c} (C_{m_{T_u}} + 2C_{m_{T_1}})}{I_{yy} U_1}$$ — Pitch angular acceleration per unit change in speed (due to thrust) — rad/sec/ft

$$M_{\dot{\alpha}} = \frac{\overline{q}_1 S \overline{c}^2 C_{m_{\dot{\alpha}}}}{2 I_{yy} U_1}$$ — Pich angular acceleration per unit rate of change of angle of attack — $1/sec$

$$M_q = \frac{\overline{q}_1 S \overline{c}^2 C_{m_q}}{2 I_{yy} U_1}$$ — Pitch angular acceleration per unit pitch rate — $1/sec$

$$M_{\delta_e} = \frac{\overline{q}_1 S \overline{c} C_{m_{\delta_e}}}{I_{yy}}$$ — Pitch angular acceleration per unit elevator angle — $1/sec^2$

Symbol	Description	Unit(s)
M_A	Aerodynamic moment scalar	ftlbs
$\vec{M}_A$	Total aerodynamic moment vector	ftlbs
M_{pl}	Moment about tab hingeline due to spring pre–load	ftlbs
$\vec{M}_T$	Total thrust moment vector	ftlbs
M_{tab}	Tab moment about its own hingeline	ftlbs

Symbol	Description	Unit(s)
n	Real part of complex root	1/sec
n	Fraction number, also load factor, $n = L/W$	——
n_{limit}	Limit load factor	——
$\overline{n}$	Quantity defined in Eqn (4.218)	——
$\hat{n}$	Quantity defined on page 283	——
$n_\alpha = n/\alpha = \frac{\partial n}{\partial \alpha}$	Variation of load factor with angle of attack	1/rad
n_j	Number of jet engines per airplane	——
n_p	Number of propellers per airplane	——

Symbol	Description	Unit(s)

Regular (Continued)

Symbol	Description	Unit(s)
n_{prpm}	Propeller r.p.m.	1/min
n_{prps}	Propeller r.p.s.	1/sec
N_D	Drag induced yawing moment due to O.E.I.	ftlbs
NP	Neutral point	fraction m.g.c.
N_j	Inlet normal force	lbs
N_p	Propeller normal force	lbs
N_u	Numerator of speed–to–elevator transfer function	ft^2rad^2/sec^6
N_α	Numerator of angle–of–attack–to–elevator transfer function	$ftrad^2/sec^5$
N_β	Numerator of sideslip to aileron or rudder transfer function	$ftrad^3/sec^6$
N_θ	Numerator of pitch–attitude–to–elevator transfer function	$ftrad^2/sec^5$
N_ϕ	Numerator of bank angle to aileron or rudder transfer function	$ftrad^3/sec^6$
N_ψ	Numerator of heading angle to aileron or rudder transfer function	$ftrad^3/sec^6$
$N_\beta = \dfrac{\overline{q}_1 Sb C_{n_\beta}}{I_{zz}}$	Yaw angular acceleration per unit sideslip angle	$rad/sec^2/rad$
$N_{T_\beta} = \dfrac{\overline{q}_1 Sb C_{n_{T_\beta}}}{I_{zz}}$	Yaw angular acceleration per unit sideslip angle (due to thrust)	$rad/sec^2/rad$
$N_p = \dfrac{\overline{q}_1 Sb^2 C_{n_p}}{2I_{zz}U_1}$	Yaw angular acceleration per unit roll rate	1/sec
$N_r = \dfrac{\overline{q}_1 Sb^2 C_{n_r}}{2I_{zz}U_1}$	Yaw angular acceleration per unit yaw rate	1/sec
$N_{\delta_a} = \dfrac{\overline{q}_1 Sb C_{n_{\delta_a}}}{I_{zz}}$	Yaw angular acceleration per unit aileron angle	$rad/sec^2/rad$
$N_{\delta_r} = \dfrac{\overline{q}_1 Sb C_{n_{\delta_r}}}{I_{zz}}$	Yaw angular acceleration per unit rudder angle	$rad/sec^2/rad$

Symbol	Description	Unit(s)

Regular (Continued)

Symbol	Description	Unit(s)
p , q , r	Perturbed values of P, Q and R	rad/sec
P , Q , R	Airplane angular velocity components about XYZ	rad/sec
$\bar{q} = 0.5\varrho V_P^2 = 1,482\delta M^2$	Airplane dynamic pressure	lbs/ft^2
$\vec{r}$	Vector which connects the c.g. with a mass element	ft
$\vec{r}'$	Vector which connects the origin of X'Y'Z' with an airplane mass element	ft
$\vec{r}_P'$	Vector which connects the origin of X'Y'Z' with airplane c.g.	ft
$R_N = \dfrac{\varrho V_P l}{\mu}$	Reynolds number	——
$\overline{R}_y$	Dimensionless radius of gyration about the Y–axis	——
s	Laplace domain variable	rad/sec
S	Area	ft^2
SM	Static margin	fraction mgc
S_p	Propeller disk area	ft^2
S_{w_f}	Flapped wing area	ft^2
S_{wet}	Airplane wetted area	ft^2
t	Thickness	ft
T	Thrust	lbs
$T_{1/2}$	Time to half amplitude	sec
T_2	Time to double amplitude	sec
T_s , T_r	Time constant of spiral and roll mode respectively	sec
$T_n = 2\pi/\omega_n$	Normalized time	sec
$(t/c)_{max}$	Maximum thickness ratio	——

Symbol	Description	Unit(s)
Regular (Continued)		
u , v , w	Perturbed value of U, V and W	ft/sec
$\dot{u}$, $\dot{v}$, $\dot{w}$	Accelerations in X,Y and Z directions	ft/sec^2
U , V , W	Components of $\vec{V}_P$ along XYZ	ft/sec
$\dot{U}$	Forward acceleration along the ground	ft/sec^2
$\overline{V}_{h \text{ or } v}$	Horizontal or vertical tail volume coefficient	——
V_{mc}	Minimum control speed (engine out)	ft/sec
$\vec{V}_P$	Airplane velocity (true airspeed)	ft/sec
V_s	Stall speed	ft/sec
$V_{s_{OEI}}$	Stall speed with one engine inoperative	ft/sec
W	Airplane weight	lbs
W_{bw}	Weight of bobweight	lbs
x , y , z	Components of $\vec{r}$ along XYZ	ft
$\dot{x}'$, $\dot{y}'$, $\dot{z}'$	Components of $\vec{V}_P$ along X'Y'Z'	ft/sec
x_{ac}	A.C. location relative to l.e. of chord	ft
$\overline{x}_{ac}$	Aerodynamic center location as fraction of mgc	——
$\overline{x}_{cp}$	C.P. location relative to l.e. of chord	ft
x_h	Distance from the 3/4 mgc point on the wing to the horizontal tail a.c.	ft
x_j	Distance from the inlet normal force to the c.g. measured along the X–stability axis	ft
$x_{ac_{h_g}}$	Distance defined in Figure 4.51	ft
$x_{ac_{wf_g}}$	Distance defined in Figure 4.51	ft
x_{cg_g}	Distance defined in Figure 4.51	ft

Symbol	Description	Unit(s)
x_{mg_g}	Distance defined in Figure 4.51	ft
x_p	Distance from the propeller normal force to the c.g. measured along the X–stability axis	ft
x_T	Distance from a thrust line attachment point to the c.g. measured along the stability X–axis	ft
$\overline{x}_{ac_A}$	Aerodynamic center location as a fraction of the mgc and measured from the leading edge of the mgc, positive aft	———
$\overline{x}_{cg}$	Center of gravity location as a fraction of the mgc and measured from the leading edge of the mgc, positive aft	———
$\overline{x}_{ref}$	Reference point location relative to l.e. of chord	ft
x_{v_s}	Distance between the vertical tail a.c. and the c.g. measured along the stability x–axis	ft
$X_\alpha = \dfrac{-\overline{q}_1 S(C_{D_\alpha} - C_{L_1})}{m}$	Forward acceleration per unit angle of attack	ft/sec^2/rad
$X_u = \dfrac{-\overline{q}_1 S(C_{D_u} + 2C_{D_1})}{mU_1}$	Forward acceleration per unit change in speed	1/sec
$X_{T_u} = \dfrac{\overline{q}_1 S(C_{T_{x_u}} + 2C_{T_{x_1}})}{mU_1}$	Forward acceleration per unit change in speed (due to thrust)	1/sec
$X_{\delta_e} = \dfrac{-\overline{q}_1 S C_{D_{\delta_e}}}{m}$	Forward acceleration per unit elevator angle	ft/sec^2/rad

Symbol	Description	Unit(s)
y_a	Distance from aileron center of load to the airplane centerline	ft
y_{dr}	Distance between the drag rudder c.p. and the c.g. measured along the stability y–axis	ft
y_T	Distance from a thrust line attachment point to the c.g. measured along the stability Y–axis	ft
$Y_\beta = \dfrac{-\overline{q}_1 S C_{y_\beta}}{m}$	Lateral acceleration per unit sideslip angle	ft/sec^2/rad
$Y_p = \dfrac{-\overline{q}_1 S b C_{y_p}}{2mU_1}$	Lateral acceleration per unit roll rate	ft/sec/rad

Symbol	Description	Unit(s)
	Regular (Continued)	
$Y_r = \dfrac{-\bar{q}_1 SbC_{y_r}}{2mU_1}$	Lateral acceleration per unit yaw rate	ft/sec/rad
$Y_{\delta_a} = \dfrac{-\bar{q}_1 SC_{y_{\delta_a}}}{m}$	Lateral acceleration per unit aileron angle	ft/sec^2/rad
$Y_{\delta_r} = \dfrac{-\bar{q}_1 SC_{y_{\delta_r}}}{m}$	Lateral acceleration per unit rudder angle	ft/sec^2/rad
z_{cg_g}	Distance defined in Figure 4.51	ft
z_{D_g}	Distance defined in Figure 4.51	ft
z_{mg_g}	Distance defined in Figure 4.51	ft
z_{T_g}	Distance defined in Figure 4.51	ft
z_{v_s}	Distance between the vertical tail a.c. and the stability x–axis	ft
$Z_\alpha = \dfrac{-\bar{q}_1 S(C_{L_\alpha} + C_{D_1})}{m}$	Vertical acceleration per unit angle of attack	ft/sec^2/rad
$Z_u = \dfrac{-\bar{q}_1 S(C_{L_u} + 2C_{L_1})}{mU_1}$	Vertical acceleration per unit change in speed	1/sec
$Z_{\dot{\alpha}} = \dfrac{-\bar{q}_1 S\bar{c}C_{L_{\dot{\alpha}}}}{2mU_1}$	Vertical acceleration per unit rate of change of angle of attack	ft/sec/rad
$Z_q = \dfrac{-\bar{q}_1 S\bar{c}C_{L_q}}{2mU_1}$	Vertical acceleration per unit pitch rate	ft/sec/rad
$Z_{\delta_e} = \dfrac{-\bar{q}_1 SC_{L_{\delta_e}}}{m}$	Vertical acceleration per unit elevator angle	ft/sec^2/rad
	Greek	
α	Angle of attack	deg or rad
$\dot{\alpha}$	Rate of change of angle of attack	rad/sec
α_0	Angle of attack at zero lift (section)	deg or rad
α_{0_L}	Angle of attack at zero lift (planform or airplane)	deg or rad

Symbol	Description	Unit(s)

Greek (Continued)

Symbol	Description	Unit(s)
$\alpha *$	Angle of attack value at end of linear range	deg or rad
$\alpha_\delta = \partial\alpha/\partial\delta$	Angle of attack effectiveness derivative	——
$\alpha_{c_{l_{max}}}$	Angle of attack at maximum lift coefficient	deg or rad
β	Angle of sideslip	deg or rad
γ	Flight path angle	deg or rad
Γ	Geometric dihedral angle	deg or rad
δ	Control surface deflection angle	deg or rad
δ_t	Control surface tab deflection angle	deg or rad
δ_{t_0}	Control surface tab deflection angle when up against a mechanical stop	deg or rad
Δ	Determinant of a matrix or increment of a parameter	——
$\Delta\bar{x}_{ac_{fus}}$	Shift in wing+fuselage aerodynamic center from the wing aerodynamic center in fractions of the m.g.c.	——
Δy	Leading edge shape parameter	——
ε	Downwash angle	deg or rad
ε_0	Downwash angle at zero angle of attack	deg or rad
ε_j	Upwash angle at inlet	deg or rad
ε_p	Upwash angle at propeller disk	deg or rad
ε_T	Twist angle	deg or rad
η	Spanwise station in fraction of b/2	——
$\eta_h,\ \eta_v,\ \eta_c$	Dynamic pressure ratio at h.t., v.t. or canard resp.	——
η_p	Propeller efficiency	——
θ	Perturbed value of Θ	rad
Θ	Airplane pitch attitude angle (See Figure 1.6)	rad
Θ	Angle in s–plane, see Fig. 5.7	rad

Symbol	Description	Unit(s)
Greek (Continued)		
λ	Taper ratio	——
λ	Root of characteristic equation	1/sec
Λ	Sweep angle	deg or rad
μ	Coefficient of viscosity	lbs–sec/ft^2
μ_g	Wheel–to–ground friction coefficient	1/lbs
ζ	Damping ratio	——
ζ_α	Damping ratio of an airplane free to oscillate in pitch only	——
ζ_β	Damping ratio of an airplane free to oscillate in yaw only	——
π	3.14	——
ϱ	Air density	slugs/ft^3
ϱ_A	Airplane mass density	slugs/ft^3
ϱ_i	Air density in inlet	slugs/ft^3
σ	Sidewash angle	deg or rad
$\tau_{e \text{ or } r} = \partial\alpha/\partial\delta_{e \text{ or } r}$	Angle of attack effectiveness factor	
ϕ	Perturbed value of Φ	rad
ϕ_{TE}	Trailing edge angle	deg
Φ	Airplane bank angle (See Figure 1.6)	rad
ϕ_T	Thrust line inclination angle w.r.t. YX–plane	rad
ψ	Perturbed value of Ψ	rad
Ψ	Airplane heading angle (See Figure 1.6)	rad
ψ_T	Inclination angle of the projection of a thrust line on the XZ–plane w.r.t the XY–plane	rad
$\vec{\omega}$	Airplane angular velocity vector	rad/sec
ω_n	Undamped natural frequency	rad/sec

Symbol	**Description**	**Unit(s)**
Greek (Continued)		
ω_{n_α}	Undamped natural frequency of an airplane free to oscillate in pitch only	rad/sec
ω_{n_β}	Undamped natural frequency of an airplane free to oscillate in yaw only	rad/sec
$\vec{\omega}_R$	Angular velocity of rotor about its spin axis	rad/sec

Subscripts

Note: A, S, b and $\bar{c}$ without a subscript indicates a wing property!

1	Steady state quantity
a	Aileron
ac or a.c. or A.C.	Aerodynamic center
artificial	Quantity obtained artificially (for example, in control forces)
A	Aerodynamic or airplane
B	Body–fixed axes
c	Canard
cg	Center of gravity
c/4	Relative to the quarter chord
cp or c.p. or C.P.	Center of pressure
CAP	Control anticipation parameter
d	Dutch roll
dr	Drag rudder
e	Elevator
f	Fuselage
ff	Fowler flap
fix	Stick (or controls) fixed
fk	Krueger flap
free	Stick (or controls) free
fus	Fuselage
g	Gust
ground	Quantity determined in ground effect
h	Horizontal tail
i	Item number i
i_h	Horizontal tail (stabilizer) incidence angle
inb'd	Inboard
j	Jet

Subscripts (Continued)

max	Maximum
mg	Main gear, about or relative to main gear
min	Minimum
l	Left
L	Landing
LE	Leading edge
M	At some Mach number
M=0	At zero Mach number
MP	Maneuver point
n	Normal to
outb'd	Outboard
OWE	Operating weight empty
p	Pylon, also: propeller
ph	Phugoid
PA	Powered Approach
r	Right or rudder
reqd	Required
t	Tip or tab
trim	trimmed
T	Thrust
r	Root or rudder or roll
rs	Roll–spiral
s	Spiral, store or spoiler or stability axes
sp	Short period
ss	Steady state
TO	Takeoff
v	Vertical tail
w	Wing
wf	Wing+fuselage
x, y or z	In the x, y or z–direction

Acronyms

ac or a.c. or A.C.	Aerodynamic center
BPR	Bypass ratio
c.g.	Center of gravity
cp or c.p. or C.P.	Center of pressure
EMP	Electromagnetic pulse
FBL	Fly–by–light
FBW	Fly–by–wire

Acronyms (Continued)

h.t.	Horizontal tail
irrev.	Irreversible
l.e.	Leading edge
l.e.r.	Leading edge radius (ft)
l.h.s.	Left hand side
mgc or MGC	Mean geometric chord (ft)
MM	Maneuver margin
NP	Neutral point
O.E.I.	One engine inoperative
P.F.C.S.	Primary flight control system
r.h.s.	Right hand side
r.p.s.	Rotations per second
S.A.S.	Stability augmentation system
SM	Static margin
v.t.	Vertical tail
w.r.t.	With respect to

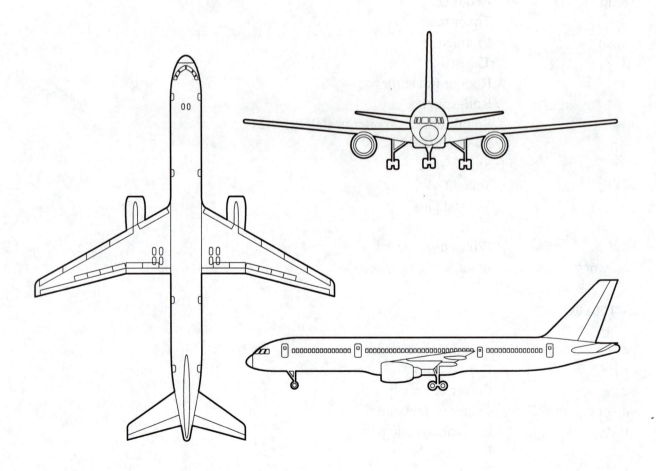

INTRODUCTION

In this two–part textbook, methods are presented for analysis and synthesis of the steady state and perturbed state (open and closed loop) stability and control of fixed wing aircraft.

Part I contains Chapters 1–6 and Appendices A–D. Part II contains Chapters 7–12 as well as Appendix E.

The book is aimed at junior, senior and first level graduate students of aeronautical engineering. Aeronautical engineers working in the aircraft industry will also find this book useful.

Throughout this text the practical (design) applications of the theory are stressed with many examples. Aircraft stability and control characteristics are all heavily regulated by civil as well as by military airworthiness authorities for reasons of safety. The role of these safety regulations in the application of the theory is therefore stressed throughout.

Many of the examples used to illustrate the application of the theory were generated with the help of a computer program called: AAA (Advanced Aircraft Analysis). This program is compatible with most Apollo, Sun, Silicon Graphics, IBM and DEC work–stations as well as with certain types of personal computers. The AAA program can be purchased from DARCorporation, 120 East Ninth Street, Suite 2, Lawrence, Kansas 66044, USA.

In Chapter 1 the general equations of motion are developed for a rigid airplane. These equations are then specialized into sets which apply to steady state and perturbed state flight conditions respectively. Before these equations can be used to help in the analysis and design of airplanes it is necessary to develop mathematical models for the aerodynamic and thrust forces and moments which act on an airplane.

Chapter 2 provides an overview of aerodynamic fundamentals needed to understand and use aerodynamic force and moment models. Several important properties of airfoils and lifting surfaces are reviewed. The effect of the fuselage on aerodynamic center is discussed and some fundamental aspects of control surface and flap characteristics are covered.

The actual modelling of aerodynamic and thrust forces and moments is discussed in Chapter 3. The reader is introduced to the concept and use of stability and control derivatives. Physical explanations and examples of signs and magnitudes of these derivatives are given.

Chapter 4 contains a discussion of the steady state equations of motion of airplanes. Solutions and applications are presented particularly from a viewpoint of how this material is used in airplane analysis and design. The relationship to handling quality regulations is pointed out. The airplane trim problem, take–off rotation problem and engine–out control problem are given significant emphasis.

In Chapter 5 the perturbed equations of motion of airplanes are discussed. The reader is introduced to the concept of airplane open loop transfer functions. The fundamental dynamic modes of airplanes (phugoid, short period, roll, spiral and dutch roll) are analyzed. Approximations to these modes are derived and typical 'drivers' of good and bad dynamic stability properties are identified. The idea of equivalent stability derivatives is introduced and the relation to automatic control of unstable airplanes is pointed out. Derivative sensitivity analyses are also discussed.

In Chapter 6 an introduction is given to the subject of airplane flying qualities. The reader is introduced to the Cooper–Harper scale and to various civil and military regulations for flying qualities. The relationship to airplane design is pointed out.

The subject of elastic airplane stability and control is taken up in Chapter 7 (in Part II). Finite element methods are used to determine stability and control coefficients and derivatives for elastic airplanes. A method for determining the equilibrium and jig (i.e. manufacturing) shape of an elastic airplane is also presented. Several numerical examples of the effect of aeroelasticity on stability and control derivatives are given for a subsonic and for a supersonic transport.

Chapter 8 presents an introduction to the construction and interpretation of Bode plots with open and closed loop airplane applications. An important inverse application is also given.

In Chapter 9 an overview is given of so–called classical control theory. The use of the root–locus method and the Bode method are illustrated with examples.

It is shown in Chapter 10 that classical control theory can be used to predict whether or not an airplane can be controlled by a human pilot. This is done with the aid of human pilot transfer functions for compensatory situations.

In Chapter 11 the reader is introduced to various aspects of automatic control of airplanes. It is shown why certain airplanes require stability augmentation. Pitch dampers, yaw dampers and roll dampers are discussed. The reader is familiarized with the basic synthesis concepts of automatic flight control modes such as: control–stick steering, various auto–pilot hold modes, speed control, navigation modes and automatic landing modes. Applications to various airplane types are also included.

In Chapter 12 a brief introduction to digital control systems using classical control theory is provided. Applications of the Z–transformation method are also included.

CHAPTER 1:   EQUATIONS OF MOTION AND AXIS SYSTEMS

In this chapter, the general equations of motion for a rigid airplane are derived and the coordinate systems in which these equations are written are discussed. Several assumptions must be made along the way and these are carefully indicated. Applications of these equations to various airplane performance, stability and control problems are outlined.

1.1   COORDINATE SYSTEMS AND EXTERNAL FORCES

Figure 1.1 depicts two axis systems: the earth fixed system X'Y'Z' and the airplane body fixed axis system XYZ. The earth fixed axis system will be regarded as an inertial reference frame: one in which Newton's laws of motion are valid. This means that the rotational velocity of the earth is neglected. Experience indicates this to be acceptable even for supersonic airplanes but not for hypersonic vehicles. Reference 1.1 (pages 135–137) provides a detailed discussion of this assumption with numerical examples.

The airplane in Figure 1.1 is assumed to consist of a continuum of mass elements, dm. These mass elements are kept track of by the vectors $\vec{r}'$ which connect the origin of X'Y'Z' with each mass element. In the case of rigid airplanes these mass elements maintain their distance relative to each other except for mass elements which are part of rotating machinery (such as compressors, turbines and propellers) or which are part of a variable sweep wing.

Each mass element is subject to the acceleration of gravity, $\vec{g}$. As seen in Figure 1.1 the vector $\vec{g}$ is assumed to be oriented along the positive Z' axis. This is the so–called flat earth assumption. As a consequence, a force $\varrho_A \vec{g} dv = \vec{g} dm$ acts on each mass element. The quantity ϱ_A represents the local mass density of the airplane. Those mass elements located at the surface of the airplane are also subjected to a combined aerodynamic and thrust force per unit area: $\vec{F}$. Note that $\vec{F}$ has the physical unit of pressure: lbs/ft^2. The forces $\varrho_A \vec{g} dv$ and $\vec{F} ds$ are assumed to be the only external forces acting on the airplane.

1.2   DERIVATION OF THE EQUATIONS OF MOTION

At this point Newton's Second Law will be applied to the airplane of Figure 1. This law states that the time derivatives of linear and angular momenta are equal to the externally applied forces and moments respectively. This statement results in the vector–integral form of the equations of motion as given in Equations (1.1) and (1.2):

$$\frac{d}{dt}\int_v \varrho_A \frac{d\vec{r}'}{dt} dv = \int_v \varrho_A \vec{g} dv + \int_S \vec{F} ds \qquad \text{Total Linear Momentum} \qquad (1.1)$$

linear   *velocity*   applied forces
momentum

Total Weight   *Aero & Thrust*

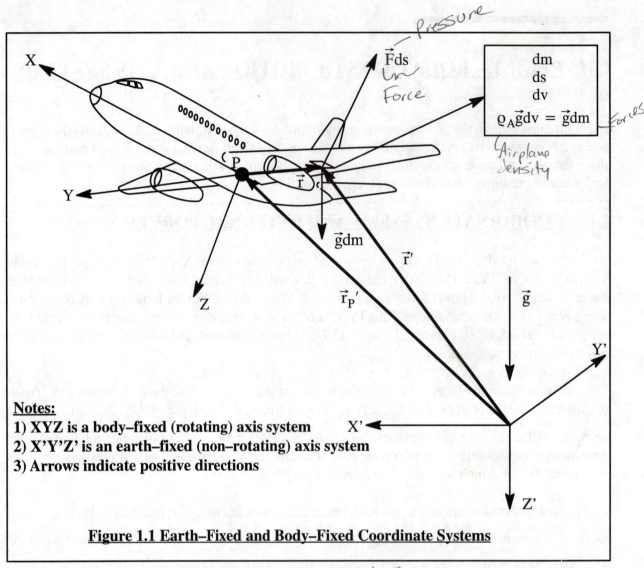

Notes:
1) XYZ is a body–fixed (rotating) axis system
2) X'Y'Z' is an earth–fixed (non–rotating) axis system
3) Arrows indicate positive directions

Figure 1.1 Earth–Fixed and Body–Fixed Coordinate Systems

$$\frac{d}{dt}\int_v \vec{r}' \times \varrho_A \frac{d\vec{r}'}{dt} dv = \int_v \vec{r}' \times \varrho_A \vec{g} dv + \int_S \vec{r}' \times \vec{F} ds \qquad (1.2)$$

angular   applied moments
momentum

The integrals $\int_v$ and $\int_s$ represent volume and surface integrals for the entire airplane. These integrals can be evaluated only if the external geometry of the airplane is known. This will be the case if the airplane is rigid. If the airplane is elastic then an aeroelastic equilibrium must be established from which the external shape of the airplane can be determined. Methods for accomplishing this are discussed in Chapter 7.

The total mass of the airplane is found from:

$$m = \int_v \varrho_A dv \qquad (1.3)$$

At this point it will be assumed that the total mass of the airplane remains constant with time:

$$\frac{dm}{dt} = 0 \tag{1.4}$$

This assumption is justified as long as the mass change is sufficiently small over a time period of 30 – 60 seconds. This time period is typical of the time duration over which airplane responses are evaluated. If a mass change is within about 5% of the begin mass after a 60 second period, the constant mass assumption is considered acceptable. Table 1.1 shows the mass change (but in lbs of weight!) during a 60 second period for airplanes and rockets. It may be seen that the constant mass assumption is reasonable for airplanes but not for rockets.

Table 1.1 Examples of Mass Changes in 60 Seconds for Airplanes and Rockets

Type	Takeoff Weight (lbs)	Maximum Fuel Weight (lbs)	Cruise Fuel Consumption (lbs/hr)	Mass Change after 60 seconds (lbs)	Mass Change after 60 sec. as % of take–off weight
SST	675,000	291,000	90,000	1,500	0.22
Fighter	54,000	17,600	5,940	99	0.18
GA Twin	6,800	1,020	200	3.3	0.05
Saturn 5	6,500,000	4,500,000	————	1,800,000	27.7
Delta	112,000	100,000	————	19,300	17.2

Another assumption which will be made is that the mass distribution is also constant with time. This assumption infers that the center of gravity of the airplane stays in the same place during a 60 second interval. Phenomena such as fuel sloshing, shifting payloads and wandering passengers are therefore outside the scope of the equations which follow. Problem 1.1 requests that the reader remove this assumption.

So far, all airplane mass elements were tracked in Figure 1.1 with the help of the vectors $\vec{r}'$. It is more convenient to use the vectors $\vec{r}$ and $\vec{r}'_P$. To that end the body–fixed coordinate system XYZ is introduced. The selection of the orientation of system XYZ relative to the airframe is done quite arbitrarily. In Figure 1.1 the X–axis has been drawn parallel to the fuselage centerline. The origin of the XYZ system is point P. Point P is now assumed to be the center of mass of the airplane. The three position vectors are related as follows:

$$\vec{r}' = \vec{r}'_P + \vec{r} \tag{1.5}$$

If point P is the center of mass the following relation must be satisfied:

$$\int_V \vec{r} \rho_A dv = 0 \tag{1.6}$$

As a consequence the following relation holds for $\vec{r}'_P$:

$$r'_P = \frac{1}{m} \int_v \varrho_A \vec{r}' dv \tag{1.7}$$

It is now possible to rewrite the left hand side of the linear momentum Eqn (1.1) as:

$$\frac{d}{dt}\frac{d}{dt} \int_v \varrho_A(\vec{r}'_P + \vec{r})dv = \frac{d}{dt}\frac{d}{dt} m\vec{r}'_P = m\frac{d\vec{V}_P}{dt} \tag{1.8}$$

where:

$$\vec{V}_P = \frac{d\vec{r}'_P}{dt} \qquad \text{TRUE AIRSPEED} \tag{1.9}$$

is defined as the velocity of the airplane center of mass. The right hand side of Eqn (1.1) can now be written as:

$$\int_v \varrho_A \vec{g} dv + \int_s \vec{F} ds = m\vec{g} + \vec{F}_A + \vec{F}_T \tag{1.10}$$

where $\vec{F}_A$ represents the total aerodynamic force vector and $\vec{F}_T$ represents the total thrust force vector. Equation (1.1) can now be expressed as:

$$m\frac{d\vec{V}_P}{dt} = m\vec{g} + \vec{F}_A + \vec{F}_T \tag{1.11}$$

Equation (1.11) proclaims that the time rate of change of linear momentum, $m\vec{V}_P$ is equal to the sum of the externally applied forces on the airplane.

Next, the angular momentum equation (1.2) needs to be further developed. Substitution of Eqn.(1.5) into Eqn.(1.2) while accounting for Eqns (1.6) and (1.1) leads to:

$$\frac{d}{dt} \int_v \vec{r} \times \frac{d\vec{r}}{dt} \varrho_A dv = \int_s \vec{r} \times \vec{F} ds = \vec{M}_A + \vec{M}_T \tag{1.12}$$

where: $\vec{M}_A$ represents the total aerodynamic moment vector and $\vec{M}_T$ represents the total thrust moment vector.

Equation (1.12) proclaims that the time rate of change of angular momentum, $\int_v \vec{r} \times \frac{d\vec{r}}{dt} \varrho_A dv$ is equal to the sum of the externally applied moments on the airplane.

Reminder: The integrals $\int_v$ and $\int_s$ in Eqns (1.10) and (1.12) represent volume and surface integrals for the entire airplane. These integrals can be evaluated only if the external geometry of the airplane is known. This is the case if the airplane is rigid. If the airplane is highly elastic then an aeroelastic equilibrium must be established before the external shape of the airplane can be determined. Methods for accomplishing this are discussed in Chapter 7.

Equation (1.12) implies that the volume integral (on the left hand side) is a time dependent function. Such time dependent integrals are awkward to work with. To eliminate the time–dependence a switch in coordinate systems will be made. It will turn out that by re–writing equations (1.10) and (1.12) with respect to coordinate system XYZ instead of X'Y'Z' (See Figure 1.1) the volume integral in Eqn (1.12) will no longer be time–dependent. A problem is that coordinate system

XYZ is a rotating (non–inertial) coordinate system. In such a system Newton's Laws do not apply as they were used earlier. However, by employing the following vector transformation relationship Newton's Laws can still be used:

$$\frac{d\vec{A}}{dt} = \frac{\partial\vec{A}}{\partial t} + \vec{\omega} \times \vec{A} = \dot{\vec{A}} + \vec{\omega} \times \vec{A} \tag{1.13}$$

fixed   rotating

X'Y'Z'   XYZ

The vector $\vec{A}$ represents any vector which is to be transformed. For proof of this vector transformation relationship the reader is referred to Ref.1.1 (pages 132–133) or Ref.1.2 (pages 96–98). The vector $\vec{\omega}$ in Eqn (1.13) is the angular rotation vector of system XYZ relative to system X'Y'Z'. This vector is also referred to as the angular velocity of the airplane relative to the earth. The latter is realistic because system XYZ was assumed to be body–fixed i.e. rigidly attached to the airplane and therefore moving with the airplane.

The transformation formula (1.13) will now be applied to the left hand side (l.h.s.) of both equations (1.10) and (1.12). **First**, for the l.h.s. of Eqn (1.10):

$$m\frac{d\vec{V}_P}{dt} = m(\frac{\partial\vec{V}_P}{\partial t} + \vec{\omega} \times \vec{V}_P) \qquad \textit{Linear Momentum} \tag{1.14}$$

This leads to:

$$m(\dot{\vec{V}}_P + \vec{\omega} \times \vec{V}_P) = m\vec{g} + \vec{F}_A + \vec{F}_T \qquad \textit{Airplane axis} \tag{1.15}$$

Second, for the l.h.s. of Eqn.(1.12):

$$\frac{d}{dt}\int_v \vec{r} \times \frac{d\vec{r}}{dt}\varrho_A dv = \int_v \vec{r} \times \frac{d}{dt}\frac{d\vec{r}}{dt}\varrho_A dv = \int_v \vec{r} \times \frac{d}{dt}(\dot{\vec{r}} + \vec{\omega} \times \vec{r})\varrho_A dv =$$

$$\int_v \vec{r} \times \{\ddot{\vec{r}} + \dot{\vec{\omega}} \times \vec{r} + 2\vec{\omega} \times \dot{\vec{r}} + \vec{\omega} \times (\vec{\omega} \times \vec{r})\}\varrho_A dv \qquad \textit{if } \dot{r}, \ddot{r} \neq 0, \textit{ unstable} \tag{1.16}$$

By assuming that all mass elements stay together and that there are no spinning rotors in the airplane [this assumption will be corrected in Section (1.3)] it is recognized that $\dot{\vec{r}} = \ddot{\vec{r}} = 0$ and therefore Eqn (1.12) can now be written as:

$$\int_v \vec{r} \times \{\dot{\vec{\omega}} \times \vec{r} + \vec{\omega} \times (\vec{\omega} \times \vec{r})\}\varrho_A dv = \vec{M}_A + \vec{M}_T \tag{1.17}$$

Note, that since the vector $\dot{\vec{\omega}}$ {(angular acceleration of axis system XYZ relative to axis system X'Y'Z') = (angular acceleration of the airplane relative to the earth)} is a property of system XYZ it can be taken outside the volume integral sign. That makes the volume integral time–independent which was the objective of the proposed switch in coordinate system.

Equations (1.15) and (1.17) represent the so–called vector forms of the airplane equations of motion. These forms are useful in arriving at generally valid results and at physical interpretations. However, these forms cannot be used to study the steady state equilibrium and time–history response behavior of an airplane. To accomplish the latter it is necessary to write the vector forms in their scalar (component) equivalents. Before this can be done it is necessary to define the components of all vectors which appear in equations (1.15) and (1.17). These components are defined in Table 1.2. The quantities i, j and k are defined as the unit vectors along the axes X, Y and Z respectively. The positive sense and the physical meaning of these vectors are indicated in Figure 1.2.

By using Equations (1.18) it is possible to cast the linear momentum equation, Eqn (1.15), in the following scalar format:

$$m(\dot{U} - VR + WQ) = mg_x + F_{A_x} + F_{T_x} \qquad \text{DRAG} \qquad (1.19a)$$

$$m(\dot{V} + UR - WP) = mg_y + F_{A_y} + F_{T_y} \qquad \text{SIDE FORCE} \qquad (1.19b)$$

$$m(\dot{W} - UQ + VP) = mg_z + F_{A_z} + F_{T_z} \qquad \text{LIFT} \qquad (1.19c)$$

FORCE EQUATIONS

Because of the volume integration Eqn (1.17) is more difficult to expand. The expansion will be done in three steps. **In Step 1** the l.h.s. of Eqn (1.17) is rewritten as follows with the help of the so–called vector–triple–product–expansion:

$$\int_v \vec{r} \times (\vec{\omega} \times \vec{r} + \vec{\omega} \times (\vec{\omega} \times \vec{r}))\varrho_A dv = \int_v \vec{\omega}(\vec{r}\cdot\vec{r})\varrho_A dv - \int_v \vec{r}(\vec{r}\cdot\vec{\omega})\varrho_A dv +$$

$$+ \int_v \vec{r} \times \vec{\omega}(\vec{\omega}\cdot\vec{r})\varrho_A dv - [\int_v \vec{r} \times \vec{r}(\vec{\omega}\cdot\vec{\omega})\varrho_A dv = 0] \qquad (1.20)$$

In Step 2 the first two terms of Eqn.(1.20) are expanded as follows:

and:
$$\int_v \vec{\omega}(\vec{r}\cdot\vec{r})\varrho_A dv = (i\dot{P} + j\dot{Q} + k\dot{R})\int_v (x^2 + y^2 + z^2)\varrho_A dv$$

$$- \int_v \vec{r}(\vec{r}\cdot\vec{\omega})\varrho_A dv = - \int_v (ix + jy + kz)(x\dot{P} + y\dot{Q} + z\dot{R})\varrho_A dv$$

By combining these two expressions they can be shown to yield:

$$i[\dot{P}\int_v (y^2 + z^2)\varrho_A dv - \dot{Q}\int_v xy\varrho_A dv - \dot{R}\int_v xz\varrho_A dv] +$$

$$j[\dot{Q}\int_v (x^2 + z^2)\varrho_A dv - \dot{P}\int_v yx\varrho_A dv - \dot{R}\int_v yz\varrho_A dv] +$$

$$k[\dot{R}\int_v (x^2 + y^2)\varrho_A dv - \dot{P}\int_v zx\varrho_A dv - \dot{Q}\int_v zy\varrho_A dv] \qquad (1.21)$$

The volume integrals in expression (1.21) are referred to as the moments and products of inertia of the airplane. Common symbols used for these integral quantities (inertias) are as follows:

$$\int_v (y^2 + z^2)\varrho_A dv = I_{xx} \qquad \int_v xy\varrho_A dv = I_{xy} \qquad \int_v xz\varrho_A dv = I_{xz} \qquad (1.22a)$$

$$\int_v (x^2 + z^2)\varrho_A dv = I_{yy} \qquad \int_v yx\varrho_A dv = I_{yx} = I_{xy} \qquad \int_v yz\varrho_A dv = I_{yz} = I_{zy} \qquad (1.22b)$$

$$\int_v (x^2 + y^2)\varrho_A dv = I_{zz} \qquad \int_v zx\varrho_A dv = I_{zx} = I_{xz} \qquad \int_v zy\varrho_A dv = I_{zy} = I_{yz} \qquad (1.22c)$$

Table 1.2 Definitions of Vector Components for Equations (1.15) and (1.17)

Forces:

$$\vec{F}_A = iF_{A_x} + jF_{A_y} + kF_{A_z} \tag{1.18a}$$

for the aerodynamic force components. By a special orientation of the XYZ coordinate system relative to the airplane these forces will be shown to be the drag, side–force and lift forces respectively.

$$\vec{F}_T = iF_{T_x} + jF_{T_y} + kF_{T_z} \tag{1.18b}$$

for the thrust force components.

$$\vec{g} = ig_x + jg_y + kg_z \tag{1.18c}$$

for the components of gravitational acceleration.

Moments:

$$\vec{M}_A = i\underset{\text{roll}}{L_A} + j\underset{\text{pitch}}{M_A} + k\underset{\text{yaw}}{N_A} \tag{1.18d}$$

for the aerodynamic moment components: rolling moment, pitching moment and yawing moment respectively.

$$\vec{M}_T = i\underset{\text{roll}}{L_T} + j\underset{\text{pitch}}{M_T} + k\underset{\text{yaw}}{N_T} \tag{1.18e}$$

for the thrust moment components: rolling moment, pitching moment and yawing moment respectively.

Velocities:

$$\vec{\omega} = i\underset{\text{roll rate}}{P} + j\underset{\text{pitch rate}}{Q} + k\underset{\text{yaw rate}}{R} \tag{1.18f}$$

for the angular velocity components: roll rate, pitch rate and yaw rate respectively.

$$\vec{V}_P = iU + jV + kW \tag{1.18g}$$

for the linear velocity components: forward velocity, side velocity and downward velocity respectively.

Distances:

$$\vec{r} = ix + jy + kz \tag{1.18h}$$

for the distance components which locate mass elements in the airplane.

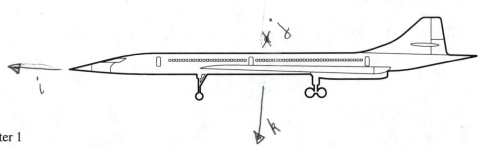

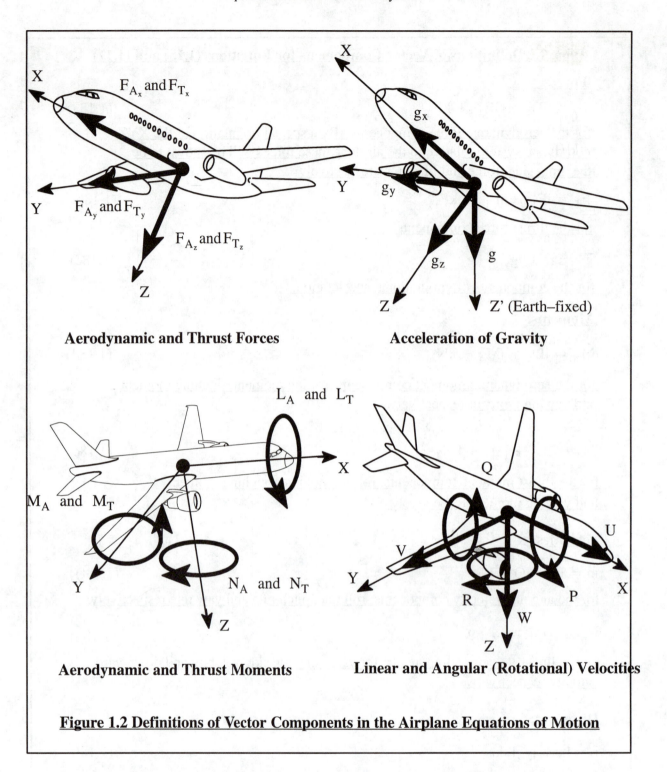

Figure 1.2 Definitions of Vector Components in the Airplane Equations of Motion

In Chapter 6 it will be shown that many of these inertial properties have a very significant influence on the response behavior of the airplane in flight as well as on the flying qualities of the airplane. With the help of Eqns.(1.22) the expression (1.21) can be written as:

$$i(\dot{P}I_{xx} - \dot{Q}I_{xy} - \dot{R}I_{xz}) + j(\dot{Q}I_{yy} - \dot{P}I_{xy} - \dot{R}I_{yz}) + k(\dot{R}I_{zz} - \dot{P}I_{xz} - \dot{Q}I_{yz}) \qquad (1.23)$$

In Step 3 the third term in Eqn (1.20) yields:

$$\int_v \vec{r} \times \vec{\omega}(\vec{\omega} \cdot \vec{r})\varrho_A dv = \int_v \{(ix + jy + kz) \times (iP + jQ + kR)(Px + Qy + Rz)\}\varrho_A dv =$$

$$i[I_{xy}PR + I_{yz}(R^2 - Q^2) - I_{xz}PQ + (I_{zz} - I_{yy})RQ] +$$

$$j[(I_{xx} - I_{zz})PR + I_{xz}(P^2 - R^2) - I_{xy}QR + I_{yz}PQ] +$$

$$k[(I_{yy} - I_{xx})PQ + I_{xy}(Q^2 - P^2) + I_{xz}QR - I_{yz}PR] \tag{1.24}$$

At this point it is recognized that most airplanes are symmetrical about the XZ plane. If that is (even approximately) the case it automatically follows that: $I_{xy} = I_{yz} = 0$. Figure 1.3 shows examples of airplanes for which this mass symmetry assumption is not satisfied.

The reader is asked to observe that most missiles have two planes of symmetry (or approximately so): the XZ and the XY plane. For such vehicles $I_{xz} = 0$ is also satisfied.

All ingredients needed to cast the angular momentum equation (1.17) into its scalar component form are now available. By using expressions (1.23) and (1.24) it is found that:

$$I_{xx}\dot{P} - I_{xz}\dot{R} - I_{xz}PQ + (I_{zz} - I_{yy})RQ = L_A + L_T \qquad \text{Rolling Moment} \tag{1.25a}$$

$$I_{yy}\dot{Q} + (I_{xx} - I_{zz})PR + I_{xz}(P^2 - R^2) = M_A + M_T \qquad \text{Pitching Moment} \tag{1.25b}$$

$$I_{zz}\dot{R} - I_{xz}\dot{P} + (I_{yy} - I_{xx})PQ + I_{xz}QR = N_A + N_T \qquad \text{Yawing Moment} \tag{1.25c}$$

Moment Eqtns.

Equations (1.19) and (1.25) form six differential equations of motion with U, V, W, P, Q and R as the dependent variables. Time is the independent variable. At this point it is not yet possible to solve these equations for the time histories of motion U(t) through R(t). The reasons for this are:

1) The aerodynamic and thrust forces and moments {r.h.s. in Eqns (1.19) and (1.25)} vary with time and with the dependent variables U, V, W, P, Q and R. These dependencies will be explored and defined in Chapter 3.

2) The gravity force components in Eqns (1.19) depend on the orientation of the airplane relative to the earth–fixed coordinate system X'Y'Z'. This dependency will be derived and discussed in Section 1.6.

There is one problem which was introduced with the assumptions: $\vec{r} = \dot{\vec{r}} = 0$ on page 7.

These assumptions also rule out any existence of spinning rotors (such as propellers and turbines) or a sweeping wing in the airplane. The effect of spinning rotors on the airplane equations of motion will be discussed in Section 1.3. In the case of a sweeping wing it will be assumed that the wing sweep motion is slow enough to be neglected. To account for the aerodynamic effect and the c.g. shift effect the airplane will be studied at various intermediate sweep angles which will be fixed in time.

Examples of moment and product of inertia data for a range of airplanes are presented in Appendix B. Rapid methods for estimating the moments and products of inertia airplanes are given in Part V of Reference 1.3: pages 17 – 23.

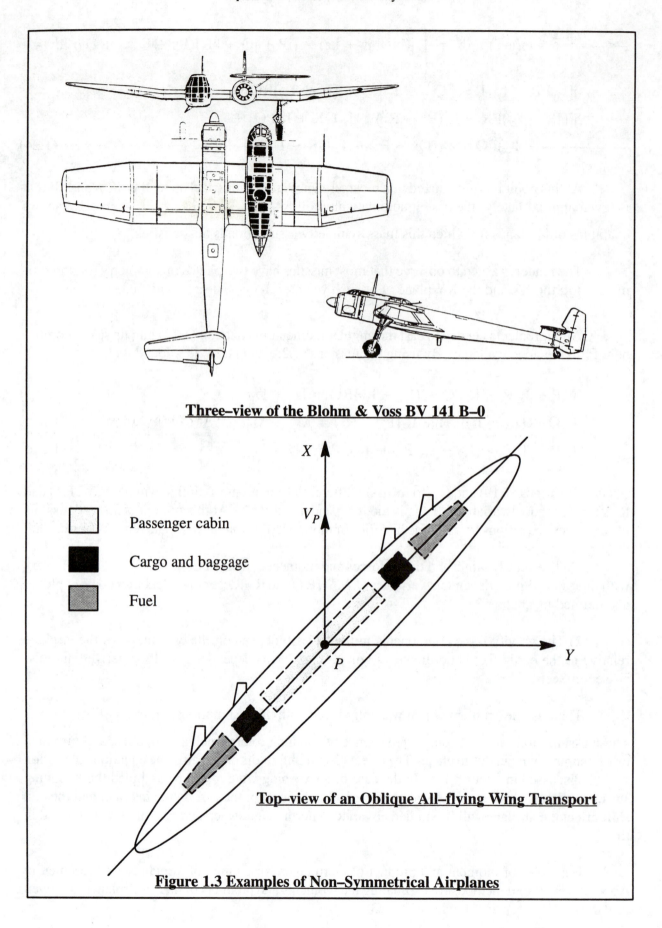

Three–view of the Blohm & Voss BV 141 B–0

Passenger cabin

Cargo and baggage

Fuel

Top–view of an Oblique All–flying Wing Transport

Figure 1.3 Examples of Non–Symmetrical Airplanes

1.3 EFFECT OF SPINNING ROTORS

Most airplanes are equipped with propellers and/or turbine engines which act like spinning rotors. Such spinning rotors exert gyroscopic moments on the body to which they are attached. Figure 1.4 shows an example of an airplane where the rotor orientation relative to the airplane can in fact be varied.

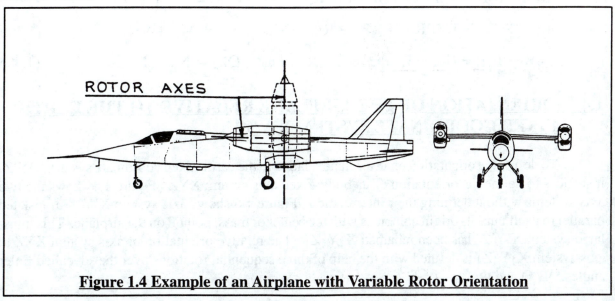

Figure 1.4 Example of an Airplane with Variable Rotor Orientation

In many airplanes these gyroscopic moments tend to be negligible (counter–rotating propellers, twin spool turbines which rotate in opposite directions, etc.) but this is not always the case. The gyroscopic moments due to spinning rotors can be accounted for by a simple addition to the angular momentum equation (1.12). To accomplish this, it is assumed that an airplane is equipped with one or more spinning rotors with a total angular momentum:

$$\vec{h} = \sum_{i=1}^{i=n} \vec{h}_i \qquad (1.26)$$

The rotor i is assumed to have a moment of inertia I_{R_i} about its own spin axis. It is also assumed that the rotor spins with angular velocity $\vec{\omega}_{R_i}$. Eqn.(1 26) can thus be written as:

$$\vec{h} = \sum_{i=1}^{i=n} I_{R_i} \vec{\omega}_{R_i} \qquad (1.27)$$

Or, in component form:

$$\vec{h} = ih_x + jh_y + kh_z \qquad (1.28)$$

It is now possible to rewrite Eqn (1.12) as follows:

$$\frac{d}{dt} \int_v \vec{r} \times \frac{d\vec{r}}{dt} \varrho_A dv + \frac{d\vec{h}}{dt} = \vec{M}_A + \vec{M}_T \qquad (1.29)$$

Angular momentum of airplane
with rotors fixed.

When the $\dfrac{d\vec{h}}{dt}$ terms in Eqn (1.29) are expanded by using Eqn (1.13) and by assuming that all spinning rotors in the airplane operate at constant angular velocity ($\dot{\vec{\omega}}_{R_i} = 0$) the airplane angular momentum equations (1.25) become:

$$I_{xx}\dot{P} - I_{xz}\dot{R} - I_{xz}PQ + (I_{zz} - I_{yy})RQ + Qh_z - Rh_y = L_A + L_T \tag{1.30a}$$

$$I_{yy}\dot{Q} + (I_{xx} - I_{zz})PR + I_{xz}(P^2 - R^2) + Rh_x - Ph_z = M_A + M_T \tag{1.30b}$$

$$I_{zz}\dot{R} - I_{xz}\dot{P} + (I_{yy} - I_{xx})PQ + I_{xz}QR + Ph_y - Qh_x = N_A + N_T \tag{1.30c}$$

1.4 ORIENTATION OF THE AIRPLANE RELATIVE TO THE EARTH FIXED COORDINATE SYSTEM X'Y'Z'

To define the orientation of an airplane relative to the earth–fixed coordinate system X'Y'Z' it suffices to define the orientation of its body–fixed axis system XYZ. Figure 1.1 shows the two axis systems without defining their interrelation. Figure 1.5 shows axis system X'Y'Z' translated parallel to itself until its origin coincides with the center of mass, point P on the airplane. This translated system X'Y'Z' has been renamed $X_1Y_1Z_1$. The relative orientation of axis system XYZ to axis system $X_1Y_1Z_1$ is defined with the help of three sequential rotations over the so–called Euler angles: Ψ, Θ and Φ:

Rotation 1:   Coordinate system $X_1Y_1Z_1$ is rotated about its $\mathbf{Z}_1$ axis over an angle Ψ which is called the heading angle. The angle is positive as shown in Figure 1.5. After rotation over the angle Ψ the coordinate system is re–labeled: $X_2Y_2Z_2$.

Rotation 2: Coordinate system $X_2Y_2Z_2$ is rotated about its $\mathbf{Y}_2$ axis over an angle Θ which is called the pitch attitude angle. The angle is positive as shown in Figure 1.5. After rotation over the angle Θ the coordinate system is re–labeled: $X_3Y_3Z_3$.

Rotation 3: Coordinate system $X_3Y_3Z_3$ is rotated about its $\mathbf{X}_3$ axis over an angle Φ which is called the bank (or roll) angle. The angle is positive as shown in Figure 1.5. After rotation over the angle Φ the coordinate system is re–labeled: XYZ. Note: the notation $X_4Y_4Z_4$ is not used in favor of XYZ.

The reader should refer to Figure 1.6. This figure shows why the definition of the axes about which the angular rotations are made is indeed important. As Figure 1.6 illustrates: finite angular rotations do **NOT** behave as vectors which have the commutative property expressed as:

$$\vec{A} + \vec{B} = \vec{B} + \vec{A} \tag{1.31}$$

The reader should keep in mind that whereas finite angular rotations do not behave as vectors, infinitesimally small angular rotations certainly do! A formal proof for these properties may be found in Reference 1.1, pages 124–129.

A problem with the use of the Euler angles Ψ, Θ and Φ is that for $\Theta = 90)$ the bank angle, Φ looses its meaning. In simulations where complete looping maneuvers may have to be performed that is not acceptable. To overcome this the so–called quaternion method may be used. A good summary of the quaternion method may be found in Reference 1.4 (pages 47 – 50).

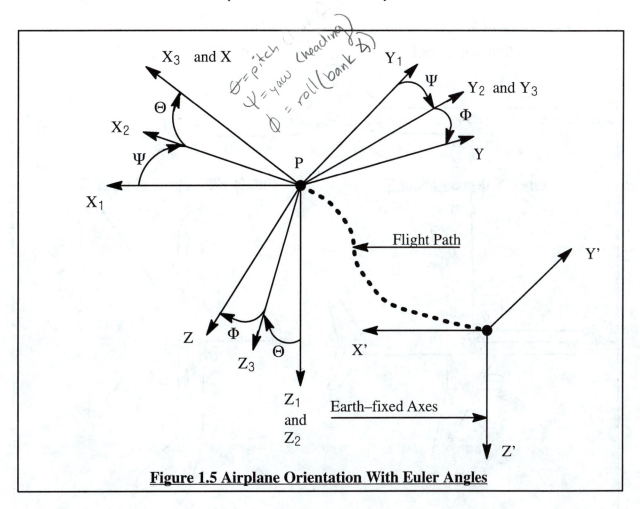

Figure 1.5 Airplane Orientation With Euler Angles

1.5   THE AIRPLANE FLIGHT PATH RELATIVE TO THE EARTH

It is now possible to determine the flight path of an airplane relative to the fixed earth from knowledge of the velocity components U, V and W in the airplane body–fixed axis system XYZ and the three Euler angles of Section 1.4. This will be done by establishing relationships between the velocity components U, V and W (velocity components of $\vec{V}_P$ in XYZ) and the velocity components $\dot{x}'$, $\dot{y}'$ and $\dot{z}'$ (velocity components of $\vec{V}_P$ in X'Y'Z'). Because $X_1Y_1Z_1$ and X'Y'Z' are parallel to each other it follows that:

$$U_1 = \dot{x}' \qquad V_1 = \dot{y}' \qquad W_1 = \dot{z}' \qquad (1.32)$$

Referring to Figure 1.7 it is possible to verify that the following relationships hold between U_1, V_1, W_1 and U_2, V_2, W_2 (= velocity components of $\vec{V}_P$ in $X_2Y_2Z_2$):

$$\begin{bmatrix} U_1 \\ V_1 \\ W_1 \end{bmatrix} = \begin{bmatrix} \cos\Psi & -\sin\Psi & 0 \\ \sin\Psi & \cos\Psi & 0 \\ 0 & 0 & 1 \end{bmatrix} \begin{bmatrix} U_2 \\ V_2 \\ W_2 \end{bmatrix} \qquad (1.33)$$

With a similar orthogonal transformation it is possible to relate U_2, V_2 and W_2 to U_3, V_3 and W_3 (velocity components of $\vec{V}_P$ in $X_3Y_3Z_3$):

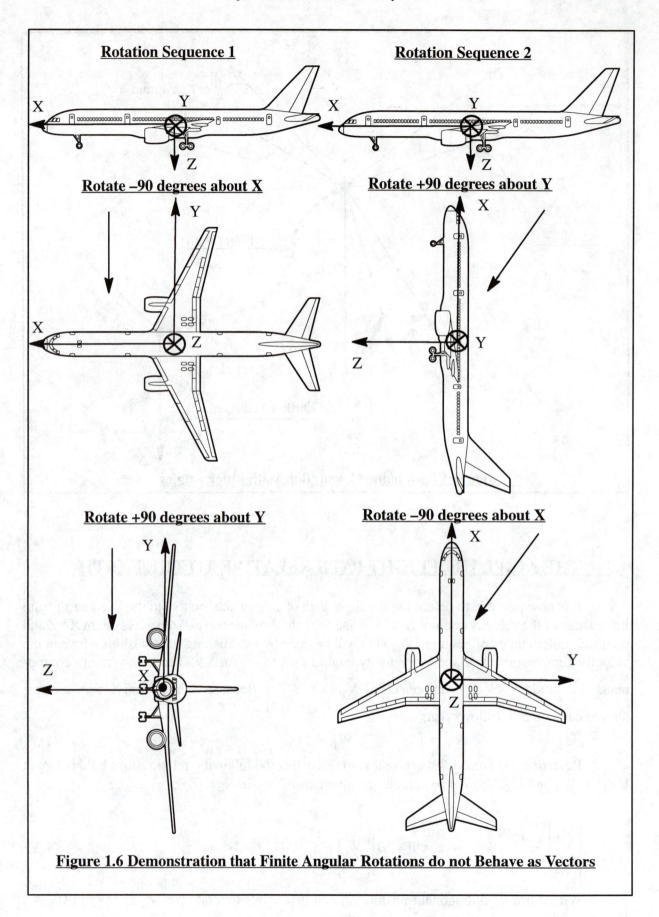

Figure 1.6 Demonstration that Finite Angular Rotations do not Behave as Vectors

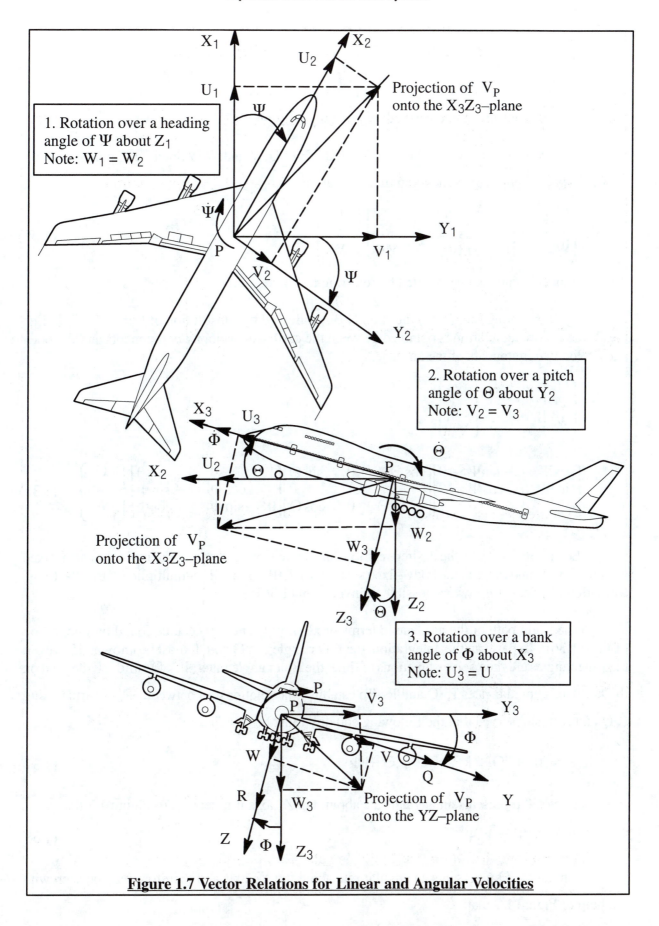

Figure 1.7 Vector Relations for Linear and Angular Velocities

$$\begin{Bmatrix} U_2 \\ V_2 \\ W_2 \end{Bmatrix} = \begin{bmatrix} \cos\Theta & 0 & \sin\Theta \\ 0 & 1 & 0 \\ -\sin\Theta & 0 & \cos\Theta \end{bmatrix} \begin{Bmatrix} U_3 \\ V_3 \\ W_3 \end{Bmatrix} \tag{1.34}$$

Again, this relationship can be verified by referring to Figure 1.7.

Finally, it is possible to relate U_3, V_3 and W_3 to U, V and W (velocity components of $\vec{V}_P$ in XYZ) by the following orthogonal transformation:

$$\begin{Bmatrix} U_3 \\ V_3 \\ W_3 \end{Bmatrix} = \begin{bmatrix} 1 & 0 & 0 \\ 0 & \cos\Phi & -\sin\Phi \\ 0 & \sin\Phi & \cos\Phi \end{bmatrix} \begin{Bmatrix} U \\ V \\ W \end{Bmatrix} \tag{1.35}$$

This relationship can also be verified by referring to Figure 1.7.

By substituting Eqn (1.35) into Eqn (1.34) followed by substitution of Eqn (1.34) into Eqn (1.33) the following relation is obtained between the earth axes velocity components and the body axes velocity components of the airplane:

$$\begin{Bmatrix} U_1 \\ V_1 \\ W_1 \end{Bmatrix} = \begin{Bmatrix} \dot{x}' \\ \dot{y}' \\ \dot{z}' \end{Bmatrix} =$$

$$\begin{bmatrix} \cos\Psi & -\sin\Psi & 0 \\ \sin\Psi & \cos\Psi & 0 \\ 0 & 0 & 1 \end{bmatrix} \begin{bmatrix} \cos\Theta & 0 & \sin\Theta \\ 0 & 1 & 0 \\ -\sin\Theta & 0 & \cos\Theta \end{bmatrix} \begin{bmatrix} 1 & 0 & 0 \\ 0 & \cos\Phi & -\sin\Phi \\ 0 & \sin\Phi & \cos\Phi \end{bmatrix} \begin{Bmatrix} U \\ V \\ W \end{Bmatrix} \tag{1.36}$$

Eqn (1.36) provides the desired relationship between velocity components in the earth–fixed system X'Y'Z' and those in the body–fixed system XYZ. By proper pre–multiplication of the transformation matrices it is always possible to invert Eqn (1.36).

The flight path of the airplane in terms of x'(t), y'(t) and z'(t) can be found by integration of Eqn (1.36). To perform this integration, the Euler angles Ψ, Θ and Φ must be known. However, the Euler angles are themselves functions of time: the Euler angle rates $\dot{\Psi}$, $\dot{\Theta}$ and $\dot{\Phi}$ depend on the body axis angular rates P, Q and R. To establish the relationship between $\dot{\Psi}$, $\dot{\Theta}$ and $\dot{\Phi}$ and P, Q and R it is observed that the following equality must be satisfied:

$$\vec{\omega} = iP + jQ + kR = \vec{\dot{\Psi}} + \vec{\dot{\Theta}} + \vec{\dot{\Phi}} \tag{1.37}$$

Since $\vec{\dot{\Psi}}$ represents an angular rate about the Z_1 axis it is seen from Figure 1.7 that:

$$\vec{\dot{\Psi}} = k_1\dot{\Psi} = k_2\dot{\Psi} \tag{1.38}$$

Similarly, $\vec{\dot{\Theta}}$ represents an angular rate about the Y_2 axis and therefore may be seen with the help of Figure 1.7 that:

$$\vec{\Theta} = j_2 \dot{\Theta} = j_3 \dot{\Theta} \qquad (1.39)$$

Finally, $\vec{\Phi}$ represents an angular rate about the X_3 axis and so it follows from Figure 1.7:

$$\vec{\Phi} = i_3 \dot{\Phi} = i \dot{\Phi} \qquad (1.40)$$

By substitution of Eqns (1.38) – (1.40) into Eqn (1.37) it is seen that:

$$\vec{\omega} = k_2 \dot{\Psi} + j_3 \dot{\Theta} + i \dot{\Phi} \qquad (1.41)$$

By now using transformations similar to those of Eqns (1.34) and (1.35) it can be shown that:

$$k_2 = -i_3 \sin\Theta + k_3 \cos\Theta = -i\sin\Theta + \cos\Theta(j\sin\Phi + k\cos\Phi) \qquad (1.42)$$

From a transformation similar to Eqn (1.35) it can also be shown that:

$$j_3 = j\cos\Phi - k\sin\Phi \qquad (1.43)$$

After substituting Eqns (1.42) and (1.43) into Eqn (1.41) and some re–arrangement it is seen that:

$$\vec{\omega} = i(-\dot{\Psi}\sin\Theta + \dot{\Phi}) + j(\dot{\Psi}\cos\Theta\sin\Phi + \dot{\Theta}\cos\Phi) +$$
$$k(\dot{\Psi}\cos\Theta\cos\Phi - \dot{\Theta}\sin\Phi) \qquad (1.44)$$

Comparison with Eqn (1.37) now yields the so–called airplane ==kinematic equations:==

$$P = \dot{\Phi} - \dot{\Psi}\sin\Theta \qquad (1.45a)$$
$$Q = \dot{\Theta}\cos\Phi + \dot{\Psi}\cos\Theta\sin\Phi \qquad (1.45b)$$
$$R = \dot{\Psi}\cos\Theta\cos\Phi - \dot{\Theta}\sin\Phi \qquad (1.45c)$$

For the flight path integration problem it is desirable to invert these equations to yield:

$$\dot{\Phi} = P + Q\sin\Phi\tan\Theta + R\cos\Phi\tan\Theta \qquad (1.46a)$$
$$\dot{\Theta} = Q\cos\Phi - R\sin\Phi \qquad (1.46b)$$
$$\dot{\Psi} = (Q\sin\Phi + R\cos\Phi)\sec\Theta \qquad (1.46c)$$

The body axis rates P, Q and R are found by integration of the airplane equations of motion: Eqns (1.25). By integrating Equations (1.46) the Euler angles Ψ, Θ and Φ are obtained so that the integration of the flight path equations (1.36) can be completed. The actual integration is performed with numerical analysis methods. Reference 1.5 can be consulted for methods of integrating sets of differential equations.

The following interpretation of Equations (1.45) is important to keep in mind:

(1.45a): Body axis roll rate, P IS NOT THE SAME as rate of change of bank angle, $\vec{\Phi}$.

(1.45b): Body axis pitch rate, Q IS NOT THE SAME as rate of change of pitch attitude angle, $\vec{\Theta}$.

(1.45c): Body axis yaw rate, R IS NOT THE SAME as rate of change of heading angle, $\vec{\Psi}$.

Later, in Chapter 5 it will be shown that in the case of the small perturbation equations of motion (relative to a wings level and horizontal steady state flight path) the approximations:

$$p = \dot{\phi}, \qquad q = \dot{\theta} \text{ and} \qquad r = \dot{\psi} \tag{1.47}$$

are acceptable. The reader should keep in mind the fact that in general these approximations are not correct!

1.6   THE COMPONENTS OF THE GRAVITATIONAL FORCE

The reader is asked to return to Eqns.(1.19) where it is seen that the following three components of the gravitational force appear: mg_x, mg_y and mg_z. By referring to Figure 1.2 the components of gravitational acceleration can be written as follows:

$$\vec{g} = k \cdot g = k_1 g \equiv ig_x + jg_y + kg_z \tag{1.48}$$

These components of gravitational acceleration can be written as functions of the Euler angles by recognizing that: $k_1 = k_2$. Since k_2 was already expressed in terms of i, j and k by Eqn (1.42) it follows that:

$$i(-g\sin\Theta) + j(g\sin\Phi\cos\Theta) + k(g\cos\Phi\cos\Theta) \equiv ig_x + jg_y + kg_z \tag{1.49}$$

From this in turn it is seen that:

$$g_x = -g\sin\Theta \tag{1.50a}$$

$$g_y = g\sin\Phi\cos\Theta \tag{1.50b}$$

$$g_z = g\cos\Phi\cos\Theta \tag{1.50c}$$

The reader should observe that the heading angle Ψ does not appear in Eqns (1.50). The reason for this is the 'flat earth' assumption made in Section 1.1.

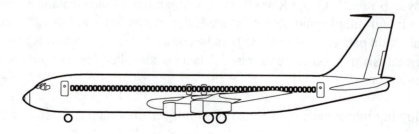

1.7   REVIEW OF THE EQUATIONS OF MOTION

At this point it is useful to review the airplane equations of motion as derived so far. There are three sets of equations:

1. The force equations obtained by substituting Eqns (1.50) into Eqns (1.19).

2. The moment equations as stated in Eqns (1.25). Note that the effect of spinning rotors (Eqns (1.30) has been omitted!

3. The kinematic equations as expressed by Eqns (1.45).

These three sets are repeated here for convenience:

1. For the force equations in the airplane body–fixed axis system XYZ:

Force along X: $m(\dot{U} - VR + WQ) = -mg\sin\Theta + F_{A_x} + F_{T_x}$ (1.51a)

Force along Y: $m(\dot{V} + UR - WP) = mg\sin\Phi\cos\Theta + F_{A_y} + F_{T_y}$ (1.51b)

Force along Z: $m(\dot{W} - UQ + VP) = mg\cos\Phi\cos\Theta + F_{A_z} + F_{T_z}$ (1.51c)

2. For the moment equations in the airplane body–fixed axis system XYZ:

Rolling moment about X: $I_{xx}\dot{P} - I_{xz}\dot{R} - I_{xz}PQ + (I_{zz} - I_{yy})RQ = L_A + L_T$ (1.52a)

Pitching moment about Y: $I_{yy}\dot{Q} + (I_{xx} - I_{zz})PR + I_{xz}(P^2 - R^2) = M_A + M_T$ (1.52b)

Yawing moment about Z: $I_{zz}\dot{R} - I_{xz}\dot{P} + (I_{yy} - I_{xx})PQ + I_{xz}QR = N_A + N_T$ (1.52c)

3. For the kinematic equations:

Roll rate about X: $P = \dot{\Phi} - \dot{\Psi}\sin\Theta$ (1.53a)

Pitch rate about Y: $Q = \dot{\Theta}\cos\Phi + \dot{\Psi}\cos\Theta\sin\Phi$ (1.53b)

Yaw rate about Z: $R = \dot{\Psi}\cos\Theta\cos\Phi - \dot{\Theta}\sin\Phi$ (1.53c)

Equations (1.51) and (1.52) are referred to as the general airplane equations of motion. That is a rather generous description since many assumptions have been made in their derivation. Many of these assumptions serve to reduce the 'generality' of these equations!

Equations (1.51) and (1.52) are as yet incomplete: the aerodynamic and thrust forces and moments in their right hand sides must still be expressed in terms of the motion variables. That will be done in Chapter 3.

From a mathematical viewpoint the equations (1.51), (1.52) and (1.53) form a set of nine differential equations in nine variables: the velocity components U, V and W, the angular rate components P, Q and R and the Euler angles Ψ, Θ and Φ. By a process of elimination of variables it is also possible to think of these equations as a set of six differential equations of motion in six variables: either U, V, W, P, Q and R or U, V, W, Ψ, Θ and Φ.

In either case, general solutions to the equations can be obtained only by numerical integration. However, from an airplane design and from a handling qualities viewpoint there are two special flight conditions for which solutions of these equations are of primary interest:

      1. Steady state flight conditions   2. Perturbed state flight conditions

The remainder of this text is primarily concerned with the study and applications of the 'general' airplane equations of motion to these two sets of flight conditions. Before specializing the equations of motion to these two sets of flight conditions it is useful to state the definition of these flight conditions:

Definition 1: Steady State Flight

A steady state flight condition is defined as one for which ALL motion variables remain constant with time relative to the body–fixed axis system XYZ.

Mathematically speaking, steady state flight implies that:

$$\vec{V}_P = 0 \quad \text{and} \quad \vec{\omega} = 0 \tag{1.54}$$

Equations (1.54) imply that $\vec{V}_P$ and $\vec{\omega}$ are constant with time relative to axis system XYZ. Figure 1.8 illustrates three typical steady state flight conditions.

It should be observed that (strictly speaking) the definition for steady state flight applies only in an atmosphere of constant density. Since in reality the atmospheric density varies with altitude, only flight at constant altitude (Example 2 in Figure 1.8) satisfies the definition of steady state flight. The reason for this is the fact that aerodynamic forces and moments are all proportional to the dynamic pressure: $\bar{q} = \frac{1}{2}\varrho V_P^2$. As the density varies, so do the aerodynamic forces and moments and that in turn would violate Eqn (1.54)!

Pragmatically speaking, as long as the density does not vary by more than about 5% during a 30–60 second time interval it is acceptable to assume that examples 1 and 3 in Figure 1.8 qualify as steady state flight conditions. Figure 1.9 shows that the flight path angles for which the steady state assumption applies are not very steep!

Definition 2: Perturbed State Flight

A perturbed state flight condition is defined as one for which ALL motion variables are defined relative to a known steady state flight condition.

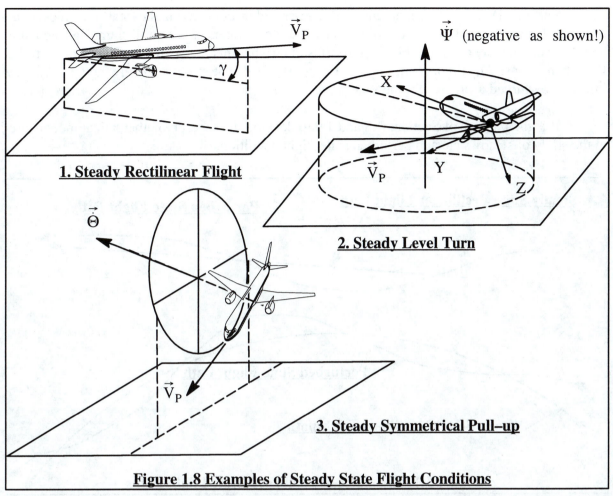

Figure 1.8 Examples of Steady State Flight Conditions

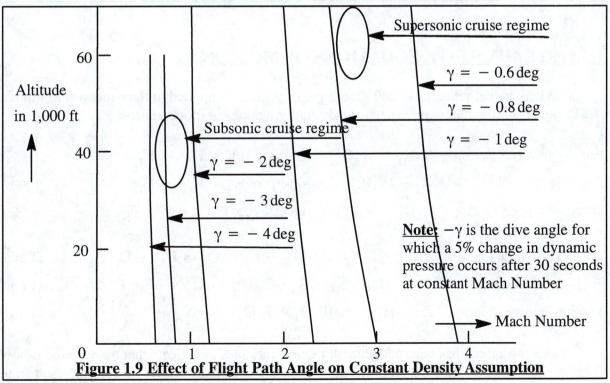

Figure 1.9 Effect of Flight Path Angle on Constant Density Assumption

Perturbed state flight is mathematically described by considering the total state of each motion variable to be equal to the sum of a steady state (or reference, or equilibrium flight) quantity and a perturbed state quantity. Figure 1.10 illustrates what this means for two types of perturbed flight conditions. Any flight condition which is not steady can be mathematically thought of as having been perturbed away from some steady state.

It is the purpose of Sections 1.8 and 1.9 to develop the specific mathematical models used in the study of steady state and perturbed state flight conditions.

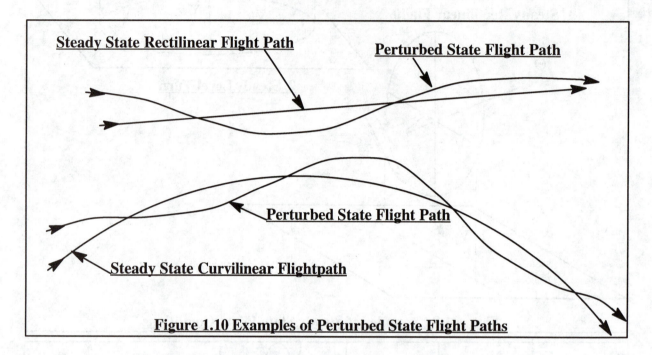

Steady State Rectilinear Flight Path

Perturbed State Flight Path

Perturbed State Flight Path

Steady State Curvilinear Flightpath

Figure 1.10 Examples of Perturbed State Flight Paths

1.8   STEADY STATE EQUATIONS OF MOTION

When the definition of steady state flight of page 22 is applied to the equations of motion (1.51) and (1.52) the following general steady state equations of motion ensue:

Force along X: $\quad m(-V_1 R_1 + W_1 Q_1) = -mg\sin\Theta_1 + F_{A_{x_1}} + F_{T_{x_1}}$ $\qquad$ (1.55a)

Force along Y: $\quad m(U_1 R_1 - W_1 P_1) = mg\sin\Phi_1\cos\Theta_1 + F_{A_{y_1}} + F_{T_{y_1}}$ $\qquad$ (1.55b)

Force along Z: $\quad m(-U_1 Q_1 + V_1 P_1) = mg\cos\Phi_1\cos\Theta_1 + F_{A_{z_1}} + F_{T_{z_1}}$ $\qquad$ (1.55c)

Rolling moment about X: $\quad -I_{xz}P_1 Q_1 + (I_{zz} - I_{yy})R_1 Q_1 = L_{A_1} + L_{T_1}$ $\qquad$ (1.56a)

Pitching moment about Y: $\quad (I_{xx} - I_{zz})P_1 R_1 + I_{xz}(P_1^2 - R_1^2) = M_{A_1} + M_{T_1}$ $\qquad$ (1.56b)

Yawing moment about Z: $\quad (I_{yy} - I_{xx})P_1 Q_1 + I_{xz}Q_1 R_1 = N_{A_1} + N_{T_1}$ $\qquad$ (1.56c)

The subscript 1 has been added to all motion variables to indicate that the variable is now a steady state variable. This notation will be consistently used unless no confusion can result from dropping the subscript. Since the kinematic equations (1.53) do not contain any accelerations they remain unchanged except for the addition of the subscript 1:

Roll rate about X : $\quad P_1 = \dot{\Phi}_1 - \dot{\Psi}_1 \sin \Theta_1$ $\hfill$ (1.57a)

Pitch rate about Y : $\quad Q_1 = \dot{\Theta}_1 \cos \Phi_1 + \dot{\Psi}_1 \cos \Theta_1 \sin \Phi_1$ $\hfill$ (1.57b)

Yaw rate about Z : $\quad R_1 = \dot{\Psi}_1 \cos \Theta_1 \cos \Phi_1 - \dot{\Theta}_1 \sin \Phi_1$ $\hfill$ (1.57c)

The three steady state flight cases depicted in Figure 1.8 are of special interest:

Case 1) Steady state rectilinear flight (straight line flight)

Case 2) Steady state turning flight (steady level turn)

Case 3) Steady symmetrical pull–up

For each of these types of steady state flight conditions the general equations of steady state motion, Eqns (1.55) through (1.57) take on special forms. These special forms will now be derived. A detailed discussion of the application of these forms to the problems of steady state controllability is presented in Chapter 4.

1.8.1 CASE 1: EQUATIONS OF MOTION FOR STEADY STATE RECTILINEAR FLIGHT

Steady state rectilinear flight as suggested by Figure 1.8 is characterized by the following condition: $\vec{\omega} = 0$ which in turn implies that: $P_1 = Q_1 = R_1 = 0$. Therefore, the kinematic equations (1.57) become trivial and the force and moment equations are:

Force along X : $\quad 0 = -mg \sin \Theta_1 + F_{A_{x_1}} + F_{T_{x_1}}$ $\hfill$ (1.58a)

Force along Y : $\quad 0 = mg \sin \Phi_1 \cos \Theta_1 + F_{A_{y_1}} + F_{T_{y_1}}$ $\hfill$ (1.58b)

Force along Z : $\quad 0 = mg \cos \Phi_1 \cos \Theta_1 + F_{A_{z_1}} + F_{T_{z_1}}$ $\hfill$ (1.58c)

Rolling moment about X : $\quad 0 = L_{A_1} + L_{T_1}$ $\hfill$ (1.59a)

Pitching moment about Y : $\quad 0 = M_{A_1} + M_{T_1}$ $\hfill$ (1.59b)

Yawing moment about Z : $\quad 0 = N_{A_1} + N_{T_1}$ $\hfill$ (1.59c)

Equations (1.58) and (1.59) form the basis for studying airplane controllability problems in the following flight conditions:

* Cruise $\qquad\qquad\qquad$ * Engine(s) inoperative flight
* Shallow climbs, dives and glides $\qquad$ * Steady state flight with certain failed systems

Applications are discussed in Chapter 4.

1.8.2 CASE 2: EQUATIONS OF MOTION FOR STEADY STATE, LEVEL TURNING FLIGHT

Steady state turning flight is characterized by the fact that $\vec{\omega}$ is vertical in the earth–fixed X'Y'Z' axis system. From Figure 1.8, Case 2 it follows that:

$$\vec{\omega} = k'\dot{\Psi} = k_1\dot{\Psi} \tag{1.60}$$

Evidently, in a steady level turn only the heading angle, Ψ changes while the pitch attitude angle, Θ and the bank angle Φ remain constant. The kinematic equations (1.57) therefore become:

Roll rate about X: $\quad P_1 = -\dot{\Psi}_1 \sin\Theta_1$ \hfill (1.61a)

Pitch rate about Y: $\quad Q_1 = \dot{\Psi}_1 \cos\Theta_1 \sin\Phi_1$ \hfill (1.61b)

Yaw rate about Z: $\quad R_1 = \dot{\Psi}_1 \cos\Theta_1 \cos\Phi_1$ \hfill (1.61c)

The airplane force and moment equations of motion remain as stated in Eqns (1.55) and (1.56) respectively. Equations (1.55), (1.56) and (1.61) are used to study airplane controllability problems in the following conditions:

* Steady turning flight with all engines operating
* Steady turning flight with one or more engines inoperative
* Ability to maintain steady state turning flight with certain failed systems

Applications are discussed in Chapter 4.

1.8.3 CASE 3: EQUATIONS OF MOTION FOR STEADY SYMMETRICAL PULL–UP

Referring to Figure 1.8, Case 3 it is seen that for a steady, symmetrical pull–up maneuver the following conditions apply:

$$\vec{\omega} = k\dot{\Theta}, \quad V_1 = P_1 = R_1 = 0 \quad \text{and} \quad \Phi_1 = 0 \tag{1.62}$$

The only non–zero rotational velocity component is therefore the pitch rate, Q_1. The force and moment equations of motion (1.55) and (1.56) therefore become:

Force along X: $\quad mW_1 Q_1 = -mg\sin\Theta_1 + F_{A_{x_1}} + F_{T_{x_1}}$ \hfill (1.63a)

Force along Y: $\quad 0 = F_{A_{y_1}} + F_{T_{y_1}}$ \hfill (1.63b)

Force along Z: $\quad -mU_1 Q_1 = mg\cos\Theta_1 + F_{A_{z_1}} + F_{T_{z_1}}$ \hfill (1.63c)

Rolling moment about X: $\quad 0 = L_{A_1} + L_{T_1}$ \hfill (1.64a)

Pitching moment about Y: $\quad 0 = M_{A_1} + M_{T_1}$ \hfill (1.64b)

Yawing moment about Z: $\quad 0 = N_{A_1} + N_{T_1}$ \hfill (1.64c)

The kinematic equations (1.57) reduce to:

$$Q_1 = \dot{\Theta} \tag{1.65}$$

Equations (1.63), (1.64) and (1.65) are used to study airplane controllability problems in the following conditions:

* Symmetrical pull–up flight with all engines operating
* Symmetrical pull–up flight with one or more engines inoperative
* Ability to perform pull–up flight with certain failed systems

Applications are discussed in Chapter 4.

1.9   PERTURBED STATE EQUATIONS OF MOTION

According to the definition of perturbed state flight (page 22) the following substitutions are applied to all motion variables and to all forces and moments:

Motion Variables:

$$U = U_1 + u \qquad V = V_1 + v \qquad W = W_1 + w \tag{1.66a}$$

$$P = P_1 + p \qquad Q = Q_1 + q \qquad R = R_1 + r \tag{1.66b}$$

$$\Psi = \Psi_1 + \psi \qquad \Theta = \Theta_1 + \theta \qquad \Phi = \Phi_1 + \phi \tag{1.66c}$$

Forces:

$$F_{A_x} = F_{A_{x_1}} + f_{A_x} \qquad F_{A_y} = F_{A_{y_1}} + f_{A_y} \qquad F_{A_z} = F_{A_{z_1}} + f_{A_z} \tag{1.67a}$$

$$F_{T_x} = F_{T_{x_1}} + f_{T_x} \qquad F_{T_y} = F_{T_{y_1}} + f_{T_y} \qquad F_{T_z} = F_{T_{z_1}} + f_{T_z} \tag{1.67b}$$

Moments:

$$L_A = L_{A_1} + l_A \qquad M_A = M_{A_1} + m_A \qquad N_A = N_{A_1} + n_A \tag{1.68a}$$

$$L_T = L_{T_1} + l_T \qquad M_T = M_{T_1} + m_T \qquad N_T = N_{T_1} + n_T \tag{1.68b}$$

These substitutions are referred to as the **'Perturbation Substitutions'**. At this stage, the magnitude of these perturbations is quite arbitrary! Carrying out these perturbation substitutions into the general airplane equations of motion (1.51) and (1.52) results in:

$$\text{Force along } X: \ m[\dot{u} - (V_1 + v)(R_1 + r) + (W_1 + w)(Q_1 + q)] =$$
$$- mg\sin(\Theta_1 + \theta) + F_{A_{x_1}} + f_{A_x} + F_{T_{x_1}} + f_{T_x} \tag{1.69a}$$

$$\text{Force along } Y: \ m[\dot{v} + (U_1 + u)(R_1 + r) - (W_1 + w)(P_1 + p)] =$$
$$mg\sin(\Phi_1 + \phi)\cos(\Theta_1 + \theta) + F_{A_{y_1}} + f_{A_y} + F_{T_{y_1}} + f_{T_y} \tag{1.69b}$$

$$\text{Force along } Z: \ m[\dot{w} - (U_1 + u)(Q_1 + q) + (V_1 + v)(P_1 + p)] =$$
$$mg\cos(\Phi_1 + \phi)\cos(\Theta_1 + \theta) + F_{A_{z_1}} + f_{A_z} + F_{T_{z_1}} + f_{T_z} \tag{1.69c}$$

Moment about X: $I_{xx}\dot{p} - I_{xz}\dot{r} - I_{xz}(P_1 + p)(Q_1 + q) + (I_{zz} - I_{yy})(R_1 + r)(Q_1 + q) =$

$$L_{A_1} + l_A + L_{T_1} + l_T \tag{1.70a}$$

Moment about Y: $I_{yy}\dot{q} + (I_{xx} - I_{zz})(P_1 + p)(R_1 + r) + I_{xz}[(P_1 + p)^2 - (R_1 + r)^2] =$

$$M_{A_1} + m_A + M_{T_1} + m_T \tag{1.70b}$$

Moment about Z: $I_{zz}\dot{r} - I_{xz}\dot{p} + (I_{yy} - I_{xx})(P_1 + p)(Q_1 + q) + I_{xz}(Q_1 + q)(R_1 + r) =$

$$N_{A_1} + n_A + N_{T_1} + n_T \tag{1.70c}$$

To allow for a simple expansion of the trigonometric quantities in Eqns (1.69) the first restriction to the allowable magnitude of the motion perturbations is now introduced. The perturbation values of θ and ϕ are selected un such a way that the following approximations apply:

$$\cos\theta = \cos\phi \approx 1.0 \qquad \sin\theta \approx \theta \qquad \sin\phi \approx \phi \tag{1.71}$$

These approximations give quite acceptable results even for perturbed angles as large as 15 degrees. With these approximations it can be shown that the following expansions for the trigonometric quantities in Eqns (1.69) can be used:

$$\sin(\Theta_1 + \theta) \approx \sin\Theta_1 + \theta\cos\Theta_1 \tag{1.72a}$$

$$\sin(\Phi_1 + \phi)\cos(\Theta_1 + \theta) \approx$$

$$\sin\Phi_1\cos\Theta_1 - \theta\sin\Phi_1\sin\Theta_1 + \phi\cos\Phi_1\cos\Theta_1 - \phi\theta\cos\Phi_1\sin\Theta_1 \tag{1.72b}$$

$$\cos(\Phi_1 + \phi)\cos(\Theta_1 + \theta) \approx$$

$$\cos\Phi_1\cos\Theta_1 - \theta\cos\Phi_1\sin\Theta_1 - \phi\sin\Phi_1\cos\Theta_1 + \phi\theta\sin\Phi_1\sin\Theta_1 \tag{1.72c}$$

By expanding equations (1.69) and (1.70) while utilizing the approximations (1.72) the force and moment equations take on the form shown in Table 1.3: Eqns (1.73) and (1.74).

Observe that the **thin** underlined terms in Table 1.3 represent the general steady state equations of motion (1.55) and (1.56). Since the steady state equations of motion are assumed to be inherently satisfied they can be eliminated from Table 1.3 without loss of generality.

Observe that the **fat** underlined terms in Table 1.3 all contain products or cross products of perturbed motion variables. These terms are also referred to as non–linear terms. At this point the so–called **small perturbation assumption** will be made: the non–linear terms will be assumed to

Table 1.3 Perturbed Equations of Motion

Force along X:

$$m(-V_1R_1 + W_1Q_1) + m(\dot{u} - V_1r - R_1v + W_1q + Q_1w) + m(-vr + wq) =$$

$$-mg\sin\Theta_1 + F_{A_{x_1}} + F_{T_{x_1}} - mg\theta\cos\Theta_1 + f_{A_x} + f_{T_x} \qquad (1.73a)$$

Force along Y:

$$m(U_1R_1 - W_1P_1) + m(\dot{v} + U_1r + R_1u - W_1p - P_1w) + m(ur - wp) = mg\sin\Phi_1\cos\Theta_1 +$$

$$F_{A_{y_1}} + F_{T_{y_1}} - mg\theta\sin\Phi_1\sin\Theta_1 + mg\phi\cos\Phi_1\cos\Theta_1 + f_{A_y} + f_{T_y} - mg\phi\theta\cos\Phi_1\sin\Theta_1 \quad (1.73b)$$

Force along Z:

$$m(-U_1Q_1 + V_1P_1) + m(\dot{w} - U_1q - Q_1u + V_1p + P_1v) + m(-uq + vp) = mg\cos\Phi_1\cos\Theta_1 +$$

$$F_{A_{z_1}} + F_{T_{z_1}} - mg\theta\cos\Phi_1\sin\Theta_1 - mg\phi\sin\Phi_1\cos\Theta_1 + f_{A_z} + f_{T_z} + mg\phi\theta\sin\Phi_1\sin\Theta_1 \quad (1.73c)$$

Moment about X:

$$-I_{xz}P_1Q_1 + (I_{zz} - I_{yy})R_1Q_1 + I_{xx}\dot{p} - I_{xz}\dot{r} - I_{xz}(P_1q + Q_1p) + (I_{zz} - I_{yy})(R_1q + Q_1r) +$$

$$-I_{xz}pq + (I_{zz} - I_{yy})rq = L_{A_1} + L_{T_1} + l_A + l_T \qquad (1.74a)$$

Moment about Y:

$$(I_{xx} - I_{zz})P_1R_1 + I_{xz}(P_1^2 - R_1^2) + I_{yy}\dot{q} + (I_{xx} - I_{zz})(P_1r + R_1p) + I_{xz}(2P_1p - 2R_1r) +$$

$$(I_{xx} - I_{zz})pr + I_{xz}(p^2 - r^2) = M_{A_1} + M_{T_1} + m_A + m_T \qquad (1.74b)$$

Moment about Z:

$$(I_{yy} - I_{xx})P_1Q_1 + I_{xz}Q_1R_1 + I_{zz}\dot{r} - I_{xz}\dot{p} + (I_{yy} - I_{xx})(P_1q + Q_1p) + I_{xz}(Q_1r + R_1q) +$$

$$(I_{yy} - I_{xx})pq + I_{xz}qr = N_{A_1} + N_{T_1} + n_A + n_T \qquad (1.74c)$$

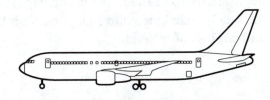

be negligible compared with the linear terms. Therefore the fat underlined terms in Table 1.3 will also be dropped. The result is Eqns (1.75) and (1.76):

$$m(\dot{u} - V_1r - R_1v + W_1q + Q_1w) = -mg\theta\cos\Theta_1 + f_{A_x} + f_{T_x} \tag{1.75a}$$

$$m(\dot{v} + U_1r + R_1u - W_1p - P_1w) = -mg\theta\sin\Phi_1\sin\Theta_1 +$$
$$mg\phi\cos\Phi_1\cos\Theta_1 + f_{A_y} + f_{T_y} \tag{1.75b}$$

$$m(\dot{w} - U_1q - Q_1u + V_1p + P_1v) = -mg\theta\cos\Phi_1\sin\Theta_1 +$$
$$- mg\phi\sin\Phi_1\cos\Theta_1 + f_{A_z} + f_{T_z} \tag{1.75c}$$

$$I_{xx}\dot{p} - I_{xz}\dot{r} - I_{xz}(P_1q + Q_1p) + (I_{zz} - I_{yy})(R_1q + Q_1r) = l_A + l_T \tag{1.76a}$$

$$I_{yy}\dot{q} + (I_{xx} - I_{zz})(P_1r + R_1p) + I_{xz}(2P_1p - 2R_1r) = m_A + m_T \tag{1.76b}$$

$$I_{zz}\dot{r} - I_{xz}\dot{p} + (I_{yy} - I_{xx})(P_1q + Q_1p) + I_{xz}(Q_1r + R_1q) = n_A + n_T \tag{1.76c}$$

The reader should realize that the small perturbation assumption limits the validity of Equations (1.75) and (1.76) to small perturbations only! Because airplanes are supposed to fly with as much comfort to the passengers as possible (very small perturbations!) this assumption is not very restrictive from a pragmatic viewpoint. Even fighter and attack airplanes operate mostly under conditions where small perturbations are desired: ordnance delivery accuracy partly depends on that! Exceptions to this behavior are when airplanes are intentionally maneuvered to the edge of their flight envelope and/or airplanes which are encountering gust upsets.

The perturbation substitution must also be made in the kinematic equations (1.45). Doing so results in:

$$P_1 + p = (\dot{\Phi}_1 + \dot{\phi}) - (\dot{\Psi}_1 + \dot{\psi})\sin(\Theta_1 + \theta) \tag{1.77a}$$

$$Q_1 + q = (\dot{\Theta}_1 + \dot{\theta})\cos(\Phi_1 + \phi) + (\dot{\Psi}_1 + \dot{\psi})\cos(\Theta_1 + \theta)\sin(\Phi_1 + \phi) \tag{1.77b}$$

$$R_1 + r = (\dot{\Psi}_1 + \dot{\psi})\cos(\Theta_1 + \theta)\cos(\Phi_1 + \phi) - (\dot{\Theta}_1 + \dot{\theta})\sin(\Phi_1 + \phi) \tag{1.77c}$$

When these equations are expanded the equations of Table 1.4 are obtained.

Observe that the **thin** underlined terms in Table 1.4 represent the steady state kinematic equations of motion (1.57). Since the steady state kinematic equations are inherently satisfied they can be eliminated from Table 1.4 without loss of generality.

Table 1.4 Perturbed Kinematic Equations

$$P_1 + p = \dot{\Phi}_1 + \dot{\phi} - \dot{\Psi}_1 \sin\Theta_1 - \dot{\Psi}_1\theta\cos\Theta_1 - \dot{\psi}\sin\Theta_1 - \dot{\psi}\theta\cos\Theta_1 \qquad (1.78a)$$

$$Q_1 + q = \dot{\Theta}_1\cos\Phi_1 - \dot{\Theta}_1\phi\sin\Phi_1 + \dot{\theta}\cos\Phi_1 - \dot{\theta}\phi\sin\Phi_1 + \dot{\Psi}_1\cos\Theta_1\sin\Phi_1 +$$
$$\dot{\Psi}_1\phi\cos\Theta_1\cos\Phi_1 - \dot{\Psi}_1\theta\sin\Theta_1\sin\Phi_1 - \dot{\Psi}_1\theta\phi\sin\Theta_1\cos\Phi_1 + \dot{\psi}\cos\Theta_1\sin\Phi_1 +$$
$$\dot{\psi}\phi\cos\Theta_1\cos\Phi_1 - \dot{\psi}\theta\sin\Theta_1\sin\Phi_1 - \dot{\psi}\theta\phi\sin\Theta_1\cos\Phi_1 \qquad (1.78b)$$

$$R_1 + r = \dot{\Psi}_1\cos\Theta_1\cos\Phi_1 - \dot{\Psi}_1\phi\cos\Theta_1\sin\Phi_1 - \dot{\Psi}_1\theta\sin\Theta_1\cos\Phi_1 - \dot{\Psi}_1\theta\phi\sin\Theta_1\sin\Phi_1 +$$
$$\dot{\psi}\cos\Theta_1\cos\Phi_1 - \dot{\psi}\phi\cos\Theta_1\sin\Phi_1 - \dot{\psi}\theta\sin\Theta_1\cos\Phi_1 + \dot{\psi}\theta\phi\sin\Theta_1\sin\Phi_1 -$$
$$\dot{\Theta}_1\sin\Phi_1 - \dot{\Theta}_1\phi\cos\Phi_1 - \dot{\theta}\sin\Phi_1 - \dot{\theta}\phi\cos\Phi_1 \qquad (1.78c)$$

Observe that the **fat** underlined terms in Table 1.4 all contain products or cross products of perturbed Euler angles or rates. These terms are also referred to as non–linear terms. At this point the so–called **small perturbation assumption** will be made: the non–linear terms will be assumed to be negligible compared with the linear terms. Therefore the fat underlined terms in Table 1.4 will also be dropped. The result is Eqns (1.79):

$$p = \dot{\phi} - \dot{\Psi}_1\theta\cos\Theta_1 - \dot{\psi}\sin\Theta_1 \qquad (1.79a)$$

$$q = -\dot{\Theta}_1\phi\sin\Phi_1 + \dot{\theta}\cos\Phi_1 + \dot{\Psi}_1\phi\cos\Theta_1\cos\Phi_1 +$$
$$- \dot{\Psi}_1\theta\sin\Theta_1\sin\Phi_1 + \dot{\psi}\cos\Theta_1\sin\Phi_1 \qquad (1.79b)$$

$$r = -\dot{\Psi}_1\phi\cos\Theta_1\sin\Phi_1 - \dot{\Psi}_1\theta\sin\Theta_1\cos\Phi_1 + \dot{\psi}\cos\Theta_1\cos\Phi_1 +$$
$$- \dot{\Theta}_1\phi\cos\Phi_1 - \dot{\theta}\sin\Phi_1 \qquad (1.79c)$$

The combined equations (1.75), (1.76) and (1.79) are the nine perturbed equations of motion relative to a very general steady state: i.e. one for which all motion variables are allowed to have non–zero steady state values. It turns out that the majority of airplane dynamic stability problems are concerned with perturbed motions relative to a wings level, steady state, straight line flight condition with a relatively small flight path angle. For such a steady state the following conditions hold:

a) no initial steady state side velocity exists: $V_1 = 0$ $\qquad (1.80)$
b) no initial bank angle exists: $\Phi_1 = 0$ $\qquad (1.80)$
c) no initial angular velocities exist: $P_1 = Q_1 = R_1 = \dot{\Psi}_1 = \dot{\Theta}_1 = \dot{\Phi}_1 = 0$ $\qquad (1.80)$

When the special steady state conditions (1.80) are introduced into Eqns (1.75), (1.76) and (1.79) these equations become:

$$m(\dot{u} + W_1 q) = - mg\theta \cos \Theta_1 + f_{A_x} + f_{T_x} \quad \text{Drag-Force} \tag{1.81a}$$

$$m(\dot{v} + U_1 r - W_1 p) = mg\phi \cos \Theta_1 + f_{A_y} + f_{T_y} \quad \text{Side-Force} \tag{1.81b}$$

$$m(\dot{w} - U_1 q) = - mg\theta \sin \Theta_1 + f_{A_z} + f_{T_z} \quad \text{Lift-Force} \tag{1.81c}$$

$$I_{xx}\dot{p} - I_{xz}\dot{r} = l_A + l_T \quad \text{Roll Moments} \tag{1.82a}$$

$$I_{yy}\dot{q} = m_A + m_T \quad \text{Pitch Moments} \tag{1.82b}$$

$$I_{zz}\dot{r} - I_{xz}\dot{p} = n_A + n_T \quad \text{Yaw Moments} \tag{1.82c}$$

$$p = \dot{\phi} - \dot{\psi} \sin \Theta_1 \quad \text{Roll Rate} \tag{1.83a}$$

$$q = \dot{\theta} \quad \text{Pitch Rate} \tag{1.83b}$$

$$r = \dot{\psi} \cos \Theta_1 \quad \text{Yaw Rate} \tag{1.83c}$$

Equations (1.81), (1.82) and (1.83) form the basis for the airplane dynamic stability and response discussion presented in Chapter 5. They also form the basis for the discussion of automatic flight control theory and applications which are presented in Chapter 8.

1.10 SUMMARY FOR CHAPTER 1

In this chapter the airplane equations of motion were developed by applying the Newtonian principles of conservation of linear and angular momentum. The equations were written for a body–fixed axis system, XYZ which moves with the airplane and which has its origin at the airplane center of mass. First, the equations were written in a general vector–integral format: Eqns (1.14) and (1.17). Second, these equations were expanded into a scalar format to yield Eqns (1.19) and (1.25).

To account for the motion of the airplane relative to an earth–fixed coordinate system X'Y'Z' the so–called Euler angles were introduced: Ψ for heading, Θ for pitch attitude and Φ for bank angle. A relationship was developed which relates the velocity components in the airplane body–fixed axis system XYZ to those in the earth–fixed axis system X'Y'Z': Eqns (1.36). These equations are used to solve navigational problems. The Euler angles were also used to find expressions for the components of gravitational acceleration along the airplane body–fixed axes. This resulted in the six general equations of motion: (1.51) and (1.52).

By relating the Euler angle rates to the airplane body axis rates the so–called airplane kinematic equations were obtained: (1.53).

The equations of motion were next specialized to cope with two sets of flight conditions: Equations (1.55) through (1.57) for steady state and Equations (1.81) through (1.83) for perturbed state flight conditions.

Before solutions of the various equations of motion can be discussed and interpreted it is necessary to express the aerodynamic and thrust forces and moments in terms of pertinent motion variables. In Chapter 2, a review is presented of important aerodynamic effects which are used in obtaining such relations. Expressions relating the aerodynamic forces and moments to the pertinent motion variables are developed in Chapter 3.

1.11 PROBLEMS FOR CHAPTER 1

1.1   The following sketch shows a moving mass inside a cargo airplane. The mass, m_{pl} moves along the airplane X–axis with constant velocity $\partial \vec{r}_1 / \partial t$ (no friction). The total mass of the airplane is now: $m = \displaystyle\int_v \varrho_A dv + m_{pl}$. Rewrite equations (1.1) and (1.2) to account for the effect of this moving payload mass.

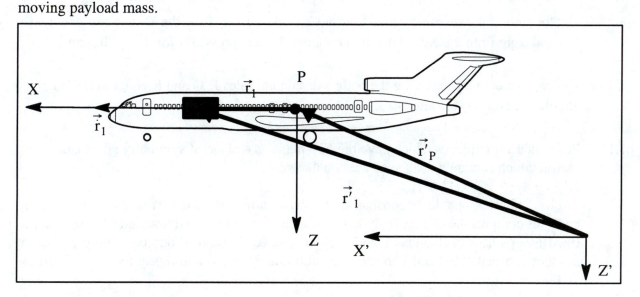

1.2   Carry out the operations needed to demonstrate that Equation (1.12) is correct.

1.3   Carry out the operations needed to demonstrate that Equations (1.19) are correct.

1.4   To what form do Eqns.(1.19) and (1.25) reduce if the airplane is not rotating? ($\vec{\omega} = 0$)

1.5   To what form do Equations (1.19) and (1.25) reduce if the airplane is restrained to move only in a vertical plane?

1.6   Rederive Equations (1.10) and (1.12) for the situation defined in Problem 1.1.

1.7   This problem assumes that Part V of Reference 1.3 is available. Use the radius of gyration method to predict the moments of inertia I_{xx} , I_{yy} and I_{zz} for the following airplanes: Boeing 737–100 and Boeing 737–400; McDonnell–Douglas DC–10–30 and MD–11;

Cessna 208 and the Piaggio P–180. Use the appropriate issue of Jane's All the World Aircraft (McGraw–Hill publication) to find three–views of these airplanes.

1.8   Show step–by–step that Equations (1.25) are correct.

1.9   Rewrite Equations (1.19) and (1.25) for a bullet.

1.10   Consider two imaginary airplanes which have the same weight. One looks like a Vickers VC–10, the other looks like a Convair 880. State why and how their moments of inertia I_{xx} , I_{yy} and I_{zz} differ.

1.11   Using some sketches, explain how rolling and yawing moments due to thrust can arise on airplanes configured like a Boeing 767 and like a Fokker F–50 after one engine has failed.

1.12   An airplane has two jet engines, each with a positive angular momentum of $I_R \omega_R$. Assume that the rotor spin axes are oriented at an angle 30 degrees up from the X–axis and 20 degrees left and right from the XZ–plane of symmetry. Find expressions for h_x , h_y and h_z .

1.13   Under what circumstances are the body axis angular rates P, Q and R equal to the Euler angular rates $\dot{\Psi}$, $\dot{\Theta}$ and $\dot{\Phi}$?

1.14   Prove that for airplanes which have the XZ–plane as a plane of symmetry all products of inertia which contain a distance y are equal to zero.

1.15   To check how reasonable the constant air density assumption is for use in stability and control analyses compute the change in dynamic pressure for a 60 second time interval for straight line flight paths with flight path angles of –0.5, –1.0, –2.0 and –4 degrees. Keep the Mach number constant at 0.8 and start the calculations at 35,000 ft and repeat them for a start at 70,000 ft.

1.12 REFERENCES FOR CHAPTER 1

1.1   Goldstein, H; Classical Mechanics; Addison–Wesley; 1959.

1.2   Landau, L.D. and Lifshitz, E.M.; Mechanics; Pergamon Press; 1960.

1.3   Roskam, J.; Airplane Design, Parts I through VIII; Roskam Aviation and Engineering Corporation, 2550 Riley Road, Ottawa, Kansas, 66067, USA; 1990.

1.4   Rolfe, J.M. and Staples, K.J.; Flight Simulation; Cambridge University Press; 1988.

1.5   Todd, J.; A Survey of Numerical Analysis; McGraw Hill Book Co., Inc., N.Y.; 1962.

CHAPTER 2:   REVIEW OF AERODYNAMIC FUNDAMENTALS

In this chapter a review is presented of those aerodynamic fundamentals which are important in understanding aircraft stability and control concepts. The assumption is made that the reader is reasonably familiar with fundamental aerodynamic theory such as discussed in Reference 2.1.

2.1   DEFINITION OF AIRFOIL PARAMETERS

The following geometric airfoil parameters have been found to be important in affecting aerodynamic characteristics of airfoils:

1) maximum thickness ratio, $(t/c)_{max}$

2) shape of the mean line (also referred to as camber). If the mean line is a straight line, the airfoil is said to be symmetrical.

3) leading edge shape or Δy parameter and leading edge radius (l.e.r.)

4) trailing edge angle, ϕ_{TE}

Figure 2.1 provides a geometric interpretation for these parameters.

The reader should consult Reference 2.2 for a detailed discussion of airfoil parameters and airfoil characteristics. Reference 2.2 also contains a large body of experimental data on a variety of NACA (National Advisory Committee on Aeronautics, predecessor of NASA, the National Aeronautics and Space Administration) airfoils. In addition, this reference contains explanations for the numerical designations used with NACA airfoils.

2.2   AIRFOIL AERODYNAMIC CHARACTERISTICS

Part VI of Reference 2.3 may be consulted for rapid empirical methods used to predict section lift, drag and pitching moment characteristics from the basic geometric parameters seen in Figure 2.1.

Figure 2.2 shows a typical graphical representation of those airfoil characteristics which are of prime importance in the analysis of airplane stability and control properties. Table 2.1 summarizes the principal effect of the geometric parameters of Figure 2.1 on the aerodynamic characteristics of Figure 2.2.

Because lifting surfaces (such as wings, tails, canards and pylons) can be thought of as spanwise arrangements of airfoils, the basic characteristics of airfoils have a major effect on the behavior of lifting surfaces. It is therefore important to be aware of those airfoil characteristics which have the potential of being 'driving' factors in airplane stability and control.

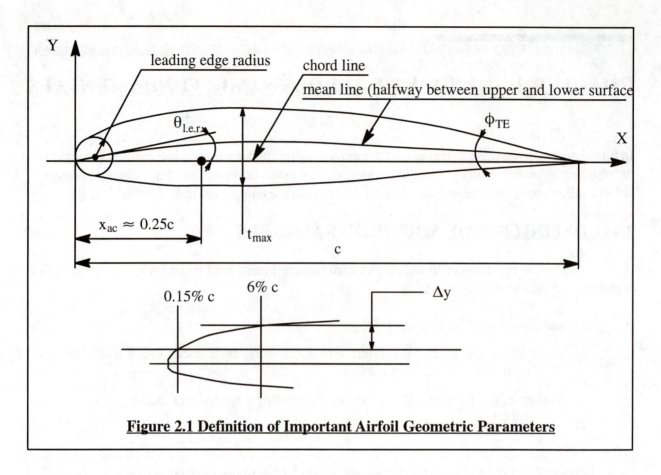

Figure 2.1 Definition of Important Airfoil Geometric Parameters

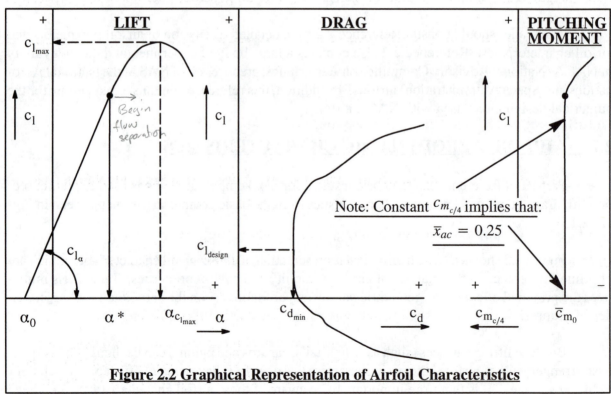

Figure 2.2 Graphical Representation of Airfoil Characteristics

Table 2.1 Summary of Principal Effects of Geometric Airfoil Parameters on Aerodynamic characteristics of Airfoils

Geometric Airfoil Parameter	Principal Effect on Aerodynamic Characteristics other than Drag
Maximum Thickness ratio, t/c_{max} *best usually ~14-15%*	Maximum lift coefficient, $c_{l_{max}}$ Aerodynamic center, $\overline{x}_{ac} = \dfrac{x_{ac}}{c}$
Shape of the mean line	Zero lift angle of attack, α_0 Maximum lift coefficient, $c_{l_{max}}$ Pitching moment coefficient at zero lift coefficient, $\overline{c}_{m_0}$
Leading edge radius, l.e.r. and leading edge shape parameter, Δy	Maximum lift coefficient, $c_{l_{max}}$ and end of the linear angle of attack range, $\alpha *$
Trailing edge angle, ϕ_{TE}	Aerodynamic center, $\overline{x}_{ac} = \dfrac{x_{ac}}{c}$

Note: References 2.2 and Part VI of 2.3 should be consulted for theoretical, empirical and experimental details.

The following airfoil (two–dimensional) properties of Figure 2.2 will have a significant effect on their lifting surface (three–dimensional) counterparts.

In Lift:
* angle of attack for zero lift: α_0
* lift curve slope: c_{l_α}
* maximum lift coefficient: $c_{l_{max}}$ (function of Reynolds Number, R_N)
* angle of attack at $c_{l_{max}}$, $\alpha_{c_{l_{max}}}$
* end of the linear angle of attack range: $\alpha *$

In Drag:
* lift coefficient for minimum drag or design lift coefficient: $c_{l_{design}}$
* minimum drag coefficient: $c_{d_{min}}$ (function of R_N)

In Pitching Moment:
* pitching moment coefficient at zero lift coefficient: $\overline{c}_{m_0}$
* aerodynamic center (i.e. that point on the airfoil chord where the variation of pitching moment coefficient with angle of attack is zero). Figure 2.3 shows how the aerodynamic center is located geometrically. The following notation is normally used: $\overline{x}_{ac} = \dfrac{x_{ac}}{c}$

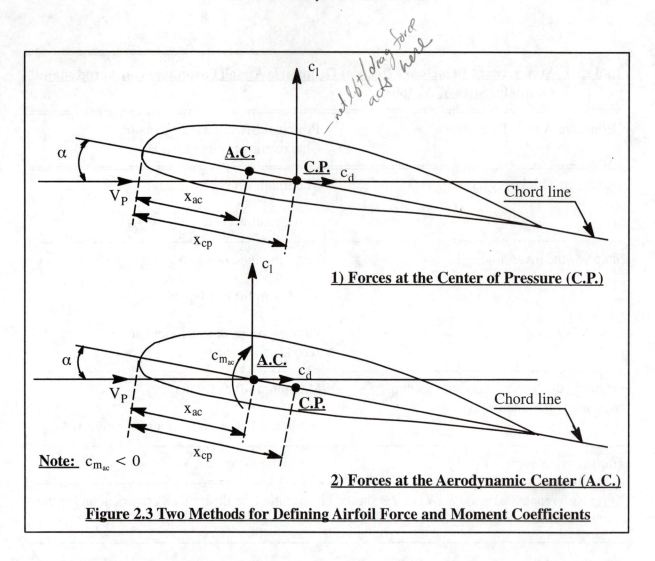

1) **Forces at the Center of Pressure (C.P.)**

Note: $c_{m_{ac}} < 0$

2) **Forces at the Aerodynamic Center (A.C.)**

Figure 2.3 Two Methods for Defining Airfoil Force and Moment Coefficients

Table 2.2 gives an overview of typical numerical values associated with some of these quantities. It will be noted that the airfoil lift–curve–slope, c_{l_α} typically has a value of approximately 2π (roughly 6.3 per rad or 0.110 per deg). Note also that the location of airfoil aerodynamic center is typically close to the quarter chord point: $\bar{x}_{ac} = 0.25$. The reader should be aware of the fact that most of these quantities are also a strong function of Mach Number, M. The dependence on Mach Number of the aerodynamic center location, $\bar{x}_{ac}$ and the lift–curve–slope c_{l_α} of airfoils is of particular significance to airplane stability and control. For that reason these characteristics are discussed in more detail in Sub–sections 2.2.1 and 2.2.2 respectively.

2.2.1 AIRFOIL AERODYNAMIC CENTER

Definition: The aerodynamic center of an airfoil is defined as that point on its chord about which the pitching moment coefficient is invariant with angle of attack.

In other words: $\bar{x}_{ac} = \frac{x_{ac}}{c}$ is that point for which: $c_{m_\alpha} = 0$. The aerodynamic center of an airfoil should not be confused with its center of pressure.

Table 2.2 Experimental, Low Speed NACA Airfoil Data for Smooth Leading Edges
(Note: Data reproduced from Reference 2.1 for $R_N = 9 \times 10^6$)

Airfoil	α_0 (deg)	$\bar{c}_{m_0}$	c_{l_α} (1/deg)	$\bar{x}_{ac}$	$\alpha_{c_{l_{max}}}$ (deg)	$c_{l_{max}}$	α^* (deg)
0006	0	0	0.108	0.250	9.0	0.92	9.0
0009	0	0	0.109	0.250	13.4	1.32	11.4
1408	0.8	−0.023	0.109	0.250	14.0	1.35	10.0
1410	−1.0	−0.020	0.108	0.247	14.3	1.50	11.0
1412	−1.1	−0.025	0.108	0.252	15.2	1.58	12.0
2412	−2.0	−0.047	0.105	0.247	16.8	1.68	9.5
2415	−2.0	−0.049	0.106	0.246	16.4	1.63	10.0
2418	−2.3	−0.050	0.103	0.241	14.0	1.47	10.0
2421	−1.8	−0.040	0.103	0.241	16.0	1.47	8.0
2424	−1.8	−0.040	0.098	0.231	16.0	1.29	8.4
23012	−1.4	−0.014	0.107	0.247	18.0	1.79	12.0
23015	−1.0	−0.007	0.107	0.243	18.0	1.72	10.0
23018	−1.2	−0.005	0.104	0.243	16.0	1.60	11.8
23021	−1.2	0	0.103	0.238	15.0	1.50	10.3
23024	−0.8	0	0.097	0.231	15.0	1.40	9.7
64–006	0	0	0.109	0.256	9.0	0.80	7.2
64–009	0	0	0.110	0.262	11.0	1.17	10.0
64_1–012	0	0	0.111	0.262	14.5	1.45	11.0
64_1–212	−1.3	−0.027	0.113	0.262	15.0	1.55	11.0
64_1–412	−2.6	−0.065	0.112	0.267	15.0	1.67	8.0
64–206	−1.0	−0.040	0.110	0.253	12.0	1.03	8.0
64–209	−1.5	−0.040	0.107	0.261	13.0	1.40	8.9
64–210	−1.6	−0.040	0.110	0.258	14.0	1.45	10.8
64A010	0	0	0.110	0.253	12.0	1.23	10.0
64A210	−1.5	−0.040	0.105	0.251	13.0	1.44	10.0
64A410	−3.0	−0.080	0.100	0.254	15.0	1.61	10.0
64_1A212	−2.0	−0.040	0.100	0.252	14.0	1.54	11.0
64_2A215	−2.0	−0.040	0.095	0.252	15.0	1.50	12.0

Note: For definition of symbols, see Figure 2.2 and the list of Symbols

Definition: The center of pressure of an airfoil is that point on its chord where the resultant of the pressure distribution (resultant aerodynamic force) acts.

The lift distribution on any non–symmetrical (cambered) airfoil can be shown to be the sum of two types of lift distribution:

1.) the <u>basic lift distribution</u> which depends on the shape (camber) of the mean line. This basic lift distribution has zero net lift but non–zero pitching moment: $\bar{c}_{m_0} < 0$ for air-foils with positive camber.

2.) the <u>additional lift distribution</u> which depends linearly on the angle of attack, α.

The net lift of an airfoil is due to this additional lift distribution.

Apparently, the aerodynamic center of an airfoil can also be thought of as the centroid of the additional lift distribution. Therefore, for a symmetrical airfoil the center of pressure and the aerodynamic center coincide!

Figure 2.3 presents two methods used to resolve the force and moment coefficients which act on an airfoil. In this text the second method will be used. Expressing the center of pressure and aerodynamic center locations relative to the leading edge of the airfoil as: x_{ac} and x_{cp} respectively it is found that for small angles of attack and for negligible drag contribution to the pitching moment:

$$c_{m_{ac}} = - c_l(x_{cp} - x_{ac})/c \qquad (2.1)$$

From this the location of the airfoil center of pressure can be solved:

$$x_{cp} = x_{ac} - (c_{m_{ac}}c)/(c_l) \qquad (2.2)$$

Because the quantity $c_{m_{ac}}$ is negative for positively cambered airfoils, the center of pressure is behind the aerodynamic center. Note that:

$$c_{m_{ac}} = \bar{c}_{m_0} \qquad (2.3)$$

Because a symmetrical airfoil has no net pitching moment at zero lift: $c_{m_{ac}} = 0$. As symm.airfoil

a consequence, for a symmetrical airfoil: $x_{ac} = x_{cp}$. Do not forget that this property does **NOT** apply to cambered (un–symmetrical airfoils).

The data in Table 2.2 indicate that the aerodynamic center location for airfoils is roughly at the quarter chord. Actually, the airfoil thickness ratio and trailing edge angle together define where the aerodynamic center is located. Figure 2.4 (reproduced from Reference 2.4) shows this. Note that the data in Figure 2.4 straddle the 25% chord location!

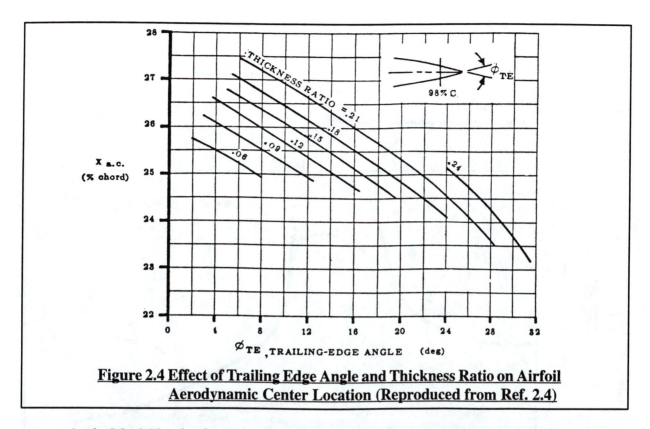

Figure 2.4 Effect of Trailing Edge Angle and Thickness Ratio on Airfoil Aerodynamic Center Location (Reproduced from Ref. 2.4)

As the Mach Number increases from low sub sonic to transonic the airfoil center of pressure and aerodynamic center tend to move aft (not necessarily at the same rate). For a thin, symmetrical airfoil at exactly M=1 the center of pressure tends to be at the semi–chord (50%) position. An example of how the aerodynamic center moves aft with Mach Number is shown in Figure 2.5. This aft shift of the aerodynamic center will be shown (Chapters 4 and 5) to have significant consequences to the stability and controllability of airplanes.

2.2.2 AIRFOIL LIFT CURVE SLOPE

According to thin airfoil theory, the lift–curve slope of an airfoil, c_{l_α} increases with Mach Number in the subsonic speed range as follows:

$$c_{l_{\alpha_M}} = \frac{c_{l_{\alpha_{M=0}}}}{\sqrt{1 - M^2}} \qquad M < 1 \tag{2.4}$$

This in accordance with the so–called Prandtl–Glauert transformation as explained in detail in Reference 2.5 (pages 200–203). Figure 2.5 shows a graphical representation of Eqn.(2.4). According to Reference 2.6 (Chapter 3), in the supersonic speed range this relationship becomes:

$$c_{l_{\alpha_M}} = \frac{4}{\sqrt{M^2 - 1}} \qquad M > 1 \tag{2.5}$$

Note that both Equations (2.4) and (2.5) predict the lift–curve slope to extend to infinity around M=1.0. This does not happen in reality because the theories used to derive these equations become invalid in the Mach range around M=1.0. The 'faired' curve shown in Figure 2.5 represents more closely what really happens.

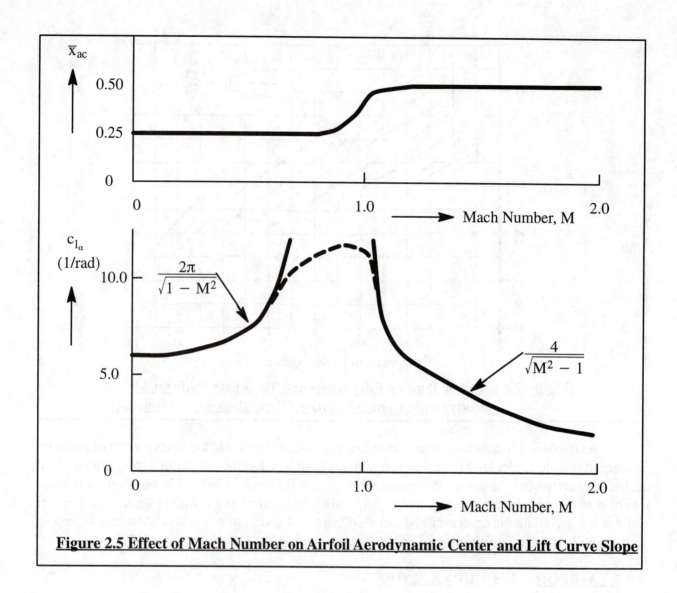

Figure 2.5 Effect of Mach Number on Airfoil Aerodynamic Center and Lift Curve Slope

2.3   PLANFORM PARAMETERS

As indicated before, airfoils are integrated in a spanwise manner to form lifting surfaces such as wings, tails, canards and pylons. The planform geometry of these lifting surfaces plays a major role in determining their aerodynamic characteristics. In the following it is assumed that most of these planforms can be approximated by a so–called straight tapered form as shown in Figure 2.6. The following planform quantities are important in stability and control analyses:

Taper ratio, $\lambda = \dfrac{c_t}{c_r}$ (2.6)

Aspect ratio, $A = \dfrac{b^2}{S} = \dfrac{2b}{c_r(1 + \lambda)}$ (2.7)

Area, $S = \dfrac{b}{2}c_r(1 + \lambda)$ (2.8)

Mean geometric chord (mgc), $\bar{c} = \dfrac{2}{3}c_r\left(\dfrac{1 + \lambda + \lambda^2}{1 + \lambda}\right)$ (2.9)

Lateral location of the mgc, $\quad y_{mgc} = \dfrac{b(1 + 2\lambda)}{6(1 + \lambda)}$ (2.10)

Longitudinal location of the mgc, $\quad x_{mgc} = \dfrac{b(1 + 2\lambda)}{6(1 + \lambda)} \tan \Lambda_{LE}$ (2.11)

Sweep Angle of the n fraction locus : $\quad \tan \Lambda_n = \tan \Lambda_{LE} - \dfrac{4n(1 - \lambda)}{A(1 + \lambda)}$ (2.12)

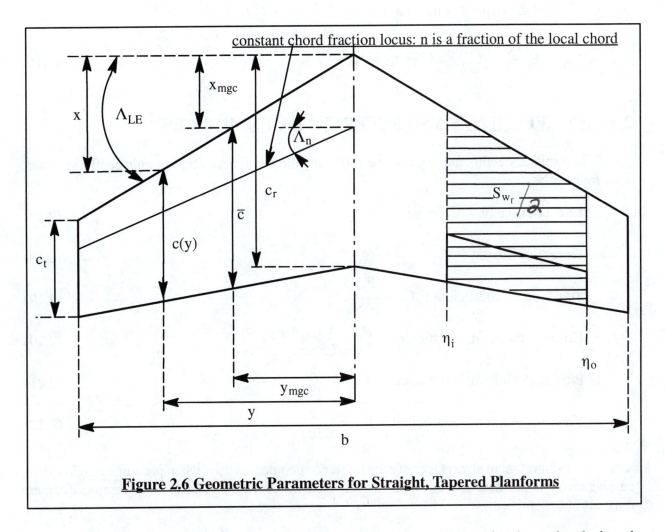

Figure 2.6 Geometric Parameters for Straight, Tapered Planforms

For a more general planform, the following integrals can be used to determine the length and location of the mean geometric chord:

Mean geometric chord : $\quad \overline{c} = \dfrac{1}{S} \displaystyle\int_{-b/2}^{+b/2} c^2(y)\,dy$ (2.13)

Lateral location of the mgc, $\quad y_{mgc} = \dfrac{2}{S} \displaystyle\int_{-b/2}^{+b/2} y c(y)\,dy$ (2.14)

Longitudinal location of the mgc, $x_{mgc} = \dfrac{1}{S} \displaystyle\int_{-b/2}^{+b/2} xc(y)dy$ (2.15)

Many lifting surfaces are equipped with trailing edge flaps and /or trailing edge control surfaces. The inboard and outboard stations of flaps and/or control surfaces are identified by semi–span fractions called η_i and η_o respectively. Such flaps and/or control surfaces affect an area of the planform called the flapped wing area, S_{w_f} :

$$S_{w_f} = \frac{S}{2(1 + \lambda)}(1 - \lambda)(2 - \eta_o - \eta_i + 2\lambda)$$ (2.16)

2.4 COEFFICIENTS AND REFERENCE GEOMETRIES

In airplane stability and control, the following dimensionless aerodynamic coefficients are used frequently:

Lift coefficient : $C_L = \dfrac{L}{qS}$ (2.17)

Drag coefficient : $C_D = \dfrac{D}{qS}$ (2.18)

Side force coefficient : $C_y = \dfrac{F_{A_y}}{qS}$ (2.19)

Rolling moment coefficient : $C_l = \dfrac{L_A}{qSb}$ (2.20)

Pitching moment coefficient : $C_m = \dfrac{M_A}{qS\bar{c}}$ (2.21)

Yawing moment coefficient : $C_n = \dfrac{N_A}{qSb}$ (2.22)

It is important to always identify the reference geometries used when presenting and/or discussing aerodynamic data! For the moment coefficients, the location of the moment reference center must also be identified!

2.5   AERODYNAMIC CHARACTERISTICS OF PLANFORMS AND FUSELAGE

In this section a very condensed discussion is presented of those aerodynamic characteristics of planforms which are of major concern in the prediction and analysis of airplane stability and control behavior. These characteristics are:

2.5.1 Lift–curve slope, C_{L_α}

2.5.2 Aerodynamic center, x_{ac}

2.5.3 Zero–lift angle of attack, α_0

2.5.4 Moment coefficient about the aerodynamic center, $C_{m_{ac}}$

2.5.5 Downwash (and upwash), ε and its rate of change with angle of attack, $d\varepsilon/d\alpha$

2.5.6 Effect of the fuselage on planform aerodynamic center,

All characteristics discussed in this section apply to a variety of lifting surfaces such as: wings, horizontal tails, canards, vertical tails, pylons, etc. To distinguish the aerodynamic characteristics of one lifting surface from another, subscripts are used. The following subscripts are used:

w for wing	h for horizontal tail	p for pylon
c for canard	v for vertical tail	s for store

2.5.1   LIFT–CURVE SLOPE

The lift–curve slope of planforms, C_{L_α} has been found to depend primarily on the following parameters:

* Aspect ratio	* Sweep angle	* Taper ratio
* Section lift–curve slope		* Mach number

Part VI of Reference 2.3 contains methods for estimating planform C_{L_α} values (Pages 248–255). These methods have been programmed in the Advanced Aircraft Analysis (AAA) program which is described in Appendix A. Figure 2.7 shows how planform lift–curve slope varies with Mach number, sweep angle and aspect ratio. Note the following behaviors:

In the subsonic to transonic speed range:

* C_{L_α} increases with increasing aspect ratio

* C_{L_α} decreases with increasing sweep angle

* C_{L_α} increases with increasing Mach number

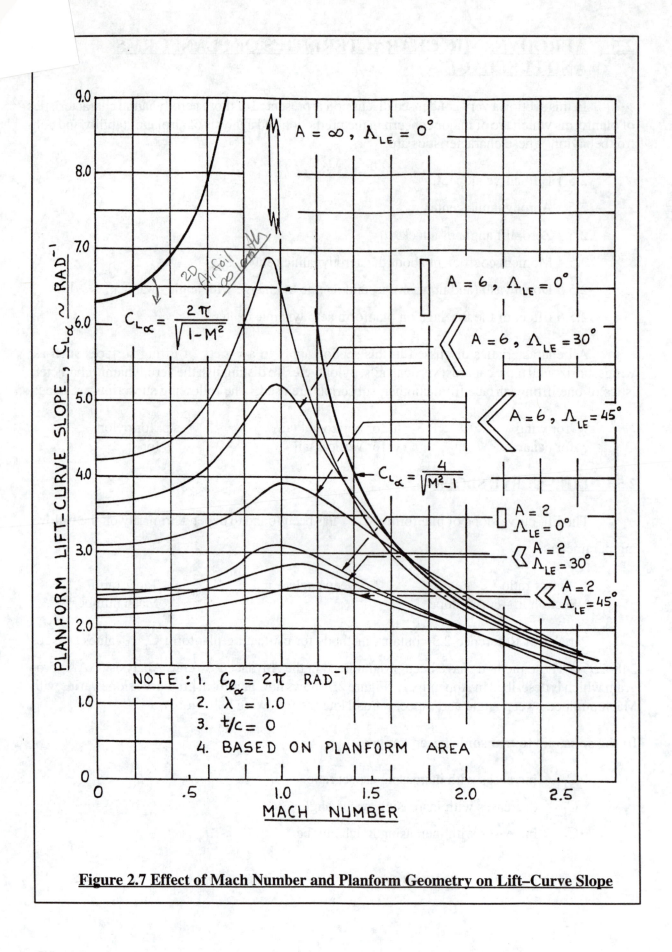

Figure 2.7 Effect of Mach Number and Planform Geometry on Lift–Curve Slope

Observe that below M=1.0 the trend of C_{L_α} with Mach number follows the Prandtl–Glauert transformation of Eqn (2.3).

In the supersonic speed range:

* C_{L_α} increases with increasing aspect ratio

* C_{L_α} tends to follow the supersonic Prandtl–Glauert transformation Eqn (2.5). Note that sweep angle does not matter very much in that speed range.

When estimating planform values for lift–curve slope it is a good idea to perform a 'sanity' check on the answers by comparing with Figure 2.7.

2.5.2   AERODYNAMIC CENTER

Definition: the aerodynamic center of a planform is defined as that point about which the pitching moment coefficient with angle of attack is in variant: $C_{m_\alpha} = 0$.

The planform aerodynamic center will be assumed to be located on its mean geometric chord (mgc). For planforms with moderate sweep angle and moderate to high aspect ratios the aerodynamic center is often close to the 25% chord point on the mgc. For other points on the mgc, the variation of pitching moment coefficient with angle of attack may be found from:

$$C_{m_\alpha} = C_{L_\alpha}(x_{ref} - x_{ac})\frac{1}{\overline{c}} = C_{L_\alpha}(\overline{x}_{ref} - \overline{x}_{ac}) \qquad (2.23)$$

The geometric definition of the parameters x_{ref} and x_{ac} is given in Figure 2.8. This figure also shows a simple geometric construction which can be used to determine the location of the mean geometric chord (mgc).

The aerodynamic center of a planform has been found to be primarily a function of the following parameters:

* Aspect ratio   * Sweep angle   * Taper ratio
* Section lift–curve slope   * Mach number

Methods for estimating planform aerodynamic center locations may be found in Part VI of Reference 2.3 (pages 305–308). Figure 2.9 shows an example of how the a.c. location varies with planform geometry. Until compressibility effects begin to play a role, it is seen that the planform aerodynamic center ranges from 25% to about 30% of the mgc. In the transonic speed range the aerodynamic center tends to move aft. For very thin wings, at supersonic speeds, the aerodynamic center moves close to the 50% chord point on the mgc. Figure 2.10 shows an example of how the aerodynamic center moves with sweep angle, taper ratio and Mach number.

For a given center of gravity location Eqn (2.23) suggests that the variation of pitching moment coefficient with angle of attack is strongly influenced by the location of the aerodynamic center. This will turn out to have a major influence on airplane controllability.

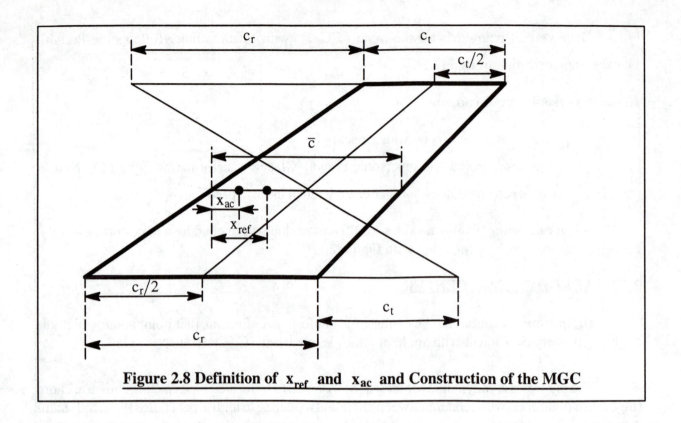

Figure 2.8 Definition of x_{ref} and x_{ac} and Construction of the MGC

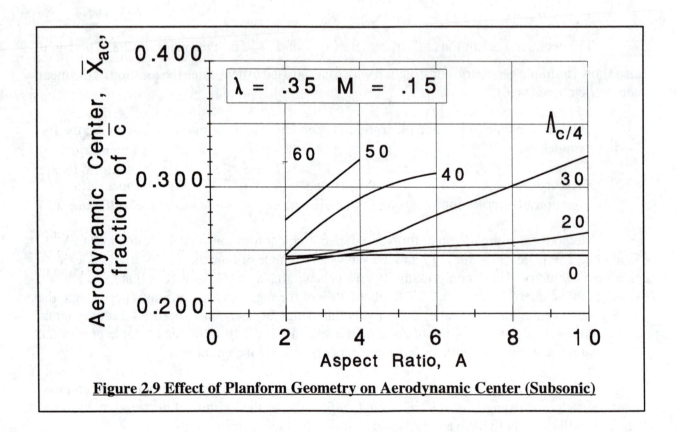

Figure 2.9 Effect of Planform Geometry on Aerodynamic Center (Subsonic)

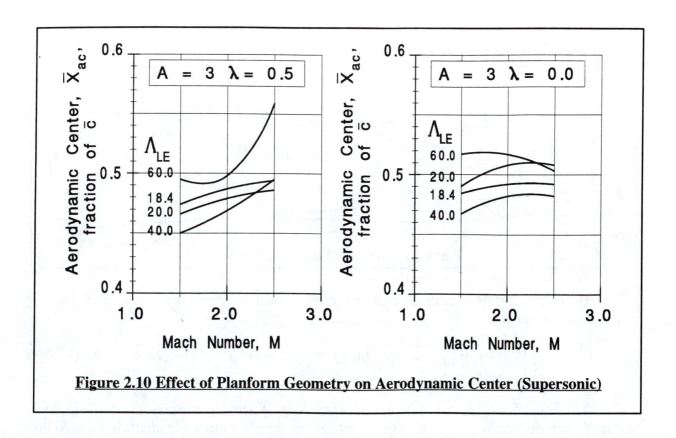

Figure 2.10 Effect of Planform Geometry on Aerodynamic Center (Supersonic)

2.5.3   ZERO–LIFT ANGLE OF ATTACK

The angle of attack of a planform is arbitrarily defined as the angle of attack of its root–chord. As the wording implies, the zero–lift angle of attack of a planform is that angle of attack for which the total planform lift equals zero. This quantity plays an important role in determining the required wing incidence angle for cruise and/or for approach flight conditions. The following parameters have been found to be instrumental in determining the zero–lift angle of attack of a planform:

* Aspect ratio	* Sweep angle	* Taper ratio
* Airfoil zero–lift angle of attack		* Planform twist

The planform twist angle at a given spanwise station, y, $\varepsilon_T(y)$ is defined in Figure 2.11.

Note, that positive twist is defined as leading edge UP. Wings are typically twisted leading edge down at outboard wing stations to prevent the tip from stalling before the root. Another reason for twisting wing planforms is to tailor the spanwise load distribution such as to achieve certain induced drag or air–load distribution objectives.

The root angle of attack for which zero lift occurs at an intermediate span station, y is found from:

$$\alpha_{r_{l=0 \text{ at } y}} = \alpha_0(y) - \varepsilon_T(y) \tag{2.24}$$

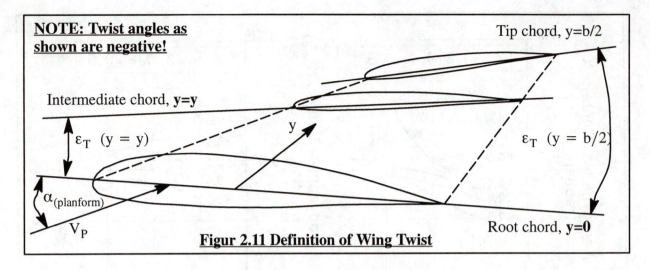

Figur 2.11 Definition of Wing Twist

By integrating this quantity over the planform, the value of planform angle of attack for zero planform lift is found as:

$$\alpha_{0_L} = \frac{1}{S} \int_{-b/2}^{b/2} c(y)[\alpha_0(y) - \varepsilon_T(y)]dy \qquad (2.25)$$

This equation applies only to wings without sweep. When flaps are present anywhere along the span, their deflection can cause a significant shift in the planform angle of attack for zero lift. Methods for computing the effect of sweep and flaps on α_{0_L} are found in Part VI of Reference 2.3 (pages 245–247).

2.5.4 MOMENT COEFFICIENT ABOUT THE AERODYNAMIC CENTER

The pitching moment about the aerodynamic center of a wing has significant consequences for the trimmability of an airplane. In Sub–section 2.2.1 it was seen that positively cambered airfoils tend to have negative pitching moments about their aerodynamic centers (See Table 2.2). A planform consisting of positively cambered airfoils can therefore be expected to also have a negative value for its pitching moment coefficient about the aerodynamic center: $C_{m_{ac}}$. Methods for determining $C_{m_{ac}}$ for various planforms and Mach numbers are found in Part VI of Reference 2.3. It is noted that the value of $C_{m_{ac}}$ of a planform is the same as the pitching moment coefficient for zero lift (not zero angle of attack!), $\overline{C}_{m_0}$: see Eqn (2.3) where this is stated for airfoils. For a swept wing, the value of $C_{m_{ac}}$ is a strong function of the sweep angle, the spanwise twist distribution and the spanwise variation of airfoil zero–lift angle of attack. This can be seen from the following equation:

$$C_{m_{ac}} = \frac{1}{S\bar{c}}\left[\int_{-b/2}^{b/2} [c_{m_{ac}}(y)c(y)^2]dy + \pi \int_{-b/2}^{b/2} [\alpha_{0_L} + \varepsilon_T(y) - \alpha_0(y)]c(y)x_1(y)dy\right] \qquad (2.26)$$

Figure 2.12 shows the definition of the geometric terms in Eqn (2.26).

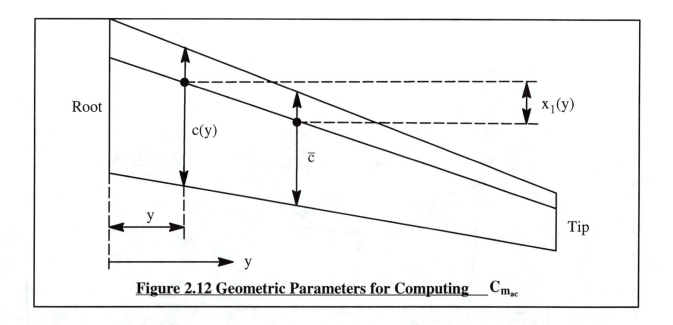

Figure 2.12 Geometric Parameters for Computing __ $C_{m_{ac}}$

2.5.5 DOWNWASH, UPWASH AND DYNAMIC PRESSURE RATIO (Adapted from Reference 2.4)

In Subsonic Flow

The downwash behind a wing is a consequence of the wing trailing vortex system. A typical wing trailing vortex system is pictured in Figure 2.13. A vortex sheet is shed behind the lifting wing. This vortex sheet is deflected downward (downwash) by the bound (or lifting) vortex and by the tip vortices which together comprise the wing vortex system. In general, the vortex sheet will not be flat although the curvature around the mid–span area is very small for large span wings. This is particularly true for high aspect ratio, low sweep angle wings. For such wings it has been found that considering the vortex sheet to be approximately flat is a good approximation. Wings with considerable trailing edge sweep angles tend to produce a vortex sheet which is bowed upward near the plane of symmetry.

The tip vortices normally do not experience a vertical displacement of the same magnitude as the central portion of the vortex sheet. In general they trail back comparatively close to the streamwise direction. Furthermore, as the vortex system moves downstream, the tip vortices tend to move inboard. Also, with increasing distance behind the wing, the trailing–sheet vorticity tends to be transferred to the tip vortices. This transfer of vorticity and the inboard movement of the tip vortices takes place in such a way that the lateral center of gravity of the vorticity remains at a fixed spanwise location. When all of the vorticity of the trailing–sheet has been transferred to the tip vortices, the vortex system is considered top be fully rolled –up. In a non–viscous fluid this vortex system would extend to infinity. This way of looking at the vortex system is consistent with the vortex laws formulated by Helmholtz (See Ref. 2.5.).

Ahead of the downstream station of complete roll–up, the spanwise downwash distribution is dependent on the spanwise lift distribution of the wing. However, when the roll–up is complete, the downwash angles for all planforms of equal lift and equal effective span are identical!

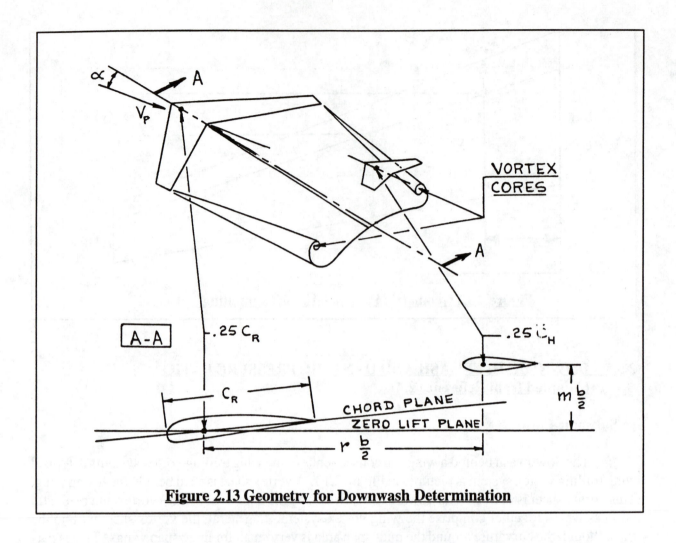

Figure 2.13 Geometry for Downwash Determination

As suggested by Figure 2.13, the shape of the vortex sheet will have a significant effect on the downwash experienced by a horizontal tail placed in the flow field behind a wing. The location of such a tail (vertical and horizontal) relative to the wing is therefore very important. Because the wing–tip vortices are somewhat above the wing vortex sheet, the downwash above the sheet is somewhat larger than the downwash below the vortex sheet. The rate at which the downwash angle changes with angle of attack is the so–called downwash gradient, $d\epsilon/d\alpha$. The numerical value of

this downwash gradient <u>in the zero–lift plane</u> ranges from 1.0 at the wing trailing edge to $2C_{L_\alpha}/\pi A$

at infinity. Figure 2.14 shows an example of how the downwash gradient varies for various horizontal tail locations behind an unswept wing of different aspect ratios.

In stability considerations (as shown in Chapter 3) the parameter $(1 - d\epsilon/d\alpha)$ frequently occurs. Figure 2.15 shows how this parameter varies for locations in front of and behind wings with elliptical planforms. In front of the wing the term upwash is used instead of downwash. Upwash is particularly important in the case of canard airplanes.

In subsonic flow the downwash gradient tends to vary with Mach number as predicted by the Prandtl–Glauert transformation:

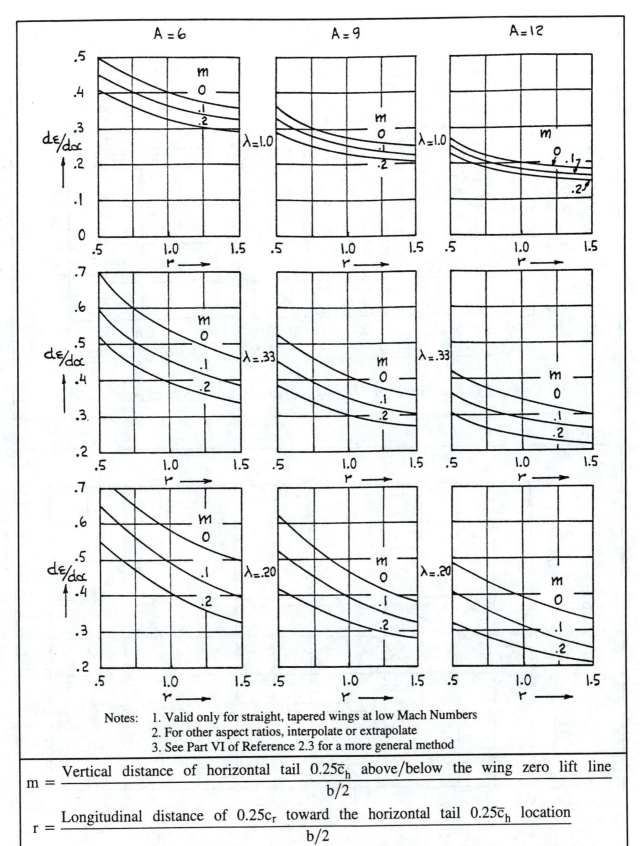

Notes: 1. Valid only for straight, tapered wings at low Mach Numbers
2. For other aspect ratios, interpolate or extrapolate
3. See Part VI of Reference 2.3 for a more general method

$$m = \frac{\text{Vertical distance of horizontal tail } 0.25\overline{c}_h \text{ above/below the wing zero lift line}}{b/2}$$

$$r = \frac{\text{Longitudinal distance of } 0.25c_r \text{ toward the horizontal tail } 0.25\overline{c}_h \text{ location}}{b/2}$$

Figure 2.14 Effect of Wing Aspect Ratio and Horizontal Tail Location on the Downwash Gradient

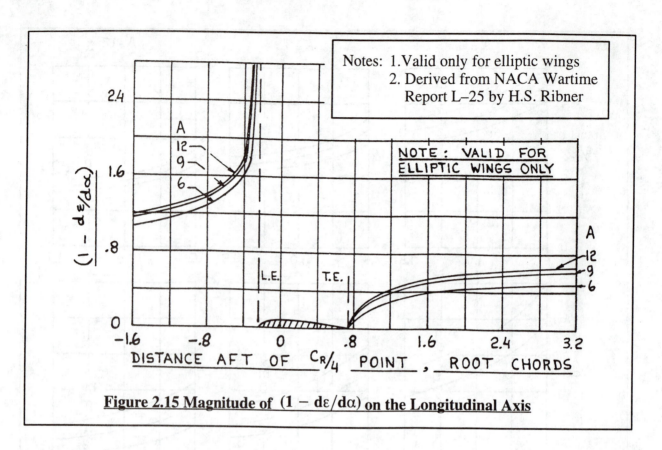

Figure 2.15 Magnitude of $(1 - d\varepsilon/d\alpha)$ on the Longitudinal Axis

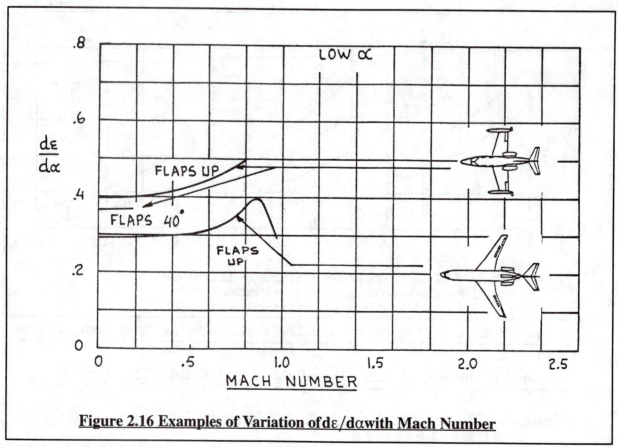

Figure 2.16 Examples of Variation of $d\varepsilon/d\alpha$ with Mach Number

$$(d\varepsilon/d\alpha)_M = (d\varepsilon/d\alpha)_{M=0}\sqrt{(1 - M^2)} \tag{2.27}$$

A method for calculating the downwash gradient behind arbitrary wings is given in Part VI of Reference 2.3. Figure 2.16 shows an example of how the downwash gradient varies with Mach number for several airplanes.

In the case of low aspect ratio wings and in the case of a canard configuration the tip vortex of the wing or the canard may impinge on the the aft surface. Reference 2.7 contains a method to account for that.

Upwash is induced ahead of a wing in a manner similar to that for downwash. To account for the aerodynamic forces on propellers, nacelles and/or stores ahead of a wing due to this upwash the design charts of Reference 2.7 may be used.

<u>Dynamic Pressure Ratio</u>

The aerodynamic forces on lifting surfaces are proportional to the local dynamic pressure of the flow field. The reference (or free stream) dynamic pressure used in computing aerodynamic forces and moments on the entire airplane is that based on airplane true air speed: $\overline{q} = 0.5\rho V_P^2$.

The dynamic pressure in the downwash wake of a wing can be reduced by friction losses and/or by separation phenomena. However, if an aft surface is mounted in the propeller wake it is possible that (depending on engine power) the dynamic pressure is in fact larger than the free–stream dynamic pressure. The change in local dynamic pressure is expressed in terms of a ratio of dynamic pressures. For example, in the case of horizontal and vertical tails these ratios are expressed as: $\eta_h = \overline{q}_h/\overline{q}$ and $\eta_v = \overline{q}_v/\overline{q}$ respectively. Part VI of Reference 2.3 (Pages 269–271) contains methods for estimating these dynamic pressure ratios.

In Transonic Flow

In transonic flow no accurate methods are available as yet to estimate downwash characteristics. When estimates (or tunnel data) are available for wing lift–curve slope in the transonic region, a first order approximation for estimating the downwash gradient is to use the lift–curve slope ratio:

$$(d\varepsilon/d\alpha)_M = (d\varepsilon/d\alpha)_{M=0}\frac{C_{L_{\alpha_M}}}{C_{L_{\alpha_{M=0}}}} \tag{2.28}$$

In Supersonic Flow

At supersonic speeds downwash is caused by two factors. First, the region behind the trailing–edge shock or expansion wave is distorted by the wing vortex system in a manner similar to that which occurs at subsonic speeds. Because of the variation of span load, a vortex sheet is shed which rolls up with increasing downstream distance from the trailing edge. Tip vortices similar to their subsonic counterparts are also present. At supersonic Mach numbers the entire flow field is swept back and isolated regions of influence may exist over certain portions of the wing surface and in the flow field behind it. For instance, regions not affected by the wing tip are generally present.

Second, a change in flow direction occurs in the flow region between the leading edge shock or expansion waves as shown in Figure 2.17. Since this region of the flow does not 'see' the wing vortex system, numerical values for downwash can be calculated with shock–expansion theory. To simplify the calculations it is standard practice to perform these calculations with the geometry of the wing root and to assume two–dimensional flow. For configurations where the tail span is less than the wing span, this assumption is justified.

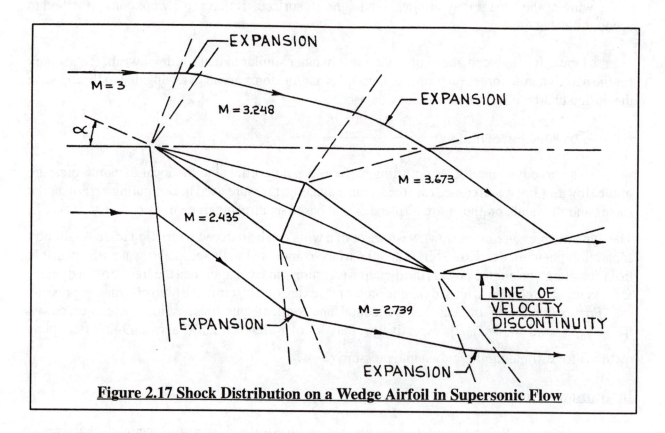

Figure 2.17 Shock Distribution on a Wedge Airfoil in Supersonic Flow

2.5.6 EFFECT OF THE FUSELAGE ON WING AERODYNAMIC CENTER

When a fuselage is added to a wing, the aerodynamic center of the wing+fuselage shifts forward compared to that of the wing alone. A physical explanation for this effect can be seen from Figure 2.18. Considering the fuselage to be represented by a body of revolution placed in a potential flow field the pressure distribution is roughly as indicated by the + and – signs in Figure 2.19.

In potential flow, at a given angle of attack, α the following observations can be made:

* net pressure drag is zero   *** net lift is zero**   *** net pitching moment is positive.**

As a consequence the fuselage will add a positively increasing pitching moment with each increase of angle of attack: the fuselage adds an increment $\Delta C_{m_{\alpha_{fus}}} > 0$ to the wing. This increment

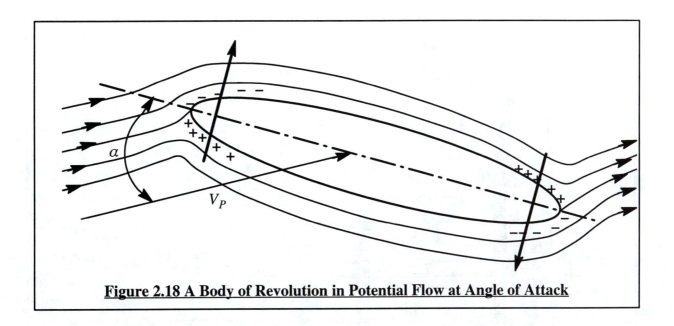

Figure 2.18 A Body of Revolution in Potential Flow at Angle of Attack

in the static longitudinal stability derivative, C_{m_α} can be interpreted as a forward shift in aerodynamic center: $\Delta \overline{x}_{ac_{fus}}$ which is negative. This fuselage effect is also called the Munk effect (after its discoverer, Max Munk). Part VI of Reference 2.3 contains a numerical integration method for estimating the fuselage induced shift of the aerodynamic center. This method accounts for the effect of wing up–wash and wing down–wash on the fuselage. It is based on a method first developed by Multhopp in Reference 2.10.

Figure 2.19 shows three numerical examples of this fuselage induced a.c. shift as computed for different airplanes. It is shown in Part II of Reference 2.3 that typical center–of–gravity shifts in airplanes range from 10%–25% of the mgc. The 4%, 14% and 32% fuselage induced shifts in aerodynamic center location are therefore very important and must be accounted for in the design of a new airplane!

It has been found that the fuselage induced a.c. shift is essentially independent of Mach number for moderate to high fuselage slenderness ratios. Therefore, the aerodynamic center of a wing+fuselage tends to shift aft with Mach number more or less like that of a wing alone.

It should be noted that nacelles and stores when mounted under a wing such that they protrude forward from the wing leading edge, also cause a shift in a.c. These shifts can also be predicted with the Multhopp method.

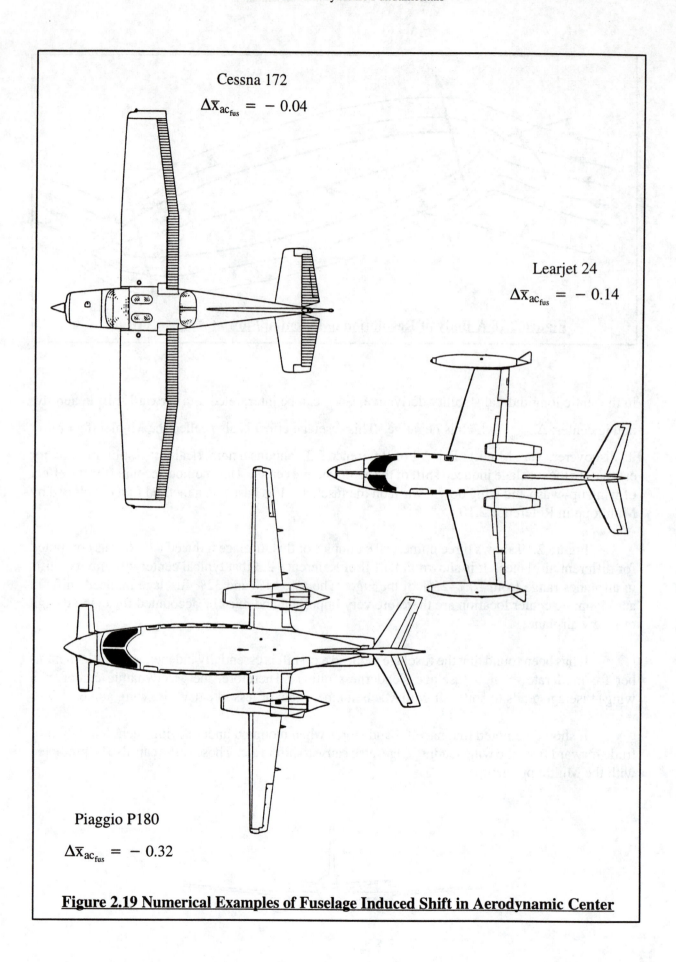

Cessna 172

$$\Delta \bar{x}_{ac_{fus}} = -0.04$$

Learjet 24

$$\Delta \bar{x}_{ac_{fus}} = -0.14$$

Piaggio P180

$$\Delta \bar{x}_{ac_{fus}} = -0.32$$

Figure 2.19 Numerical Examples of Fuselage Induced Shift in Aerodynamic Center

2.6 EFFECTIVENESS OF CONTROL SURFACES

The controllability of airplanes depends on the lift and moment effectiveness of flight control surfaces. Most control surfaces are designed as plain flaps (with open or closed gap) as illustrated in Figure 2.20. Closed gap configurations have greater effectiveness than open gap configurations. Note that a control surface deflection **is defined as positive** when the trailing edge is down.

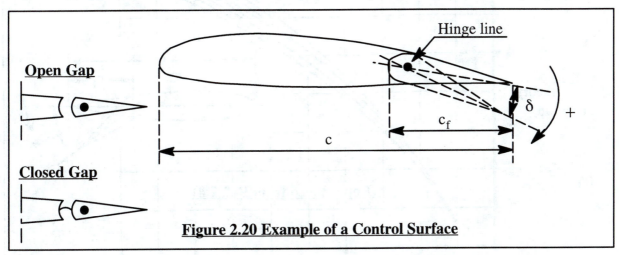

Figure 2.20 Example of a Control Surface

The lift effectiveness of a control surface is designated by $c_{l_\delta} = \dfrac{\partial c_l}{\partial \delta}$ for an airfoil and $C_{L_\delta} = \dfrac{\partial C_L}{\partial \delta}$ for a planform. For an airfoil section, the magnitude of c_{l_δ} depends primarily on the following parameters:

* control surface chord ratio, c_f/c * section thickness ratio, t/c

* control surface deflection, δ * Mach number

Figure 2.21 shows an example of how c_{l_δ} depends on the first two parameters. It is seen that the chord ratio has primary influence while the thickness ratio has only secondary influence on lift effectiveness. It will be shown in Chapter 3 that in most airplane control power derivatives the lift effectiveness appears in product form with the moment arm of the control surface to the center of gravity. Methods for estimating C_{L_δ} from c_{l_δ} are found in Part VI of Reference 2.3. Factors which affect the numerical magnitude of C_{L_δ} are, in addition to those mentioned for c_{l_δ}:

* Sweep angle   * Control surface inboard and outboard span stations, η_i and η_o.

The latter two quantities are defined in Figure 2.6. Figure 2.22 shows a typical plot of planform lift versus angle of attack, cross–plotted for control surface deflections. It is important to understand the graphical interpretation for C_{L_δ}:

$$C_{L_\delta} = (\frac{\partial C_L}{\partial \delta})_{\alpha = \text{constant}} \qquad (2.29)$$

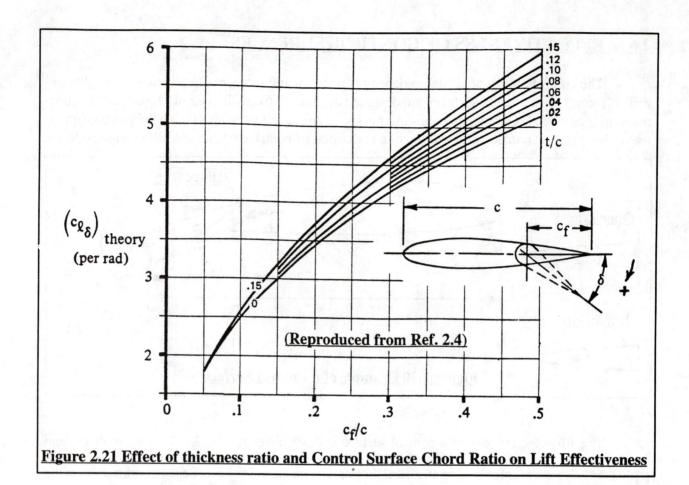

Figure 2.21 Effect of thickness ratio and Control Surface Chord Ratio on Lift Effectiveness

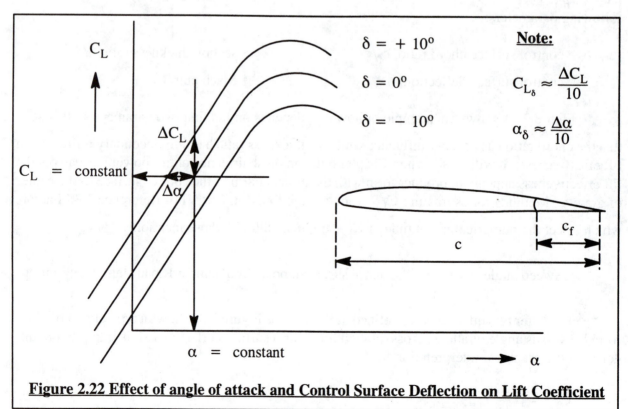

Figure 2.22 Effect of angle of attack and Control Surface Deflection on Lift Coefficient

This quantity can be viewed as the change in lift coefficient due to control surface def. at constant angle of attack. In many stability and control expressions in Chapter 3 the foll quantity (called angle–of–attack effectiveness) is also important:

$$\alpha_\delta = \left(\frac{\partial \alpha}{\partial \delta}\right)_{C_L = constant} \qquad (\smile)$$

(2.30)

This quantity can be viewed as the change in angle of attack due to control surface deflection at constant lift coefficient. It may be seen that as long as $\alpha < \alpha^*$ the following holds:

$$\alpha_\delta = \frac{C_{L_\delta}}{C_{L_\alpha}}$$

(2.31)

Figure 2.23 shows how α_δ varies with c_f/c. It is seen that a control surface with a 30% chord has 50% of the effectiveness of an all–moving (100% chord or variable incidence) planform. This is the reason why hinged control surfaces have been used on so many airplanes: per unit chord length they are very effective!

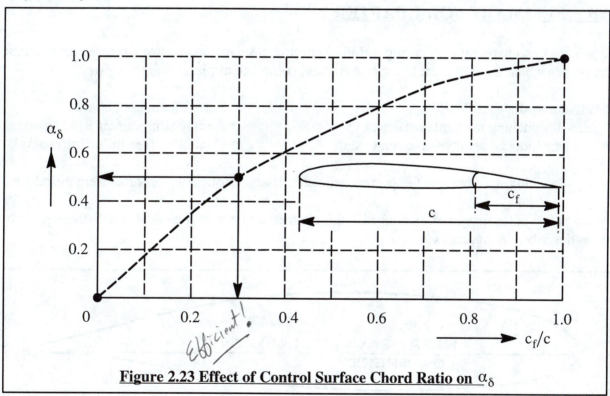

Figure 2.23 Effect of Control Surface Chord Ratio on α_δ

For a three–dimensional control surface at very low sweep angles, a good approximation for α_δ is:

$$\alpha_\delta = \frac{1}{S} \int_{-b/2}^{b/2} \alpha_\delta(y)c(y)dy$$

(2.32)

For variations with Mach number in subsonic flow, the Prandtl–Glauert transformation can be used again to yield:

$$c_{l_\delta} = \frac{c_{l_{\delta M = 0}}}{\sqrt{1 - M^2}} \qquad \text{and} \qquad C_{L_\delta} = \frac{C_{L_{\delta M = 0}}}{\sqrt{1 - M^2}} \qquad (2.33)$$

More general methods which account for the effect of sweep angle and for transonic and super sonic flow are found in Part VI of Reference 2.3.

2.7 MODERN AIRFOILS COMPARED TO NACA AIRFOILS

Since the advent of reliable computational methods for the prediction of airfoil behavior and for the design of airfoils (for example, References 2.8 and 2.9) it is possible to develop airfoils with lift, drag and pitching moment characteristics which are tailored to specific applications and specific flight conditions.   Figure 2.24 shows a geometric comparison between older and newer airfoils. Figure 2.25 show example data comparing modern airfoils with NACA type airfoils.

2.8 SUMMARY FOR CHAPTER 2

In this chapter the following airfoil, planform, fuselage and control surface aerodynamic properties which are important to the stability and control of airplanes were reviewed:

* Lift–curve slope
* Zero–lift pitching moment coefficient
* Fuselage induced aerodynamic center shift

* Zero–lift angle of attack
* Aerodynamic center
* Control surface lift effectiveness

In addition, a number of important geometric characteristics of planforms were introduced.

Most of the quantities mentioned in this chapter can be rapidly evaluated with the AAA program described in Appendix A.

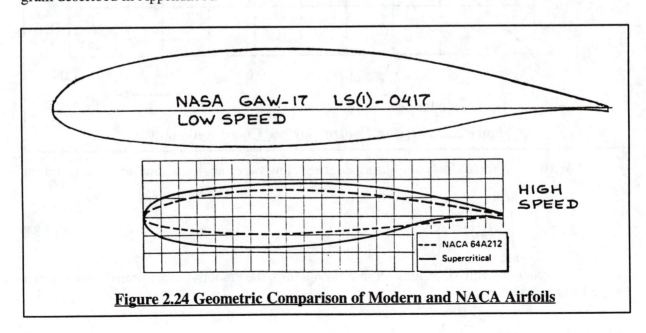

Figure 2.24 Geometric Comparison of Modern and NACA Airfoils

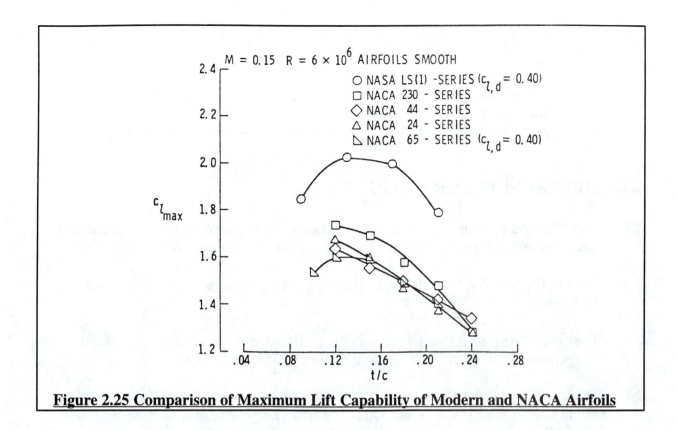

Figure 2.25 Comparison of Maximum Lift Capability of Modern and NACA Airfoils

2.9   PROBLEMS FOR CHAPTER 2

2.1   For a thin airfoil, calculate and plot the theoretical section lift–curve slope for $0 < M < 2.0$.

2.2   Using data from Reference 2.2 plot section lift–curve slope versus thickness ratio for NACA 44XX and 23YYY series airfoils.

2.3   Make accurate sketches of wing planforms, characterized by the following parameters:
Leading edge sweep angle: 0 degrees:

a) $\lambda = 0$ $A = 2, 4, 6, 8, 10$ b) $\lambda = 0.35 A = 2, 4, 6, 8, 10$
b) $\lambda = 1.0$ $A = 2, 4, 6, 8, 10$ d) $\lambda = 1.35 A = 2, 4, 6, 8, 10$

Repeat this assignment for leading edge sweep angles of 30 and 60 degrees.

2.4   Consult recent and older versions of Jane's All The World Aircraft to find examples of air–planes with wings which approximately fit some of the planforms sketched in Problem 2.3.

2.5   Calculate and plot the planform lift curve slope versus Mach number for the following two families of wings:
Leading edge sweep angle: 0, 20, 40 and 60 degrees
Aspect ratio: 2, 6 and 10
Taper ratio: 0.35
Note: The method of Part VI of Ref.2.3 or any other suitable method can be used.

2.6   Calculate and plot the planform aerodynamic center location versus Mach number for the following two families of wings:

   Leading edge sweep angle: 0, 20, 40 and 60 degrees
   Aspect ratio: 2, 6 and 10
   Taper ratio: 0.35

Note: The method of Part VI of Ref.2.3 or any other suitable method can be used.

2.10   REFERENCES FOR CHAPTER 2

2.1   Lan, C.E. and Roskam, J.; <u>Airplane Aerodynamics and Performance</u>; Roskam Aviation and Engineering Corporation, 2550 Riley Road, Ottawa, Kansas, 66067, USA; 1988.

2.2   Abbott, I.H. and Von Doenhoff, A.E.; <u>Theory of Wing Sections</u>; Dover Publications, N.Y.; 1959.

2.3   Roskam, J.; <u>Airplane Design</u>, Parts I through VIII; Roskam Aviation and Engineering Corporation, 2550 Riley Road, Ottawa, Kansas, 66067, USA; 1990.

2.4   Hoak, D.E. and Ellison, D.E. et al; USAF Stability and Control DATCOM; 1968 edition, Flight Control Division, Air Force Flight Dynamics Laboratory, Wright Patterson Air Force Base, Ohio.

2.5   Kuethe, A.M. and Schetzer, J.D.; <u>Foundations of Aerodynamics</u>; J. Wiley & Sons, New York, 1959.

2.6   Bonney, E.A.; <u>Engineering Supersonic Aerodynamics</u>; McGraw–Hill, New York, 1950.

2.7   Alford, W.J., Jr.; Theoretical and Experimental Investigation of the Subsonic Flow Fields Beneath Swept and Unswept Wings with Tables of Vortex–Induces Velocities; NACA TN 3738, August 1956.

2.8   Bauer, F., Garabedian, P. and Korn, D.; A Theory of Supercritical Wing Sections II; Lecture Notes in Economic and Mathematical Systems, Volume 108, Springer Verlag, N.Y., 1975.

2.9   Eppler, R. and Sommers, D.M.; A Computer Program for the Design and Analysis of Low Speed Airfoils, NACA TM–80210, 1980.

2.10   Multhopp, H.; Aerodynamics of the Fuselage; NACA Technical Memorandum No. 1036, December 1942.

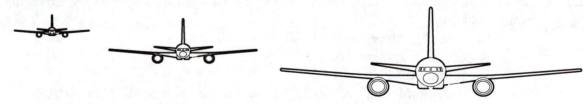

CHAPTER 3:   AERODYNAMIC AND THRUST FORCES AND MOMENTS

The purpose of this chapter is to present approaches to the modelling of aerodynamic and thrust forces and moments for the following two types of flight conditions:

1) Steady state: see Section 3.1   2) Perturbed state: see Section 3.2

Aerodynamic and thrust forces and moments can be determined in two ways:

* by experimental methods (flight test or tunnel test)
* by computational and/or empirical methods

Experimental methods have the great advantage of allowing rather accurate predictions of full scale airplane aerodynamic behavior over a wide range of flight conditions, including nonlinear effects. A disadvantage of experimental methods is that they tend to be very costly, both in calendar time and money. For these reasons, experimental methods are used primarily in research and in design verification prior to committing to building flying hardware. In most preliminary design and parametric design studies theoretical and/or empirical methods are used.

In this chapter, relatively simple mathematical models for aerodynamic and thrust forces and moments are developed by means of a combination of theoretical and empirical methods. The main emphasis is on the so–called component build–up method for modelling aerodynamic and thrust forces and moments. In this method the airplane is assumed to be built up from a number of components. The total forces and moments which act on the airplane are then assumed to follow from summing the forces and moments which act on these components. For example, in the case of the total aerodynamic force the following type of expression will be used:

$$F_{A_{airplane}} = F_{A_{wing}} + F_{A_{fuselage}} + F_{A_{hor.tail}} + F_{A_{vert.tail}} + \text{etc.} \tag{3.1}$$

Interference effects are accounted for by using empiricism. The number of components which should be used depends on the airplane configuration and on the level of accuracy desired. In the presentations which follow, emphasis is placed on gaining a physical understanding of the fundamental mechanisms which cause forces and moments to act on airplanes.

The axis system used in modelling all forces and moments is a modification of the body–fixed axis system: XYZ (See Figure 1.1), called the stability axis system $X_s Y_s Z_s$. Figure 3.1 shows how the stability axis system is defined for an airplane in a steady state, wings level, straight line flight condition with NO initial sideslip. Figure 3.2 shows how the stability axis system is defined incase initial sideslip is not zero. Note that the stability X–axis in that case is defined along the projection of the total airplane velocity vector onto the airplane XZ–plane.

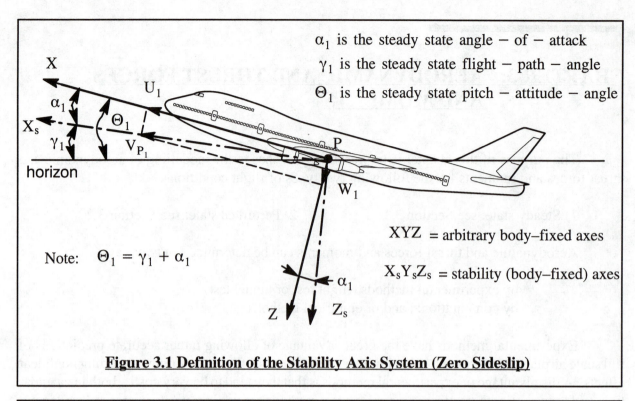

α_1 is the steady state angle $-$ of $-$ attack

γ_1 is the steady state flight $-$ path $-$ angle

Θ_1 is the steady state pitch $-$ attitude $-$ angle

Note: $\Theta_1 = \gamma_1 + \alpha_1$

XYZ = arbitrary body–fixed axes

$X_sY_sZ_s$ = stability (body–fixed) axes

Figure 3.1 Definition of the Stability Axis System (Zero Sideslip)

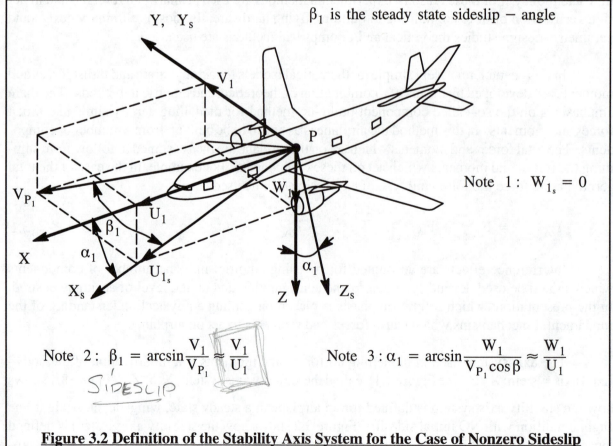

β_1 is the steady state sideslip $-$ angle

Note 1: $W_{1_s} = 0$

Note 2: $\beta_1 = \arcsin \dfrac{V_1}{V_{P_1}} \approx \dfrac{V_1}{U_1}$

SIDESLIP

Note 3: $\alpha_1 = \arcsin \dfrac{W_1}{V_{P_1} \cos \beta} \approx \dfrac{W_1}{U_1}$

Figure 3.2 Definition of the Stability Axis System for the Case of Nonzero Sideslip

NOTE: the reader should not loose sight of the fact that the stability axis system still is a body–fixed axis system. Therefore, the equations of motion developed in Chapter 1 can be applied directly to the stability axis system. Note from Figures 3.1 and 3.2 that in the stability axis system:

$$V_{P_1} = U_{1_s} \qquad \text{and}: \qquad W_{1_s} = 0 \qquad\qquad (3.2)$$

In developing the mathematical models for aerodynamic and thrust forces and moments, intensive use will be made of the idea of stability and control derivatives. Several of these were already encountered in Chapter 2: C_{L_α} and C_{L_δ} are typical examples. To illustrate typical magnitudes and trends for airplane stability and control derivatives, example plots of derivatives (and their variation with Mach number) are presented. Figures 3.3 through 3.6 show three–views of four airplanes for which data will be presented. These figures also present the reference geometries on which all derivatives are based.

3.1 STEADY STATE FORCES AND MOMENTS

Since airplanes differ from one another in configuration, shape and size, it should be expected that it is not feasible to develop a mathematical model for airplane steady state forces and moments which applies to all airplanes. The approach taken here is to first list the forces and moments to be modeled. Second, those variables of motion which experience shows to have a significant effect on the forces and moments, are also listed. For the aerodynamic forces and moments, this is done in the form of a table such as Table 3.1.

Table 3.1 Dependence of Steady State Aerodynamic Forces and Moments on Variables						
Variable	all = 0	α	β	δ_a	δ_e	δ_r
$F_{Ax_{1_s}}$	drag at zero value for all variables	induced drag	negligible for small: β	negligible for small: δ_a	negligible for small: δ_e	negligible for small: δ_r
$F_{Ay_{1_s}}$	zero	negligible for small: α	side force due to: β	zero	zero	side force due to: δ_r
$F_{Az_{1_s}}$	lift at zero value for all variables	lift due to: α	negligible for small: β	negligible	lift due to: δ_e	negligible
$L_{A_{1_s}}$	zero	rolling moment due to sideslip is affected by: α	rolling moment due to: β	rolling moment due to: δ_a	zero	rolling moment due to: δ_r
$M_{A_{1_s}}$	pitching moment at zero value for all variables	pitching moment due to: α	negligible for small: β	negligible	pitching moment due to: δ_e	negligible
$N_{A_{1_s}}$	zero	yawing moment due to sideslip is affected by: α	yawing moment due to: β	yawing moment due to: δ_a	zero	yawing moment due to: δ_r

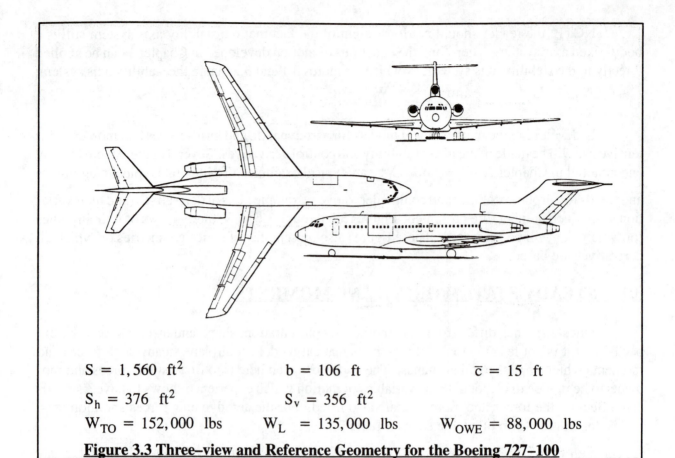

$S = 1,560 \text{ ft}^2$ $\qquad$ $b = 106 \text{ ft}$ $\qquad$ $\bar{c} = 15 \text{ ft}$

$S_h = 376 \text{ ft}^2$ $\qquad$ $S_v = 356 \text{ ft}^2$

$W_{TO} = 152,000 \text{ lbs}$ $\qquad$ $W_L = 135,000 \text{ lbs}$ $\qquad$ $W_{OWE} = 88,000 \text{ lbs}$

Figure 3.3 Three–view and Reference Geometry for the Boeing 727–100

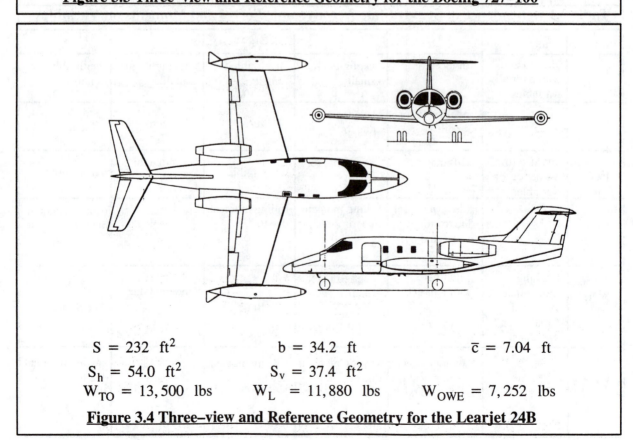

$S = 232 \text{ ft}^2$ $\qquad$ $b = 34.2 \text{ ft}$ $\qquad$ $\bar{c} = 7.04 \text{ ft}$

$S_h = 54.0 \text{ ft}^2$ $\qquad$ $S_v = 37.4 \text{ ft}^2$

$W_{TO} = 13,500 \text{ lbs}$ $\qquad$ $W_L = 11,880 \text{ lbs}$ $\qquad$ $W_{OWE} = 7,252 \text{ lbs}$

Figure 3.4 Three–view and Reference Geometry for the Learjet 24B

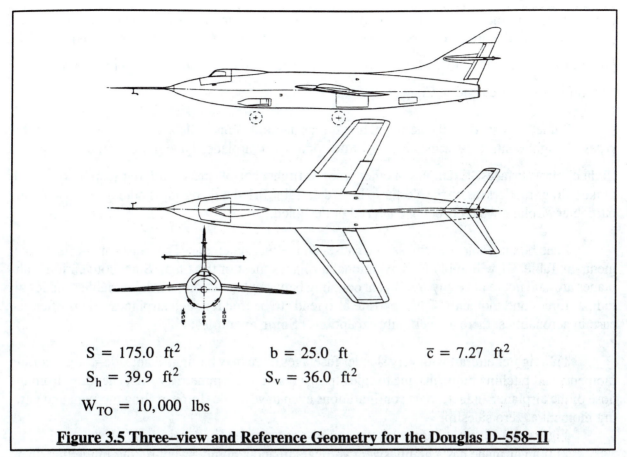

$S = 175.0 \ \text{ft}^2$ $b = 25.0 \ \text{ft}$ $\bar{c} = 7.27 \ \text{ft}^2$

$S_h = 39.9 \ \text{ft}^2$ $S_v = 36.0 \ \text{ft}^2$

$W_{TO} = 10,000 \ \text{lbs}$

Figure 3.5 Three–view and Reference Geometry for the Douglas D–558–II

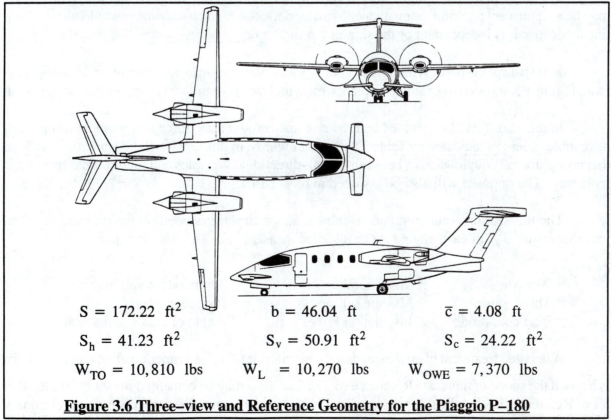

$S = 172.22 \ \text{ft}^2$ $b = 46.04 \ \text{ft}$ $\bar{c} = 4.08 \ \text{ft}$

$S_h = 41.23 \ \text{ft}^2$ $S_v = 50.91 \ \text{ft}^2$ $S_c = 24.22 \ \text{ft}^2$

$W_{TO} = 10,810 \ \text{lbs}$ $W_L = 10,270 \ \text{lbs}$ $W_{OWE} = 7,370 \ \text{lbs}$

Figure 3.6 Three–view and Reference Geometry for the Piaggio P–180

Note: in the model of Table 3.1 it is assumed that all steady state angular rates, P_1, Q_1 and R_1 are zero: in other words, the steady state is a straight line flight condition. The effect of non–zero P_1, Q_1 and R_1 (i.e. curvilinear steady state flight) on aerodynamic forces and moments is discussed in Chapter 4.

Table 3.1 lists only the aerodynamic forces and moments. Also, Table 3.1 lists only three types of flight control surfaces: δ_a, δ_e and δ_r. Most airplanes have more than three types of flight control surfaces. Examples of other types of flight control surface are: flaps, spoilers, speed-brakes, drag–rudders (as on the Northrop B–2) etc. Table 3.1 should be adjusted/expanded to fit any particular airplane which is being analyzed or designed.

Each box in Table 3.1 represents a cause–and–effect statement. The cause–and–effect statements in Table 3.1 will apply to conventional airplanes most of the time. Such conventional airplanes are said not to have any significant coupling between lateral–directional variables and longitudinal forces and moments. The opposite also tends to be true for such airplanes. As is often the case in aeronautics: there are certainly exceptions. **Some examples:**

1) In fighter aircraft with very slender fuselages there may be significant side–forces, rolling moments and pitching moments due to sideslip as a result of asymmetric vortex shedding from the nose of the airplane. In fact, some configurations even have a side–force, rolling moment and yawing moment at zero sideslip!

2) If an airplane has a highly swept vertical tail and a highly swept rudder hinge line, there may be a significant pitching moment due to rudder deflection. Such a moment would also be non-linear because it is independent of the sign of the rudder deflection!

3) If an airplane is not symmetrical about its XZ–plane, significant coupling effects may prevail. Figure 1.3 shows two example airplanes for which aerodynamic coupling effects are present.

In this text it will be assumed that the airplane aerodynamic force and moment models behave more or less as indicated by Table 3.1. In other words, in this text it will be generally assumed that no significant coupling exists between lateral–directional variables and longitudinal forces and moments. The opposite will also be assumed in most cases.

The thrust forces and moments which act on an airplane depend on the magnitude of the installed thrust, T_i, of each engine.. The installed thrust, T_i, is itself a function of:

* Altitude   * Mach number   * Temperature and humidity
* Thrust setting   * Mixture setting   * Propeller setting
* Inlet conditions   * Installation losses   * Angle of attack and sideslip

A detailed treatment of how to predict the magnitude of T_i as a function of all these variables is beyond the scope of this text. References 3.1, 3.2 and 3.3 may be consulted for such details. Part VI of Reference 3.1 contains step–by–step methods for estimating these effects in the preliminary design stage. In this text it will be assumed that the magnitude of the installed thrust of each engine, T_i is known.

Depending on the placement of propellers and/or jet exhausts, there may be significant interference effects between aerodynamic and thrust forces and moments. These interference effects are also considered to be beyond the scope of this text. The reader may wish to consult References 3.4 and 3.5 for further study of such interference effects.

Because it is assumed that little coupling between the longitudinal variables and the lateral–directional variables exists, the modelling of forces and moments will be discussed in two independent sets in the following Sub–sections:

3.1.1 through 3.1.6   Longitudinal Forces and Moments

3.1.7 through 3.1.12   Lateral–Directional Forces and Moments

3.1.1   LONGITUDINAL AERODYNAMIC FORCES AND MOMENTS

Figure 3.7 illustrates the longitudinal aerodynamic forces and moments which act on an airplane in a steady state flight condition. In the stability axis system, these forces and moments are written as follows:

$$F_{A_{x_{1_s}}} = -D$$
$$F_{A_{z_{1_s}}} = -L \tag{3.3}$$
$$M_{A_{1_s}} = M_A$$

[handwritten: F_{Aero} x-axis / 1-ss / s-stability]

In the development of models for drag, lift and pitching moment, the subscripts 1 and s will be dropped for the remainder of this section. This can be done without ambiguity because it is understood that the material deals only with steady state effects in the stability axis system!

The modelling of drag, lift and pitching moment is discussed in Sub–sections 3.1.2 through 3.1.4 respectively.

3.1.2   AIRPLANE DRAG

Airplane drag, D, is non–dimensionalized as follows:

$$D = C_D \overline{q} S \tag{3.4}$$

where: C_D is the total airplane drag coefficient.

The steady state airplane drag coefficient depends on the following factors:

* airplane wetted area   * airplane average skin friction coefficient
* angle of attack, α * control surface deflection(s), δ_e, i_h, etc.

* dynamic pressure, $\overline{q}$ * Mach number and Reynolds number

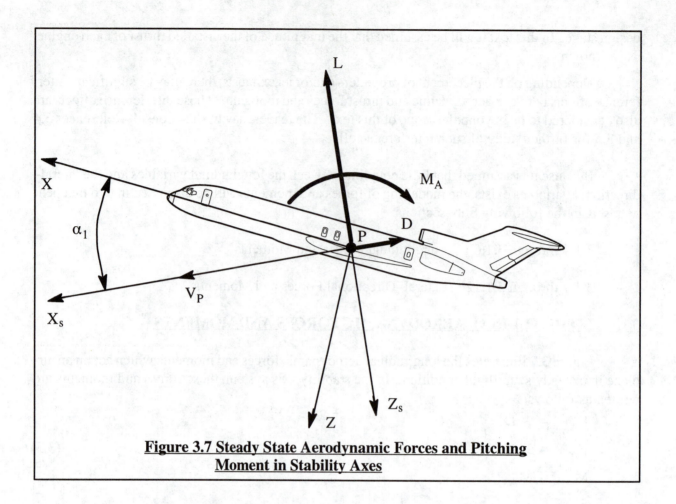

Figure 3.7 Steady State Aerodynamic Forces and Pitching Moment in Stability Axes

For an airplane equipped with an elevator and a variable incidence horizontal tail, the drag coefficient, C_D, is expressed with the help of a first order Taylor series:

$$C_D = C_{D_0} + C_{D_\alpha}\alpha + C_{D_{i_h}}i_h + C_{D_{\delta_e}}\delta_e \qquad (3.5)$$

The coefficient and derivatives in Eqn (3.5) are to be evaluated at constant Mach number and Reynolds number. The terms in Eqn (3.5) have the following meanings:

C_{D_0} is the value of C_D for: $\alpha = i_h = \delta_e = 0$

$C_{D_\alpha} = \partial C_D/\partial\alpha$ is the change in airplane drag due to a change in airplane angle of attack, α

$C_{D_{i_h}} = \partial C_D/\partial i_h$ is the change in airplane drag due to a change in stabilizer incidence angle, i_h, for: $\alpha = \delta_e = 0$

$C_{D_{\delta_e}} = \partial C_D/\partial\delta_e$ is the change in airplane drag due to a change in elevator angle, δ_e, for: $\alpha = i_h = 0$

Figure 3.8 shows a graphical interpretation of C_{D_0} and C_{D_α}. Note that the numerical values for C_{D_0} and C_{D_α} depend on the steady state itself! For most stability and control applications

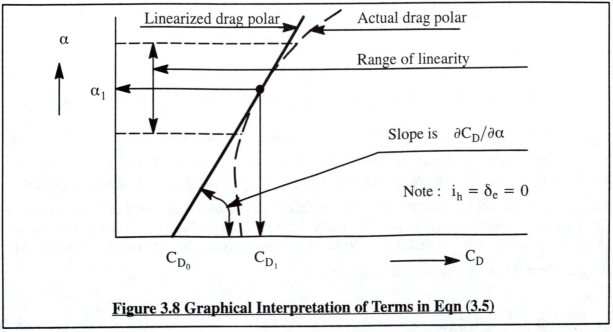

Figure 3.8 Graphical Interpretation of Terms in Eqn (3.5)

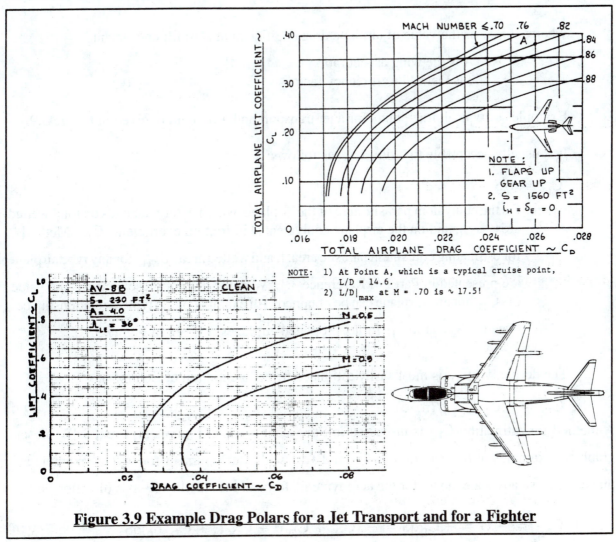

NOTE: 1) At Point A, which is a typical cruise point, L/D = 14.6.
2) $L/D|_{max}$ at M = .70 is ∿ 17.5!

Figure 3.9 Example Drag Polars for a Jet Transport and for a Fighter

it has been found acceptable to neglect drag changes due to control surface deflections (one of several exceptions to this is the so–called minimum control speed problem to be discussed in Chapter 4). Therefore, usually:

$$C_{D_{i_h}} = C_{D_{\delta_e}} = 0 \tag{3.6}$$

In performance problems where trim drag is important, Eqn(3.6) should NOT be used!

There is a notational problem with C_{D_0} in Eqn (3.5): the symbol C_{D_0} as used here is the value of airplane drag coefficient for zero angle of attack, zero elevator deflection and zero stabilizer incidence angle. In performance applications, the symbol C_{D_0} stands for the value of airplane drag coefficient at zero lift coefficient, zero elevator deflection and zero stabilizer incidence deflection. To avoid confusion between these two physically different drag coefficients in this text, the notation $\overline{C}_{D_0}$ will be used for the zero–lift drag coefficient. Therefore, in this text the standard parabolic form of the airplane drag polar will be written as:

$$C_D = \overline{C}_{D_0} + \frac{C_L^2}{\pi Ae} \tag{3.7}$$

where: $\overline{C}_{D_0}$ is the value of airplane drag coefficient at zero lift coefficient

              A is the wing aspect ratio
              e is Oswald's efficiency factor

Examples of typical drag polars for a jet transport and a fighter are given in Figure 3.9.

It is usually acceptable to write $\overline{C}_{D_0}$ as follows:

$$\overline{C}_{D_0} = f/S \tag{3.8}$$

where: f is the equivalent parasite area of the airplane, which in turn depends on total wetted area S_{wet}, and on the airplane equivalent skin friction coefficient, C_f . Methods for estimating equivalent parasite area, f, and wetted area, S_{wet} , for any type airplane are presented in Part I of Reference 3.1. With the help of those methods the value of $\overline{C}_{D_0}$ for any airplane can be obtained. An example of the typical relationship be–tween f, S_{wet} and C_f for jet propelled airplanes is given in Figure 3.10.

The derivative C_{D_α} is most easily estimated by differentiation of Eqn (3.7):

$$C_{D_\alpha} = (2C_{L_1}C_{L_\alpha})/(\pi Ae) \tag{3.9}$$

A method for estimating C_{L_α} is discussed in Sub–section 3.1.3. Figures 3.11 and 3.12 present graphical examples of the variation of C_D and C_{D_α} with Mach number for several example airplanes. The steady state model for the aerodynamic force in the stability X–axis direction is:

$$F_{A_{x_{1_s}}} = -D = -C_D \overline{q}S = -(C_{D_0} + C_{D_\alpha}\alpha + C_{D_{i_h}}i_h + C_{D_{\delta_e}}\delta_e)\overline{q}S \tag{3.10}$$

This figure was generated with the Advanced Aircraft Analysis (AAA) Program described in Appendix A

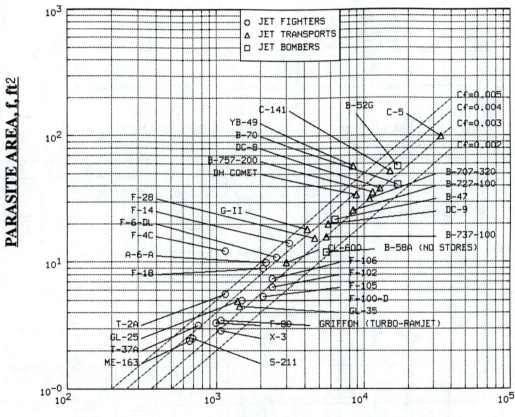

Figure 3.10 Effect of Wetted Area and Equivalent Skin Friction on Parasite Area of Jet Powered Airplanes

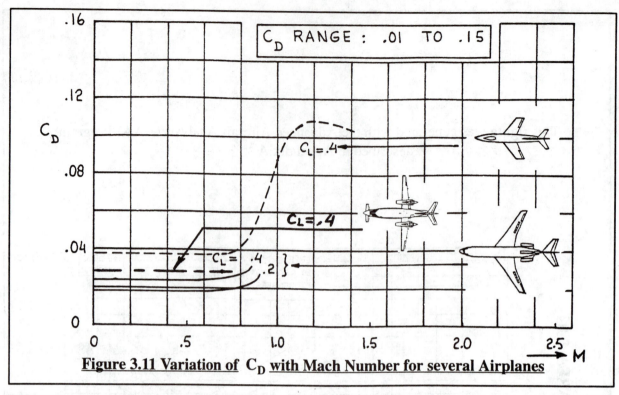

Figure 3.11 Variation of C_D with Mach Number for several Airplanes

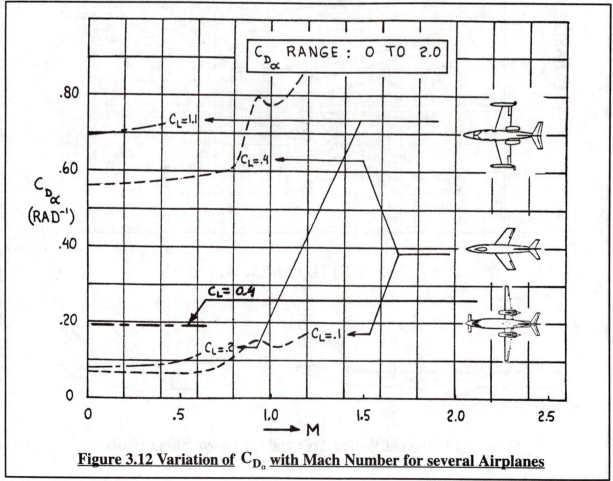

Figure 3.12 Variation of C_{D_α} with Mach Number for several Airplanes

3.1.3 AIRPLANE LIFT

Airplane lift is non–dimensionalized as follows:

$$L = C_L \bar{q} S \tag{3.11}$$

where: C_L is the total airplane lift coefficient.

The steady state airplane lift coefficient depends on the following factors:

* angle of attack, α * control surface deflection(s), δ_e, i_h, etc.

* dynamic pressure, $\bar{q}$ * Mach number and Reynolds number

For an airplane equipped with an elevator and variable incidence horizontal tail (stabilizer) the lift coefficient, C_L, is expressed with the help of a first order Taylor series:

$$C_L = C_{L_0} + C_{L_\alpha}\alpha + C_{L_{i_h}}i_h + C_{L_{\delta_e}}\delta_e \tag{3.12}$$

The coefficient and derivatives in Eqn (3.12) are to be evaluated at constant Mach number and Reynolds number. The terms in Eqn (3.12) have the following meanings:

C_{L_0} is the value of C_L for: $\alpha = i_h = \delta_e = 0$

$C_{L_\alpha} = \partial C_L/\partial\alpha$ is the change in airplane lift due to a change in airplane angle of attack, α

$C_{L_{i_h}} = \partial C_L/\partial i_h$ is the change in airplane lift due to a change in stabilizer incidence angle, i_h for: $\alpha = \delta_e = 0$

$C_{L_{\delta_e}} = \partial C_L/\partial\delta_e$ is the change in airplane lift due to a change in elevator angle, δ_e for: $\alpha = i_h = 0$

In the following, it will be shown how the coefficients and derivatives in Eqn (3.12) can be estimated using the airplane component build–up philosophy. To keep the development simple, a conventional (tail–aft) airplane will be used as an example. Figure 3.13 shows the definition of geometric parameters to be used.

It will be assumed that the drag forces acting on the wing–fuselage and the horizontal tail are negligible. The total lift which acts on the airplane is then found from:

$$L \approx L_{wf} + L_h \cos\varepsilon \approx L_{wf} + L_h \tag{3.13}$$

This can be written in coefficient form:

$$C_L\bar{q}S = C_{L_{wf}}\bar{q}S + C_{L_h}\bar{q}_h S_h \tag{3.14}$$

Due to Propeller Slipstream, Dynamic Pressure Has Increased.

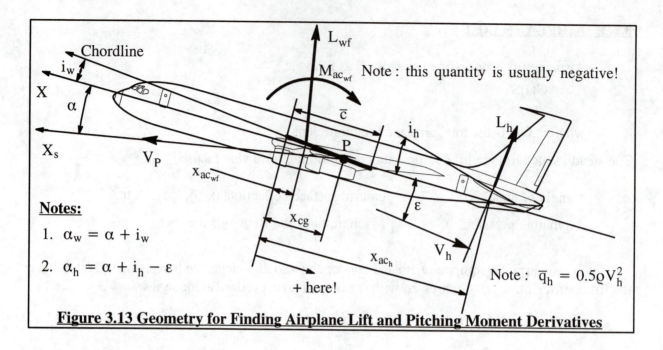

Figure 3.13 Geometry for Finding Airplane Lift and Pitching Moment Derivatives

Note that the dynamic pressure at the horizontal tail, $\bar{q}_h$ is potentially different from that at the wing–fuselage, $\bar{q}$. Reasons for this difference can be that the tail is affected by propeller slipstream, by jet exhaust effects and by fuselage boundary layer effects. The difference in dynamic pressure is accounted for by the introduction of the so–called dynamic pressure ratio, η_h :

$$\eta_h = \bar{q}_h / \bar{q} \qquad \text{Note}: \bar{q}_h = 0.5 \varrho V_h^2 \tag{3.15}$$

Eqn (3.14) can be rewritten as:

$$C_L = C_{L_{wf}} + C_{L_h} \eta_h \frac{S_h}{S} \tag{3.16}$$

The wing–fuselage lift coefficient, $C_{L_{wf}}$ can be expressed as follows:

$$C_{L_{wf}} = C_{L_{0_{wf}}} + C_{L_{\alpha_{wf}}} \alpha \tag{3.17}$$

The wing–fuselage lift–curve slope, $C_{L_{\alpha_{wf}}}$ differs from the wing lift–curve slope, $C_{L_{\alpha_w}}$ because of the wing–to–fuselage interference effect. Methods for accounting for this effect are presented in Part VI of Reference 3.1. For airplanes with a wing span to fuselage diameter ratio of six or higher it is usually acceptable to assume: $C_{L_{\alpha_{wf}}} \approx C_{L_{\alpha_w}}$.

Observe from Figure 3.13 that airplane angle of attack, α is not the same as wing angle of attack, α_w :

$$\alpha_w = \alpha + i_w \tag{3.18}$$

The wing incidence angle, i_w is determined by factors such as cruise drag, maintaining a level cabin floor in cruise and/or visibility on approach to landing. Part III of Reference 3.1 contains more detailed discussions on this subject.

The horizontal tail lift coefficient, C_{L_h}, is determined from:

$$C_{L_h} = C_{L_{0_h}} + C_{L_{\alpha_h}}\alpha_h + C_{L_{\alpha_h}}\tau_e\delta_e \qquad (3.19)$$

where: $C_{L_{0_h}}$ equals 0 for tails with symmetrical airfoils. It should be noted that many airplanes have negatively cambered tails. For such airplanes $C_{L_{0_h}}$ is negative!

α_h is the horizontal tail angle of attack:

$$\alpha_h = \alpha + i_h - \varepsilon \qquad (3.20)$$

where: i_h is the horizontal tail incidence angle. In many high performance airplanes this angle is controllable from the cockpit. It is defined as positive, trailing edge down (=leading edge up!). In such an operating mode the surface is referred to as a stabilator or variable incidence stabilizer.

ε is the average downwash angle induced by the wing on the tail and often expressed as:

$$\varepsilon = \varepsilon_0 + \frac{d\varepsilon}{d\alpha}\alpha \qquad (3.21)$$

where: ε_0 is the downwash angle at zero airplane angle of attack

τ_e is the elevator angle of attack effectiveness

δ_e is the elevator deflection angle, positive trailing edge down.

Methods for estimating the various quantities introduced here are found in Part VI of Reference 3.1. By substituting Eqns (3.17) through (3.21) into Eqn (3.16) and rearranging it follows:

$$C_L = C_{L_{0_{wf}}} + C_{L_{\alpha_{wf}}}\alpha + C_{L_{\alpha_h}}\eta_h\frac{S_h}{S}[\alpha - (\varepsilon_0 + \frac{d\varepsilon}{d\alpha}\alpha) + i_h + \tau_e\delta_e] + C_{L_{0_h}} \qquad (3.22)$$

Wing fuselag &
Horiz Tail

By comparing this equation with Eqn (3.12) the following equations for the airplane coefficient and derivatives are found by partial differentiation:

$$C_{L_0} = C_{L_{0_{wf}}} - C_{L_{\alpha_h}}\eta_h\frac{S_h}{S}\varepsilon_0 + C_{L_{0_h}} \approx C_{L_{0_{wf}}} \quad \text{in many airplanes} \qquad (3.23)$$

$$C_{L_\alpha} = C_{L_{\alpha_{wf}}} + C_{L_{\alpha_h}}\eta_h\frac{S_h}{S}(1 - \frac{d\varepsilon}{d\alpha}) \qquad (3.24)$$

$$C_{L_{i_h}} = C_{L_{\alpha_h}}\eta_h\frac{S_h}{S} \qquad (3.25)$$

$$C_{L_{\delta_e}} = C_{L_{\alpha_h}}\eta_h\frac{S_h}{S}\tau_e \qquad (3.26)$$

The derivative C_{L_α} is called the total airplane lift–curve slope. It is of major importance to stability, control and response to turbulence of airplanes.

Figure 3.14 shows how airplane lift coefficient is related to angle of attack and stabilizer incidence angle for a flaps up and flaps down case. Typical magnitudes of the coefficient and derivatives of Eqns (3.23) through (3.26) are presented in Figures 3.15 through 3.18. Observe that the only difference between $C_{L_{i_h}}$ and $C_{L_{\delta_e}}$ is the elevator angle of attack effectiveness parameter, τ_e. This parameter is called α_δ in Figure 2.23. For airplanes with roughly 30% chord elevators it is seen from Figure 2.23 that $C_{L_{i_h}}$ will therefore be about twice the value of $C_{L_{\delta_e}}$. Note from Equation (3.24) that the magnitude of airplane lift–curve slope can be significantly higher than the magnitude for wing–fuselage lift–curve slope for airplanes with a large horizontal tail.

The steady state model for the aerodynamic force in the stability Z–axis direction is:

$$F_{A_{z_{1_s}}} = -L = -C_L\overline{q}S = -(C_{L_0} + C_{L_\alpha}\alpha + C_{L_{i_h}}i_h + C_{L_{\delta_e}}\delta_e)\overline{q}S \qquad (3.27)$$

3.1.4   AIRPLANE AERODYNAMIC PITCHING MOMENT

The airplane aerodynamic pitching moment, M_A, is non–dimensionalized as follows:

$$M_A = C_m\overline{q}S\overline{c} \qquad (3.28)$$

where: C_m is the total airplane aerodynamic pitching moment coefficient.

The steady state airplane aerodynamic pitching moment coefficient depends on the following factors:

* angle of attack, α * control surface deflection(s), δ_e, i_h, etc.

* dynamic pressure, $\overline{q}$ * Mach number and Reynolds number

* moment reference center (usually the center of gravity) location

For an airplane with an elevator and a variable incidence horizontal tail, the aerodynamic pitching moment coefficient C_m is expressed in the form of a first order Taylor series as:

$$C_m = C_{m_0} + C_{m_\alpha}\alpha + C_{m_{i_h}}i_h + C_{m_{\delta_e}}\delta_e \qquad (3.29)$$

The coefficient and derivatives in Eqn (3.29) are to be evaluated at constant Mach number and Reynolds number. The terms in Eqn (3.29) have the following meanings:

C_{m_0} is the value of C_m for: $\alpha = i_h = \delta_e = 0$

$C_{m_\alpha} = \partial C_m/\partial\alpha$ is the change in airplane aerodynamic pitching moment coefficient due to a change in angle of attack

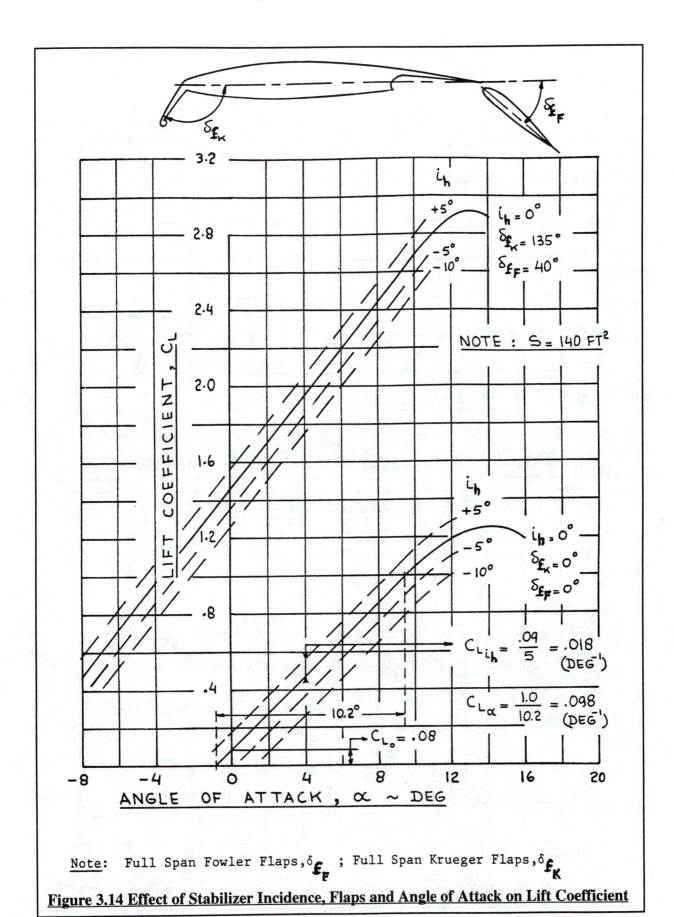

Figure 3.14 Effect of Stabilizer Incidence, Flaps and Angle of Attack on Lift Coefficient

Note: Full Span Fowler Flaps, δ_{f_F} ; Full Span Krueger Flaps, δ_{f_K}

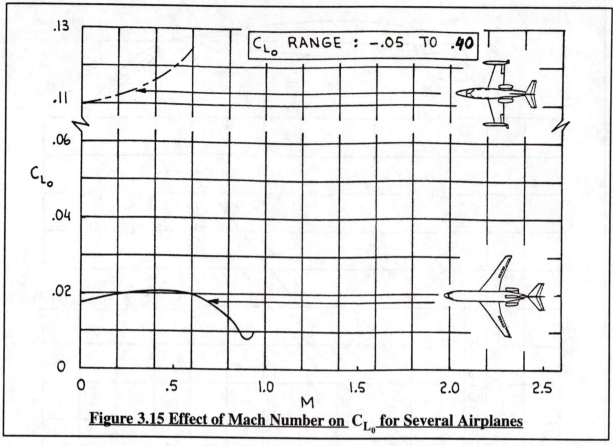

Figure 3.15 Effect of Mach Number on C_{L_0} for Several Airplanes

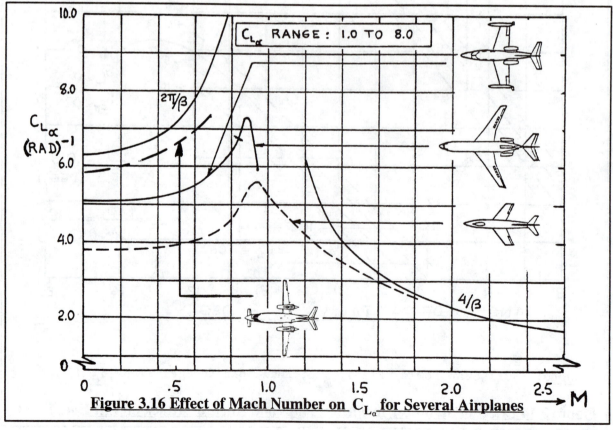

Figure 3.16 Effect of Mach Number on C_{L_α} for Several Airplanes

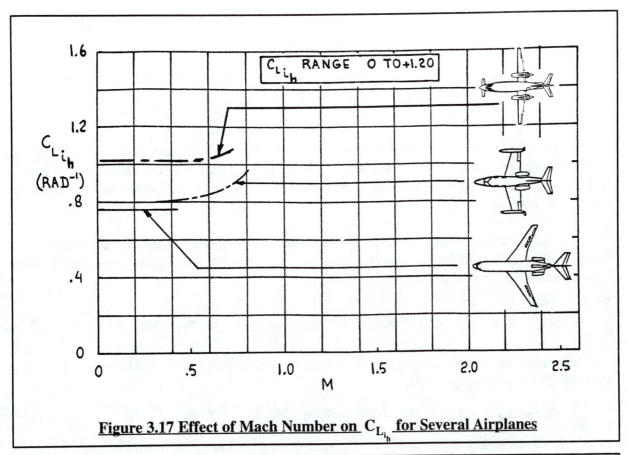

Figure 3.17 Effect of Mach Number on $C_{L_{i_h}}$ for Several Airplanes

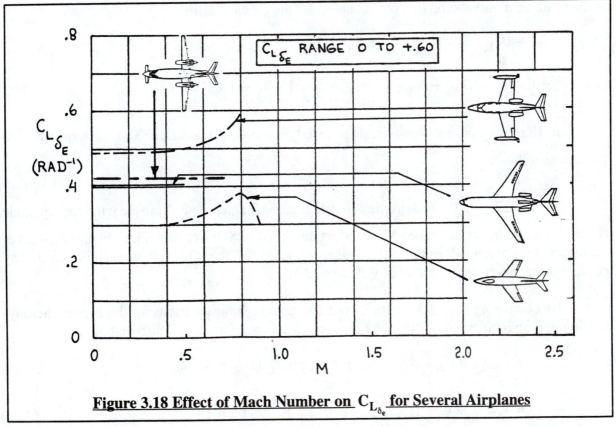

Figure 3.18 Effect of Mach Number on $C_{L_{\delta_e}}$ for Several Airplanes

$C_{m_{i_h}} = \partial C_m / \partial i_h$ is the change in airplane aerodynamic pitching moment coefficient due to a change in stabilizer incidence angle, i_h for: $\alpha = \delta_e = 0$

$C_{m_{\delta_e}} = \partial C_m / \partial \delta_e$ is the change in airplane aerodynamic pitching moment coefficient due to a change in elevator angle, δ_e for: $\alpha = i_h = 0$

In the following, it will be shown how the coefficient and derivatives in Eqn (3.29) can be estimated using the airplane component build–up idea. To keep the development simple, the tail–aft airplane geometry of Figure 3.13 will again be used. Point P in Figure 3.13 acts as the moment reference center (usually the center of gravity).

It will be assumed that the effect of wing–fuselage drag and tail drag on airplane pitching moment is negligible. Referring back to Figure 3.13, it is seen that the airplane aerodynamic pitching moment about point P can be expressed as:

$$M_A = M_{ac_{wf}} + L_{wf}(x_{cg} - x_{ac_{wf}})\cos(\alpha + i_w) - L_h(x_{ac_h} - x_{cg})\cos(\alpha + i_w - \varepsilon) \quad (3.30)$$

In most instances it is acceptable to set the cosines in Eqn (3.30) equal to 1.0. Doing that and non–dimensionalizing yields:

$$C_m = C_{m_{ac_{wf}}} + C_{L_{wf}}\frac{(x_{cg} - x_{ac_{wf}})}{\overline{c}} - C_{L_h}\eta_h\frac{S_h}{S}\frac{(x_{ac_h} - x_{cg})}{\overline{c}} \quad (3.31)$$

At this point Equations (3.17), (3.19), (3.20) and (3.21) are substituted in Eqn (3.31) while at the same time introducing the 'bar' notation for the moment arms:

$$C_m = (C_{L_{0_{wf}}} + C_{L_{\alpha_{wf}}}\alpha)(\overline{x}_{cg} - \overline{x}_{ac_{wf}}) +$$

$$- C_{L_{\alpha_h}}\eta_h\frac{S_h}{S}(\overline{x}_{ac_h} - \overline{x}_{cg})[\alpha - (\varepsilon_0 + \frac{d\varepsilon}{d\alpha}\alpha) + i_h + \tau_e\delta_e] \quad (3.32)$$

In this equation, the wing–fuselage aerodynamic center location, $\overline{x}_{ac_{wf}}$, is normally expressed as follows:

$$\overline{x}_{ac_{wf}} = \overline{x}_{ac_w} + \Delta\overline{x}_{ac_{fus}} \quad (3.33)$$

where: $\Delta\overline{x}_{ac_{fus}}$ is the shift in wing+fuselage aerodynamic center from the wing aerodynamic center as caused by the so–called Munk effect discussed in Sub–section 2.5.6. Figure 2.19 gives examples of the magnitude of this shift for three airplanes. Methods for computing this shift for any configuration are given in Part VI of Reference 3.1.

By comparing Eqn (3.33) with Eqn (3.29) the following equations for the airplane aerodynamic pitching moment coefficient and derivatives are found by partial differentiation:

$$C_{m_0} = C_{m_{ac_{wf}}} + C_{L_{0_{wf}}}(\overline{x}_{cg} - \overline{x}_{ac_{wf}}) + C_{L_{\alpha_h}}\eta_h\frac{S_h}{S}(\overline{x}_{ac_h} - \overline{x}_{cg})\varepsilon_0 \approx$$

$$\approx C_{m_{ac_{wf}}} + C_{L_{0_{wf}}}(\overline{x}_{cg} - \overline{x}_{ac_{wf}}) \quad \text{if } \varepsilon_0 \text{ is negligible} \quad (3.34)$$

$$C_{m_\alpha} = C_{L_{\alpha_{wf}}}(\bar{x}_{cg} - \bar{x}_{ac_{wf}}) - C_{L_{\alpha_h}}\eta_h\frac{S_h}{S}(\bar{x}_{ac_h} - \bar{x}_{cg})(1 - d\varepsilon/d\alpha) \qquad (3.35)$$

Sor transport ~ 0.8 stable
, 6 nuetrally stable

$$C_{m_{i_h}} = -C_{L_{\alpha_h}}\eta_h\frac{S_h}{S}(\bar{x}_{ac_h} - \bar{x}_{cg}) = -C_{L_{\alpha_h}}\eta_h\bar{V}_h \qquad (3.36)$$

$$\text{where}: \quad \bar{V}_h = (S_h/S)(\bar{x}_{ac_h} - \bar{x}_{cg}) \qquad (3.36a)$$

is the horizontal tail volume coefficient. This volume coefficient is useful in preliminary tail–sizing which is used in the early aircraft design process. A detailed explanation is found in Part II of Reference 3.1.

$$C_{m_{\delta_e}} = -C_{L_{\alpha_h}}\eta_h\bar{V}_h\tau_e \qquad (3.37)$$

The derivatives $C_{m_{i_h}}$ and $C_{m_{\delta_e}}$ are referred to as longitudinal control power derivatives. They are of major importance in airplane controllability considerations as will become clear in Chapters 4 and 5.

Figure 3.19 shows how airplane aerodynamic pitching moment coefficient is related to angle of attack and stabilizer incidence angle. Figures 3.20 through 3.23 present typical magnitude of the coefficient and derivatives represented by Eqns (3.34) through (3.37). Several observations are in order:

1) Note that the only difference between $C_{m_{i_h}}$ and $C_{m_{\delta_e}}$ (Figures 3.22 and 3.23) is the angle of attack effectiveness of the elevator, τ_e. For airplanes with roughly 30% chord elevators it is seen from Figure 3.22 that $C_{m_{i_h}}$ will therefore be about twice the value of $C_{m_{\delta_e}}$.

2) Note from Figure 3.20 that the zero–angle–of–attack pitching moment coefficient, C_{m_0} can be negative as well a positive. From a trim point of view, a positive value is to be preferred.

3) Note from Figure 3.20 that C_{m_0} tends to change in the negative (i.e. nose–down) direction with increasing Mach number. This phenomenon is referred to as 'tuck'. It can lead to handling quality problems during recoveries from a high speed dive.

4) Note the 'stable' and 'unstable' breaks in the pitching moment coefficient at high angle of attack. Whether a stable or an unstable break occurs, depends on the detail design of the configuration. For a detailed discussion, see Part III of Reference 3.1.

The derivative C_{m_α} is called the static longitudinal stability derivative. It is of major importance to airplane stability and control as will become clear in Chapters 4 and 5. By introducing the idea of total airplane aerodynamic center it is possible to simplify Eqn (3.35).

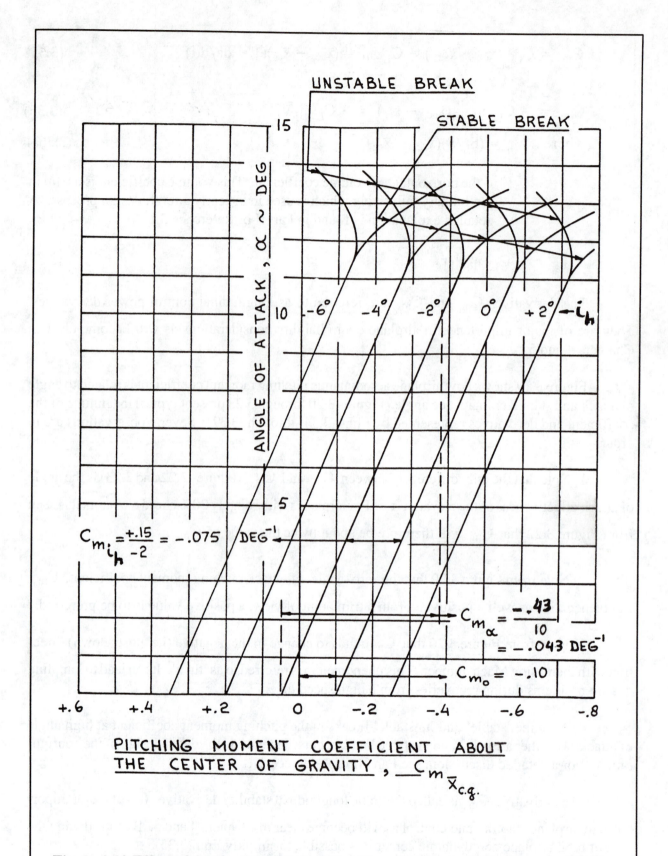

Figure 3.19 Effect of Angle of Attack and Stabilizer Incidence Angle on Aerodynamic Pitching Moment Coefficient

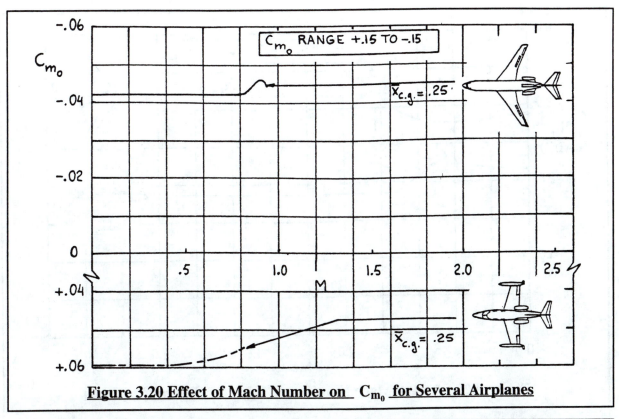

Figure 3.20 Effect of Mach Number on C_{m_0} for Several Airplanes

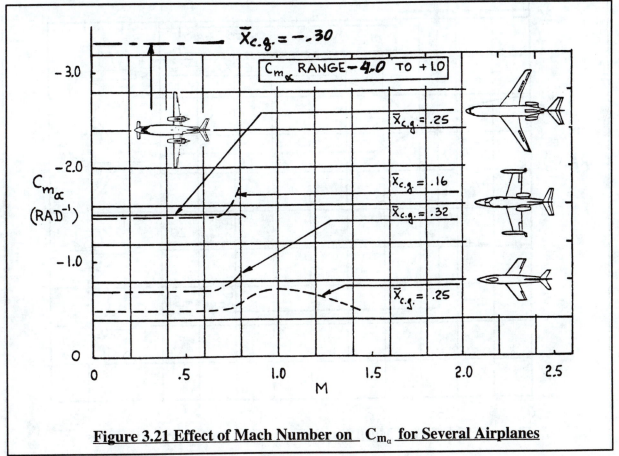

Figure 3.21 Effect of Mach Number on C_{m_α} for Several Airplanes

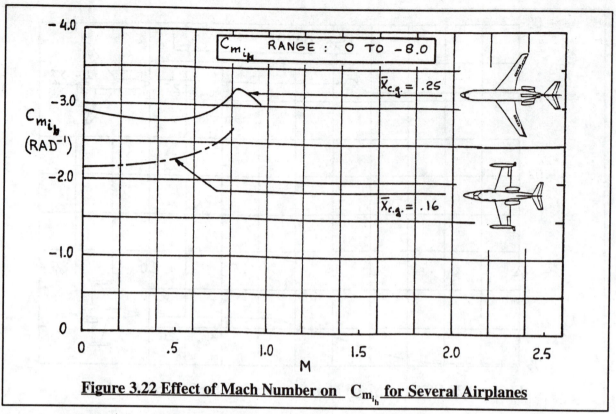

Figure 3.22 Effect of Mach Number on $C_{m_{i_h}}$ for Several Airplanes

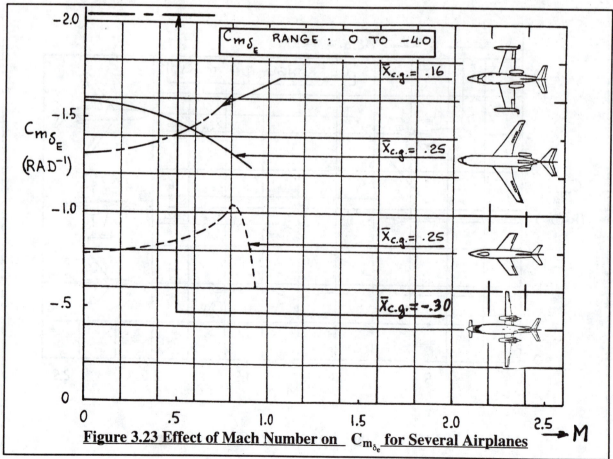

Figure 3.23 Effect of Mach Number on $C_{m_{\delta_e}}$ for Several Airplanes

[handwritten: x_{ac} behind x_{cg} for stability]

Definition: The aerodynamic center of an airplane is defined as that point on the wing mean geometric chord about which the variation of pitching moment coefficient with angle of attack is zero.

The location of airplane aerodynamic center on the wing mean geometric chord is normally expressed as a fraction of the mgc, $\overline{x}_{ac_A}$, and is also referred to as the airplane (stick–fixed) neutral point. The significance of the 'stick–fixed' addition will be made clear in Chapter 4.

The definition of airplane aerodynamic center, when applied to Eqn (3.35), leads to the condition: $C_{m_\alpha} = 0$ and $\overline{x}_{cg} \mapsto \overline{x}_{ac_A}$ so that:

$$\overline{x}_{ac_A} = \frac{\overline{x}_{ac_{wf}} + \dfrac{C_{L_{\alpha_h}}}{C_{L_{\alpha_{wf}}}}\eta_h \dfrac{S_h}{S}\overline{x}_{ac_h}(1 - \dfrac{d\varepsilon}{d\alpha})}{1 + \dfrac{C_{L_{\alpha_h}}}{C_{L_{\alpha_{wf}}}}\eta_h \dfrac{S_h}{S}(1 - \dfrac{d\varepsilon}{d\alpha})}$$ (3.38)

[handwritten: ~1.1]

The reader is asked to show that Equations (3.35) and (3.38) can be combined to yield:

$$C_{m_\alpha} = C_{L_\alpha}(\overline{x}_{cg} - \overline{x}_{ac_A})$$ (3.39)

At this point the reader is reminded of two facts:

1) Equations (3.38) and (3.39) do not include the pitching moment contribution due to the propulsive installation. Particularly in propeller driven airplanes there can exist a significant shift in aerodynamic center due to the so–called propeller normal force as well as due to propeller tilt angle. See Part VI of Reference 3.1 for more details.

2) Equation (3.38) applies to tail–aft airplanes only. For canard and for three–surface airplanes (such as the Beech Starship I and the Piaggio P–180 Avanti) Eqn (3.38) must be modified. For airplanes where the canard does NOT SIGNIFICANTLY interfere with the wing (or tail) flow–field it is possible to show that Eqn (3.38) when applied to a three–surface airplane becomes:

$$\overline{x}_{ac_A} = \frac{\overline{x}_{ac_{wf}} - \dfrac{C_{L_{\alpha_c}}}{C_{L_{\alpha_{wf}}}}\eta_c \dfrac{S_c}{S}\overline{x}_{ac_c}(1 + \dfrac{d\varepsilon_c}{d\alpha}) + \dfrac{C_{L_{\alpha_h}}}{C_{L_{\alpha_{wf}}}}\eta_h \dfrac{S_h}{S}\overline{x}_{ac_h}(1 - \dfrac{d\varepsilon}{d\alpha})}{1 + \dfrac{C_{L_{\alpha_c}}}{C_{L_{\alpha_{wf}}}}\eta_c \dfrac{S_c}{S}(1 + \dfrac{d\varepsilon_c}{d\alpha}) + \dfrac{C_{L_{\alpha_h}}}{C_{L_{\alpha_{wf}}}}\eta_h \dfrac{S_h}{S}(1 - \dfrac{d\varepsilon}{d\alpha})}$$ (3.40)

For a pure canard airplane the horizontal tail term in Eqn (3.40) must be stricken. Figure 3.24 shows how $\overline{x}_{ac_c}$ is defined in relationship to $\overline{x}_{ac_h}$ for a three–surface airplane. The quantity η_c represents the dynamic pressure ratio, $\overline{q}_c/\overline{q}$, at the canard location. The angle ε_c is the up–wash angle caused by the wing at the canard location. Methods for determining the various quantities in Eqn (3.40) are contained in Part VI of Reference 3.1.

The steady state model for the aerodynamic pitching moment about the stability Y–axis (same as body–fixed Y–axis!) is:

$$M_{A_{1_s}} = M_A = C_m\overline{q}S\overline{c} = (C_{m_0} + C_{m_\alpha}\alpha + C_{m_{i_h}}i_h + C_{m_{\delta_e}}\delta_e)\overline{q}S\overline{c}$$ (3.41)

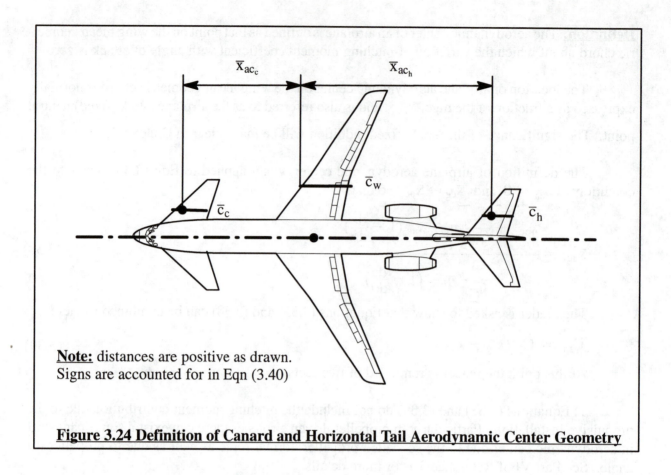

Note: distances are positive as drawn.
Signs are accounted for in Eqn (3.40)

Figure 3.24 Definition of Canard and Horizontal Tail Aerodynamic Center Geometry

3.1.5   LONGITUDINAL THRUST FORCES AND MOMENTS

Most airplanes are equipped with one or more engines. The number of engines and their disposition over the airplane depends on many mission and airworthiness related factors. For a discussion of these factors, the reader may consult Parts II and III of Reference 3.1. In this text it will be assumed that the number and disposition of the engines over the airplane is given.

The effect of thrust on the airplane forces and moments will be assumed to be comprised of:

1) Direct thrust effects   2) Indirect thrust effects

1) Direct thrust effects can be modeled in the body–fixed XYZ axis system as illustrated in Figure 3.25. The thrust output of each engine is referred to as the installed thrust. Installed thrust is computed from engine manufacturer's thrust data by accounting for various installation losses as described in Part VI of Reference 3.1. In this text it is assumed that the installed thrust for each engine is a given.

2) Indirect thrust effects occur when propeller flow fields or jet exhausts interfere with lifting surfaces, for example, by impinging on them. These effects will not be modelled in detail because they tend to be strongly configuration dependent which makes a generalized modelling approach of questionable value. Specific examples of indirect thrust effects are:

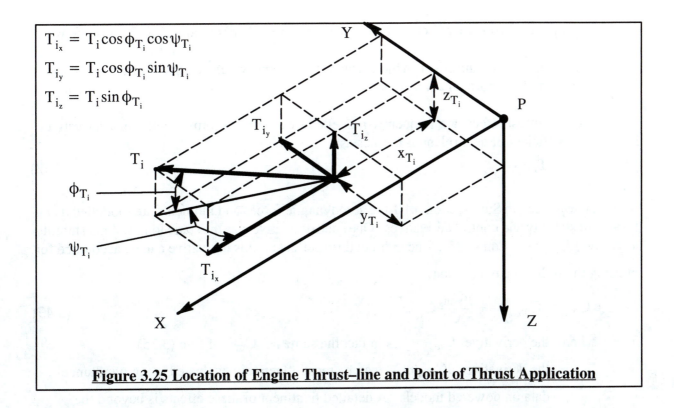

$$T_{i_x} = T_i \cos\phi_{T_i} \cos\psi_{T_i}$$
$$T_{i_y} = T_i \cos\phi_{T_i} \sin\psi_{T_i}$$
$$T_{i_z} = T_i \sin\phi_{T_i}$$

Figure 3.25 Location of Engine Thrust–line and Point of Thrust Application

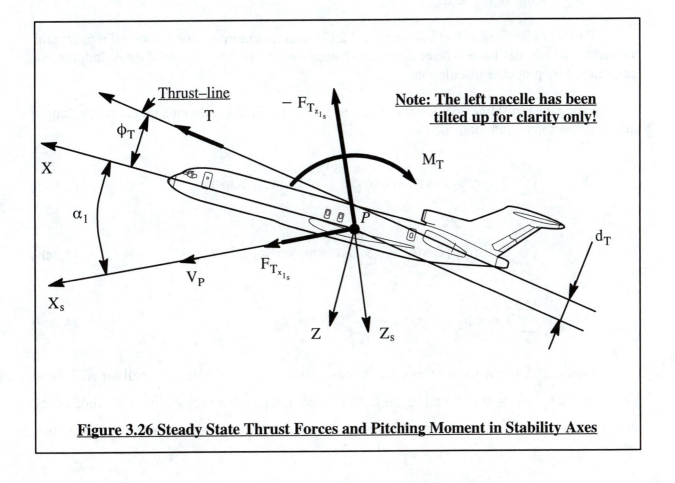

Figure 3.26 Steady State Thrust Forces and Pitching Moment in Stability Axes

a) propeller slipstream effect on a wing when the propeller is mounted in front of the wing

b) propeller slipstream effect on the downwash of a wing which in turn can affect the aerodynamics of the horizontal and/or vertical tail

Indirect thrust effects are frequently modelled by the use of thrust coefficient derivatives. The thrust coefficient of an airplane is defines as:

$$C_T = T/\overline{q}S \tag{3.42}$$

As was seen in Sub–section 3.1.1 the aerodynamic forces and moments are modelled using the idea of stability and control derivatives. One such derivative was the static longitudinal stability derivative, C_{m_α} : see Eqn (3.35). The indirect thrust effect on this derivative can be accounted for by using the following expression:

$$C_{m_\alpha} = C_{m_{\alpha_{C_T=0}}} + \frac{\partial C_{m_\alpha}}{\partial C_T} C_T \qquad \xrightarrow{} \begin{array}{l} \text{Term} = 0 \\ \text{for jet a/c} \end{array} \tag{3.43}$$

where: the derivative $C_{m_{\alpha_{C_T=0}}}$ is in fact the same as C_{m_α} of Eqn (3.35).

the derivative $\partial C_{m_\alpha}/\partial C_T$ can be most effectively evaluated using windtunnel

data on powered models. A detailed treatment of these effects is beyond the scope of this text.

Part VI of Reference 3.1 (Sub–section 8.2.8) contains a more detailed discussion of several corrections which may have to be made to aerodynamic derivatives as a result of thrust induced effects caused by propeller installations.

Using the thrust line orientations of Figure 3.25 results in the following model for the longitudinal thrust forces and moments:

$$F_{T_{x_{1_s}}} = (\sum_{i=1}^{i=n} T_i \cos\phi_{T_i} \cos\psi_{T_i})\cos\alpha_1 + (\sum_{i=1}^{i=n} T_i \sin\phi_{T_i})\sin\alpha_1 \tag{3.44a}$$

$$F_{T_{z_{1_s}}} = (\sum_{i=1}^{i=n} T_i \sin\phi_{T_i})\cos\alpha_1 - (\sum_{i=1}^{i=n} T_i \cos\phi_{T_i} \cos\psi_{T_i})\sin\alpha_1 \tag{3.44b}$$

$$M_{T_{1_s}} = \sum_{i=1}^{i=n} T_i \cos\phi_{T_i} \cos\psi_{T_i} z_{T_i} + \sum_{i=1}^{i=n} T_i \sin\phi_{T_i} x_{T_i} \tag{3.44c}$$

Figure 3.26 shows the net thrust for the case where ψ_{T_i} is negligibly small for ALL i engines and where $\phi_{T_i} = \phi_T$ for all engines. The thrust, T, then is the vector sum of the thrust vectors of all i engines. This results in the following model for the longitudinal thrust forces and moment:

$$F_{T_{x_{1_s}}} = T\cos(\phi_T + \alpha_1) \tag{3.45a}$$

$$F_{T_{z_{1_s}}} = -T\sin(\phi_T + \alpha_1) \tag{3.45b}$$

$$M_{T_{1_s}} = M_{T_1} = -Td_T \tag{3.45c}$$

3.1.6 ASSEMBLING THE STEADY STATE LONGITUDINAL FORCES AND MOMENTS

It is now possible to assemble all expressions for the longitudinal steady state forces and moments in matrix format. This is done in Table 3.2. Note that the aerodynamic forces and moments are treated as linear. The thrust terms still contain transcendental terms. Later, in the discussion of the equations of motion in Chapter 4, it will be shown that by the introduction of iteration schemes or by using the small angle assumption this problem will fade away.

Table 3.2 Matrix Format for Steady State Longitudinal Forces and Moments

$$\begin{Bmatrix} F_{A_{x_{1_s}}} \\ F_{A_{z_{1_s}}} \\ M_{A_{1_s}} \end{Bmatrix} = \begin{Bmatrix} -D \\ -L \\ M_A \end{Bmatrix} = \begin{Bmatrix} -C_D \bar{q} S \\ -C_L \bar{q} S \\ C_m \bar{q} S \bar{c} \end{Bmatrix} \qquad \textbf{with:}$$

$$\begin{Bmatrix} C_D \\ C_L \\ C_m \end{Bmatrix} = \begin{bmatrix} C_{D_0} & C_{D_\alpha} & C_{D_{i_h}} & C_{D_{\delta_e}} \\ \text{drag polar} & \text{drag polar} & \text{small} & \text{small} \\ C_{L_0} & C_{L_\alpha} & C_{L_{i_h}} & C_{L_{\delta_e}} \\ (3.23) & (3.24) & (3.25) & (3.26) \\ C_{m_0} & C_{m_\alpha} & C_{m_{i_h}} & C_{m_{\delta_e}} \\ (3.34) & (3.35) & (3.36) & (3.37) \end{bmatrix} \begin{Bmatrix} 1 \\ \alpha \\ i_h \\ \delta_e \end{Bmatrix} \tag{3.46a}$$

$$\begin{Bmatrix} F_{T_{x_{1_s}}} \\ F_{T_{z_{1_s}}} \\ M_{T_{1_s}} \end{Bmatrix} = \begin{Bmatrix} T\cos(\phi_T + \alpha) \\ -T\sin(\phi_T + \alpha) \\ -Td_T \end{Bmatrix} \tag{3.46b}$$

3.1.7 LATERAL–DIRECTIONAL AERODYNAMIC FORCES AND MOMENTS

When an airplane is in a steady state flight condition such that $V_1 \neq 0$, the airplane is said to be side–slipping. The sideslip angle, β_1 is defined in Figure 3.27. As seen in Table 3.1 this sideslip gives rise to an aerodynamic rolling moment, $L_{A_{1_s}}$, an aerodynamic side force, $F_{A_{y_{1_s}}}$, and an aerodynamic yawing moment, $N_{A_{1_s}}$. In addition (as also suggested by Table 3.1), any lateral–directional control surface deflections will contribute to this force and to these moments. Figure 3.27, where the subscript 1 has been deleted, shows how the side force, rolling and yawing moments are oriented relative to the airplane.

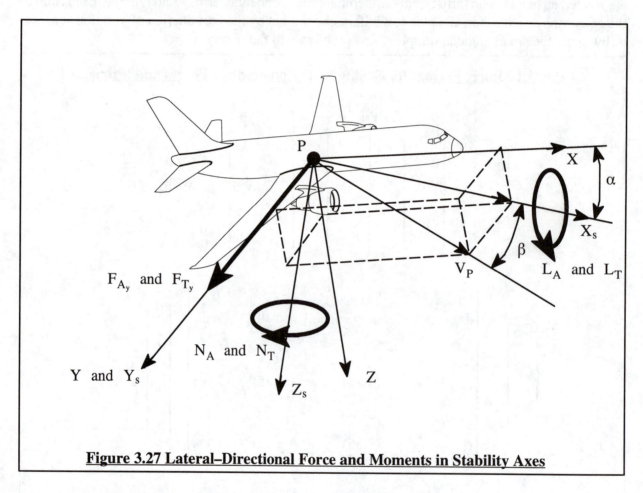

Figure 3.27 Lateral–Directional Force and Moments in Stability Axes

In the stability axis system they are written as follows:

$$L_{A_{1_s}} = L_A \tag{3.47}$$

$$F_{A_{y_{1_s}}} = F_{A_y} \tag{3.48}$$

$$N_{A_{1_s}} = N_A \tag{3.49}$$

As indicated before, the stability axis system will be used and all force and moment expressions are defined in the steady state and therefore, the subscripts 1 and s will be dropped without ambiguity.

3.1.8 AIRPLANE AERODYNAMIC ROLLING MOMENT

The steady state airplane aerodynamic rolling moment, L_A, is non–dimensionalized as:

$$L_A = C_l \bar{q} S b \qquad (3.50)$$

where: C_l is the airplane aerodynamic rolling moment coefficient.

The steady state airplane aerodynamic rolling moment coefficient, C_l, depends on the following factors:

* angle of sideslip, β * deflection of lateral control surface(s)

* angle of attack, α * deflection of directional control surface(s)

* dynamic pressure, $\bar{q}$ (see p.103)   * Mach number and Reynolds number

* moment reference center (usually the center of gravity) location

For an airplane equipped with ailerons and rudder, the rolling moment coefficient is expressed in first order Taylor series form:

$$C_l = C_{l_0} + C_{l_\beta}\beta + C_{l_{\delta_a}}\delta_a + C_{l_{\delta_r}}\delta_r \qquad (3.51)$$

The coefficient and derivatives in Eqn (3.51) are to be evaluated at constant Mach number and Reynolds number. The terms in Eqn (3.51) have the following meanings:

C_{l_0} is the value of C_l for: $\beta = \delta_a = \delta_r = 0$

$C_{l_\beta} = \partial C_l / \partial \beta$ is the change in airplane rolling moment coefficient due to a change in airplane sideslip angle, β

$C_{l_{\delta_a}} = \partial C_l / \partial \delta_a$ is the change in airplane rolling moment coefficient due to a change in aileron deflection, δ_a

$C_{l_{\delta_r}} = \partial C_l / \partial \delta_r$ is the change in airplane rolling moment coefficient due to a change in rudder deflection, δ_r

The coefficient C_{l_0} tends to be equal to zero for symmetrical airplane configurations. Exceptions to this are found in airplanes (such as fighters) with very slender, long fore–bodies. In such cases it is possible that the flow–field around the nose becomes dominated by asymmetrically shed vortices which can cause C_{l_0} to have nonzero values. For asymmetrical airplanes such as those shown in Figure 1.3, the coefficient C_{l_0} also tends to have a non– zero value.

The derivative C_{l_β} is called the airplane dihedral effect. This derivative plays a major role in determining airplane stability. The control power derivative $C_{l_{\delta_a}}$ is a dominant factor in the bank angle maneuverability of airplanes. The control power derivative $C_{l_{\delta_r}}$ is a so–called cross–control derivative. The magnitude of this derivative should preferably be close to zero.

In the following, it will be shown how the derivatives in Eqn (3.51) can be determined by using the component build–up philosophy.

Rolling Moment Coefficient Derivative Due to Sideslip, C_{l_β}

The rolling moment coefficient due to sideslip (dihedral effect) derivative, C_{l_β}, may be estimated by summing the individual dihedral effect of the airplane components. For a conventional airplane this yields:

$$C_{l_\beta} = C_{l_{\beta_{wf}}} + C_{l_{\beta_h}} + C_{l_{\beta_v}} \tag{3.52}$$

For non–conventional airplanes the reader should adjust this equation accordingly. A physical explanation for the dihedral effect of the wing–fuselage, the horizontal tail and the vertical tail will be given next.

Wing–fuselage Contribution, $C_{l_{\beta_{wf}}}$

The dihedral effect of the wing–fuselage combination is caused primarily by three factors:

1) Wing geometric dihedral effect
2) Effect of wing position on the fuselage (high or low)
3) Effect of wing sweep angle

1) Wing geometric dihedral effect

Figure 3.28 illustrates how the geometric dihedral angle, Γ, of a wing, can cause a rolling moment due to sideslip. Observe the right wing panel. As a result of the combination of angle of attack and sideslip, a normal velocity, V_n, is induced on that panel. This normal velocity is:

$$V_n = W\cos\Gamma + V\sin\Gamma \approx W + V\Gamma \tag{3.53}$$

If $\Gamma > 0$ (as shown in Figure 3.28) it is called positive. If $\Gamma < 0$, it is called negative. The latter is also referred to as 'anhedral'. As a result of a positive dihedral angle, the right wing sees a positive increase in angle of attack given by:

$$\Delta\alpha \approx \frac{V\Gamma}{U} \approx \frac{U\beta\Gamma}{U} \approx \beta\Gamma \tag{3.54}$$

It is this increment in angle of attack which produces a corresponding increment in lift. This in turn results in a negative rolling moment contribution. Note that the left wing panel experiences

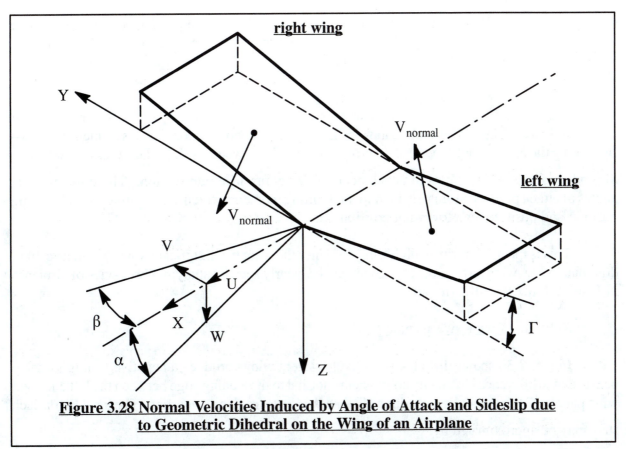

Figure 3.28 Normal Velocities Induced by Angle of Attack and Sideslip due to Geometric Dihedral on the Wing of an Airplane

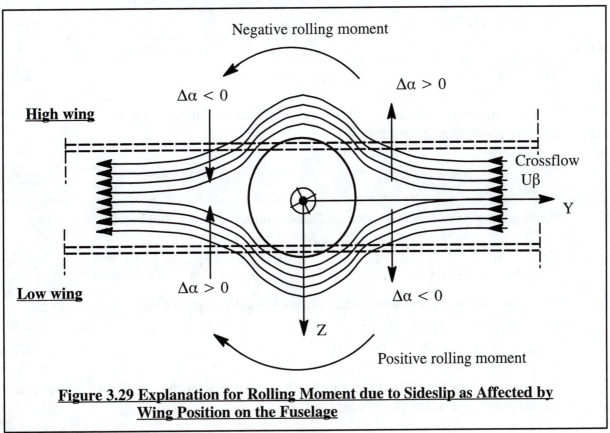

Figure 3.29 Explanation for Rolling Moment due to Sideslip as Affected by Wing Position on the Fuselage

exactly the opposite effect which also results in a negative rolling moment. The rolling moment due to sideslip due to geometric wing dihedral is therefore proportional to the geometric dihedral angle itself! Part VI of Reference 3.1 contains detailed methods for estimating this contribution.

2) Effect of wing position on the fuselage (high or low)

In Figure 3.29 the flow–field in sideslip is split into two components: a symmetrical flow–field along the X–axis (not shown) and a cross–flow field with velocity $U\beta$. This cross–flow is seen to produce incremental angles of attack near the wing–fuselage intersection. These incremental angles of attack produce ultimately incremental rolling moments which are negative for a high wing position and positive for a low wing position.

This is the reason why in high wing airplanes the wing has significantly less geometric dihedral than in low wing airplanes. This effect can be clearly seen by studying three–vies of airplanes in Jane's All the World's Aircraft.

3) Effect of wing sweep angle

Figure 3.30 shows that aft (= positively) swept wings produce a negative rolling moment because of a difference in velocity components normal to the leading edge between the left and right wing panels. Consider two wing strips at distances +/– y_i from the centerline. The local lift on each strip may be approximated by:

$$\Delta L_i = C_{L_i}\overline{q}_i S_i \tag{3.55}$$

where:

$$\overline{q}_i = 0.5\varrho V_{n_i}^2 \tag{3.56}$$

As shown in Figure 3.30, the velocity component normal to the leading edge is larger for the right wing strip than for the left wing strip:

$$[V_{n_{i_{l.h.s.}}} = V_P\cos(\Lambda_{LE} + \beta)] < [V_{n_{i_{r.h.s.}}} = V_P\cos(\Lambda_{LE} - \beta)] \tag{3.57}$$

The two wing strips together cause a negative rolling moment which is:

$$\Delta L_{A_{strips}} = -y_i C_{L_i}\frac{1}{2}\varrho S_i V_P^2[\cos^2(\Lambda_{LE} - \beta) - \cos^2(\Lambda_{LE} + \beta)] \tag{3.58}$$

This result, when expanded for small values of sideslip angle yields:

$$\Delta L_{A_{strips}} = -y_i C_{L_i}\overline{q}S_i(2\beta\sin 2\Lambda_{LE}) \tag{3.59}$$

The reader is asked to show that for forward swept wings the sign of Eqn (3.59) reverses! It is of interest to note from Eqn (3.59) that:

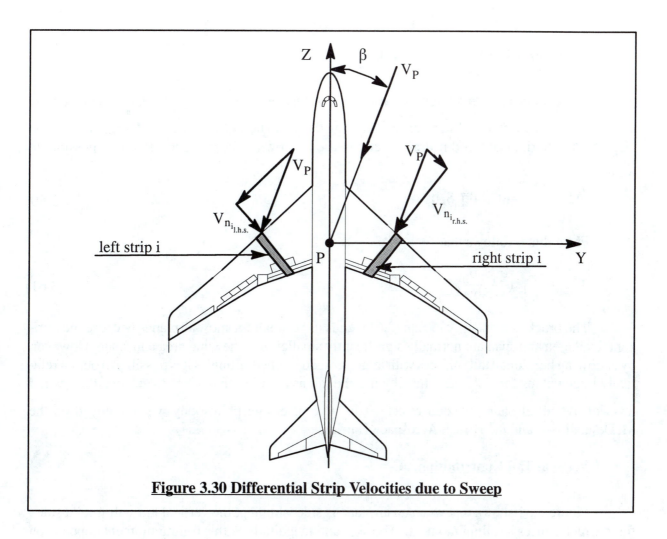

Figure 3.30 Differential Strip Velocities due to Sweep

a)   rolling moment due to sideslip, due to sweep (aft) is negative

b)   the rolling moment due to sideslip, due to sweep (aft) is proportional to lift coefficient

c)   the rolling moment due to sideslip, due to sweep (aft) is proportional to the sine of twice the leading edge sweep angle

It will be shown later that the overall airplane dihedral effect, C_{l_β}, is of major significance to stability and controllability of airplanes. The fact that this important derivative itself, for swept wing airplanes is proportional to the lift coefficient (and therefore dependent on wing–loading and dynamic pressure) also has significant consequences to configuration design.

In Chapter 4, it will be shown that making the dihedral effect, C_{l_β}, more negative will make an airplane more spirally stable. At the same time, the dutch–roll damping ratio tends to decrease. This presents a design conflict which must be resolved through some compromise.

Methods for predicting numerical values of $C_{l_{\beta_w}}$ are found in Part VI of Reference 3.1.

Horizontal Tail Contribution, $C_{l_{\beta_h}}$

The explanations given for the various wing–fuselage contributions to C_{l_β} can be directly applied to the horizontal tail by merely considering the tail to be a lifting surface. Using the notation $\overline{C}_{l_{\beta_h}}$ for the horizontal tail dihedral effect based on its own reference geometry it is possible to write:

$$\Delta L_{A_{h_{sideslip}}} = \overline{C}_{l_{\beta_h}} \beta \overline{q}_h S_h b_h \qquad (3.60)$$

From this it follows that:

$$C_{l_{\beta_h}} = \overline{C}_{l_{\beta_h}} \left(\frac{\overline{q}_h S_h b_h}{\overline{q} S b} \right) \qquad (3.61)$$

The bracketed quantity in Eqn (3.61) tends to be small for most airplanes because the horizontal tail area and span are normally significantly smaller than the wing area and span. However, by endowing horizontal tail surfaces with large geometric dihedral angles it is possible to obtain relatively large values for $\overline{C}_{l_{\beta_h}}$ and thereby use the tail as a 'tailoring device' to achieve the desired level of overall airplane dihedral effect. This type of design philosophy was employed on the McDonnell F–4 and the British Aerospace Harrier.

Vertical Tail Contribution, $C_{l_{\beta_v}}$

Figure 3.31 shows that when an airplane is side–slipping, the vertical tail will 'see' a side–force which causes a rolling moment. The sign and magnitude of this rolling moment depends on the 'vertical' moment arm of the vertical tail.

First, consider the lift coefficient which acts on the vertical tail:

$$C_{L_v} = C_{L_{\alpha_v}} (\beta - \sigma) = C_{L_{\alpha_v}} \left(1 - \frac{d\sigma}{d\beta} \right) \beta \qquad (3.62)$$

where: $C_{L_{\alpha_v}}$ is the lift–curve slope of the vertical tail, based on its own reference geometry

σ is the side–wash angle induced at the vertical tail by the fact that the wing–fuselage combination will itself be generating a side–force which creates side–wash. This effect is the aerodynamic equivalent of horizontal tail down–wash created by the wing.

The 'lift' on the vertical tail causes a negative rolling moment which can be expressed by:

$$\Delta L_{A_v} = - z_{v_s} C_{L_{\alpha_v}} (\beta - \sigma) \overline{q}_v S_v \qquad (3.63)$$

By non–dimensionalizing and by using the notation of Eqn (3.62):

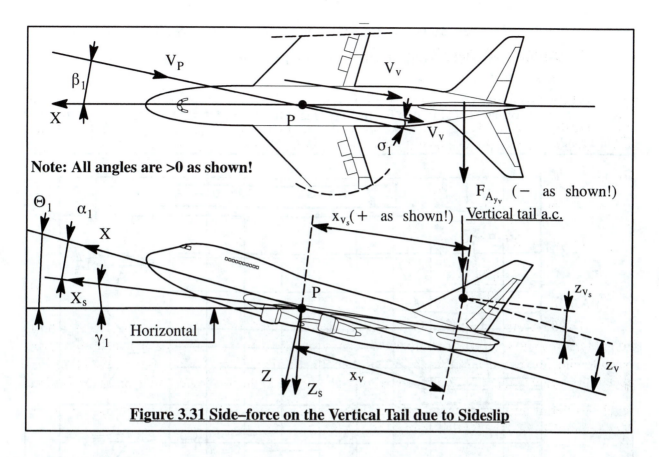

Note: All angles are >0 as shown!

Figure 3.31 Side–force on the Vertical Tail due to Sideslip

$$C_{l_{\beta_v}} \beta \overline{q} S b = - z_{v_s} C_{L_{\alpha_v}} (1 - \frac{d\sigma}{d\beta}) \beta \overline{q}_v S_v \qquad (3.64)$$

From this it follows for the vertical tail contribution to airplane dihedral effect:

$$C_{l_{\beta_v}} = - C_{L_{\alpha_v}} (1 - \frac{d\sigma}{d\beta}) \eta_v \frac{S_v z_{v_s}}{S b} \qquad (3.65)$$

It is seen that the vertical tail contribution to the derivative C_{l_β} depends on five factors:

1) the geometry of the vertical tail: aspect ratio and sweep angle determine $C_{L_{\alpha_v}}$

2) the side–wash derivative $d\sigma/d\beta$ which is normally rather small

3) the dynamic pressure ratio at the vertical tail, η_v , which tends to have a value close to 1.0 except in the case of propeller driven airplanes with the vertical tail immersed in the propeller slipstream

4) the vertical tail moment arm, z_{v_s} . Note in Figure 3.31 that this moment arm depends on the steady state angle of attack! In extreme high angle of attack cases it is possible for this moment arm to reverse sign!

5) the size of the vertical tail in relation to the size of the wing: S_v/S . An example of an airplane with a large vertical tail relative to the wing is the Boeing 747–SP: see Figure 3.31.

Examples of numerical trends for the airplane dihedral effect derivative, C_{l_β} are given in Figure 3.32.

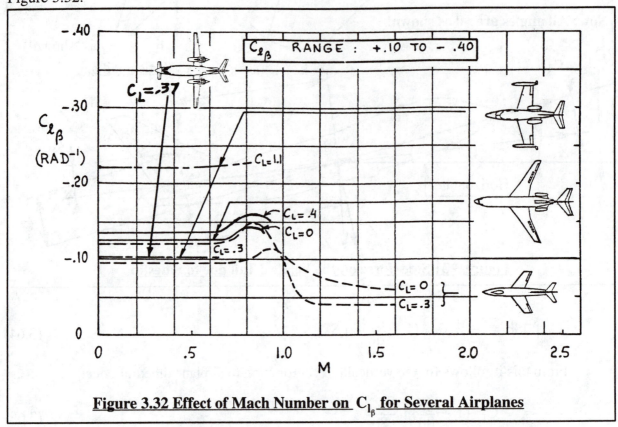

Figure 3.32 Effect of Mach Number on C_{l_β} for Several Airplanes

Roll Control Derivatives, $C_{l_{\delta_a}}$ and $C_{l_{\delta_r}}$

Lateral control (about the X–axis, body or stability) of airplanes can be accomplished with a number of devices:

* ailerons, $C_{l_{\delta_a}}$ * flaperons, $C_{l_{\delta_a}}$ * spoilers, $C_{l_{\delta_s}}$

* differential stabilizer, $C_{l_{i_h}}$ * combination of previous devices   * other devices

Several generic properties of ailerons, spoilers and differential stabilizers will be discussed. A mathematical model used when combinations of these devices are employed is also discussed.

Nearly all airplanes employ some form of directional (yaw) control, usually a rudder. Although undesirable, rudders also tend to produce a rolling moment. This rolling moment must be compensated for by either the pilot or some automatic mechanism. The generic properties of a rudder in generating an undesirable rolling moment are also discussed.

Aileron Rolling Moment Coefficient Derivative, $C_{l_{\delta_a}}$

Figure 3.33 illustrates how ailerons produce a rolling moment. A positive aileron deflection is referred to as one which results in a positive rolling moment about the X–axis. Because ailerons also produce an undesirable yawing moment (See Sub–section 3.1.8), most ailerons are deflected differentially (i.e. one more than the other) to minimize this yawing moment. For that reason an aileron deflection, δ_a , is usually defined as:

$$\delta_a = \tfrac{1}{2}(\delta_{a_{l.h.s.}} + \delta_{a_{r.h.s.}}) \tag{3.66}$$

The derivative $C_{l_{\delta_a}}$ depends on the following factors:

* aileron chord to wing chord ratio   * aileron inboard and outboard span location
* wing sweep angle   * aileron deflection
* Mach number

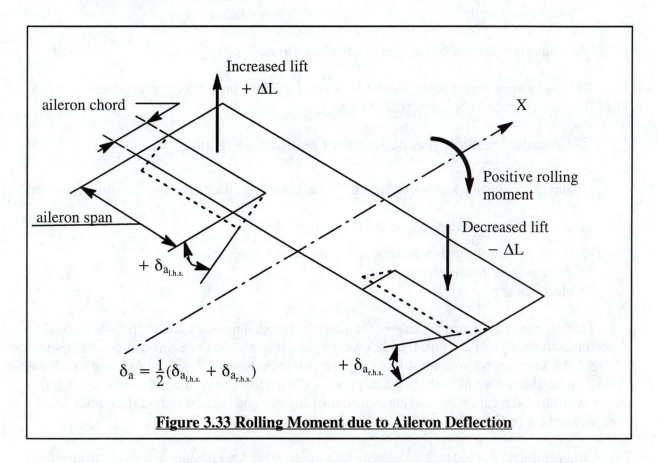

Figure 3.33 Rolling Moment due to Aileron Deflection

When ailerons are deflected more than about 20–25 degrees flow separation tends to occur. The ailerons then loose their effectiveness. Also, close to wing stall, even small downward aileron deflections can produce separation and loss of control effectiveness. In addition, aileron control power is very sensitive to dynamic pressure because of aero–elastic effects. Most high performance airplanes have a so–called aileron reversal speed beyond which the ailerons induce so much elastic wing twist that the sign of the derivative reverses! This effect is discussed in detail in Chapter 7.

At wing sweep angles beyond about 55 degrees, ailerons loose effectiveness because of out-board flow which tends to become parallel to the aileron hinge lines.

In several airplanes, the flaps are moved differentially to act as ailerons. Such devices are referred to as flaperons. They are analyzed as if they are ailerons.

Spoiler Rolling Moment Coefficient Derivative, $C_{l_{\delta_s}}$

Figure 3.34 shows how a spoiler produces a rolling moment. Spoilers when used for roll control are usually deflected on one side only.

The derivative $C_{l_{\delta_s}}$ depends on the following factors:

* spoiler chord to wing chord ratio   * spoiler inboard and outboard span location
* spoiler hingeline location   * spoiler deflection
* wing sweep angle   * Mach number

Maximum spoiler deflections range anywhere from 30–60 degrees.

At wing sweep angles beyond about 55 degrees spoilers loose effectiveness because of out-board flow which tends to become parallel to the spoiler hinge lines.

Differential Stabilizer Rolling Moment Coefficient Derivative, $C_{l_{i_h}}$

Figure 3.35 illustrates how a differentially deflected stabilizer generates a rolling moment.

The derivative $C_{l_{i_h}}$ depends on the following factors:

* stabilizer geometry: aspect ratio, sweep angle and taper ratio
* stabilizer size relative to the wing
* Mach number

Differential stabilizers, because of their relatively small moment arm to the X–axis tend to be used mostly on fighter aircraft: the high wing sweep angle makes ailerons and/or spoilers less effective. In addition, because most fighters have tail–span–to–wing–span ratios close to 1.0 the relative rolling moment arm is still reasonably good. Add the fact that both stabilizer halves on fighters are controlled separately for longitudinal control anyway and the ability for differential deflection (required for roll) comes at little additional weight penalty!

Many airplanes of today employ more than one of these lateral control devices. In airplanes with a mixture of lateral control devices, it is necessary to 'gear' the various lateral control devices together so that they are simultaneously activated when the cockpit controls (lateral stick or left/right wheel deflection are activated by the pilot.

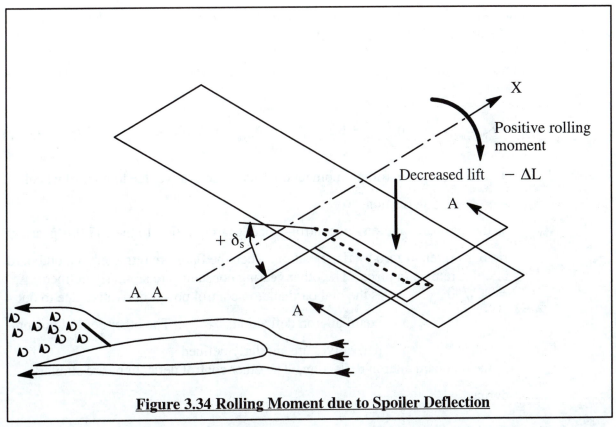

Figure 3.34 Rolling Moment due to Spoiler Deflection

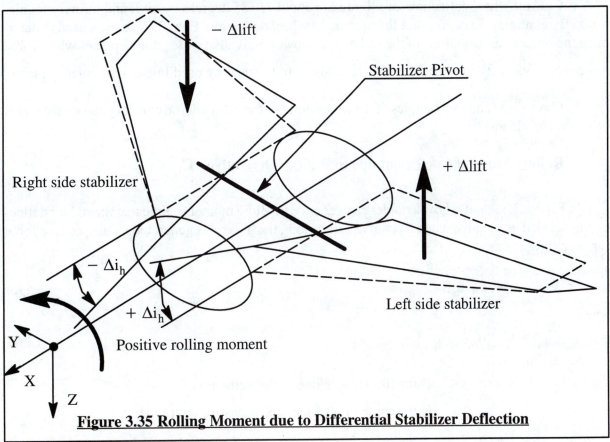

Figure 3.35 Rolling Moment due to Differential Stabilizer Deflection

An example is the Boeing 747 which has three different types of roll control devices: inboard ailerons, outboard ailerons and spoilers: see Figure 3.36.

These three roll control devices are 'geared' to the control wheel in the cockpit. The following equation expresses this gearing:

Gearing Const.

$$C_{l_{\delta_w}}\delta_w = K_{aw_{outb'd}}C_{l_{\delta_{a_{outb'd}}}}\delta_{a_{outb'd}} + K_{aw_{inb'd}}C_{l_{\delta_{a_{inb'd}}}}\delta_{a_{inb'd}} + K_{sw}C_{l_{\delta_s}}\delta_s \qquad (3.67)$$

where: $C_{l_{\delta_w}} = \partial C_l/\partial\delta_w$ is the rolling moment coefficient derivative due to control wheel deflection, δ_w

$K_{aw_{outb'd}}$ is the outboard–aileron–to–control–wheel gearing ratio. In the 747 this gearing ratio is driven to zero by flap position: when the flaps are retracted, the outboard ailerons remain in place. The other gearing constants are similarly defined.

$C_{l_{\delta_{a_{outb'd}}}} = \partial C_l/\partial\delta_{a_{outb'd}}$ is the outboard aileron control power derivative due to out-board aileron deflection, $\delta_{a_{outb'd}}$. The other control power derivatives are similarly defined.

$\delta_{a_{outb'd}}$ is the outboard aileron deflection. The other control deflections are similarly defined.

Cockpit wheel deflections are limited to about +/– 85 degrees by civil and military regulations. By assuming 85 degrees for the maximum wheel deflection, Eqn (3.67) can be used to determine the numerical magnitude of the roll control power derivative $C_{l_{\delta_w}}$ for airplanes with geared roll control systems. Eqn (3.67) has to be adjusted to the gearing used in any particular airplane.

Figure 3.37 shows examples of the Mach number trend for aileron control power derivatives of several airplanes.

Rolling Moment Coefficient due to Rudder Derivative, $C_{l_{\delta_r}}$

Figure 3.38 shows how a rudder can generate a rolling moment. Note that the rudder deflection is defined as positive when a positive force along the Y–axis is generated. This positive force can be expressed as:

$$F_{A_{y_{v_{rudder}}}} = C_{L_v}\bar{q}_v S_v \qquad (3.68)$$

where:

$$C_{L_v} = C_{L_{\alpha_v}}\alpha_{\delta_r}\delta_r \qquad (3.69)$$

where: $C_{L_{\alpha_v}}$ is the lift–curve slope of the vertical tail

α_{δ_r} is the angle of attack effectiveness of the rudder

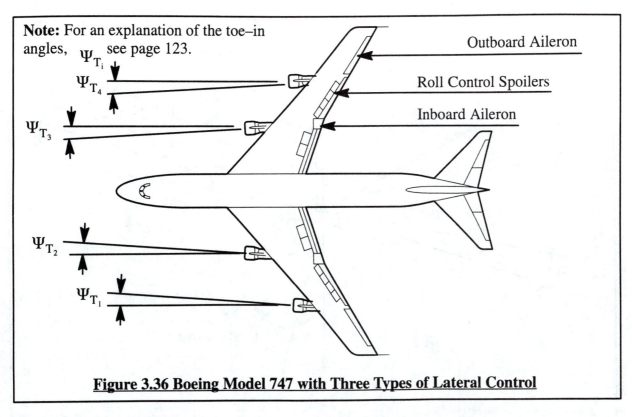

Figure 3.36 Boeing Model 747 with Three Types of Lateral Control

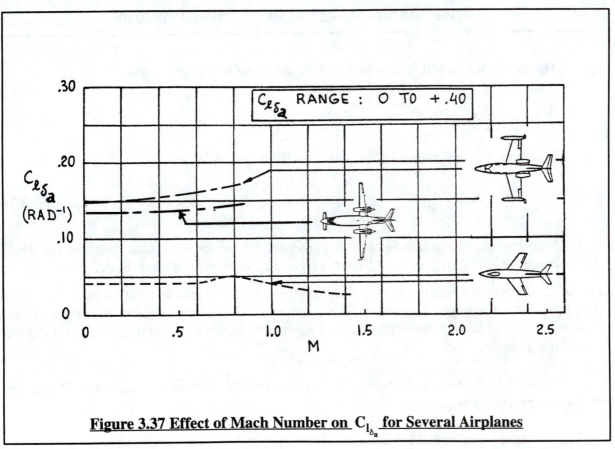

Figure 3.37 Effect of Mach Number on $C_{l_{\delta_a}}$ for Several Airplanes

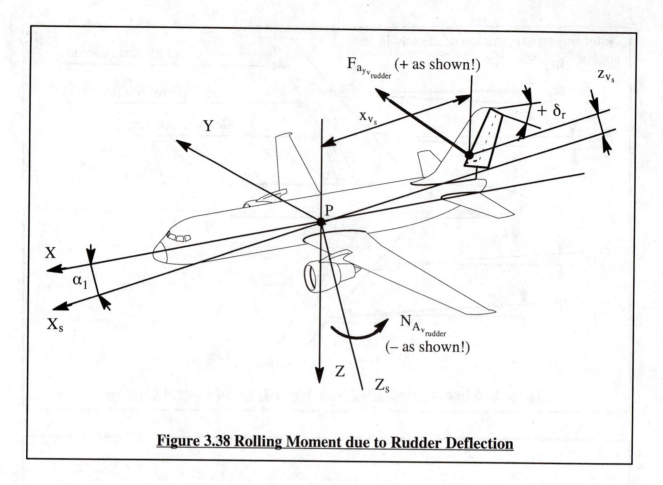

Figure 3.38 Rolling Moment due to Rudder Deflection

The rolling moment due to rudder deflection can be written as:

$$L_{A_{rudder}} = F_{A_{y_{v_{rudder}}}} z_{v_s} = C_{l_{\delta_r}} \delta_r \bar{q} S b \qquad (3.70)$$

By combining equations (3.68) through (3.70) it is found that:

$$C_{l_{\delta_r}} = C_{L_{\alpha_v}} \alpha_{\delta_r} \bar{q}_v \frac{S_v x_{v_s}}{S b} \qquad (3.71)$$

Note that this derivative is normally positive. However, at angles of attack for which z_{v_s} becomes negative, so does $C_{l_{\delta_r}}$. From a handling qualities viewpoint the derivative $C_{l_{\delta_r}}$ is a problem: particularly positive values of this derivative tend to interfere with a pilot's ability to carry out lateral–directional maneuvers. This is one reason why many airplanes have some type of flight control interconnect between the roll and yaw axis to compensate for the rolling moment due to rudder deflection.

Figure 3.39 shows how the rolling moment due to rudder derivative varies with Mach number for several airplanes.

The steady state model for the airplane aerodynamic rolling moment now is:

$$L_{A_{1_s}} = L_A = (C_{l_\beta}\beta + C_{l_{\delta_a}}\delta_a + C_{l_{\delta_r}}\delta_r) \qquad (3.72)$$

For airplanes with a combination of roll control devices it is recommended to replace the term $C_{l_{\delta_a}}\delta_a$ with the term $C_{l_{\delta_w}}\delta_w$ as defined by Eqn (3.67).

Methods for predicting the magnitudes of the derivatives which appear in Eqn (3.72) can be found in Part VI of Reference 3.1.

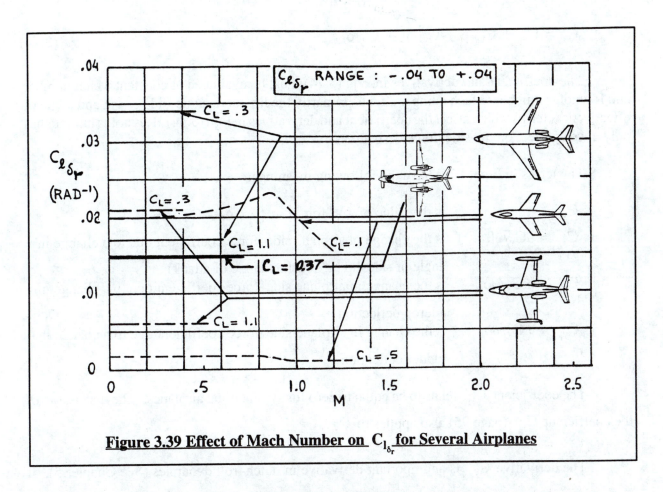

Figure 3.39 Effect of Mach Number on $C_{l_{\delta_r}}$ for Several Airplanes

3.1.9 AIRPLANE AERODYNAMIC SIDE–FORCE

The steady state airplane aerodynamic side–force, F_{A_y}, is non–dimensionalized as:

$$F_{A_y} = C_y \overline{q} S \qquad (3.73)$$

where: C_y is the airplane aerodynamic side–force coefficient.

This steady state airplane aerodynamic side–force coefficient depends on the following factors:

* angle of sideslip, β * deflection of directional control surface(s)

* deflection of lateral control surface   * angle of attack

* Mach number and Reynolds number

For an airplane equipped with ailerons and rudder the side–force coefficient is expressed in first order Taylor series form:

$$C_y = C_{y_0} + C_{y_\beta} \beta + C_{y_{\delta_a}} \delta_a + C_{y_{\delta_r}} \delta_r \qquad (3.74)$$

usually → 0

The coefficient and derivatives in Eqn (3.74) must be evaluated at constant Mach number and Reynolds number. Mach number affects primarily the lift curve slope, side–wash and angle of effectiveness terms which affect the coefficient and derivatives in Eqn (3.34). Reynolds number has only a weak effect on the side–force derivatives.

The terms in Eqn (3.74) have the following meanings:

C_{y_0} is the value of C_y for: $\alpha = \beta = \delta_a = \delta_r = 0$

$C_{y_\beta} = \partial C_y/\partial \beta$ is the change in airplane side–force coefficient due to a change in angle of sideslip (at constant angle of attack)

$C_{y_{\delta_a}} = \partial C_y/\partial \delta_a$ is the change in airplane side–force coefficient due to a change in aileron deflection

$C_{y_{\delta_r}} = \partial C_y/\partial \delta_r$ is the change in airplane side–force coefficient due to a change in rudder deflection

The coefficient C_{y_0} tends to be equal to zero for symmetrical airplanes. The discussion of the coefficient C_{l_0} (page 95) also applies to C_{y_0}.

The derivative C_{y_β} is an important derivative in dutch–roll dynamics (See Chapter 5). It is also important in flight path control when making s–turns without banking at very low height above the ground. The control derivative $C_{y_{\delta_a}}$ is normally negligible. The side force control derivative $C_{y_{\delta_r}}$ is of major importance in determining the yaw control derivative, $C_{n_{\delta_r}}$, as will be seen in Sub–section 3.1.10.

Side–Force Coefficient Due to Sideslip Derivative, C_{y_β}

The side–force due to sideslip may be estimated by summing the effects of various airplane components. For conventional airplanes this yields:

$$C_{y_\beta} = C_{y_{\beta_w}} + C_{y_{\beta_f}} + C_{y_{\beta_v}} \qquad (3.75)$$

Wing Contribution, $C_{y_{\beta_w}}$ and Fuselage Contribution, $C_{y_{\beta_f}}$

The wing contribution to C_{y_β} depends primarily on the geometric dihedral angle of the wing. For small geometric dihedral angles the wing contribution is usually negligible.

The fuselage contribution depends strongly on the shape and size of the fuselage in relation to the wing and on the placement of the wing on the fuselage. Methods for estimating the wing/fuselage contributions to C_{y_β} may be found in Part VI of Reference 3.1. For most airplanes these contributions tend to be small.

Vertical Tail Contribution, $C_{y_{\beta_v}}$

The vertical tail contribution to C_{y_β} was explained as part of the discussion of the rolling moment due to sideslip contribution of the vertical tail in Sub–sub–section 3.1.8.1: see Figure 3.31. With the help of Eqn (3.62) it is seen that:

$$F_{A_{y_v}} = C_{y_\beta}\beta\overline{q}S = -C_{L_{\alpha_v}}(1 - \frac{d\sigma}{d\beta})\overline{q}_v S_v \qquad (3.76)$$

From this it follows that:

$$C_{y_{\beta_v}} = -C_{L_{\alpha_v}}(1 - \frac{d\sigma}{d\beta})\eta_v \frac{S_v}{S} \qquad (3.77)$$

Note that the vertical tail contribution depends strongly on the vertical tail size in relation to the wing as well as on the lift–curve slope of the vertical tail. The latter in turn depends mostly on aspect ratio and sweep angle of the vertical tail.

Figure 3.40 shows how C_{y_β} varies with Mach number for several airplanes.

Side Force Control Derivatives, $C_{y_{\delta_a}}$ and $C_{y_{\delta_r}}$

Aileron Side Force Coefficient Derivative, $C_{y_{\delta_a}}$

This derivative is normally negligible. However, in the case of airplanes where the rolling moment controls are in close proximity to a vertical surface (fuselage or vertical tail) a side force which is not negligible may well be generated. Figure 3.41 illustrates an example of how this can occur in the case of a differential stabilizer which is located close to a vertical tail. Whenever this is suspected to be the case windtunnel tests are the only reliable way of obtaining data.

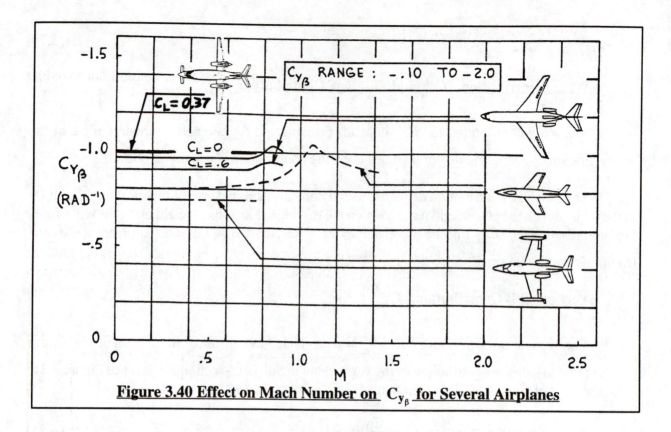

Figure 3.40 Effect on Mach Number on C_{y_β} for Several Airplanes

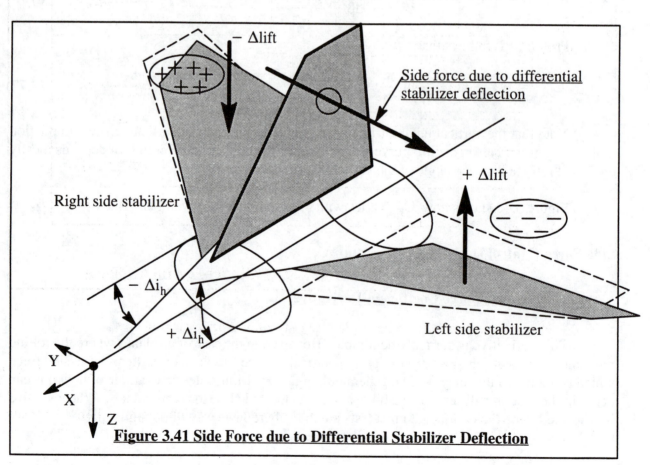

Figure 3.41 Side Force due to Differential Stabilizer Deflection

Rudder Side–Force Coefficient Derivative, $C_{y_{\delta_r}}$

Figure 3.38 shows how a positive rudder deflection yields a positive side–force due to rudder deflection. This side–force is written as:

$$F_{A_{y_{v_{rudder}}}} = C_{y_{\delta_r}} \delta_r \, \overline{q}S \qquad (3.78)$$

Now, by combining Eqns (3.78), (3.68) and (3.69) it is seen that:

$$C_{y_{\delta_r}} = C_{L_{\alpha_v}} \alpha_{\delta_r} \, \eta_v \frac{S_v}{S} \qquad (3.79)$$

Note that the side–force due to rudder derivative depends strongly on the vertical tail size in relation to the wing as well as on the lift–curve slope of the vertical tail. The latter in turn depends mostly on aspect ratio and sweep angle of the vertical tail. Figure 3.42 shows how $C_{y_{\delta_r}}$ varies with Mach number for several airplanes.

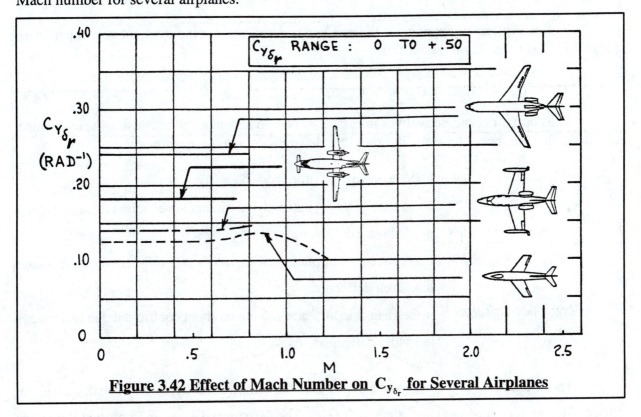

Figure 3.42 Effect of Mach Number on $C_{y_{\delta_r}}$ for Several Airplanes

The steady state model for the airplane aerodynamic side force now is:

$$F_{A_{y_{1_s}}} = F_{A_y} = (C_{y_\beta}\beta + C_{y_{\delta_a}}\delta_a + C_{y_{\delta_r}}\delta_r) \qquad (3.80)$$

Methods for predicting the magnitudes of the derivatives which appear in Eqn (3.72) can be found in Part VI of Reference 3.1.

3.1.10 AIRPLANE AERODYNAMIC YAWING MOMENT

The steady state airplane aerodynamic yawing moment, N_A, is non–dimensionalized as:

$$N_A = C_n \bar{q} S b \tag{3.81}$$

where: C_n is the airplane aerodynamic yawing moment coefficient.

The steady state airplane aerodynamic yawing moment coefficient, C_n, depends on the following factors:

* angle of sideslip, β * deflection of directional control surface(s)

* angle of attack, α * deflection of lateral control surface(s)

* Mach number and Reynolds number   * moment reference center (usually the c.g.) location

For an airplane equipped with ailerons and rudders, the yawing moment coefficient is expressed in first order Taylor series form:

$$C_n = C_{n_0} + C_{n_\beta} \beta + C_{n_{\delta_a}} \delta_a + C_{n_{\delta_r}} \delta_r \tag{3.82}$$

The coefficient and derivatives in Eqn (3.82) are to be evaluated at constant Mach number and Reynolds number. The terms in Eqn (3.82) have the following meanings:

C_{n_0} is the value of C_n for: $\beta = \delta_a = \delta_r = 0$

✱ $C_{n_\beta} = \partial C_n / \partial \beta$ is the change in airplane yawing moment coefficient due to a change

     min: +.0010/degree   in airplane sideslip angle, β *+ for stability*

$C_{n_{\delta_a}} = \partial C_n / \partial \delta_a$ is the change in airplane yawing moment coefficient due to a change

                  in aileron deflection, δ_a

$C_{n_{\delta_r}} = \partial C_n / \partial \delta_r$ is the change in airplane yawing moment coefficient due to a change

                  in rudder deflection, δ_r

The coefficient C_{n_0} tends to be equal to zero for symmetrical airplanes. The discussion of the coefficient C_{l_0} (page 95) also applies to C_{n_0}. The derivative C_{n_β} is an important derivative in dutch roll and spiral dynamics. The derivative C_{n_β} is referred to as the static directional stability derivative. The control derivative $C_{n_{\delta_a}}$ plays a nuisance role. Ideally its value would be zero or perhaps slightly positive. As will be shown, for most ailerons its value is negative. For that reason it is referred to as the adverse aileron–yaw effect. The control derivative $C_{n_{\delta_r}}$ is the rudder control derivative. It is very important in coordinating turns and in helping to overcome asymmetric thrust (or power) situations.

Yawing Moment Coefficient Due to Sideslip Derivative, C_{n_β}

The yawing moment due to sideslip (directional stability) derivative, C_{n_β}, may be estimated by summing the effects of various airplane components. For conventional airplanes this yields:

$$C_{n_\beta} = C_{n_{\beta_w}} + C_{n_{\beta_f}} + C_{n_{\beta_v}} \tag{3.83}$$

Wing Contribution, $C_{n_{\beta_w}}$ and Fuselage Contribution, $C_{n_{\beta_f}}$

The wing contribution to C_{n_β} tends to be negligible, except at high angles of attack.

The fuselage contribution depends strongly on the shape of the fuselage and the amount of projected side area forward and aft of the center of gravity. The so–called Munk effect discussed in Sub–section 2.5.6 also applies to a fuselage in sideslip. For that reason the fuselage contribution to directional stability tends to be strongly negative. Methods for computing the fuselage contribution to C_{n_β} are presented in Part VI of Reference 3.1.

Vertical Tail Contribution, $C_{n_{\beta_v}}$

A physical explanation for the directionally stabilizing effect of a vertical tail may be gleaned from Figure 3.31. The yawing moment due to the vertical tail me be written as:

$$N_v = - F_{A_{y_v}} x_{v_s} = C_{n_{\beta_v}} \beta \overline{q} S b \tag{3.84}$$

where: $F_{A_{y_v}}$ is the side–force due to sideslip as determined from Eqn (3.76).

x_{v_s} is the distance along the stability x–axis from the vertical tail aerodynamic center to the airplane center of gravity.

By combining Eqn (3.76) and Eqn (3.84) it follows that:

$$C_{n_{\beta_v}} = C_{L_{\alpha_v}}(1 - \frac{d\sigma}{d\beta})\eta_v \frac{S_v \, x_{v_s}}{Sb} \tag{3.85}$$

Note that the vertical tail contribution depends strongly on the vertical tail size in relation to the wing as well as on the lift–curve slope of the vertical tail. The latter depends mostly on aspect ratio and sweep angle of the vertical tail. Also, it is seen that the 'moment–arm', x_{v_s}, is important to directional stability.

Figure 3.43 shows how C_{n_β} varies with Mach number for several airplanes.

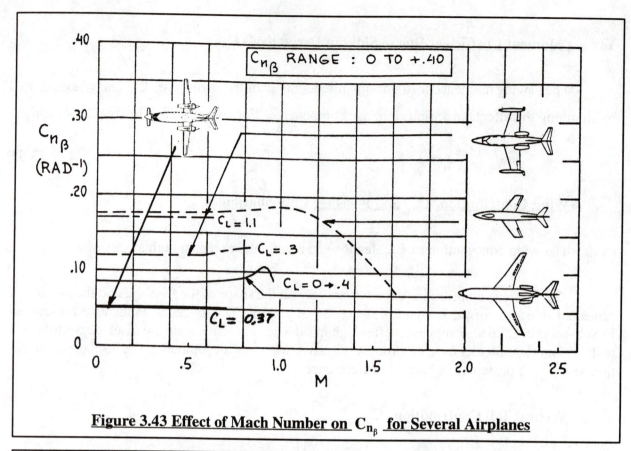

Figure 3.43 Effect of Mach Number on C_{n_β} for Several Airplanes

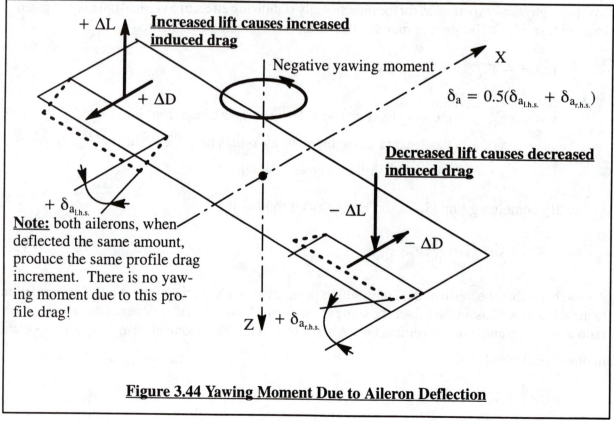

Figure 3.44 Yawing Moment Due to Aileron Deflection

Yawing Moment Control Derivatives, $C_{n_{\delta_a}}$, $C_{n_{\delta_s}}$, $C_{n_{i_h}}$, $C_{n_{\delta_r}}$ and $C_{n_{\delta_{r_{drag}}}}$

Nearly all airplanes employ some form of lateral control as discussed in Sub–section 3.1.8. A problem is, that most roll control devices also introduce a yawing moment. The generic properties of roll control devices which lead to generating yawing moments are now briefly discussed.

Aileron Yawing Moment Coefficient Derivative, $C_{n_{\delta_a}}$

Figure 3.44 shows how conventional ailerons create a negative (called adverse) yawing moment. Note that this yawing moment is caused by the differential induced drag which in turn is caused by the changes in local lift created by the ailerons. The reason the aileron induced yawing moment is called adverse is because it tends to yaw an airplane out of an intended turn.

To eliminate the negative yawing moment due to aileron deflection, either Frise ailerons or differentially deflected (or a combination of both) are used. Figure 3.45 illustrates the effect of Frise ailerons as well as of differentially deflected ailerons. Note, that in both cases a differential profile drag component is produced which is used to off–set the adverse (negative) aileron yaw.

Spoiler Yawing Moment Coefficient Derivative, $C_{n_{\delta_s}}$

Figure 3.34 shows how a spoiler generates a rolling moment. Figure 3.46 shows how a spoiler causes a positive yawing moment. This is referred to as proverse yaw. This is preferred over adverse yaw unless it becomes too proverse!

Methods for computing the yawing moment due to aileron and spoiler control derivatives are found in Part VI of Reference 3.1.

Figure 3.47 shows how $C_{n_{\delta_a}}$ varies with Mach number for several airplanes.

Differential Stabilizer Yawing Moment Coefficient Derivative, $C_{n_{i_h}}$

Figure 3.41 illustrates how a differentially deflected stabilizer generates a side force. Since the center of gravity of the airplane is usually forward of the vertical tail, a yawing moment due to differential stabilizer deflection will also be generated. If this is suspected to be significant, it is advisable to run windtunnel tests to establish the magnitude.

Directional control (about the Z–axis, body or stability) of airplanes can be accomplished with a number of devices:

     * rudders ($C_{n_{\delta_r}}$)   * drag rudders ($C_{n_{\delta_{r_{drag}}}}$)   * other devices

Some of the generic properties of rudders and drag rudders will now be discussed.

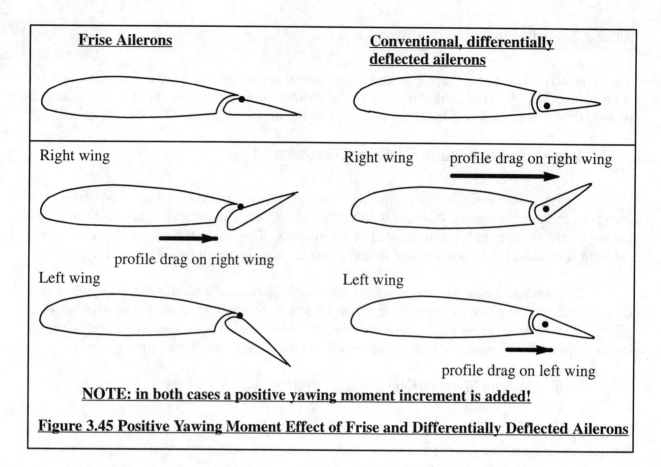

Frise Ailerons

Conventional, differentially deflected ailerons

Right wing

Right wing

profile drag on right wing

profile drag on right wing

Left wing

Left wing

profile drag on left wing

NOTE: in both cases a positive yawing moment increment is added!

Figure 3.45 Positive Yawing Moment Effect of Frise and Differentially Deflected Ailerons

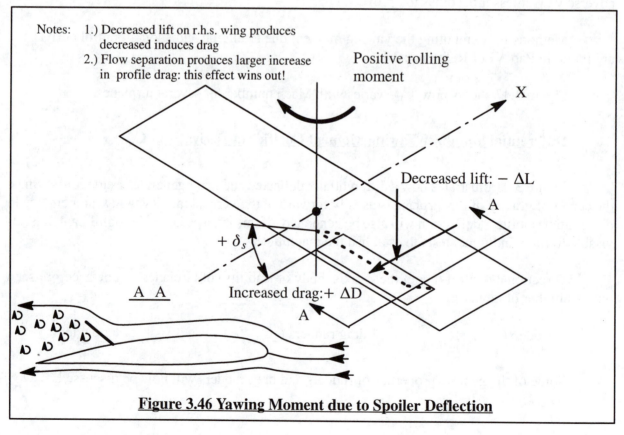

Notes: 1.) Decreased lift on r.h.s. wing produces decreased induces drag
2.) Flow separation produces larger increase in profile drag: this effect wins out!

Positive rolling moment

X

Decreased lift: $- \Delta L$

A

$+ \delta_s$

$\underline{A \ A}$

Increased drag: $+ \Delta D$

A

Figure 3.46 Yawing Moment due to Spoiler Deflection

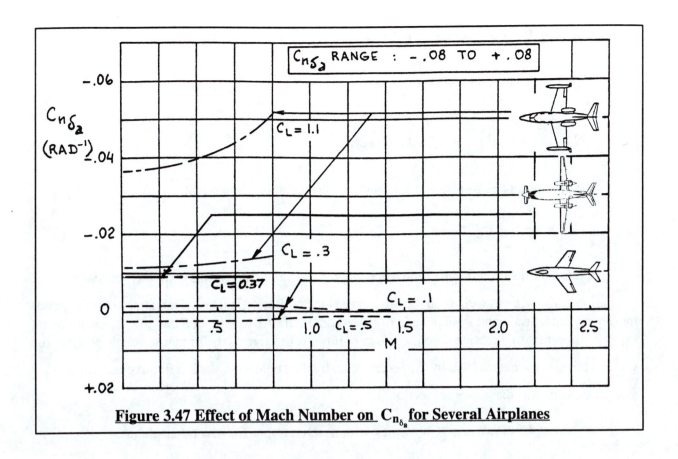

Figure 3.47 Effect of Mach Number on $C_{n_{\delta_a}}$ for Several Airplanes

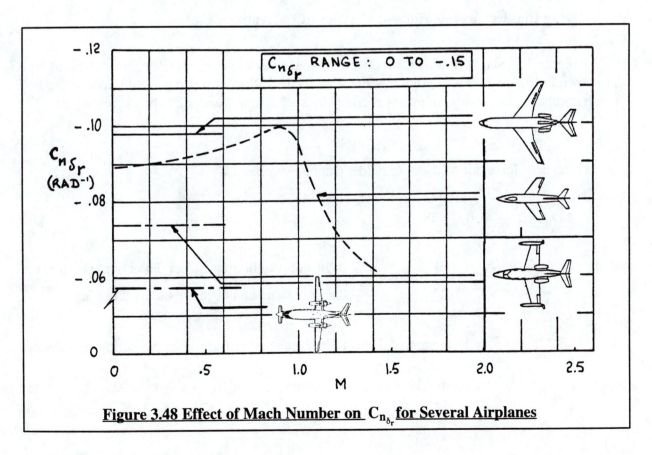

Figure 3.48 Effect of Mach Number on $C_{n_{\delta_r}}$ for Several Airplanes

Rudder Yawing Moment Coefficient Derivative, $C_{n_{\delta_r}}$

Figure 3.38 shows how the side–force due to rudder deflection generates a negative yawing moment:

$$N_{A_{v_{rudder}}} = -F_{a_{y_{v_{rudder}}}} x_{v_s} = C_{n_{\delta_r}} \delta_r \,\overline{q}Sb \tag{3.86}$$

By combining Eqns (3.85), (3.68) and (3.69) it can be shown that:

$$C_{n_{\delta_r}} = -C_{L_{\alpha_v}} \alpha_{\delta_r} \,\eta_v \frac{S_v \, x_{v_s}}{Sb} \tag{3.87}$$

Note that the directional control derivative, $C_{n_{\delta_r}}$, depends strongly on the vertical tail size in relation to the wing as well as on the lift–curve slope of the vertical tail. The latter in turn depends mostly on aspect ratio and sweep angle of the vertical tail. Also, it is seen that the 'moment–arm', x_{v_s}, is important to directional control power. Finally, the size of the rudder in relationship to the vertical tail size (as determined by S_v) is reflected by the angle–of–attack–effectiveness term α_{δ_r}. The latter term was discussed in Section 2.6.

Figure 3.48 shows how $C_{n_{\delta_r}}$ varies with Mach number for several airplanes.

Drag Rudder Yawing Moment Coefficient Derivative, $C_{n_{\delta_{r_{drag}}}}$

Figure 3.49 shows how a drag rudder generates a yawing moment. The particular drag rudder shown in Figure 3.49 was originally invented by Jack Northrop and is used today in the B–2 stealth bomber. The yawing moment generated by such a drag–rudder can be expressed as:

$$N_{A_{dr}} = \Delta D_{dr} \, y_{dr} = C_{n_{\delta_{r_{drag}}}} \delta_{r_{drag}} \,\overline{q}Sb \tag{3.88}$$

The drag force due to the drag rudder can be modelled as:

$$\Delta D_{dr} = \frac{\partial C_{D_{dr}}}{\partial \delta_{dr}} \delta_{r_{drag}} \,\overline{q}S \tag{3.89}$$

where: $\delta_{r_{drag}} = 0.5(\delta_{r_{drag_{upper}}} + \delta_{r_{drag_{lower}}})$ is the equivalent drag rudder deflection, positive on the right wing and negative on the left wing.

$\dfrac{\partial C_{D_{dr}}}{\partial \delta_{r_{drag}}}$ is the incremental drag rudder drag due to drag rudder deflection. In subsonic flight this derivative may be approximated by: $\dfrac{\partial C_{D_{dr}}}{\partial \delta_{r_{drag}}} = 0.025 \dfrac{b_{dr} \, c_{dr}}{S}$ 1/deg

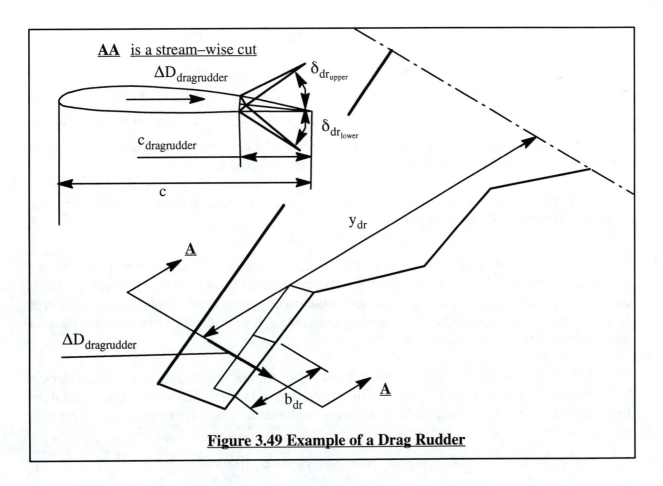

Figure 3.49 Example of a Drag Rudder

where: b_{dr} is the span of the drag rudder and,

c_{dr} is the chord of the drag rudder.

The drag–rudder yawing moment coefficient derivative can now be written as:

$$C_{n_{\delta_{r_{drag}}}} = \frac{0.025 b_{dr} c_{dr} y_{dr}}{Sb} \tag{3.90}$$

In Eqn (3.90) the assumption is made that at 60 degree deflection the drag rudder drag coefficient increment is 0.8 based on its own area. It is also assumed that the drag rudder drag increment varies linearly with drag rudder deflection.

The steady state model for the airplane aerodynamic yawing moment now is:

$$N_{A_{y_{1_s}}} = N_A = (C_{n_\beta}\beta + C_{n_{\delta_a}}\delta_a + C_{n_{\delta_r}}\delta_r) \tag{3.91}$$

Methods for predicting the magnitudes of the derivatives which appear in Eqn (3.72) can be found in Part VI of Reference 3.1.

3.1.11 LATERAL–DIRECTIONAL THRUST FORCES AND MOMENTS

Depending on airplane configuration, failure state of the propulsion system and on the cockpit thrust or power setting(s), there may also be a thrust induced rolling moment, $L_{T_{1_s}}$, a thrust induced side force, $F_{T_{y_{1_s}}}$, and a thrust induced yawing moment, $N_{T_{1_s}}$, acting on the airplane. For these force and moments, the subscripts 1 and s will also be dropped. Furthermore, it will be assumed that the installed values of thrust are known for each engine.

Flight condition and design parameters on which the steady state installed thrust vectors, T_i, depend are defined on page 70.

As mentioned on page 92, whenever airplane components are affected by propeller slipstream and/or by jet exhausts, the aerodynamic, lateral force and moments are all affected. For the lateral directional aerodynamic force and moments corrections for these propulsive installation effects can be made with models as suggested by Eqn (3.43). A more detailed discussion of these effects is beyond the scope of this text.

Figure 3.25 shows how the installed thrust vector for one engine is oriented in the airplane body–fixed axis system. Figure 3.27 shows the orientation and sense of the lateral–directional thrust force and moments. Therefore, the lateral–directional thrust force and moments can be written as:

$$L_{T_{1_s}} = L_T = [\sum_{i=0}^{i=n} T_i(z_{T_i}\cos\phi_{T_i}\sin\psi_{T_i} - y_{T_i}\sin\phi_{T_i})]\cos\alpha_1 +$$
$$+ [\sum_{i=0}^{i=n} T_i(x_{T_i}\cos\phi_{T_i}\sin\psi_{T_i} - y_{T_i}\cos\phi_{T_i}\cos\psi_{T_i})]\sin\alpha_1 \qquad (3.92a)$$

$$F_{T_{y_1}} = F_{T_y} = \sum_{i=0}^{i=n} T_i(\cos\phi_{T_i}\sin\psi_{T_i}) \qquad (3.92b)$$

$$N_{T_{1_s}} = N_T = [\sum_{i=0}^{i=n} T_i(x_{T_i}\cos\phi_{T_i}\sin\psi_{T_i} - y_{T_i}\cos\phi_{T_i}\cos\psi_{T_i})]\cos\alpha_1 +$$
$$- [\sum_{i=0}^{i=n} T_i(z_{T_i}\cos\phi_{T_i}\sin\psi_{T_i} - y_{T_i}\sin\phi_{T_i})]\sin\alpha_1 \qquad (3.92c)$$

It is to be noted that whenever the engine installation is symmetrical with respect to the airplane XZ–plane AND whenever the thrust output of the engine installation is also symmetrical with respect the airplane XZ–plane, all lateral–directional force and moments are zero!

Assuming that for the case of a symmetrical engine installation, one engine is inoperative (OEI), the lateral force and moments due to the one (asymmetrically) operating engine can be expressed as:

$$L_T = [T_i(z_{T_i}\cos\phi_{T_i}\sin\psi_{T_i} - y_{T_i}\sin\phi_{T_i})]\cos\alpha_1 +$$

$$+ \ [T_i(x_{T_i}\cos\phi_{T_i}\sin\psi_{T_i} - y_{T_i}\cos\phi_{T_i}\cos\psi_{T_i})]\sin\alpha_1 \qquad (3.93a)$$

$$F_{T_y} = T_i(\cos\phi_{T_i}\sin\psi_{T_i}) \qquad (3.93b)$$

$$N_T = [T_i(x_{T_i}\cos\phi_{T_i}\sin\psi_{T_i} - y_{T_i}\cos\phi_{T_i}\cos\psi_{T_i})]\cos\alpha_1 \ +$$

$$- \ [T_i(z_{T_i}\cos\phi_{T_i}\sin\psi_{T_i} - y_{T_i}\sin\phi_{T_i})]\sin\alpha_1 + \Delta N_{D_i} \qquad (3.93c)$$

Whenever an engine or propeller is inoperative, some type of incremental drag arises on that engine. That increase in drag results in an additional drag–induced side force, rolling moment and yawing moment. In many instances only the drag induced yawing moment turns out to be significant from a stability and control viewpoint. That is the reason for the appearance of the ΔN_{D_i} term in Eqn (3.93c). This extra drag due to the inoperative engine must also be accounted for in any climb performance calculations with one (or more) engines inoperative. A method to account for ΔN_{D_i} is presented on page 216.

The lateral thrust–line off–set angle, ψ_{T_i}, and the thrust–line inclination angle ϕ_{T_i}, are small, but not equal to zero in most modern transport airplanes. In such cases these angles are referred to as the engine toe–in angle and toe–up angles respectively. The reason for these angles is to minimize engine nacelle drag in their local flow–field. Figure 3.36 shows the toe–in angles on the Boeing 747. Assuming that the steady state angle of attack and both the toe–in and the toe–up angles are small, equations (3.93) simplify to:

$$L_T \approx T_i(z_{T_i}\psi_{T_i} - y_{T_i}\phi_{T_i}) - T_i y_{T_i}\alpha_1 \qquad (3.94a)$$

$$F_{T_y} = T_i\psi_{T_i} \qquad (3.94b)$$

$$N_T \approx T_i(x_{T_i}\psi_{T_i} - y_{T_i}) + \Delta N_{D_i} \qquad (3.94c)$$

3.1.12 ASSEMBLING THE STEADY STATE LATERAL–DIRECTIONAL FORCES AND MOMENTS

It is now possible to assemble all expressions for the lateral–directional force and moments in matrix format. This is done in Table 3.3: Eqns (3.95a) and (3.95b). Note that the aerodynamic force and moments are treated as linear terms. The thrust terms contain transcendental terms in the steady state angle of attack. Later, in the discussion of the equations of motion in Chapter 4, it will be shown that by introduction of iteration schemes or by using the small angle assumption this problem will fade away.

Table 3.3 Matrix Format for Steady State Lateral–Directional Forces and Moments

$$
\begin{Bmatrix} L_{A_{1_s}} \\ F_{A_{y_{1_s}}} \\ N_{A_{1_s}} \end{Bmatrix} = \begin{Bmatrix} L_A \\ F_{A_y} \\ N_A \end{Bmatrix} = \begin{Bmatrix} C_l \bar{q} S b \\ C_y \bar{q} S \\ C_n \bar{q} S b \end{Bmatrix} \quad \textbf{with:}
$$

$$
\begin{Bmatrix} C_l \\ C_y \\ C_n \end{Bmatrix} = \begin{bmatrix} C_{l_\beta} & C_{l_{\delta_a}} & C_{l_{\delta_r}} \\ (3.52) & (\text{See p.104}) & (\text{See p.106}) \\ C_{y_\beta} & C_{y_{\delta_a}} & C_{y_{\delta_r}} \\ (3.75) & (\text{See p.111}) & (\text{See p.113}) \\ C_{n_\beta} & C_{n_{\delta_a}} & C_{n_{\delta_r}} \\ (3.82) & (\text{See p.117}) & (\text{See p.120}) \end{bmatrix} \begin{Bmatrix} \beta \\ \delta_a \\ \delta_r \end{Bmatrix} \tag{3.95a}
$$

$$
\begin{Bmatrix} L_T \\ F_{T_y} \\ N_T \end{Bmatrix} = \begin{Bmatrix} \sum\limits_{i=0}^{i=n} T_i (z_{T_i} \psi_{T_i} - y_{T_i} \phi_{T_i}) - T_i y_{T_i} \alpha_1 \\ \\ \sum\limits_{i=0}^{i=n} T_i \psi_{T_i} \\ \\ \sum\limits_{i=0}^{i=n} T_i (x_{T_i} \psi_{T_i} - y_{T_i}) + \Delta N_{D_i} \end{Bmatrix} \tag{3.95b}
$$

3.2   PERTURBED STATE FORCES AND MOMENTS

Since airplanes differ from one another in configuration, shape and size, it should be expected that it is not feasible to develop a mathematical model for airplane perturbed state force and moments which applies to all airplanes. The approach taken here is to first list the forces and moments to be modeled. Second, those variables of motion which experience shows to have a significant effect on the forces and moments are also listed. For the aerodynamic forces and moments, this is done in the form of a table such as Table 3.4.

The meaning of several perturbed state variables is illustrated in Figure 3.50. This figure should be used in conjunction with Table 3.4. In this table it is assumed that all perturbations are defined relative to a steady state for which: $V_1 = P_1 = R_1 = 0$. If the various thrust vectors which act on the airplane are symmetrical about the XZ–plane, this also means that: $F_{A_{y_{1_s}}} = L_{A_{1_s}} = N_{A_{1_s}} = 0$ is satisfied. Practical experience shows that these are not very restrictive conditions in terms of the validity of the resulting small perturbation equations. In other words, when these conditions are not exactly satisfied, the basic structure of Table 3.4 still applies.

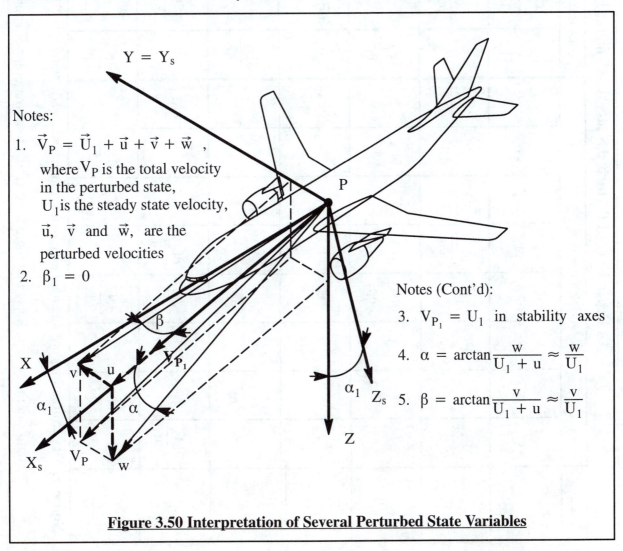

Notes:

1. $\vec{V}_P = \vec{U}_1 + \vec{u} + \vec{v} + \vec{w}$,

   where V_P is the total velocity in the perturbed state,
   U_1 is the steady state velocity,
   $\vec{u}, \vec{v}$ and $\vec{w}$, are the perturbed velocities

2. $\beta_1 = 0$

Notes (Cont'd):

3. $V_{P_1} = U_1$ in stability axes

4. $\alpha = \arctan\dfrac{w}{U_1 + u} \approx \dfrac{w}{U_1}$

5. $\beta = \arctan\dfrac{v}{U_1 + u} \approx \dfrac{v}{U_1}$

Figure 3.50 Interpretation of Several Perturbed State Variables

Table 3.4 Dependence of Perturbed State Aerodynamic Forces and Moments on Variables

Variable	Direct Variables								Derived Variables				Control Variables			
	u	v	w	p	q	r	$\dot{v}$	$\dot{w}$	$\beta = \dfrac{v}{U_1}$	$\alpha = \dfrac{w}{U_1}$	$\dot{\beta} = \dfrac{\dot{v}}{U_1}$	$\dot{\alpha} = \dfrac{\dot{w}}{U_1}$	δ_a	δ_e	δ_r	δ_f
f_{A_x}	$\dfrac{\partial F_{A_x}}{\partial u}$		$\dfrac{\partial F_{A_x}}{\partial w}$		$\dfrac{\partial F_{A_x}}{\partial q}$			$\dfrac{\partial F_{A_x}}{\partial \dot{w}}$		$\dfrac{\partial F_{A_x}}{\partial \alpha}$		$\dfrac{\partial F_{A_x}}{\partial \dot{\alpha}}$		$\dfrac{\partial F_{A_x}}{\partial \delta_e}$		$\dfrac{\partial F_{A_x}}{\partial \delta_f}$
f_{A_y}		$\dfrac{\partial F_{A_y}}{\partial v}$		$\dfrac{\partial F_{A_y}}{\partial p}$		$\dfrac{\partial F_{A_y}}{\partial r}$	$\dfrac{\partial F_{A_y}}{\partial \dot{v}}$		$\dfrac{\partial F_{A_y}}{\partial \beta}$		$\dfrac{\partial F_{A_y}}{\partial \dot{\beta}}$		$\dfrac{\partial F_{A_y}}{\partial \delta_a}$		$\dfrac{\partial F_{A_y}}{\partial \delta_r}$	
f_{A_z}	$\dfrac{\partial F_{A_z}}{\partial u}$		$\dfrac{\partial F_{A_z}}{\partial w}$		$\dfrac{\partial F_{A_z}}{\partial q}$			$\dfrac{\partial F_{A_z}}{\partial \dot{w}}$		$\dfrac{\partial F_{A_z}}{\partial \alpha}$		$\dfrac{\partial F_{A_z}}{\partial \dot{\alpha}}$		$\dfrac{\partial F_{A_z}}{\partial \delta_e}$		$\dfrac{\partial F_{A_z}}{\partial \delta_f}$
l_A		$\dfrac{\partial L_A}{\partial v}$		$\dfrac{\partial L_A}{\partial p}$		$\dfrac{\partial L_A}{\partial r}$	$\dfrac{\partial L_A}{\partial \dot{v}}$		$\dfrac{\partial L_A}{\partial \beta}$		$\dfrac{\partial L_A}{\partial \dot{\beta}}$		$\dfrac{\partial L_A}{\partial \delta_a}$		$\dfrac{\partial L_A}{\partial \delta_r}$	
m_A	$\dfrac{\partial M_A}{\partial u}$		$\dfrac{\partial M_A}{\partial w}$		$\dfrac{\partial M_A}{\partial q}$			$\dfrac{\partial M_A}{\partial \dot{w}}$		$\dfrac{\partial M_A}{\partial \alpha}$		$\dfrac{\partial M_A}{\partial \dot{\alpha}}$		$\dfrac{\partial M_A}{\partial \delta_e}$		$\dfrac{\partial M_A}{\partial \delta_f}$
n_A		$\dfrac{\partial N_A}{\partial v}$		$\dfrac{\partial N_A}{\partial p}$		$\dfrac{\partial N_A}{\partial r}$	$\dfrac{\partial N_A}{\partial \dot{v}}$		$\dfrac{\partial N_A}{\partial \beta}$		$\dfrac{\partial N_A}{\partial \dot{\beta}}$		$\dfrac{\partial N_A}{\partial \delta_a}$		$\dfrac{\partial N_A}{\partial \delta_r}$	

Notes: 1. All perturbations are taken relative to a symmetrical steady state: $V_1 = P_1 = R_1 = 0$

2. Blanks in the table indicate that there is no effect, to a first order of approximation

The basic structure of Table 3.4 is based on the following assumptions:

1) blanks in Table 3.4 indicate that a particular perturbed variable has NO effect on a particular perturbed force or moment.

2) partial derivatives in Table 3.4 indicate the slope by which a a particular perturbed force or moment is affected by a particular perturbed variable.

Whether or not these assumptions are satisfied depends largely on the symmetry (or lack thereof) of the airplane configuration being considered. With the exception of airplanes such as shown in Figure 1.3 the assumptions 1) and 2) are generally considered to be reasonable.

Next, an outline of the effect of the perturbed motion variables on the perturbed aerodynamic forces and moments is given.

Effect of a forward speed perturbation, u:

The consequence of a forward speed perturbation is two–fold: the dynamic pressure, $\bar{q} = \frac{1}{2}\varrho V_P^2$, and the Mach number, $M = V_P/c$, both change. As a result, the following longitudinal aerodynamic forces and moment will change: F_{A_x}, F_{A_z} and M_A. These changes are ex–pressed with the help of the derivatives: $\frac{\partial F_{A_x}}{\partial u}$, $\frac{\partial F_{A_z}}{\partial u}$ and $\frac{\partial M_A}{\partial u}$ in Table 3.4. Because the steady state lateral–directional force and moments: $F_{A_{y_{1s}}} = L_{A_{1s}} = N_{A_{1s}} = 0$, there will be no changes in F_{A_y}, L_A and N_A due to a forward speed perturbation, u. Therefore, the corresponding rectangles in Table 3.4 have been left blank.

Effect of a lateral speed (or side velocity) perturbation, v:

The effect of a side velocity perturbation, v, can be thought of as a perturbed sideslip angle, $\beta = \frac{v}{U_1}$, as shown in Figure 3.50. The effect of v on dynamic pressure is considered negligible. It was already shown in Section 3.1 that the effect of a change in sideslip angle is to change the lateral–directional force and moments: F_{A_y}, L_A and N_A. These changes are expressed through the derivatives: $\frac{\partial F_{A_y}}{\partial v}$, $\frac{\partial L_A}{\partial v}$ and $\frac{\partial N_A}{\partial v}$ or $\frac{\partial F_{A_y}}{\partial \beta}$, $\frac{\partial L_A}{\partial \beta}$ and $\frac{\partial N_A}{\partial \beta}$ in Table 3.4. As long as the sideslip angle is small, its effect on the longitudinal forces and moment: F_{A_x}, F_{A_z} and M_A is assumed to be negligible. That explains the corresponding blank rectangles in Table 3.4.

Effect of a downward speed (or downward velocity) perturbation, w:

The effect of a downward velocity perturbation, w, can be thought of as a perturbed angle of attack, $\alpha = \frac{w}{U_1}$, as shown in Figure 3.50. The effect of w on dynamic pressure is considered to be negligible. It was already shown in Section 3.1 that the effect of a change in angle of attack is to change the longitudinal forces and moment: F_{A_x}, F_{A_z} and M_A. These changes are ex–

pressed with the aid of the derivatives: $\dfrac{\partial F_{A_x}}{\partial w}$, $\dfrac{\partial F_{A_z}}{\partial w}$ and $\dfrac{\partial M_A}{\partial w}$ or $\dfrac{\partial F_{A_x}}{\partial \alpha}$, $\dfrac{\partial F_{A_z}}{\partial \alpha}$ and $\dfrac{\partial M_A}{\partial \alpha}$ in Table 3.4. As long as the angle of attack is small, its effect on the lateral–directional force and moments: F_{A_y}, L_A and N_A is negligible. That explains the corresponding blank rectangles in Table 3.4.

Effect of a roll rate perturbation, p:

The effect of a small perturbation in roll rate, p, is to cause non–symmetrical changes in local angles of attack over the wing, canard and tail surfaces. It is assumed that these changes take place in an anti–symmetrical manner so that there are negligible effects on the longitudinal aerodynamic forces and moment: F_{A_x}, F_{A_z} and M_A. Strictly speaking, this argument is not valid for a vertical tail. However, in most conventional airplanes the vertical tail effect due to roll rate perturbations is small anyway. The changes in the lateral–directional force and moments: F_{A_y}, L_A and N_A are accounted for through the derivatives: $\dfrac{\partial F_{A_y}}{\partial p}$, $\dfrac{\partial L_A}{\partial p}$ and $\dfrac{\partial N_A}{\partial p}$ as indicated in Table 3.4.

Effect of a pitch rate perturbation, q:

A pitch rate perturbation causes a symmetrical change in angles of attack over the wing, canard, horizontal tail and fuselage. The effect of this is to change the longitudinal aerodynamic forces and moment: F_{A_x}, F_{A_z} and M_A. These changes are expressed with the help of the derivatives: $\dfrac{\partial F_{A_x}}{\partial q}$, $\dfrac{\partial F_{A_z}}{\partial q}$ and $\dfrac{\partial M_A}{\partial q}$, as shown in Table 3.4. The effect of perturbed pitch rate on the lateral–directional force and moments: F_{A_y}, L_A and N_A is assumed to be negligible.

Effect of a yaw rate perturbation, r:

A yaw rate perturbation causes a non–symmetrical change in the local velocities of the wing, canard and horizontal tail. In addition, it causes a non–symmetrical change in local angles of attack over the vertical tail. These changes will generally affect the lateral–directional force and moments: F_{A_y}, L_A and N_A. This is expressed by the derivatives: $\dfrac{\partial F_{A_y}}{\partial r}$, $\dfrac{\partial L_A}{\partial r}$ and $\dfrac{\partial N_A}{\partial r}$ in Table 3.4.

Effect of rate of change of angle of attack, $\dot{\alpha}$

When the angle of attack of an airplane changes with time, the wing produces a vortex field which changes with time. That changing vortex field can have a significant effect on the aerodynamics of the horizontal tail. Such an effect is accounted for by means of so–called $\dot{\alpha}$ derivatives which affect the longitudinal forces and moment: F_{A_x}, F_{A_z} and M_A. The corresponding derivatives: $\dfrac{\partial F_{A_x}}{\partial \dot{\alpha}}$, $\dfrac{\partial F_{A_z}}{\partial \dot{\alpha}}$ and $\dfrac{\partial M_A}{\partial \dot{\alpha}}$ are also shown in Table 3.4. The effect of $\dot{\alpha}$ on the lateral–directional force and moments: F_{A_y}, L_A and N_A is considered negligible.

Effect of rate of change of angle of sideslip, $\dot{\beta}$

When the angle of sideslip of an airplane changes with time, the wing–fuselage combination produces a vortex field which changes with time. That changing vortex field can have a significant effect on the vertical tail. Such an effect is accounted for by means of so–called $\dot{\beta}$ derivatives which affect the lateral–directional force and moments, F_{A_y}, L_A and N_A. The corresponding derivatives: $\dfrac{\partial F_{A_y}}{\partial\dot{\beta}}$, $\dfrac{\partial L_A}{\partial\dot{\beta}}$ and $\dfrac{\partial N_A}{\partial\dot{\beta}}$ are also shown in Table 3.4.

Effect of control surface perturbations, δ_a, δ_e, δ_r and δ_f

It will be assumed that perturbations in longitudinal control surface deflections, such as δ_e and δ_f only affect the longitudinal forces and moment: F_{A_x}, F_{A_z} and M_A through the derivatives: $\dfrac{\partial F_{A_x}}{\partial\delta_e}$, $\dfrac{\partial F_{A_z}}{\partial\delta_e}$ and $\dfrac{\partial M_A}{\partial\delta_e}$ and $\dfrac{\partial F_{A_x}}{\partial\delta_f}$, $\dfrac{\partial F_{A_z}}{\partial\delta_f}$ and $\dfrac{\partial M_A}{\partial\delta_f}$. For other control surfaces, similar derivatives should be substituted.

It will also be assumed that perturbations in lateral–directional control surface deflections, such as δ_a and δ_r only affect the lateral–directional force and moments: F_{A_y}, L_A and N_A. The corresponding derivatives: $\dfrac{\partial F_{A_y}}{\partial\delta_a}$, $\dfrac{\partial L_A}{\partial\delta_a}$ and $\dfrac{\partial N_A}{\partial\delta_a}$ and $\dfrac{\partial F_{A_y}}{\partial\delta_r}$, $\dfrac{\partial L_A}{\partial\delta_r}$ and $\dfrac{\partial N_A}{\partial\delta_r}$ are also shown in Table 3.4.

Whether or not these explanations are applicable depends largely on the symmetry (or lack thereof) of the airplane configuration being considered. With the exception of airplanes such as shown in Figure 1.3 the explanations given before are considered to be reasonable.

Another important assumption which is made at this point is that all perturbed forces and moments are a function of the instantaneous values of the perturbed motion variables only. This assumption is also known as the quasi–steady assumption. It has been pointed out by Etkin in Reference 3.6 that this assumption is not always realistic, depending on the motion frequencies of an airplane. Very roughly, for frequencies above about 10 radians per second the effect of motion frequency on the perturbed forces and moments does become important. In such cases, Etkin and Rodden (References 3.6 and 3.7) have developed alternate formulations for the perturbed forces and moments. Experience has shown that the great majority of rigid airplane stability and control problems can be adequately analyzed with the quasi–steady assumption.

Finally, it will also be assumed that higher order derivatives than the first derivatives accounted for in this text are negligible.

Table 3.5 shows the mathematical model used to represent the perturbed aerodynamic forces and moments, based on these explanations. Where applicable, the derived instead of the direct variables have been used.

Table 3.5 Dimensional Quasi–Steady Model for Perturbed Aerodynamic Forces and Moments

Longitudinal:

$$f_{A_x} = \frac{\partial F_{A_x}}{\partial u}u + \frac{\partial F_{A_x}}{\partial \alpha}\alpha + \frac{\partial F_{A_x}}{\partial \dot{\alpha}}\dot{\alpha} + \frac{\partial F_{A_x}}{\partial q}q + \frac{\partial F_{A_x}}{\partial \delta_e}\delta_e + \frac{\partial F_{A_x}}{\partial \delta_f}\delta_f \tag{3.96a}$$

$$f_{A_z} = \frac{\partial F_{A_z}}{\partial u}u + \frac{\partial F_{A_z}}{\partial \alpha}\alpha + \frac{\partial F_{A_z}}{\partial \dot{\alpha}}\dot{\alpha} + \frac{\partial F_{A_z}}{\partial q}q + \frac{\partial F_{A_z}}{\partial \delta_e}\delta_e + \frac{\partial F_{A_z}}{\partial \delta_f}\delta_f \tag{3.96b}$$

$$m_A = \frac{\partial M_A}{\partial u}u + \frac{\partial M_A}{\partial \alpha}\alpha + \frac{\partial M_A}{\partial \dot{\alpha}}\dot{\alpha} + \frac{\partial M_A}{\partial q}q + \frac{\partial M_A}{\partial \delta_e}\delta_e + \frac{\partial M_A}{\partial \delta_f}\delta_f \tag{3.96c}$$

Lateral–Directional:

$$f_{A_y} = \frac{\partial F_{A_y}}{\partial \beta}\beta + \frac{\partial F_{A_y}}{\partial \dot{\beta}}\dot{\beta} + \frac{\partial F_{A_y}}{\partial p}p + \frac{\partial F_{A_y}}{\partial r}r + \frac{\partial F_{A_y}}{\partial \delta_a}\delta_a + \frac{\partial F_{A_y}}{\partial \delta_r}\delta_r \tag{3.97a}$$

$$l_A = \frac{\partial L_A}{\partial \beta}\beta + \frac{\partial L_A}{\partial \dot{\beta}}\dot{\beta} + \frac{\partial L_A}{\partial p}p + \frac{\partial L_A}{\partial r}r + \frac{\partial L_A}{\partial \delta_a}\delta_a + \frac{\partial L_A}{\partial \delta_r}\delta_r \tag{3.97b}$$

$$n_A = \frac{\partial N_A}{\partial \beta}\beta + \frac{\partial N_A}{\partial \dot{\beta}}\dot{\beta} + \frac{\partial N_A}{\partial p}p + \frac{\partial N_A}{\partial r}r + \frac{\partial N_A}{\partial \delta_a}\delta_a + \frac{\partial N_A}{\partial \delta_r}\delta_r \tag{3.97c}$$

The mathematical model of Table 3.5 has a problem: the variables have physical units ranging from radians to radians/second and ft/sec. For reasons of uniformity it is preferred to make all variables dimensionless. This is achieved as follows:

1) by dividing the speed perturbation u by: U_1

2) by multiplying longitudinal perturbed angular rates by: $\frac{\bar{c}}{2U_1}$

3) by multiplying lateral–directional angular rates by: $\frac{b}{2U_1}$

The effect of this is to alter the model of Table 3.5 to that of Table 3.6. That model will be used in this text.

Table 3.6 Non–Dimensional Quasi–Steady Model for Perturbed Aerodynamic Forces and Moments

Longitudinal:

$$f_{A_x} = \frac{\partial F_{A_x}}{\partial(\frac{u}{U_1})}(\frac{u}{U_1}) + \frac{\partial F_{A_x}}{\partial\alpha}\alpha + \frac{\partial F_{A_x}}{\partial(\frac{\dot\alpha\bar c}{2U_1})}(\frac{\dot\alpha\bar c}{2U_1}) + \frac{\partial F_{A_x}}{\partial(\frac{q\bar c}{2U_1})}(\frac{q\bar c}{2U_1}) + \frac{\partial F_{A_x}}{\partial\delta_e}\delta_e + \frac{\partial F_{A_x}}{\partial\delta_f}\delta_f \quad (3.98a)$$

$$f_{A_z} = \frac{\partial F_{A_z}}{\partial(\frac{u}{U_1})}(\frac{u}{U_1}) + \frac{\partial F_{A_z}}{\partial\alpha}\alpha + \frac{\partial F_{A_z}}{\partial(\frac{\dot\alpha\bar c}{2U_1})}(\frac{\dot\alpha\bar c}{2U_1}) + \frac{\partial F_{A_z}}{\partial(\frac{q\bar c}{2U_1})}(\frac{q\bar c}{2U_1}) + \frac{\partial F_{A_z}}{\partial\delta_e}\delta_e + \frac{\partial F_{A_z}}{\partial\delta_f}\delta_f \quad (3.98b)$$

$$m_A = \frac{\partial M_A}{\partial(\frac{u}{U_1})}(\frac{u}{U_1}) + \frac{\partial M_A}{\partial\alpha}\alpha + \frac{\partial M_A}{\partial(\frac{\dot\alpha\bar c}{2U_1})}(\frac{\dot\alpha\bar c}{2U_1}) + \frac{\partial M_A}{\partial(\frac{q\bar c}{2U_1})}(\frac{q\bar c}{2U_1}) + \frac{\partial M_A}{\partial\delta_e}\delta_e + \frac{\partial M_A}{\partial\delta_f}\delta_f \quad (3.98c)$$

Lateral–Directional:

$$f_{A_y} = \frac{\partial F_{A_y}}{\partial\beta}\beta + \frac{\partial F_{A_y}}{\partial(\frac{\dot\beta b}{2U_1})}(\frac{\dot\beta b}{2U_1}) + \frac{\partial F_{A_y}}{\partial(\frac{pb}{2U_1})}(\frac{pb}{2U_1}) + \frac{\partial F_{A_y}}{\partial(\frac{rb}{2U_1})}(\frac{rb}{2U_1}) + \frac{\partial F_{A_y}}{\partial\delta_a}\delta_a + \frac{\partial F_{A_y}}{\partial\delta_r}\delta_r \quad (3.99a)$$

$$l_A = \frac{\partial L_A}{\partial\beta}\beta + \frac{\partial L_A}{\partial(\frac{\dot\beta b}{2U_1})}(\frac{\dot\beta b}{2U_1}) + \frac{\partial L_A}{\partial(\frac{pb}{2U_1})}(\frac{pb}{2U_1}) + \frac{\partial L_A}{\partial(\frac{rb}{2U_1})}(\frac{rb}{2U_1}) + \frac{\partial L_A}{\partial\delta_a}\delta_a + \frac{\partial L_A}{\partial\delta_r}\delta_r \quad (3.99b)$$

$$n_A = \frac{\partial N_A}{\partial\beta}\beta + \frac{\partial N_A}{\partial(\frac{\dot\beta b}{2U_1})}(\frac{\dot\beta b}{2U_1}) + \frac{\partial N_A}{\partial(\frac{pb}{2U_1})}(\frac{pb}{2U_1}) + \frac{\partial N_A}{\partial(\frac{rb}{2U_1})}(\frac{rb}{2U_1}) + \frac{\partial N_A}{\partial\delta_a}\delta_a + \frac{\partial N_A}{\partial\delta_r}\delta_r \quad (3.99c)$$

Expressions for the partial force and moment derivatives in Table 3.6 will be developed in Sub–sections 3.2.1 through 3.2.13.

3.2.1 PERTURBED STATE, LONGITUDINAL AERODYNAMIC FORCES AND MOMENTS

The perturbed state, longitudinal aerodynamic forces and moments are stated in Table 3.6 Eqns (3.98) and (3.99) in their dimensionless form. It is seen that the partial derivatives of the longitudinal forces and moment with respect to the dimensionless motion and control variables play the key role. The purpose of Sub–sections 3.2.2 through 3.2.13 is to show how these force and moment derivatives may be determined with the help of various stability and control derivatives. The dependence of these stability and control derivatives on airplane configuration design parameters will also be discussed.

3.2.2 AERODYNAMIC FORCE AND MOMENT DERIVATIVES WITH RESPECT TO FORWARD SPEED

According to Table 3.6, the following forces and moment are affected by changes in forward speed, u: F_{A_x}, F_{A_z} and M_A. These forces and moment are non–dimensionalized as follows:

$$F_{A_x} = C_x \overline{q} S \tag{3.100a}$$

$$F_{A_z} = C_z \overline{q} S \tag{3.100b}$$

$$M_A = C_m \overline{q} S \overline{c} \tag{3.100c}$$

The reader is reminded of the fact that F_{A_x}, F_{A_z} and M_A are defined in the stability axis system. Next, the partial differentiations implied by Table 3.6 will be systematically performed for Equations (3.100a) through (3.100c).

Partial Differentiation of Equation (3.100a) with respect to u/U_1

Partial differentiation of Eqn (3.100a) with respect to (u/U_1), leads to:

$$\frac{\partial F_{A_x}}{\partial (\frac{u}{U_1})} = \frac{\partial C_x}{\partial (\frac{u}{U_1})} \overline{q} S + C_x S \frac{\partial \overline{q}}{\partial (\frac{u}{U_1})} \tag{3.101}$$

At this point it should be recognized that the partial differentiations in Eqn (3.101) carry the following significance:

$$\frac{\partial F_{A_x}}{\partial (\frac{u}{U_1})} \quad \text{implies :} \quad \frac{\partial F_{A_x}}{\partial (\frac{u}{U_1})}\bigg|_1$$

In other words, both partial differentiations and the coefficient C_x in Eqn (3.101) must be evaluated in the steady state flight condition for which all perturbed quantities are equal to zero! For the partial differentiation of $\overline{q}$ this has the following consequence:

$$\frac{\partial \overline{q}}{\partial (\frac{u}{U_1})} = U_1 \frac{\partial \overline{q}}{\partial u}\bigg|_1 = U_1 \frac{\partial \frac{1}{2}\varrho[(U_1 + u)^2 + v^2 + w^2]}{\partial u}\bigg|_1 =$$

$$= U_1 \varrho (U_1 + u)\bigg|_1 = \varrho U_1^2 \tag{3.102}$$

Before carrying out the partial differentiation of C_x it is necessary to refer to Figure 3.51 to relate C_x to C_L and C_D. By using the 'small angle' assumption:

$$C_x = -C_D + C_L \alpha \tag{3.103a}$$

Partial differentiation of C_x yields:

$$\frac{\partial C_x}{\partial (\frac{u}{U_1})}\bigg|_1 = -\frac{\partial C_D}{\partial (\frac{u}{U_1})}\bigg|_1 + \frac{\partial C_L}{\partial (\frac{u}{U_1})}\alpha\bigg|_1 = -\frac{\partial C_D}{\partial (\frac{u}{U_1})}\bigg|_1 \tag{3.103b}$$

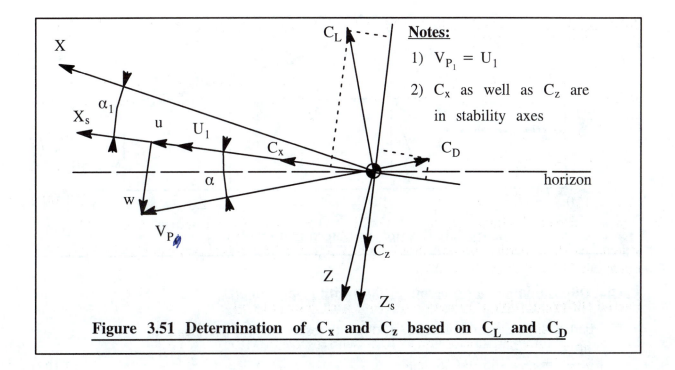

Figure 3.51 Determination of C_x and C_z based on C_L and C_D

From Eqn (3.103a) it follows that in the steady state:

$$C_{x_1} = - C_{D_1} \qquad (3.104)$$

The following notation is now introduced:

$$C_{D_u} = \frac{\partial C_D}{\partial(\frac{u}{U_1})}\Big|_1 \qquad (3.105)$$

With this notation it is possible to rewrite Eqn (3.101) as:

$$\frac{\partial F_{A_x}}{\partial(\frac{u}{U_1})} = - (C_{D_u} + 2C_{D_1})\bar{q}_1 S \qquad (3.106)$$

The derivative C_{D_u} is referred to as the speed–damping derivative. The sign and magnitude of C_{D_u} depends on the steady state Mach number of the airplane. Figure 3.52 shows a typical plot of the steady state drag coefficient versus Mach number (at constant angle of attack!). Since:

$$C_{D_u} = \frac{\partial C_D}{\partial(\frac{u}{U_1})} = \frac{U_1}{a}\frac{\partial C_D}{\partial \frac{u}{a}} = M_1 \frac{\partial C_D}{\partial M} \qquad (3.107)$$

The quantity 'a' represents the speed of sound for the steady state flight condition being considered. The numerical magnitude and sign of $\partial C_D/\partial M$ can be determined from a figure like Figure 3.52. Note that $\partial C_D/\partial M$ is generally >0 for M<1 while it is <0 for M>1. Figure 3.53 gives examples of the variation of C_{D_u} with Mach number for several airplanes.

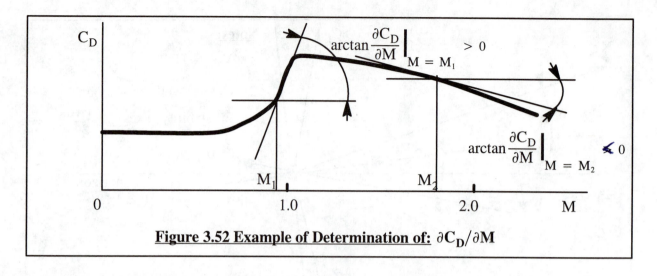

Figure 3.52 Example of Determination of: $\partial C_D / \partial M$

Partial Differentiation of Equation (3.100b) with respect to u/U$_1$

Partial differentiation of Eqn (3.100b) with respect to (u/U_1), leads to:

$$\frac{\partial F_{A_z}}{\partial(\frac{u}{U_1})} = \frac{\partial C_z}{\partial(\frac{u}{U_1})}\overline{q}S + C_z S\frac{\partial \overline{q}}{\partial(\frac{u}{U_1})} \tag{3.108}$$

Referring to Figure 3.51 it may be seen that (for small angle α):

$$C_z = -C_L - C_D\alpha \tag{3.109}$$

In the steady state this means:

$$C_{z_1} = -C_{L_1} \tag{3.110}$$

Differentiation of Eqn (3.109) yields:

$$\frac{\partial C_z}{\partial(\frac{u}{U_1})} = -\frac{\partial C_L}{\partial(\frac{u}{U_1})} - \alpha\frac{\partial C_D}{\partial(\frac{u}{U_1})} \tag{3.111}$$

Evaluated at the steady state, this condition produces:

$$C_{z_u} = -C_{L_u} \tag{3.112}$$

Note that:

$$C_{L_u} = \frac{\partial C_L}{\partial(\frac{u}{U_1})}\Bigg|_1 \tag{3.113}$$

By using Equations (3.112) and (3.110) it follows for Eqn (3.108) that:

$$\frac{\partial F_{A_z}}{\partial(\frac{u}{U_1})} = -(C_{L_u} + 2C_{L_1})\overline{q}_1 S \tag{3.114}$$

The derivative C_{L_u} can be evaluated for high aspect ratio wings as follows. At subsonic speeds, according to the Prandtl–Glauert transformation it is found that:

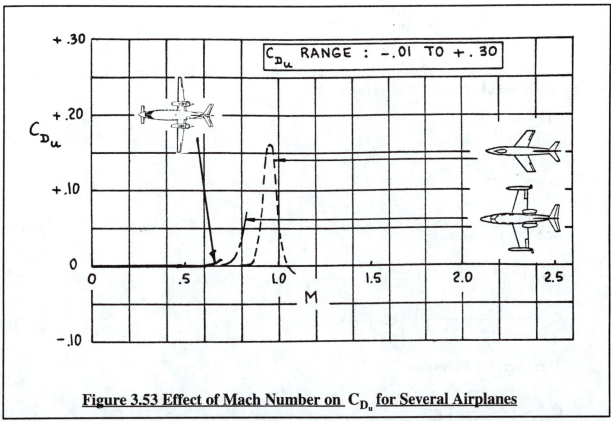

Figure 3.53 Effect of Mach Number on C_{D_u} for Several Airplanes

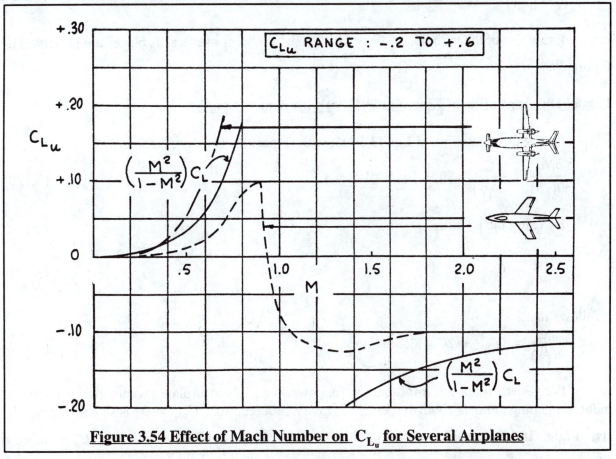

Figure 3.54 Effect of Mach Number on C_{L_u} for Several Airplanes

$$C_L = \frac{C_{L_0} + (C_{L_\alpha}|_{M=0})\alpha}{\sqrt{(1 - M^2)}} \tag{3.115}$$

This expression must now be differentiated with respect to M. For most airplanes, the following first order of approximation is reasonable:

$$\frac{\partial C_{L_0}}{\partial(\frac{u}{U_1})} \approx 0 \tag{3.116}$$

In that case:

$$\frac{\partial C_L}{\partial M} = \frac{M}{(1 - M^2)}C_L \tag{3.117}$$

Recalling Eqn (3.107) it follows that:

$$C_{L_u} = \frac{\partial C_L}{\partial(\frac{u}{U_1})} = \frac{U_1}{a}\frac{\partial C_L}{\partial \frac{u}{a}} = M_1\frac{\partial C_L}{\partial M} \tag{3.118}$$

Therefore, it follows that:

$$C_{L_u} = \frac{M_1^2}{(1 - M_1^2)}C_L \tag{3.119}$$

Examples of the variation of C_{L_u} with Mach number for several airplanes are presented in Figure 3.54.

Partial Differentiation of Equation (3.100c) with respect to u/U_1

Partial differentiation of Eqn (3.100c) with respect to (u/U_1), leads to:

$$\frac{\partial M_A}{\partial(\frac{u}{U_1})} = \frac{\partial C_m}{\partial(\frac{u}{U_1})}\bar{q}_1 S\bar{c} + C_{m_1}S\bar{c}\varrho U_1^2 \tag{3.120}$$

By using the notation:

$$\frac{\partial C_m}{\partial(\frac{u}{U_1})} = C_{m_u} \tag{3.121}$$

it follows that:

$$\frac{\partial M}{\partial(\frac{u}{U_1})} = (C_{m_u} + 2C_{m_1})\bar{q}_1 S\bar{c} \qquad \text{Airplane Tuck Derivative} \tag{3.122}$$

For gliders, for power–off flight and for power–on flight in airplanes where there is no thrust induced pitching moment about the center of gravity, the condition: $C_{m_1} = 0$ is satisfied in steady state flight. If thrust does contribute to pitching moment, the condition: $C_{m_1} = -C_{m_{T_1}}$ applies and this term must be accounted for in Eqn (3.122).

For reasons similar to those leading to Eqn (3.118):

$$C_{m_u} = M_1 \frac{\partial C_m}{\partial M} \tag{3.123}$$

The change in pitching moment coefficient due to Mach number is caused by changes in C_{m_0} and by the aft shift in aerodynamic center (and center of pressure) which tend to occur in the high subsonic speed range. If changes in C_{m_0} with Mach number are negligible, it is possible to compute $\partial C_m/\partial M$ from the following equation:

$$\frac{\partial C_m}{\partial M}(\Delta M) = -\Delta \overline{x}_{ac_A} C_{L_1} \tag{3.124}$$

where: $\Delta \overline{x}_{ac_A}$ is the aft shift in airplane aerodynamic center for a change in Mach number, ΔM. In that case, using Eqn (3.123):

$$C_{m_u} = -M_1 C_{L_1} \frac{\partial x_{ac_A}}{\partial M} \tag{3.125}$$

Note that in Eqns (3.124) and (3.125) an aft shift in a.c. is counted as positive! Shifts in a.c. with Mach number can be determined theoretically (See Ref.1, Part VI) or from windtunnel data. It is seen from Eqn (3.125) that in the transonic speed range below M=1, $C_{m_u} < 0$. This implies that for an increase in Mach number, the airplane has a tendency to put the nose down. This phenomenon is referred to as transonic 'tuck'. It can result in unacceptable handling quality behavior. Such behavior can be corrected by careful attention to airfoil design, wing planform design and/or by the introduction of Mach–trim systems.

Figure 3.55 presents examples of the variation of C_{m_u} with Mach number for several example airplanes. Note that the D–558–II 'bucks' the subsonic trend. The reason for this is not known to the author.

3.2.3 AERODYNAMIC FORCE AND MOMENT DERIVATIVES WITH RESPECT TO ANGLE OF ATTACK

According to Table 3.6 the following forces and moment are affected by changes in forward speed, u: F_{A_x}, F_{A_z} and M_A. These quantities were non–dimensionalized in Eqns (3.100).

Partial Differentiation of Equation (3.100a) with respect to α

Partial differentiation of Eqn (3.100a) with respect to α, leads to:

$$\frac{\partial F_{A_x}}{\partial \alpha} = \frac{\partial C_x}{\partial \alpha}\overline{q}S \tag{3.126}$$

By invoking Eqn (3.102) it follows that:

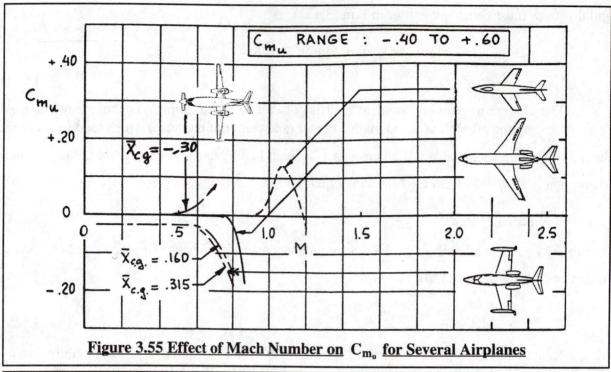

Figure 3.55 Effect of Mach Number on C_{m_u} for Several Airplanes

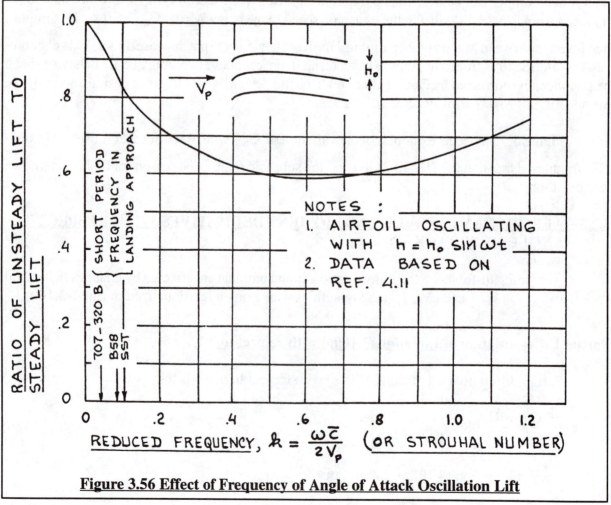

Figure 3.56 Effect of Frequency of Angle of Attack Oscillation Lift

$$C_{x_\alpha} = \frac{\partial C_x}{\partial \alpha} = -\frac{\partial C_D}{\partial \alpha} + \frac{\partial C_L}{\partial \alpha}\alpha + C_L \qquad (3.127)$$

After evaluating this result in the steady state flight condition:

$$C_{x_\alpha} = -C_{D_\alpha} + C_{L_1} \qquad (3.128)$$

And thus, Eqn (3.126) yields:

$$\frac{\partial F_{A_x}}{\partial \alpha} = (-C_{D_\alpha} + C_{L_1})\bar{q}_1 S \qquad (3.129)$$

where the derivative C_{D_α} is obtained from Eqn (3.9).

Partial Differentiation of Equation (3.100b) with respect to α

Partial differentiation of Eqn (3.100b) with respect to α, leads to:

$$\frac{\partial F_{A_z}}{\partial \alpha} = \frac{\partial C_z}{\partial \alpha}\bar{q}S \qquad (3.130)$$

From Eqn (3.109) it is found that:

$$C_{z_\alpha} = \frac{\partial C_z}{\partial \alpha} = -\frac{\partial C_L}{\partial \alpha} - \frac{\partial C_D}{\partial \alpha}\alpha - C_D \qquad (3.131)$$

After evaluating this result in the steady state flight condition:

$$C_{z_\alpha} = -C_{L_\alpha} - C_{D_1} \qquad (3.132)$$

And thus, Eqn (3.130) yields:

$$\frac{\partial F_{A_x}}{\partial \alpha} = -(C_{L_\alpha} + C_{D_1})\bar{q}_1 S \qquad (3.133)$$

where the derivative C_{L_α} is obtained from Eqn (3.24).

Partial Differentiation of Equation (3.100c) with respect to α

Partial differentiation of Eqn (3.100c) with respect to α and evaluating the result in the steady state flight condition leads to:

$$\frac{\partial M_A}{\partial \alpha} = \frac{\partial C_m}{\partial \alpha}\bar{q}S\bar{c} = C_{m_\alpha}\bar{q}_1 S\bar{c} \qquad (3.134)$$

The derivative C_{m_α} is obtained from Eqn (3.35).

Examples of the variation of C_{D_α}, C_{L_α} and C_{m_α} with Mach number are presented in Figures (3.12), (3.16) and (3.21) respectively.

3.2.4 AERODYNAMIC FORCE AND MOMENT DERIVATIVES WITH RESPECT TO ANGLE OF ATTACK RATE

According to Table 3.6 the following forces and moment are affected by changes in angle of attack rate: F_{A_x} , F_{A_z} and M_A. These quantities were non–dimensionalized in Eqns (3.98).

Introduction of angle of attack rate derivatives rests upon the assumption that, as a result of a change in $\dot{\alpha}$ the aerodynamic pressure distribution over the airplane adjusts itself instantaneously to α .

This so–called quasi–steady assumption has been shown to be reasonable (Ref. 3.6) as long as the following condition is satisfied:

$$\begin{bmatrix} \text{reduced} \\ \text{frequency} \end{bmatrix} = k = \frac{\dot{\alpha}\bar{c}}{2U_1} < 0.04 \qquad (3.135)$$

An example of the ratio of unsteady lift to steady lift for a thin airfoil which oscillates up and down in subsonic flow is shown in Figure 3.56. The data in Figure 3.56 suggest that criterion (3.135) is indeed reasonable.

Methods for computing the $\dot{\alpha}$ effect for arbitrary airplane configurations are not yet available. In the mean time the so–called 'lag–of–downwash' method can be used to obtain estimates for the derivatives of F_{A_x}, F_{A_z} and M_A with respect to $\dot{\alpha}$. In this method it is assumed that downwash behind a wing (or other lifting surface) is dependent primarily on the strength of the trailing vortices of the wing in the vicinity of the horizontal tail.

Because vorticity is transported with the flow, a change in downwash at the wing trailing edge (due to a change in angle of attack) will not be felt as a change in downwash at the horizontal tail until a time increment $\Delta t = x_h/U_1$ has elapsed. The quantity x_h is the distance from the 3/4 mgc point on the wing to the aerodynamic center of the horizontal tail.

Depending on overall airplane layout, the following approximation is often satisfied:

$$x_h \approx x_{ac_h} - x_{cg} \qquad (3.136)$$

It will be assumed that the downwash at the horizontal tail, ε (t), equals that downwash which corresponds to the wing angle of attack $\alpha(t - \Delta t)$. Therefore, a correction to the horizontal tail angle of attack can be made as follows:

$$\Delta\varepsilon = -\frac{d\varepsilon}{d\alpha}\dot{\alpha}\Delta t = -\frac{d\varepsilon}{d\alpha}\dot{\alpha}\frac{(\bar{x}_{ac_h} - \bar{x}_{cg})}{U_1} \qquad (3.137)$$

Next, the partial derivatives of F_{A_x}, F_{A_z} and M_A will be taken one–by one.

Partial Differentiation of Equation (3.100a) with respect to $(\dot{\alpha}\bar{c}/2U_1)$

Partial differentiation of Eqn (3.100a) with respect to $(\dot{\alpha}\bar{c}/2U_1)$ leads to:

$$\frac{\partial F_{A_x}}{\partial(\frac{\dot{\alpha}\bar{c}}{2U_1})} = C_{x_{\dot{\alpha}}}\bar{q}S = -C_{D_{\dot{\alpha}}}\bar{q}S = 0 \tag{3.138}$$

where it is assumed that the effect of downwash lag on drag can be neglected: $C_{D_{\dot{\alpha}}} \approx 0$

Partial Differentiation of Equation (3.100b) with respect to $(\dot{\alpha}\bar{c}/2U_1)$

Partial differentiation of Eqn (3.100b) with respect to $(\dot{\alpha}\bar{c}/2U_1)$, leads to:

$$\frac{\partial F_{A_z}}{\partial(\frac{\dot{\alpha}\bar{c}}{2U_1})} = \frac{\partial C_Z}{\partial(\frac{\dot{\alpha}\bar{c}}{2U_1})}\bar{q}_1 S = C_{Z_{\dot{\alpha}}}\bar{q}_1 S \tag{3.139}$$

Since:

$$C_{Z_{\dot{\alpha}}} = -C_{L_{\dot{\alpha}}} \tag{3.140}$$

The derivative $C_{L_{\dot{\alpha}}}$ is found by observing the fact that $\Delta\varepsilon$ of Eqn (3.137) causes a change in horizontal tail lift coefficient which can be expressed as follows:

$$\Delta C_{L_h} = -C_{L_{\alpha_h}}\Delta\varepsilon = C_{L_{\alpha_h}}\frac{d\varepsilon}{d\alpha}\dot{\alpha}\frac{(x_{ac_h} - x_{cg})}{U_1} \tag{3.141}$$

For the entire airplane this yields:

$$\Delta C_L \text{ airplane, caused by } \dot{\alpha} = C_{L_{\alpha_h}}\frac{d\varepsilon}{d\alpha}\dot{\alpha}\frac{(x_{ac_h} - x_{cg})}{U_1}\eta_h\frac{S_h}{S} \tag{3.142}$$

Partial differentiation w.r.t $(\dot{\alpha}\bar{c}/2U_1)$ and using Eqn (3.140) produces:

$$C_{Z_{\dot{\alpha}}} = -C_{L_{\dot{\alpha}}} = -2C_{L_{\alpha_h}}\frac{d\varepsilon}{d\alpha}\frac{(x_{ac_h} - x_{cg})}{\bar{c}}\eta_h\frac{S_h}{S} \tag{3.143}$$

Introducing the concept of horizontal tail volume coefficient first used in Eqn (3.36):

$$C_{L_{\dot{\alpha}}} = 2C_{L_{\alpha_h}}\eta_h\bar{V}_h\frac{d\varepsilon}{d\alpha} \tag{3.144}$$

Combining Eqn (3.139) with (3.140) and (3.144) results in:

$$\frac{\partial F_{A_z}}{\partial(\frac{\dot{\alpha}\bar{c}}{2U_1})} = -2C_{L_{\alpha_h}}\eta_h\bar{V}_h\frac{d\varepsilon}{d\alpha}\bar{q}_1 S \tag{3.145}$$

Figure 3.57 shows how $C_{L_{\dot{\alpha}}}$ varies with Mach number for several airplanes.

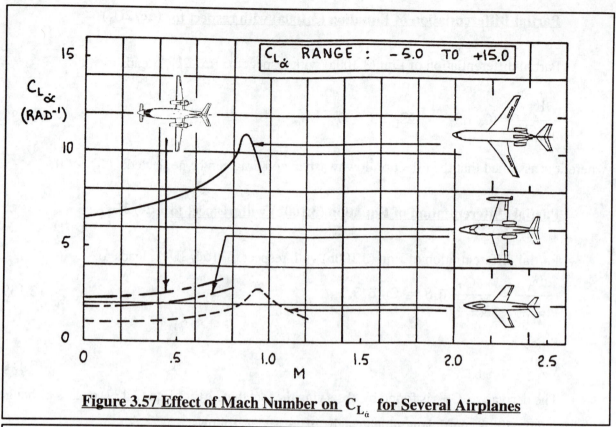

Figure 3.57 Effect of Mach Number on $C_{L_{\dot{\alpha}}}$ **for Several Airplanes**

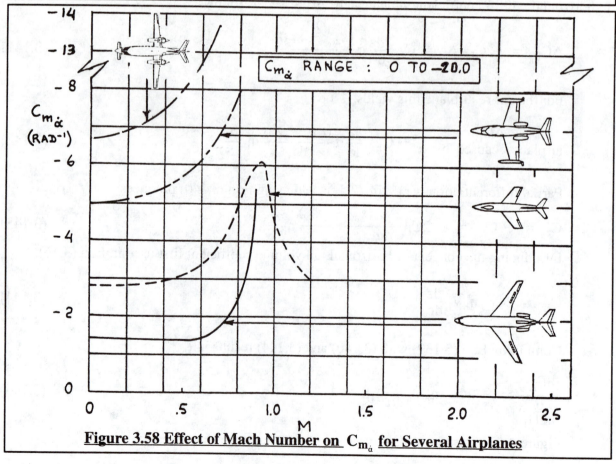

Figure 3.58 Effect of Mach Number on $C_{m_{\dot{\alpha}}}$ **for Several Airplanes**

Partial Differentiation of Equation (3.100c) with respect to $(\dot{\alpha}\bar{c}/2U_1)$

Partial differentiation of Eqn (3.98c) with respect to $(\dot{\alpha}\bar{c}/2U_1)$ and evaluation at the steady state leads to:

$$\frac{\partial M_A}{\partial(\frac{\dot{\alpha}\bar{c}}{2U_1})} = C_{m_{\dot{\alpha}}}\bar{q}_1 S\bar{c} \tag{3.146}$$

The derivative $C_{m_{\dot{\alpha}}}$ is found from Eqn (3.144) by multiplying by the dimensional moment arm of the horizontal tail, $(\bar{x}_{ac_h} - \bar{x}_{cg})$ and accounting for the fact that up–lift on the horizontal tail produces a nose–down pitching moment. This yields:

$$C_{m_{\dot{\alpha}}} = -2C_{L_{\alpha_h}}\eta_h \bar{V}_h(\bar{x}_{ac_h} - \bar{x}_{cg})\frac{d\varepsilon}{d\alpha} \tag{3.147}$$

Figure 3.58 shows how $C_{m_{\dot{\alpha}}}$ varies with Mach number for several airplanes.

3.2.5 AERODYNAMIC FORCE AND MOMENT DERIVATIVES WITH RESPECT TO PITCH RATE

According to Table 3.6 the following forces and moment are affected by changes in pitch rate, q: F_{A_x} , F_{A_z} and M_A. These quantities were non–dimensionalized in Eqns (3.100).

Figure 3.59 shows that the effect of a pitch rate perturbation about the airplane center of gravity is to create 'slewing' velocities at all lifting surfaces. These slewing velocities induce local changes in angle of attack which in turn create lift changes on all lifting surfaces. These lift changes in turn cause increments in induced drag and in pitching moment. It is generally assumed that the pitch rate effect on induced drag is negligible. The effect of pitch rate on lift is not always negligible. The effect of pitch rate on pitching moment is nearly always very important as will be seen in the following derivation for a conventional airplane (wing + tail aft).

Methods for determining pitch rate derivatives for an arbitrary airplane configuration are presented in Part VI of Ref.3.1.

Partial Differentiation of Equation (3.100a) with respect to $(q\bar{c}/2U_1)$

Partial differentiation of Eqn (3.100a) with respect to $(q\bar{c}/2U_1)$, leads to:

$$\frac{\partial F_{A_x}}{\partial(\frac{q\bar{c}}{2U_1})} = C_{x_q}\bar{q}S = -C_{D_q}\bar{q}S = 0 \tag{3.148}$$

where it is assumed that the effect of pitch rate on drag can be neglected: $C_{D_q} \approx 0$

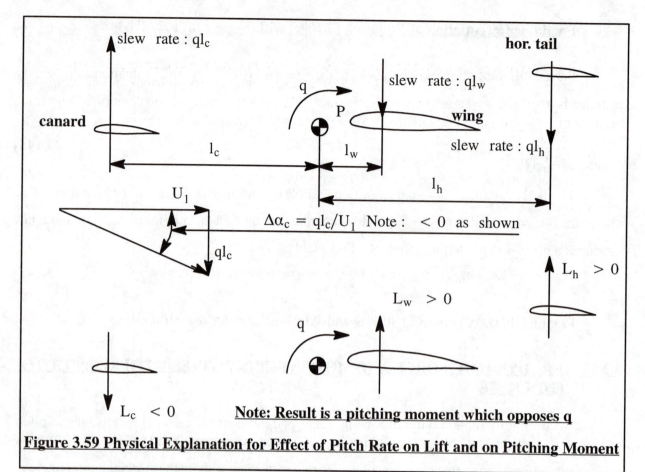

Figure 3.59 Physical Explanation for Effect of Pitch Rate on Lift and on Pitching Moment

Partial Differentiation of Equation (3.100b) with respect to $(q\bar{c}/2U_1)$

Partial differentiation of Eqn (3.100b) with respect to $(q\bar{c}/2U_1)$, leads to:

$$\frac{\partial F_{A_z}}{\partial(\frac{q\bar{c}}{2U_1})} = \frac{\partial C_z}{\partial(\frac{q\bar{c}}{2U_1})}\bar{q}_1 S = C_{z_q}\bar{q}_1 S \qquad (3.149)$$

Since:

$$C_{z_q} = -C_{L_q} \qquad (3.150)$$

It is seen in Figure 3.59 that pitch rate, q, induces an angle of attack at the canard. Although not shown in Figure 3.59, there is also an induced angle of attack at the horizontal tail:

$$\Delta\alpha_h = \frac{ql_h}{U_1} \qquad (3.151)$$

This induced angle of attack at the horizontal tail results in the following induced lift coefficient for the airplane:

$$\left(\begin{array}{c}\Delta C_L\\ \text{airplane, caused by q}\end{array}\right) = C_{L_{\alpha_h}}\frac{ql_h}{U_1}\eta_h\frac{S_h}{S} \qquad (3.152)$$

After partial differentiation with respect to $(q\bar{c}/2U_1)$, it follows:

$$C_{L_q} = 2C_{L_{\alpha_h}}\frac{l_h}{\bar{c}}\eta_h\frac{S_h}{S} \tag{3.153}$$

For conventional (i.e. no canard) airplanes, it is found that the center of gravity is located close to the wing aerodynamic center. In that case, there is no canard contribution, the wing contribution is negligible because of its small slew rate BUT, the horizontal tail contribution is important because of its significant moment arm. For such cases it is acceptable to write:

$$l_h = (x_{ac_h} - x_{cg}) \tag{3.154}$$

The consequence of this for conventional airplanes is:

$$\frac{\partial F_{A_z}}{\partial(\frac{q\bar{c}}{2U_1})} = -C_{L_q}\bar{q}_1 S = -2C_{L_{\alpha_h}}\eta_h\bar{V}_h\bar{q}_1 S \tag{3.155}$$

Figure 3.60 shows trends of C_{L_q} with Mach number for several airplanes.

Partial Differentiation of Equation (3.100c) with respect to $(q\bar{c}/2U_1)$

Partial differentiation of Eqn (3.100c) with respect to $(q\bar{c}/2U_1)$ leads to:

$$\frac{\partial M_A}{\partial(\frac{q\bar{c}}{2U_1})} = \frac{\partial C_m}{\partial(\frac{q\bar{c}}{2U_1})}\bar{q}_1 S = C_{m_q}\bar{q}_1 S \tag{3.156}$$

Pitch Damping for Conventional A/c.

Pitch Damping ∝ to (tail moment arm)²

By using reasoning similar to what lead to Eqn (3.147), the reader is asked to show that:

$$C_{m_q} = -2C_{L_{\alpha_h}}\eta_h\bar{V}_h(\bar{x}_{ac_h} - \bar{x}_{cg}) \tag{3.157}$$

Since in many conventional airplanes the wing contribution to C_{m_q} is not entirely negligible, a 'fudge–factor' is often used to produce for the entire airplane (conventional only!):

$$C_{m_q} = -2.2C_{L_{\alpha_h}}\eta_h\bar{V}_h(\bar{x}_{ac_h} - \bar{x}_{cg}) \tag{3.158}$$

2.2 → 10% ↑ for wing effect

It should be observed that the derivative, C_{m_q}, is proportional to the square of the moment arm of the horizontal tail. This is why this derivative is often rather large. The derivative, C_{m_q} is referred to as the pitch–damping derivative. It is very important to the flying qualities of an airplane. Figure 3.61 shows trends of C_{m_q} with Mach number for several airplanes.

3.2.6 AERODYNAMIC FORCE AND MOMENT DERIVATIVES WITH RESPECT TO LONGITUDINAL CONTROL SURFACE AND FLAP DEFLECTIONS

According to Table 3.6 the following forces and moments are affected by changes in control surface and flap deflections, δ_e and δ_f : F_{A_x} , F_{A_z} and M_A. These forces and moment were non–dimensionalized in Eqns (3.100).

Partial differentiation of F_{A_x}, F_{A_z} and M_A with respect to δ_e and δ_f leads to the following expressions:

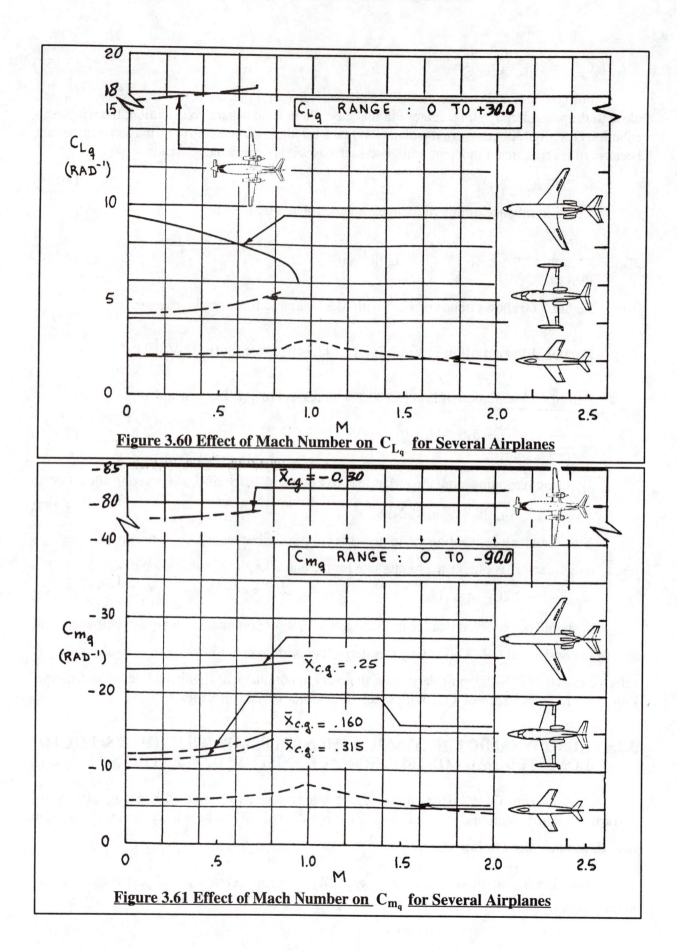

Figure 3.60 Effect of Mach Number on C_{L_q} for Several Airplanes

Figure 3.61 Effect of Mach Number on C_{m_q} for Several Airplanes

$$\frac{\partial F_{A_x}}{\partial \delta} = \frac{\partial C_x}{\partial \delta}\overline{q}_1 S = C_{x_\delta}\overline{q}_1 S = -C_{D_\delta}\overline{q}_1 S \tag{3.159}$$

$$\frac{\partial F_{A_z}}{\partial \delta} = \frac{\partial C_z}{\partial \delta}\overline{q}_1 S = C_{z_\delta}\overline{q}_1 S = -C_{L_\delta}\overline{q}_1 S \tag{3.160}$$

$$\frac{\partial M_A}{\partial \delta} = \frac{\partial C_m}{\partial \delta}\overline{q}_1 S\overline{c} = C_{m_\delta}\overline{q}_1 S\overline{c} \tag{3.161}$$

The subscripts used to indicate the control surface type were dropped from Eqns (3.159) through (3.161). Expressions for the elevator and stabilizer control surface derivatives were derived in Sub–sections 3.1.2, 3.1.3 and 3.1.4. For more general control surface derivatives and for flap derivatives the reader may wish to consult Part VI of Ref.3.1.

3.2.7 ASSEMBLING THE PERTURBED LONGITUDINAL AERODYNAMIC FORCES AND MOMENTS

At this point the perturbed, longitudinal aerodynamic forces and moment are assembled in matrix format in Table 3.7.

Table 3.7 Matrix Format for Perturbed State Longitudinal Aerodynamic Forces and Moment

$$
\begin{Bmatrix} \dfrac{f_{A_x}}{\overline{q}_1 S} \\[3ex] \dfrac{f_{A_z}}{\overline{q}_1 S} \\[3ex] \dfrac{m_A}{\overline{q}_1 S\overline{c}} \end{Bmatrix}
=
\begin{bmatrix}
\overset{(3.106)}{-(C_{D_u}+2C_{D_1})} & \overset{(3.128)}{(-C_{D_\alpha}+C_{L_1})} & \overset{(3.138)}{-C_{D_{\dot\alpha}}} & \overset{(3.148)}{-C_{D_q}\approx 0} & \overset{(3.6)}{-C_{D_{\delta_e}}} \\[3ex]
\overset{(3.114)}{-(C_{L_u}+2C_{L_1})} & \overset{(3.132)}{(-C_{L_\alpha}-C_{D_1})} & \overset{(3.144)}{-C_{L_{\dot\alpha}}} & \overset{(3.153)}{-C_{L_q}} & \overset{(3.26)}{-C_{L_{\delta_e}}} \\[3ex]
\overset{(3.122)}{(C_{m_u}+2C_{m_1})} & \overset{(3.134)}{C_{m_\alpha}} & \overset{(3.147)}{C_{m_{\dot\alpha}}} & \overset{(3.158)}{C_{m_q}} & \overset{(3.37)}{C_{m_{\delta_e}}}
\end{bmatrix}
\begin{Bmatrix} \dfrac{u}{U_1} \\[2ex] \alpha \\[2ex] \dfrac{\dot\alpha\overline{c}}{2U_1} \\[2ex] \dfrac{q\overline{c}}{2U_1} \\[2ex] \delta_e \end{Bmatrix}
\tag{3.162}
$$

Notes: 1) Airplanes may have more than one longitudinal control surface. Only the elevator have been included in Eqn (3.162). Additional control surfaces simply expand the size of the matrices.
2) Bracketed numbers refer to equations in the text.
3) All stability derivatives may be computed with the methods of Part VI of Ref.3.1 and/or with the AAA program (Appendix A)

3.2.8 PERTURBED STATE, LATERAL–DIRECTIONAL, AERODYNAMIC FORCES AND MOMENTS

The perturbed state, lateral–directional, aerodynamic forces and moments are defined in Table 3.6 , Eqns (3.99) in their dimensionless form. It is seen that the partial derivatives of the lateral–directional force and moments with respect to dimensionless motion and control variables play the key role. The purpose of Sub–sections 3.2.9 through 3.2.14 is to show how these force and moment derivatives may be determined with the help of various stability and control derivatives.

3.2.9 AERODYNAMIC FORCE AND MOMENT DERIVATIVES WITH RESPECT TO SIDESLIP

According to Table 3.6 the following force and moments are affected by changes in sideslip angle, β: F_{A_y} , L_A and N_A. These force and moments are non–dimensionalized as follows:

$$F_{A_y} = - C_y \overline{q} S \tag{3.163a}$$

$$L_A = - C_l \overline{q} S b \tag{3.163b}$$

$$N_A = - C_n \overline{q} S b \tag{3.163c}$$

The reader is reminded of the fact that F_{A_y} , L_A and N_A are defined in the stability axis system. Next, the partial differentiations implied by Table 3.6 will be systematically performed for Equations (3.163a) through (3.163c). Partial differentiation of Eqns (3.163) with respect to sideslip angle, β, leads to the following expressions:

$$\frac{\partial F_{A_y}}{\partial \beta} = \frac{\partial C_y}{\partial \beta} \overline{q}_1 S = C_{y_\beta} \overline{q}_1 S \tag{3.164}$$

$$\frac{\partial L_A}{\partial \beta} = \frac{\partial C_l}{\partial \beta} \overline{q}_1 S b = C_{l_\beta} \overline{q}_1 S b \tag{3.165}$$

$$\frac{\partial N_A}{\partial \beta} = \frac{\partial C_n}{\partial \beta} \overline{q}_1 S b = C_{n_\beta} \overline{q}_1 S b \tag{3.166}$$

The stability derivatives C_{y_β}, C_{l_β} and C_{n_β} were already discussed in Sub–sections 3.1.9, 3.1.8 and 3.1.10 respectively.

3.2.10 AERODYNAMIC FORCE AND MOMENT DERIVATIVES WITH RESPECT TO SIDESLIP RATE

According to Table 3.6 the following force and moments are affected by changes in sideslip, β: F_{A_y} , L_A and N_A. These force and moments were non–dimensionalized in Eqns (3.163).

Partial differentiation of Eqns (3.163) with respect to sideslip angle, β, leads to the following expressions:

$$\frac{\partial F_{A_y}}{\partial(\frac{\dot{\beta}b}{2U_1})} = \frac{\partial C_y}{\partial(\frac{\dot{\beta}b}{2U_1})}\bar{q}_1 S = C_{y_{\dot{\beta}}}\bar{q}_1 S \qquad (3.167)$$

$$\frac{\partial L_A}{\partial(\frac{\dot{\beta}b}{2U_1})} = \frac{\partial C_l}{\partial(\frac{\dot{\beta}b}{2U_1})}\bar{q}_1 Sb = C_{l_{\dot{\beta}}}\bar{q}_1 Sb \qquad (3.168)$$

$$\frac{\partial N_A}{\partial(\frac{\dot{\beta}b}{2U_1})} = \frac{\partial C_n}{\partial(\frac{\dot{\beta}b}{2U_1})}\bar{q}_1 Sb = C_{n_{\dot{\beta}}}\bar{q}_1 Sb \qquad (3.169)$$

The stability derivatives $C_{y_{\dot{\beta}}}$, $C_{l_{\dot{\beta}}}$ and $C_{n_{\dot{\beta}}}$ are physically analogous to the $\dot{\alpha}$ – derivatives which were discussed in Sub–section 3.2.4. Methods for numerically predicting these $\dot{\beta}$ – derivatives are given in Part VI of Reference 3.1. Except for airplanes in the high subsonic speed range, the $\dot{\beta}$ – derivatives are frequently considered negligible.

3.2.11 AERODYNAMIC FORCE AND MOMENT DERIVATIVES WITH RESPECT TO ROLL RATE

According to Table 3.6 the following force and moments are affected by changes in perturbed roll rate, p: F_{A_y}, L_A and N_A. These force and moments were non–dimensionalized in Eqns (3.163).

Partial differentiation of Eqns (3.163) with respect to roll rate, p, leads to the following expressions:

$$\frac{\partial F_{A_y}}{\partial(\frac{pb}{2U_1})} = \frac{\partial C_y}{\partial(\frac{pb}{2U_1})}\bar{q}_1 S = C_{y_p}\bar{q}_1 S \qquad (3.170)$$

$$\frac{\partial L_A}{\partial(\frac{pb}{2U_1})} = \frac{\partial C_l}{\partial(\frac{pb}{2U_1})}\bar{q}_1 Sb = C_{l_p}\bar{q}_1 Sb \qquad (3.171)$$

$$\frac{\partial N_A}{\partial(\frac{pb}{2U_1})} = \frac{\partial C_n}{\partial(\frac{pb}{2U_1})}\bar{q}_1 Sb = C_{n_p}\bar{q}_1 Sb \qquad (3.172)$$

A physical explanation for how the roll–rate derivatives C_{y_p}, C_{l_p} and C_{n_p} occur is presented in the following.

Side–force coefficient due to roll rate derivative, C_{y_p}

This derivative is usually made up of two components:

$$C_{y_p} = C_{y_{p_{wfh}}} + C_{y_{pv}} \tag{3.173}$$

The contribution due to the wing–fuselage–horizontal tail, $C_{y_{p_{wfh}}}$, is generally negligible for conventional configurations, particularly when compared to the contribution due to the vertical tail, $C_{y_{pv}}$. A physical explanation for the aerodynamic mechanism responsible for $C_{y_{pv}}$ is presented in Figure 3.62. It is seen that due to roll rate p, about the stability X–axis, a force $F_{y_{pv}}$ is induced on the vertical tail in the negative Y–direction. Note that this force acts at a point, a distance z_{v_s} away from the X–stability axis. That point is assumed to be the vertical tail aerodynamic center due to the additional pressure distribution caused by the roll rate, p. In principle, this distance z_{v_s} is not the same as the distance of the same name–tag in Figure 3.31. However, this difference is usually ignored. Assuming z_{v_s} is known, the local angle of attack due to roll rate induced on the vertical tail is: $\Delta \alpha_v = p z_{v_s}/U_1$. Therefore, the side force on the vertical tail may be modelled as:

$$F_{y_{pv}} = C_{L_{\alpha_v}}(\frac{p z_{v_s}}{U_1})\overline{q}_v S_v \tag{3.174}$$

The side–force due to roll rate on the entire airplane can be written as:

$$F_{y_p} = C_y \overline{q} S = - C_{L_{\alpha_v}}(\frac{p z_{v_s}}{U_1})\overline{q}_v S_v \tag{3.175}$$

From this, by partial differentiation w.r.t. $\frac{pb}{2U_1}$ it follows that:

$$C_{y_p} \approx C_{y_{pv}} = - 2C_{L_{\alpha_v}}(\frac{z_{v_s}}{b})\eta_v(\frac{S_v}{S}) \tag{3.176}$$

Although Eqn (3.176) suggests that the sign of C_{y_p} is generally negative, it is evident from Figure 3.62 that the sign of the moment arm, z_{v_s} can reverse at high angles of attack. Figure 3.63 shows examples of the variation of C_{y_p} with Mach number for several airplanes.

The derivative C_{y_p} is normally not a very important derivative in terms of its effect on air-plane dynamic stability. However, in the synthesis of turn–coordination modes in auto–pilots, this derivative should not be neglected.

Rolling moment coefficient due to roll rate derivative, C_{l_p}

This derivative is usually made up of three components:

$$C_{l_p} = C_{l_{p_{wf}}} + C_{l_{p_h}} + C_{l_{pv}} \tag{3.177}$$

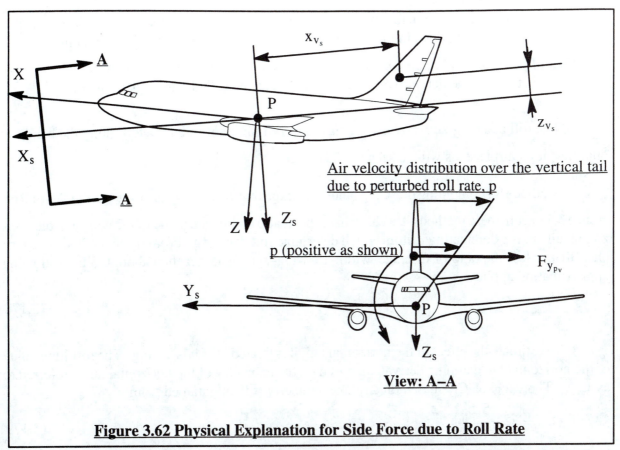

Figure 3.62 Physical Explanation for Side Force due to Roll Rate

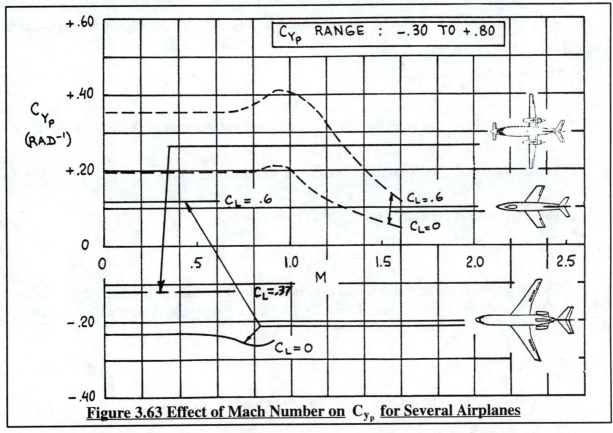

Figure 3.63 Effect of Mach Number on C_{y_p} for Several Airplanes

A physical explanation for the principal aerodynamic mechanism which is responsible for $C_{l_{p_{wf}}}$ and $C_{l_{p_h}}$ is provided in Figure 3.64. It is seen that, as long as the flow remains attached, the effect of perturbed roll rate, p, is to create an asymmetrical lift distribution which opposes the roll rate. That is why the derivative C_{l_p} is referred to as the roll–damping derivative.

The roll damping derivative, C_{l_p}, plays a very important role in determining the handling qualities of an airplane, as will be seen in Chapter 5.

Methods for computing the $C_{l_{p_{wf}}}$ and $C_{l_{p_h}}$ contributions to C_{l_p} are given in Part VI of Reference 3.1. From these methods it is clear that aspect ratio and sweep angle of the wing and the horizontal tail are the dominating factors which determine roll damping. From these methods it is also clear that unless the ratio of fuselage–width–to–wing–span is larger than about 0.3 the following approximation applies:

$$C_{l_{p_w}} \approx C_{l_{p_{wf}}} \tag{3.178}$$

To estimate the effect of the horizontal tail, it is treated as if it is a wing. The resulting value of the horizontal tail damping derivative, based on the geometry of the horizontal tail is referred to as $\overline{C}_{l_{p_h}}$. The value of $C_{l_{p_h}}$ based on airplane geometry is then obtained from:

$$C_{l_{p_h}} = \overline{C}_{l_{p_h}} \frac{S_h b_h^2}{S b^2} \tag{3.179}$$

An expression for $C_{l_{p_v}}$ can be found with the help of Eqn (3.176). The reader is asked to show that:

$$C_{l_{p_v}} = -2 C_{L_{\alpha_v}} \left(\frac{z_{v_s}}{b}\right)^2 \eta_v \left(\frac{S_v}{S}\right) \tag{3.180}$$

Figure 3.65 shows examples of how C_{l_p} varies with Mach number for several airplanes.

Yawing moment coefficient due to roll rate derivative, C_{n_p}

This derivative is normally made up of two components:

$$C_{n_p} = C_{n_{p_{wf}}} + C_{n_{p_v}} \tag{3.181}$$

The horizontal tail contribution tends to be insignificant for conventional airplanes with tails which are small compared to the wing. The wing–fuselage contribution is normally dominated by the wing and is caused by three mechanisms:

1) wing drag increase   2) wing lift vector tilting   3) wing tip suction

A physical explanation for these three effects follows.

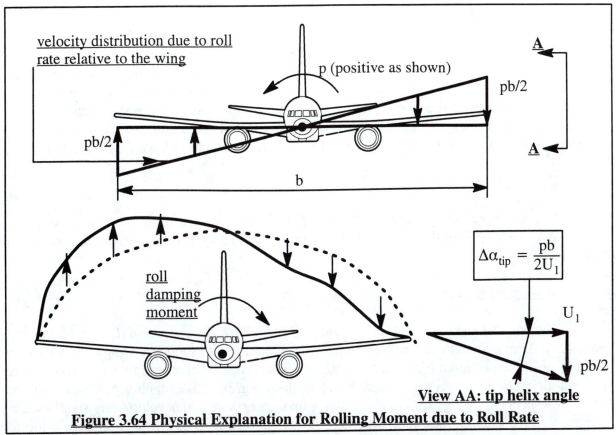

velocity distribution due to roll rate relative to the wing

p (positive as shown)

pb/2

pb/2

b

roll damping moment

$$\Delta\alpha_{tip} = \frac{pb}{2U_1}$$

U_1

pb/2

View AA: tip helix angle

Figure 3.64 Physical Explanation for Rolling Moment due to Roll Rate

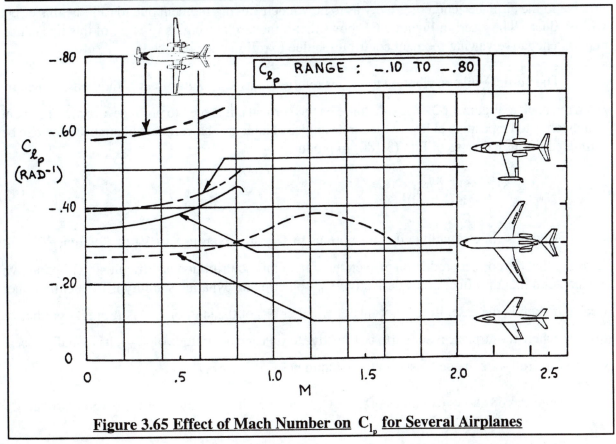

C_{ℓ_p} RANGE : $-.10$ TO $-.80$

C_{ℓ_p} (RAD^{-1})

Figure 3.65 Effect of Mach Number on C_{l_p} for Several Airplanes

1) wing drag increase

Figure 3.66 shows that as a result of the rolling motion of the wing the local angles of attack over the wing span are altered. For a positive roll rate (right wing down) the right wing experiences an increase in local angle of attack while the left wing experiences a similar decrease in local angle of attack. Figure 3.66 illustrates this for spanwise stations +y and −y. These angle of attack changes are seen to produce changes in local lift and drag. It is seen that the effect of the increase in drag at spanwise stations +/− y is to generate a positive increment in the yawing moment due to roll rate.

2) wing lift vector tilting

It is seen from Figure 3.66 that the changes in lift produced by roll rate at spanwise stations +/− y result in a 'tilting' of the total local lift vectors in such a way as to produce a negative yawing moment due to roll rate.

3) wing tip suction

The wing tip suction effect is illustrated in Figure 3.67. It is seen that if a wing is carrying no net lift, there is no net side force due to roll rate. However, as soon as a wing carries a certain amount of lift, the addition of a positive roll rate causes a net positive side force due to the effect of wing–tip suction. Clearly the magnitude of this tip suction effect is a function of the wing geometry. Low aspect ratio wings with relatively large tip thickness tend to develop fairly significant net suction forces due to roll rate. It all depends on where the center of this tip suction force is located relative to the airplane center of gravity as to how much yawing moment due to roll rate this effect will produce. The insert in Figure 3.67 shows that if the airplane c.g. is forward of this tip suction center, a negative yawing moment contribution due to roll rate is produced.

The vertical tail contribution to C_{n_p} is referred to as $C_{n_{p_v}}$. Its effect is most easily seen by referring back to Figure 3.62. The side force on the vertical tail is seen to produce a yawing moment which tends to be positive at low to moderate angles of attack. The vertical tail contribution can be estimated through the use of Eqn (3.180) to produce:

$$C_{n_{p_v}} = 2C_{L_{\alpha_v}}(\frac{z_{v_s}}{b})(\frac{x_{v_s}}{b})\eta_v(\frac{S_v}{S})$$

(3.182)

Methods for estimating all contributions to C_{n_p} are given in Part VI of Reference 3.1. It turns out that the correct prediction of even the sign of this contribution is difficult. It will be shown in Chapter 5 that the effect of the derivative C_{n_p} on airplane dynamic stability is frequently rather weak. If such is the case, it may not matter whether or not the sign of C_{n_p} is properly predicted. In cases where the airplane is shown to be sensitive to sign and magnitude of C_{n_p}, it is usually necessary to run 'roll–rate–model–tests' in the windtunnel.

Figure 3.68 shows examples of how C_{n_p} varies with Mach number for several airplanes.

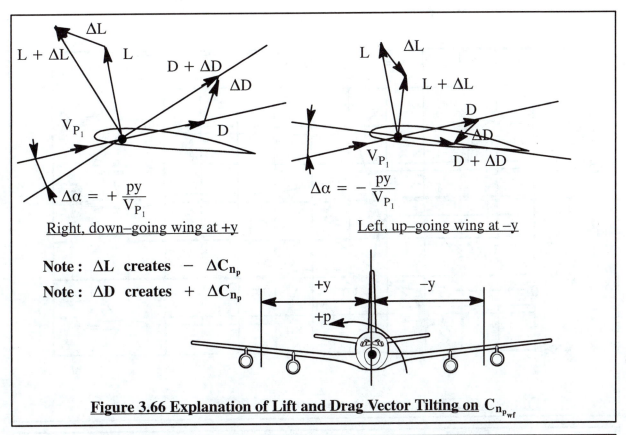

$$\Delta\alpha = + \frac{py}{V_{P_1}}$$

Right, down–going wing at +y

$$\Delta\alpha = - \frac{py}{V_{P_1}}$$

Left, up–going wing at –y

Note : ΔL creates $- \Delta C_{n_p}$

Note : ΔD creates $+ \Delta C_{n_p}$

Figure 3.66 Explanation of Lift and Drag Vector Tilting on $C_{n_{p_{wf}}}$

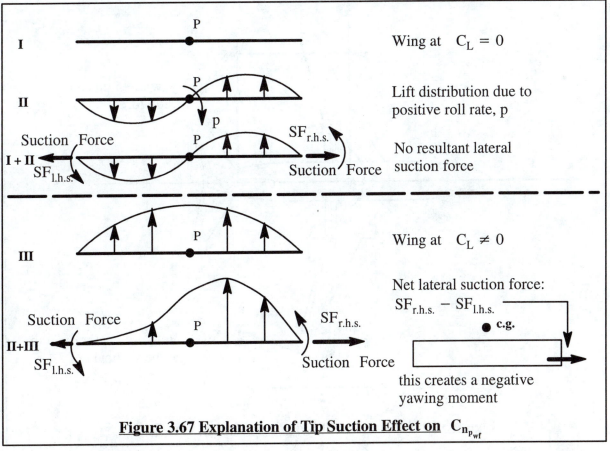

I — Wing at $C_L = 0$

II — Lift distribution due to positive roll rate, p

I + II — No resultant lateral suction force

III — Wing at $C_L \neq 0$

II+III — Net lateral suction force: $SF_{r.h.s.} - SF_{l.h.s.}$

this creates a negative yawing moment

Figure 3.67 Explanation of Tip Suction Effect on $C_{n_{p_{wf}}}$

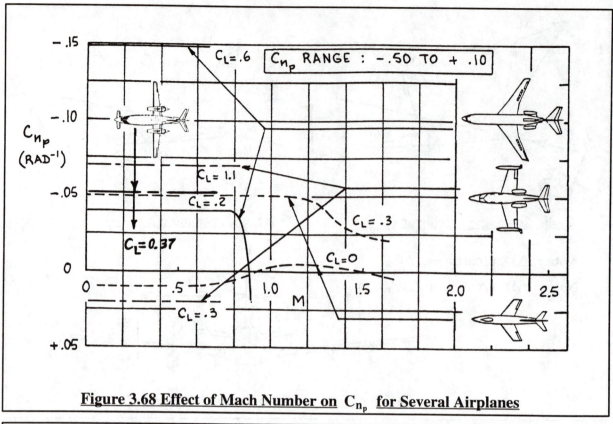

Figure 3.68 Effect of Mach Number on C_{n_p} for Several Airplanes

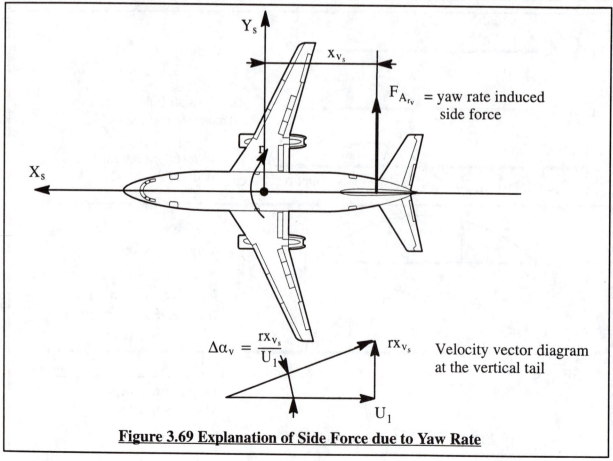

$$\Delta\alpha_v = \frac{rx_{v_s}}{U_1}$$

Velocity vector diagram at the vertical tail

Figure 3.69 Explanation of Side Force due to Yaw Rate

3.2.12 AERODYNAMIC FORCE AND MOMENT DERIVATIVES WITH RESPECT TO YAW RATE

According to Table 3.6 the following force and moments are affected by changes in perturbed yaw rate, r: F_{A_y}, L_A and N_A. These force and moments were non–dimensionalized in Eqns (3.163). Partial differentiation of Eqns (3.163) with respect to yaw rate, r, leads to the following expressions:

$$\frac{\partial F_{A_y}}{\partial(\frac{rb}{2U_1})} = \frac{\partial C_y}{\partial(\frac{rb}{2U_1})}\overline{q}_1 S = C_{y_r}\overline{q}_1 S \tag{3.183}$$

$$\frac{\partial L_A}{\partial(\frac{rb}{2U_1})} = \frac{\partial C_l}{\partial(\frac{rb}{2U_1})}\overline{q}_1 Sb = C_{l_r}\overline{q}_1 Sb \tag{3.184}$$

$$\frac{\partial N_A}{\partial(\frac{rb}{2U_1})} = \frac{\partial C_n}{\partial(\frac{rb}{2U_1})}\overline{q}_1 Sb = C_{n_r}\overline{q}_1 Sb \tag{3.185}$$

A physical explanation for how the yaw–rate derivatives C_{y_r}, C_{l_r} and C_{n_r} occur is presented in the following.

Side–force coefficient due to yaw rate derivative, C_{y_r}

This derivative is usually made up of two components:

$$C_{y_r} = C_{y_{r_{wfh}}} + C_{y_{r_v}} \tag{3.186}$$

The contribution due to the wing–fuselage–horizontal tail, $C_{y_{r_{wfh}}}$, is generally negligible for conventional configurations, particularly when compared to the contribution due to the vertical tail, $C_{y_{r_v}}$. A physical explanation for the aerodynamic mechanism responsible for $C_{y_{r_v}}$ is presented in Figure 3.69. It is seen that the effect of yaw rate is to induce an angle of attack at the vertical tail which gives rise to the following side force:

$$F_{A_{y_v}} = C_{L_{\alpha_v}}(\frac{rx_{v_s}}{U_1})\overline{q}_v S_v \tag{3.187}$$

In this expression, the side–wash due to yaw rate has been neglected. In terms of total airplane side force it is also possible to write:

$$F_{A_{y_v}} = C_{y_v}\overline{q}S \tag{3.188}$$

By differentiating the coefficient C_{y_v} with respect to $rb/2U_1$ it is possible to show:

$$C_{y_r} \approx C_{y_{r_v}} = C_{L_{\alpha_v}}(\frac{2x_{v_s}}{U_1})\eta_v(\frac{S_v}{S}) \tag{3.189}$$

Examples of the trend of C_{y_v} with Mach number are given in Figure 3.70.

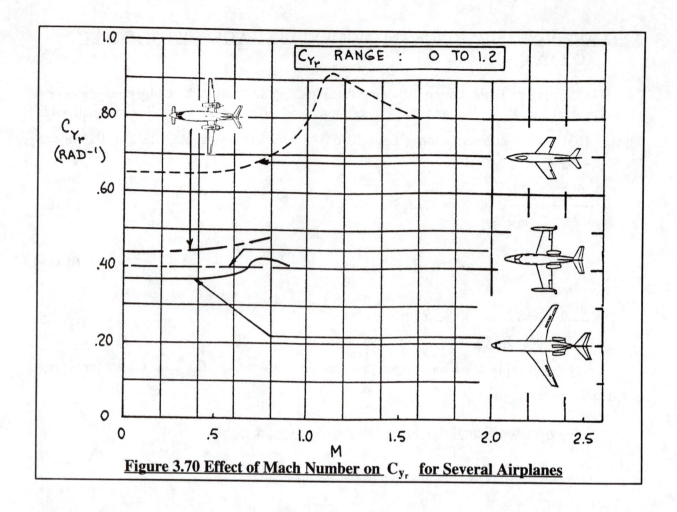

Figure 3.70 Effect of Mach Number on C_{y_r} for Several Airplanes

Rolling moment coefficient due to yaw rate derivative, C_{l_r}

This derivative is generally made up of the following contributions:

$$C_{l_r} = C_{l_{r_{wf}}} + C_{l_{r_h}} + C_{l_{r_v}}$$ (3.190)

The contribution of the horizontal tail is frequently neglected. Figure 3.71 contains the physical explanation for the occurrence of the wing–fuselage contribution, $C_{l_{r_{wf}}}$, and the vertical tail contribution, $C_{l_{r_v}}$. Methods for estimating the numerical magnitude of $C_{l_{r_{wf}}}$ are presented in Part VI of Reference 3.1. The reader is asked to show that the vertical tail contribution can be expressed as:

$$C_{l_{r_v}} = C_{L_{\alpha_v}}(\frac{2x_{v_s}z_{v_s}}{b^2})\eta_v \frac{S_v}{S}$$ (3.191)

Observe that, depending on the magnitude of the airplane steady state angle of attack, α_1, the sign of $C_{l_{r_v}}$ can be either positive or negative. The wing–fuselage contribution, $C_{l_{r_{wf}}}$, is always

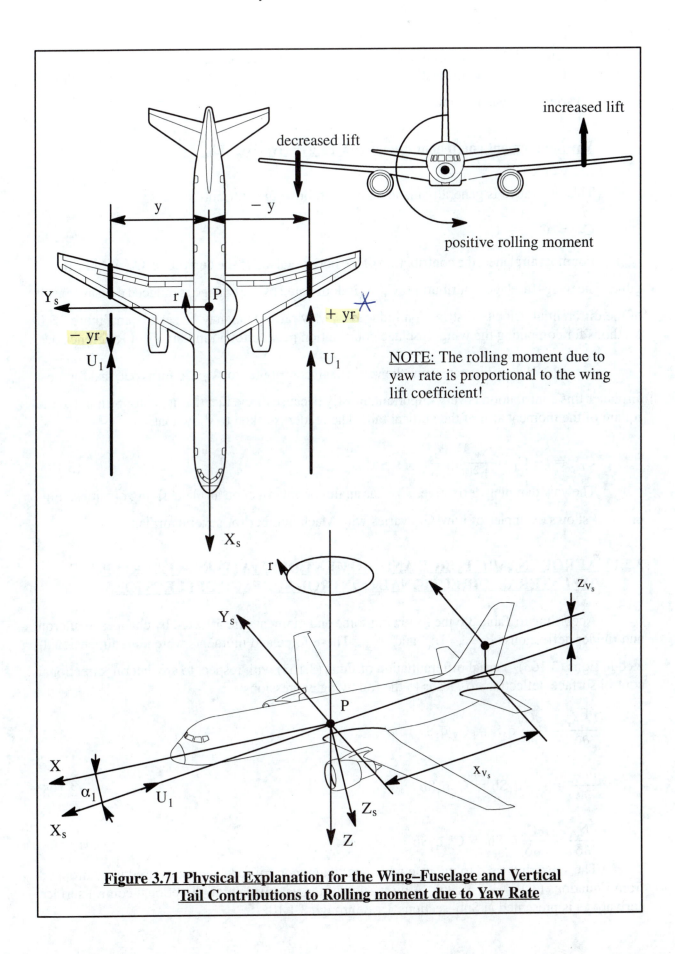

Figure 3.71 Physical Explanation for the Wing–Fuselage and Vertical Tail Contributions to Rolling moment due to Yaw Rate

positive for attached flow situations and normally outweighs the magnitude of the vertical tail contribution. This makes the derivative C_{l_r} usually positive. Figure 3.72 presents examples of how C_{l_r} varies with Mach number for several airplanes.

Yawing moment coefficient due to yaw rate derivative, C_{n_r}

This derivative is generally made up of the following contributions:

$$C_{n_r} = C_{n_{r_{wf}}} + C_{n_{r_v}}$$ (3.192)

For most airplanes, the contribution of the horizontal tail to the derivative C_{n_r} is quite negligible. The wing–fuselage contribution, $C_{n_{r_{wf}}}$, is dominated by the change in induced drag as a result of the differential velocity distribution induced by yaw rate. This may be seen from Figure 3.71. Methods for computing the wing–fuselage contribution may be found in Part VI of Reference 3.1.

Figure 3.71 also illustrates how the vertical tail contributes to C_{n_r}. It turns out, that for most airplanes this contribution is very important, mostly because of the fact that it is proportional to the square of the moment arm of the vertical tail. The reader is asked to show that:

$$C_{n_{r_v}} = - C_{L_{\alpha_v}} \left(\frac{2x_{v_s}^2}{b^2} \right) \eta_v \frac{S_v}{S}$$ (3.193)

The yaw damping derivative, C_{n_r} has an important effect on airplane flying qualities. Figure 3.73 shows examples of how C_{n_r} varies with Mach number for several airplanes.

3.2.13 AERODYNAMIC FORCE AND MOMENT DERIVATIVES WITH RESPECT TO LATERAL–DIRECTIONAL CONTROL SURFACE DEFLECTIONS

According to Table 3.6 the following force and moments are affected by changes in aileron and rudder deflections: F_{A_y}, L_A and N_A. These force and moments were non–dimensionalized in Eqns (3.163). Partial differentiation of Eqns (3.163) with respect to any lateral–directional control surface deflection, δ, leads to the following expressions:

$$\frac{\partial F_{A_y}}{\partial \delta} = \frac{\partial C_y}{\partial \delta} \bar{q}_1 S = C_{y_\delta} \bar{q}_1 S$$ (3.194)

$$\frac{\partial L_A}{\partial \delta} = \frac{\partial C_l}{\partial \delta} \bar{q}_1 Sb = C_{l_\delta} \bar{q}_1 Sb$$ (3.195)

$$\frac{\partial N_A}{\partial \delta} = \frac{\partial C_n}{\partial \delta} \bar{q}_1 Sb = C_{n_\delta} \bar{q}_1 Sb$$ (3.196)

The subscripts used to indicate which particular control surface type is used were dropped from Equations (3.194) – (3.196). A discussion of the various lateral–directional control surface derivatives is presented in Sub–sections 3.1.8 through 3.1.10.

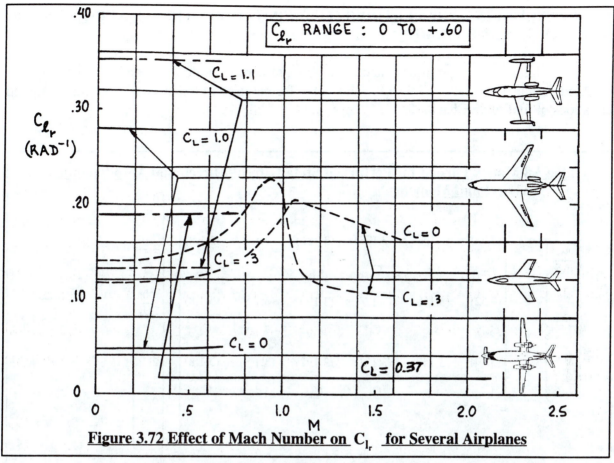

Figure 3.72 Effect of Mach Number on C_{l_r} for Several Airplanes

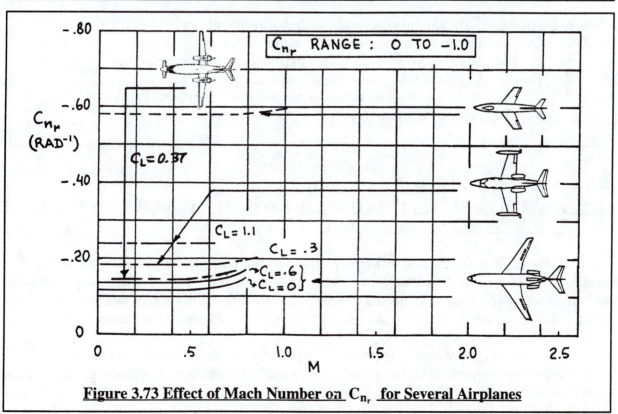

Figure 3.73 Effect of Mach Number on C_{n_r} for Several Airplanes

3.2.14 ASSEMBLING THE PERTURBED LATERAL–DIRECTIONAL AERODYNAMIC FORCES AND MOMENTS

At this point the perturbed, lateral–directional aerodynamic force and moments are assembled in matrix format in Table 3.8. This is the format used in the discussion of the perturbed equations of motion in Chapter 5.

Table 3.8 Matrix Format for Perturbed State Lateral–Directional Aerodynamic Force and Moments

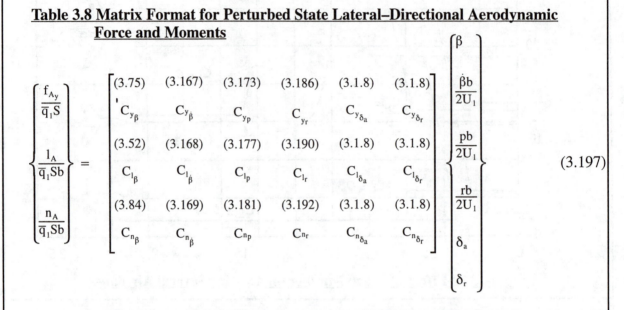

$$
\left\{
\begin{array}{c}
\dfrac{f_{A_y}}{\overline{q}_1 S} \\[2ex]
\dfrac{l_A}{\overline{q}_1 Sb} \\[2ex]
\dfrac{n_A}{\overline{q}_1 Sb}
\end{array}
\right\}
=
\begin{bmatrix}
\overset{(3.75)}{C_{y_\beta}} & \overset{(3.167)}{C_{y_{\dot\beta}}} & \overset{(3.173)}{C_{y_p}} & \overset{(3.186)}{C_{y_r}} & \overset{(3.1.8)}{C_{y_{\delta_a}}} & \overset{(3.1.8)}{C_{y_{\delta_r}}} \\[2ex]
\overset{(3.52)}{C_{l_\beta}} & \overset{(3.168)}{C_{l_{\dot\beta}}} & \overset{(3.177)}{C_{l_p}} & \overset{(3.190)}{C_{l_r}} & \overset{(3.1.8)}{C_{l_{\delta_a}}} & \overset{(3.1.8)}{C_{l_{\delta_r}}} \\[2ex]
\overset{(3.84)}{C_{n_\beta}} & \overset{(3.169)}{C_{n_{\dot\beta}}} & \overset{(3.181)}{C_{n_p}} & \overset{(3.192)}{C_{n_r}} & \overset{(3.1.8)}{C_{n_{\delta_a}}} & \overset{(3.1.8)}{C_{n_{\delta_r}}}
\end{bmatrix}
\left\{
\begin{array}{c}
\beta \\[2ex]
\dfrac{\dot\beta b}{2U_1} \\[2ex]
\dfrac{pb}{2U_1} \\[2ex]
\dfrac{rb}{2U_1} \\[2ex]
\delta_a \\[2ex]
\delta_r
\end{array}
\right\}
\qquad (3.197)
$$

Notes: 1) Airplanes may have more than one lateral–directional control surface. Only the aileron and rudder have been included in Eqn (3.197). For additional control surfaces simply expand the size of the matrices.
2) Bracketed numbers refer to equations and/or sections in the text.
3) All stability derivatives may be computed with the methods of Part VI of Ref. 3.1 and/or with the AAA program (Appendix A)

3.2.15 PERTURBED STATE LONGITUDINAL AND LATERAL–DIRECTIONAL THRUST FORCES AND MOMENTS

It is possible to make a case for the existence of perturbed thrust forces and moments as functions of all perturbed motion variables: u, v, w, p, q and r. As it turns out, for most airplanes only the variables u, v and w have significant effects on the perturbed thrust forces and moments. The reader is cautioned however, not to take this for granted for all future configurations!

The consequence of assuming that only the perturbed motion variables u, v and w have significant effects on the perturbed thrust forces and moments is the mathematical model given in Equations (3.198) through (3.203):

$$f_{T_x} = \frac{\partial F_{T_x}}{\partial(\frac{u}{U_1})}(\frac{u}{U_1}) + \frac{\partial F_{T_x}}{\partial\alpha}\alpha \tag{3.198}$$

$$f_{T_z} = \frac{\partial F_{T_z}}{\partial(\frac{u}{U_1})}(\frac{u}{U_1}) + \frac{\partial F_{T_z}}{\partial\alpha}\alpha \tag{3.199}$$

$$m_T = \frac{\partial M_T}{\partial(\frac{u}{U_1})}(\frac{u}{U_1}) + \frac{\partial M_T}{\partial\alpha}\alpha \tag{3.200}$$

$$f_{T_y} = \frac{\partial F_{T_y}}{\partial\beta} \tag{3.201}$$

$$l_T = \frac{\partial L_T}{\partial\beta} \tag{3.202}$$

$$n_T = \frac{\partial N_T}{\partial\beta} \tag{3.203}$$

Detailed expressions for the perturbed thrust force and moment derivatives are developed in Sub–sections 3.2.16 through 3.2.18.

3.2.16 THRUST FORCE AND MOMENT DERIVATIVES WITH RESPECT TO FORWARD SPEED

Based on Sub–section 3.2.2 the perturbed longitudinal, thrust forces and moment are non–dimensionalized as follows:

$$F_{T_x} = C_{T_x}\overline{q}S \tag{3.204a}$$

$$F_{T_z} = C_{T_z}\overline{q}S \tag{3.204b}$$

$$M_T = C_{m_T}\overline{q}S\overline{c} \tag{3.204c}$$

The reader is reminded of the fact that F_{T_x}, F_{T_z} and M_T are defined in the stability axis system. Next, the partial differentiations implied by Equations (3.198) – (3.200) will be systematically performed for Equations (3.204a) – (3.204c).

Partial Differentiation of Equation (3.204a) with Respect to u/U_1

Partial differentiation of Equation (3.204a) with respect to u/U_1, leads to:

$$\frac{\partial F_{T_x}}{\partial(\frac{u}{U_1})} = \frac{\partial C_{T_x}}{\partial(\frac{u}{U_1})}\overline{q}S + C_{T_x}S\frac{\partial\overline{q}}{\partial(\frac{u}{U_1})} \tag{3.205}$$

Evaluation at the steady state, recalling Eqn (3.102) and using the following notation: $C_{T_{x_u}} = \dfrac{\partial C_{T_x}}{\partial(\frac{u}{U_1})}$, it can be shown that:

$$\frac{\partial F_{T_x}}{\partial(\frac{u}{U_1})} = C_{T_{x_u}}\bar{q}_1 S + 2C_{T_{x_1}}\bar{q}_1 S \tag{3.206}$$

The steady state thrust coefficient, $C_{T_{x_1}}$ is normally equal to the steady state drag coefficient because T=D in level steady state flight. The derivative $C_{T_{x_u}}$ depends on the characteristics of the propulsion system. Five cases will be considered:

Case 1: Gliders or power–off flight

Case 2: Airplanes equipped with rockets

Case 3: Airplanes equipped with pure jets and fan jets

Case 4: Airplanes equipped with variable pitch propellers

Case 5: Airplanes equipped with fixed pitch propellers

Case 1: Gliders or power–off flight

Since there is no thrust in this case: $C_{T_{x_u}} = C_{T_{x_1}} = 0$, so that:

$$\frac{\partial F_{T_x}}{\partial(\frac{u}{U_1})} = 0 \tag{3.207}$$

Case 2: Airplanes equipped with rockets

The installed thrust output of a rocket engine does **not** (to a first order approximation) depend on the flight speed: $C_{T_{x_u}} = 0$. Therefore:

$$\frac{\partial F_{T_x}}{\partial(\frac{u}{U_1})} = 2C_{T_{x_1}}\bar{q}_1 S \tag{3.208}$$

Case 3: Airplanes equipped with pure jets and fan jets

In this case it is necessary to establish the variation of installed thrust with Mach number, with altitude and with fuel flow (or throttle position). Methods for determining installed thrust from engine manufacturer's thrust data are found in Part VI of Reference 3.1.

Figure 3.74 shows an example of estimated installed thrust data for a small, single engine fan–jet trainer. The slope $\partial F_{T_x}/\partial M$ may be measured directly from graphs such as presented in Figure 3.74. Having done so, the following is obtained:

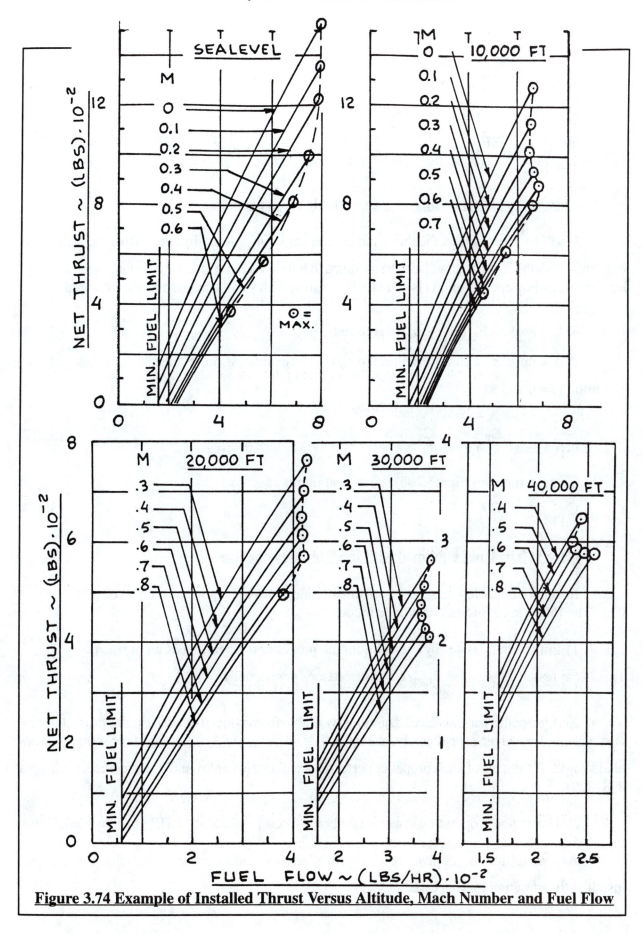

Figure 3.74 Example of Installed Thrust Versus Altitude, Mach Number and Fuel Flow

$$C_{T_{x_u}} = \frac{M_1}{\bar{q}_1 S} \frac{\partial F_{T_x}}{\partial M} - 2C_{T_{x_1}} \qquad (3.209)$$

With Eqn (3.206) it is now found that:

$$\frac{\partial F_{T_x}}{\partial(\frac{u}{U_1})} = M_1 \frac{\partial F_{T_x}}{\partial M} \qquad (3.210)$$

Case 4: Airplanes equipped with variable pitch propellers

It will be assumed that the thrust inclination angle, ϕ_T, is negligible, so that the thrust axis is aligned with the X–axis. It will also be assumed that for a variable pitch (= constant speed) propeller, the thrust–horsepower output is essentially constant with small changes in forward speed. Thus:

$$T(U_1 + u) \approx F_{T_x}(U_1 + u) \approx constant \qquad (3.211)$$

Partial differentiation with respect to u/U_1 and evaluating the result at the steady state flight condition (u=0) yields:

$$\frac{\partial F_{T_x}}{\partial(\frac{u}{U_1})} = - F_{T_{x_1}} = - C_{T_{x_1}}\bar{q}_1 S \qquad (3.212)$$

Comparison with Eqn (3.206) shows that in this case:

$$C_{T_{x_u}} = - 3C_{T_{x_1}} \qquad (3.213)$$

Case 5: Airplanes equipped with fixed pitch propellers

In general, only low cost, low performance airplanes are equipped with fixed pitch propellers. The following assumptions will be made:

1) In the steady state flight condition, the propeller is operating at a known rpm, n_{prpm} This is expressed as $n_{prps} = n_{rpm}/60$ rps (rotations per second).

2) A propeller performance diagram is available from which the variation of propeller efficiency, η_p, for a given propeller advance ratio, $J = U_1/(n_{prps}D_p)$, is known at constant propeller blade angle. Examples of such propeller performance diagrams are found in Reference 3.9 (pages 298–329).

3) The engine is operating at a constant brake–horsepower level, BHP, as set by the throttle.

Assuming that the airplane has n_p propellers, the following relation holds for the total installed thrust output for this case:

$$F_{T_x} = \frac{n_p 550 \eta_p BHP}{U_1} \tag{3.214}$$

Partial differentiation with respect to u/U_1 now yields after evaluating the result at the steady state flight condition:

$$\frac{\partial F_{T_x}}{\partial(\frac{u}{U_1})} = n_p[\frac{-550\eta_p(BHP)}{U_1} + 550(BHP)\frac{\partial\eta_p}{\partial u}] \tag{3.215}$$

The derivative $\partial\eta_p/\partial u$ can be expressed as follows,:

$$\frac{\partial\eta_p}{\partial u} = (\frac{\partial\eta_p}{\partial J})(\frac{\partial J}{\partial u}) \tag{3.216}$$

where: the propeller advance ratio, $J = U_1/(n_{prps}D_p)$, so that $\partial J/\partial u = 1/n_{prps}D_p$. Therefore it is found that:

$$\frac{\partial F_{T_x}}{\partial(\frac{u}{U_1})} = n_p[\frac{-550\eta_{p_1}(BHP)}{U_1} + \frac{550(BHP)}{n_{prps}D_p}\frac{\partial\eta_p}{\partial J}] \tag{3.217}$$

This can be rewritten as follows:

$$\frac{\partial F_{T_x}}{\partial(\frac{u}{U_1})} = -C_{T_{x_1}}\bar{q}_1 S + \frac{T_1 U_1}{\eta_{p_1}n_{prps}D_p}\frac{\partial\eta_p}{\partial J} \tag{3.218}$$

The derivative $\partial\eta_p/\partial J$ can be obtained from the propeller performance diagram mentioned before under 2). Comparison with Eqn (3.206) shows that:

$$C_{T_{x_u}} = -3C_{T_{x_1}} + \frac{C_{T_{x_1}}U_1}{\eta_{p_1}n_{prps}D_p}\frac{\partial\eta_p}{\partial J} \tag{3.219}$$

Partial Differentiation of Equation (3.204b) with Respect to u/U_1

Partial differentiation of Equation (3.204a) with respect to u/U_1 leads to:

$$\frac{\partial F_{T_z}}{\partial(\frac{u}{U_1})} = C_{T_{z_u}}\bar{q}_1 S + 2C_{T_{z_1}}\bar{q}_1 S \tag{3.220}$$

The derivative $C_{T_{z_u}}$ and the coefficient $C_{T_{z_1}}$ are negligible for most conventional airplane configurations. It should be kept in mind that for airplanes with vectorable thrust this is definitely not the case! For conventional airplanes it will be assumed that:

$$\frac{\partial F_{T_z}}{\partial(\frac{u}{U_1})} = 0 \tag{3.221}$$

Partial Differentiation of Equation (3.204c) with Respect to u/U_1

Partial differentiation of Eqn (3.204c) with respect to u/U_1 yields:

$$\frac{\partial M_T}{\partial(\frac{u}{U_1})} = C_{m_{T_u}}\bar{q}_1 S\bar{c} + 2C_{m_{T_1}}\bar{q}_1 S\bar{c} \qquad (3.222)$$

For conventional propulsive arrangements the derivative $C_{m_{T_u}}$ is obtained from the derivative $C_{x_{T_u}}$ by multiplying with the non–dimensional moment arm of the thrust–line relative to the center of gravity, $d_T/\bar{c}$:

$$C_{m_{T_u}} = -C_{x_{T_u}}\frac{d_T}{\bar{c}} \qquad (3.223)$$

where: d_T is defined in Figure 3.26. Note that d_T is counted as positive if the thrust–line
is above the center of gravity.

The value of the steady state thrust–pitching moment coefficient, $C_{m_{T_1}}$, depends on the airplane trim state. For pitching moment equilibrium in the steady state flight condition, the following condition should be met:

$$C_{m_{T_1}} + C_{m_1} = 0 \qquad (3.224)$$

Since the aerodynamic and the thrust pitching moment coefficients apparently cancel each other in steady state flight, the total variation of airplane pitching moment with perturbed speed, u, is given by:

$$\frac{\partial(M_A + M_T)}{\partial\frac{u}{U_1}} = (C_{m_u} + C_{m_{T_u}})\bar{q}_1 S\bar{c} \qquad (3.225)$$

The numerical magnitude of $C_{m_{T_u}}$ is negligible for those airplane configurations where the thrust–line passes close by the center of gravity.

3.2.17 THRUST FORCE AND MOMENT DERIVATIVES WITH RESPECT TO ANGLE OF ATTACK

The perturbed longitudinal, thrust forces and moment are non–dimensionalized as shown in Equations (3.204). In the following, these expressions will be partially differentiated with respect to the perturbed airplane angle of attack, α.

Partial Differentiation of Equation (3.204a) with Respect to α

Partial differentiation of Equation (3.204a) with respect to α leads to:

$$\frac{\partial F_{T_x}}{\partial \alpha} = C_{T_{x_\alpha}} \bar{q}_1 S \tag{3.226}$$

For the normal range of angles of attack and for most conventional airplanes the derivative $C_{T_{x_\alpha}}$ is negligible:

$$C_{T_{x_\alpha}} \approx 0 \tag{3.227}$$

Partial Differentiation of Equation (3.204b) with Respect to α

Partial differentiation of Equation (3.204b) with respect to α leads to:

$$\frac{\partial F_{T_z}}{\partial \alpha} = C_{T_{z_\alpha}} \bar{q}_1 S \tag{3.228}$$

The physical cause of the derivative $C_{T_{z_\alpha}}$ is the so-called propeller and/or inlet normal force which occur as a result of perturbations in angle of attack. The physical reason for such normal forces is the change in flow momentum in a direction perpendicular to the spin axis of the propeller or turbine. The corresponding flow geometry of these effects is illustrated in Figure 3.75. The magnitudes of these normal forces are normally sufficiently small that they can be be neglected when compared to changes in aerodynamic lift due to angle of attack perturbations. Therefore:

$$C_{T_{z_\alpha}} \approx 0 \tag{3.229}$$

Partial Differentiation of Equation (3.204c) with Respect to α

Despite the assumption which leads to Eqn (3.229), the pitching moment contribution due to this derivative may not be negligible at all! Partial differentiation of Equation (3.204c) with respect to α leads to:

$$\frac{\partial M_T}{\partial \alpha} = C_{m_{T_\alpha}} \bar{q}_1 S \bar{c} \tag{3.230}$$

In the following, expressions will be derived from which $C_{m_{T_\alpha}}$ may be estimated. This will be done for two cases:

Case 1) Propeller driven airplanes
Case 2) Jet driven airplanes

Case 1) Propeller Driven Airplanes

Figure 3.75 shows the propeller normal force, N_p, as well as the moment arm of this force about the center of gravity. The propeller normal force, N_p, may be expressed as:

$$N_p = C_{N_p} \bar{q} S_p \tag{3.231}$$

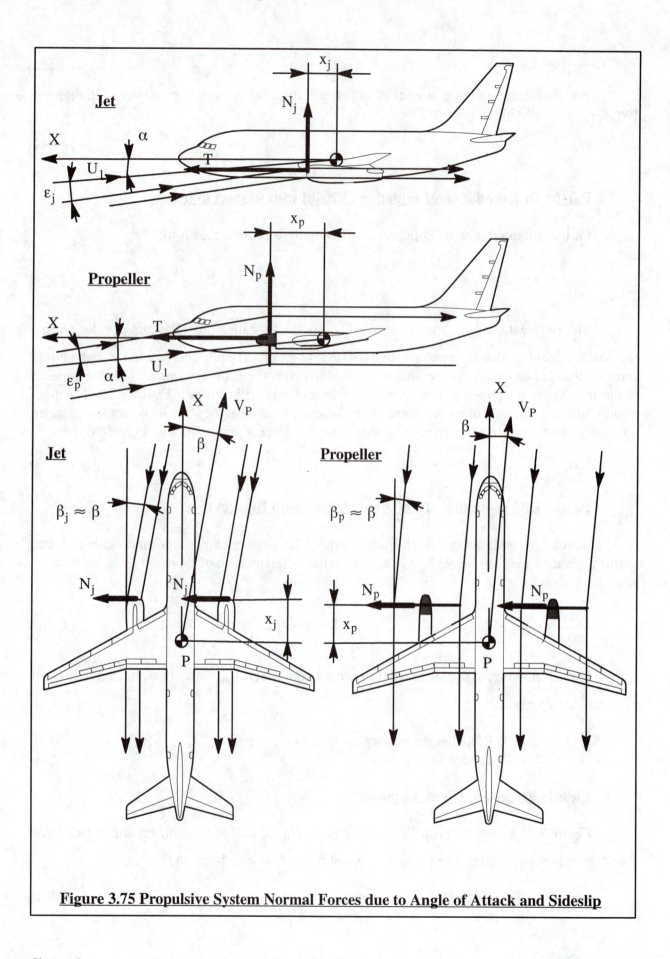

Figure 3.75 Propulsive System Normal Forces due to Angle of Attack and Sideslip

The pitching moment coefficient due to the propeller normal force can be written as:

$$C_{m_{T_{N_p}}} = n_p C_{N_p} \frac{x_p S_p}{\bar{c}S}$$

(3.232)

where: n_p is the number of propellers

x_p is the moment arm of the propeller disk

$S_p = \frac{\pi}{4}D_p^2$ is the propeller disk area

D_p is the propeller diameter

For tractor propellers, the propeller plane is usually in the wing up–wash field. Therefore, the propeller normal force coefficient, C_{N_p}, is proportional to the propeller angle of attack, α_p (this is the angle between the propeller spin axis and the free stream velocity vector in the steady state). Differentiating Eqn (3.232) with respect to α_p yields:

$$C_{m_{T_\alpha}} = n_p \frac{x_p S_p}{\bar{c}S} \frac{\partial C_{N_p}}{\partial \alpha_p} \frac{\partial \alpha_p}{\partial \alpha}$$

(3.233)

Since:

$$\alpha_p = \alpha + \varepsilon_p + \begin{matrix} \text{some constant} \\ \text{incidence } \measuredangle \end{matrix}$$

(3.234)

where: ε_p is the wing induced up–wash at the propeller

it follows that:

$$\frac{\partial \alpha_p}{\partial \alpha} = 1 + \frac{\partial \varepsilon_p}{\partial \alpha}$$

(3.235)

Therefore:

$$C_{m_{T_\alpha}} = n_p \frac{x_p S_p}{\bar{c}S} \frac{\partial C_{N_p}}{\partial \alpha_p}(1 + \frac{\partial \varepsilon_p}{\partial \alpha})$$

(3.236)

Methods for determining $\partial C_{N_p}/\partial \alpha$ and the up–wash gradient, $\partial \varepsilon_p/\partial \alpha$, may be found in References 3.4, 3.5 and 3.10. The reader should keep in mind that the propeller flow downstream of the propeller plane may in turn affect the downwash at the horizontal tail. Reference 3.4 contains an approach for computing these effects.

Case 2) Jet Driven Airplanes

Figure 3.75 also shows the jet engine normal force, N_j, and the moment arm of the jet engine nacelle inlet about the center of gravity. The jet engine normal force, N_j, may be expressed as:

$$N_j = \dot{m}'V_i \sin(\alpha + \varepsilon_j + \begin{matrix} \text{someconstant} \\ \text{incidence } \measuredangle \end{matrix})$$

(3.237)

where: $\dot{m}'$ is the mass flow rate through the engine

V_i is the inlet flow velocity

ε_j is the wing induced up–wash at the inlet

The inlet flow velocity, V_i , may be determined from:

$$V_i = \frac{\dot{m}'}{A_i \; \varrho_i} \tag{3.238}$$

where: A_i is the inlet cross sectional area

ϱ_i is the inlet air density

The pitching moment contribution due the normal forces from n_j jet engines is:

$$C_{m_{T_N}} = n_j \frac{(\dot{m}')^2 x_j}{A_i \; \varrho_i \; \overline{q}_1 S \overline{c}} (\alpha + \varepsilon_j + \begin{array}{c} \text{some constant} \\ \text{incidence} \end{array} \not{\,}) \tag{3.239}$$

where: n_j is the number jet engines

x_j is the moment arm of the engine inlet

Upon differentiation with respect to α, it follows that:

$$C_{m_{T_\alpha}} = n_j \frac{(\dot{m}')^2 x_j}{A_i \; \varrho_i \; \overline{q}_1 S \overline{c}} (1 + \frac{\partial \varepsilon_j}{\partial \alpha}) \tag{3.240}$$

Methods for determining the up–wash gradient $\partial \varepsilon_j / \partial \alpha$ may be found in Part VI of Ref. 3.1.

The reader should observe that the derivative, $C_{m_{T_\alpha}}$ {of Eqn (3.236) or (3.240)} when added to the derivative, C_{m_α} {of Eqn (3.35)} yields the so–called power–on value of the static longitudinal stability derivative. It is suggested that the reader use the procedure of page 89 to redefine the aerodynamic center of an airplane with power on.

Note that Eqn (3.240) yields a positive (unstable) contribution to longitudinal stability. The reader should observe that a tractor installation tends to reduce overall airplane longitudinal stability whereas a pusher installation tends to enhance longitudinal stability.

3.2.18 THRUST FORCE AND MOMENT DERIVATIVES WITH RESPECT TO ANGLE OF SIDESLIP

Based on Sub–section 3.2.9 the perturbed longitudinal, thrust forces and moment are non–dimensionalized as follows:

$$F_{T_y} = C_{T_y} \overline{q} S \tag{3.241a}$$

$$L_T = C_{l_T} \bar{q} S b \qquad (3.241b)$$

$$N_T = C_{n_T} \bar{q} S b \qquad (3.241c)$$

The physical cause of the derivatives in Eqns (3.241) is the so–called propeller and/or inlet normal force which occur as a result of perturbations in angle of sideslip. The physical reason for such normal forces is the change in flow momentum in a direction perpendicular to the spin axis of the propeller or turbine. The corresponding flow geometry of these effects is shown in Figure 3.75. The magnitudes of these normal forces are normally sufficiently small that they can be be neglected when compared to changes in aerodynamic side–force due to angle of sideslip perturbations.

The reader is reminded of the fact that F_{T_y}, L_T and N_T are defined in the stability axis system. Next, the partial differentiations implied by Equations (3.164) – (3.166) will be systematically performed for Equations (3.241a) – (3.241c).

Partial Differentiation of Equation (3.241a) with Respect to β

Partial differentiation of Equation (3.241a) with respect to β leads to:

$$\frac{\partial F_{T_y}}{\partial \beta} = C_{T_{y_\beta}} \bar{q}_1 S \qquad (3.242)$$

For the normal range of angles of attack and for most conventional airplanes the derivative $C_{T_{y_\beta}}$ is negligible:

$$C_{T_{y_\beta}} \approx 0 \qquad (3.243)$$

Partial Differentiation of Equation (3.241b) with Respect to β

Partial differentiation of Equation (3.241b) with respect to β leads to:

$$\frac{\partial L_T}{\partial \beta} = C_{l_{T_\beta}} \bar{q}_1 S b \qquad (3.244)$$

For the normal range of angles of attack and for most conventional airplanes the derivative $C_{l_{T_\beta}}$ is negligible:

$$C_{l_{T_\beta}} \approx 0 \qquad (3.245)$$

Partial Differentiation of Equation (3.241c) with Respect to β

Partial differentiation of Equation (3.241c) with respect to β leads to:

$$\frac{\partial N_T}{\partial \beta} = C_{n_{T_\beta}} \bar{q}_1 Sb \tag{3.246}$$

The reader is asked to show that, by analogy to the development in Sub–section 3.2.17 for the pitching moment, it follows that the derivative $C_{n_{T_\beta}}$ may be written as:

$$C_{n_{T_\beta}} = - n_j \frac{(\dot{m}')^2 x_j}{A_i \, \varrho_i \, \bar{q}_1 Sb} \tag{3.247}$$

Note the minus sign in Eqn (3.247). The reader should observe, that a tractor installation tends to reduce overall airplane directional stability whereas a pusher installation tends to enhance directional stability.

3.2.19 ASSEMBLING THE PERTURBED STATE LONGITUDINAL AND LATERAL–DIRECTIONAL THRUST FORCES AND MOMENTS

At this point the perturbed, longitudinal and lateral–directional thrust forces and moments are assembled in matrix format in Table 3.9.

Table 3.9 Matrix Format for Perturbed State Longitudinal and Lateral–Directional Thrust Forces and Moments

$$\begin{Bmatrix} \dfrac{f_{T_x}}{\bar{q}_1 S} \\[2mm] \dfrac{f_{T_z}}{\bar{q}_1 S} \\[2mm] \dfrac{m_T}{\bar{q}_1 S\bar{c}} \end{Bmatrix} = \begin{bmatrix} (C_{T_{x_u}} + 2C_{T_{x_1}}) & 0_{0_0} \\ 0 & 0 \\ (C_{m_{T_u}} + 2C_{m_{T_1}}) & C_{m_{T_\alpha}} \end{bmatrix} \begin{Bmatrix} \dfrac{u}{U_1} \\[2mm] \alpha \end{Bmatrix} \tag{3.248}$$

$$\begin{Bmatrix} \dfrac{f_{T_y}}{\bar{q}_1 S} \\[2mm] \dfrac{l_T}{\bar{q}_1 Sb} \\[2mm] \dfrac{n_T}{\bar{q}_1 Sb} \end{Bmatrix} = \begin{Bmatrix} 0 \\ 0 \\ C_{n_{T_\beta}} \end{Bmatrix} \beta \tag{3.249}$$

Note: bracketed numbers refer to equations in the text

3.3   OVERVIEW OF USUAL SIGNS FOR AERODYNAMIC COEFFICIENTS AND DERIVATIVES

To enable the reader to quickly review the various sign conventions and 'usual' signs which occur for the many aerodynamic coefficients and derivatives, Figures 3.76 through 3.79 are included in this Section.

These figures also allow the reader to review the pertinent perturbations which are associated with various aerodynamic derivatives. It is hoped that these figures will be useful when reviewing the material presented in Sections 3.1 and 3.2.

3.4   SUMMARY FOR CHAPTER 3

To solve the airplane equations of motion developed in Chapter 1, it is necessary to have available a set of mathematical models which relate the aerodynamic and thrust forces and moments to the appropriate motion and control surface variables. The purpose of this Chapter was to develop and discuss these models.

The equations of motion in Chapter 1 are divided into two sets: equations for steady state and equations for perturbed state flight respectively. Similarly, the mathematical models for aerodynamic and thrust forces and moments are also divided into steady state models (Section 3.1) and perturbed state models (Section 3.2).

In estimating the magnitudes of the various coefficients and derivatives, it is important to account for the effect of major airplane components, such as: wing/fuselage, vertical tail, horizontal tail, canard, nacelles etc. In all cases, physical explanations and derivations were presented to provide the reader with an appreciation for the relative contributions of these components. To acquaint the reader with typical numerical magnitudes for these coefficients and derivatives, numerical examples for the most important stability and control derivatives are given for four different airplanes.

Finally, the propulsive installation of an airplane can have significant effects on several coefficients and derivatives. The most important of these effects were also discussed.

Appendix B contains a listing of stability and control derivatives for several flight conditions and for a range of different airplanes.

A question which always arises is: how important is any given stability and control derivative to the in–flight behavior of a given airplane? That question is addressed in Chapter 5. It is shown in Chapter 5, that by carrying out a so–called derivative sensitivity analysis, it is possible to determine the importance of any derivative and inertial parameter.

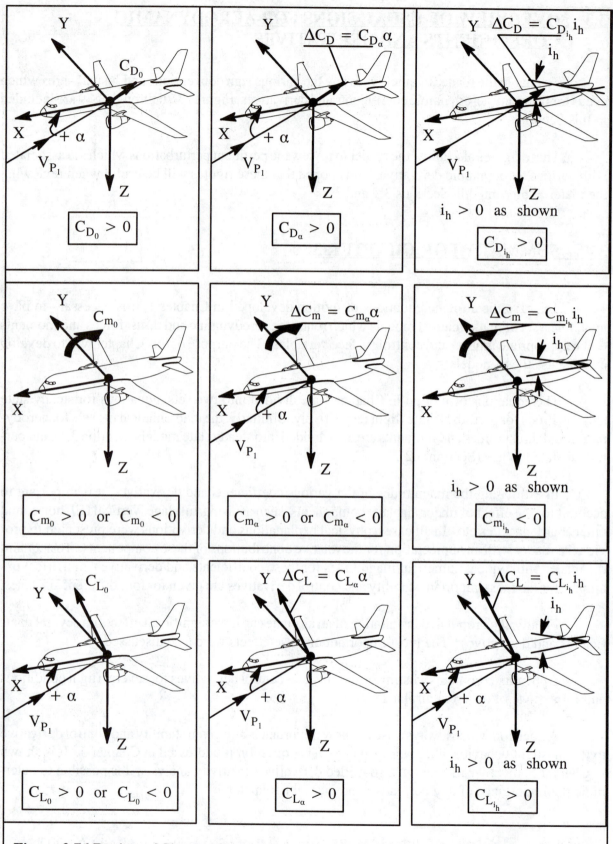

Figure 3.76 Review of Signs of Steady State Longitudinal Force and Moment Derivatives

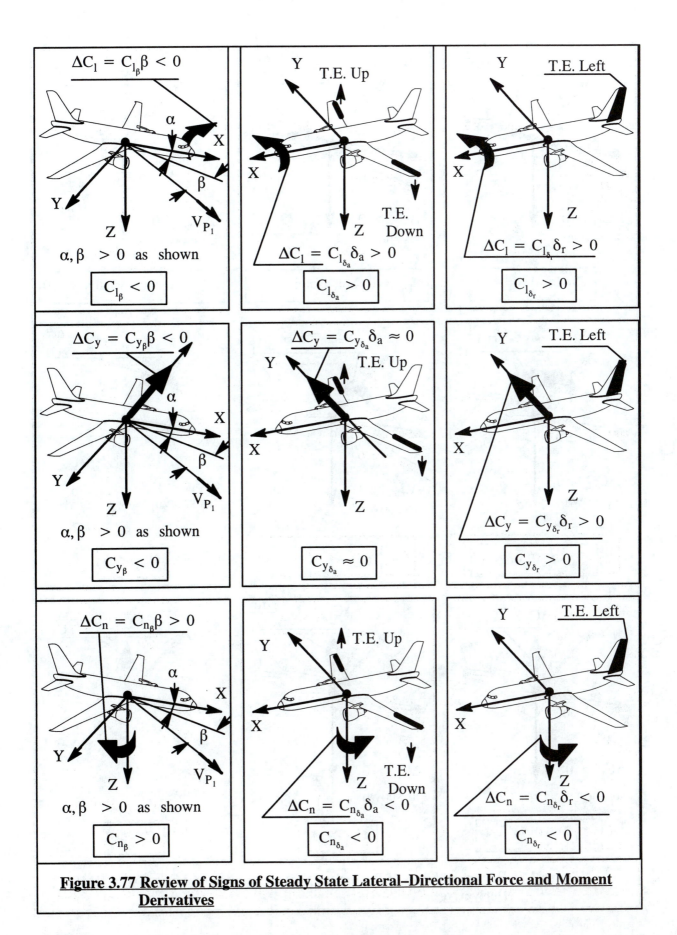

Figure 3.77 Review of Signs of Steady State Lateral–Directional Force and Moment Derivatives

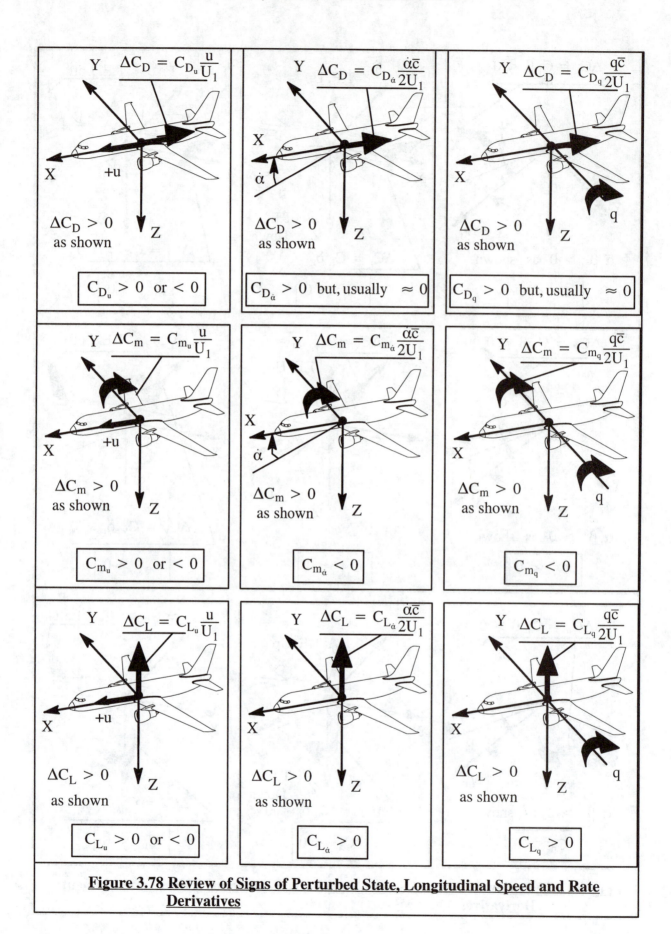

Figure 3.78 Review of Signs of Perturbed State, Longitudinal Speed and Rate Derivatives

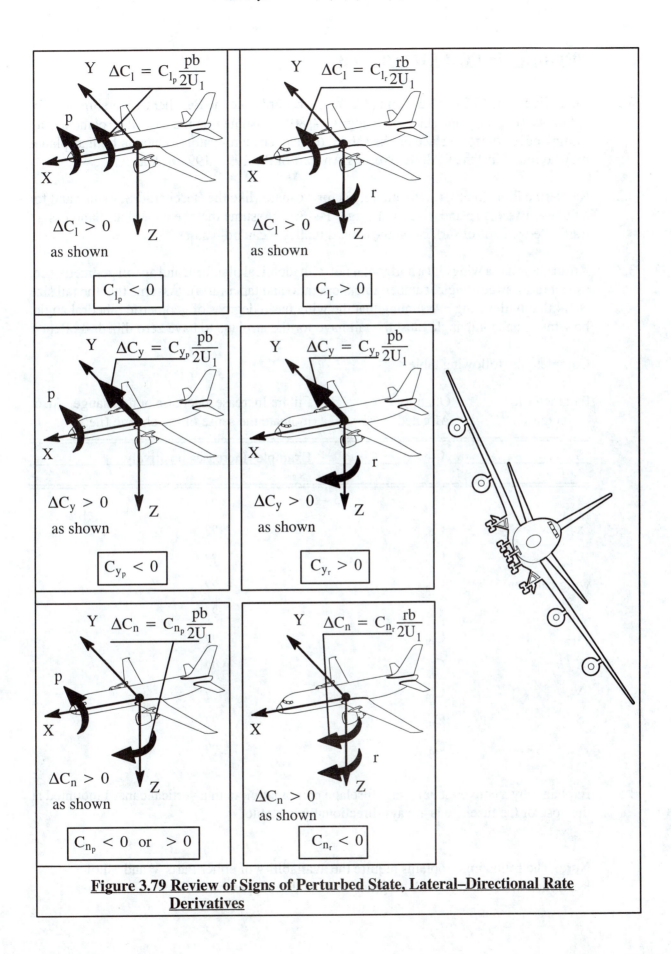

Figure 3.79 Review of Signs of Perturbed State, Lateral–Directional Rate Derivatives

3.5   PROBLEMS FOR CHAPTER 3

3.1   Re–derive Eqns (3.24), (3.25) and (3.26) for a canard (like the Beechcraft Starship) and for a three–surface airplane (like the Piaggio P–180). Assume that the canard airplane has a trailing edge control surface on the canard (called a canard–vator). Data on both airplanes may be found in Jane's All the World's Aircraft of the 1991–1994 period.

3.2   Re–derive Eqns (3.35), (3.36) and (3.37) for a canard (like the Beechcraft Starship) and for a three–surface airplane (like the Piaggio P–180). Assume that the canard airplane has a trailing edge control surface on the canard (called a canard–vator).

3.3   An airplane has a wing and a horizontal tail with identical planform and airfoil geometry (i.e. aspect ratio, sweep angle, camber, thickness ratio and taper ratio). Assume that the tail size is 1/4 that of the wing. Assuming that the wing has 3 degrees of geometric dihedral angle, how much anhedral angle must the tail have for the airplane to have zero dihedral effect?

3.4   Complete the following table.

Parameter to be increased	Quantity Affected	Fill in: Increase, decrease or no change. Also: indicate the sense of the change (i.e. + or –)
S_v	C_{n_β}	Example: Increases positively.
x_{V_s}	C_{n_β}	??
x_{V_s}	$C_{n_{\delta_r}}$	??
$C_{L_{\alpha_h}}$	$C_{m_{i_h}}$	??
wing camber	C_{m_0}	??
S_h	x_{ac_A}	??
$\overline{x}_{cg}$	C_{m_α}	??
S_v	C_{l_β}	??
$\overline{V}_h$	C_{m_q}	??
S_v	C_{n_r}	??
x_{V_s}	C_{n_r}	??

3.5   Explain why a conventional wing–fuselage combination with a vertical canard mounted at the nose of the fuselage is always directionally unstable.

Note: The following problems require the availability of either Parts V and VI of Reference 3.1 or of the AAA program described in Appendix A.

3.6   Find a three–view for the Fokker F–100 jet transport (see Jane's All the World's Aircraft of the 1991–1994 period). Calculate all stability derivatives in Eqn (3.46a). Do this for the following flight conditions:

* high altitude cruise at design cruise weight
* takeoff at sea–level and at maximum takeoff weight
* landing approach and at design landing weight

Perform sanity checks on your answers by comparing with suitable graphs in this chapter.

3.7   Find a three–view for the Fokker F–100 jet transport (see Jane's All the World's Aircraft of the 1991–1994 period). Calculate all stability derivatives in Eqn (3.95a). Do this for the following flight conditions:

* high altitude cruise at design cruise weight
* takeoff at sea–level and at maximum takeoff weight
* landing approach and at design landing weight

Perform sanity checks on your answers by comparing with suitable graphs in this chapter.

3.8   Find a three–view for the Boeing 777 jet transport (see Jane's All the World's Aircraft of the 1993+ period). Calculate all stability derivatives in Eqn (3.162). Do this for the following flight conditions:

* high altitude cruise at design cruise weight
* takeoff at sea–level and at maximum takeoff weight
* landing approach and at design landing weight

Perform sanity checks on your answers by comparing with suitable graphs in this chapter.

3.9   Find a three–view for the Boeing 777 jet transport (see Jane's All the World's Aircraft of the 1993+ period). Calculate all stability derivatives in Eqn (3.197). Do this for the following flight conditions:

* high altitude cruise at design cruise weight
* takeoff at sea–level and at maximum takeoff weight
* landing approach and at design landing weight

Perform sanity checks on your answers by comparing with suitable graphs in this chapter.

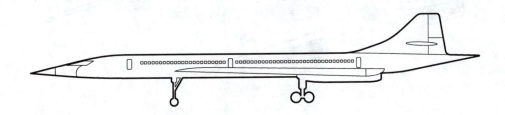

3.6   REFERENCES FOR CHAPTER 3

3.1   Roskam, J.; <u>Airplane Design</u>, Parts I through VIII; Roskam Aviation and Engineering Corporation, 2550 Riley Road, Ottawa, Kansas, 66067, USA; 1990.

3.2   Mattingly, J.D.; Heiser, W.H. and Daley, D.H.; <u>Aircraft Engine Design</u>; AIAA Education Series, 1987.

3.3   Kerrebrock, J.L.; <u>Aircraft Engines and Gas Turbines</u>; MIT Press, Cambridge, MA, 1977.

3.4   Wolowics, C.H. and Yancey, R.B.; Longitudinal Aerodynamic Characteristics of Light, Twin–engine Propeller Driven Airplanes; NASA TN D–6800; 1972.

3.5   Perkins, C.D. and Hage, R.E.; <u>Airplane Performance, Stability and Control</u>; J. Wiley & Sons; 1949.

3.6   Etkin, B.; <u>Dynamics of Flight</u>; J. Wiley & Sons; 1959.

3.7   Rodden, W.P. and Giesing, W.P.; Application of Oscillatory Aerodynamic Theory for Estimation of Dynamic Stability Derivatives; Journal of Aircraft, Vol. 7, No. 3, May–June 1970, pp 272–275.

3.8   Fung, Y.C.; <u>An Introduction to the Theory of Aeroelasticity</u>; J. Wiley & Sons;1955.

3.9   Lan, C.E. and Roskam, J.; <u>Airplane Aerodynamics and Performance</u>; Roskam Aviation and Engineering Corporation, 2550 Riley Road, Ottawa, Kansas, 66067, USA; 1988.

3.10   Ribner, H.S.; Notes on the Propeller and Slipstream in Relation to Stability; NACA WR L–25, 1944 (Formerly NACA ARR L4I12a).

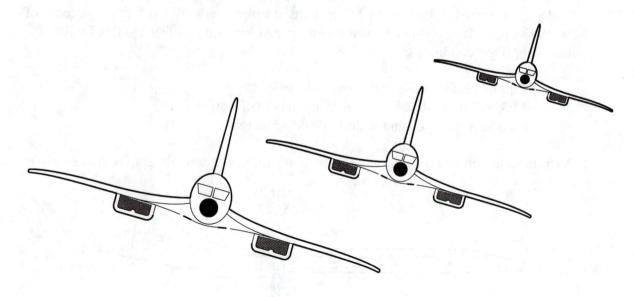

CHAPTER 4: STABILITY AND CONTROL DURING STEADY STATE FLIGHT

Airplanes must have the following general flight characteristics:

1. The airplane must have sufficient control power to maintain steady state, straight line flight throughout the design flight envelope.

2. It must be possible for the airplane to be safely maneuvered from one steady state flight condition to another.

3. Cockpit control forces should be within acceptable upper and lower limits under all expected conditions throughout the design flight envelope. This includes changes in airplane configuration such as: flaps up/down, landing gear up/down, weapons launch etc.

4. The airplane must be trimmable in certain flight conditions.

These four very general flight characteristics are a subset of the so–called 'flying or handling qualities' of the airplane. Requirements for good flying qualities of airplanes are qualitatively and quantitatively specified in the so–called airworthiness requirements: FAR 23, FAR 25 and JAR–VLA (for civil airplanes); Mil–F–8785C and Mil–Std–1797A (for military airplanes). These requirements are given in References 4.1 – 4.4 and will be referred to as the 'regulations' in this text.

To predict whether or not an airplane meets the regulations, the airplane designer/analyst employs mathematical models which are based on the equations of motion (as derived in Chapter 1) and on certain relationships between aerodynamic and thrust forces and moments and the motion variables (as discussed in Chapter 3). The purpose of this chapter is to combine the results of Chapters 1 and 3 to form mathematical models from which the stability and control characteristics of an airplane in steady state flight can be predicted. This will be done in such a way that it is clear what design 'fixes' the designer must make to ensure that the airplane meets the intent of the regulations.

Section 4.1 contains a derivation and discussion of static stability criteria for airplanes.

A discussion of the most important steady state stability and controllability characteristics of airplanes in steady, straight line flight and in maneuvering flight is contained in Sections 4.2 and 4.3 respectively. The effect of airplane configuration on airplane trim is discussed in Section 4.4.

The effect of reversible flight control systems on stability and control is covered in Sections 4.5 and 4.6. A more general, matrix based approach to the steady state stability and control properties of airplanes is given in Section 4.7 and 4.8. In Section 4.9, the topic of airplane takeoff rotation is taken up. Finally, Section 4.10 contains a brief discussion of irreversible flight control systems.

4.1 INTRODUCTION TO STATIC STABILITY AND ITS CRITERIA

The following definitions are used for static stability and for static stability criteria:

Definition of Static Stability:

> Static stability is defined as the tendency of an airplane to develop forces or moments which directly oppose an instantaneous perturbation of a motion variable from a steady–state flight condition.

Definition of Static Stability Criterion:

> A static stability criterion is defined as a rule by which steady state flight conditions are separated into the categories of stable, unstable or neutrally stable..

Figures 4.1 and 4.2 contain examples of what is meant by static stability, neutral stability and static instability for a mechanical system and an airplane in pitch respectively.

The steady state motion of an airplane was defined in Chapter 1 as that motion for which the linear velocity vector, $\vec{V}_P$, and the angular velocity vector, $\vec{\omega}$, remain constant with time in a body–fixed axis system XYZ. In more common language, steady state flight is thought of as having constant speed, constant rotational velocities and constant load factor. This type of flight condition is encountered frequently in straight, wings level flight, in steady turns and in steady pull–ups or push–overs.

It is observed that the momentary position of the airplane center of mass in inertial space, $\vec{r}_P{}'$, is not important in determining stability behavior. The state vector components $X_1{}', Y_1{}', Z_1{}'$ will therefore not be included in stability considerations and therefore, **neutral static stability** with respect to changes in these motion variables is accepted. A similar statement can be made with respect to the Euler angles Ψ_1, Θ_1, Φ_1 : **neutral static stability** with respect to changes in heading angle, pitch attitude angle and bank angle will also be accepted. All this makes sense if it is recalled that no aerodynamic forces arise as a result of any changes in the motion variables $X_1{}', Y_1{}', Z_1{}'$ and Ψ_1, Θ_1, Φ_1.

For determination of static stability, it therefore suffices to consider only the components of $\vec{V}_P$ and $\vec{\omega}$ which (in the steady state) respectively are: U_1, V_1, W_1 and P_1, Q_1, R_1. The perturbations relative to these steady state motion variables are: u, v, w and p, q, r.

The definition of static stability will now be applied by using the instantaneous force and moment behavior to these instantaneous perturbations. In determining which combinations of forces , moments and perturbations are to be singled out, the following arbitrary rules have been followed:

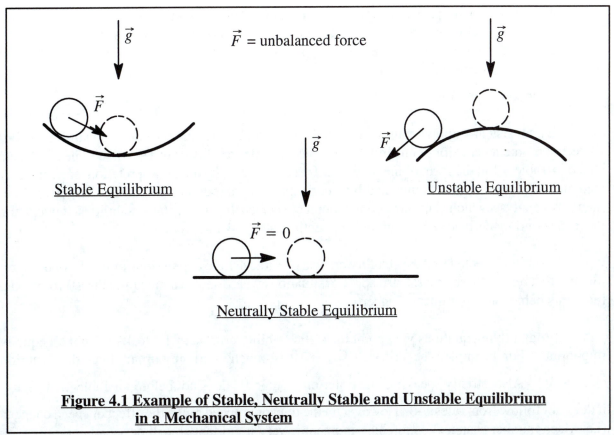

Figure 4.1 Example of Stable, Neutrally Stable and Unstable Equilibrium in a Mechanical System

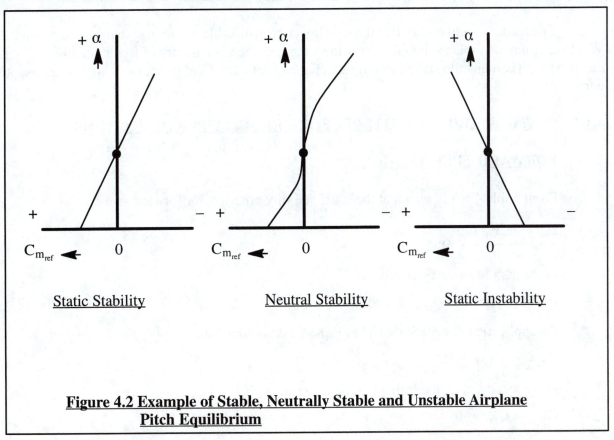

Figure 4.2 Example of Stable, Neutrally Stable and Unstable Airplane Pitch Equilibrium

1. Linear velocity perturbations are initially opposed only by forces.
2. Angular velocity perturbations are initially opposed only by moments.
3. Angle of sideslip and angle of attack perturbations obtained by interpreting the velocity perturbations v and w as $\beta = v/U_1$ and $\alpha = w/U_1$ are initially opposed only by moments.

By consistently applying these rules and the definition of static stability to the instantaneous force and moment behavior of an airplane, a series of static stability criteria evolve. The results are stated in Table 4.1 in the form of inequalities. To assist in the physical interpretation, each stability statement in Table 4.1 is accompanied by a corresponding aerodynamic stability derivative statement. An analysis which shows the connection between each general static stability statement and its corresponding derivative is given in Sub–sections 4.1.1–4.1.4.

It should be noted that the stability criteria of Table 4.1 are expressions of local slope behavior. For that reason these criteria also apply to situations where aerodynamic (and thrust) forces and moments behave in a nonlinear manner.

From a flying qualities viewpoint the static stability criteria in Table 4.1 are not all equally important. For example, the criterion $C_{m_\alpha} < 0$ is much more important than the criterion $C_{y_\beta} < 0$. Also, strictly speaking, the criterion $C_{m_u} > 0$ does not belong in Table 4.1 because it does not follow from rules 1–3. However, in the transonic speed range the effect of speed changes (i.e. Mach number changes) on pitching moment is very important as will be seen later.

The reader should realize that the stability criteria of Table 4.1 are just that, stability criteria. Whether or not an airplane should always meet these criteria is a matter of flying qualities. Pilots can cope with certain mild static instabilities. The regulations of References 4.1 – 4.4 take this into consideration.

4.1.1   STATIC STABILITY CRITERIA FOR VELOCITY PERTURBATIONS

FORWARD SPEED STABILITY

From Table 4.1 it is seen that the static stability criterion for forward speed is:

$$\frac{\partial(F_{A_x} + F_{T_x})}{\partial u} < 0 \tag{4.1}$$

In the stability axis system:

$$F_{A_x} + F_{T_x} = (-C_D + C_{T_x})\overline{q}S \tag{4.2}$$

By application of criterion (4.1) to Eqn (4.2) it is found that:

$$(C_{T_{x_u}} - C_{D_u}) + (C_{T_{x_1}} - C_{D_1})\frac{2}{U_1} < 0 \tag{4.3}$$

In the steady state, the following must be satisfied:

$$C_{T_{x_1}} - C_{D_1} = 0 \tag{4.4}$$

Table 4.1 Criteria for Static Stability of Airplanes

Forces and moments	Perturbed Variables							
	u	v	w	$\beta = \dfrac{v}{U_1}$	$\alpha = \dfrac{w}{U_1}$	p	q	r
$F_{A_x} + F_{T_x}$	$\dfrac{\partial(F_{A_x} + F_{T_x})}{\partial u} < 0$ $\approx C_{D_u} > 0$							
$F_{A_y} + F_{T_y}$		$\dfrac{\partial(F_{A_y} + F_{T_y})}{\partial v} < 0$ $\approx C_{y_\beta} < 0$						
$F_{A_z} + F_{T_z}$			$\dfrac{\partial(F_{A_z} + F_{T_z})}{\partial w} < 0$ $\approx C_{L_\alpha} > 0$					
$L_A + L_T$				$\dfrac{\partial(L_A + L_T)}{\partial \beta} < 0$ $\approx C_{l_\beta} < 0$		$\dfrac{\partial(L_A + L_T)}{\partial p} < 0$ $\approx C_{l_p} < 0$		
$M_A + M_T$	$\dfrac{\partial(M_A + M_T)}{\partial u} < 0$ $\approx C_{m_u} > 0$				$\dfrac{\partial(M_A + M_T)}{\partial \alpha} < 0$ $\approx C_{m_\alpha} < 0$		$\dfrac{\partial(M_A + M_T)}{\partial q} < 0$ $\approx C_{m_q} < 0$	
$N_A + N_T$				$\dfrac{\partial(N_A + N_T)}{\partial \beta} > 0$ $\approx C_{n_\beta} > 0$				$\dfrac{\partial(N_A + N_T)}{\partial r} < 0$ $\approx C_{n_r} < 0$

Notes: 1. All perturbations are taken relative to a steady state: $U_1, V_1, W_1, P_1, Q_1, R_1$

2. Blanks in the table indicate that there is no stability consequence

Therefore, static stability criterion (4.1) reduces to:

$$(C_{T_{x_u}} - C_{D_u}) < 0 \tag{4.5}$$

Intuitively, the stability criterion as expressed by (4.1) or (4.5) is a very desirable characteristic. It means that an airplane which satisfies these criteria has the inherent tendency to return to its equilibrium speed when perturbed in either direction. This behavior is considered particularly critical on final approach to landing.

Figure 4.3 illustrates the fact, well known to pilots, that airplanes tend to be speed–stable at high speed (point A) but become speed–unstable at low speed (point B). Flying at point B is referred to as flying on the 'backside' of the thrust–required (or power required) curve.

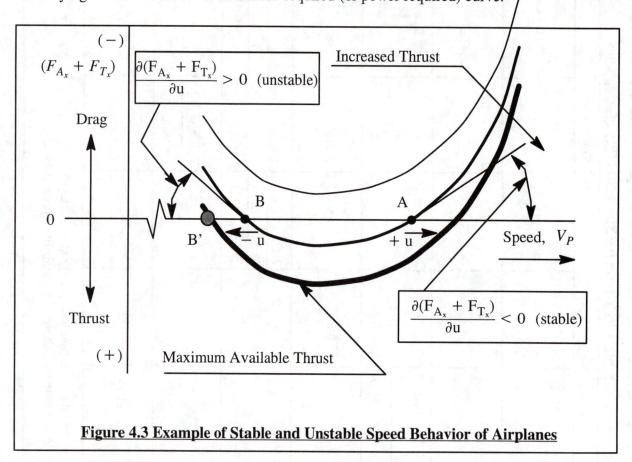

Figure 4.3 Example of Stable and Unstable Speed Behavior of Airplanes

Consider what happens at point A, when the airplane is perturbed by a positive shear gust, +u. At constant thrust, the drag will increase which tends to drive the airplane back to its equilibrium speed at point A.

Next, consider what happens at point B, when the airplane is perturbed by a negative shear gust, –u. At constant thrust, the drag will increase which in this case drives the airplane further away from its equilibrium speed at point B. To recover from such a perturbation a pilot would have to command added thrust. The success of that command depends on how much extra thrust is still available AND on how rapidly the propulsive system reacts to a thrust command. In many jet engines, because of the relatively slow spool–up time, this can create problems.

Note that when flying at point B' there no longer is added thrust available. If the speed corresponding to point B' is above the stall speed, the airplane will be driven into the stall. Recovery from an impending stall is then possible only by pushing the nose of the airplane down (diving). However, when flying close to the ground this may not be a viable alternative!

For a more detailed discussion of the derivatives C_{D_u} and $C_{T_{x_u}}$, see Sub–sections 3.2.2 and 3.2.16 respectively.

SIDE SPEED STABILITY

From Table 4.1 it is seen that the static stability criterion for side speed is:

$$\frac{\partial(F_{A_y} + F_{T_y})}{\partial v} < 0 \tag{4.6}$$

In the stability axis system:

$$F_{A_y} + F_{T_y} = (-C_y + C_{T_y})\overline{q}S \tag{4.7}$$

By application of criterion (4.1) to Eqn (4.7) while assuming that the side speed perturbation, v, does not affect dynamic pressure in an appreciable manner, it is found that:

$$C_{y_\beta} + C_{T_{y_\beta}} < 0 \tag{4.8}$$

In most instances, the approximation $C_{T_{y_\beta}} \approx 0$ is acceptable so that (4.8) reduces to:

$$C_{y_\beta} < 0 \tag{4.9}$$

As long as the flow around an airplane is attached, this condition is satisfied by current configurations. To meet the civil and military handling quality requirements in sideslip, condition (4.9) must be satisfied. It also has two very practical side effects:

1) Whether or not an airplane is flying at or near zero sideslip angle is very difficult to perceive by a pilot. Condition (4.9) increases the 'visibility' of sideslip by forcing airplanes to bank

in steady sideslips. References 4.1 (Subsection 3.6) and 4.2 (Sub–section 23.177 and 25.177) specifically require this characteristic.

2) Condition (4.9) allows pilots to perform skidding turns at very low altitude where bank angle restrictions may have to be observed because of clearance to the terrain. This ability is particularly important when performing so–called side–step maneuvers when misaligned with the runway on final approach.

For a more detailed discussion of the derivative C_{y_β}, see Sub–section 3.1.9.

VERTICAL SPEED STABILITY

From Table 4.1 it is seen that the static stability criterion for vertical speed is:

$$\frac{\partial(F_{A_z} + F_{T_z})}{\partial w} < 0 \tag{4.10}$$

In the stability axis system:

$$F_{A_z} + F_{T_z} = (- C_L + C_{T_z})\overline{q}S \tag{4.11}$$

By application of criterion (4.1) to Eqn (4.11), while using the approximation: $w = \alpha U_1$ it is found that:

$$\frac{1}{U_1}(- C_{L_\alpha} + C_{T_{z_\alpha}})\overline{q}S < 0 \tag{4.12}$$

The derivative $C_{z_{T_\alpha}}$ reflects the behavior of the inlet (or propeller) normal force with angle of attack. These effects were discussed in Sub–section 3.2.17. For many airplanes and flight conditions it is acceptable to assume: $C_{z_{T_\alpha}} \ll C_{L_\alpha}$ so that condition (4.12) can usually be written as:

$$C_{L_\alpha} > 0 \tag{4.13}$$

This condition states that the lift–curve slope of an airplane must be positive for static stability against perturbations in vertical velocity. As long as the airplane angle of attack is below the stall angle of attack, condition (4.13) is always satisfied.

A detailed discussion of the derivative C_{L_α} is provided in Sub–section 3.1.3. Airplane lift–curve slope, C_{L_α}, has long been recognized as a very important derivative mostly because of two effects on airplane behavior in flight:

1) When flying through turbulence, changes in angle of attack are continuously induced on an airplane. The load factor, n, which an airplane experiences in flight is defined as:

$$n = \frac{L}{W} \approx \frac{(C_{L_0} + C_{L_\alpha}\alpha)\overline{q}S}{W} \tag{4.14}$$

By differentiating this expression with respect to angle of attack it follows that:

$$\frac{\partial n}{\partial \alpha} = n_\alpha = \frac{\overline{q}C_{L_\alpha}}{(W/S)} \tag{4.15}$$

The derivative n_α is referred to as the load–factor–due–to–gust–induced–angle–of–attack effect. If its numerical value is large, an airplane will give a rough ride through turbulence. If its numerical value is small, an airplane will ride smoothly through turbulence. Observe that the derivative C_{L_α} plays a key role in the gust responsiveness of an airplane. From Figure 2.7 it is known that wings with high aspect ratio and low sweep angle yield large value of C_{L_α}. Many low speed airplanes combine a high value of C_{L_α} with a low value of wing loading, W/S. As Eqn (4.15) shows, that leads to a rough ride. For more information on the calculation of airplane ride characteristics the reader should consult Part VII of Reference 3.

2) It will be shown in Chapter 5 that the derivative C_{L_α} also plays an important role in determining the damping ratio of the so–called short period oscillation of an airplane. Relatively high damping ratios in that oscillatory mode is also a flying quality requirement as seen in Ref. 4.1.

It will be shown in Chapter 7, that aeroelastic effects on the derivative C_{L_α} can be very large. In aft swept wings the effect of aeroelasticity is to reduce C_{L_α} while in forward swept wings the opposite is true.

4.1.2   STATIC STABILITY CRITERIA FOR ANGLE OF ATTACK AND SIDESLIP ANGLE PERTURBATIONS

ANGLE OF ATTACK STABILITY

According to Table 4.1 the static stability criterion for perturbations in angle of attack is:

$$\frac{\partial(M_A + M_T)}{\partial \alpha} < 0 \tag{4.16}$$

The physical significance of this stability criterion is that an airplane will 'weathercock' into the new relative wind as a result of a perturbation in angle of attack. A certain amount of weathercocking behavior of airplanes is generally desirable.

In the stability axis system:

$$M_A + M_T = (C_m + C_{m_T})\bar{q}S\bar{c} \tag{4.17}$$

By application of criterion (4.16) to Eqn (4.17) it is found that:

$$C_{m_\alpha} + C_{m_{T_\alpha}} < 0 \tag{4.18}$$

It is shown in Sub–section 3.2.17 that the sign and magnitude of $C_{m_{T_\alpha}}$ depends not only on the magnitude of $C_{z_{T_\alpha}}$ but also on the moment arm of the engine inlet (or propeller plane) from the center of gravity. In cases where the derivative $C_{m_{T_\alpha}}$ is negligible compared with C_{m_α} the static stability condition (4.18) reduces to:

$$C_{m_\alpha} < 0 \tag{4.19}$$

Inequality (4.19) represents the familiar requirement for static longitudinal stability. From Eqn (3.39) it is seen that this requirement is satisfied as long as the aerodynamic center is located behind the center of gravity.

The reader should realize that as the c.g. of an airplane is moved aft toward the 'stability boundary' defined by $C_{m_\alpha} = 0$ nothing disastrous happens. What has been found from flight tests and simulator tests is that the precision of control over the airplane and the forgiveness of the airplane to pilot mistakes in control input steadily decrease as the c.g. moves aft. As a result pilots are required to 'lead' the airplane which causes a significant increase in pilot workload until the pilot is no longer able to control the airplane. Then disastrous things can indeed happen!

Nevertheless, simulator studies have shown that flying slightly unstable airplanes with a very large pitching moment of inertia is quite possible. This behavior can be connected to the idea of 'time–to–double–amplitude–in–pitch'. As long as the time to double the amplitude in pitch is large, pilots can control the airplane. Airplanes with a large pitching moment of inertia satisfy this condition. The Boeing 747 and the Lockheed C–5 are in this category of airplanes.

By incorporating certain automatic feedback control systems in an airplane it is possible to develop airplanes with inherently unstable C_{m_α} behavior. However, including the effects of the feedback control system, such airplanes still behave as an inherently stable airplane as far as the pilot is concerned. This will be referred to as 'de–facto' stability.

In Sections 4.4 and 4.5 as well as in Section 5.2 it will be shown that the derivative C_{m_α} is directly tied to several very important handling quality parameters.

Mach number and aeroelastic effects on the sign and magnitude of C_{m_α} can be very important and must be accounted for in airplanes where this is the case. For additional discussions of C_{m_α} see Sub–section 3.1.4.

ANGLE OF SIDESLIP STABILITY

From Table 4.1 it follows that the static stability criterion for perturbations in angle of sideslip is:

$$\frac{\partial(N_A + N_T)}{\partial\beta} > 0 \qquad (4.20)$$

The physical significance of this stability criterion is that an airplane will 'weathercock' into the new relative wind as a result of a perturbation in sideslip angle. Because of the difficulties a pilot has in identifying sideslip, this form of stability is very desirable. It is commonly referred to as directional stability, although that is a poor choice of words! Directional stability would seem to imply stability in heading angle, Ψ. However, it was already stipulated that airplanes have neutral stability in heading.

In the stability axis system:

$$N_A + N_T = (C_n + C_{T_n})\bar{q}Sb \qquad (4.21)$$

By application of criterion (4.20) to Eqn (4.21) it is found that:

$$C_{n_\beta} + C_{n_{T_\beta}} > 0 \qquad (4.22)$$

If the thrust contribution to directional stability is negligible ($C_{n_{T_\beta}} \ll C_{n_\beta}$), then condition

(4.22) reduces to the following requirement:

$$C_{n_\beta} > 0 \tag{4.23}$$

When an airplane is flying in symmetrical, straight and level flight, the steady state yawing moment coefficient is zero. However, when an airplane is flying at a nonzero sideslip angle, the steady state yawing moment coefficient is NOT zero: $C_{n_1} \neq 0$. In that case the requirement for directional stability becomes:

$$(C_{n_\beta})_{\beta \neq 0} > 0 \tag{4.24}$$

This implies that the LOCAL slope of yawing moment coefficient with respect to sideslip angle must be positive. This is in fact what is required by the military flying quality requirements of Ref. 4.1. It is noted that the civil flying quality requirements as expressed by Ref. 4.3 in paragraphs 23.177 and 25.177 also require this BUT in addition, require condition (4.23) to be met.

Note that condition (4.24) applies specifically to cases where the variation of yawing moment coefficient with sideslip angle is nonlinear. This occurs in many airplane configurations. The XB–70 was a typical example.

Mach number and aeroelastic effects on the sign and magnitude of C_{n_β} can be very important and must be accounted for in airplanes where this is the case. For additional discussions of C_{n_β} see Sub–section 3.1.10.

4.1.3 STATIC STABILITY CRITERIA FOR ANGULAR VELOCITY PERTURBATIONS

Static stability against the following angular velocity perturbations will be considered: roll rate, p, pitch rate, q, and yaw rate, r.

ROLL RATE STABILITY

From Table 4.1 it follows that the static stability criterion for perturbations in roll rate is:

$$\frac{\partial(L_A + L_T)}{\partial p} < 0 \tag{4.25}$$

The physical meaning of this criterion is that as a result of a change in roll rate, p, a rolling moment must be generated which tends to oppose the increase in rolling velocity. In the stability axis system:

$$L_A + L_T = (C_l + C_{l_T})\overline{q}Sb \tag{4.26}$$

Neglecting the thrust term in Eqn (4.26) it follows that Criterion (4.25) implies that:

$$C_{l_p} < 0 \tag{4.27}$$

The derivative C_{l_p} is recognized as the roll damping derivative. For a rigid airplane in attached flow conditions, this criterion is always satisfied. Mach number, aspect ratio, sweep angle and aeroelastic effects all affect the roll damping derivative. For a discussion of which factors affect the magnitude of C_{l_p}, the reader is referred to Section 3.2.11.

Roll damping is an important handling quality parameter. Even though the magnitude of C_{l_p} is not specified in any handling quality requirements, it will be seen in Chapter 5 that it plays a significant role in affecting the roll performance and sometimes even the Dutch roll characteristics of an airplane.

PITCH RATE STABILITY

From Table 4.1 it follows that the static stability criterion for perturbations in pitch rate is:

$$\frac{\partial(M_A + M_T)}{\partial q} < 0 \tag{4.28}$$

The physical meaning of this criterion is that as a result of a change in pitch rate, q, a pitching moment must be generated which tends to oppose the increase in pitching velocity. In the stability axis system:

$$M_A + M_T = (C_m + C_{m_T})\overline{q}S\overline{c} \tag{4.29}$$

Neglecting the effect of thrust, criterion (4.28) implies that:

$$C_{m_q} < 0 \tag{4.30}$$

The derivative C_{m_q} is the pitch damping derivative which is discussed in Section 3.2.5. It has a major effect on the short period damping ratio of airplanes as will be seen in Chapter 5.

Aeroelasticity and Mach number both affect this derivative. As long as the flow over the airplane is attached this derivative is always negative so that criterion (4.28) is normally satisfied.

YAW RATE STABILITY

From Table 4.1 it follows that the static stability criterion for perturbations in yaw rate is:

$$\frac{\partial(N_A + N_T)}{\partial r} < 0 \tag{4.31}$$

The physical meaning of this criterion is that as a result of a change in yaw rate, r, a yawing moment must be generated which tends to oppose the increase in yawing velocity. In stability axes:

$$N_A + N_T = (C_n + C_{n_T})\overline{q}Sb \tag{4.32}$$

Neglecting the effect of thrust, criterion (4.29) implies that:

$$C_{n_r} < 0 \tag{4.33}$$

The derivative C_{n_r} is the yaw damping derivative which is discussed in Section 3.2.5. This derivative has a very significant effect on the Dutch roll damping ratio of airplanes as will become clear in Chapter 5. Aeroelasticity and Mach number both affect this derivative. As long as the flow over the airplane is attached this derivative is always negative so that criterion (4.28) is normally satisfied.

4.1.4   DISCUSSION OF PITCHING MOMENT DUE TO SPEED AND ROLLING MOMENT DUE TO SIDESLIP STABILITY

Under the adopted definition of static stability at the beginning of this chapter, the effect of speed on pitching moment and the effect of sideslip on rolling moment do not qualify as static stability effects. Nevertheless, experience shows that both are very important from a handling qualities viewpoint. For that reason they will be discussed.

EFFECT OF FORWARD SPEED ON PITCHING MOMENT

According to Table 5.1 the desired behavior of an airplane when perturbed in forward speed, u, is that:

$$\frac{\partial(M_A + M_T)}{\partial u} > 0 \qquad (4.34)$$

The implication of this requirement is that when an airplane experiences an increase in speed, u, relative to its steady state speed, U_1, it should react with a positive increase (i.e. nose up) in pitching moment. Obviously, the latter would tend to slow the airplane down again, making it statically stable. In the stability axis system:

$$M_A + M_T = (C_m + C_{m_T})\overline{q}S\overline{c} \qquad (4.35)$$

Application of the stability criterion (4.34) now yields:

$$(C_{m_u} + C_{m_{T_u}}) + (C_{m_1} + C_{m_{T_1}})\frac{2}{U_1} > 0 \qquad (4.36)$$

Since in steady state flight $(C_{m_1} + C_{m_{T_1}} = 0)$ it follows that:

$$(C_{m_u} + C_{m_{T_u}}) > 0 \qquad (4.37)$$

In many airplanes the thrust contribution can be neglected so that:

$$C_{m_u} > 0 \qquad (4.38)$$

The derivative C_{m_u} is the so–called tuck derivative discussed in Section 3.2.2. It tends to have the value of zero in the low subsonic speed regime. However, as the subsonic Mach number increases and the airplane center of pressure shifts aft, this derivative has a tendency to take on the 'wrong' sign, giving some airplanes a Mach–tuck problem.

An unstable sign of C_{m_u} can be acceptable if the airplane also has a steep drag–rise which would tend to prevent large forward speed disturbances from developing. It turns out that the magnitude of an unstable C_{m_u} depends strongly on airfoil and planform design parameters. Most of the current generation of transports tend to have rather mild forms of tuck whereas the earlier generations of jet transports had fairly severe tuck.

EFFECT OF SIDESLIP ON ROLLING MOMENT

According to Table 5.1 the desired behavior of an airplane when perturbed by a small sideslip angle, β is:

$$\frac{\partial(L_A + L_T)}{\partial\beta} < 0 \qquad (4.39)$$

The physical significance is, that for a positive sideslip (nose left of the oncoming airspeed vector), the airplane tends to roll away from the disturbance, i.e. roll to the left. By checking with Figure 4.4 it is seen that in the extreme case, the sideslip angle disappears and becomes an angle of attack: the effective sideslip angle is diminished by a roll to the left. For this reason, an airplane which satisfies stability criterion (4.39) is referred to as having lateral stability. In the stability axis system:

$$L_A + L_T = (C_l + C_{l_T})\bar{q}Sb \qquad (4.40)$$

Neglecting the effect of thrust, application of criterion (4.39) results in:

$$C_{l_\beta} < 0 \qquad (4.41)$$

The derivative C_{l_β} is also known as the airplane dihedral effect. It must be negative for airplanes to meet the lateral stability requirements of References 4.1 – 4.4. However, as will be shown in Chapter 5, if C_{l_β} takes on too large a negative magnitude it can result in lowering the damping ratio of the Dutch roll mode. Which aspects of airplane configuration design affect the sign and magnitude of C_{l_β} is discussed in Section 3.2.9.

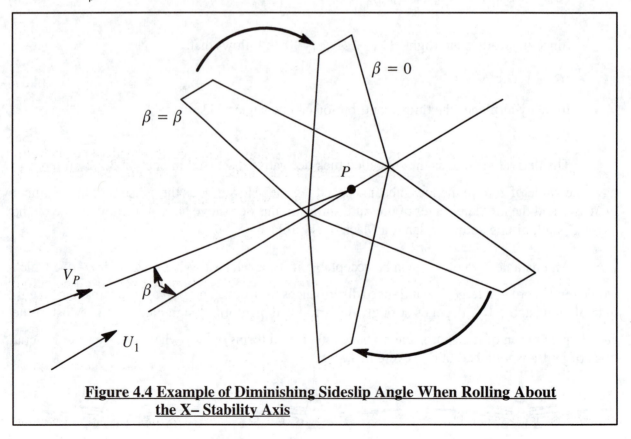

Figure 4.4 Example of Diminishing Sideslip Angle When Rolling About the X– Stability Axis

4.2 STABILITY AND CONTROL CHARACTERISTICS FOR STEADY STATE, STRAIGHT LINE FLIGHT

To keep an airplane in a given steady state flight condition and to allow it to be maneuvered from one flight condition to another, including the effect of certain configuration changes, it is necessary that the following conditions be satisfied:

1. The airplane must have adequate control power

2. No extraordinary pilot effort must be required

The objective of this section is to analyze these conditions in sufficient detail so that the designer can decide whether or not a given airplane design meets the pertinent civil and military handling quality requirements. To carry out such an analysis the appropriate equations of motion must be invoked. From Chapter 1, the steady state, straight line equations of motion (1.58) and (1.59) and from Chapter 3 the corresponding aerodynamic and thrust force and moment equations (3.46) and (3.95) are combined to give the following set of six equations:

$$mg\sin\gamma_1 = -(C_{D_0} + C_{D_\alpha}\alpha_1 + C_{D_{i_h}}i_{h_1} + C_{D_{\delta_e}}\delta_{e_1})\overline{q}_1 S + T_1\cos(\phi_T + \alpha_1) \qquad (4.42a)$$

$$-mg\sin\phi_1\cos\gamma_1 = (C_{y_\beta}\beta_1 + C_{y_{\delta_a}}\delta_{a_1} + C_{y_{\delta_r}}\delta_{r_1})\overline{q}_1 S + F_{y_{T_1}} \qquad (4.42b)$$

$$mg\cos\phi_1\cos\gamma_1 = (C_{L_0} + C_{L_\alpha}\alpha_1 + C_{L_{i_h}}i_{h_1} + C_{L_{\delta_e}}\delta_{e_1})\overline{q}_1 S + T_1\sin(\phi_T + \alpha_1) \qquad (4.42c)$$

$$0 = (C_{l_\beta}\beta_1 + C_{l_{\delta_a}}\delta_{a_1} + C_{l_{\delta_r}}\delta_{r_1})\overline{q}_1 Sb + L_{T_1} \qquad (4.42d)$$

$$0 = (C_{m_0} + C_{m_\alpha}\alpha_1 + C_{m_{i_h}}i_{h_1} + C_{m_{\delta_e}}\delta_{e_1})\overline{q}_1 S\overline{c} - T_1 d_T \qquad (4.42e)$$

$$0 = (C_{n_\beta}\beta_1 + C_{n_{\delta_a}}\delta_{a_1} + C_{n_{\delta_r}}\delta_{r_1})\overline{q}_1 Sb + N_{T_1} \qquad (4.42f)$$

These equations are written in the stability axis system. Therefore, the steady state pitch attitude angle, θ_1, is set equal to the steady state flight path angle, γ_1. Assuming that the dynamic pressure, q_1, is known, these six equations have the following nine unknowns:

$$\gamma_1, \quad \phi_1, \quad \alpha_1, \quad \beta_1, \quad \delta_{a_1}, \quad i_{h_1}, \quad \delta_{e_1}, \quad \delta_{r_1}, \quad \text{and} \quad T_1$$

Since there are only six equations, three of these variables will have to be specified before the others can be solved for. In most applications, this is done by specifying the steady state bank angle, ϕ_1, the steady state thrust, T_1, and the steady state stabilizer incidence angle, i_{h_1}.

It will be shown later, that in many situations the pilot will set the value of i_{h_1} such as to drive the cockpit control force (which is required to hold the elevator, δ_e, at a deflection which guarantees pitching moment equilibrium) to zero. Having selected any three of the nine variables, the equations (4.22) can now be used to solve for the other six. This is typically done by using an iterative matrix method. Such a method is used in Section 4.7 to solve the airplane force and moment equations adjoined by the stick force equation.

The reader will observe that by selecting the bank angle (which appears only in Eqns (4.42b) and (4.42c) the six equations conveniently split into two independent sets:

1) The longitudinal equations: (4.42a), (4.42c) and (4.42e)

and:

2) The lateral–directional equations: (4.42b), (4.42d) and (4.42f)

Solutions to the longitudinal equations are discussed in Sub–sections 4.2.1 through 4.2.5 and solutions to the lateral–directional equations are discussed in Sub–section 4.2.6.

4.2.1 LONGITUDINAL STABILITY AND CONTROL CHARACTERISTICS FOR STEADY STATE, STRAIGHT LINE FLIGHT

Separating the longitudinal equations from Eqns (4.42) and assuming wings–level flight yields:

$$mg \sin\gamma_1 = -(C_{D_0} + C_{D_\alpha}\alpha_1 + C_{D_{i_h}}i_{h_1} + C_{D_{\delta_e}}\delta_{e_1})\bar{q}_1 S + T_1 \cos(\phi_T + \alpha_1) \qquad (4.43a)$$

$$mg \cos\gamma_1 = (C_{L_0} + C_{L_\alpha}\alpha_1 + C_{L_{i_h}}i_{h_1} + C_{L_{\delta_e}}\delta_{e_1})\bar{q}_1 S + T_1 \sin(\phi_T + \alpha_1) \qquad (4.43b)$$

$$0 = (C_{m_0} + C_{m_\alpha}\alpha_1 + C_{m_{i_h}}i_{h_1} + C_{m_{\delta_e}}\delta_{e_1})\bar{q}_1 S\bar{c} - T_1 d_T \qquad (4.43c)$$

Observe that Eqns (4.43) pre–suppose that the bank angle, $\phi_1 = 0$. Assuming that T_1 and i_{h_1} are pre–selected, the variables α_1, γ_1 and δ_{e_1} can be solved for using iterative matrix techniques. Iterative techniques are required because of the non–linear nature of Eqns (4.43).

With the iterative solutions available, the engineer can form a judgment about the 'sanity' of these solutions. For example, if one of the solutions is 45 degrees for the elevator deflection, there is clearly a problem: tails with elevator deflections much beyond 25–30 degrees would stall. Although a solution may be mathematically acceptable, it may not pass such a 'sanity' check.

What these iterative solutions do not allow the engineer to do is to obtain immediate insight into what the 'design drivers' are which make the numerical solutions small or large, negative or positive. Such insight can be obtained by introducing three assumptions:

a) assume that there is always sufficient thrust to balance the drag equation (4.43a), making it superfluous

b) assume that the thrust–line passes through the center of gravity: $d_T = 0$.

c) assume that the term $T_1 \sin(\phi_T + \alpha_1)$ is negligible in the lift equation (4.43b)

With these assumptions, Eqns (4.43) simplify to the following form which is also the form applicable to power–off flight:

$$mg \cos\gamma_1 = (C_{L_0} + C_{L_\alpha}\alpha_1 + C_{L_{i_h}}i_{h_1} + C_{L_{\delta_e}}\delta_{e_1})\bar{q}_1 S \tag{4.44a}$$

$$0 = (C_{m_0} + C_{m_\alpha}\alpha_1 + C_{m_{i_h}}i_{h_1} + C_{m_{\delta_e}}\delta_{e_1})\bar{q}_1 S\bar{c} \tag{4.44b}$$

When an airplane satisfies the pitching moment equation (4.44b) it is said to be in moment equilibrium or in moment trim. It is useful to write Eqns (4.44) in a matrix format:

$$\begin{bmatrix} C_{L_\alpha} & C_{L_{\delta_e}} \\ C_{m_\alpha} & C_{m_{\delta_e}} \end{bmatrix} \begin{Bmatrix} \alpha_1 \\ \delta_{e_1} \end{Bmatrix} = \begin{Bmatrix} C_{L_1} - C_{L_0} - C_{L_{i_h}}i_{h_1} \\ -C_{m_0} - C_{m_{i_h}}i_{h_1} \end{Bmatrix} \tag{4.45}$$

where: $C_{L_1} = \dfrac{mg}{\bar{q}_1 S}$, which is the airplane steady state lift coefficient. Solutions to matrix Eqn (4.45) are the following:

$$\alpha_1 = \frac{(C_{L_1} - C_{L_0} - C_{L_{i_h}}i_{h_1})C_{m_{\delta_e}} + (C_{m_0} + C_{m_{i_h}}i_{h_1})C_{L_{\delta_e}}}{(C_{L_\alpha}C_{m_{\delta_e}} - C_{m_\alpha}C_{L_{\delta_e}})} \tag{4.46}$$

$$\delta_{e_1} = \frac{-C_{L_\alpha}(C_{m_0} + C_{m_{i_h}}i_{h_1}) - C_{m_\alpha}(C_{L_1} - C_{L_0} - C_{L_{i_h}}i_{h_1})}{(C_{L_\alpha}C_{m_{\delta_e}} - C_{m_\alpha}C_{L_{\delta_e}})} \tag{4.47}$$

A very useful way of writing these solutions is the following:

$$\alpha_1 = \alpha_{C_{L_1}=0} + \frac{\partial\alpha}{\partial C_L}C_{L_1} \tag{4.48}$$

$$\delta_{e_1} = \delta_{e_{C_{L_1}=0}} + \frac{\partial\delta_e}{\partial C_L}C_{L_1} \tag{4.49}$$

The constant terms in Eqns (4.48) and (4.49) have the following physical significance:

$\alpha_{C_{L_1}=0}$ is the angle of attack at which the airplane is trimmed with $C_{L_1} = 0$

$\delta_{e_{C_{L_1}=0}}$ is the elevator angle for which the airplane is trimmed with $C_{L_1} = 0$

$\dfrac{\partial\alpha}{\partial C_L}$ is the rate of change of trim angle of attack with lift coefficient

$\dfrac{\partial\delta_e}{\partial C_L}$ is the rate of change of elevator trim angle with lift coefficient

From Eqns (4.46) and (4.47) it can be deduced that:

$$\alpha_{C_{L_1}=0} = \frac{(-C_{L_0} - C_{L_{i_h}}i_{h_1})C_{m_{\delta_e}} + (C_{m_0} + C_{m_{i_h}}i_{h_1})C_{L_{\delta_e}}}{(C_{L_\alpha}C_{m_{\delta_e}} - C_{m_\alpha}C_{L_{\delta_e}})} \tag{4.50}$$

$$\delta_{e_{C_{L_1}=0}} = \frac{-C_{L_\alpha}(C_{m_0} + C_{m_{i_h}}i_{h_1}) - C_{m_\alpha}(-C_{L_0} - C_{L_{i_h}}i_{h_1})}{(C_{L_\alpha}C_{m_{\delta_e}} - C_{m_\alpha}C_{L_{\delta_e}})} \tag{4.51}$$

$$\frac{\partial\alpha}{\partial C_L} = \frac{C_{m_{\delta_e}}}{(C_{L_\alpha}C_{m_{\delta_e}} - C_{m_\alpha}C_{L_{\delta_e}})} \tag{4.52}$$

$$\frac{\partial\delta_e}{\partial C_L} = \frac{-C_{m_\alpha}}{(C_{L_\alpha}C_{m_{\delta_e}} - C_{m_\alpha}C_{L_{\delta_e}})} \tag{4.53}$$

Figure 4.5 shows a graphical solution of Eqn (4.45) for the case of an airplane where the elevator throw has been limited to a range of +10 deg to –20 deg. Note from the upper part of this figure that trim (i.e. $C_m = 0$) occurs only for points A, B, C and D. Transferring points A,B,C and D to the lower part of this figure (also labeled points A, B, C and D) results in the so–called 'trimmed lift coefficient versus angle of attack line'. The slope of this line corresponds to the inverse slope of Eqn (4.52). The intercept with $C_L = 0$ in turn corresponds to Eqn (4.50).

Observe the insert plot in the lower part of Figure 4.5: the slope of that line corresponds to Eqn (4.53) and the intercept of that line with $C_L = 0$ corresponds to Eqn (4.51).

Observe that at Point D in Figure 4.5 the lift coefficient is 1.0. Therefore, in this case, 1.0 is the maximum trimmable lift coefficient! The airplane can not be trimmed at a speed below that corresponding to this lift coefficient value!

Observe that at Point A in Figure 4.5 the lift coefficient is 0.57. Therefore, in this case, 0.57 is the minimum trimmable lift coefficient! The airplane can not be trimmed at a speed above that corresponding to this lift coefficient value!

Two factors are primarily responsible for these findings:

first, the imposed elevator deflection range of +10 deg to –20 deg

and

second, the magnitude of control power which is proportional to the vertical distances between the constant elevator lines in the upper part of Figure 4.5.

During the preliminary design of an airplane, both factors are under the control of the designer and must be selected in such a way that trim is not a limiting factor anywhere in the intended flight envelope of the airplane!

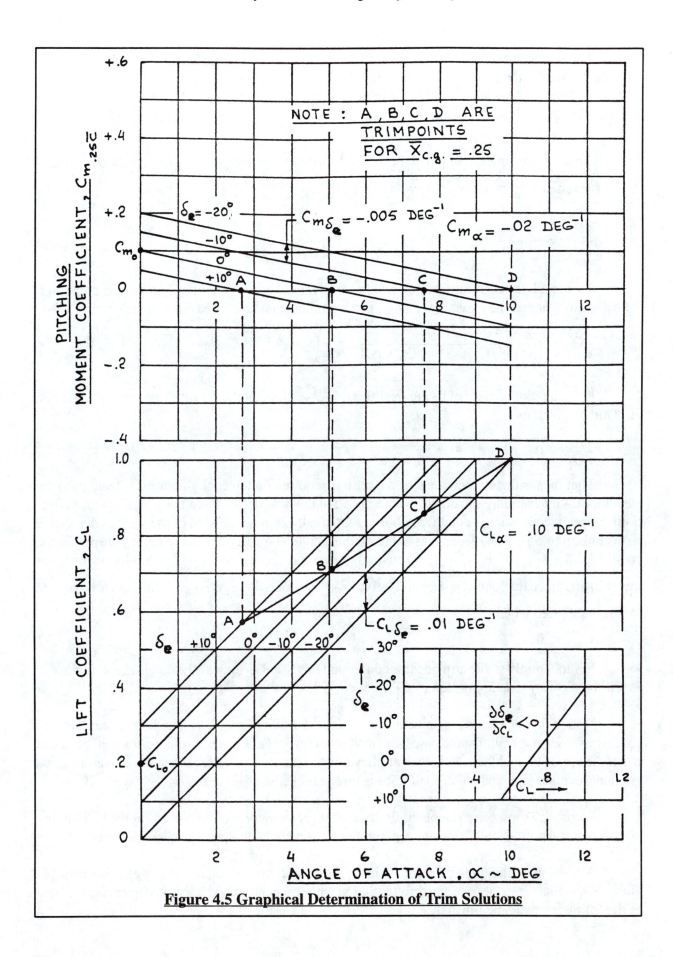

Figure 4.5 Graphical Determination of Trim Solutions

The elevator–versus–lift–coefficient gradient of Eqn (4.53) can be determined in flight test as a function of center of gravity location. By plotting such data as shown in Figure 4.6 it is possible by extrapolation to determine the location of airplane aerodynamic center. This point is also referred to as the 'neutral–point–stick–fixed', or NP_{fix} .

An important interpretation of the derivative of elevator deflection with respect to lift coefficient is given next. Since $C_{L_1} = \dfrac{mg}{\bar{q}_1 S}$ it is seen that:

$$\frac{\partial C_L}{\partial U_1} = -\frac{4W}{\varrho S U_1^3} \tag{4.54}$$

This result is also referred to as the elevator–versus–speed–gradient. As long as compressibility is not a factor, the elevator–versus–speed–gradient can also be expressed as:

$$\frac{\partial \delta_e}{\partial U_1} = (\frac{4W}{\varrho S U_1^3}) \frac{C_{m_\alpha}}{(C_{L_\alpha} C_{m_{\delta_e}} - C_{m_\alpha} C_{L_{\delta_e}})} \tag{4.55}$$

Elevator Speed Gradient

From a point of view of flying qualities it is essential that the elevator–speed gradient of an airplane be positive:

$$\frac{\partial \delta_e}{\partial U_1} > 0 \tag{4.56}$$

That means that to increase speed a push is required on the cockpit controls, leading to the elevator moving trailing edge down. Remember that this was defined as a positive elevator deflection! To see whether or not condition (4.56) is satisfied, examine the sign of the various derivative terms in Eqn (4.55). The reader is asked to do this and to show that for many current airplanes the condition: $|C_{L_\alpha} C_{m_{\delta_e}}| \gg |C_{m_\alpha} C_{L_{\delta_e}}|$ is satisfied. Since the derivative C_{L_α} is generally positive below stall and since the control power derivative $C_{m_{\delta_e}}$ is generally negative, it follows that condition (4.56) is satisfied when:

$$C_{m_\alpha} < 0 \tag{4.57}$$

For inherently stable airplane this condition is satisfied as long as the c.g. is ahead of the a.c. as will be clear by examining Eqn (3.39) in Section 3.1.4.

Notice that when the c.g. is behind the a.c., condition (4.56) is violated. This can be very confusing to a pilot and in some cases can lead to a crash. As a general rule, pilots cannot detect when the c.g. is behind the a.c. However, they most certainly can detect when the elevator–speed gradient reverses sign and condition (4.56) is no longer satisfied.

Figure 4.7 shows an example of flight test data of elevator–versus–speed for the F–27 twin–turboprop transport. Note that as the c.g. moves aft, the elevator–speed gradient decreases.

A problem with Eqn (4.55) is that it is valid only as long as compressibility effects are negligible. When that is not the case any differentiation with respect to speed becomes more complicated as the following example illustrates.

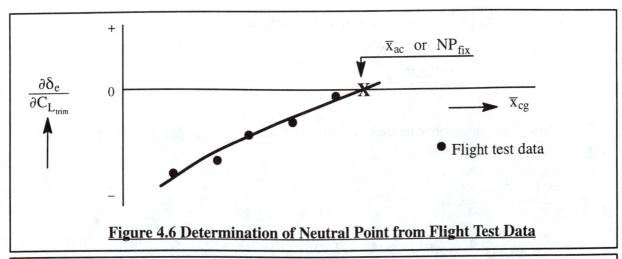

Figure 4.6 Determination of Neutral Point from Flight Test Data

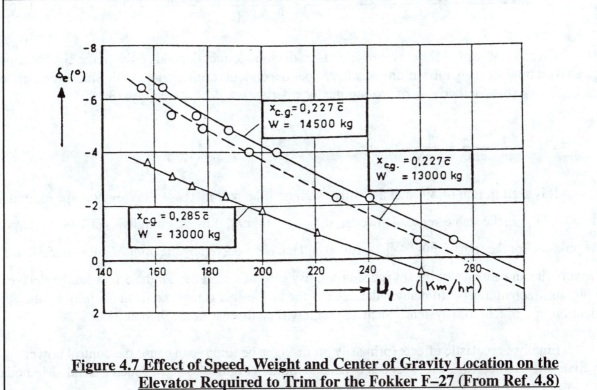

Figure 4.7 Effect of Speed, Weight and Center of Gravity Location on the Elevator Required to Trim for the Fokker F-27 (From Ref. 4.8)

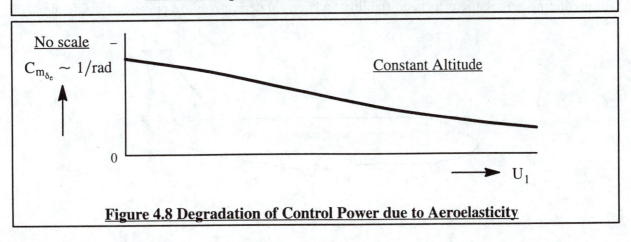

Figure 4.8 Degradation of Control Power due to Aeroelasticity

Consider Eqn (4.44b) and assume that the stabilizer incidence angle, $i_{h_1} \approx 0$ and that the trimmed angle of attack, α_1, is known. The elevator required to trim can now be written as:

$$\delta_{e_{trim}} = \frac{-(C_{m_0} + C_{m_\alpha}\alpha_{trim})}{C_{m_{\delta_e}}} \tag{4.58}$$

Partial differentiation with respect to speed while allowing for Mach number variations now produces the following result:

$$\frac{\partial \delta_{e_{trim}}}{\partial V_P} = \frac{1}{a}\frac{\partial \delta_{e_{trim}}}{\partial M} =$$

$$= -\frac{1}{a}\frac{\left(\dfrac{\partial C_{m_0}}{\partial M} + \dfrac{\partial C_{m_\alpha}}{\partial M}\alpha_{trim} + C_{m_\alpha}\dfrac{\partial \alpha_{trim}}{\partial M}\right)}{C_{m_{\delta_e}}} + \frac{1}{a}\frac{(C_{m_0} + C_{m_\alpha}\alpha_{trim})}{(C_{m_{\delta_e}})^2}\frac{\partial C_{m_{\delta_e}}}{\partial M} \tag{4.59}$$

Clearly, the sign of the elevator–speed–gradient no longer depends only on the c.g. location but also on how strongly the various Mach number dependent terms change with Mach number. It can be shown that another way of writing the tuck derivative, C_{m_u}, (see Eqn (3.125) is:

$$C_{m_u} \approx \frac{1}{a}\left(\frac{\partial C_{m_0}}{\partial M} + \frac{\partial C_{m_\alpha}}{\partial M}\alpha_{trim}\right) \tag{4.60}$$

It is seen in Eqn (4.59) that a positive sign of C_{m_u} will increase the elevator–speed gradient $\partial \delta_e / \partial V_p$ in the stable sense. However, if $C_{m_u} < 0$ and if its magnitude is sufficiently large, it is possible for the sign of $\partial \delta_e / \partial V_p$ to reverse. That is perceived by the pilot as 'tuck–under' and, if severe, it can cause a significant speed upset. By careful airfoil design the effect can be delayed to higher Mach numbers. In many older designs the tuck effect is masked from the pilot by the application of a Mach–trim system. Such a system will be discussed in Chapter 11.

Finally, aeroelastic effects (primarily aft fuselage bending) can cause the control power derivative $C_{m_{\delta_e}}$ to decrease with speed at constant altitude. Figure 4.8 shows such a trend. Methods for predicting aeroelastic effects on stability and control derivatives are presented in Chapter 7.

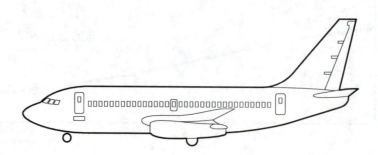

4.2.2 THE AIRPLANE TRIM DIAGRAM

The graphical solution of Eqns (4.44) as depicted in Figure 4.5 changes with a shift in the location of the center of gravity, $\overline{x}_{cg}$. The C_m − versus − α lines on the top graph of Figure 4.5 could, of course, be re–drawn for each new c.g. location. To avoid such a cumbersome process, the following (slightly different) form for Eqns (4.44) will be adopted:

$$C_L = C_{L_0} + C_{L_\alpha}\alpha + C_{L_{i_h}}i_h + C_{L_{\delta_e}}\delta_e \tag{4.61a}$$

$$0 = \overline{C}_{m_0} + \frac{dC_m}{dC_L}C_L + \overline{C}_{m_{i_h}}i_h + \overline{C}_{m_{\delta_e}}\delta_e \tag{4.61b}$$

In this format it has also been assumed that the flight path angle, γ , is very small. Also, the subscript 1 has been dropped even though the solutions are still meant to correspond to a steady state.

The derivative dC_m/dC_L is obtained by dividing C_{m_α} by C_{L_α} . An airplane is said to have a positive static margin, SM, if the derivative $dC_m/dC_L < 0$. As a consequence, by invoking Eqn (3.39):

$$SM = -\frac{dC_m}{dC_L} = -\frac{C_{m_\alpha}}{C_{L_\alpha}} = -(\overline{x}_{cg} - \overline{x}_{ac}) = (\overline{x}_{ac} - \overline{x}_{cg}) \tag{4.62}$$

The static margin therefore is the non–dimensional distance (in fractions of the m.g.c) of the a.c. behind the c.g.

The barred quantities in Eqn (4.61b) have the following meanings:

$$\overline{C}_{m_0} = C_{m_{(C_L = i_h = \delta_e = 0)}} \quad (\text{Remember}: C_{m_0} = C_{m_{(\alpha = i_h = \delta_e = 0)}}) \tag{4.63a}$$

$$\overline{C}_{m_{i_h}} = (\frac{\partial C_m}{\partial i_h})_{(\text{constant } C_L \text{ and constant } \delta_e)} \tag{4.63b}$$

$$\overline{C}_{m_{\delta_e}} = (\frac{\partial C_m}{\partial \delta_e})_{(\text{constant } C_L \text{ and constant } i_h)} \tag{4.63c}$$

The reader is asked to verify that C_{m_0} , $C_{m_{\delta_e}}$ and $C_{m_{i_h}}$ are related to $\overline{C}_{m_0}$, $\overline{C}_{m_{\delta_e}}$ and $\overline{C}_{m_{i_h}}$ in the following manner:

$$\overline{C}_{m_0} = C_{m_0} - \frac{C_{m_\alpha}}{C_{L_\alpha}}C_{L_0} \tag{4.64a}$$

$$\overline{C}_{m_{i_h}} = C_{m_{i_h}} - \frac{C_{m_\alpha}}{C_{L_\alpha}}C_{L_{i_h}} \tag{4.64b}$$

$$\overline{C}_{m_{\delta_e}} = C_{m_{\delta_e}} - \frac{C_{m_\alpha}}{C_{L_\alpha}}C_{L_{\delta_e}} \tag{4.64c}$$

The barred quantities (defined at constant lift coefficient) are equal to the unbarred quantities (defined at constant angle of attack) for airplanes where: $C_{L_0} \approx C_{L_{\delta_e}} \approx C_{L_{i_h}} \approx 0$ is satisfied.

Figure 4.9 presents a graphical solution of Eqns (4.61). Observe that the moment reference point for the pitching moment coefficient is arbitrarily selected to be at the 0.25 mgc point. In the form of Figure 4.9 the graph is referred to as an **airplane trim diagram**. It is useful in determining:

1) whether or not an airplane can be trimmed at **any** center of gravity location with reasonable control surface deflections

2) whether or not tail stall is a limiting factor in trim

These features will now be illustrated with three examples.

Example 1: Trim at any c.g. location

Assume that the following question is asked: What is the range of trimmable lift coefficients with the center of gravity moved forward to the 0.15 mgc point?

To answer this question, consider the fact that if the airplane is flying at a lift coefficient of 1.0 with the c.g. shifted over $(0.25 - 0.15)\overline{c} = 0.10\overline{c}$, an incremental pitching moment coefficient is introduced which is equal to $-(1.0 \text{x} 0.10) = -0.10$. This must be 'trimmed' (cancelled) with an incremental pitching moment coefficient equal to $+0.10$.

Therefore, the new $C_m = 0$ line with the c.g. at the 0.15 m.g.c point is the line so labeled in Figure 4.10. Points A, B', C', D' are used to find the values of trimmed lift coefficients for this c.g. location.

The reader is asked to show that if the c.g. is moved aft to the 0.30 mgc point, a similar line of reasoning can be used to find the $C_m = 0$ line with the c.g. at the 0.30 mgc point. Points A, B", C", D" (only A, B" and C" are shown) are now used to find the corresponding values of trimmed lift coefficients for this c.g. location.

Example 2: The trim triangle

Consider Figures 4.11a and 4.11b.

In Figure 4.11a it is assumed that the stabilizer incidence angle, i_h is the primary control surface. Lines for $C_m = 0$ at forward and at aft center of gravity locations have been drawn in (using the procedure illustrated in Example 1. The trim triangle is defined as the triangular area (shaded grey in Figure 4.11a) bounded by the forward and aft c.g. lines and by the maximum airplane angle of attack line. An airplane must be trimmable inside this triangle with reasonable stabilizer incidence values. That appears to be the case in Figure 4.11a.

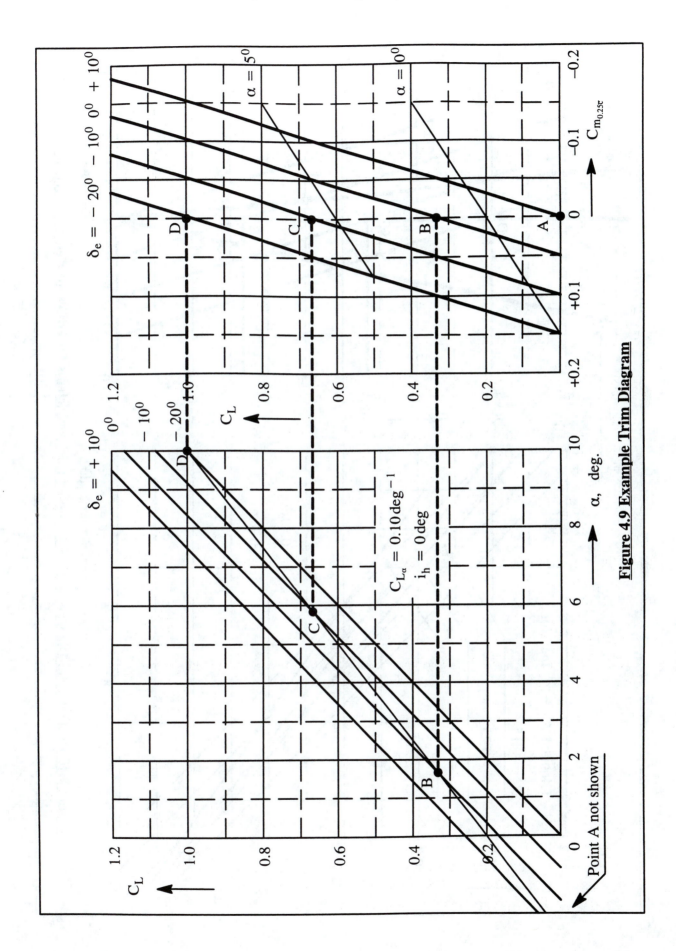

Figure 4.9 Example Trim Diagram

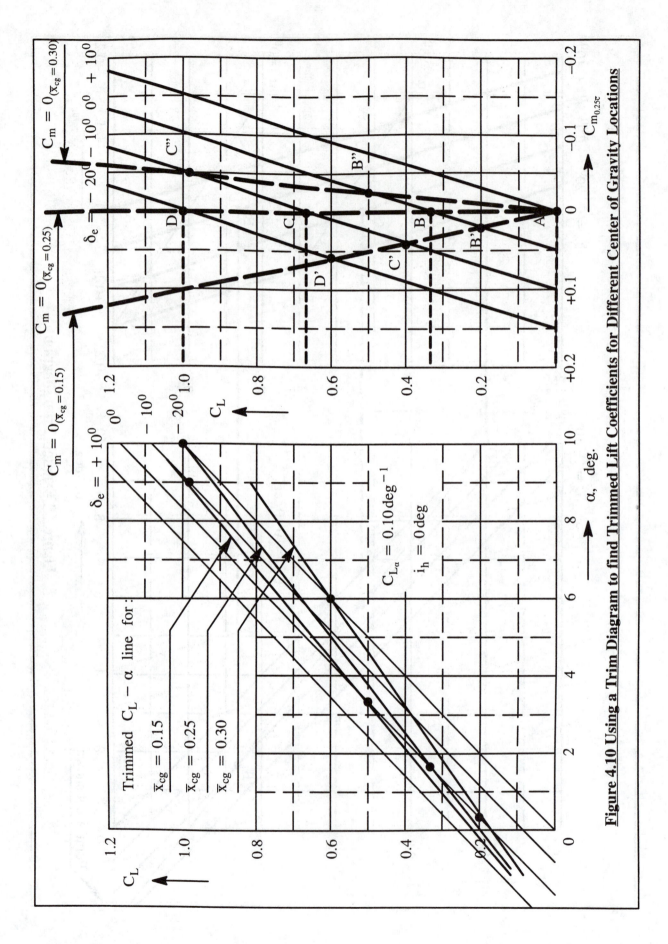

Figure 4.10 Using a Trim Diagram to find Trimmed Lift Coefficients for Different Center of Gravity Locations

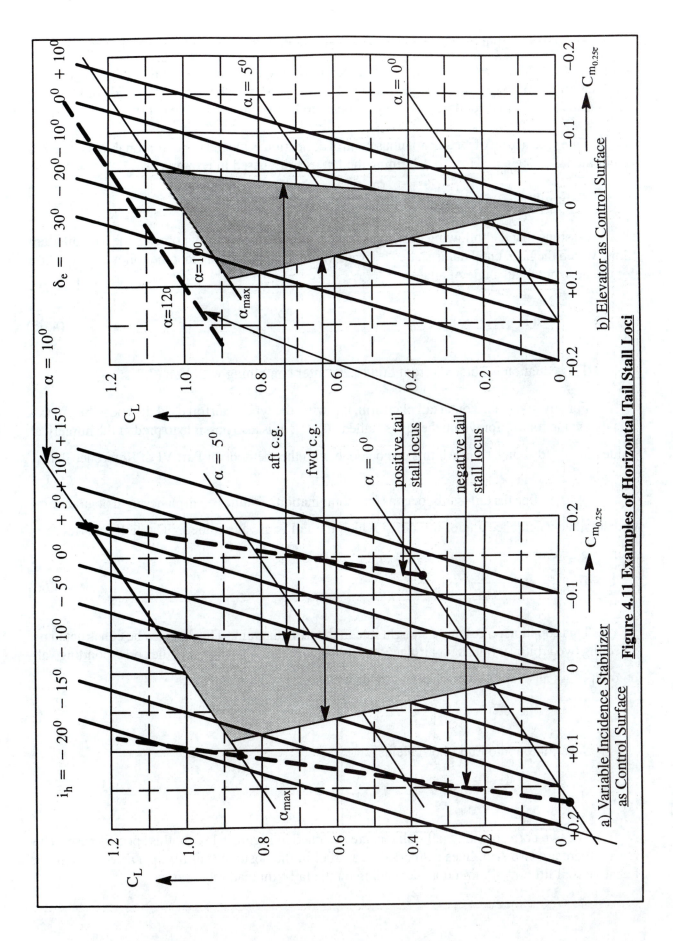

Figure 4.11 Examples of Horizontal Tail Stall Loci

a) Variable Incidence Stabilizer as Control Surface

b) Elevator as Control Surface

In Figure 4.11b it is assumed that the elevator with deflection angle, δ_e, is the primary control surface. Again, lines for forward and aft center of gravity have been drawn in and again, the trim triangle has been identified by grey shading. An airplane must be trimmable inside this triangle with reasonable elevator deflections. That appears to be the case in Figure 4.11b.

One vital aspect of whether or not a control deflection is judged to be 'reasonable' is whether or not the tail is stalled. How to determine the latter is discussed in Example 3.

Example 3: Tail stall as a limiting factor

Assume that the following question is asked: What is the locus of points in the trim diagram along which the horizontal tail is stalled? To answer this question, consider the following equation for the horizontal tail angle of attack:

$$\alpha_h = \alpha(1 - \frac{d\varepsilon}{d\alpha}) + i_h - \varepsilon_0 \tag{4.65}$$

This equation is obtained from Eqn (3.20) after combining with Eqn (3.21).

For any given horizontal tail planform, knowing the type of airfoil used, it is possible to predict that value for α_h for which the tail is stalled: $\alpha_{h_{stall}}$. It is also possible to predict the numerical values for $d\varepsilon/d\alpha$ and ε_0. All this can be done with the methods of Part VI of Reference 4.1.

Next, define the tail–stall–locus as that combination of values of airplane angle of attack, α, and stabilizer incidence angle, i_h, along which the tail is always stalled. The tail–stall–locus is therefore given by:

$$\alpha_{h_{stall}} = \alpha(1 - \frac{d\varepsilon}{d\alpha}) + i_h - \varepsilon_0 \tag{4.66}$$

This equation represents a straight line in the trim diagram. This line can be constructed by selecting two arbitrary values for airplane angle of attack, α, and computing the corresponding value of i_h. As an example, consider a case for which:

$$\alpha_{h_{stall}} = \pm 12 \, deg \ , \quad d\varepsilon/d\alpha = 0.35 \quad \text{and} \quad \varepsilon_0 = 0 \, deg.$$

Substitution into Eqn (4.66) yields:

$$\pm 12 = 0.65\alpha + i_h$$

The two corresponding tail stall loci are sketched in Figure 4.11a for this specific case. The reason there are **two** such lines is, that tails can stall in the positive (tail lift up!) as well as in the negative (tail lift down!) direction, depending on the tail trim load required.

Next, assume that the stabilizer angle is fixed at an angle i_h, and that longitudinal control is accomplished with an elevator. Since the elevator can be thought of as a plain flap attached to the stabilizer, it may be assumed that to a first order of approximation, the tail stall angle is independent of the elevator deflection. This assumption is acceptable up to about 25 degrees of elevator deflection. In that case, Eqn (4.66) may be solved for the airplane angle of attack for which the tail is always stalled: $\alpha_{tail-stall}$. That angle of attack is given by

$$\alpha_{tail-stall} = \frac{(\alpha_{h_{stall}} - i_h + \varepsilon_0)}{(1 - \frac{d\varepsilon}{d\alpha})} \tag{4.67}$$

As an example, consider the case where:

$$\alpha_{h_{stall}} = \pm 12 \deg \ , \ d\varepsilon/d\alpha = 0.35 \ , \ i_h = -4 \deg \ \text{and} \ \varepsilon_0 = 0 \deg$$

The corresponding values for airplane angle of attack for which the tail is stalled are given by: $\alpha_{tail-stall} \approx 12 \deg$ and $\alpha_{tail-stall} \approx 25 \deg$ respectively. Figure 4.11b shows only the negative tail stall locus because the positive locus is outside the diagram. Observe that the tail–stall loci in this case are merely constant airplane angle of attack lines. The location of these lines depends strongly on the fixed stabilizer incidence angle as seen from Eqn (4.67).

The triangular shapes shown in Figure 4.11 were referred to as trim triangles. Their boundaries were formed by three lines:

1) locus of zero pitching moment coefficient at forward c.g. (left boundary)

2) locus of zero pitching moment coefficient at aft c.g. (right boundary)

3) maximum allowable airplane angle of attack locus ($\alpha = 10 \deg$)

The maximum airplane angle of attack locus is formed EITHER by the airplane stall angle of attack locus OR by that angle of attack locus along which the airplane pitching moment becomes unmanageable. The meaning of this will be discussed in Sub–section 4.2.3.

As indicated under Example 3, tail stall **should not occur within** the so–called trim triangle. This trim–triangle is identified in Figure 4.11 by the filled–in area. If tail stall is predicted to occur within the trim–triangle a design 'fix' is required. Three examples of potential design 'fixes' which move the location of tail–stall loci are:

a) Use of a negatively cambered airfoil in the tail.

This has the effect of increasing the negative magnitude of $\alpha_{h_{stall}}$ while decreasing the positive magnitude of $\alpha_{h_{stall}}$. Many current jet transports employ negatively cambered tails for this reason.

b) Use of a fixed slot in the leading edge of the tail.

This has the effect of increasing the negative magnitude of $\alpha_{h_{stall}}$ while decreasing the positive magnitude of $\alpha_{h_{stall}}$. The Cessna Cardinal is an example of an airplane utilizing this type of 'fix'.

c) Use of leading edge blowing.

This has the effect of increasing the negative magnitude of $\alpha_{h_{stall}}$ while decreasing the positive magnitude of $\alpha_{h_{stall}}$. This type of 'fix' was used on several early F–4 fighters.

The trim diagrams discussed so–far suggest that the relationship between lift–coefficient, pitching–moment–coefficient and angle–of–attack is a linear one. This does not correspond to reality in most cases. The effect of nonlinear relations is briefly discussed in Sub–section 4.2.3.

All trim diagram examples discussed in this section, apply only to airplanes with conventional (i.e. tail–aft) configurations. Examples of trim diagrams for non–conventional airplanes are shown on page 354 of Part VI of Reference 4.5. Methods for constructing such trim diagrams are also contained in Part VI of Reference 4.5. Several important aspects of trim associated with pure–canard and with three–surface airplanes are discussed in Section 4.4.

4.2.3 STABLE AND UNSTABLE PITCH BREAKS

When flow separation starts to occur (usually first on the top surface of the inboard wing) the assumed linear relations between lift–coefficient, pitching–moment–coefficient and angle–of–attack no longer apply. Figure 4.12 shows an example of typical non–linear effects.

Note that when the pitching moment lines break to the right (i.e airplane nose down), this is called a 'stable pitch break'. Conversely, when the pitching moment lines break to the left (i.e airplane nose up), this is called an 'unstable pitch break'. The maximum allowable angle–of–attack of an airplane with an unstable pitch break can be significantly less than that of an airplane with a stable pitch break. The difference in α_{max} depends on pitch controllability in that region.

The reader should be aware of the fact that lower α_{max} values also imply higher reference speeds and therefore longer field–lengths. That is because performance reference speeds are all based on the higher of the stall speed or that minimum speed below which the airplane becomes uncontrollable.

Whether or not an airplane has a stable or an unstable pitch break and whether or not the airplane remains controllable in case of an unstable pitch break is strongly dependent on the details of the configuration design of the airplane. Part III of Reference 4.5 (pages 263–270) contains more detailed discussions of these effects.

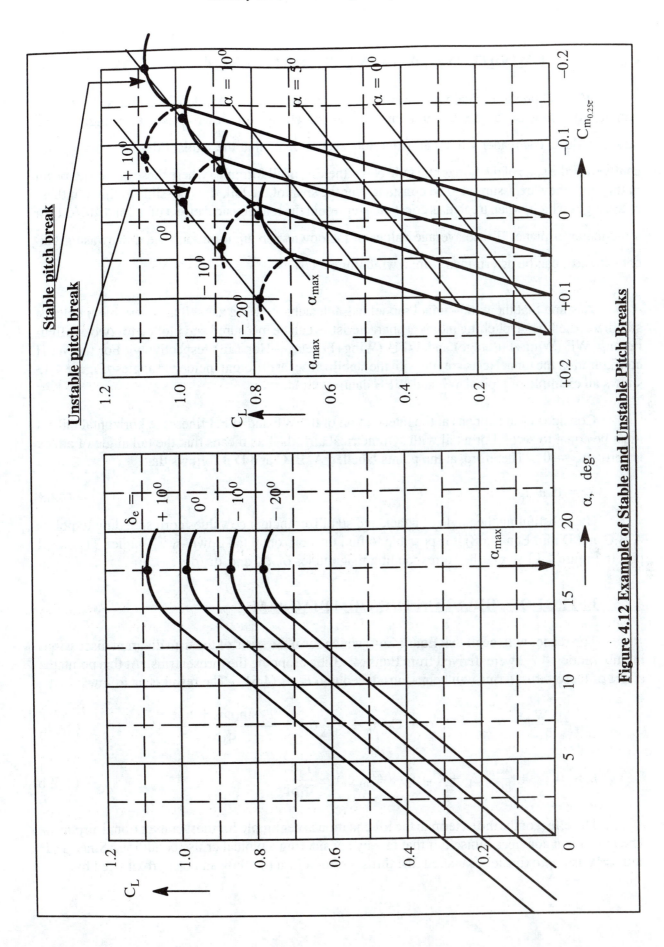

Figure 4.12 Example of Stable and Unstable Pitch Breaks

4.2.4   USE OF WINDTUNNEL DATA IN DETERMINING $d\varepsilon/d\alpha$

Many expressions dealing with airplane lift, pitching moment and longitudinal stability contain the down–wash angle, ε, and /or the rate of change of down–wash with angle of attack, $d\varepsilon/d\alpha$. The reader will recall from Sub–section 2.5.5 that these quantities can vary significantly over the span of the horizontal tail. Nevertheless, in all formulas where these quantities occur in this text, they are assumed to be constant over the span of the tail. It is possible to think of these as averages which, when treated as constants, represent the real physical effect of ε and $d\varepsilon/d\alpha$ for a particular airplane. These average values of the downwash angle, ε and the downwash gradient, $d\varepsilon/d\alpha$, can be determined from a wind–tunnel test.

Assume that the wind–tunnel model has a detachable wing as well as a variable incidence stabilizer, the lift and pitching moment characteristics can be measured and plotted for two configurations: WF (Wing+Fuselage) and WFH (Wing+Fuselage+Hor.Tail) respectively. For the WFH configuration the tunnel tests are run with the stabilizer set at different incidence angles. Figure 4.13 shows an example of typical WF and WFH data.

Consider what happens at the intersection of the WF and WFH lines: the horizontal tail lift must be equal to zero! For a tail with symmetrical airfoils, this means that the tail angle of attack is zero: $\alpha_h = 0$. Therefore, at the points labelled A, B, C and D it follows that:

$$\varepsilon = \alpha + i_h \qquad (4.68)$$

By substituting the angle of attack and stabilizer incidence values corresponding to points A,B,C and D into Eqn (4.68) it is possible to find the horizontal tail down–wash angle. The insert plot in Figure 4.13 shows the corresponding magnitudes of ε_0 and $d\varepsilon/d\alpha$.

4.2.5   EFFECT OF THRUST ON THE TRIM DIAGRAM

The reader will recall that Eqns (4.44) which form the basis of the trim diagram discussions in Sub–section 4.2.2 were derived from Eqns (4.43) by dropping the thrust terms. At this point, the effect of these thrust terms will be re–introduced into Eqns (4.61). The result is as follows:

$$C_L = \frac{W}{\overline{q}_1 S} = (C_{L_0} + C_{L_\alpha}\alpha + C_{L_{i_h}}i_h + C_{L_{\delta_e}}\delta_e) + \frac{T_1 \sin(\phi_T + \alpha_1)}{\overline{q}_1 S} \qquad (4.69a)$$

$$0 = (\overline{C}_{m_0} + \frac{dC_m}{dC_L}C_L + \overline{C}_{m_{i_h}}i_h + \overline{C}_{m_{\delta_e}}\delta_e) - \frac{T_1 d_T}{\overline{q}_1 S\overline{c}} \qquad (4.69b)$$

The effect of the thrust term in the lift equation is negligible for most conventional airplanes. The reader can convince himself of that fact by considering a typical cruise condition. Since T=D and L=W is approximately satisfied, the thrust–term in Eqn (4.69a) can be approximated by:

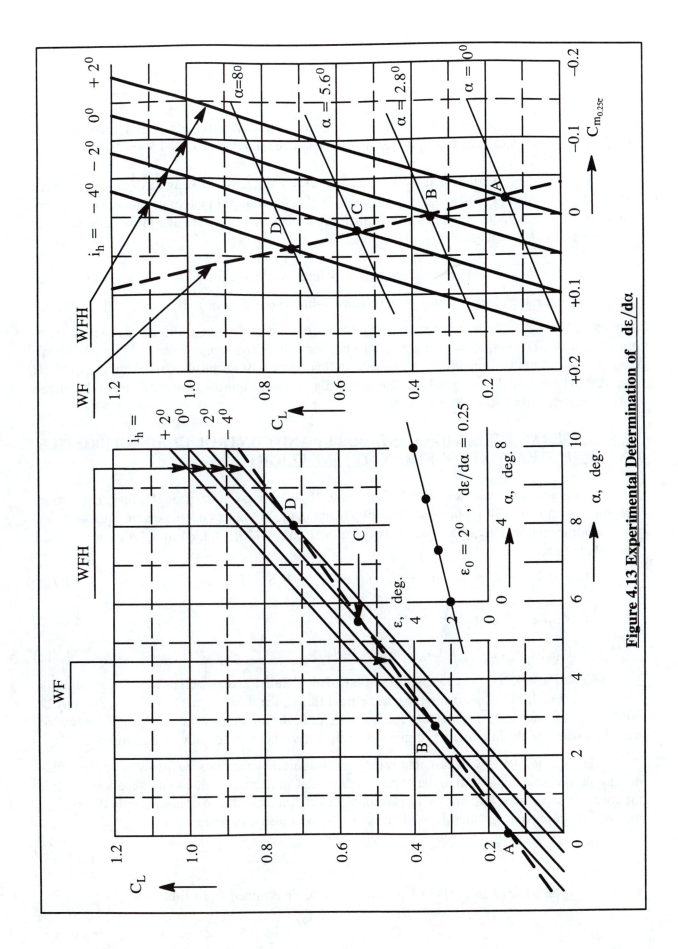

Figure 4.13 Experimental Determination of $d\varepsilon/d\alpha$

$$\frac{T_1 \sin(\phi_T + \alpha_1)}{\bar{q}_1 S} \approx \frac{1}{L/D} \sin(\phi_T + \alpha_1) \tag{4.70}$$

Assuming a typical cruise lift–to–drag ratio of 15 and a value of nine degrees for the sum of thrust inclination angle and angle of attack, the thrust term can be thought of as a 'change' in lift coefficient of 0.01. Compared to typical cruise lift coefficient ranges of $0.3 - 0.5$, this is quite small!

If an airplane is cruising at a lift coefficient of 0.5 and a lift–to–drag ratio of 15, while the ratio of thrust moment arm to m.g.c. is assumed to be 0.3, the change in pitching moment coefficient due to the thrust moment effect is 0.01. In many instances this small change in pitching moment coefficient can also be neglected.

Figure 4.14 shows an example of two trim diagrams: one with $d_T = 0$ (thrust–line passes through the c.g.), the other with $d_T = 3$ ft (thrust–line above the c.g.). Because, with the thrust-line above the c.g., a nose–down moment is generated, more negative stabilizer deflection is required to trim. The nonlinear character of the constant–stabilizer–angle lines in Figure 4.14b are caused by the fact that thrust is not a constant in this figure. At each lift coefficient, the thrust is assumed to be adjusted to satisfy T=D. Both trim diagrams of Figure 4.14 were generated with the AAA program described in Appendix A..

4.2.6 LATERAL–DIRECTIONAL STABILITY AND CONTROL CHARACTERISTICS FOR STEADY STATE, STRAIGHT LINE FLIGHT

On page 198 it was seen that by assuming flight at a given bank angle, the steady state, straight line equations of motion split into two mathematically independent sets of equations. At this point, the lateral directional equations of motion, Eqns (4.42b), (4.42d) and (4.42f) are recalled and re–numbered:

$$- mg\sin\phi_1 \cos\gamma_1 = (C_{y_\beta}\beta_1 + C_{y_{\delta_a}}\delta_{a_1} + C_{y_{\delta_r}}\delta_{r_1})\bar{q}_1 S + F_{y_{T_1}} \tag{4.71a}$$

$$0 = (C_{l_\beta}\beta_1 + C_{l_{\delta_a}}\delta_{a_1} + C_{l_{\delta_r}}\delta_{r_1})\bar{q}_1 Sb + L_{T_1} \tag{4.71b}$$

$$0 = (C_{n_\beta}\beta_1 + C_{n_{\delta_a}}\delta_{a_1} + C_{n_{\delta_r}}\delta_{r_1})\bar{q}_1 Sb + N_{T_1} \tag{4.71c}$$

Equations (4.71) apply to flight situations with symmetrical as well as asymmetrical thrust (or power). For flight situations with symmetrical thrust, the thrust terms in Eqns (4.71) may be omitted. The reader should be aware of the fact, that for flight situations with one engine inoperative, a drag increase on the inoperative engine side usually results in an added yawing moment, ΔN_{D_1}.

This additional yawing moment is physically caused by the drag due to a stopped or wind–milling propeller, a wind–milling jet engine and/or inlet spillage drag due to an expelled shock in the case of a supersonic airplane. The additional yawing moment due to drag evidently depends on the type of propulsive installation used. It is usually acceptable to write:

$$N_{T_1} + \Delta N_{D_1} \approx (F_{OEI})N_{T_1} \tag{4.72}$$

where: F_{OEI} is a factor, larger than 1.0, which may be determined from Table 4.2.

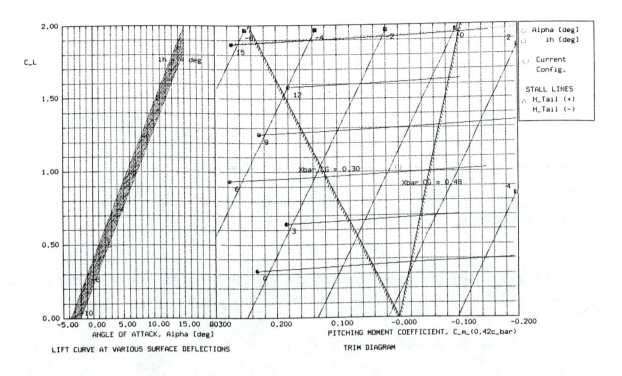

$$d_T = 0 \text{ ft}$$

Figure 4.14a Trim Diagram Without Effect of Thrust

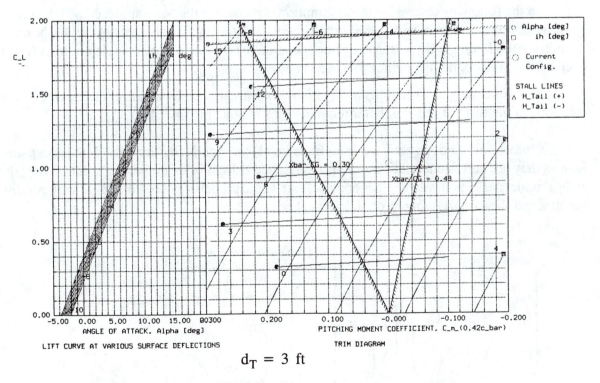

$$d_T = 3 \text{ ft}$$

Figure 4.14b Trim Diagram Including Effect of Thrust

Table 4.2 Effect of the Propulsive Installation on F_{OEI} Eqn (4.72)

Type of Powerplant	Fixed Pitch	Variable Pitch	Low BPR	High BPR
F_{OEI}	1.25	1.10	1.15	1.25

For a given thrust level, T, and for a given flight path angle, γ, (both as used in the longitudinal equations) the following variables remain in Eqns (4.71):

$$\phi , \quad \beta , \quad \delta_a \text{ and } \delta_r$$

Since there are four variables and only three equations, one needs to be specified. This is normally done by selecting one the following possibilities:

$$\text{select}: \quad \phi \text{ and solve for } \beta , \quad \delta_a \text{ and } \delta_r$$

or $\qquad \text{select}: \quad \beta \text{ and solve for } \phi , \quad \delta_a \text{ and } \delta_r$

or $\qquad \text{select}: \quad \delta_a \text{ and solve for } \phi , \quad \beta \text{ and } \delta_r$

or $\qquad \text{select}: \quad \delta_r \text{ and solve for } \phi , \quad \beta \text{ and } \delta_a$

In the following discussion the assumption is made that the bank angle, ϕ, will be selected. This case is important because it is specifically required in the regulations that an airplane be controllable in a straight line flight with one engine inoperative (OEI) and a bank angle not to exceed five degrees (into the operating engine) for speeds above 1.2 $F_{S_{TO}}$.

It is customary to write Eqns (4.71) in matrix format: as shown in Eqn (4.73) and to cast its solutions in the form of ratios of determinants. This is done in Table 4.3.

Numerical solutions obtained from Eqns (4.74) through (4.76) are considered acceptable as long as they are consistent with conditions of attached flow. For example, if a solution for aileron and/or rudder deflection is 25 degrees or more, that would probably not be consistent with conditions for attached flow on the wing or on the vertical tail.

$$\begin{bmatrix} C_{y_\beta} & C_{y_{\delta_a}} & C_{y_{\delta_r}} \\ C_{l_\beta} & C_{l_{\delta_a}} & C_{l_{\delta_r}} \\ C_{n_\beta} & C_{n_{\delta_a}} & C_{n_{\delta_r}} \end{bmatrix} \begin{Bmatrix} \beta \\ \delta_a \\ \delta_r \end{Bmatrix} = \begin{Bmatrix} \dfrac{-(mg\sin\phi\cos\gamma + F_{y_{T_1}})}{\overline{q}_1 S} \\[2ex] \dfrac{-L_{T_1}}{\overline{q}_1 Sb} \\[2ex] \dfrac{-N_{T_1} - \Delta N_{D_1}}{\overline{q}_1 Sb} \end{Bmatrix} \qquad (4.73)$$

Table 4.3 Solutions for the Steady State Lateral–Directional Equations of Motion

$$\beta_1 = \frac{\begin{vmatrix} \dfrac{-(mg\sin\phi\cos\gamma + F_{y_{T_1}})}{\overline{q}_1 S} & C_{y_{\delta_a}} & C_{y_{\delta_r}} \\[2em] \dfrac{-L_{T_1}}{\overline{q}_1 Sb} & C_{l_{\delta_a}} & C_{l_{\delta_r}} \\[2em] \dfrac{-N_{T_1} - \Delta N_{D_1}}{\overline{q}_1 Sb} & C_{n_{\delta_a}} & C_{n_{\delta_r}} \end{vmatrix}}{\Delta} \tag{4.74}$$

$$\delta_{a_1} = \frac{\begin{vmatrix} C_{y_\beta} & \dfrac{-(mg\sin\phi\cos\gamma + F_{y_{T_1}})}{\overline{q}_1 S} & C_{y_{\delta_r}} \\[2em] C_{l_\beta} & \dfrac{-L_{T_1}}{\overline{q}_1 Sb} & C_{l_{\delta_r}} \\[2em] C_{n_\beta} & \dfrac{-N_{T_1} - \Delta N_{D_1}}{\overline{q}_1 Sb} & C_{n_{\delta_r}} \end{vmatrix}}{\Delta} \tag{4.75}$$

$$\delta_{a_1} = \frac{\begin{vmatrix} C_{y_\beta} & C_{y_{\delta_a}} & \dfrac{-(mg\sin\phi\cos\gamma + F_{y_{T_1}})}{\overline{q}_1 S} \\[2em] C_{l_\beta} & C_{l_{\delta_a}} & \dfrac{-L_{T_1}}{\overline{q}_1 Sb} \\[2em] C_{n_\beta} & C_{n_{\delta_a}} & \dfrac{-N_{T_1} - \Delta N_{D_1}}{\overline{q}_1 Sb} \end{vmatrix}}{\Delta} \tag{4.76}$$

$$\text{where:} \quad \Delta = \begin{vmatrix} C_{y_\beta} & C_{y_{\delta_a}} & C_{y_{\delta_r}} \\ C_{l_\beta} & C_{l_{\delta_a}} & C_{l_{\delta_r}} \\ C_{n_\beta} & C_{n_{\delta_a}} & C_{n_{\delta_r}} \end{vmatrix} \tag{4.77}$$

Another consideration in any existing airplane is the fact that all control surfaces have limited deflection ranges imposed by 'hard' mechanical stops.

A problem with the solutions given in Table 4.3 is that they are not very transparent in identifying 'design drivers'. To determine which aspects of a design are driven by OEI considerations, it is instructive to examine simplified forms of Eqn (4.73).

As a first example, consider the moment equilibrium about the Z–axis only, as represented by Eqn (4.71c), but rewritten as follows:

$$C_{n_\beta}\beta + C_{n_{\delta_r}}\delta_r + \frac{N_{T_1} + \Delta N_{D_1}}{\bar{q}_1 Sb} = 0 \tag{4.78}$$

This equation can be solved for the amount of rudder deflection required to cope with a one–engine–inoperative (OEI) flight condition:

$$\delta_r = \frac{-C_{n_\beta}\beta - \dfrac{N_{T_1} + \Delta N_{D_1}}{\bar{q}_1 Sb}}{C_{n_{\delta_r}}} \tag{4.79}$$

Figure 4.15 shows an unscaled plot of how the rudder deflection varies with speed and with sideslip. Particularly at low speed, it is desirable to fly as close to zero sideslip angle as possible because otherwise the drag of the airplane could compromise the ability to climb out on the remaining engine(s). Assuming the sideslip angle to be negligible:

$$\delta_r = -\left(\frac{N_{T_1} + \Delta N_{D_1}}{C_{n_{\delta_r}}\bar{q}_1 Sb}\right) \tag{4.80}$$

It is seen from Eqn (4.80) that as the speed of the airplane decreases, the amount of rudder deflection required to control the OEI flight situation becomes very large. Conventional rudders should not be deflected more than about 25 degrees or the vertical tail may stall. If the maximum rudder deflection available is designated to be $\delta_{r_{max}}$, the minimum speed at which the OEI condition can be controlled is:

$$V_{mc} = \sqrt{\frac{2(N_{T_1} + \Delta N_{D_1})}{\varrho C_{n_{\delta_r}}\delta_{r_{max}}\bar{q}_1 Sb}} \tag{4.81}$$

The regulations of References 4.1 through 4.4 require that this minimum control speed be larger than the stall speed of the airplane in that configuration:

$$V_{mc} \leq 1.2 V_{s_{OEI}} \quad (FAR\ 23\ and\ FAR\ 25)$$

$$V_{mc} \leq highest\ of\ 1.1V_s\ or\ V_s + 10\ keas\ (Mil - F - 8785C) \tag{4.82}$$

For a given combination of takeoff speed, engine thrust and engine y–moment arm, the ability to control the OEI flight condition is dependent on the magnitude of the rudder control power

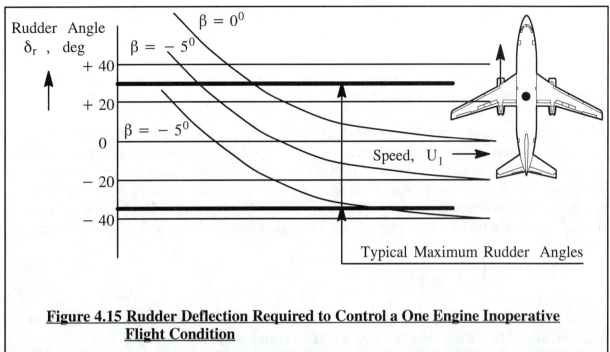

Figure 4.15 Rudder Deflection Required to Control a One Engine Inoperative Flight Condition

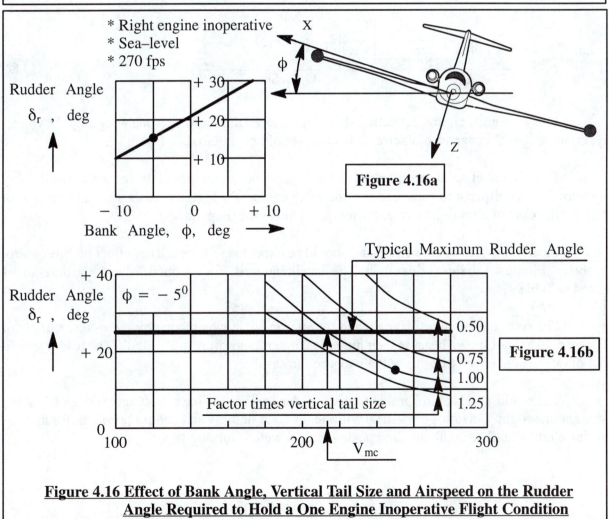

Figure 4.16 Effect of Bank Angle, Vertical Tail Size and Airspeed on the Rudder Angle Required to Hold a One Engine Inoperative Flight Condition

derivative $C_{n_{\delta_r}}$. Equation (3.87) shows which design aspects of the vertical tail and rudder affect this derivative.

It should be obvious that to attempt flight in a multi–engine airplane at speeds below the minimum control speed is asking for trouble.

After an engine failure has occurred, a certain amount of time must be allowed to elapse before control action is taken. The reason for this is the fact that it takes some time before a pilot has recognized which engine has failed and then it takes some time to initiate the appropriate action. This amount of time is typically one to two seconds. During that time the airplane will begin to yaw and, because of its dihedral effect, it will also begin to roll. Returning to Eqn (4.78) and assuming no pilot action, the maximum amount of sideslip angle which will be reached is found from:

$$\beta_{max} = -\left(\frac{N_{T_1} + \Delta N_{D_1}}{C_{n_\beta}\bar{q}_1 Sb}\right) \tag{4.83}$$

Next, consider the equilibrium about the X–axis. To keep the wings level, the amount of required aileron deflection is found from Eqns (4.73) and (4.83) as:

$$\delta_a = \frac{-C_{l_\beta}\beta_{max} - \dfrac{L_{T_1}}{\bar{q}_1 Sb}}{C_{l_{\delta_a}}} = \frac{\left\{\dfrac{C_{l_\beta}}{C_{n_\beta}}(N_{T_1} + \Delta N_{D_1}) - L_{T_1}\right\}}{C_{l_{\delta_a}}\bar{q}_1 Sb} \tag{4.84}$$

This amount of aileron deflection should not exceed that for which one wing stalls. Typically, no more than 25 degrees of aileron deflection should be required.

The amount of rudder required to hold an engine–out condition can be reduced considerably by allowing the airplane to bank into the operating engine(s). Figure 4.16a shows an example of this for the case of a small jet airplane with the right engine inoperative.

Clearly, the size of the vertical tail should be expected to have a large effect on this control problem. Figure 4.16b shows this effect. The data in Figure 4.16 were obtained with the derivatives listed in Table 4.4.

The solutions for sideslip angle and for aileron angle which correspond to the example of Figure 4.16 are not shown because their numerical magnitudes were quite small. The reader should not draw the conclusion that this will always be the case!

The stability and control problems discussed in this Section have dealt only with steady state, straight line flight. Section 4.3 will deal with steady state stability and control problems for maneuvering flight situations: pull–up (and push–over) as well as turning flight.

Table 4.4 Data Required to Produce Figures 4.16a and 4.16b

a) Flight Condition and Derivative Data Required to Produce Figure 4.16a:

$W = 8,750$ lbs $\varrho = 0.002378$ slugs/ft^3 (S.L.) $U_1 = 270$ fps $S = 253$ ft^2

$L_{T_1} = 1682$ ftlbs $N_{T_1} = 10,940$ ftlbs $\Delta N_{D_1} = 1,000$ ftlbs   'b = 38 ft

$C_{y_\beta} = -0.0105$ deg^{-1} $C_{y_{\delta_a}} = 0$ deg^{-1} $C_{y_{\delta_r}} = +0.0021$ deg^{-1}

$C_{l_\beta} = -0.0029$ deg^{-1} $C_{l_{\delta_a}} = +0.0024$ deg^{-1} $C_{l_{\delta_r}} = +0.0002$ deg^{-1}

$C_{n_\beta} = +0.0018$ deg^{-1} $C_{n_{\delta_a}} = +0.0005$ deg^{-1} $C_{n_{\delta_r}} = -0.0010$ deg^{-1}

b) Flight Condition and Derivative Data Required to Produce Figure 4.16b:

Relative Vertical Tail Size	C_{n_β} deg^{-1}	$C_{y_{\delta_r}}$ deg^{-1}	$C_{l_{\delta_r}}$ deg^{-1}	$C_{n_{\delta_r}}$ deg^{-1}
0.50	–0.00010	+0.00105	–0.00048	+0.00008
0.75	–0.00085	+0.00158	–0.00072	+0.00011
1.00	+0.00180	+0.00210	–0.00096	+0.00015
1.25	+0.00275	+0.00263	–0.00120	+0.00019

Note: For the wing–fuselage: $C_{n_{\beta_{WF}}} = -0.0020$ deg^{-1} is used with all tail sizes

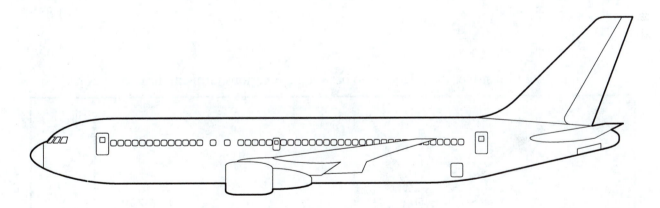

4.3 STABILITY AND CONTROL CHARACTERISTICS FOR STEADY STATE, MANEUVERING FLIGHT

In transitioning from one steady state flight condition to another and in maneuvering to change flight path or to avoid traffic, an airplane must be able to perform steady turning maneuvers as well as pull–up and push–over maneuvers. The objective of this section is to develop mathematical models for such maneuvers and to discuss their application. The material is organized as follows:

4.3.1. Stability and Control for Steady State Turning Flight

4.3.2. Stability and Control for Steady Symmetrical Pull–ups (and Push–overs)

4.3.1 STABILITY AND CONTROL CHARACTERISTICS FOR STEADY STATE, TURNING FLIGHT

The general, steady state equations of motion, including the effect of angular rates, were derived in Chapter 1 as Eqns (1.55) and (1.56). These equations were written in the body fixed axis system. By using the stability axis system as defined in Chapter 3 (Figure 3.1) it is found that the component of velocity, W_1, disappears: $W_{1_s} = 0$. It will be assumed that the turning maneuver takes places in a horizontal plane. The consequence of this assumption is that the stability X–axis will lie in the same horizontal plane. Since the rate–of–turn vector $\vec{\psi}_1$ is perpendicular to this horizontal plane (See Figure 1.8) it follows that the steady state roll rate, P_1, also vanishes: $P_{1_s} = 0$. The kinematic equations (1.57) written in stability axes (but without the subscript 's') now yield:

$$P_1 = 0 \tag{4.85a}$$

$$Q_1 = \dot{\psi}_1 \sin\phi_1 \tag{4.85b}$$

$$R_1 = \dot{\psi}_1 \cos\phi_1 \tag{4.85c}$$

Figure 4.17 illustrates the relationship between the various terms in these equations.

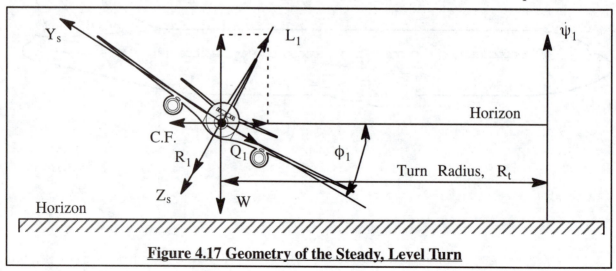

Figure 4.17 Geometry of the Steady, Level Turn

By combining Eqns (1.55) and (1.56) with the aerodynamic and thrust force and moment equations (3.46) and (3.95), while at the same time observing that in this flight condition $\theta_1 = \gamma_1 = 0$ is satisfied, the equations of motion take the following form:

$$0 = -(C_{D_0} + C_{D_\alpha}\alpha_1 + C_{D_{i_h}}i_{h_1} + C_{D_{\delta_e}}\delta_{e_1})\overline{q}_1 S + T_1 \cos(\phi_T + \alpha_1) \tag{4.86a}$$

$$mU_1 R_1 - mg\sin\phi_1 = (C_{y_\beta}\beta_1 + C_{Y_r}\frac{R_1 b}{2U_1} + C_{y_{\delta_a}}\delta_{a_1} + C_{y_{\delta_r}}\delta_{r_1})\overline{q}_1 S \tag{4.86b}$$

$$-mU_1 Q_1 - mg\cos\phi_1 = -(C_{L_0} + C_{L_\alpha}\alpha_1 + C_{L_q}\frac{Q_1\overline{c}}{2U_1} + C_{L_{i_h}}i_{h_1} + C_{L_{\delta_e}}\delta_{e_1})\overline{q}_1 S +$$
$$-T_1\sin(\phi_T + \alpha_1) \tag{4.86c}$$

$$(I_{zz} - I_{yy})R_1 Q_1 = (C_{l_\beta}\beta_1 + C_{l_r}\frac{R_1 b}{2U_1} + C_{l_{\delta_a}}\delta_{a_1} + C_{l_{\delta_r}}\delta_{r_1})\overline{q}_1 Sb \tag{4.86d}$$

$$-I_{xz}R_1^2 = (C_{m_0} + C_{m_\alpha}\alpha_1 + C_{m_q}\frac{Q_1\overline{c}}{2U_1} + C_{m_{i_h}}i_{h_1} + C_{m_{\delta_e}}\delta_{e_1})\overline{q}_1 S\overline{c} \tag{4.86e}$$

$$I_{xz}Q_1 R_1 = (C_{n_\beta}\beta_1 + C_{n_r}\frac{R_1 b}{2U_1} + C_{n_{\delta_a}}\delta_{a_1} + C_{n_{\delta_r}}\delta_{r_1})\overline{q}_1 Sb \tag{4.86f}$$

Note the inclusion of a number of rate derivative forces and moments. This accounts for the fact that in a steady level turn the pitch rate and the yaw rate are not zero: see Eqns (4.85). Therefore, the corresponding aerodynamic forces and moments must be included. It has been assumed in these equations that there is no asymmetric thrust and that the net thrust line passes through the center of gravity: $M_{T_1} = L_{T_1} = N_{T_1} = F_{T_{y_1}} = 0$.

It will be observed, that these six equations are all coupled together because of the various angular rate terms. Assuming that the dynamic pressure, q_1, is known, these six equations have the following ten unknowns:

$$\phi_1, \quad \alpha_1, \quad \beta_1, \quad \delta_{a_1}, \quad i_{h_1}, \quad \delta_{e_1}, \quad \delta_{r_1}, \quad Q_1, \quad R_1, \quad \text{and } T_1$$

Since there are only six equations, three of these variable will have to be specified before the others can be solved for. In most applications this is done by specifying the steady state thrust, T_1, and the stabilizer incidence angle, i_{h_1}. Since the steady state pitch rate and the steady state yaw rate, R_1, are related to the steady state bank angle, $\vec{\phi}_1$, there are now six equations left, with six variables. These equations can therefore be solved.

It is instructive to analyze the relationship between Q_1, R_1 and $\vec{\phi}_1$. This is accomplished by referring to Figure 4.17 and observing that the following equilibrium conditions must hold:

$$\text{C.F.} = mR_t\dot{\psi}_1^{\,2} = L\sin\phi_1 \tag{4.87a}$$

$$W = L\cos\phi_1 \tag{4.87b}$$

Observe that the following kinematic relationship must also be satisfied:

$$U_1 = R_t\dot{\psi}_1 \tag{4.88}$$

From equations (4.87) and (4.88) it follows that the turn radius can be written as:

$$R_t = \frac{U_1^{\,2}\tan\phi_1}{g} \tag{4.89}$$

The corresponding turn rate, $\vec{\dot{\psi}}_1$, is found by eliminating the turn radius from Eqns (4.88) and (4.89). This yields:

$$\dot{\psi}_1 = \frac{g\tan\phi_1}{U_1} \tag{4.90}$$

The turn radius and the turn rate of a military airplane are important performance parameters. For civilian airplanes which must operate into and out of areas with physical obstructions (box canyons are one example!) the turn radius can be a matter of life or death.

At this point, the concept of load factor, n is introduced:

$$L = nW \tag{4.91}$$

By referring to Equation (4.87b) it is seen that:

$$n = 1/\cos\phi_1 \tag{4.92}$$

By combining Eqns (4.85b,c with Eqns (4.90) and (4.91) it can be shown that:

$$Q_1 = \frac{g\sin^2\phi_1}{U_1\cos\phi_1} = \frac{g}{U_1}\left(n - \frac{1}{n}\right) \tag{4.93}$$

and

$$R_1 = \frac{g\sin\phi_1}{U_1} = \frac{g}{nU_1}\sqrt{n^2 - 1} \tag{4.94}$$

The steady pitch and yaw rate in this type of turning maneuver are therefore simple functions of the load factor, n.

Another important property which can be deduced is that the left hand side of Eqn (4.86b) is zero because:

$$mU_1R_1 = \frac{g\sin\phi_1}{U_1} \tag{4.95}$$

This can be seen from Eqn (4.94). This result implies that in a steady, level turn the aerodynamic side force is equal to zero. The turn is said to be **coordinated**: no net lateral acceleration acts on the airplane. From Eqn (4.86b), in such a coordinated turn:

$$0 = (C_{y_\beta}\beta_1 + C_{Y_r}\frac{R_1 b}{2U_1} + C_{y_{\delta_a}}\delta_{a_1} + C_{y_{\delta_r}}\delta_{r_1})\overline{q}_1 S \tag{4.96}$$

The reader should observe that this equation can be satisfied with a non–zero sideslip angle!

An important consequence of these developments is that the lateral–directional equations (4.86b), (4.86d) and (4.86f) can be separated from the total set to yield:

$$\begin{bmatrix} C_{y_\beta} & C_{y_{\delta_a}} & C_{y_{\delta_r}} \\ C_{l_\beta} & C_{l_{\delta_a}} & C_{l_{\delta_r}} \\ C_{n_\beta} & C_{n_{\delta_a}} & C_{n_{\delta_r}} \end{bmatrix} \begin{Bmatrix} \beta \\ \delta_a \\ \delta_r \end{Bmatrix} = \begin{Bmatrix} -C_{y_r}\dfrac{bg\sin\phi}{2U_1^2} \\[2mm] \dfrac{(I_{zz}-I_{yy})g^2\sin^3\phi}{\overline{q}_1 SbU_1^2\cos\phi} - C_{l_r}\dfrac{bg\sin\phi}{2U_1^2} \\[2mm] \dfrac{I_{xz}g^2\sin^3\phi}{\overline{q}_1 SbU_1^2\cos\phi} - C_{n_r}\dfrac{bg\sin\phi}{2U_1^2} \end{Bmatrix} \tag{4.97}$$

The subscripts 1 have been dropped from Eqn (4.97), except in the steady state speed terms. Solutions to these equations can again be written in determinant format as shown in Table 4.5.

The solutions as represented by Eqns (4.98)–(4.102) in Table 4.5 are considered 'acceptable' as long as they are consistent with conditions of attached flow. For example, if a solution for aileron/rudder deflection is 25 degrees or more, that would probably not be consistent with conditions of attached flow over the wing or vertical tail. In such a case, the aileron and/or rudder control power would have to be increased to solve the problem.

The remaining longitudinal equations: (4.86a, c and e) can be rewritten as:

$$0 = -(C_{D_0} + C_{D_\alpha}\alpha_1 + C_{D_{i_h}}i_{h_1} + C_{D_{\delta_e}}\delta_{e_1})\overline{q}_1 S + T_1\cos(\phi_T + \alpha_1) \tag{4.103a}$$

$$-\frac{mg}{\cos\phi} = -(C_{L_0} + C_{L_\alpha}\alpha_1 + C_{L_{i_h}}i_{h_1} + C_{L_q}\frac{g\overline{c}\sin^2\phi}{2U_1^2\cos\phi} + C_{L_{\delta_e}}\delta_{e_1})\overline{q}_1 S +$$
$$- T_1\sin(\phi_T + \alpha_1) \tag{4.103b}$$

$$- I_{xz}\frac{g^2\sin^2\phi}{U_1^2} = (C_{m_0} + C_{m_\alpha}\alpha_1 + C_{m_q}\frac{g\overline{c}\sin^2\phi}{2U_1^2\cos\phi} + C_{m_{i_h}}i_{h_1} + C_{m_{\delta_e}}\delta_{e_1})\overline{q}_1 S\overline{c} +$$
$$- T_1 d_T \tag{4.103c}$$

These equations will be treated in a manner similar to what was done in Sub–section 4.2.1: the stabilizer incidence angle, i_{h_1}, and the bank angle, ϕ_1, are assumed to be known. Also, the thrust, T_1, is assumed to be sufficient to sustain the airplane in its steady state banked flight. This implies that the drag equation (4.103a) is assumed to be satisfied. That leaves the lift and pitching moment equations (4.103b) and (4.103c) to be considered.

Table 4.5 Solutions for the Steady State Lateral–Directional Equations of Motion for Turning Flight

$$\beta_1 = \frac{\begin{vmatrix} a_{11} & C_{y_{\delta_a}} & C_{y_{\delta_r}} \\ b_{11} & C_{l_{\delta_a}} & C_{l_{\delta_r}} \\ c_{11} & C_{n_{\delta_a}} & C_{n_{\delta_r}} \end{vmatrix}}{\Delta} \tag{4.98}$$

$$\delta_{a_1} = \frac{\begin{vmatrix} C_{y_\beta} & a_{11} & C_{y_{\delta_r}} \\ C_{l_\beta} & b_{11} & C_{l_{\delta_r}} \\ C_{n_\beta} & c_{11} & C_{n_{\delta_r}} \end{vmatrix}}{\Delta} \tag{4.99}$$

$$\delta_{a_1} = \frac{\begin{vmatrix} C_{y_\beta} & C_{y_{\delta_a}} & a_{11} \\ C_{l_\beta} & C_{l_{\delta_a}} & b_{11} \\ C_{n_\beta} & C_{n_{\delta_a}} & c_{11} \end{vmatrix}}{\Delta} \tag{4.100}$$

$$\text{where}: \quad \Delta = \begin{vmatrix} C_{y_\beta} & C_{y_{\delta_a}} & C_{y_{\delta_r}} \\ C_{l_\beta} & C_{l_{\delta_a}} & C_{l_{\delta_r}} \\ C_{n_\beta} & C_{n_{\delta_a}} & C_{n_{\delta_r}} \end{vmatrix} \tag{4.101}$$

$$\text{and}: \quad a_{11} = -C_{y_r}\frac{bg\sin\phi}{2U_1^{\,2}} \tag{4.102a}$$

$$b_{11} = \frac{(I_{zz} - I_{yy})g^2\sin^3\phi}{\bar{q}_1 SbU_1^{\,2}\cos\phi} - C_{l_r}\frac{gb\sin\phi}{2U_1^{\,2}} \tag{4.102b}$$

$$c_{11} = \frac{I_{xz}g^2\sin^3\phi}{\bar{q}_1 SbU_1^{\,2}\cos\phi} - C_{n_r}\frac{gb\sin\phi}{2U_1^{\,2}} \tag{4.102c}$$

It can be numerically verified, that the derivative C_{L_q} in Eqn (4.103b) can nearly always be neglected. Neglecting also the effect of thrust in Eqns (4.103b) and (4.103c) while writing:

$$\frac{mg}{qS} = C_{L_{trim}} \qquad \cos\phi = \frac{1}{n} \qquad \sin^2\phi = 1 - \frac{1}{n^2} \tag{4.104}$$

it is possible to cast the solutions to Eqns (4.103b) and (4.103c) in the following matrix form:

$$\begin{bmatrix} C_{L_\alpha} & C_{L_{\delta_e}} \\ C_{m_\alpha} & C_{m_{\delta_e}} \end{bmatrix} \begin{Bmatrix} \alpha_1 \\ \delta_{e_1} \end{Bmatrix} = \begin{Bmatrix} nC_{L_{trim}} - C_{L_o} - C_{L_{i_h}}i_{h_1} \\ -C_{m_o} - C_{m_{i_h}}i_{h_1} - C_{m_q}\dfrac{\bar{c}g}{2U_1^{\;2}}(n - \frac{1}{n}) \end{Bmatrix} \tag{4.105}$$

Solutions to matrix Eqn (4.105) are the following:

$$\alpha_1 = \frac{n(C_{L_{trim}} - C_{L_o} - C_{L_{i_h}}i_{h_1})C_{m_{\delta_e}} + \left\{ C_{m_o} + C_{m_{i_h}}i_{h_1} + C_{m_q}\dfrac{\bar{c}g}{2U_1^{\;2}}(n - \frac{1}{n}) \right\}C_{L_{\delta_e}}}{(C_{L_\alpha}C_{m_{\delta_e}} - C_{m_\alpha}C_{L_{\delta_e}})} \tag{4.106}$$

$$\delta_{e_1} = \frac{-C_{L_\alpha}\left\{ C_{m_o} + C_{m_{i_h}}i_{h_1} + C_{m_q}\dfrac{\bar{c}g}{2U_1^{\;2}}(n - \frac{1}{n}) \right\} - C_{m_\alpha}(nC_{L_{trim}} - C_{L_o} - C_{L_{i_h}}i_{h_1})}{(C_{L_\alpha}C_{m_{\delta_e}} - C_{m_\alpha}C_{L_{\delta_e}})} \tag{4.107}$$

The reader should compare these solutions with those of Eqns (4.46) and (4.47) for steady state, straight line flight. It is seen that flight in a steady level turn takes place at a higher angle of attack and requires a larger (negatively speaking!) elevator deflection angle. Pilots are well acquainted with this characteristic.

The reader should observe that the amount of elevator required to trim the airplane in a turn is strongly dependent on the load factor, n, associated with the turn. Of particular interest is the so-called elevator–versus–load–factor gradient, $\partial\delta_e/\partial n$. This gradient can be obtained by differentiating Eqn (4.107):

$$\frac{\partial\delta_e}{\partial n} = \frac{-C_{L_\alpha}C_{m_q}\dfrac{\bar{c}g}{2U_1^{\;2}}(1 + \frac{1}{n^2}) - C_{m_\alpha}C_{L_{trim}}}{C_{L_\alpha}C_{m_{\delta_e}} - C_{L_{\delta_e}}C_{m_\alpha}} \tag{4.108}$$

For acceptable flying qualities, this gradient (which is also referred to as the 'elevator–per–'g'–gradient') must always be negative:

$$\frac{\partial\delta_e}{\partial n} < 0 \tag{4.109}$$

Figure 4.18 shows the result of flight test measurements of elevator required versus load factor carried out during a turning maneuver in a small single–engine, propeller driven airplane.

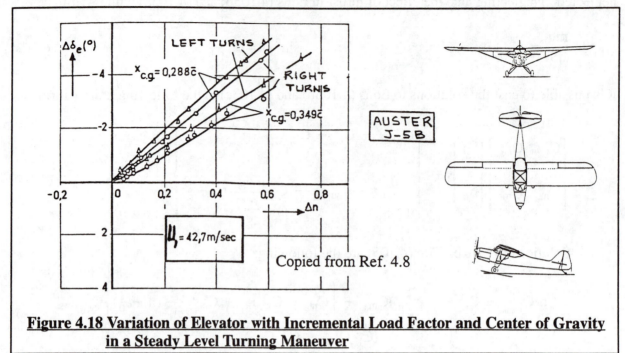

Figure 4.18 Variation of Elevator with Incremental Load Factor and Center of Gravity in a Steady Level Turning Maneuver

It is of interest to consider the situation where the elevator–per–'g' gradient disappears. This would occur whenever the following condition is satisfied:

$$0 = - C_{L_\alpha} C_{m_q} \frac{\overline{c}g}{2U_1^2}(1 + \frac{1}{n^2}) - C_{m_\alpha} C_{L_1} \qquad (4.110)$$

Next, recall Eqn (4.62). By combining Eqns (4.62) and (4.110) it can be shown that the elevator–per–'g' gradient vanishes if the following condition is satisfied:

$$\overline{x}_{cg_{\text{for: }\frac{\partial \delta_e}{\partial n}=0}} = \overline{x}_{ac} - \frac{C_{m_q}}{C_{L_1}}\frac{\overline{c}g}{2U_1^2}(1 + \frac{1}{n^2}) \qquad (4.111a)$$

This particular c.g. location is referred to as the maneuver–point–stick–fixed, or MP_{fix}, of the airplane. The significance of the subscript 'fix' will become clear in Section 4.5. Note that the maneuver point is behind the aerodynamic center as long as the pitch damping derivative, C_{m_q}, is negative. Because $C_{L_{trim}} = W/\overline{q}S$ it is possible to rewrite Eqn (4.111a) as:

$$\overline{x}_{cg_{\text{for: }\frac{\partial \delta_e}{\partial n}=0}} = MP_{fix} = \overline{x}_{ac} - \frac{C_{m_q}\varrho S\overline{c}g}{4W}(1 + \frac{1}{n^2}) = NP_{fix} - \frac{C_{m_q}\varrho S\overline{c}g}{4W}(1 + \frac{1}{n^2}) \quad (4.111b)$$

From the latter it is seen that the distance between the maneuver point and the aerodynamic center is a function of altitude: at high altitude the maneuver point tends to move toward the aerodynamic center (also called: NP_{fix} on page 203).

At this point, the concept of maneuver margin, MM is introduced by using as an analogy the idea of static margin, SM, of Eqn (4.62). The maneuver margin, MM is defined as:

$$MM = MP_{fix} - \overline{x}_{cg} \tag{4.112}$$

An airplane will have the correct sign of the elevator–per–'g'–gradient {see: Eqn (4.109)} if its maneuver margin is positive.

This sub–section has dealt with control and stability during turning flight. Turning can be viewed as a way of re–orienting the flight path in a horizontal plane. Pilots also have to be able to re–orient the flight path in a vertical plane. The maneuver which can accomplish this is the pull–up (or push–over) maneuver. Sub–section 4.3.2 deals with stability and control properties for pull–ups.

4.3.2 STABILITY AND CONTROL CHARACTERISTICS FOR STEADY STATE, SYMMETRICAL PULL–UP (PUSH–OVER) FLIGHT

Figure 4.19 depicts an airplane in a steady symmetrical pull–up maneuver. In such a maneuver the only angular rate present is the steady state pitch rate, Q_1. The lateral–directional equations

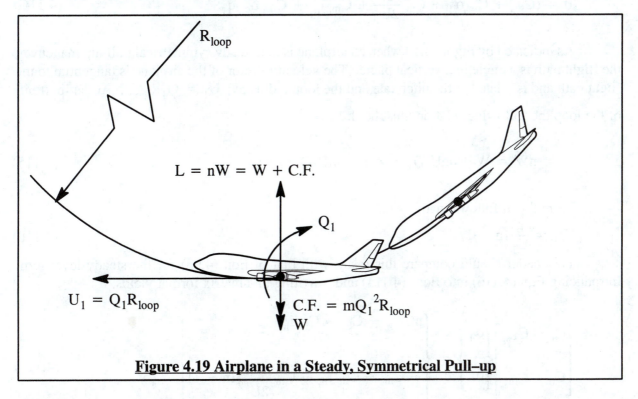

Figure 4.19 Airplane in a Steady, Symmetrical Pull–up

are not needed in this case. The longitudinal (drag, lift and pitching moment) equations are obtained from Eqns (1.55) and (1.56). These are adjoined by the aerodynamic force and moment equations (3.46) and (3.93). The resulting equations are:

$$0 = -(C_{D_0} + C_{D_\alpha}\alpha_1 + C_{D_{i_h}}i_{h_1} + C_{D_{\delta_e}}\delta_{e_1})\overline{q}_1 S + T_1 \cos(\phi_T + \alpha_1) \tag{4.113a}$$

$$- mU_1Q_1 - mg\cos\gamma_1 = -(C_{L_0} + C_{L_\alpha}\alpha_1 + C_{L_{i_h}}i_{h_1} + C_{L_q}\frac{Q_1\bar{c}}{2U_1} + C_{L_{\delta_e}}\delta_{e_1})\bar{q}_1 S +$$
$$- T_1\sin(\phi_T + \alpha_1) \qquad (4.113b)$$

$$0 = (C_{m_0} + C_{m_\alpha}\alpha_1 + C_{m_q}\frac{Q_1\bar{c}}{2U_1} + C_{m_{i_h}}i_{h_1} + C_{m_{\delta_e}}\delta_{e_1})\bar{q}_1 S\bar{c} \qquad (4.113c)$$

For given values of: $\bar{q}_1$, T_1 and i_{h_1} these equations can be solved for α_1, Q_1 and δ_{e_1}. Consider again the case where the steady state thrust, T_1, is selected to satisfy the drag equation. Next, the effect of thrust in Eqns (4.113b) and (4.113c) and the derivative C_{L_q} will be neglected. As a result, Eqns (4.113b) and (4.113c) become:

$$- mU_1Q_1 - mg\cos\gamma_1 = -(C_{L_0} + C_{L_\alpha}\alpha_1 + C_{L_{i_h}}i_{h_1} + C_{L_{\delta_e}}\delta_{e_1})\bar{q}_1 S \qquad (4.114a)$$

$$0 = (C_{m_0} + C_{m_\alpha}\alpha_1 + C_{m_q}\frac{Q_1\bar{c}}{2U_1} + C_{m_{i_h}}i_{h_1} + C_{m_{\delta_e}}\delta_{e_1})\bar{q}_1 S\bar{c} \qquad (4.114b)$$

As indicated by Figure 4.19 when an airplane is in a steady symmetrical pull–up maneuver, the flight path is a circle in a vertical plane. The velocity vector of the airplane is tangential to the flight path and is related to the pitch rate and the loop radius by: $U_1 = Q_1 R_{loop}$. At the 'bottom' of the loop the following relation must hold:

$$L = nW = W + mU_1Q_1 = mg + mU_1Q_1 \qquad (4.115)$$

From this it follows that:
$$Q_1 = \frac{g}{U_1}(n - 1) \qquad (4.116)$$

The reader should compare this result with that of Eqn (4.93) for the steady level turn. Introducing Eqn (4.116) into Eqns (4.114) and rewriting in a matrix format yields:

$$\begin{bmatrix} C_{L_\alpha} & C_{L_{\delta_e}} \\ C_{m_\alpha} & C_{m_{\delta_e}} \end{bmatrix}\begin{Bmatrix} \alpha_1 \\ \delta_{e_1} \end{Bmatrix} = \begin{Bmatrix} nC_{L_{trim}} - C_{L_0} - C_{L_{i_h}}i_{h_1} \\ -C_{m_0} - C_{m_{i_h}}i_{h_1} - C_{m_q}\frac{\bar{c}g}{2U_1^2}(n - 1) \end{Bmatrix} \qquad (4.117)$$

The solutions to Eqn (4.117) can be written as:

$$\alpha_1 = \frac{(nC_{L_{trim}} - C_{L_0} - C_{L_{i_h}}i_{h_1})C_{m_{\delta_e}} + \left\{ C_{m_0} + C_{m_{i_h}}i_{h_1} + C_{m_q}\frac{\bar{c}g}{2U_1^2}(n - 1) \right\}C_{L_{\delta_e}}}{(C_{L_\alpha}C_{m_{\delta_e}} - C_{m_\alpha}C_{L_{\delta_e}})} \qquad (4.118)$$

$n =$ load factor

$$\delta_{e_1} = \frac{- C_{L_\alpha}\left\{ C_{m_0} + C_{m_{i_h}} i_{h_1} + C_{m_q} \frac{\overline{c}g}{2U_1^2}(n - 1) \right\} - C_{m_\alpha}(nC_{L_{trim}} - C_{L_0} - C_{L_{i_h}} i_{h_1})}{(C_{L_\alpha} C_{m_{\delta_e}} - C_{m_\alpha} C_{L_{\delta_e}})} \qquad (4.119)$$

These equations represent the solutions for α_1 and δ_{e_1} required to maintain the airplane in a symmetrical pull–up. Of interest is again the change in elevator angle required as a result of a change in load factor. By differentiation of Eqn (4.119) it is found that:

$$\frac{\partial \delta_e}{\partial n} = \frac{- C_{L_\alpha} C_{m_q} \frac{\overline{c}g}{2U_1^2} - C_{m_\alpha} C_{L_{trim}}}{C_{L_\alpha} C_{m_{\delta_e}} - C_{L_{\delta_e}} C_{m_\alpha}} \qquad (4.120)$$

Figure 4.20 shows the result of flight test measurements of elevator required versus load factor carried out during a pull–up maneuver in a small single–engine, propeller driven airplane.

The maneuver point for the pull–up maneuver is defined in a manner similar to that for the steady turning maneuver: see Eqn (4.112). For the maneuver point in a pull–up maneuver it is found that:

$$\overline{x}_{cg_{\;for:\;\frac{\partial \delta_e}{\partial n}=0}} = MP_{fix} = \overline{x}_{ac} - \frac{C_{m_q}\varrho S\overline{c}g}{4W} = NP_{fix} - \frac{C_{m_q}\varrho S\overline{c}g}{4W} \qquad (4.121)$$

The significance of the subscript 'fix' will become clear in Section 4.5. Comparison of Eqns (4.111b) and (4.121) shows that the MP in a steady turn is always forward of the MP in a symmetrical pull–up. In both cases the MP approaches the NP at very high altitudes.

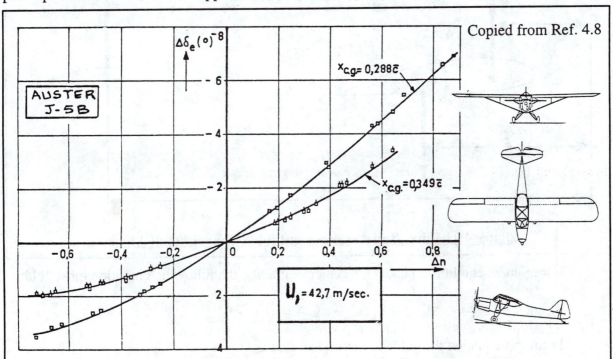

Figure 4.20 Variation of Elevator with Incremental Load Factor and Center of Gravity in a Steady, Symmetrical Pull–up Maneuver

4.4   TRIM COMPARISONS FOR CONVENTIONAL, CANARD AND THREE–SURFACE CONFIGURATIONS

The discussion of stability and trim has so–far been limited to conventional (i.e. tail aft) airplane configurations. It is not difficult (albeit laborious) to rederive all equations of Sections 4.2 and 4.3 so that they apply to three–surface configurations. One example of such an equation is Eqn (3.40) for the aerodynamic center location of a three–surface airplane. By striking the horizontal tail terms in Eqn (3.40) it applies to pure canard airplanes.

A frequently asked question is: "To trim an airplane, is the lift on the tail (or canard) in the up or down direction?" The answer to this question can be discerned from simple equilibrium calculations. Examples will be given for a conventional, canard and a three–surface configuration in Sub–sections 4.4.1 – 4.4.3 respectively.

4.4.1   TRIM OF A CONVENTIONAL CONFIGURATION

Figure 4.21 shows a wing–tail arrangement for a conventional airplane. The fuselage has been omitted for clarity. The effect of the fuselage is accounted for by placing the wing–fuselage lift vector at the wing–fuselage aerodynamic center. The following assumptions are made:

$$C_{m_{ac_{wf}}} < 0 \quad \text{and} \quad C_{m_{ac_h}} \approx 0 \tag{4.122}$$

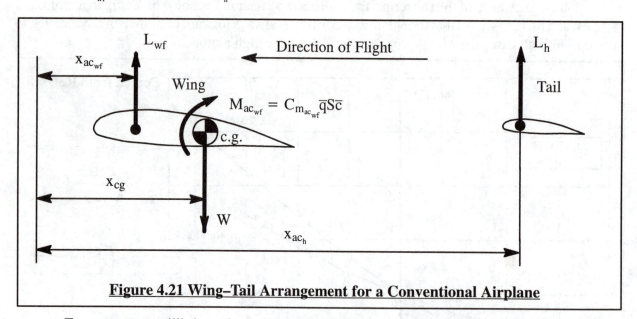

Figure 4.21 Wing–Tail Arrangement for a Conventional Airplane

For moment equilibrium about the center of gravity, the following condition must hold:

$$L_{wf}(x_{cg} - x_{ac_{wf}}) + M_{ac_{wf}} - L_h(x_{ac_h} - x_{cg}) = 0 \tag{4.123}$$

From this equation the tail load to trim is found as:

$$L_h = \frac{L_{wf}(x_{cg} - x_{ac_{wf}}) + M_{ac_{wf}}}{(x_{ac_h} - x_{cg})} \tag{4.124}$$

It is observed that for a conventional airplane the following inequalities hold:

$$(x_{ac_h} - x_{cg}) > 0 \qquad\qquad M_{ac_{wf}} < 0 \qquad\qquad L_{wf} > 0 \qquad\qquad (4.125)$$

Therefore, the following conclusions for the 'sign' of the tail lift (load), L_h, may be drawn, depending on the location of the center of gravity:

Case 1: $\quad x_{cg} > x_{ac_{wf}}$ (unstable wing–fuselage combination) leads to:

$\qquad\qquad\qquad L_h > 0$ or $L_h < 0$ 'up' load or 'down' load,

$\qquad\qquad\qquad$ depending on the negative magnitude of $M_{ac_{wf}}$

Case 2: $\quad x_{cg} = x_{ac_{wf}}$ (neutrally stable wing–fuselage combination) leads to:

$\qquad\qquad\qquad L_h < 0$ 'down' load

Case 3: $\quad x_{cg} < x_{ac_{wf}}$ (stable wing–fuselage combination) leads to:

$\qquad\qquad\qquad L_h < 0$ 'down' load

Conclusion: the tail load to trim will generally be in the 'down' direction, unless the wing–fuselage itself is unstable AND at the same time:

$$|M_{ac_{wf}}| > L_{wf}(x_{cg} - x_{ac_{wf}}) \text{ is satisfied.}$$

4.4.2   TRIM OF A CANARD CONFIGURATION

Figure 4.22 shows a canard–wing arrangement for a canard airplane. The fuselage has been omitted for clarity. The effect of the fuselage is accounted for by placing the wing–fuselage lift vector at the wing–fuselage aerodynamic center. The following assumptions are made:

$$C_{m_{ac_{wf}}} < 0 \quad \text{and} \quad C_{m_{ac_c}} \approx 0 \qquad\qquad (4.126)$$

For moment equilibrium about the center of gravity the following condition must hold:

$$L_c(x_{cg} - x_{ac_c}) + M_{ac_{wf}} - L_{wf}(x_{ac_{wf}} - x_{cg}) = 0 \qquad\qquad (4.127)$$

From this equation the canard load to trim is found as:

$$L_c = \frac{L_{wf}(x_{ac_{wf}} - x_{cg}) - M_{ac_{wf}}}{(x_{cg} - x_{ac_c})} \qquad\qquad (4.128)$$

It is observed that for a conventional airplane the following inequalities hold:

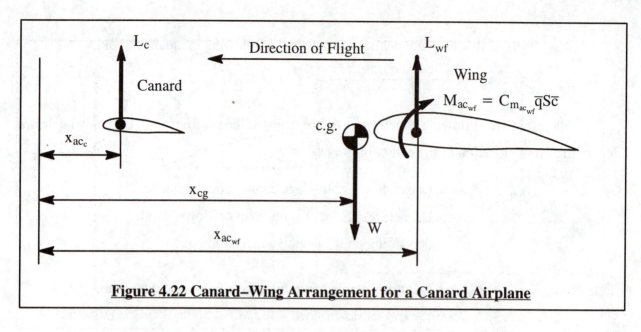

Figure 4.22 Canard–Wing Arrangement for a Canard Airplane

$$(x_{cg} - x_{ac_c}) > 0 \qquad M_{ac_{wf}} < 0 \qquad L_{wf} > 0 \qquad\qquad (4.129)$$

Therefore, the following conclusions for the 'sign' of the canard–lift, L_c , may be drawn, depending on the location of the center of gravity:

Case 1: $\quad x_{cg} > x_{ac_{wf}}$ (unstable wing–fuselage combination) leads to:

$L_c > 0$ or $L_c < 0$ 'up' load or 'down' load,

depending on the negative magnitude of $M_{ac_{wf}}$

Case 2: $\quad x_{cg} = x_{ac_{wf}}$ (neutrally stable wing–fuselage combination) leads to:

$L_c > 0$ 'up' load

Case 3: $\quad x_{cg} < x_{ac_{wf}}$ (stable wing–fuselage combination) leads to:

$L_c > 0$ 'up' load

Conclusion: the canard load to trim will generally be in the 'up' direction, unless the wing–fuselage itself is unstable AND at the same time:

$$|M_{ac_{wf}}| > L_{wf}(x_{cg} - x_{ac_{wf}}) \text{ is satisfied.}$$

4.4.3   TRIM OF A THREE–SURFACE CONFIGURATION

Figure 4.23 shows a canard–wing–tail arrangement for a three–surface airplane. The fuselage has been omitted for clarity. The effect of the fuselage is accounted for by placing the wing–fuselage lift vector at the wing–fuselage aerodynamic center. The following assumptions are made:

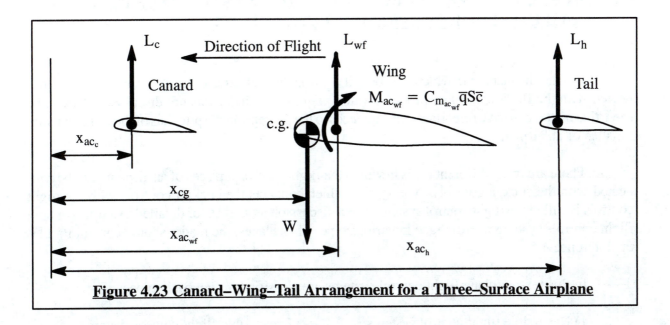

Figure 4.23 Canard–Wing–Tail Arrangement for a Three–Surface Airplane

$$C_{m_{ac_{wf}}} < 0 \quad , \quad C_{m_{ac_h}} \approx 0 \quad \text{and} \quad C_{m_{ac_c}} \approx 0 \tag{4.130}$$

For moment equilibrium about the center of gravity the following condition must hold:

$$L_c(x_{cg} - X_{ac_c}) - L_{wf}(x_{ac_{wf}} - x_{cg}) + M_{ac_{wf}} - L_h(x_{ac_h} - x_{cg}) = 0 \tag{4.131}$$

In the case of three–surface airplanes the following inequalities are normally satisfied:

$$(x_{cg} - x_{ac_c}) > 0 \qquad M_{ac_{wf}} < 0 \qquad L_{wf} > 0 \qquad (x_{ac_h} - x_{cg}) > 0 \tag{4.132}$$

In addition, $x_{ac_{wf}} - x_{cg} > 0$ is usually satisfied in the case of a three–surface airplane.

Since there are now two different trim–loads to solve for in Eqn (4.10) one of the two must be selected. Solving for the canard trim load:

$$L_c = \frac{- M_{ac_{wf}} + L_{wf}(x_{ac_{wf}} - x_{cg}) + L_h(x_{ac_h} - x_{cg})}{(x_{cg} - x_{ac_c})} \tag{4.133}$$

From Eqn (4.133) it may be concluded that as long as L_h is positive (i.e. 'up') the canard load to trim, L_c , will also be positive (i.e. 'up').

Note: if the answer to any of the trim solutions in Sub–sections 4.4.1 – 4.4.3 is that all trim loads are in the 'up' direction, that does not imply that the airplane trim drag is minimized. The latter depends on whether or not the net span loading of the trimmed configuration is elliptical!

4.5 EFFECTS OF THE FLIGHT CONTROL SYSTEM ON STABILITY AND CONTROL IN STEADY STATE FLIGHT

So–far, the manner in which the cockpit controls (wheel, stick or rudder) are physically connected with the flight control surfaces (elevator, aileron or rudder) was not discussed. As will be seen, this matter can have important consequences to the perception the pilot has of the flying characteristics of an airplane.

There are many different ways in which the flight control surfaces of an airplane can be connected with the cockpit controls. The system which connects the cockpit controls with the flight controls is called the flight control system. For a discussion as well as for detailed examples of how flight controls systems are arranged in various types of airplanes, the reader should consult Part IV of Reference 4.5.

In this text, airplane flight control systems are classified in two basic types:

1) Reversible flight control systems   2) Irreversible flight control systems

In a reversible flight control system the cockpit controls are mechanically linked to the flight control surfaces in such a way that any movement of the cockpit controls results in a movement of the flight controls AND VICE VERSA! These mechanical systems typically consist of a system of push–rods and/or cables. Figure 4.24 is an example of such a reversible, mechanical system.

It can be seen from Figure 4.24, that any changes in aerodynamic pressure distribution over a flight control surface will result in a feedback to the cockpit controls. This feedback will be shown to have important consequences to the flying characteristics of airplanes.

In an irreversible system any movement of the cockpit controls signals the flight control system to position the flight controls according to some control law. The flight control systems holds the flight control surfaces at a deflection angle which is determined by the control law. Figure 4.25 shows an example of such an irreversible system. A detailed description of irreversible flight control systems is beyond the scope of this text. Part IV of Reference 4.5 contains examples and discussions of such systems, including the hydraulic system which is normally used to power such systems.

It can be seen from Figure 4.25, that any changes in aerodynamic pressure distribution will not result in a feedback to the cockpit controls.

Hybrid systems which possess some of the characteristics of either system also exist. The effects such hybrid systems may have on airplane flying qualities are not discussed in this text.

Reversible, irreversible and hybrid flight control systems all serve to transmit pilot induced forces or movements of the cockpit controls to the flight control surfaces. For a pilot to be able to properly and predictably control an airplane, it is necessary that certain relationships between cockpit control forces and/or movements and flight control surfaces movements are satisfied.

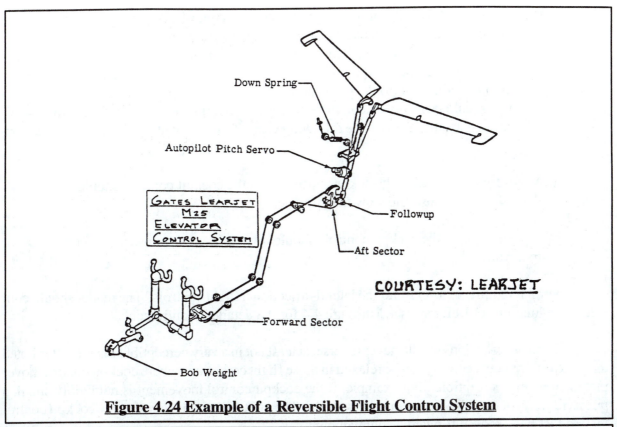

Figure 4.24 Example of a Reversible Flight Control System

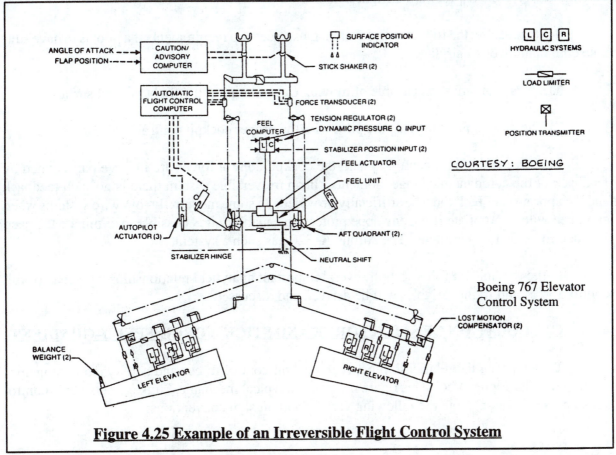

Figure 4.25 Example of an Irreversible Flight Control System

In some flight conditions the movement of the cockpit controls can be considerable. Examples are the movement of the lateral cockpit controls when maneuvering close to the ground in the presence of severe turbulence. However, in most cases the movement of the cockpit controls is barely perceptible. For that reason, the cockpit control forces (rather than the cockpit control movement) are the most important indication (to the pilot) of the severity of a particular maneuver. It follows from this that there should be no reversal in these forces which might require the pilot to reverse his thinking. This line of reasoning leads to the following general requirements for the longitudinal controls:

a) A pull force (defined in this text as positive) on the cockpit controls should always raise the nose and slow the airplane.

b) A push force on the cockpit controls should always lower the nose and speed up the airplane.

Similar requirements exist for the lateral–directional flight controls. The reader should consult the regulations of References 4.1 through 4.4 for the detailed requirements.

Control deflections should never reverse, at least not in a very perceptible manner. It is noted that this requirement certainly can be relaxed in those flight conditions where cockpit control movement is not very perceptible. For example, if the cockpit control movement is negligibly small, a pilot will sense that a pull is required to slow down. The pilot will be unaware that the cockpit control may in fact have moved forward a slight amount.

To summarize, the flight control system must meet two requirements if a pilot is to have suitable command over an airplane:

1) The system must be capable of moving (repositioning) the flight control surfaces

2) The system must provide the pilot with the proper cockpit control force 'feel'

In a reversible flight control system the cockpit control forces are in large part created by feedback of the aerodynamic hinge moments. In an irreversible system there is no such feedback and the appropriate 'feel' must be artificially provided. In some modern fly–by–wire systems when equipped with appropriate flight envelope protection capability it is possible to eliminate the need for such force feel requirement. The Airbus A–320 has such a system.

In the remainder of this section several important analytical relationships between cockpit control forces and flight variables will be derived and discussed.

4.5.1 CALCULATION OF STICK FORCE AND STICK–FORCE–SPEED–GRADIENT

To determine the relationship between cockpit control forces and aerodynamic hingemoments, consider Figure 4.26. This figure illustrates a typical mechanical linkage between a control stick and an elevator. Note the following very important sign conventions:

1) A pull force on the control stick is called positive

2) A trailing edge up deflection of the elevator is called negative

3) The elevator hingemoment is called positive if it tends to drive the elevator trailing edge down, which is called a positive deflection

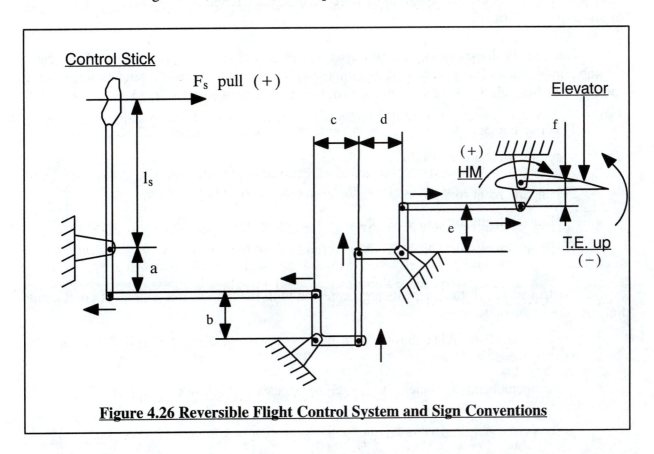

Figure 4.26 Reversible Flight Control System and Sign Conventions

Neglecting control system friction, the amount of work performed by the pilot on the stick must equal the amount of work performed by the aerodynamic hingemoment on the flight control surface. By tracing through the example system of Figure 4.26 it is found that:

$$F_s = \frac{a}{l_s} \frac{c}{b} \frac{e}{d} \frac{}{f} HM = G_e HM \qquad (4.134)$$

The moment arms associated with the stick, the elevator and the various system bell–cranks are lumped together in the quantity called the system gearing ratio, G_e :

$$G_e = \frac{a}{l_s} \frac{c}{b} \frac{e}{d} \frac{}{f} \qquad (4.135)$$

Observe that because of the 'equal work' condition used in deriving Eqn (4.134) the physical unit of the gearing ratio, G_e , is rad/ft. Typical values for control system gearing ratios may be found on page 203 of Part IV, Reference 4.5. Because of ergonomic considerations, the designer does not have much choice when selecting the numerical value of l_s . Because of physical space limitations, the designer does not have much leeway in selecting a, b, c, d, e and f either. For these reasons the magnitude of the gearing ratio is about the same for most airplanes: it ranges roughly from 0.7 to 1.7. This fact has important repercussions to the aerodynamic design of control surfaces. It should be obvious that control stick forces can be neither too large nor too small. With the value of G_e

limited to a narrow range, the designer must focus his attention on designing the control surface such that the aerodynamic hingemoment about the control surface hinge line is consistent with a range of allowable stick forces.

Figure 4.27 illustrates various aerodynamic pressure distributions over a stabilizer–elevator–tab combination. Each pressure distribution can be integrated to yield a hingemoment **about the elevator hingeline**. There are four types of hingemoment to be considered:

1) Hingemoment for: $\alpha_h = \delta_e = \delta_{t_e} = 0$ (Not shown in Figure 4.27 because of the symmetrical airfoil used.)

2) Hingemoment for: $\alpha_h \neq 0$, $\delta_e = 0$ and $\delta_{t_e} = 0$

3) Hingemoment for: $\alpha_h = 0$, $\delta_e \neq 0$ and $\delta_{t_e} = 0$

4) Hingemoment for: $\alpha_h = 0$, $\delta_e = 0$ and $\delta_{t_e} \neq 0$

Control surface hingemoments are expressed with the help of hingemoment coefficients. For the case of an elevator:

$$HM = C_h \overline{q} S_e \overline{c}_e \qquad (4.136)$$

The hingemoment coefficient, C_h, itself is expressed as follows:

$$C_h = C_{h_0} + C_{h_\alpha} \alpha_h + C_{h_{\delta_e}} \delta_e + C_{h_{\delta_{t_e}}} \delta_{t_e} \qquad (4.137)$$

where: C_{h_0} is the elevator hingemoment coefficient for $\alpha_h = \delta_e = \delta_{t_e} = 0$

C_{h_α} is the partial derivative of elevator hingemoment coefficient with angle of attack

$C_{h_{\delta_e}}$ is the partial derivative of elevator hingemoment coefficient with elevator angle

$C_{h_{\delta_{t_e}}}$ is the partial derivative of elevator hingemoment coefficient with elevator tab angle

By referring to Figure 4.27 it may be seen that the hingemoment derivatives will normally be negative. The following parameters tend to affect the numerical value of the hingemoment coefficient and its derivatives for a flight control surface:

* Reynolds number   * Mach number   * Angle of attack
* Control surface deflection   * Chord ratio   * Overhang
* Nose shape   * Gap   * Trailing edge angle
* Horn geometry   * Tab geometry

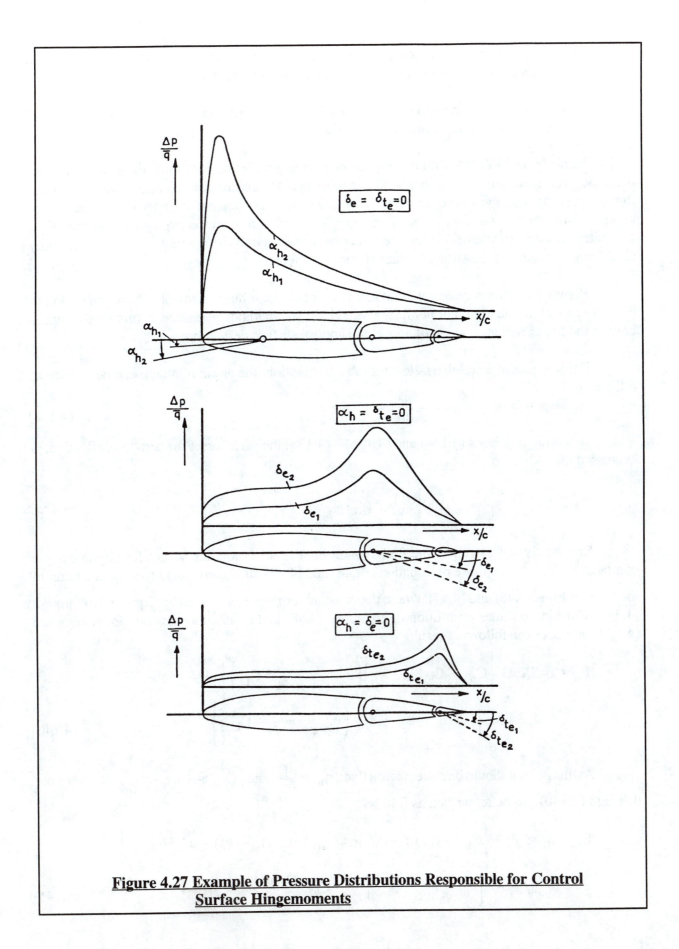

Figure 4.27 Example of Pressure Distributions Responsible for Control Surface Hingemoments

Figure 4.28 presents a geometrical interpretation for these parameters. Hingemoments tend to become nonlinear even at moderate angles of attack and control surface deflection.

Methods for estimating hingemoment coefficients and their derivatives are found in Part VI of Reference 4.5 as well as in References 4.6 and 4.7.

Experience indicates that even with the best of prediction methods hingemoments can often be predicted only to within +/- 30% accuracy! The reason for this poor state of affairs is that the pressure distributions over the aft part of a control surface are strongly influenced by the characteristics of the boundary layer. Therefore, Reynolds number effects play an important role. If greater accuracy (than 30%) is required, it is recommended to run a windtunnel test, preferably at full scale because of the strong Reynolds number effects.

Figure 4.29 shows typical windtunnel data for elevator hingemoments. Note the region of linearity as well as the region of nonlinear behavior! The methods presented in this Section apply only in the linear region of angle of attack and control surface deflection.

For the case of a stabilizer/elevator/tab combination, the angle of attack can be written as follows:

$$\alpha_h = \alpha - \varepsilon + i_h = \alpha(1 - \frac{d\varepsilon}{d\alpha}) + i_h - \varepsilon_0 \tag{4.138}$$

By combining Eqns (4.134) and (4.136) – (4.138) the stick force, for zero tab deflection, is expressed as:

$$F_s = \bar{q}_h S_e \bar{c}_e G_e \left[C_{h_o} + C_{h_\alpha}\left\{\alpha\left(1 - \frac{d\varepsilon}{d\alpha}\right) + i_h - \varepsilon_0\right\} + C_{h_{\delta_e}}\delta_e \right] \tag{4.139}$$

In a steady state, straight line flight condition, the corresponding values for airplane angle of attack, α and δ_e are those of Equations (4.46) and (4.47). It is convenient to write the latter in the form of Eqns (4.48) and (4.49), where the constant terms are expressed by Eqns (4.50) through (4.53). Carrying out the substitution of equations (4.48) and (4.49) into the stick force equation (4.139) produces the following result:

$$F_s = \bar{q}_h S_e \bar{c}_e G_e \left\{ C_{h_o} + C_{h_\alpha}\left(1 - \frac{d\varepsilon}{d\alpha}\right)\left(\alpha_{C_{L_1}=0} + \frac{\partial\alpha}{\partial C_L}C_{L_1}\right)\right\} +$$
$$+ \bar{q}_h S_e \bar{c}_e G_e \left\{ C_{h_\alpha}(i_h - \varepsilon_0) + C_{h_{\delta_e}}\left(\delta_{e_{C_{L_1}=0}} + \frac{\partial\delta_e}{\partial C_L}C_{L_1}\right)\right\} \tag{4.140}$$

At this point it should be remembered that: $\eta_h = \frac{\bar{q}}{\bar{q}_h}$ and $C_{L_1} = C_{L_{trim}} = \frac{W}{\bar{q}S}$. Therefore that Eqn (4.140) can be re–written as follows:

$$F_s = \eta_h \bar{q} S_e \bar{c}_e G_e \left\{ C_{h_o} + C_{h_\alpha}\left(1 - \frac{d\varepsilon}{d\alpha}\right)\alpha_{C_{L_1}=0} + C_{h_\alpha}(i_h - \varepsilon_0) + C_{h_{\delta_e}}\delta_{e_{C_{L_1}=0}}\right\} +$$
$$+ \eta_h S_e \bar{c}_e G_e \left\{ C_{h_\alpha}\frac{\partial\alpha}{\partial C_L}\frac{W}{S}(1 - \frac{d\varepsilon}{d\alpha}) + C_{h_{\delta_e}}\frac{\partial\delta_e}{\partial C_L}\frac{W}{S}\right\} \tag{4.141}$$

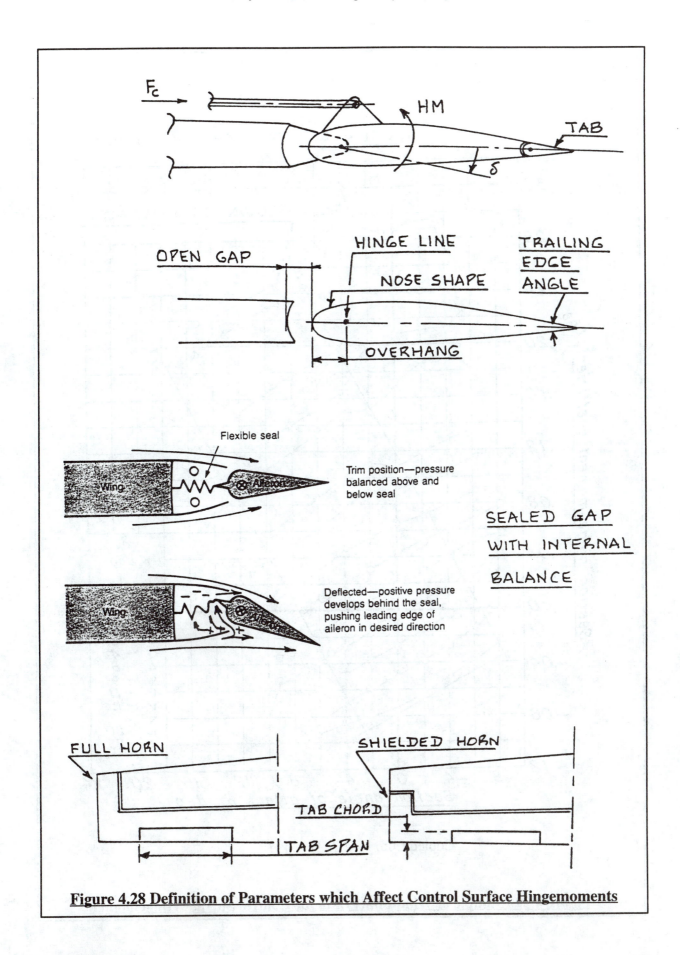

Figure 4.28 Definition of Parameters which Affect Control Surface Hingemoments

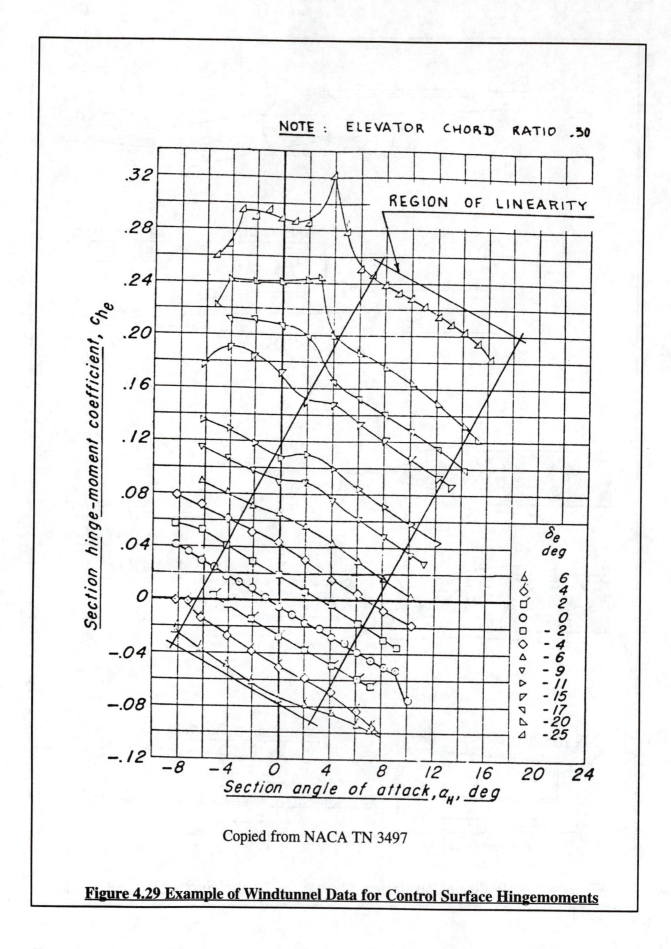

Copied from NACA TN 3497

Figure 4.29 Example of Windtunnel Data for Control Surface Hingemoments

The maximum allowable stick forces are defined in the regulations (References 4.1 – 4.4) Typically, the regulations define all allowable cockpit control forces in terms of temporary and prolonged flight conditions.

A temporary flight condition is one which occurs shortly following a failure which requires a major adjustment in cockpit control force to keep the airplane under control. Examples are:

      * rudder pedal force required following a sudden outboard engine failure

      * elevator stick force required following a sudden flap failure

A prolonged flight condition is one that occurs either in normal flight or after the airplane has been re–trimmed by the pilot following some failure.

Table 4.6 defines the allowable cockpit control forces according to FAR 23 and FAR 25. The military specifications have more extensive requirements, particularly for naval aircraft on final approach to a carrier.

Table 4.6 Maximum Cockpit Control Forces Allowed by FAR 23 and FAR 25			
Cockpit control forces are given in (pounds) lbs as applied to the stick, control wheel or rudder pedal(s)	Pitch	Roll	Yaw
a) For temporary application:			
Stick	60	30	
Wheel (applied to rim)	75	60	
Rudder pedal(s)			150
b) For prolonged application:	10	5	20

Detailed inspection of Eqn (4.141) reveals the fact that the stick force magnitude is strongly dependent on the c.g. location. This can be seen by recalling Eqn (4.53) and Eqn (3.39). The stick forces tend to be higher at forward c.g. and lower at aft c.g.

The reader should recognize the fact that the stick force equation (4.141) contains two terms:

      * the first term is **dependent** on the dynamic pressure

and

      * the second term is **independent** of the dynamic pressure.

In the steady state: $\bar{q} = \frac{1}{2}\varrho U_1^2$ and therefore, the stick force can be expected to vary parabolically with speed in a manner indicated in Figure 4.30. Observe that the stick force can be cast in the following form:

$$F_s = F_{s_{V_P=0}} + \frac{1}{2}\frac{\partial F_s}{\partial V_P}V_P \qquad (4.142)$$

where: $F_{s_{V_P=0}}$ is the stick force magnitude at zero speed. This quantity has meaning only during flight. Clearly, on the ground and at zero speed, the stick force would be also zero.

$\frac{\partial F_s}{\partial V_P}$ is the so–called stick–force–speed–gradient. This stick–force–speed–gradient is very important to a pilot. This gradient is obtained by differentiation of Eqn (4.141) with respect to speed. At constant Mach number this yields:

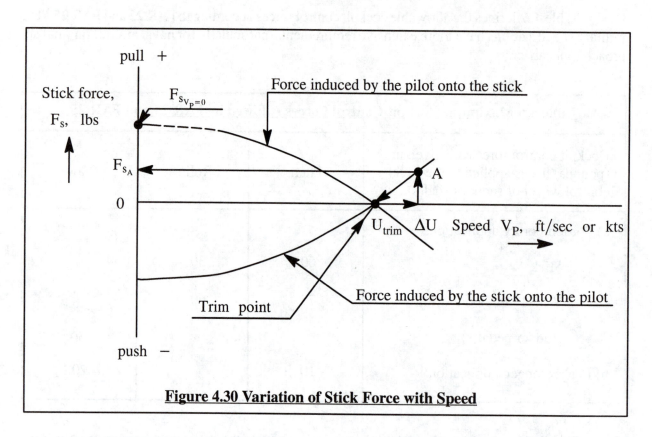

Figure 4.30 Variation of Stick Force with Speed

$$\frac{\partial F_s}{\partial V_P} = \varrho\eta_h V_P S_e \bar{c}_e G_e\left[C_{h_o} + C_{h_\alpha}\left\{\alpha_{C_{L_1}=0}\left(1 - \frac{d\varepsilon}{d\alpha}\right) + i_h - \varepsilon_0\right\} + C_{h_{\delta_e}}\delta_{e_{C_{L_1}=0}}\right] \qquad (4.143)$$

The stick–force–speed–gradient is seen to depend on a large number of parameters. Most prominent are the flight speed, V_P itself, the c.g. location (through $\delta_{e_{C_{L_1}=0}}$, which in turn depends on C_{m_α}, which in turn depends on the c.g. location!) and the various hingemoment coefficient derivatives. All regulations require the stick–force–speed–gradient to be negative:

$$\frac{\partial F_s}{\partial V_P} < 0 \qquad\qquad (4.144)$$

As long as this gradient is negative, the airplane has what is referred to as **speed–stability**, also known as **return–to–trim–speed–stability**. The latter characteristic can be deduced from Figure 4.30. Assume that the airplane is perturbed by a horizontal (or shear) gust of magnitude, ΔU. As shown by point A and the corresponding pull–force on the stick, F_{s_A}, the airplane is driven back toward its trimspeed, U_{trim}. As shown in Chapter 6, the stick–force–speed–gradient may not be so small as to become un–perceptible.

A typical minimum allowable slope is **1 lbs per 6 knots of speed**. Inspection of Eqn (4.143) shows that the stick–force–speed–gradient becomes lower as the c.g. is moved aft. At some point the flight path becomes difficult to control and the airplane develops a tendency toward speed divergence. Such a characteristic can be dangerous.

The return–to–trim–speed–stability behavior of an airplane can be masked by friction in the flight control system which causes the friction bandwidth shown in Figure 4.31.

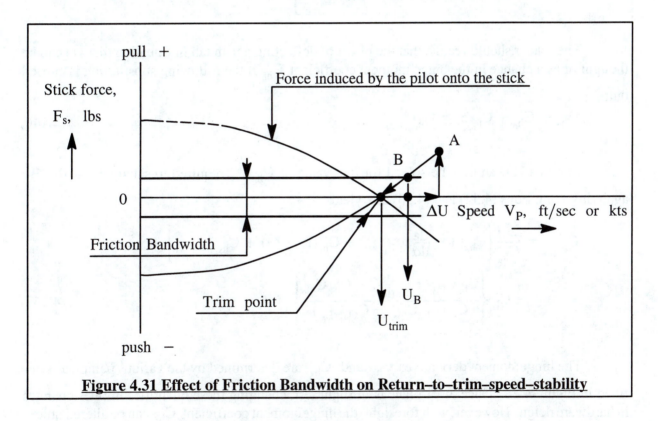

Figure 4.31 Effect of Friction Bandwidth on Return–to–trim–speed–stability

As a result of control system friction the airplane will not quite return to the original trim–speed but to a speed dictated by the friction bandwidth. Clearly there must be limits on allowable control system friction. These limits are expressed in the regulations as maximum allowable break-out forces and are defined in Chapter 6. In addition, the return–to–trim–speed–stability behavior of an airplane is expressed **in terms of a percentage of the original trim–speed**. Chapter 6 specifies what these percentages should be.

For long term (prolonged) flight it must be possible to maintain steady state flight with zero stick force. To satisfy this requirement the pilot must be given control over a term in Eqn (4.141) so that $F_s = 0$ can be satisfied. In many airplanes, this stick force trim requirement is met by giving the pilot direct control over the stabilizer incidence angle, i_h, (trimmable stabilizer) or by giving the pilot direct control over a trim tab deflection angle, δ_t. Figure 4.32 shows a layout example of an elevator trim tab system.

Using a trimmable stabilizer to set $F_s = 0$, Eqn (4.141) in combination with Eqns (4.52) and (4.53) yields:

$$i_{h_{F_s=0}} = \frac{-1}{C_{h_\alpha}}\left\{C_{h_0} + C_{h_\alpha}\left(1 - \frac{d\varepsilon}{d\alpha}\right)\alpha_{C_{L_1}=0} - C_{h_\alpha}\varepsilon_0 + C_{h_{\delta_e}}\delta_{e_{C_{L_1}=0}}\right\} +$$
$$- C_{L_1}\left\{\frac{C_{h_\alpha}C_{m_{\delta_e}}(1 - \frac{d\varepsilon}{d\alpha}) - C_{h_{\delta_e}}C_{m_\alpha}}{C_{h_\alpha}(C_{L_\alpha}C_{m_{\delta_e}} - C_{m_\alpha}C_{L_{\delta_e}})}\right\} \qquad (4.145)$$

The reader should realize that the effect of deflecting a trim tab in Equation (4.141) can be thought of as a change in the hinge moment coefficient C_{h_0} if the following substitution is carried out:

$$C_{h_0} \rightarrow C_{h_0} + C_{h_{\delta_t}}\delta_t = C_{h_{0_{trim}}} \qquad (4.146)$$

Eqn (4.141) can then be solved for that value of $C_{h_{0_{trim}}}$ required to satisfy $F_s = 0$. By again invoking Eqns (4.52) and (4.53) this yields:

$$C_{h_{0_{trim}}} = \frac{-1}{C_{h_\alpha}}\left\{C_{h_\alpha}\left(1 - \frac{d\varepsilon}{d\alpha}\right)\alpha_{C_{L_1}=0} + C_{h_\alpha}(i_h - \varepsilon_0) + C_{h_{\delta_e}}\delta_{e_{C_{L_1}=0}}\right\} +$$
$$- C_{L_1}\left\{\frac{C_{h_\alpha}C_{m_{\delta_e}}(1 - \frac{d\varepsilon}{d\alpha}) - C_{h_{\delta_e}}C_{m_\alpha}}{C_{h_\alpha}(C_{L_\alpha}C_{m_{\delta_e}} - C_{m_\alpha}C_{L_{\delta_e}})}\right\} \qquad (4.147)$$

The hingemoment derivatives C_{h_α} and $C_{h_{\delta_e}}$ are determined by the various parameters defined in Figure 4.28. Once an airplane is in flight test, changing these quantities implies changes in hardware design. However, with foresight, the hingemoment coefficient C_{h_0} can be altered quickly by changing the gearing ratio on a geared tab. This is particularly important during flight testing because all other parameters are not easily changed once the airplane has reached the flight test stage. Geared (or) balance tabs are discussed in Sub–section 4.5.5.

The reversibility of the flight control systems has a significant effect on static longitudinal stability as will be shown in Sub–section 4.5.2

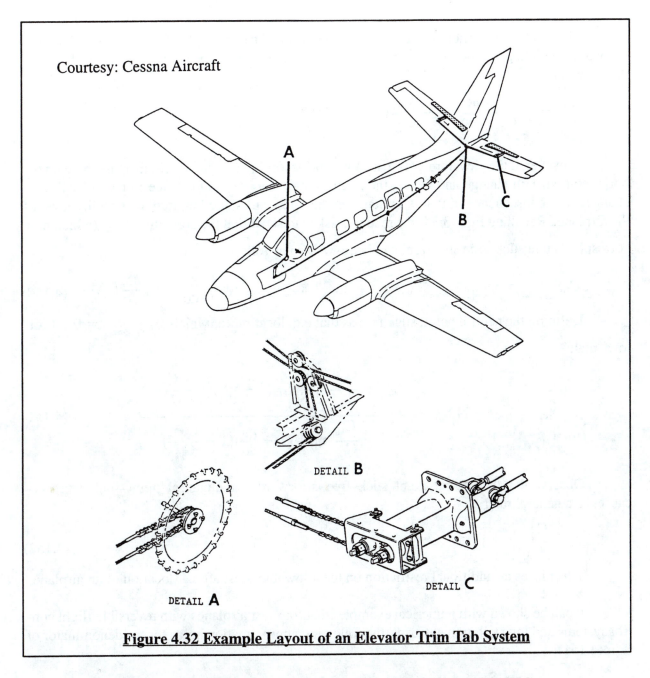

Courtesy: Cessna Aircraft

DETAIL B

DETAIL A

DETAIL C

Figure 4.32 Example Layout of an Elevator Trim Tab System

4.5.2 EFFECT OF CONTROL SURFACE REVERSIBILITY ON STATIC LONGITUDINAL STABILITY

An important consequence of having a reversible flight control system is that the definition of the airplane aerodynamic center (or neutral point), as given by Eqn (3.38) must be revised. The reason is the 'floatation behavior' of the elevator. To understand this floatation behavior, consider an airplane to be in moment trim as well as in stick force trim. When a gust hits the horizontal tail, the tail angle of attack will change. That causes the elevator to 'float' to a new angle. The relationship between tail angle of attack and elevator floatation angle is defined by the flotation condition:

$$C_h = 0 = C_{h_0} + C_{h_\alpha}\alpha_h + C_{h_{\delta_e}}\delta_e \qquad (4.148)$$

The floatation relation between elevator angle and airplane angle of attack is found by partially differentiating Eqn (4.148) with respect to the elevator angle. The reader is asked to show that this results in:

$$\frac{\partial \delta_e}{\partial \alpha} = -\frac{C_{h_\alpha}}{C_{h_{\delta_e}}}\frac{\partial \alpha_h}{\partial \alpha} = -\frac{C_{h_\alpha}}{C_{h_{\delta_e}}}(1-\frac{d\varepsilon}{d\alpha}) \sim \text{usually} \sim .7 . \tag{4.149}$$

However, if the elevator floats to a new angle according to Eqn (4.148) then the force on the horizontal tail will change and hence, the pitching moment contribution due to the tail will also change. The consequence of that is a change in the **apparent** static longitudinal stability level of the airplane. Recalling Eqn (3.35) the reader is asked to show that the derivative C_{m_α} (which now corresponds to a stick–free situation) can be re–written as follows:

$$C_{m_{\alpha_{stick-free}}} = C_{L_{\alpha_{wf}}}(\overline{x}_{cg} - \overline{x}_{wf}) - C_{L_{\alpha_h}}\eta_h\frac{S_h}{S}(\overline{x}_{ac_h} - \overline{x}_{cg})[(1-\frac{d\varepsilon}{d\alpha}) + \tau_e\frac{\partial \delta_e}{\partial \alpha}] \tag{4.150}$$

Defining the neutral point, stick free as that c.g. location for which $C_{m_{\alpha_{stick-free}}} = 0$, it follows that:

$$\overline{x}_{cg} = NP_{free} = \frac{\overline{x}_{ac_{wf}} + \dfrac{C_{L_{\alpha_h}}}{C_{L_{\alpha_{wf}}}}\eta_h\dfrac{S_h}{S}\overline{x}_{ac_h}(1-\dfrac{d\varepsilon}{d\alpha})(1-\dfrac{C_{h_\alpha}\tau_e}{C_{h_{\delta_e}}})}{1 + \dfrac{C_{L_{\alpha_h}}}{C_{L_{\alpha_{wf}}}}\eta_h\dfrac{S_h}{S}(1-\dfrac{d\varepsilon}{d\alpha})(1-\dfrac{C_{h_\alpha}\tau_e}{C_{h_{\delta_e}}})} \tag{4.151}$$

(for $C_{m_{\alpha_{stick-free}}}$)

Observe that the neutral–point–stick–free is forward of the neutral–point–stick–fixed because, as a general rule: $(\overline{x}_{ac})$

$$(1-\frac{C_{h_\alpha}\tau_e}{C_{h_{\delta_e}}}) < 1.0 \tag{4.152}$$

This places an additional restriction on the allowable most aft c.g. location of an airplane.

It can be shown with numerical examples that for most airplanes with reversible flight control systems and long tail moment arms, the following approximation holds for the denominator of Eqn (4.151):

$$\left[1 + \frac{C_{L_{\alpha_h}}}{C_{L_{\alpha_{wf}}}}\eta_h\frac{S_h}{S}(1-\frac{d\varepsilon}{d\alpha})(1-\frac{C_{h_\alpha}\tau_e}{C_{h_{\delta_e}}})\right] \approx 1.1 \approx 1.0 \tag{4.153}$$

Using the approximation suggested by Eqn (4.153) it is possible to cast Eqn (4.151) in the following format:

$$NP_{free} \approx \overline{x}_{ac_{wf}} + \frac{C_{L_{\alpha_h}}}{C_{L_{\alpha_{wf}}}}\eta_h\frac{S_h}{S}\overline{x}_{ac_h}(1-\frac{d\varepsilon}{d\alpha})(1-\frac{C_{h_\alpha}\tau_e}{C_{h_{\delta_e}}}) \approx$$

$$\approx NP_{fix} - \frac{C_{L_{\alpha_h}}}{C_{L_{\alpha_{wf}}}}\eta_h\frac{S_h}{S}\overline{x}_{ac_h}(1-\frac{d\varepsilon}{d\alpha})\frac{C_{h_\alpha}\tau_e}{C_{h_{\delta_e}}} \approx$$

$$\approx NP_{fix} + \frac{C_{m_{\delta_e}}}{C_{L_\alpha}}(1-\frac{d\varepsilon}{d\alpha})\frac{C_{h_\alpha}\tau_e}{C_{h_{\delta_e}}} \tag{4.154}$$

To justify Eqn (4.154), the equation for the elevator control power derivative, $C_{m_{\delta_e}}$ {see Eqn (3.37)} has been written as follows:

$$C_{m_{\delta_e}} = -C_{L_{\alpha_h}}\eta_h\overline{V}_h\tau_e = -C_{L_{\alpha_h}}\eta_h\frac{S_h}{S}(\overline{x}_{ac_h} - \overline{x}_{cg})\tau_e \approx -C_{L_{\alpha_h}}\eta_h\frac{S_h}{S}\overline{x}_{ac_h}\tau_e \qquad (4.155)$$

At this point the following definitions are introduced:

Definition 1:

$$\text{Static Margin Stick Fixed} = SM_{fix} = NP_{fix} - \overline{x}_{cg} = \overline{x}_{ac_A} - \overline{x}_{cg} \qquad (4.156)$$

Definition 2:

$$\text{Static Margin Stick Free} = SM_{free} = NP_{free} - \overline{x}_{cg} \qquad (4.157)$$

By combining these two definitions with Eqn (4.154), it follows that:

$$SM_{fix} - SM_{free} = NP_{fix} - NP_{free} = -\left\{\frac{C_{m_{\delta_e}}}{C_{L_\alpha}}(1 - \frac{d\varepsilon}{d\alpha})\frac{C_{h_\alpha}\tau_e}{C_{h_{\delta_e}}}\right\} \qquad (4.158)$$

These definitions will be used in Sub–section 4.5.3 to derive an alternate expression for the stick–force–versus–speed–gradient and in Sub–section 4.5.4 to derive an expression for the variation of stick–force with load–factor.

4.5.3   ANOTHER LOOK AT THE STICK–FORCE–VERSUS–SPEED GRADIENT

With the help of Definition 2 in Sub–section 4.5.2 the stick force equation (4.141) can now be approximated in the following manner:

$$F_s \approx \eta_h G_e S_e \overline{c}_e(\overline{q}A + \frac{W}{S}\frac{C_{h_{\delta_e}}}{C_{m_{\delta_e}}}SM_{free}) \qquad (4.159)$$

where:

$$A = \left[C_{h_0} + C_{h_\alpha}\left\{(i_h - \varepsilon_0) + (1 - \frac{d\varepsilon}{d\alpha})\alpha_{C_{L_1}=0}\right\} + \delta_{e_{C_{L_1}=0}}C_{h_{\delta_e}}\right] \qquad (4.160)$$

Note from Eqn (4.160) that the stick force depends on the c.g. location, $\overline{x}_{cg}$ through two terms: SM_{free} and $\delta_{e_{C_{L_1}=0}}$. From a pragmatic viewpoint, the SM_{free} term is the stronger effect. Figure 4.33 shows how the quantities A and SM_{free} influence the variation of stick force with speed.

The stick–force–speed–gradient at any speed, V_P can be found by by differentiation of Eqn (4.159):

$$\frac{\partial F_s}{\partial V_P} = \varrho \eta_h G_e S_e \overline{c}_e V_P A \tag{4.161}$$

By carefully selecting aerodynamic balance of a flight control surface, the designer can influence the various hingemoment coefficients and derivatives which make up the quantity A, such that the stick–force–speed–gradient is adequate and such that trim can be achieved within the appropriate range of c.g. locations and within the required range of speeds. Aerodynamic balance of the hingemoments is most often done with the help of tabs. The effect of several types of tabs is discussed in Sub–section 4.5.5.

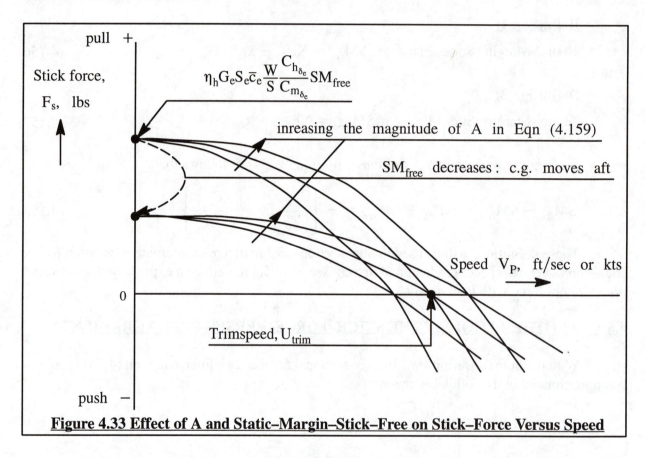

Figure 4.33 Effect of A and Static–Margin–Stick–Free on Stick–Force Versus Speed

4.5.4 CALCULATION OF STICK–FORCE–PER–'g'

Another way in which the pilot can 'feel' the relationship between stick force and the severity of a commanded maneuver is in the stick–force required to produce a change in load factor, n. This relationship is referred to as the 'stick–force–per–'g' and is given the symbol $\partial F_s/\partial n$. The following derivation shows how the 'stick–force–per–'g' can be calculated. Two types of maneuver will be considered: steady symmetrical pull–up and steady level turn.

Stick–force–per–'g' in a steady, symmetrical pull–up

The stick–force equation to be used here is re–written from Eqn (4.139) as follows:

$$F_s = \eta_h \bar{q} S_e \bar{c}_e G_e (C_{h_0} + C_{h_\alpha} \alpha_h + C_{h_{\delta_e}} \delta_e) \tag{4.162}$$

In a steady symmetrical pull–up, the angle of attack of the horizontal tail can be written as:

$$\alpha_h = \alpha - \varepsilon + i_h + Q_1 \left(\frac{x_{ac_h} - x_{cg}}{U_1} \right) \tag{4.163}$$

By using Eqn (4.116) and (3.21) this can be changed to:

$$\alpha_h = \alpha \left(1 - \frac{d\varepsilon}{d\alpha} \right) - \varepsilon_0 + i_h + (n - 1)g \frac{(x_{ac_h} - x_{cg})}{U_1^2} \tag{4.164}$$

The airplane angle of attack in such a maneuver can be written as:

$$\alpha = \alpha_{0_L} + \frac{n C_{L_{trim}}}{C_{L_\alpha}} \tag{4.165}$$

By combining Eqns (4.164) and (4.165), the horizontal tail angle of attack becomes:

$$\alpha_h = \alpha_{0_L} \left(1 - \frac{d\varepsilon}{d\alpha} \right) - \varepsilon_0 + i_h + \left(1 - \frac{d\varepsilon}{d\alpha} \right) \frac{n C_{L_{trim}}}{C_{L_\alpha}} + (n - 1)g \frac{(x_{ac_h} - x_{cg})}{U_1^2} \tag{4.166}$$

The elevator angle required to trim in this case is obtained from Eqn (4.119) by also assuming that $C_{m_\alpha} C_{L_{\delta_e}} \ll C_{L_\alpha} C_{m_{\delta_e}}$ is normally satisfied:

$$\delta_e = \delta_{e_{(n=1 \text{ and } C_{L_{trim}} = 0)}} - \frac{C_{m_q}(n - 1)\left(\dfrac{\bar{c}g}{2U_1^2} \right)}{C_{m_{\delta_e}}} - \frac{C_{m_\alpha} n C_{L_{trim}}}{C_{L_\alpha} C_{m_{\delta_e}}} \tag{4.167}$$

By introducing Eqns (3.158) and (3.37) into Eqn (4.167) the latter can be re–written as:

$$\delta_e = \delta_{e_{(n=1 \text{ and } C_{L_{trim}} = 0)}} - (n - 1)\left[\frac{1.1g(x_{ac_h} - x_{cg})}{\tau_e U_1^2} \right] + \frac{n C_{L_{trim}}}{C_{m_{\delta_e}}} SM_{fix} \tag{4.168}$$

Next, substitute Eqns (4.166) and (4.168) into Eqn (4.162), introduce the definition of static margin, stick free of Eqn (4.157) and differentiate with respect to load factor to obtain the stick–force–per–'g' as follows:

$$\frac{\partial F_s}{\partial n} = \eta_h \bar{q} S_e \bar{c}_e G_e \left[C_{L_{trim}} \left[\frac{C_{h_{\delta_e}}}{C_{m_{\delta_e}}} \right] SM_{free} + \left\{ \frac{g(x_{ac_h} - x_{cg})}{U_1^2} \right\} \left[C_{h_\alpha} - \frac{1.1 C_{h_{\delta_e}}}{\tau_e} \right] \right] \tag{4.169}$$

Because inherently stable airplanes must have a positive static margin, stick free it is seen from Eqn 4.169) that the stick–force–per–'g' gradient will have the proper sign as long as the condition: $(C_{h_\alpha} - C_{h_{\delta_e}}/\tau_e) > 0$ is satisfied. In some cases it is found that this condition is difficult to meet. In that case the stick–force–per–'g' gradient can be artificially augmented with the help of a bob–weight. The effect of a bob–weight is discussed in Sub–section 4.5.5.

For an airplane with a reversible flight control system, the maneuver–point–stick–free, MP_{free}, is now defined as that c.g. location for which the stick–force–per–'g' gradient, $\partial F_s/\partial n$, vanishes. With Eqn (4.169) it can be shown that:

$$MP_{free} = \overline{x}_{cg_{\partial F_s/\partial n=0}} = NP_{free} + \left[\frac{g(x_{ac_h} - x_{cg})}{C_{L_1}U_1^2}\right]\left[C_{h_\alpha} - \frac{1.1C_{h_{\delta_e}}}{\tau_e}\right]\frac{C_{m_{\delta_e}}}{C_{h_{\delta_e}}} \qquad (4.170)$$

or, after a slight re–arrangement while using Eqn (3.158):

$$MP_{free} = \overline{x}_{cg_{\partial F_s/\partial n=0}} = NP_{free} - \left[1 - \frac{C_{h_\alpha}\tau_e}{C_{h_{\delta_e}}}\right]\left(\frac{\varrho S\overline{c}g}{4W}\right)C_{m_q} \qquad (4.171)$$

Comparing this result with that of Eqn (4.121) it is seen that the maneuver points stick fixed and stick free differ by the bracketed term involving the elevator hingemoment derivatives. For the usual negative sign of the hingemoment derivatives, the maneuver point stick free will be forward of the maneuver point stick fixed! Therefore, the maneuver margin is reduced with the controls free vis–a–vis controls fixed.

Figure 4.34 shows an example of how the stick–force–per–'g' varies with incremental load factor (relative to 1.0) for a light airplane. Note the strong effect of c.g. location. This is predicted by Eqn (4.169) because the c.g. location affects the static margin stick free.

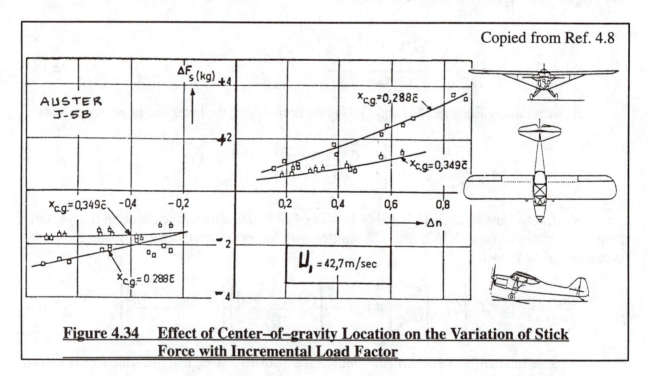

Figure 4.34   Effect of Center–of–gravity Location on the Variation of Stick Force with Incremental Load Factor

Stick–force–per–'g' in a steady, symmetrical turn

The reader is asked to modify Eqn (4.171) for the case of a steady, symmetrical turn. Hint: start with Eqn (4.163) and substitute the steady pitch rate corresponding to that in a turn.

4.5.5 EFFECT OF CONTROL SURFACE TABS, DOWN–SPRING AND BOB–WEIGHT

To assist in achieving cockpit control force trim as well as in tailoring the gradients of cockpit control forces with speed and with load factor, designers have introduced various types of control surface tabs and other control system gadgets. The following types of tab will be considered:

* Trim Tab	* Balance or Geared Tab
* Blow–down Tab	* Servo Tab

In addition, two frequently used control system gadgets, the down–spring and the bob–weight will also be discussed. For a discussion of other types of tabs, such as servo–tabs and spring–tabs, the reader may wish to consult References 4.9 and 4.10.

4.5.5.1 Effect of Trim Tabs

Trim tabs are used primarily in reversible flight control systems for the purpose of achieving moment trim with zero cockpit control forces. Figure 4.35 shows an example of three types of trim tab arrangements. Figure 4.32 showed how such a tab can be controlled from the cockpit. When the pilot is given control over tab position relative to the flight control surface to which the tab is attached, this has the effect of the pilot controlling the term C_{h_0} in the stick force equation {as seen from Eqns (4.159) and (4.160)}. At this point, the stick force Equation (4.159) is recalled:

$$F_s \approx \eta_h G_e S_e \bar{c}_e \left\{ \bar{q}(A + C_{h_t}) + \frac{W}{S} \frac{C_{h_{\delta_e}}}{C_{m_{\delta_e}}} SM_{free} \right\} \qquad (4.172)$$

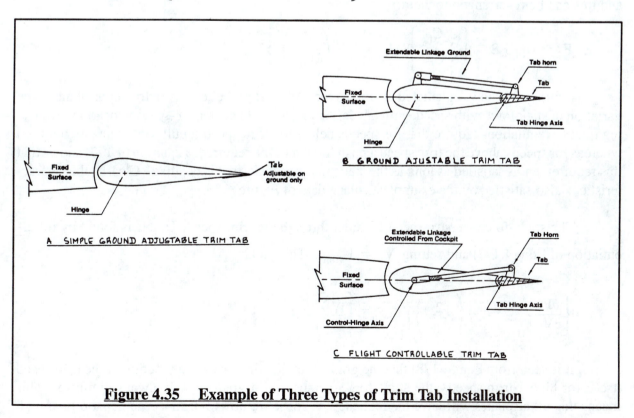

Figure 4.35   Example of Three Types of Trim Tab Installation

where: A is defined by Eqn (4.160) with the understanding that the stabilizer incidence angle, i_h,

now is set at a fixed angle.

C_{h_t} is the elevator hingemoment coefficient induced by the tab in accordance with:

$$C_{h_t} = C_{h_{\delta_{te}}} \delta_t \qquad (4.173)$$

Figure 4.27 illustrates how tab deflection is defined relative to the elevator. Note that the effect of the tab in Eqn (4.172) is to change the speed–dependent term in the stick force equation. The trim tab angle required for stick force trim can be solved from Eqns (4.173) and (4.172) by setting the stick force equal to zero:

$$\delta_{t_{trim}} = \frac{C_{h_{t_{trim}}}}{C_{h_{\delta_{te}}}} \qquad (4.174)$$

where:

$$C_{h_{t_{trim}}} = \left\{ -A - \frac{1}{\overline{q}_{trim}} \frac{W}{S} \frac{C_{h_{\delta_e}}}{C_{m_{\delta_e}}} SM_{free} \right\} \qquad (4.175)$$

The stick force at any speed, U, other than the trim speed, U_{trim}, is found by substituting Eqn (4.175) back into Eqn (4.172):

$$F_s \approx \eta_h G_e S_e \overline{c}_e \left\{ \frac{-\overline{q}}{\overline{q}_{trim}} \frac{W}{S} \frac{C_{h_{\delta_e}}}{C_{m_{\delta_e}}} SM_{free} + \frac{W}{S} \frac{C_{h_{\delta_e}}}{C_{m_{\delta_e}}} SM_{free} \right) \right\} \qquad (4.176)$$

and this can be re–arranged to yield:

$$F_s \approx (\eta_h G_e S_e \overline{c}_e) \left[\frac{W}{S} \frac{C_{h_{\delta_e}}}{C_{m_{\delta_e}}} \right] SM_{free} \left\{ 1 - \left(\frac{V_P}{U_{trim}} \right)^2 \right\} \qquad (4.177)$$

Figure 4.36 shows calculated examples for a WW–II propeller driven trainer airplane of the variation of stick force with speed, with tab deflection and with center–of–gravity location. All flying quality regulations require that for speeds below the trim speed a pull force must be required whereas for speeds above the trim speed a push force must be required. Equation (4.177) shows that this requirement is satisfied as long as the static margin, stick–free is positive! Clearly, this characteristic is also satisfied by the example airplane data of Figure 4.36.

The stick–force–versus–speed gradient through the trim speed, U_{trim}, is found by differentiation of Eqn (4.177) and setting $V_P = U_{trim}$. This yields:

$$\left\{ \frac{\partial F_s}{\partial V_P} \right\}_{U_{trim}} \approx - \left(\frac{2}{U_{trim}} \right) \eta_h G_e S_e \overline{c}_e \left\{ \frac{W}{S} \frac{C_{h_{\delta_e}}}{C_{m_{\delta_e}}} SM_{free} \right\} \qquad (4.178)$$

It is seen from Eqn (4.178) that the gradient at the trim speed is a function of the trim speed itself: for higher trim speeds, the stick–force–versus–speed gradient will always diminish. This means that all airplanes will have the tendency to 'loose' return–to–trim–speed capability at high speed. This can be particularly critical at aft center of gravity because there the static–margin–stick–free will be least.

The trim function, therefore, serves two functions: 1) it provides the ability to zero–out the stick forces and 2) it provides for speed stability at the trim speed. The reader is asked to show, that if a variable incidence stabilizer is used for the purpose of setting the stick force equal to zero, the stick–force–versus–speed gradient at the trim speed is identical to Eqn (4.178).

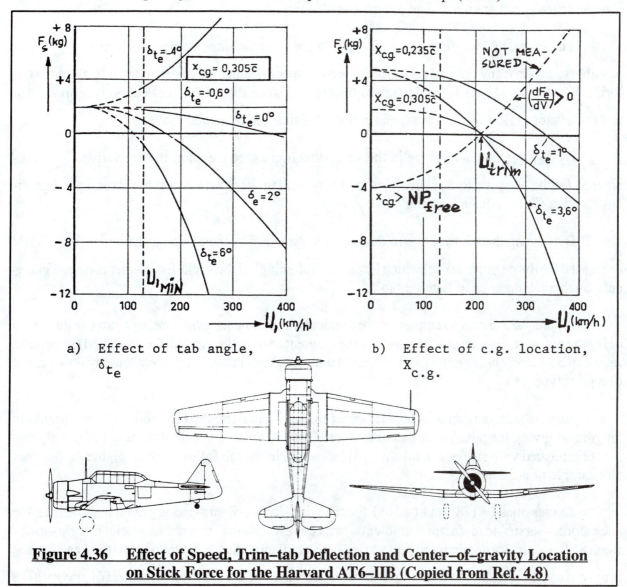

a) Effect of tab angle, δ_{t_e}

b) Effect of c.g. location, $X_{c.g.}$

Figure 4.36   Effect of Speed, Trim–tab Deflection and Center–of–gravity Location on Stick Force for the Harvard AT6–IIB (Copied from Ref. 4.8)

4.5.5.2 Effect of Balance or Geared Tabs

It is clear from Eqn (4.178) that the stick–force–versus–speed gradient at the trim speed is dependent on the product of the elevator hingemoment derivative, $C_{h_{\delta_e}}$, and the airplane static margin, stick free, SM_{free}. The latter itself is dependent on the ratio of the elevator hingemoment derivatives, $C_{h_\alpha}/C_{h_{\delta_e}}$.

Observe, that an increase in $C_{h_{\delta_e}}$ (i.e. making it more negative) 'stiffens' the stick–force–versus–speed gradient while a decrease in $C_{h_{\delta_e}}$ (i.e. making it less negative) 'softens' the stick–force–versus–speed gradient. Also, note from Eqn (4.158) that increasing $C_{h_{\delta_e}}$ (i.e. making it more negative) increases the static–margin–stick–free, SM_{free}, which in turn would 'stiffen' the stick–force–versus–speed gradient. The opposite is also true.

Therefore, by 'tailoring' the magnitude of the elevator hingemoment derivative, $C_{h_{\delta_e}}$, it is possible to achieve any desired stick–force–versus–speed gradient. A fairly simple method for tailoring $C_{h_{\delta_e}}$ is to add a trailing edge tab to the elevator such that the tab deflection is proportional to the elevator deflection. Such a tab is called a balance tab or geared tab.

By forcing the tab to move in the same direction as the elevator, the derivative $C_{h_{\delta_e}}$ is increased (in the negative sense) which leads to a 'stiffening' of the stick–force–versus–speed gradient. Such a tab is called a 'leading tab'.

By forcing the tab to move in the opposite direction as the elevator, the derivative $C_{h_{\delta_e}}$ is decreased (in the negative sense) which leads to a 'softening' of the stick–force–versus–speed gradient. Such a tab is called a 'lagging tab'.

Figure 4.37 shows examples of mechanical arrangements which cause a tab to either lead or lag the elevator. By varying the length of the moment arms in the system, the so–called tab gearing ratio can be quickly changed. That is a useful feature in flight testing to prevent lengthy down times of a prototype.

Any balance tab can also be used as a trim tab by making the tab follower arm variable in length and giving the pilot either mechanical or electrical control over that length. Frequently this is accomplished with an electro–mechanical jackscrew in the tab follower arm. Figure 4.38 shows an example of a balance–trim tab.

Expressions (4.178) and (4.169) for the stick–force–versus–speed gradient as well as the stick–force–versus–load–factor gradient respectively show that the static–margin–stick–free, SM_{free}, plays a dominant role in setting both gradients. As the center of gravity of an airplane is moved aft, the magnitude of SM_{free} eventually decreases to zero. Airplane centers of gravity have a tendency to always come out further aft than the designers intended. Therefore, it would be convenient to have available a method to 'tailor' the apparent magnitude of SM_{free}. One method for doing this without introducing artificial stability through feedback is the so–called 'blow–down' tab. The effect of a blow–down tab is discussed in Sub–section 4.5.5.3.

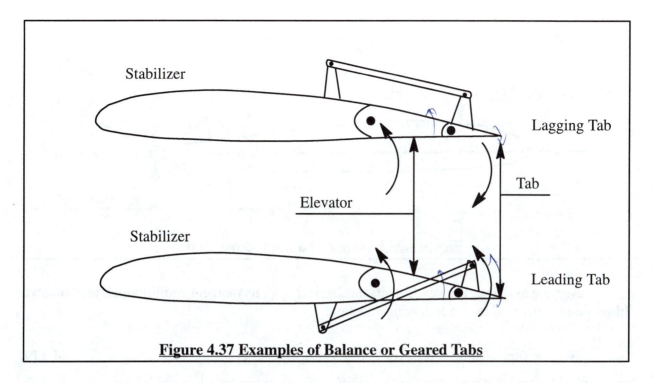

Figure 4.37 Examples of Balance or Geared Tabs

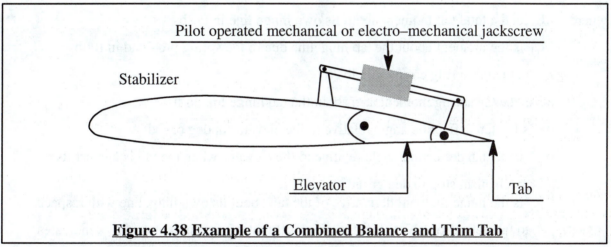

Figure 4.38 Example of a Combined Balance and Trim Tab

4.5.5.3 Effect of a Blow–down Tab

Figure 4.39 shows an example of a typical blow–down tab installation. The tab link contains a pre–loaded spring which pulls the tab against a hard stop on the elevator at zero speed. As speed, and therefore dynamic pressure builds up, the air–loads on the tab will tend to deflect the tab away from its stop. Note, that above the speed for which the tab moves away from its mechanical stop, the aerodynamic hinge–moment due to the tab about the tab hingeline is balanced by the moment due to the spring about the tab hinge line. By carefully selecting the magnitude of spring pre–load and spring constant, it is possible to make the spring moment about the tab hingeline approximately independent of the tab deflection. Assuming that the tab hingemoment derivatives about the tab hingeline and about the elevator hingeline are in a constant proportion to each other, the result is that the blow–down tab creates a hingemoment about the elevator hinge line which is constant with speed. That hinge moment is felt at the stick as a constant stick force with speed.

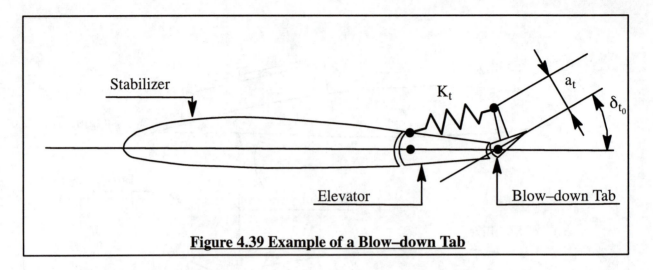

Figure 4.39 Example of a Blow–down Tab

As soon as the tab is away from its mechanical stop, its moment equilibrium **about its own hingeline** is governed by the following equation:

$$M_{tab} = 0 = -M_{pl} - K_t a_t^2 (\delta_t - \delta_{t_0}) + C^t_{h_{\delta_t}} \delta_t \eta_h \overline{q} S_t \overline{c}_t \qquad (4.179)$$

where: M_{tab} is the total tab moment about its own hinge line in ft–lbs

M_{pl} is the moment about the tab hingeline due to the spring pre–load in ft–lbs

K_t is the tab spring constant in lbs/ft

a_t is the tab spring moment arm about the tab hinge line in ft

δ_t is the tab deflection angle relative to the elevator in deg or rad

δ_{t_0} is the tab deflection angle relative to the elevator when the tab is against its

mechanical stop in deg or rad

$C^t_{h_{\delta_t}}$ is the hinge moment derivative of the tab about its own hingeline with respect

to tab deflection. Note that the previously introduced notation, $C_{h_{\delta_t}}$, indicates

the hinge moment derivative of the tab about the elevator hingeline with respect
to tab deflection!

S_t is the tab area in ft2

$\overline{c}_t$ is the tab mean geometric chord in ft

Eqn (4.179) can be solved for the equilibrium tab deflection at any dynamic pressure:

$$\delta_t = \frac{(M_{pl} - K_t a_t^2 \delta_{t_0})}{(C^t_{h_{\delta_t}} \eta_h \overline{q} S_t \overline{c}_t - K a_t^2)} \qquad (4.180)$$

By selecting the magnitudes of the tab moment arm, a_t , and the spring constant, K_t , suffi-

ciently small, such that their corresponding terms in the numerator and the denominator of Eqn 4.180) are negligible compared to their counterparts the following approximation holds:

$$\delta_t \approx \frac{M_{pl}}{C^t_{h_{\delta_t}} \eta_h \bar{q} S_t \bar{c}_t} \qquad (4.180)$$

Next, recall the the stick–force equation (4.172) and add the effect of the blow–down tab. The result is:

$$F_s \approx \eta_h G_e S_e \bar{c}_e \left\{ \bar{q}(A + C_{h_t}) + \frac{W}{S} \frac{C_{h_{\delta_e}}}{C_{m_{\delta_e}}} SM_{free} + C_{h_{\delta_t}} \frac{M_{pl}}{C^t_{h_{\delta_t}} \eta_h S_t \bar{c}_t} \right\} \qquad (4.181)$$

Observe that this equation now contains **two terms which are independent of speed**. This suggests the definition of an equivalent static margin, stick free according to:

$$SM_{free_{equivalent}} = SM_{free} + \Delta SM_{free_{blow-down-tab}} \qquad (4.182)$$

With the blow–down tab, the stick force equation (4.181) can therefore be written as:

$$F_s \approx \eta_h G_e S_e \bar{c}_e \left\{ \bar{q}(A + C_{h_t}) + \frac{W}{S} \frac{C_{h_{\delta_e}}}{C_{m_{\delta_e}}} SM_{free_{equivalent}} \right\} \qquad (4.183)$$

where:

$$SM_{free_{equivalent}} = SM_{free} + \frac{\left(C_{m_{\delta_e}} C_{h_{\delta_t}} M_{pl} \right)}{\left(C_{h_{\delta_e}} C^t_{h_{\delta_t}} S_t \bar{c}_t (W/S) \right)} \qquad (4.184)$$

The pilot therefore will experience the effect of the blow–down tab as an effective increase in longitudinal stability! The speed independent increase in the stick force due to the blow–down tab can be obtained from Eqn (4.181) as:

$$\Delta F_{s_{blow-down-tab}} = G_e M_{pl} \left(\frac{S_e \bar{c}_e}{S_t \bar{c}_t} \right) \left[\frac{C_{h_{\delta_t}}}{C^t_{h_{\delta_t}}} \right] \qquad (4.185)$$

Figure 4.40 illustrates the effect of a blow–down tab on a typical stick force versus speed plot. Comparison with Figure 4.33 also indicates that the blow–down tab has an effect similar to that of moving the center–of–gravity. The discontinuity in the stick force versus speed plot shown in Figure 4.40 is not very desirable. The effect of this discontinuity can be 'softened' by carefully selecting the speed at which it occurs. The speed at which the discontinuity occurs is evidently a function of the spring pre–load. Here is another reason to select a spring with a relatively small pre-load.

One undesirable side effect of the blow–down tab is that a 'springy' element is introduced in the flight control system. That can lead to undesirable flight control system oscillations if the system is poorly damped. By adding a viscous damper in the flight control system this effect can be effectively eliminated. Flutter of the lifting surface to which the blow–down tab equipped control surface is attached is also a potential problem. Finally, if the spring fails, the airplane could become difficult to handle. Frequent inspections of the spring are therefore required. These inspections should be easy to carry out!

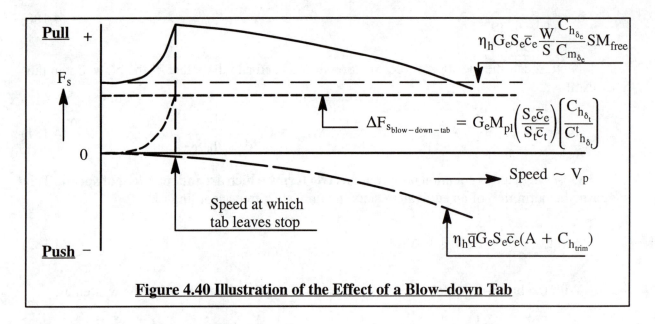

$$\eta_h G_e S_e \bar{c}_e \frac{W}{S} \frac{C_{h_{\delta_e}}}{C_{m_{\delta_e}}} SM_{free}$$

$$\Delta F_{s_{blow-down-tab}} = G_e M_{pl} \left(\frac{S_e \bar{c}_e}{S_t \bar{c}_t}\right) \left(\frac{C_{h_{\delta_t}}}{C^t_{h_{\delta_t}}}\right)$$

Speed $\sim V_p$

$$\eta_h \bar{q} G_e S_e \bar{c}_e (A + C_{h_{trim}})$$

Figure 4.40 Illustration of the Effect of a Blow−down Tab

4.5.5.4 Effect of a Down−spring

Another control system gadget which is frequently used to assist in the tailoring of stick−force−versus−speed gradients is the elevator down−spring. Such springs can be mechanically arranged almost anywhere in the flight control system but their effect is to pull the control stick forward and therefore the elevator trailing edge down. Figure 4.41 illustrates an example arrangement for a down−spring. In Figure 4.41 it is assumed that when the stick is at the forward mechanical stop, the down−spring exerts a force through a pre−load.

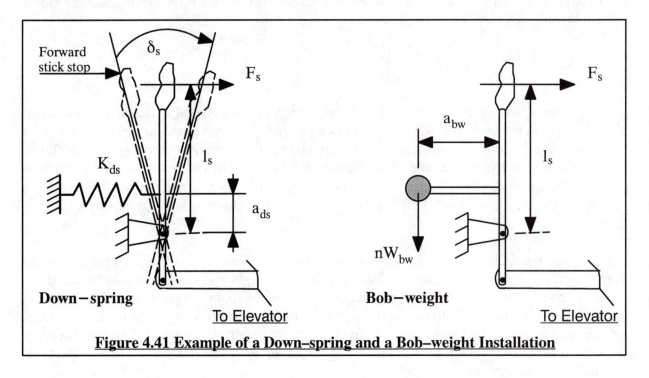

Figure 4.41 Example of a Down−spring and a Bob−weight Installation

The incremental stick force due to the down–spring at any stick deflection can thus be written as:

$$\Delta F_{s_{ds}} = f_{pl}\left(\frac{a_{ds}}{l_s}\right) + K_{ds}\left(\frac{a_{ds}{}^2 \delta_s}{l_s}\right) \qquad (4.186)$$

The gearing ratio, G_e, is used to relate the stick travel, $l_s \delta_s$, to the elevator deflection, δ_e :

$$\delta_e = G_e \delta_s l_s \qquad (4.187)$$

Therefore, Eqn (4.186) can be rewritten as:

$$\Delta F_{s_{ds}} = f_{pl}\left(\frac{a_{ds}}{l_s}\right) + K_{ds}\left(\frac{a_{ds}{}^2 \delta_e}{l_s{}^2 G_e}\right) \qquad (4.188)$$

where: f_{pl} is the pre–load of the down–spring (stick against forward stop) in lbs

K_{ds} is the spring constant of the down–spring in lbs/ft

δ_s is the stick deflection in rad

If the elevator down–spring is designed such that it has a large pre–load and a small spring constant, the second term in Eqn (4.188) becomes negligible. The stick force due to the down–spring in that case becomes independent of stick position and thus independent of elevator deflection. In such a case Eqn (4.188) becomes:

$$\Delta F_{s_{ds}} \approx f_{pl}\left(\frac{a_{ds}}{l_s}\right) \qquad (4.189)$$

In the stick–force–versus–speed diagram, this has the effect illustrated in Figure 4.42. Note, that for a given trim–tab deflection, the addition of the down–spring increases the trim speed. By re–trimming at the original trimspeed, before addition of the down–spring, it is seen that the down–spring has the effect of 'stiffening' the stick–force–versus–speed gradient.

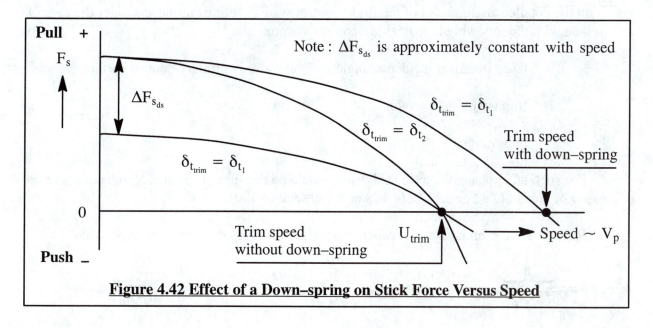

Figure 4.42 Effect of a Down–spring on Stick Force Versus Speed

4.5.5.5 Effect of a Bob–weight

Bob–weights are used primarily to tailor the stick–force–per–'g'. As a general rule, in small, highly maneuverable airplanes, a light stick–force–per–'g' is desired. On the other hand, in larger airplanes where maneuvering may be limited for reasons of passenger comfort, a fairly high stick–force–per–'g' may be desired. A bob–weight as shown in Figure 4.41 can be used to increase the stick–force–per–'g'. The incremental stick force due to the bob–weight of Figure 4.41 at a load factor of n can be written as:

$$\Delta F_{s_{bw}} \approx \frac{n W_{bw} a_{bw}}{l_s} \qquad (4.190)$$

This equation applies only for relatively shallow pitch attitude angles. At high pitch attitude angles, the moment arm of the bob–weight will be affected by the pitch attitude of the airplane because the field of gravity is assumed to always act perpendicular to the earths surface.

Clearly, the bob–weight allows the designer to alter the stick–force–per–'g' by an amount equal to:

$$\Delta \left(\frac{\partial F_s}{\partial n} \right)_{bw} \approx \frac{W_{bw} a_{bw}}{l_s} \qquad (4.191)$$

Note, that at n=1 (steady state straight line flight), the bob–weight introduces a constant (i.e. speed independent) stick force increment which has the same effect as the down–spring illustrated in Figure 4.42.

4.5.6 STICK FORCE EQUATION IN THE PRESENCE OF A TRIM TAB, DOWN–SPRING AND BOB–WEIGHT

It should be evident to the reader that the actual stick force equation for a given airplane depends on the detailed arrangement of the flight control system. For example, consider the case of an airplane with the following type of flight control system:

* fixed stabilizer incidence angle   * elevator is primary control surface

* trim tab on the elevator   * down–spring

* bob–weight

For such an airplane, the total stick force would be the sum of the stick force equations as expressed by Eqns (4.172 or 4.177), (4.188 or 4.189) and (4.190).

It is left as an exercise for the reader to develop this type of stick–force expression.

4.6   LATERAL–DIRECTIONAL COCKPIT CONTROL FORCES

The effect of control surface hinge moments on flying qualities as perceived by the pilot through the cockpit control forces is not limited to longitudinal cases. Clearly, rudder and aileron control surfaces present similar problems. In this Section, three important lateral–directional control force problems will be discussed:

* Rudder pedal control forces

* Pedal free directional stability, pedal forces in sideslip and rudder lock

* Aileron wheel (or stick) control forces

4.6.1   RUDDER PEDAL CONTROL FORCES

The rudder pedal cockpit control force needed to deflect the rudder in the presence of sideslip can be written by analogy to Eqn (4.139) and by considering the geometry of Figure 4.43:

$$F_r = G_r \eta_v \bar{q} S_r \bar{c}_r (C_{h_{\delta_r}} \delta_r + C_{h_{\delta_{r_t}}} \delta_{r_t} + C_{h_{\beta_v}} \beta_v) \tag{4.192}$$

where: F_r is the rudder pedal force. **This force is counted as positive if it causes a negative sideslip (i.e. trailing edge to right rudder = positive pedal force)**

G_r is the rudder–pedal–to–rudder gearing ratio in rad/ft

η_v is the dynamic pressure ratio at the vertical tail

S_r is the rudder area in ft2

$\bar{c}_r$ is the rudder mean geometric chord in ft

$C_{h_{\delta_r}}$ is the hinge moment derivative of the rudder about its own hingeline with respect to rudder deflection, in 1/deg or 1/rad. This derivative is normally positive!

$C_{h_{\delta_{r_t}}}$ is the hinge moment derivative of the rudder–tab about the rudder hingeline w.r.t. the rudder–tab deflection, in 1/deg or 1/rad. This derivative is normally positive!

$C_{h_{\beta_v}}$ is the hinge moment derivative of the rudder about the rudder hingeline with respect to sideslip angle, in 1/deg or 1/rad. This derivative is normally negative!

Eqn (4.192) can be used to estimate the rudder pedal force required for a number of flight situations. Some examples are:

* pedal force required to generate sideslip
* pedal force required to hold the rudder at a deflection required to meet the V_{mc}

   requirements discussed in Sub–section 4.2.6
* pedal force required to cope with a hard–over failure in the rudder tab drive mechanism

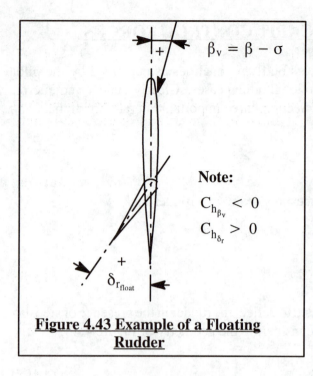

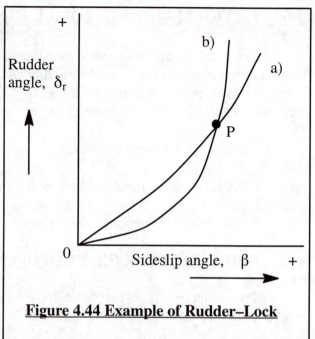

Figure 4.43 Example of a Floating Rudder

Figure 4.44 Example of Rudder–Lock

4.6.2 PEDAL–FREE DIRECTIONAL STABILITY, PEDAL FORCES IN SIDESLIP AND RUDDER LOCK

In a directionally trimmed flight condition with the rudder pedals free (feet on the cockpit floor), the rudder is free to float in accordance with the following condition:

$$0 = C_{h_{\delta_r}} \delta_r + C_{h_{\beta_v}} \beta_v \tag{4.193}$$

In this equation, the rudder tab angle is assumed to be at zero deflection. The reader will recognize the analogy with Eqn (4.148) for elevator floatation. The rudder float angle follows from Eqn (4.193) as:

$$\delta_{r_{float}} = -\frac{C_{h_{\beta_v}} \beta_v}{C_{h_{\delta_r}}} \tag{4.194}$$

A consequence of this rudder float is a reduction in the effective angle of attack of the vertical tail. The latter can be expressed as:

$$\beta_{v_{effective}} = \beta - \sigma + \tau_r \delta_{r_{float}} \tag{4.195}$$

where: σ is the sidewash angle at the vertical tail

  τ_r is the angle of attack effectiveness of the rudder (analogous to τ_e of the elevator).

The effective stabilizing yawing moment coefficient due to the vertical tail can now be written as follows:

$$C_{n_v} = C_{L_{\alpha_v}} (\beta - \sigma + \tau_r \delta_{r_{float}}) \eta_v \frac{S_v x_{v_s}}{Sb} \tag{4.196}$$

By employing Eqn (4.194) and differentiation with respect to sideslip, the directional stability contribution due to the vertical tail with the pedals free is found as:

$$C_{n_{\beta_{v_{free}}}} = C_{L_{\alpha_v}}\eta_v\frac{S_vx_{v_s}}{Sb}\left[1 - \frac{C_{h_{\beta_v}}}{C_{h_{\delta_r}}}\tau_r\right] - C_{L_{\alpha_v}}\eta_v\frac{S_vx_{v_s}}{Sb}\frac{\partial\sigma}{\partial\beta} \tag{4.197}$$

The negative contribution to directional stability due to the wing–fuselage combination is not affected by rudder floatation. Therefore, it is possible to write for the overall directional stability of the airplane:

$$C_{n_{\beta_{free}}} = C_{n_{\beta_{fix}}} - C_{L_{\alpha_v}}\eta_v\frac{S_vx_{v_s}}{Sb}\left[\frac{C_{h_{\beta_v}}}{C_{h_{\delta_r}}}\tau_r\right] \tag{4.198}$$

With the help of Eqn (3.87) this can be also written as:

$$C_{n_{\beta_{free}}} = C_{n_{\beta_{fix}}} + C_{n_{\delta_r}}\left[\frac{C_{h_{\beta_v}}}{C_{h_{\delta_r}}}\right] \tag{4.199}$$

When a pilot pushes on the rudder pedals to generate sideslip, the airplane yawing moment equilibrium requires that the following condition is satisfied:

$$C_{n_{\beta_{fix}}}\beta + C_{n_{\delta_r}}\delta_r = 0 \tag{4.200}$$

Therefore, to produce a given sideslip angle, β, requires a rudder angle given by:

$$\delta_r = \frac{-C_{n_{\beta_{fix}}}\beta}{C_{n_{\delta_r}}} \tag{4.201}$$

Neglecting the side–wash angle, σ, the rudder pedal force required to produce a given sideslip angle, β, may be found from Eqns (4.192) and (4.201) as:

$$F_r = G_r\eta_v\bar{q}S_r\bar{c}_r(C_{h_{\beta_v}}\beta - C_{h_{\delta_r}}\frac{C_{n_{\beta_{fix}}}\beta}{C_{n_{\delta_r}}} + C_{h_{\delta_{r_t}}}\delta_{r_t}) \tag{4.202}$$

In the flying quality regulations it is required that the slope of rudder pedal force with respect to sideslip angle must have the correct sign (right rudder = positive pedal force for negative sideslip) and should not be too large. The rudder–pedal–force–versus–sideslip gradient can be obtained from Eqn (4.202) by differentiation. Using Eqn (4.199) the reader is asked to show that:

$$\frac{\partial F_r}{\partial\beta} = \frac{G_r\eta_v\bar{q}S_r\bar{c}_rC_{h_{\beta_{\delta_r}}}}{C_{n_{\delta_r}}}C_{n_{\beta_{free}}} \tag{4.203}$$

Because neither directional stability, rudder control power nor the rudder hingemoment derivatives are constant with sideslip, it is often difficult to meet this requirement. Because the bottom of the rudder is often enveloped in a thick boundary layer of the fuselage (which at moderate to high angles of attack may also separate), the rudder hingemoment derivatives are often severely nonlinear with sideslip. This can give rise to the rudder lock phenomenon described next.

Consider curves a) and b) in Figure 4.44. Curve a) represents the rudder angle required to produce any given sideslip angle. If this relationship were linear it would be represented by Eqn

(4.201). Curve b) represents the rudder float angle at any given sideslip angle. If all derivatives were linear, this curve would be represented by Eqn (4.194). The difference between curves a) and b) at any given sideslip angle is that part of the rudder deflection for which the pilot must provide a force to keep it there! Clearly, when the rudder moves beyond the intersection point P, the rudder pedal force reverses and the rudder moves hard–over to its mechanical stop. That phenomenon is known as 'rudder–lock'. It is clearly unacceptable within the normal flight envelope of an airplane.

Rudder–lock can and has caused the loss of airplane and crew. An example is the Bristol Freighter (Type 170) which, during a certification flight test, experienced such large sideslip angles following rudder lock, that the vertical tail broke off rendering the airplane uncontrollable.

Since the rudder–lock problem is frequently associated with the boundary layer phenomenon mentioned before, a solution is sometimes found in re–energizing the boundary layer over the lower part of the rudder. That can be accomplished with a highly swept, sharp–edged dorsal fin as illustrated in Figure 4.45. Such fins tend to generate a significant amount of vorticity which helps in straightening–out the flow around the base of the vertical tail.

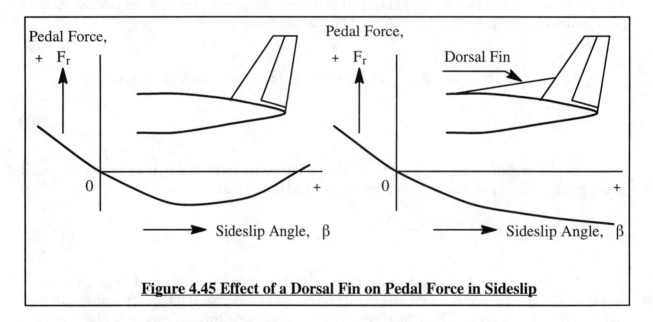

Figure 4.45 Effect of a Dorsal Fin on Pedal Force in Sideslip

4.6.3   AILERON WHEEL (OR STICK) CONTROL FORCES

Roll (or bank angle) performance capabilities of airplanes are essential for safe flight and in many military airplanes required as part of the mission. Whether or not airplanes can achieve the roll performance is based on an assumption that a given required aileron deflection can indeed be reached AND, when reached does not cause the wing to deform aero–elastically (see aileron reversal phenomenon discussion in Chapter 7, Part II of this text). Whether or not a given aileron deflection can indeed be reached depends on the aileron wheel (or stick) force required and on any elastic compliance in the flight control system itself. It will be assumed here, that the flight control system itself has no significant aeroelastic compliance.

Figure 4.46 shows how the ailerons are assumed to move as a result of deflection of the cockpit control. A positive aileron deflection is defined as one which results in a positive rolling moment.

The aileron deflection, δ_a , is defined as one half of the sum of the left and the right aileron deflections:

$$\delta_a = \frac{1}{2}(\delta_{a_l} + \delta_{a_r}) \qquad (4.204)$$

The left aileron is sometimes referred to as the down–going aileron and the right aileron as the up–going aileron. Eqn (4.204) recognizes the fact that the left and right ailerons may not move the same amount: remember the aileron–yawing moment problem discussed in Chapter 3. The aileron wheel (or stick) force required to hold both ailerons at a certain angle can be written as follows:

$$F_a = -G_{a_l}HM_{a_l} + G_{a_r}HM_{a_r} \qquad (4.205)$$

where: G_{a_l} and G_{a_r} are the gearing ratios for the left and right ailerons respectively, both counted positive and both in rad/ft

HM_{a_l} and HM_{a_r} are the hingemoments for the left and right ailerons respectively. A hin–ge–moment is defined as positive if it tends to drive the trailing edge of a control surface down and vice–versa.

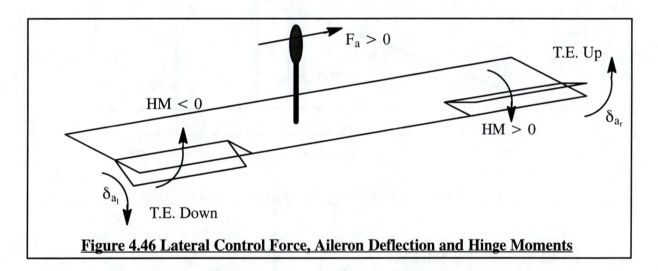

<u>Figure 4.46 Lateral Control Force, Aileron Deflection and Hinge Moments</u>

The hingemoments of the left and right ailerons can be expressed as:

$$HM_{a_l} = C_{h_{a_l}}\bar{q}S_a\bar{c}_a \quad \text{and} \quad HM_{a_r} = C_{h_{a_r}}\bar{q}S_a\bar{c}_a \qquad (4.206)$$

where it is assumed that both ailerons have the same surface area, S_a, and surface chord, $\bar{c}_a$.

The hingemoment coefficients, $C_{h_{a_l}}$ and $C_{h_{a_r}}$, are assumed to be linear functions of angle of attack and aileron deflection angles:

$$C_{h_{a_l}} = C_{h_{o_a}} + C_{h_{\alpha_a}}\alpha_{a_l} + C_{h_{\delta_a}}\delta_{a_l} \quad \text{and} \quad C_{h_{a_r}} = C_{h_{o_a}} + C_{h_{\alpha_a}}\alpha_{a_r} + C_{h_{\delta_a}}\delta_{a_r} \qquad (4.207)$$

where: δ_{a_l} and δ_{a_r} are the left and right aileron deflection angles, in deg or rad

α_{a_l} and α_{a_r} represent the 'average' angle of attack over the aileron span for the left and right aileron respectively. These angles of attack are the sum of the wing angle of attack and the angle of attack induced by steady state roll rate if the airplane is rolling. Figure 4.47 illustrates how the average angle of attack at an aileron station is defined.

Two cases will be considered:

* 4.6.3.1 Steady State Roll Rate

* 4.6.3.2 Steady State Straight Line Flight

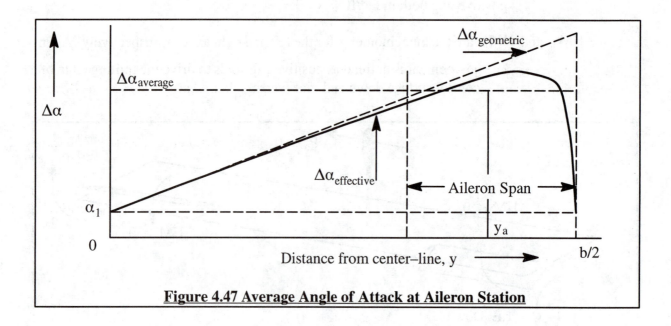

Figure 4.47 Average Angle of Attack at Aileron Station

4.6.3.1 Steady State Roll Rate

Assuming that the aileron station, where the average angle of attack is to be considered, is designated as y_a and assuming that the steady state roll rate is $\dot{\phi}_{ss}$, the following holds for the average aileron angles of attack:

$$\alpha_{a_l} = \alpha_w - \frac{\dot{\phi}_{ss} y_a}{U_1} \quad \text{and} \quad \alpha_{a_r} = \alpha_w + \frac{\dot{\phi}_{ss} y_a}{U_1} \tag{4.208}$$

where: $\dot{\phi}_{ss}$ is the steady state roll rate which corresponds to a given aileron deflection, δ_a.

An expression for the latter is derived in Chapter 5, Eqn (5.134):

$$\dot{\phi}_{ss} = \frac{L_{\delta_a} \delta_a}{-L_p} \tag{4.209}$$

For definitions of L_{δ_a} and L_p the reader should refer to Table 5.7 in Chapter 5.

The aileron wheel or stick force can therefore be written as:

$$F_a = \overline{q}S_a\overline{c}_a\left\{ - G_{a_l}\left(C_{h_{o_a}} + C_{h_{\alpha_a}}\alpha_{a_l} + C_{h_{\delta_a}}\delta_{a_l}\right) + G_{a_r}\left(C_{h_{o_a}} + C_{h_{\alpha_a}}\alpha_{a_r} + C_{h_{\delta_a}}\delta_{a_r}\right)\right\} \quad (4.210)$$

or, with Eqns (4.208) and (4.209) as:

$$F_a = \overline{q}S_a\overline{c}_a\left[- G_{a_l}\left\{C_{h_{o_a}} + C_{h_{\alpha_a}}\left(\alpha_w - \frac{\dot{\phi}_{ss}y_a}{U_1}\right) + C_{h_{\delta_a}}\delta_{a_l}\right\}\right] +$$

$$+ \overline{q}S_a\overline{c}_a\left[G_{a_r}\left\{C_{h_{o_a}} + C_{h_{\alpha_a}}\left(\alpha_w + \frac{\dot{\phi}_{ss}y_a}{U_1}\right) + C_{h_{\delta_a}}\delta_{a_r}\right\}\right] \quad (4.211)$$

At this point a simplifying assumption will be made. Assume that the left and right ailerons have the same gearing ratio: $G_{a_l} = G_{a_r} = G_a$. In that case, the left and right ailerons will move over the same angle: $\delta_a = \delta_{a_l} = -\delta_{a_r}$. Remembering that the hingemoment due to aileron deflection is positive for the right aileron and negative for the left aileron, the aileron wheel or stick force now yields:

$$F_a = \overline{q}S_a\overline{c}_aG_a\delta_a\left\{C_{h_{\alpha_a}}\left(\frac{2L_{\delta_a}y_a}{-U_1L_p}\right) - 2C_{h_{\delta_a}}\right\} \quad (4.212)$$

This can be re-written as:

$$F_a = -2\overline{q}S_a\overline{c}_aG_aC_{h_{\delta_a}}\delta_a\left\{1 - \frac{C_{h_{\alpha_a}}}{C_{h_{\delta_a}}}\left(\frac{L_{\delta_a}y_a}{-U_1L_p}\right)\right\} \quad (4.213)$$

The reader should keep in mind, that the derivatives $C_{h_{\delta_a}}$ and $C_{h_{\alpha_a}}$ apply to each aileron individually. That is the reason for the factor 2 in Eqn (4.213).

Equation (4.213) shows that the aileron floatation derivative, $C_{h_{\alpha_a}}$, can have a significant effect on the aileron control force in a steady state roll. If the ailerons are designed so that they float trailing edge up (i.e. $C_{h_{\alpha_a}}$ is large in the negative sense), the aileron control force in a steady state roll will be lower than if the ailerons are designed with less up–float tendency.

It is also seen from Eqn (4.213) that, for a given set of hingemoment derivatives, the lateral control forces increase with dynamic pressure. In airplanes with a reversible flight control system the maximum force of which a pilot is capable can therefore become a limiting factor in achieving certain roll rates. Figure 4.48 shows the generic effect of aileron wheel force on achievable roll rate for a rigid airplane. If the airplane has significant aero–elastic effects (See Chapter 7 in Part II) the achievable roll rates will be further reduced as suggested in Figure 4.48.

4.6.3.2 Steady State, Straight Line Flight

Using the same assumptions about aileron gearing made in 4.6.3.1 the reader is asked to show that in steady state straight line flight, the lateral control force equation is simplified to:

$$F_a = -2\overline{q}S_a\overline{c}_aG_aC_{h_{\delta_a}}\delta_a \tag{4.214}$$

This is the aileron wheel force equation which should be used in conjunction with the minimum control speed problem, one–engine–inoperative.

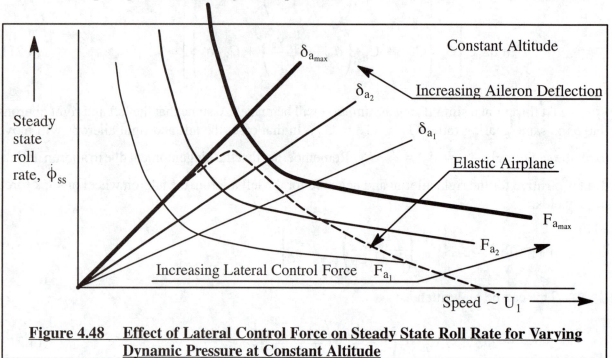

Figure 4.48   Effect of Lateral Control Force on Steady State Roll Rate for Varying Dynamic Pressure at Constant Altitude

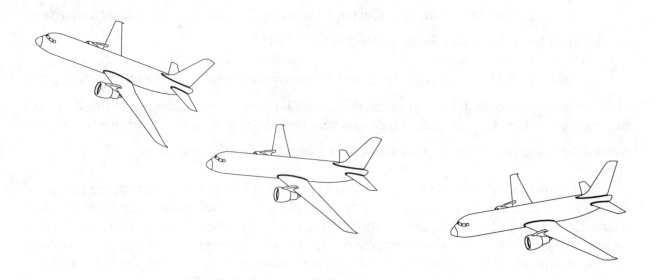

4.7 A MATRIX APPROACH TO THE GENERAL LONGITUDINAL TRIM PROBLEM

The procedure employed so–far in analyzing airplane trimmed flight situations has been:

1) determine the airplane force and moment equilibrium with Eqns (4.46) and (4.47) which results in solutions for the trimmed angle of attack and for the trimmed elevator angle.

2) these solutions were used next in the stick force equation (4.141) to find the stabilizer or tab angle {Equations (4.145) and (4.174) respectively} required to obtain stick force trim (zero stick–force).

This procedure is simple and allows clear insight into where the 'design drivers' of a trim problem are. Strictly speaking, this procedure is wrong because it neglects coupling between the lift, pitching moment and stick–force equations. The correct way to analyze airplane trim is to take the drag, lift, pitching moment AND stick–force equations and solve them simultaneously. A matrix approach to do just that will now be presented.

In the mathematical model to be developed here, the following variables will be considered:

* Angle of attack, α * Flight path angle, γ

* Stabilizer incidence angle, i_h * Elevator angle, δ_e

* Elevator tab angle, δ_t * Stick (or wheel) force, F_s

Thrust (or power) setting, speed and altitude are assumed to be pre–specified.

Because there are only four equations: drag, lift, pitching moment and stick force equations, two of these six variables have to be specified. Typical cases which need to be considered in new airplane design are:

Case 1: Specify flight path angle, γ (level flight), and stick force, F_s (zero if trimmed)

       Solve for: α , i_h , δ_e and δ_t

Case 2: Specify stabilizer incidence angle, i_h , and stick force, F_s (zero if trimmed)

       Solve for: α , γ , δ_e and δ_t

Case 3: Specify stabilizer incidence angle, i_h , and (run–away) tab angle, δ_t

       Solve for: α , γ , δ_e and F_s

Solutions to these problems must then be subjected to an 'acceptability check' similar to that mentioned on page 227. Solutions make sense only if they are consistent with 'attached flow' conditions.

The mathematical model for generalized trim should be sufficiently general to cover straight line as well as maneuvering flight cases. For that reason, the general, steady state longitudinal equations (1.55a), (1.55c) and (1.56b) will be invoked and renumbered:

Force along X: $m(-V_1R_1 + W_1Q_1) = -mg\sin\Theta_1 + F_{A_{x_1}} + F_{T_{x_1}}$ (4.215a)

Force along Z: $m(-U_1Q_1 + V_1P_1) = mg\cos\Phi_1\cos\Theta_1 + F_{A_{z_1}} + F_{T_{z_1}}$ (4.215b)

Pitching moment about Y: $(I_{xx} - I_{zz})P_1R_1 + I_{xz}(P_1^2 - R_1^2) = M_{A_1} + M_{T_1}$ (4.215c)

For zero sideslip: $V_1 = 0$. Also, in the stability axis system, $\Theta_1 = \gamma_1$ and $W_1 = 0$. By also invoking the standard forms for drag, lift and thrust, while using $W = mg$, Eqns (4.215) are re-written as:

$$0 = -W\sin\gamma_1 - D + T\cos(\alpha_1 + \phi_T)$$ (4.216a)

$$-\frac{W}{g}U_1Q_1 = W\cos\Phi_1\cos\gamma_1 - L - T\sin(\alpha_1 + \phi_T)$$ (4.216b)

$$(I_{xx} - I_{zz})P_1R_1 + I_{xz}(P_1^2 - R_1^2) = M_{A_1} - Td_T$$ (4.216c)

The steady state angular rates in Eqns (4.216) were shown to be functions of the load factor, n, see Eqns (4.85), (4.93) and (4.116):

For the steady level turn:	**For the steady symmetrical pull–up:**	
$P_1 = 0$	$P_1 = 0$	(4.217a)
$Q_1 = \frac{g}{U_1}(n - \frac{1}{n})$	$Q_1 = \frac{g}{U_1}(n - 1)$	(4.217b)
$R_1 = \frac{g}{nU_1}\sqrt{n^2 - 1}$	$R_1 = 0$	(4.217c)
$\cos\phi_1 = \frac{1}{n}$	$\cos\phi_1 = 1.0$	(4.217d)

Equations (4.217) can be generalized by introducing the following notation:

Steady level turn : $\frac{1}{\overline{n}} = \frac{1}{n}$ Steady symmetrical pull – up : $\frac{1}{\overline{n}} = 1$ (4.218)

The result is that Eqns (4.217) are re–written as:

$$P_1 = 0 \qquad Q_1 = \frac{g}{U_1}(n - \frac{1}{n}) \qquad R_1 = \frac{g}{U_1}\sqrt{1 - \frac{1}{n^2}} \qquad \cos\phi_1 = \frac{1}{n} \qquad (4.219)$$

Using the notation of Eqns (4.219) the equations of motion and by assuming small flight path angles, γ Eqns (4.216) are written as:

$$0 = -W\gamma_1 - D + T\cos(\alpha_1 + \phi_T) \qquad (4.220a)$$

$$-nW = -L - T\sin(\alpha_1 + \phi_T) \qquad (4.220b)$$

$$-I_{xz}\frac{g^2}{U_1^2}(1 - \frac{1}{n^2}) = M_{A_1} - Td_T \qquad (4.220c)$$

The drag, lift and pitching moment in Eqns (4.220) are modelled as follows by analogy to Eqns (4.86a), (4.86c) and (4.86e) respectively:

$$D = C_D\bar{q}_1 S = (C_{D_0} + C_{D_\alpha}\alpha + C_{D_{\alpha^2}}\alpha^2 + C_{D_{i_h}}i_h + C_{D_{\delta_e}}\delta_e + C_{D_{\delta_t}}\delta_t)\bar{q}_1 S \qquad (4.221a)$$

$$L = C_L\bar{q}_1 S = (C_{L_0} + C_{L_\alpha}\alpha + C_{L_q}\frac{Q_1\bar{c}}{2U_1} + C_{L_{i_h}}i_h + C_{L_{\delta_e}}\delta_e + C_{L_{\delta_t}}\delta_t)\bar{q}_1 S \qquad (4.221b)$$

$$M_A = C_m\bar{q}_1 S\bar{c} =$$

$$= (C_{m_0} + C_{m_\alpha}\alpha + C_{m_q}\frac{Q_1\bar{c}}{2U_1} + C_{m_{i_h}}i_h + C_{m_{\delta_e}}\delta_e + C_{m_{\delta_t}}\delta_t)\bar{q}_1 S\bar{c} \qquad (4.221c)$$

To clarify some of the notation used, the symbol $\overline{C}_{D_0}$ represents the drag coefficient for zero angle of attack (as opposed to zero lift coefficient). The symbol C_{m_0} represents the pitching moment coefficient at zero angle of attack, as usual.

In airplanes with propellers which are mounted such that either the wing or the tails are embedded in the propeller slipstream, it may be that several stability and control derivatives become functions of the power dissipated by the propeller. If that is the case, one way to account for these power effects is to substitute the following for all similarly affected derivatives:

$$C_{L_{\alpha_{power-on}}} \mapsto C_{L_{\alpha_{power-off}}} + \frac{\partial C_{L_\alpha}}{\partial C_T}C_T \qquad (4.222)$$

where the thrust coefficient, C_T , is defined by:

$$C_T = \frac{T}{\bar{q}S} \qquad (4.223)$$

The derivatives $\partial C_{L_\alpha}/\partial C_T$ are difficult to predict theoretically. It is recommended to obtain these derivatives from windtunnel data with a scaled, powered propeller.

For the stick force, the following equation will be used:

$$F_s = G_e HM + F_{s_{artificial}} \tag{4.224}$$

where: G_e is the stick (or wheel) to elevator gearing ratio. This gearing ratio is assumed

to be a constant here. However, depending on the detail layout of the flight control system, the gearing ratio can be a nonlinear function of elevator deflection.

HM   is the elevator hinge moment as expressed by Eqn (4.137)

$F_{s_{artificial}}$ is the increment in stick–force caused by control system gadgetry such as:

down–spring, bob–weight etc. Clearly, $F_{s_{artificial}}$ depends on the detail design

of the flight control system. The following expression will be used here:

$$F_{s_{artificial}} = nW_{bw}K_1 + G_e\left\{K_2 + K_3\delta_e + K_4\delta_e^2 + K_5i_h\right\} \tag{4.225}$$

where: n   is the airplane load factor

W_{bw} is the weight of the bob–weight in lbs

K_1 is a proportionality constant which depends on the geometry of the bob–weight

installation. For the example of Figure 4.41: $K_1 = a_{bw}/l_s$.

K_2 is the hinge moment due to the down–spring pre–load, in ft–lbs

K_3 is the hinge moment due to the down–spring as a result of elevator deflection,

in ft–lbs/rad

K_4 is the hinge moment due to the down–spring as a result of the square of elevator

deflection, in ft–lbs/rad2

K_5 is the hinge moment due to the down–spring as a result of stabilizer deflection,

in ft–lbs/rad

The hingemoment equation (4.137) contains the horizontal tail angle of attack, α_h , which in turn is affected by the pitch rate as shown in Eqn (4.164). By substituting Eqn (4.164) into Eqn (4.137) and Eqn (4.225) into Eqn (4.224) the following stick force equation is obtained:

$$F_s = \eta_h \bar{q} S_e \bar{c}_e G_e \left[C_{h_o} + C_{h_\alpha}\left\{ \alpha\left(1 - \frac{d\varepsilon}{d\alpha}\right) + i_h - \varepsilon_0 + \frac{Q_1(x_{ac_h} - x_{cg})}{U_1} \right\} + C_{h_{\delta_e}}\delta_e \right] +$$

$$+ \eta_h \bar{q} S_e \bar{c}_e G_e \left[C_{h_{\delta_t}}\delta_t \right] + nW_{bw}K_1 + G_e\left\{K_2 + K_3\delta_e + K_4\delta_e^2 + K_5i_h\right\} \tag{4.225}$$

By substituting the pitch rate term of Eqn (4.219) and re–arranging to a format similar to that of Eqns (4.221) this equation becomes:

$$F_s = \eta_h \overline{q} S_e \overline{c}_e G_e \left[C_{h_o} + C_{h_\alpha} \left\{ - \varepsilon_0 + \frac{g(x_{ac_h} - x_{cg})}{U_1^2} \left(n - \frac{1}{\overline{n}} \right) \right\} \right] + n W_{bw} K_1 + G_e K_2 +$$

$$+ \eta_h \overline{q} S_e \overline{c}_e G_e \left\{ C_{h_\alpha} \left(1 - \frac{d\varepsilon}{d\alpha} \right) \right\} \alpha + \left(\eta_h \overline{q} S_e \overline{c}_e G_e C_{h_\alpha} + G_e K_5 \right) i_h +$$

$$+ \left\{ \eta_h \overline{q} S_e \overline{c}_e G_e C_{h_{\delta_e}} + G_e (K_3 + K_4 \delta_e) \right\} \delta_e + \left(\eta_h \overline{q} S_e \overline{c}_e G_e C_{h_{\delta_t}} \right) \delta_t \qquad (4.226)$$

At this point, Eqns (4.220) with Eqns (4.221) substituted in them and Eqn (4.226) are cast in the matrix format of Table 4.7.

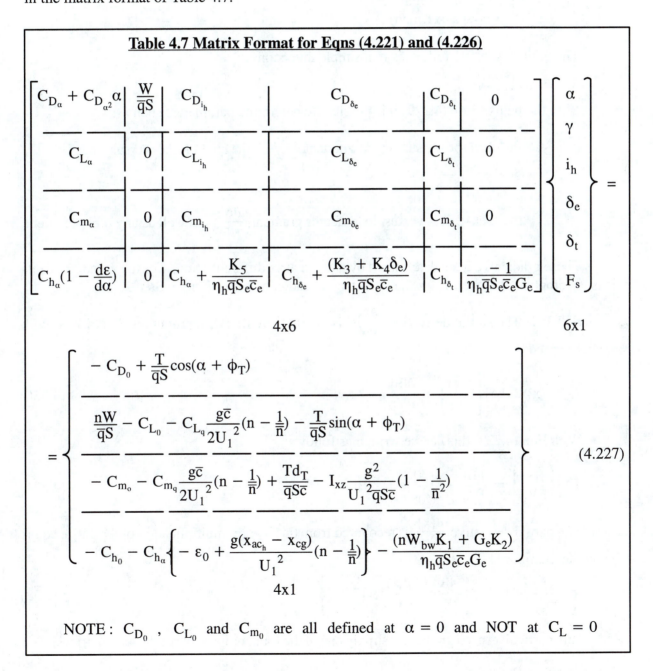

Table 4.7 Matrix Format for Eqns (4.221) and (4.226)

$$
\begin{bmatrix}
C_{D_\alpha} + C_{D_{\alpha^2}} \alpha & \dfrac{W}{\overline{q}S} & C_{D_{i_h}} & & C_{D_{\delta_e}} & C_{D_{\delta_t}} & 0 \\[2mm]
C_{L_\alpha} & 0 & C_{L_{i_h}} & & C_{L_{\delta_e}} & C_{L_{\delta_t}} & 0 \\[2mm]
C_{m_\alpha} & 0 & C_{m_{i_h}} & & C_{m_{\delta_e}} & C_{m_{\delta_t}} & 0 \\[2mm]
C_{h_\alpha}\left(1 - \dfrac{d\varepsilon}{d\alpha}\right) & 0 & C_{h_\alpha} + \dfrac{K_5}{\eta_h \overline{q} S_e \overline{c}_e} & C_{h_{\delta_e}} + \dfrac{(K_3 + K_4 \delta_e)}{\eta_h \overline{q} S_e \overline{c}_e} & C_{h_{\delta_t}} & \dfrac{-1}{\eta_h \overline{q} S_e \overline{c}_e G_e}
\end{bmatrix}
\begin{Bmatrix} \alpha \\ \gamma \\ i_h \\ \delta_e \\ \delta_t \\ F_s \end{Bmatrix} =
$$

$$4 \times 6 \qquad\qquad\qquad\qquad 6 \times 1$$

$$
= \left\{
\begin{array}{l}
- C_{D_0} + \dfrac{T}{\overline{q}S} \cos(\alpha + \phi_T) \\[3mm]
\hline
\dfrac{nW}{\overline{q}S} - C_{L_0} - C_{L_q} \dfrac{g\overline{c}}{2U_1^2}\left(n - \dfrac{1}{\overline{n}}\right) - \dfrac{T}{\overline{q}S}\sin(\alpha + \phi_T) \\[3mm]
\hline
- C_{m_0} - C_{m_q} \dfrac{g\overline{c}}{2U_1^2}\left(n - \dfrac{1}{\overline{n}}\right) + \dfrac{Td_T}{\overline{q}S\overline{c}} - I_{xz} \dfrac{g^2}{U_1^2 \overline{q}S\overline{c}}\left(1 - \dfrac{1}{\overline{n}^2}\right) \\[3mm]
\hline
- C_{h_0} - C_{h_\alpha}\left\{ - \varepsilon_0 + \dfrac{g(x_{ac_h} - x_{cg})}{U_1^2}\left(n - \dfrac{1}{\overline{n}}\right) \right\} - \dfrac{(nW_{bw} K_1 + G_e K_2)}{\eta_h \overline{q} S_e \overline{c}_e G_e}
\end{array}
\right\} \qquad (4.227)
$$

$$4 \times 1$$

NOTE: C_{D_0} , C_{L_0} and C_{m_0} are all defined at $\alpha = 0$ and NOT at $C_L = 0$

The reader will observe that Eqn (4.227) is **not linear** because the angle of attack and the elevator angle also occur in matrices [A] and {B}. In most practical applications this does not turn out to be a problem, as will be shown.

Equation (4.227) in Table 4.7 must be suitably modified to accommodate the typical user scenarios, three of which were given on page 275. When specifying any two of the six variables, the matrix equation (4.227) reduces to a conformal 4x4 set of the following general type:

$$[A]\{x\} = \{B\} \tag{4.228}$$

where: [A] is now a 4x4 matrix
{x} is now a 4x1 matrix
{B} is now a 4x1 matrix

The variables in {x} follow from a simple inversion as:

$$\{x\} = [A]^{-1}\{B\} \tag{4.229}$$

With the help of Eqn (4.229) it is possible to determine parameters such as:

* the elevator–versus–speed gradient, $\dfrac{\partial \delta_e}{\partial V_p}$; the stick–force–versus–speed gradient, $\dfrac{\partial F_s}{\partial V_p}$;

* the stick–force–versus–load–factor gradient, $\dfrac{\partial \delta_e}{\partial n}$, as well as any other gradient.

These gradients can be determined by using matrix differentiation. For the speed gradients this is accomplished in Step 1, for the load–factor gradients this is done in Step 2.

STEP 1: The partial derivative: $\dfrac{\partial \{x\}}{\partial V_p}$ is obtained by first differentiating Eqn (4.228) with respect to speed:

$$\frac{\partial [A]}{\partial V_p}\{x\} + [A]\left\{\frac{\partial \{x\}}{\partial V_p}\right\} = \frac{\partial \{B\}}{\partial V_p} \tag{4.230}$$

With Eqn (4.229) this can be written as follows:

$$[A]\left\{\frac{\partial \{x\}}{\partial V_p}\right\} = \frac{\partial \{B\}}{\partial V_p} - \frac{\partial [A]}{\partial V_p}[A]^{-1}\{B\} \tag{4.231}$$

The partial derivative $\dfrac{\partial \{x\}}{\partial V_p}$ is recovered from this by pre–multiplication of the entire equation by the matrix $[A]^{-1}$:

$$\left\{\frac{\partial \{x\}}{\partial V_p}\right\} = [A]^{-1}\left\{\frac{\partial \{B\}}{\partial V_p} - \frac{\partial [A]}{\partial V_p}[A]^{-1}\{B\}\right\} \tag{4.232}$$

Any particular speed gradient is simply one of the four components of the 4x1 matrix $\dfrac{\partial \{x\}}{\partial V_p}$.

STEP 2: The reader is asked to show by analogy to Step 1 that:

$$\left\{\frac{\partial\{x\}}{\partial n}\right\} = [A]^{-1}\left\{\frac{\partial\{B\}}{\partial n} - \frac{\partial[A]}{\partial n}[A]^{-1}\{B\}\right\} \tag{4.233}$$

Any particular load–factor gradient is simply one of the four components of the 4x1 matrix $\frac{\partial\{x\}}{\partial n}$.

It is left as an exercise to the reader to determine the differentiated matrices: $\frac{\partial[A]}{\partial V_p}$, $\frac{\partial[A]}{\partial n}$, $\frac{\partial\{B\}}{\partial V_p}$ and $\frac{\partial\{B\}}{\partial n}$.

Because of the non–linear nature of the matrices [A] and {B}, the following procedure is suggested to find the correct solution of Eqn (4.228). From the approximate equations (4.105) or (4.117), solve for the approximate values of angle of attack and elevator angle. Substitute those values in matrices [A] and {B}. Then calculate the solution {x} from Eqn (4.229). Next, re–substitute the new values for angle of attack and elevator angle in [A] and {B} and iterate until the solutions remain within 1%. It has been found that this procedure, for normal flight speeds, converges rapidly. **Warning:** for speeds below normal flight speeds convergence is not assured.

The matrix method just described has been programmed as part of the AAA program described in Appendix A. Figure 4.49 shows a screendump of this program for the case of a twin turbo-prop commuter airplane. The flight situation is a power–on landing approach at aft c.g. Power is set to result in a 3 degree glide angle. The assumption is made that the elevator tab angle is fixed at zero degrees and that the stabilizer incidence angle is fixed at –0.677 degrees. This stabilizer setting was determined so that the stick force would be zero lbs. The airplane is therefore in complete moment and stick–force trim.. This represents Case 3 on page 275. Note under output parameters the following:

1) The static margin, stick fixed is 7.00%

2) The static margin, stick free is 2.15 %

   The elevator floatation behavior therefore moves the apparent neutral point forward by roughly 5% of the m.g.c.

3) The elevator angle required is 0.954 degrees.

4) The stick–force–versus–speed gradient is –0.57 lbs/kt. This gradient has the correct sign. Since the magnitude is more than 1 lbs/6–kts this gradient also has the correct magnitude.

5) The stick–force–versus–load–factor gradient is 24.3 lbs/g. The minimum allowable value for this type of airplane is 6.8 lbs/g. This gradient is therefore also acceptable.

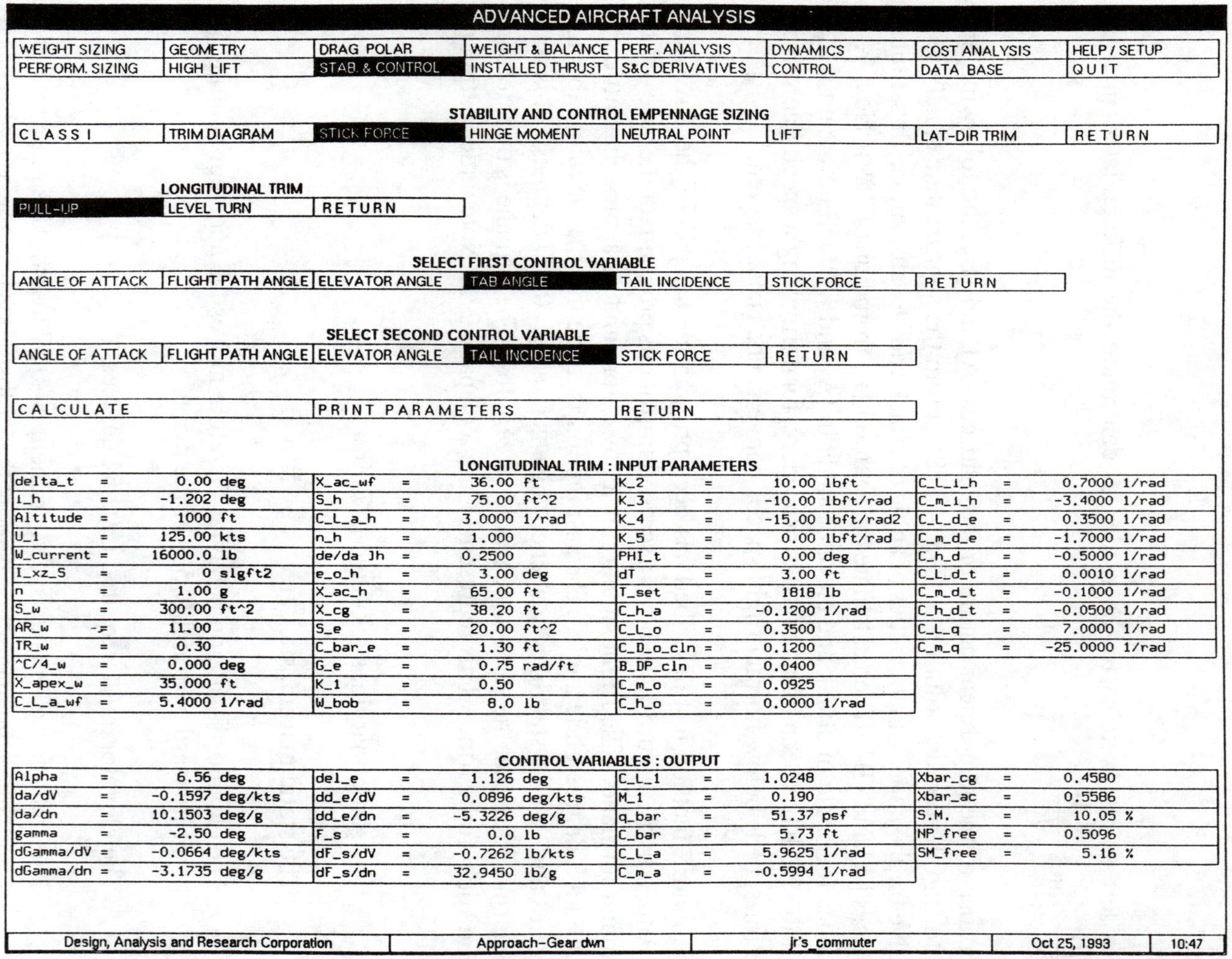

Figure 4.49   AAA Screendump of a Longitudinal Trim Solution for a Commuter Airplane in Landing Approach with One Engine Inoperative

4.8   A MATRIX APPROACH TO THE GENERAL LATERAL–DIRECTIONAL TRIM PROBLEM

To determine the lateral–directional equilibrium of an airplane, the side–force, rolling moment and yawing moment equations were used in Sub–section 4.2.6. An important case was the engine–out case leading to the amount of rudder and aileron deflection required at the minimum control speed. The method of Sub–section 4.2.6 does not account for the rudder–pedal and/or aileron–stick force required to hold the rudder and the aileron at their required angles. To account for airplane equilibrium and cockpit control forces simultaneously, clearly requires the simultaneous solution of five equations: the side force, rolling moment and yawing moment equations, the rudder pedal force equation and the aileron stick–force equation. In the remainder of this section, a matrix approach to solving these five equations simultaneously will be discussed.

The side–force, rolling moment and yawing moment equations are taken from Eqns (1.55) and (1.56) and re–numbered:

$$m(U_1 R_1 - W_1 P_1) = mg\sin\Phi_1 \cos\Theta_1 + F_{A_{y_1}} + F_{T_{y_1}} \tag{4.234a}$$

$$-I_{xz}P_1 Q_1 + (I_{zz} - I_{yy})R_1 Q_1 = L_{A_1} + L_{T_1} \tag{4.234b}$$

$$(I_{yy} - I_{xx})P_1 Q_1 + I_{xz}Q_1 R_1 = N_{A_1} + (F_{OEI})N_{T_1} \tag{4.234c}$$

where: (F_{OEI}) follows from Eqn (4.72) to account for the added drag–induced yawing moment due to flying with one engine inoperative.

The corresponding kinematic equations (1.57) are specialized for the case of a steady, level turn with the additional assumption that the steady state pitch attitude angle is small. This yields:

$$P_1 = 0 \tag{4.235a}$$
$$Q_1 = \dot{\Psi}_1 \sin\Phi_1 \tag{4.235b}$$
$$R_1 = \dot{\Psi}_1 \cos\Phi_1 \tag{4.235c}$$

The steady turn rate in Eqns (4.235) is given by Eqn (4.90) so that:

$$P_1 = 0 \tag{4.236a}$$
$$Q_1 = \frac{g}{U_1}\tan\Phi_1 \sin\Phi_1 \tag{4.236b}$$
$$R_1 = \frac{g}{U_1}\sin\Phi_1 \tag{4.236c}$$

To allow the mathematical model to be used for steady state straight line flight as well as for steady level turning flight, the parameter $\hat{n}$ is introduced:

$\hat{n} = 0$ for steady state, straight line flight

$\hat{n} = 1.0$ for steady level turning flight

Incorporating the kinematic equations (4.236) and the parameter $\hat{n}$ in Eqns (4.234) while also assuming that the steady state pitch attitude angle is small, yields:

$$\hat{n}mg\sin\phi_1 = mg\sin\phi_1 + F_{A_{y_1}} + F_{T_{y_1}} \tag{4.237a}$$

$$\hat{n}(I_{zz} - I_{yy})\frac{g^2}{U_1^2}\tan\phi_1\sin^2\phi_1 = L_{A_1} + L_{T_1} \tag{4.237b}$$

$$\hat{n}I_{xz}\frac{g^2}{U_1^2}\tan\phi_1\sin^2\phi_1 = N_{A_1} + (F_{OEI})N_{T_1} \tag{4.237c}$$

Expressions for the side–force due to thrust and the rolling and yawing moments due to thrust can be found in Eqns (3.93) – (3.95).

Expressions for the aerodynamic force and moments in Eqns (237) were previously developed as Eqns (3.197). These equations must be augmented by the appropriate tab terms in the aileron and in the rudder. This yields:

$$F_{A_{y_1}} = (C_{y_\beta}\beta + C_{y_{\delta_a}}\delta_a + C_{y_{\delta_r}}\delta_r + C_{y_{\delta_{a_t}}}\delta_{a_t} + C_{y_{\delta_{r_t}}}\delta_{r_t} + C_{y_r}\frac{\hat{n}R_1 b}{2U_1})\bar{q}_1 S \tag{4.238a}$$

$$L_{A_1} = (C_{l_\beta}\beta + C_{l_{\delta_a}}\delta_a + C_{l_{\delta_r}}\delta_r + C_{l_{\delta_{a_t}}}\delta_{a_t} + C_{l_{\delta_{r_t}}}\delta_{r_t} + C_{l_r}\frac{\hat{n}R_1 b}{2U_1})\bar{q}_1 Sb \tag{4.238b}$$

$$N_{A_1} = (C_{n_\beta}\beta + C_{n_{\delta_a}}\delta_a + C_{n_{\delta_r}}\delta_r + C_{n_{\delta_{a_t}}}\delta_{a_t} + C_{n_{\delta_{r_t}}}\delta_{r_t} + C_{n_r}\frac{\hat{n}R_1 b}{2U_1})\bar{q}_1 Sb \tag{4.238c}$$

Equations which account for the aileron wheel force and the rudder pedal force are similar to those used in Section 4.6:

For the aileron wheel–force (at zero roll rate):

$$F_a = \bar{q}_1 S_a \bar{c}_a G_a \left\{ -2C_{h_{\delta_a}}\delta_a - C_{h_{\delta_{a_t}}}\delta_{a_t} \right\} + G_a K_6 \delta_r \tag{4.239}$$

where: K_6 is a constant which depends on the mechanical installation of a rudder–aileron interconnect spring.

δ_{a_t} is the aileron tab deflection angle. The assumption is made that the tab is installed in the left aileron only and that the tab deflection is counted positive, trailing edge down relative to the aileron.

Rudder–aileron (or aileron–rudder) interconnect springs are installed in many airplanes to meet specific handling quality requirements. Examples are: compensating for excessive aileron yaw and compensating for insufficient dihedral effect.

The reader is reminded of the definition that a positive aileron wheel force is one which results in a positive rolling moment (i.e. airplane banks to the right).

For the rudder pedal force:

$$F_r = \eta_v \bar{q}_1 S_r \bar{c}_r G_r (C_{h_{\beta_r}} \beta (1 - \frac{\partial \sigma}{\partial \beta}) - \frac{C_{h_{\beta_r}} \hat{n} g(x_{ac_v} - x_{cg})}{U_1^2} + C_{h_{\delta_r}} \delta_r + C_{h_{\delta_{r_t}}} \delta_{r_t}) + G_r K_7 \delta_a \quad (4.240)$$

where: K_7 is a constant which depends on the mechanical installation of a aileron–rudder

interconnect spring in ft–lbs

The reader is reminded of the definition that a positive rudder pedal force is one which results in a positive yawing moment (i.e. airplane nose swings to the right).

Table 4.8 shows the matrix format for Equations (4.237), (4.239) and (4.240). This matrix equation must be restructured into a [5x5]{5x1}={5x1} format before solutions can be found. This requires that three of the eight variables be pre–specified. Practical examples are:

1. Specify bank angle, ϕ , aileron tab angle, δ_{a_t} , and rudder tab angle, δ_{r_t}

   Solve for: β, δ_a, δ_r, F_a and F_r

2. Specify aileron wheel force, F_a rudder pedal force, F_r , and bank angle, ϕ

   Solve for: β, δ_a, δ_r, δ_{a_t} and δ_{r_t}

An example application will now be discussed. Figure 4.50 shows a AAA screendump of the lateral–directional trim analysis of a commuter airplane. The flight situation is landing approach and the assumption is that one engine is inoperative (the right engine). Three variables must be pre–selected. In this case the aileron tab angle is set at zero degrees, the rudder tab angle is set at zero degrees and the sideslip angle is assumed to be also zero. The reason for the latter is to keep the drag as low as possible in this engine–out situation, just in case a climb is required.

Note under output parameters the following:

Phi $= -1.9$ deg. $\delta_a = -1.6$ deg $\delta_r = 10$ deg $F_a = -10.1$ lbs $F_r = -140.4$ lbs

These output data indicate that for this example airplane there is no problem controlling an engine–out situation at this speed. The rudder pedal force (although high) is less than the 150 lbs allowed for temporary application. By using rudder trim this force would have to be reduced to the allowable prolonged force level which is 20 lbs. The reader is asked to size a rudder tab with which this can be accomplished. Hint: find a value for $C_{h_{\delta_{r_t}}}$ which will reduce the rudder pedal force down to 20 lbs. Next, size the tab to produce that hingemoment derivative. Don't use more than 20 degrees of tab deflection!

Table 4.8 Matrix Format for Lateral–Directional Trim Equations

$$
\begin{bmatrix}
\dfrac{(1-\hat{n})W}{\overline{q}_1 S}+\dfrac{\hat{n}C_{y_r}bg}{2U_1^{\,2}} & C_{y_\beta} & C_{y_{\delta_a}} & C_{y_{\delta_r}} & C_{y_{\delta_{a_t}}} & C_{y_{\delta_{r_t}}} & 0 & 0 \\[2ex]
\dfrac{\hat{n}(I_{yy}-I_{zz})g^2\tan\phi\sin\phi}{\overline{q}_1 SbU_1^{\,2}}+\dfrac{\hat{n}C_{l_r}bg}{2U_1^{\,2}} & C_{l_\beta} & C_{l_{\delta_a}} & C_{l_{\delta_r}} & C_{l_{\delta_{a_t}}} & C_{l_{\delta_{r_t}}} & 0 & 0 \\[2ex]
\dfrac{-\hat{n}I_{xz}g^2\tan\phi\sin\phi}{\overline{q}_1 SbU_1^{\,2}}+\dfrac{\hat{n}C_{n_r}bg}{2U_1^{\,2}} & C_{n_\beta} & C_{n_{\delta_a}} & C_{n_{\delta_r}} & C_{n_{\delta_{a_t}}} & C_{n_{\delta_{r_t}}} & 0 & 0 \\[2ex]
0 & 0 & -2C_{h_{\delta_a}} & \dfrac{K_6}{\overline{q}_1 S_a\overline{c}_a}-C_{h_{\delta_{a_t}}} & 0 & \dfrac{-1}{\overline{q}_1 S_a\overline{c}_a G_a} & 0 \\[2ex]
-C_{h_{\beta_r}}\dfrac{\hat{n}g(x_{ac_v}-x_{cg})}{U_1^{\,2}} & C_{h_{\beta_r}}\!\left(1-\dfrac{\partial\sigma}{\partial\beta}\right)\dfrac{K_7}{\eta_v\overline{q}_1 S_r\overline{c}_r} & C_{h_{\delta_r}} & 0 & C_{h_{\delta_{r_t}}} & 0 & \dfrac{-1}{\eta_v\overline{q}_1 S_r\overline{c}_r G_r}
\end{bmatrix}
$$

5x8

$$
\times
\begin{Bmatrix}
\sin\phi \\
\beta \\
\delta_a \\
\delta_r \\
\delta_{a_t} \\
\delta_{r_t} \\
F_a \\
F_r
\end{Bmatrix}
=
\begin{Bmatrix}
-F_{T_{y_1}}/(\overline{q}_1 S) \\[1.5ex]
-L_{T_1}/(\overline{q}_1 Sb) \\[1.5ex]
-\left\{(N_{T_1})(F_{OEI})\right\}/(\overline{q}_1 Sb) \\[1.5ex]
0 \\[1.5ex]
0
\end{Bmatrix}
\qquad (4.241)
$$

8x1   5x1

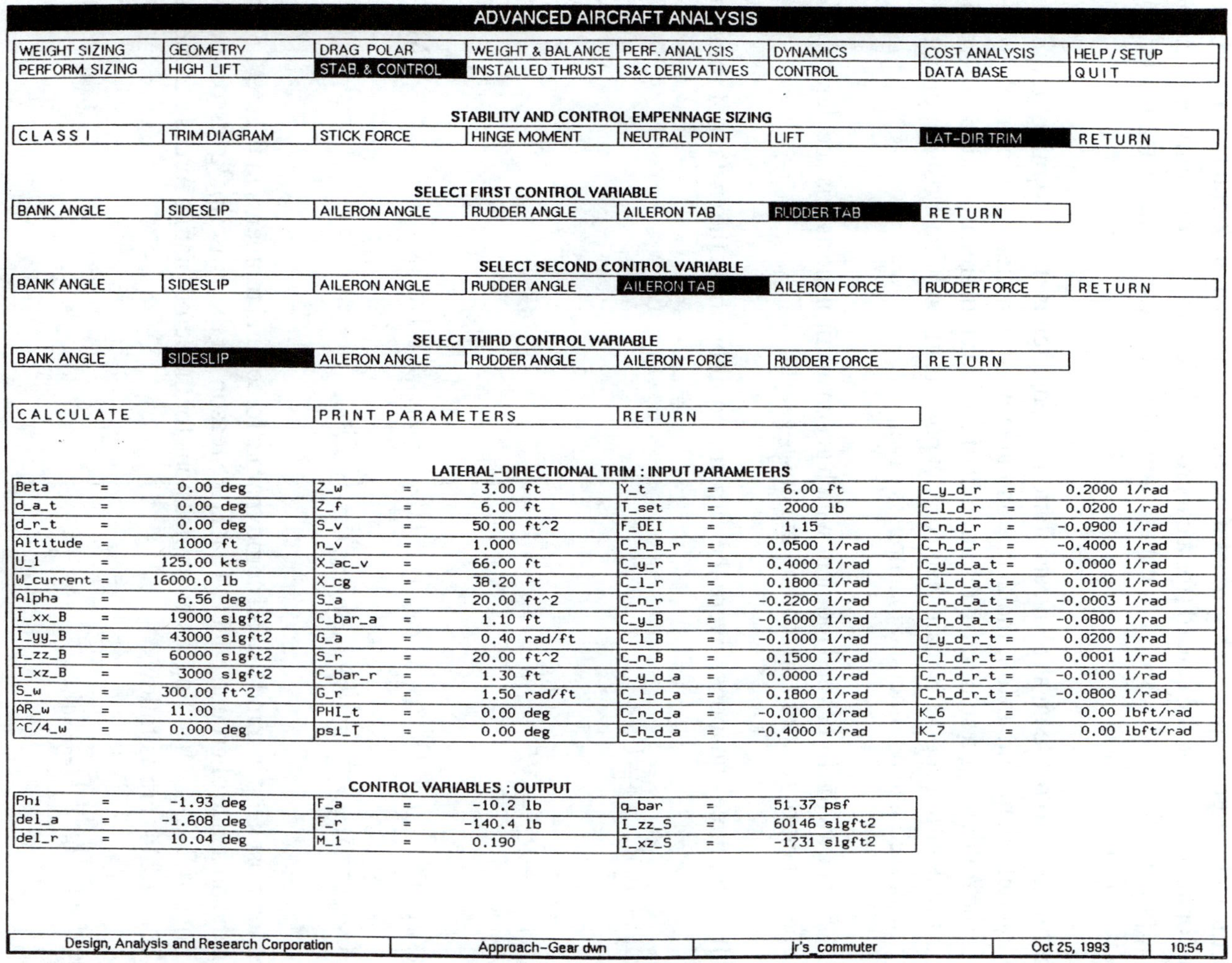

ADVANCED AIRCRAFT ANALYSIS

WEIGHT SIZING	GEOMETRY	DRAG POLAR	WEIGHT & BALANCE	PERF. ANALYSIS	DYNAMICS	COST ANALYSIS	HELP / SETUP
PERFORM. SIZING	HIGH LIFT	STAB. & CONTROL	INSTALLED THRUST	S&C DERIVATIVES	CONTROL	DATA BASE	QUIT

STABILITY AND CONTROL EMPENNAGE SIZING

CLASS I	TRIM DIAGRAM	STICK FORCE	HINGE MOMENT	NEUTRAL POINT	LIFT	LAT-DIR TRIM	RETURN

SELECT FIRST CONTROL VARIABLE

BANK ANGLE	SIDESLIP	AILERON ANGLE	RUDDER ANGLE	AILERON TAB	RUDDER TAB	RETURN

SELECT SECOND CONTROL VARIABLE

BANK ANGLE	SIDESLIP	AILERON ANGLE	RUDDER ANGLE	AILERON TAB	AILERON FORCE	RUDDER FORCE	RETURN

SELECT THIRD CONTROL VARIABLE

BANK ANGLE	SIDESLIP	AILERON ANGLE	RUDDER ANGLE	AILERON FORCE	RUDDER FORCE	RETURN

CALCULATE	PRINT PARAMETERS	RETURN

LATERAL-DIRECTIONAL TRIM : INPUT PARAMETERS

Beta	=	0.00 deg	Z_w	=	3.00 ft	Y_t	=	6.00 ft
d_a_t	=	0.00 deg	Z_f	=	6.00 ft	T_set	=	2000 lb
d_r_t	=	0.00 deg	S_v	=	50.00 ft^2	F_0EI	=	1.15
Altitude	=	1000 ft	n_v	=	1.000	C_h_B_r	=	0.0500 1/rad
U_1	=	125.00 kts	X_ac_v	=	66.00 ft	C_y_r	=	0.4000 1/rad
W_current	=	16000.0 lb	X_cg	=	38.20 ft	C_l_r	=	0.1800 1/rad
Alpha	=	6.56 deg	S_a	=	20.00 ft^2	C_n_r	=	-0.2200 1/rad
I_xx_B	=	19000 slgft2	C_bar_a	=	1.10 ft	C_y_B	=	-0.6000 1/rad
I_yy_B	=	43000 slgft2	G_a	=	0.40 rad/ft	C_l_B	=	-0.1000 1/rad
I_zz_B	=	60000 slgft2	S_r	=	20.00 ft^2	C_n_B	=	0.1500 1/rad
I_xz_B	=	3000 slgft2	C_bar_r	=	1.30 ft	C_y_d_a	=	0.0000 1/rad
S_w	=	300.00 ft^2	G_r	=	1.50 rad/ft	C_l_d_a	=	0.1800 1/rad
AR_w	=	11.00	PHI_t	=	0.00 deg	C_n_d_a	=	-0.0100 1/rad
^C/4_w	=	0.000 deg	psi_T	=	0.00 deg	C_h_d_a	=	-0.4000 1/rad

C_y_d_r	=	0.2000 1/rad
C_l_d_r	=	0.0200 1/rad
C_n_d_r	=	-0.0900 1/rad
C_h_d_r	=	-0.4000 1/rad
C_y_d_a_t	=	0.0000 1/rad
C_l_d_a_t	=	0.0100 1/rad
C_n_d_a_t	=	-0.0003 1/rad
C_h_d_a_t	=	-0.0800 1/rad
C_y_d_r_t	=	0.0200 1/rad
C_l_d_r_t	=	0.0001 1/rad
C_n_d_r_t	=	-0.0100 1/rad
C_h_d_r_t	=	-0.0800 1/rad
K_6	=	0.00 lbft/rad
K_7	=	0.00 lbft/rad

q_bar	=	51.37 psf
I_zz_S	=	60146 slgft2
I_xz_S	=	-1731 slgft2

CONTROL VARIABLES : OUTPUT

Phi	=	-1.93 deg
del_a	=	-1.608 deg
del_r	=	10.04 deg

F_a	=	-10.2 lb
F_r	=	-140.4 lb
M_l	=	0.190

Design, Analysis and Research Corporation | Approach-Gear dwn | Jr's_commuter | Oct 25, 1993 | 10:54

Figure 4.50 AAA Screendump of a Lateral-Directional Trim Solution for a Commuter Airplane in Landing Approach with One Engine Inoperative

4.9   THE TAKEOFF ROTATION PROBLEM

Most airplanes, to become airborne, must be rotated about the main gear rotation point to achieve the angle of attack required for lift–off. Exceptions to this are airplanes like to B–52. To provide an airplane with the ability to rotate at relatively low speeds (the rotation speed is normally slightly above the stall speed) requires a significant down–load on the horizontal tail (for a conventional airplane) or an up–load on the canard (for a canard airplane). In this text, only the case of the conventional airplane will be addressed. For canard and three–surface airplanes the reader should consult Part VII of Ref. 4.5.

The requirement to rotate an airplane at rotation speed often is the 'designing' requirement for the horizontal tail: planform, airfoil, incidence and area must together be compatible with this requirement. In the following, an analysis of the amount of tail area required to produce a given level of pitch angular acceleration about the main gear contact point is given. The most important design parameters are discussed and a numerical example is given.

Figure 4.51 shows the forces and moment which act on an airplane as it is accelerating down the runway at the instant of rotation: no load on the nose–gear!.

The following three equations govern the airplane equilibrium at the instant of rotation:

$$T - D_g - \mu_g R_g = \frac{W}{g}\dot{U} \tag{4.242}$$

$$L_{wf_g} + L_{h_g} + R_g = W \tag{4.243}$$

$$- W(x_{mg_g} - x_{cg_g}) + D_g(z_{D_g} - z_{mg_g}) - T(z_{T_g} - z_{mg_g}) + L_{wf_g}(x_{mg_g} - x_{ac_{wf_g}}) + M_{ac_{wf_g}} +$$

$$- L_{h_g}(x_{ac_{h_g}} - x_{mg_g}) + \frac{W}{g}\dot{U}(z_{cg_g} - z_{mg_g}) = I_{yy_{mg}}\ddot{\theta}_{mg} \tag{4.244}$$

The reader must keep in mind that all aerodynamic forces and moments in Figure 4.51 must be evaluated in the presence of ground effect. That is the reason for the subscript 'g' associated with most terms in Eqns (4.242–4.244). Suggested expressions for the aerodynamic forces and moments in Eqns (4.242) – (4.244) are as follows.

For the drag, $D_g = D_{ground}$:

$$D_g = C_{D_{ground}}\bar{q}_{rotate}S \tag{4.245}$$

where: $C_{D_{ground}}$ is the airplane drag coefficient in ground effect

$\bar{q}_{rotate}$ is the dynamic pressure at the instant of takeoff rotation

$\ddot{\theta}_{mg}$ is the angular acceleration about the main gear rotation point in rad/sec^2

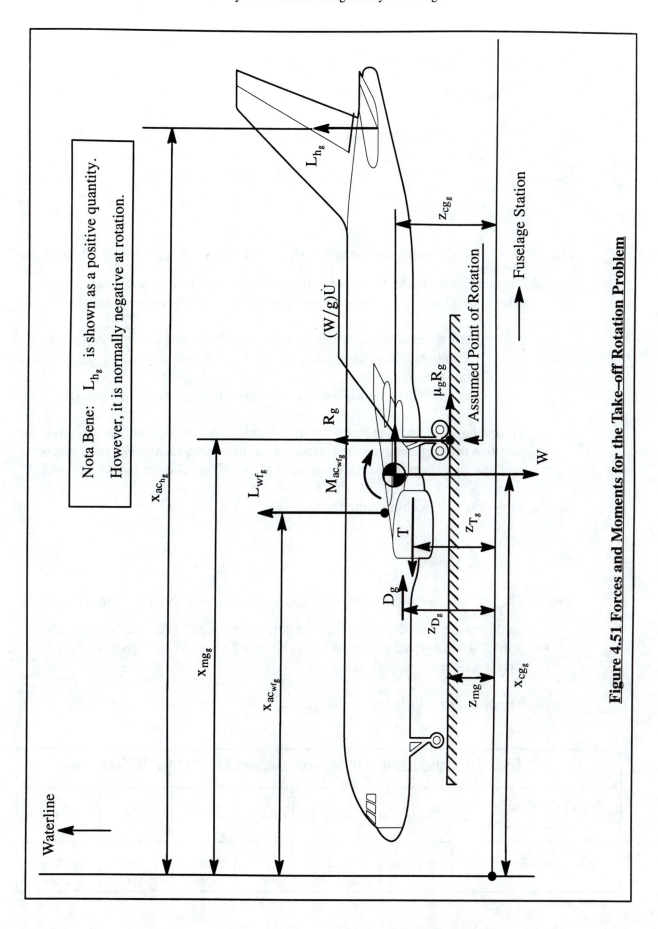

Figure 4.51 Forces and Moments for the Take–off Rotation Problem

For the wing–fuselage lift:

$$L_{wf_g} = C_{L_{wf_{ground}}} \bar{q}_{rotate} S \qquad (4.246)$$

where: $C_{L_{wf_{ground}}}$ is the airplane lift coefficient in ground effect during the takeoff run

For the tail lift:

$$L_{h_g} = C_{L_{h_{ground}}} \eta_{h_g} \bar{q}_{rotate} S_h \qquad (4.247)$$

where: $C_{L_{h_{ground}}}$ is the horizontal tail lift coefficient in ground effect during the takeoff run. This tail lift coefficient will normally be negative (tail lift acting down) to affect takeoff rotation. This lift coefficient depends on the following quantities:

* tail angle of attack which in turn depends on down–wash and on the stabilizer incidence angle.
* tail airfoils
* tail planform parameters such as aspect ratio, sweep angle and taper ratio

The methods of Part VI of Ref. 4.4 may be used to estimate the value of the maximum negative lift coefficient of the horizontal tail in ground effect. For purposes of preliminary design it is often assumed that this lift coefficient has a value of 1.0.

For the wing–fuselage pitching moment:

$$M_{ac_{wf_g}} = C_{m_{ac_{wf_{ground}}}} \bar{q}_{rotate} S \bar{c} \qquad (4.248)$$

where: $C_{m_{ac_{wf_{ground}}}}$ is the airplane pitching moment coefficient about the wing–fuselage aerodynamic center, in ground effect during the takeoff run. This coefficient will normally be negative for a positively cambered wing. With flaps down, this coefficient will be even more negative.

For the wheel–to–ground friction coefficient, μ_g , the reader should consult Table 4.9.

Table 4.9 Typical Values for Wheel–Ground Friction Coefficient						
Wheel–Ground Friction Coefficient , μ_g	0.02	0.02	0.04	0.05	0.10	0.10 – 0.30
Type of terrain	Concrete	Asphalt or Macadam	Hard Turf	Short grass	Long grass	Soft ground

The angular acceleration about the main gear rotation point, $\ddot{\theta}_{mg}$, should have a value such that the takeoff rotation process does not take more than 1–3 seconds. Suggested values in preliminary design are:

* For large transports: $\ddot{\theta}_{mg}$ = 6–8 deg/sec2

* For small transports: $\ddot{\theta}_{mg}$ = 8–10 deg/sec2

* For light airplanes and fighters: $\ddot{\theta}_{mg}$ = 10–12 deg/sec2

During preliminary design it may be assumed that the airplane rotation speed is related to the stall speed in the takeoff configuration as follows:

$$V_{rotate} = V_R \geq 1.1 V_{S_{takeoff}} \tag{4.249}$$

During the early design of an airplane it is important to assure that the tail size is adequate to achieve takeoff rotation. The amount of tail area needed for takeoff rotation at the rotation speed can be solved from Eqns (4.242) – (4.244). The result is:

$$S_h = \frac{\left[\begin{array}{c} \left\{ W(x_{cg_g} - x_{mg_g} - \mu_g z_{cg_g} + \mu_g z_{mg_g}) + D_g(z_{D_g} - z_{cg_g}) + T(z_{cg_g} - z_{T_g}) \right\} + \\ + \left\{ L_{wf_g}(x_{mg_g} - x_{ac_{wf_g}} + \mu_g z_{cg_g} - \mu_g z_{mg_g}) + M_{ac_{wf_g}} - I_{yy_{mg}} \ddot{\theta} \right\} \end{array} \right]}{(C_{L_{max_{h_{ground}}}} \eta_{h_g} \bar{q}_{rotate})(x_{ac_{h_g}} - x_{mg_g} + \mu_g z_{mg_g} - \mu_g z_{cg_g})} \tag{4.250}$$

The tail size required for takeoff rotation is quite often the requirement which sizes the horizontal tail. An example application will now be discussed.

Table 4.10 provides the input data required to carry out a takeoff rotation analysis for a twin engine commuter airplane. All pertinent input data are determined to include the effect of ground proximity. Figure 4.52 shows typical results of a trade study performed to illustrate the effect of the following parameters on the initial angular acceleration about the main gear:

Figure 4.52a shows the effect of tail area, S_h, and rotation speed, V_{rotate}, on the initial angular acceleration about the main gear, $\ddot{\theta}_{mg}$.

Figure 4.52b shows the effect of c.g. location, x_{cg_g} , and ground friction coefficient, μ_g, and thrust–line location, z_{T_g} , on the initial angular acceleration about the main gear, $\ddot{\theta}_{mg}$.

It is seen that the tail are required to rotate is very sensitive to several important design parameters. Note the effect of ground friction: if an airplane must operate out of 'soft' fields, this has a significant influence on the required tail area!

Table 4.10 Input Data Required for Takeoff Rotation Calculation

$W = 16,000$ lbs	$C_{D_{ground}} = 0.0800$	$\varrho = 0.002377$ slugs/ft^3	$\bar{c} = 5.73$ ft
$x_{cg_g} = 38.5$ ft	$C_{L_{wf_{ground}}} = 0.60$	$I_{yy_{mg}} = 58,000$ slugft^2	$\eta_{h_g} = 1.0$
$x_{mg_g} = 41.0$ ft	$x_{ac_{wf_g}} = 37.5$ ft	$C_{L_{max_{h_{ground}}}} = -0.80$	$x_{ac_{h_g}} = 65.0$ ft
$\mu_g = 0.02$			
$z_{cg_g} = 10.0$ ft	$S = 300$ ft^2	$C_{m_{ac_{wf_g}}} = -0.150$	
$z_{mg_g} = 5.5$ ft	$z_{D_g} = 9.5$ ft	$z_{T_g} = 9.0$ ft	$T = 5,000$ lbs

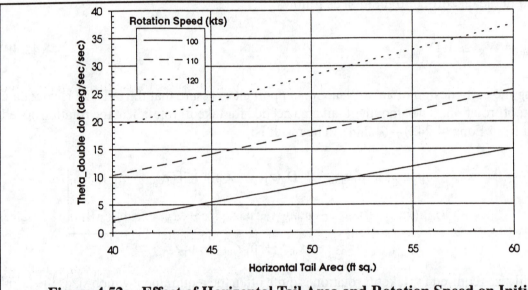

Figure 4.52a Effect of Horizontal Tail Area and Rotation Speed on Initial Angular Acceleration about the Main Gear

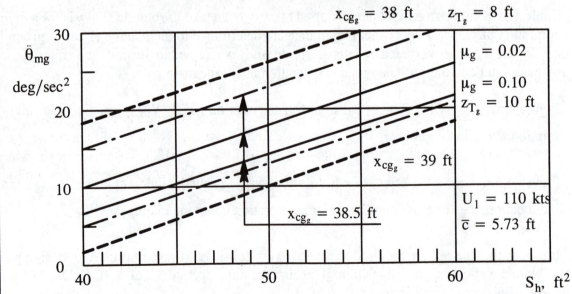

Figure 4.52b Effect of Center of Gravity Location, Ground Friction and Thrust Line Location on Initial Angular Acceleration about the Main Gear

4.10 INTRODUCTION TO IRREVERSIBLE FLIGHT CONTROL SYSTEMS

The reversible control systems discussed in Sections 4.5 through 4.8 which feature completely mechanical connections between the cockpit controls and the flight controls, have the following advantages:

* reliability (through simplicity)

* relatively maintenance free

* relatively low cost

Disadvantages are:

* serious aerodynamic problems in the very high subsonic, transonic and supersonic speed ranges

* relatively heavy

* limited to moderately sized airplanes because of magnitude of control forces

* difficult to integrate stability augmentation systems (an exception is the Separate Surface System approach discussed in Chapter 11)

Several intermediate systems between purely reversible and completely irreversible systems have been developed and flown. Reference 4.9 contains some examples of these intermediate forms.

An interesting example of an intermediate system is found in the Boeing 737 series. This airplane is equipped with two hydraulic systems with mechanical signalling for the primary controls. In case of dual engine failure and/or in case of complete hydraulic system failure the airplane has complete reversibility in the pitch and roll axis. The yaw axis in the 737 series has a third independent hydraulic system and no mechanical reversion.

The modern trend in flight control system design for high performance airplanes is to employ irreversible systems. The most common method of actuating the flight control surfaces in an irreversible system is the hydraulic system. A detailed discussion of hydraulic systems is beyond the scope of this text. Part IV of Reference 4.5 contains a chapter on hydraulic systems. For a more detailed treatment the reader should consult Reference 4.11.

Primary advantages of irreversible systems are:

* Flexibility in combining pilot control commands with automatic control and stability augmentation commands
* Ability to tailor handling qualities

    * Relatively low weight, particularly when combined with electric and/or optical signalling

Among the disadvantages of irreversible systems are:

    * Complexity   * Reliability

    * Redundancy   * Cost: development and maintenance

Cost and reliability have been the main reason why irreversible systems have not yet been used in low performance airplanes. The designer of an irreversible flight control system must prove that the probability of catastrophic failure of the system is less than once per 1,000,000,000 flight hours according to the existing airworthiness code. This is referred to as the so–called 10^9 criterion. The reader should refer to Table 6.4 and Figure 6.4 in Chapter 6 of this text for additional guidelines in regard to allowable failure rates.

In the case of electrically signalled systems, an additional disadvantage is the requirement for hardening against lightning strikes and, in military airplanes, the requirement for hardening against EMP (Electro–Magnetic Pulse).

The following general types of irreversible control systems have been developed:

* Irreversible systems with mechanical signalling

* Irreversible systems with electric (fly–by–wire) signalling

* Irreversible systems with optical (fly–by–light) signalling

Figure 4.53 shows an example of an irreversible system with mechanical signalling. In such airplanes, the cockpit controls tend to be conventional: control wheel and column as well as rudder pedals. Because there is no feedback from the aerodynamic surface controls to the cockpit controls, some form of 'artificial control force feel' system must be included, adding to the complexity of the system. Figure 4.53 shows the location of the variable feel unit.

Irreversible systems with electric signalling have been used for some time in several military airplanes. The F–16 , F–18 and F–117 are examples. The Airbus A–320 is the first commercially certified transport with irreversible flight controls and fly–by–wire signalling through a digital computer system. Figure 4.54 shows an example of a system with electrical signalling. Such a system makes it possible to use side–stick controllers without force feedback as long as some form of 'flight envelope protection' is provided. In the A–320 this is done by denying the pilot the ability to bring the airplane outside aerodynamic or structural limits.

Irreversible systems with optical signalling are still under development. The Lockheed F–22 is scheduled to have such a system which was flown also on the YF–22 prototype. Such systems have as an advantage the insensitivity to lightning and EMP strikes.

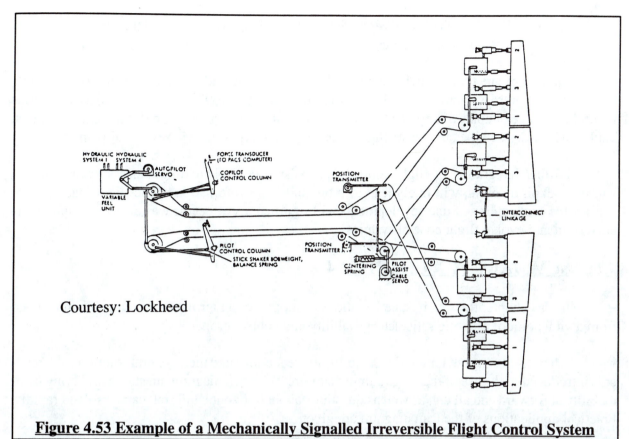

Courtesy: Lockheed

Figure 4.53 Example of a Mechanically Signalled Irreversible Flight Control System

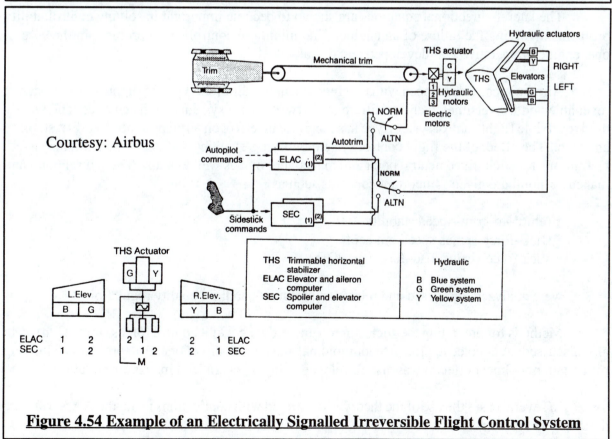

Courtesy: Airbus

THS	Trimmable horizontal stabilizer		Hydraulic
ELAC	Elevator and aileron computer	B	Blue system
SEC	Spoiler and elevator computer	G	Green system
		Y	Yellow system

Figure 4.54 Example of an Electrically Signalled Irreversible Flight Control System

A detailed discussion of the design of flight control systems is beyond the scope of this text. Part IV of Ref. 4.5 contains detailed diagrams of various types of irreversible flight control systems.

Many airplane types which are currently in production and/or development use reversible types of flight control systems. Table 4.11, taken from the 1992–1993 issue of Jane's All The Worlds Aircraft, shows examples of airplane types using reversible and irreversible flight control systems. Table 4.12 shows detail examples of flight control system types used in several airplanes.

Further integration of flight controls, propulsion controls and guidance signals with advanced cockpit displays, will likely lead to more and more automation of the flight management tasks of the cockpit crew. Such developments will significantly affect the way airplane manufacturers design and evolve flight control systems.

4.11   SUMMARY FOR CHAPTER 4

In this chapter the steady state equations of motion of an airplane were applied and solved from a viewpoint of assuring satisfactory stability and control properties.

After discussing the longitudinal equilibrium equations and their general solutions, the reader is introduced to the use of the longitudinal diagram. With this diagram questions involving trimmability at forward and aft c.g. as well as questions about horizontal tail stall can be solved rapidly. Practical applications of the trim diagram are given.

The lateral–directional equations are shown to become important in solving controllability problems involving the failure of an engine. The minimum control speed problem in the case of one–engine–inoperative was developed and discussed.

Airplanes can be equipped with two fundamentally different types of flight control systems: reversible and irreversible. Generic difference between these systems are discussed. The widely used reversible flight control system type has a significant effect on airplane controllability, stability and trim. The effect of the flight control system on flying qualities was developed and discussed. Definitions for stick–fixed neutral point and maneuver point as well as stick–free neutral point and maneuver point are given. Important concepts such as:

* return–to–trim–speed stability
* stick–force versus speed gradient
* stick force versus load–factor gradients

were analyzed, discussed and related to pertinent handling quality regulations.

Methods for predicting the stick, aileron and rudder cockpit control forces (force trim) were also discussed. A coupled approach to longitudinal and lateral–directional trim problems (allowing for certain non–linear effects) was also developed using a generalized matrix formulation.

In several cases the use of the theory is illustrated with applications using the AAA software described in Appendix A.

Table 4.11 Examples of the Use of Reversible and Irreversible Flight Control Systems		
Reversible P.F.C.S	**Reversible P.F.C.S**	**Irreversible P.F.C.S**
Beech F–33A Beech M–58 Beech King–Air all models Beech M 1900 Beech Starship I Beech M 400	EMB–120 Brasilia except for irrev. rudder EMB–312 Tucano	Boeing 747 all models Boeing 757 all models Boeing 767 all models Boeing 777 full FBW
Boeing E–3A (with power boost)	DHC–8 except for irrev. rudder	Cessna Citation 750
Cessna Caravan all models Cessna Citation 550, 525, 560	SOCATA TBM–700	Dassault Rafale
Commander 114 B	Dornier 228	Grumman A–6 Grumman F–14 Grumman E–2C
Fairchild Metro 23, C–26	SAAB 340	
Learjet M 35 and M 36 Learjet M 31 Learjet M 60	SAAB 2000 except for irrev. rudder	Lockheed F–16 full FBW Lockheed F–117 full FBW Lockheed F–22 full FBL
	Pilatus PC–9	
Mooney MSE and TLS	Shorts 330	McDD F–15 McDD AV–8B
Piper Cheyenne Piper Malibu	**Reversible/Irreversible P.F.C.S**	McDD MD–11 McDD C–17 full FBW
Swearingen SJ30	Boeing 737 all models	Northrop B–2 full FBW
Taylorcraft F22	Cessna Citation 650	Airbus A–300–600 Airbus A–320 full FBW Airbus A–340 full FBW
Fokker F–50	Gulfstream IV, C–20	
Piaggio P–180	Lockheed P–3	
CASA–IPTN CN–235	Fokker F–100	SAAB JAS –39 Gripen full FBW
Aerospatiale/Alenia ATR 42		

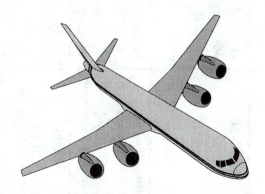
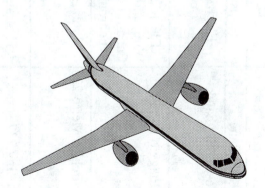

Table 4.12 Examples of Flight Control System Types

Airplane	Flaps	Longitudinal (Pitch)	Lateral (Roll)	Directional (Yaw)
Cessna Skyhawk	Electric	Elevator + manual trim tab in left elevator Reversible: Cable Driven	Frise Ailerons Reversible: Cable Driven	Rudder + Ground Adjustable Trim Tab Reversible: Cable Driven
Piaggio P–180	Electric Wing and Canard Flaps Synchronized	Elevators with geared tabs Reversible: Cable Driven Stabilizer for trim: electric	Ailerons with electric trim tab in right aileron Reversible: Cable Driven	Rudder with electric trim tab Reversible: Cable Driven
Fairchild Metro 23	Hydraulic	Elevators Reversible: Cable Driven Stabilizer for trim: electric	Ailerons + manual trim tab in each aileron Reversible: Cable Driven	Rudder + manual trim tab Reversible: Cable Driven
Boeing 737 series Two Independent Hydraulic Systems	Hydraulic	Elevators: Hydraulic + manual reversible override with geared tabs Stabilizer: dual electric with manual irreversible override	Ailerons: Hydraulic + manual reversible override with geared tabs Spoilers: Hydraulic with mechanical signalling	Rudder: Hydraulic with standby hydraulic system. Mechanical signalling
Fokker F–50	Hydraulic with electric backup	Elevators with starboard electric trim tab Reversible: Cable Driven	Ailerons with spring tab + geared tab. Right geared tab doubles as electric trim tab Reversible: Cable Driven	Rudder + manual trim tab + geared tab Reversible: Cable Driven
Airbus A–320 Sidestick control with full flight envelope protection	Hydraulic	Elevators: Hydraulic Stabilizer: Hydraulic with Mechanical Back-up Irreversible: FBW	Ailerons and Spoilers: Hydraulic Irreversible: FBW	Rudder: Hydraulic with Mechanical Back–up Irreversible: FBW
Lockheed F–22 Sidestick control with full flight envelope protection	Hydraulic	Stabilizers: Hydraulic Irreversible: FBL	Ailerons: Hydraulic Irreversible: FBL	Rudders: Hydraulic Irreversible: FBL

4.12 PROBLEMS FOR CHAPTER 4

4.1   Take any example airplane in Appendix B. Calculate and plot the maneuver point stick––fixed as a function of altitude.

4.2   Derive an equation for the neutral point stick–fixed and stick–free for a canard airplane. Assume that the canard is fixed in the first case and freely floating in the second case.

4.3   Describe how you would measure the side–wash–due–to–sideslip derivative, $d\sigma/d\beta$ from windtunnel data. Indicate the type of runs needed to get this information.

4.4   Starting with Eqn (4.141) and using Eqn (4.145) derive an expression for the tab deflection angle required to set the stick force equal to zero.

4.5   Starting with Eqn (4.141), show that Eqn (4.155) is a reasonable approximation for the stick force.

4.6   Figure 4.55 represents windtunnel data for a small jet trainer. From these data determine the following characteristics:

    a) C_{L_α} $C_{L_{\delta_e}}$ C_{L_0} α_{0_L}

    b) C_{D_0} e (assume A = 5.1) $C_{D_{\delta_e}}$ $(L/D)_{max}$ for $\delta_e = 10\,deg$

    c) $C_{m_{\delta_e}}$ $\overline{C}_{m_{\delta_e}}$ C_{m_0} $\overline{C}_{m_0}$

    d) determine C_{m_α} for $0 < C_L < 0.5$ determine $\overline{x}_{ac}$ for $0 < C_L < 0.5$

    e) If $\overline{x}_{cg_{forward}} = 0.15$ and $\overline{x}_{cg_{aft}} = 0.32$ determine $C_{L_{max_{trim}}}$ for both cg locations

4.7   For Airplanes E, F and G in Appendix B determine the minimum control speed with one engine inoperative using the single degree of freedom approximation. Assume that the maximum rudder deflection is 25 degrees.

4.8   Repeat problem 4.7 for the three–degrees–of–freedom case and find the minimum control speed as function of bank angle. Use +10, +5, 0, –5 and – 10 degrees for the bank angle.

4.9   Refer to Eqn (4.92). For $\phi_1 = 90^0$ this equation leads to the absurd conclusion that the load factor, n, becomes infinitely large. Explain what really happens in the case of an airplane flying at a bank angle of 90 degrees.

4.10   Modify Eqn (4.171) so that it applies to the case of a steady symmetrical turn.

4.11   Prove that Eqn (4.159) is correct.

4.12   Prove that Eqn (4.169) is correct.

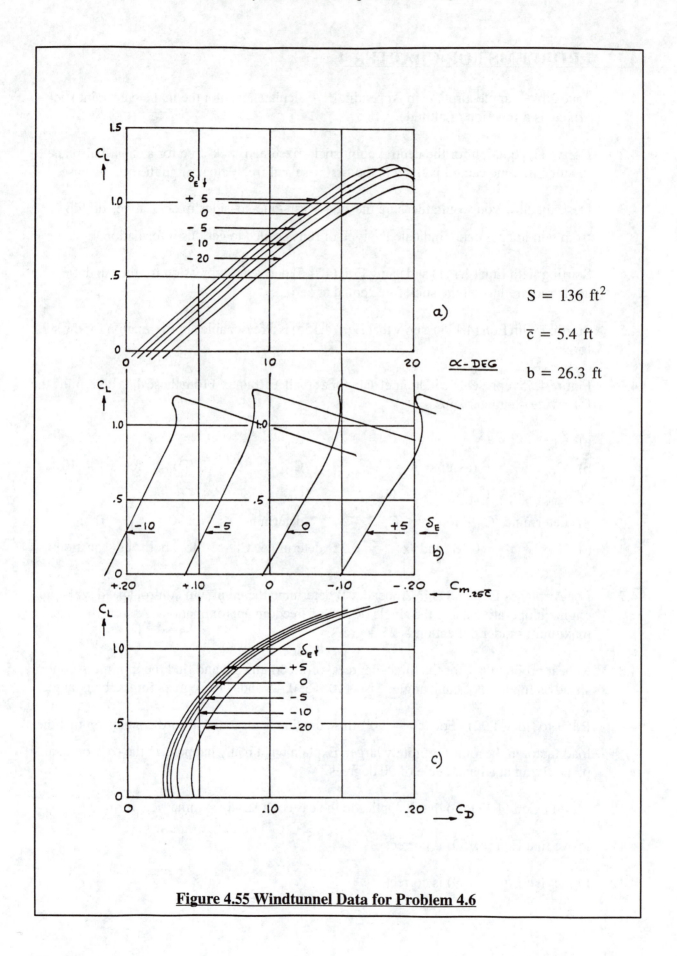

S = 136 ft^2

$\overline{c}$ = 5.4 ft

b = 26.3 ft

Figure 4.55 Windtunnel Data for Problem 4.6

4.13 A jet transport in the approach flight condition has the following geometric and aerodynamic characteristics:

$C_{L_o} = 1.4$ $\quad C_{m_\alpha} = -0.46 \text{ rad}^{-1}$ $\quad C_{L_\alpha} = 4.6 \text{ rad}^{-1}$ $\quad \bar{x}_{cg} = 0.20$

$S = 2,000 \text{ ft}^2$ $\quad \overline{C}_{m_{i_h}} = -0.01 \text{ deg}^{-1}$ $\quad C_{L_{i_h}} = 0.01 \text{ deg}^{-1}$ $\quad \dfrac{d\varepsilon}{d\alpha} = 0.5$

$\bar{c} = 19.0 \text{ ft}$ $\quad \overline{C}_{m_o} = 0$ $\quad \alpha_{max} = 10 \text{ deg}$

$d_T = -3 \text{ ft} *$ $\quad W = 125,000 \text{ lbs}$ $\quad C_{L_{max_{i_h}=0}} = 2.2$

* The thrust line is 3 ft below the c.g. $\quad \alpha_{h_{stall}} = +/- 15 \text{ deg}$

a) Assume that the forward c.g. is at 12.5 % mgc and the aft c.g. is at 22.5% of the mgc. Assume that the stabilizer incidence can move in a range of – 20 deg to + 10 deg only!. In the trim diagram plot your lines in increments of 10 deg. Label these lines!
Draw the 'trim triangle' for this airplane **without** the effect of thrust.

b) Determine the maximum trimmable lift coefficients at forward and at aft c.g. Compute the corresponding approach speeds. Discuss your results.

c) Draw in the positive and negative tail stall loci. Explain how you did that! Is the answer to a) still valid? If not, what is the new answer and why?

d) Copy your trim diagram and now indicate the effect of thrust on that trim diagram. Assume that the total approach thrust is T = 25,000 lbs.

4.14 The following three equations represent the steady state lateral–directional equations of motion for a twin–engine airplane with the engines mounted under the wings. The stall speed of the airplane in the approach configuration is: V_{s_A}. The minimum control speed for the airplane is: $V_{mc} \leq 1.2 V_{s_A}$.

$$- W \sin\phi = (C_{y_\beta}\beta + C_{y_{\delta_r}}\delta_r)\bar{q}S \qquad 0 = (C_{l_\beta}\beta + C_{l_{\delta_a}}\delta_a)\bar{q}Sb$$

$$0 = (C_{n_\beta}\beta + C_{n_{\delta_a}}\delta_a + C_{n_{\delta_r}}\delta_r)\bar{q}Sb + Ty_T$$

a) Define each quantity in these equations and indicate its usual sign.

b) Assume that the right the engine has failed. Derive an expression for the <u>allowable value</u> <u>for:</u> y_T if the objective is to fly at a five* degree bank angle and at zero sideslip angle. State the rationale behind your solution in a logical, step–by–step manner.

* Do you bank into the operating engine or into the inoperative engine? What is the the desired sign for the bank angle in this case?

4.13   REFERENCES FOR CHAPTER 4

4.1   Anon.; MIL–F–8785C, Military Specification Flying Qualities of Piloted Airplanes; November 5, 1980; Air Force Flight Dynamics Laboratory, WPAFB, Dayton, Ohio.

4.2   Anon.; MIL–STD–1797A, Flying Qualities of Piloted Aircraft; January 30, 1990; Air Force Flight Dynamics Laboratory, WPAFB, Dayton, Ohio.

4.3   Anon.; Code of Federal Regulations (CFR), Title 14, Parts 1 to 59, January 1, 1992; US Government Printing Office, Superintendent of Documents, Mail Stop SSOP, Washington DC. (Note: FAR 35 and FAR 25 are components of CFR, Title 14)

4.4   Anon.; Joint Aviation Requirements, JAR–VLA Very Light Aeroplanes; Civil Aviation Authority, January 1, 1992; Printing and Publication Services, Greville House, 37 Gratton Road, Cheltenham, Glos. GL50 2BN, United Kingdom.

4.5   Roskam, J.; Airplane Design, Parts I through VIII; (1980–1990); Roskam Aviation and Engineering Corporation, 2550 Riley Road, Ottawa, Kansas, 66067.

4.6   Anon.; Light and General Aviation Aerodynamics, Volumes 1–4, 1981; Engineering Sciences Data Unit (ESDU), London, England.

4.7   Hoak, D.E. and Ellison, D.E. et al; USAF Stability and Control DATCOM; 1968 edition; Flight Control Division, Air Force Flight Dynamics Laboratory; Wright–Patterson Air Force Base, Ohio.

4.8   Gerlach, O.H.; Airplane Handling Qualities (Vliegeigenschappen), in Dutch; Technological University of Delft, Delft, The Netherlands, February 1968.

4.9   Kolk, W.R.; Modern Flight Dynamics; Prentice Hall, Englewood Cliffs, N.J.; 1961.

4.10   Phillips, W.H.; Application of Spring Tabs to Elevator Controls; NACA Technical Report TR 755, 1943.

4.11   Neese, W.A.; Aircraft Hydraulic Systems; R.E. Krieger Publishing Co., Malabar, Florida, 1987.

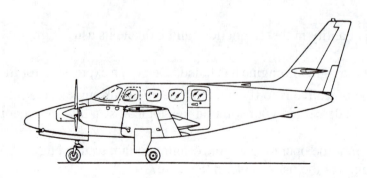

CHAPTER 5   STABILITY AND CONTROL DURING PERTURBED STATE FLIGHT

The purpose of this chapter is to examine the stability and response characteristics of airplanes in terms of small motion perturbations relative to a given (and therefore completely defined) steady state flight condition. These characteristics are also referred to as the dynamic stability and response behavior of an airplane. Before proceeding, it is useful to define precisely what is meant by dynamic stability and response.

Definition of Dynamic Stability

Dynamic stability is defined as the tendency of the amplitudes of the perturbed motion of an airplane to decrease to zero or to values corresponding to a new steady state at some time after the cause of the disturbance has stopped.

As an example, when an airplane is perturbed in pitch from a steady state flight condition and the resulting motion is damped out after some time, while the new steady state is not significantly different from the original one, the airplane is called dynamically stable.

This example and the definition indicate clearly that the subject of dynamic stability deals with the behavior of the perturbed motion of an airplane relative to some steady state flight path. The concepts of dynamic stability, neutral stability and instability (also called dynamic divergence) are illustrated in Figures 5.1 and 5.2.

As a general rule, airplanes must have some form of dynamic stability even though certain mild instabilities can be tolerated under certain conditions. The desired behavior of airplane motions under dynamic conditions (i.e. non–steady–state) is formulated with dynamic stability criteria.

Definition of Dynamic Stability Criterion

A dynamic stability criterion is defined as a rule by which perturbed motions of airplanes are separated into the categories of stable, neutrally stable or unstable.

In another context, a dynamic stability criterion can be interpreted as a requirement for specific response characteristics or for meeting specific frequency/damping relations. This type of interpretation is embodied by intent in many civil handling quality regulations and by numerical specification in many military requirements for flying qualities.

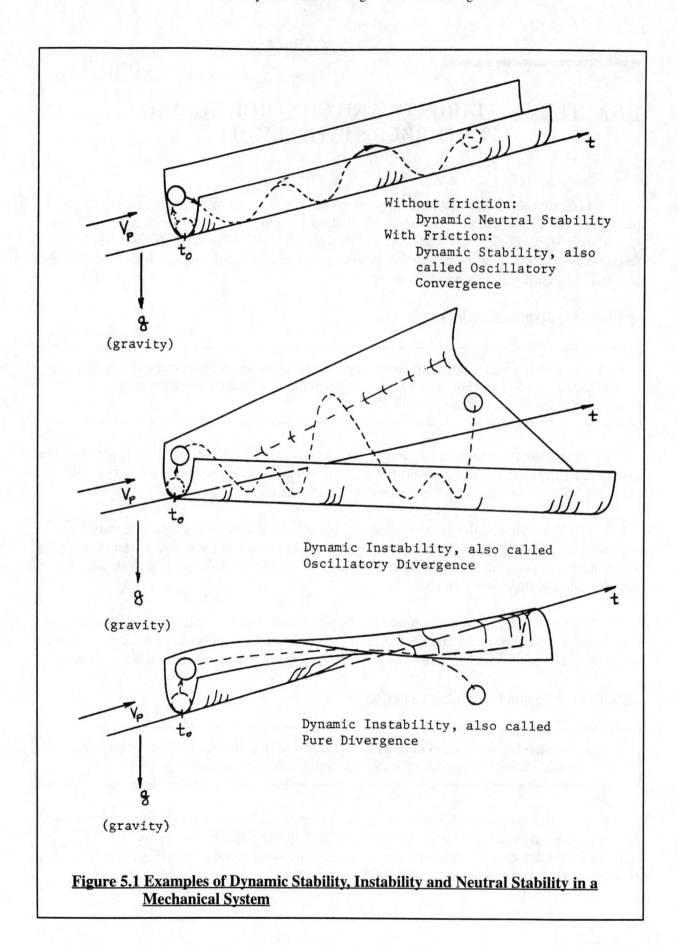

Figure 5.1 Examples of Dynamic Stability, Instability and Neutral Stability in a Mechanical System

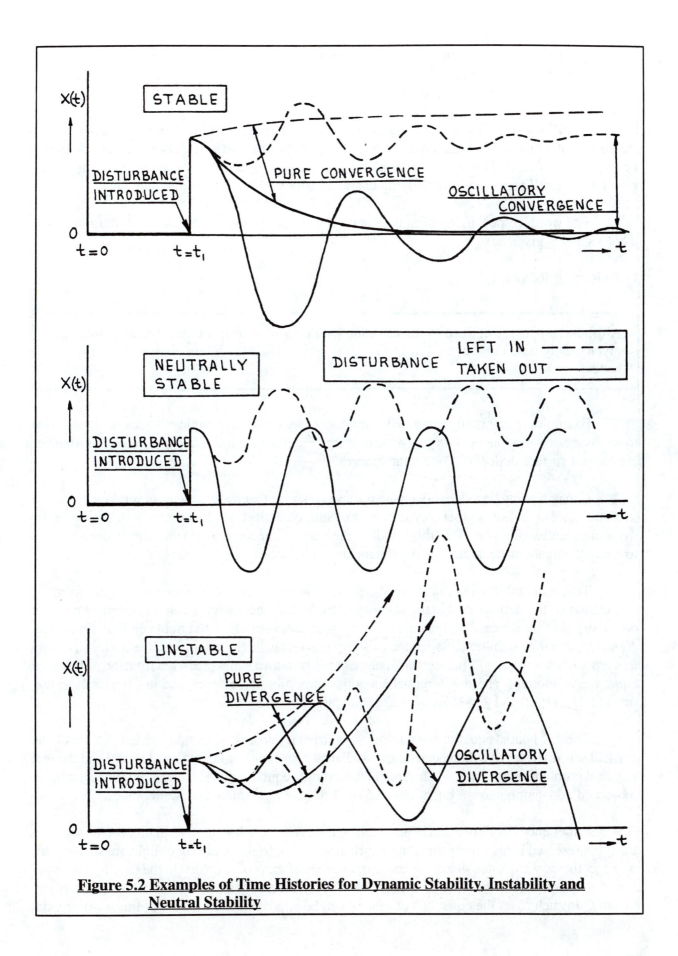

Figure 5.2 Examples of Time Histories for Dynamic Stability, Instability and Neutral Stability

The military flying quality requirements of Ref. 5.1 are viewed in this text as dynamic stability and response criteria which, when met, assure that human pilots can safely fly an airplane. Several important aspects of these requirements are included in Chapter 6.

It will be shown that there are important connections between these handling quality criteria (requirements) and purely mathematical definitions of dynamic stability. These connections will be explored in this chapter so that an airplane designer can use these connections to assure that a given design will possess adequate flying characteristics when flown by a human pilot.

The word 'response' has been used several times in the discussion so far. A definition and a discussion is given next.

Definition of Response

Airplane response is defined as the variation with time of motion variables relative to some given steady state flight condition as a result of an externally or internally generated disturbance.

Examples of externally generated disturbances are changes in angle of attack or sideslip due to atmospheric variations such as gust or turbulence. Examples of internally generated disturbances are control surface deflections or engine failures.

It may already be evident from the discussion so far that the character of airplane response to disturbances (such as a gust) and/or to control surface deflections is intimately tied up with the dynamic stability behavior. That this is indeed the case will become clear when the reader proceeds to study the mathematical analysis of airplane dynamic stability and response in this chapter.

The static stability criteria for airplanes were shown in Chapter 4 to evolve directly from the application of the definition of static stability to the instantaneous forces and moments which act on an airplane. In the case of dynamic stability, such a development has not been found possible. As stated, dynamic stability is associated with the response behavior of an airplane as a result of certain types of disturbances. This response behavior can be numerically predicted from the differential equations of motion. These differential equations of motion were developed in Chapter 1. Equations (1.51), (1.52) and (1.53) are typical examples.

The differential equations of motion of an airplane can be cast in many different forms. The particular form selected will depend on the similarity between the mathematical model and the real physical problem being analyzed. In general, differential equations can be linear, nonlinear, autonomous and non–autonomous. Equations (1.51)–(1.53) are non–linear and autonomous.

Experience has shown that in many cases, the dynamic behavior of airplanes can be satisfactorily represented by assuming that the perturbations away from steady state flight are small. This is in fact the way airplanes should behave from a point of view of comfort (in the case of passenger transports) or from a point of view of weapons delivery accuracy (in the case of certain military airplanes). In such cases the equations of motion can be approximated by a set of linear differential equations with constant coefficients. These equations are called the small perturbation equations and their basic form (relative to an arbitrary steady state) was developed in Chapter 1 as Eqns (1.75), (1.76) and (1.79).

By selecting the steady state, symmetrical, straight line flight as a special steady state condition, the perturbed equations of motion became those of Eqns (1.81) through (1.83). These equations must be augmented by using appropriate expressions for the perturbed aerodynamic and thrust forces and moments as expressed by Eqns (3.162), (3.197), (3.248) and (3.249).

Since the stability axis system was selected as the coordinate system of choice, the term W_1 (steady state velocity along the Z–axis) is by definition equal to zero. The resulting small perturbation equations of motion of the airplane are presented in two independent sets: the longitudinal equations and the lateral–directional equations. Their corresponding kinematic equations are also given.

*   — The coeff. derivatives are
size independent

For the longitudinal equations:

$$m\dot{u} = -mg\cos\theta_1 + \bar{q}_1 S\left\{ -(C_{D_u} + 2C_{D_1})\frac{u}{U_1} + (C_{T_{x_u}} + 2C_{T_{x_1}})\frac{u}{U_1} + \right.$$

$$\left. -(C_{D_\alpha} - C_{L_1})\alpha - C_{D_{\delta_e}}\delta_e \right\} \tag{5.1a}$$

$$m(\dot{w} - U_1 q) = -mg\sin\theta_1 + \bar{q}_1 S\left\{ -(C_{L_u} + 2C_{L_1})\frac{u}{U_1} - (C_{L_\alpha} + C_{D_1})\alpha + \right.$$

$$\left. -C_{L_{\dot{\alpha}}}\frac{\dot{\alpha}\bar{c}}{2U_1} - C_{L_q}\frac{q\bar{c}}{2U_1} - C_{L_{\delta_e}}\delta_e \right\} \tag{5.1b}$$

$$I_{yy}\dot{q} = \bar{q}_1 S\bar{c}\left\{ (C_{m_u} + 2C_{m_1})\frac{u}{U_1} + (C_{m_{T_u}} + 2C_{m_{T_1}})\frac{u}{U_1} + C_{m_\alpha}\alpha + C_{m_{T_\alpha}}\alpha + \right.$$

$$\left. -C_{m_{\dot{\alpha}}}\frac{\dot{\alpha}\bar{c}}{2U_1} - C_{m_q}\frac{q\bar{c}}{2U_1} - C_{m_{\delta_e}}\delta_e \right\} \tag{5.1c}$$

$$\text{where}: \quad q = \dot{\theta} \quad \text{and} \quad w = U_1\alpha \tag{5.1d}$$

For the lateral–directional equations:

$$m(\dot{v} + U_1 r) = mg\phi\cos\theta_1 + \bar{q}_1 S\left\{ C_{y_\beta}\beta + C_{y_p}\frac{pb}{2U_1} + C_{y_r}\frac{rb}{2U_1} + C_{y_{\delta_a}}\delta_a + C_{y_{\delta_r}}\delta_r \right\} \tag{5.2a}$$

$$I_{xx}\dot{p} - I_{xz}\dot{r} = \bar{q}_1 Sb\left\{ C_{l_\beta}\beta + C_{l_p}\frac{pb}{2U_1} + C_{l_r}\frac{rb}{2U_1} + C_{l_{\delta_a}}\delta_a + C_{l_{\delta_r}}\delta_r \right\} \tag{5.2b}$$

$$I_{zz}\dot{r} - I_{xz}\dot{p} = \bar{q}_1 Sb\left\{ C_{n_\beta}\beta + C_{n_{T_\beta}}\beta + C_{n_p}\frac{pb}{2U_1} + C_{n_r}\frac{rb}{2U_1} + C_{n_{\delta_a}}\delta_a + C_{n_{\delta_r}}\delta_r \right\} \tag{5.2c}$$

$$\text{where}: \quad p = \dot{\phi}, \quad r = \dot{\psi} \quad \text{and} \quad v = U_1\beta \tag{5.2d}$$

Equation sets (5.1) and (5.2) represent eight linear differential equations with constant coefficients. The reader will note, that these equations split into two (mathematically independent) sets:

Set (5.1) the small perturbation longitudinal equations

and

Set (5.2) the small perturbation lateral–directional equations.

Because of the appearance of accelerations in six of these equations they are of the second order. To solve these equations and to interpret their solutions the method of Laplace transformation will be used. References 5.2 and 5.3 provide a good overview of the theory and applications of Laplace transformation theory. Appendix C of this text contains a summary of those properties of Laplace transforms which are essential for the reader to understand.

The Laplace transforms of Equation sets (5.1) and (5.2) will be formed in such a manner as to yield the so–called open loop transfer functions of the airplane. The dynamic stability and response behavior of the airplane will then be determined from these transfer functions. It will turn out that these airplane transfer functions have properties similar to that of a simple, mechanical spring–mass–damper system. To understand airplane dynamics, it is essential that the reader understand the stability and response properties of a spring–mass–damper system. The behavior of such systems is discussed in Section 5.1.

The dynamic stability and response (to control inputs) of the airplane according to the small perturbation **longitudinal** equations of motion is discussed in Section 5.2. The dynamic stability and response (to control inputs) of the airplane according to the small perturbation **lateral–directional** equations of motion is discussed in Section 5.3.

It should be noted that equation sets (5.1) and (5.2) do not include a model of the dynamic behavior of the flight control system itself. For that reason they are referred to as 'fixed control surface' equations: they apply to airplanes with irreversible flight control systems. They also apply to airplanes with reversible flight control systems, provided the pilot (or auto–pilot) keeps the control surfaces fixed at some initial position or moves them in accordance to some fixed schedule (step–input, ramp input, sinusoidal input, etc. To account for the effect of freeing the controls (i.e. allowing the control surface to float dynamically) a change in the mathematical model is required. Reference 5.4 contains a fairly detailed discussion of the dynamic effect of freeing the controls. A summary of the required additional equations is given in Appendix D.

During the early design phases of an airplane it is important for the designer to understand the sensitivity of the dynamic stability and response behavior of an airplane to changes in various aerodynamic, geometric and inertial parameters. These effects can be studied by performing so–called sensitivity analyses. How this is done is discussed in Section 5.4.

Many high performance airplanes require an automatic feedback system to achieve acceptable flying qualities. It is possible to estimate the required feedback gains in such systems with the help of so–called equivalent stability derivatives. An introduction to equivalent stability derivatives and their role in early design is given in Section 5.5.

Fighter airplanes in particular can encounter severe inertial coupling effects when maneuvered at high roll rates and/or high pitch rates. A method for evaluating the dynamic stability of airplanes which undergo such maneuvers is discussed in Section 5.6.

Examples of how a designer might go about assuring that an airplane has certain pre–specified dynamic stability and response characteristics (such as specified in the regulations) are given in Chapter 6, Section 6.6.

5.1 DYNAMIC STABILITY AND RESPONSE BEHAVIOR OF A SPRING– MASS–DAMPER SYSTEM AND ITS STABILITY CRITERIA

Figure 5.3 shows an example of a mechanical spring–mass–damper system. The position of the mass, x(t), is considered to be the 'output' of the system. The externally applied driving force, f(t), is considered to be the 'input' to the system.

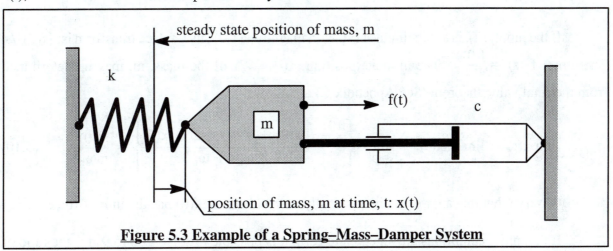

Figure 5.3 Example of a Spring–Mass–Damper System

The equation of motion for the system of Figure 5.3 can be written as follows:

$$m\ddot{x} + c\dot{x} + kx = f(t) \qquad (5.3)$$

It is useful to cast this equation in terms of accelerations rather than forces. This is done by dividing by the mass, m:

$$\ddot{x} + \frac{c}{m}\dot{x} + \frac{k}{m}x = \frac{f(t)}{m} \qquad (5.4)$$

The following two quantities will now be <u>defined</u>:

the undamped natural frequency : $\quad \omega_n = \sqrt{\dfrac{k}{m}} \qquad (5.5)$

and:

the damping ratio : $\quad \zeta = \dfrac{c}{2\sqrt{km}} \qquad (5.6)$

The physical significance of these quantities will be made clear later. Eliminating c, k and m in Eqn ((5.4) in favor of ζ and ω_n results in:

$$\ddot{x} + 2\zeta\omega_n\dot{x} + \omega_n^2x = \frac{f(t)}{m} = f_1(t) \tag{5.7}$$

Applying the Laplace transform for non–zero initial conditions yields:

$$s^2x(s) + 2\zeta\omega_nsx(s) + \omega_n^2x(s) = f_1(s) + \dot{x}(0) + sx(0) + 2\zeta\omega_nx(0) \tag{5.8}$$

Where $f_1(s)$ is defined as the Laplace transform of $f_1(t)$. The output of this system in the s–domain, $x(s)$, can now be written as:

$$x(s) = \frac{f_1(s) + \dot{x}(0) + sx(0) + 2\zeta\omega_nx(0)}{s^2 + 2\zeta\omega_ns + \omega_n^2} \tag{5.9}$$

If the input, f(t), is a step–input at t=0 with magnitude f(0), its Laplace transform is: {f(0)}/s. Therefore: $f_1(s) = \frac{f(0)}{ms}$. The ultimate position, $x(t \to \infty)$ of the mass, m, may be determined from the final value theorem (See Appendix C) as follows:

$$\lim_{t \to \infty} x(t) = \lim_{s \to 0} \{sx(s)\} = \lim_{s \to 0} s\left\{\frac{\frac{f(0)}{ms} + \dot{x}(0) + sx(0) + 2\zeta\omega_nx(0)}{s^2 + 2\zeta\omega_ns + \omega_n^2}\right\} = \frac{f(0)}{m\omega_n^2} \tag{5.10}$$

Observe that this answer is dimensionally correct because f(0) has the unit of force.

If the initial conditions are all equal to zero, it is possible to solve Eqn (5.9) for the ratio of the output Laplace transform, $x(s)$, to the input Laplace transform, $f_1(s)$:

$$\boxed{\frac{x(s)}{f_1(s)} = G(s) = \frac{1}{s^2 + 2\zeta\omega_ns + \omega_n^2}} \tag{5.11}$$

This ratio is referred to as the **open loop transfer function** of the spring–mass–damper system. The concept of open loop transfer function is very important to the study of airplane dynamics.

The response of any system with G(s) as the open loop transfer function is obtained by multiplying the open loop transfer function of the system by the Laplace transform of the input to that system. The application of this idea to the spring–mass–damper system of Figure 5.3 will now be discussed. Assume that the forcing function $f_1(t)$ is a unit step as illustrated in Figure 5.4. The Laplace transform of the unit step is:

$$f_1(s) = \frac{1}{s} \tag{5.12}$$

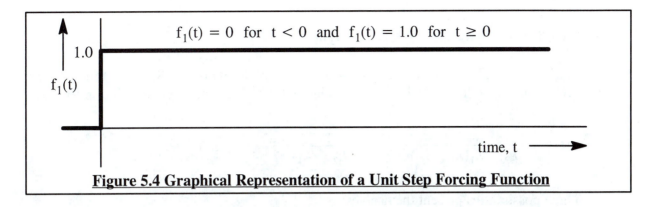

Figure 5.4 Graphical Representation of a Unit Step Forcing Function

The output of the system, in the s–domain, can now be written as:

$$x(s) = \frac{1}{s}\left(\frac{1}{s^2 + 2\zeta\omega_n s + \omega_n^2}\right) \tag{5.13}$$

To find the corresponding time domain response, $x(t)$, it is necessary to find the inverse Laplace transform of $x(s)$. This is done with the method of partial fraction expansion. How this is done is explained in detail in Ref. (5.2). The usual procedure is to first find the roots of the characteristics equation:

$$s^2 + 2\zeta\omega_n s + \omega_n^2 = 0 \tag{5.14}$$

The roots of this characteristic equation will be called λ_1 and λ_2. These roots are sometimes referred to as the 'eigen–values' of the system. It is now possible to write:

$$s^2 + 2\zeta\omega_n s + \omega_n^2 = (s - \lambda_1)(s - \lambda_2) \tag{5.15}$$

The system output in the s–domain can now be written as:

$$x(s) = \frac{1}{s}\left(\frac{1}{(s - \lambda_1)(s - \lambda_2)}\right) = \frac{A}{s} + \frac{B}{s - \lambda_1} + \frac{C}{s - \lambda_2} \tag{5.16}$$

The constants A, B and C may be determined with the theorem of residues (See Ref. 5.5). It is found that:

$$A = \frac{1}{\lambda_1\lambda_2} \qquad B = \frac{1}{\lambda_1(\lambda_1 - \lambda_2)} \qquad C = \frac{1}{\lambda_2(\lambda_2 - \lambda_1)} \tag{5.17}$$

It is now possible to rewrite Eqn (5.16) as:

$$x(s) = \frac{\frac{1}{\lambda_1\lambda_2}}{s} + \frac{\frac{1}{\lambda_1(\lambda_1 - \lambda_2)}}{s - \lambda_1} + \frac{\frac{1}{(\lambda_2(\lambda_2 - \lambda_1))}}{s - \lambda_2} \tag{5.18}$$

The roots of Eqn (5.14), λ_1 and λ_2, can be either both real or both complex. Both cases will be considered.

Case 1: Both roots of Eqn (5.14) are real

The inverse Laplace transform of the s–domain functions in Eqn (5.18) can be found directly from Table C1 in Appendix C. Doing so results in the following time–domain solution for x(t):

$$x(t) = \frac{1}{\lambda_1\lambda_2} + \frac{1}{\lambda_1(\lambda_1 - \lambda_2)}e^{\lambda_1 t} + \frac{1}{\lambda_2(\lambda_2 - \lambda_1)}e^{\lambda_2 t} \qquad (5.19)$$

Three possibilities present themselves:

1) If both roots, λ_1 and λ_2, are positive, $\lambda_1 > 0$ and $\lambda_2 > 0$, it is seen that x(t) will diverge to infinity. Such a system is said to be divergent. Note that if only one root is positive the system will still be divergent.

2) If both roots, λ_1 and λ_2, are negative, $\lambda_1 < 0$ and $\lambda_2 < 0$, it is seen that x(t) will converge toward the value x(t) = $1/(\lambda_1\lambda_2)$. Such a system is said to be convergent.

3) If both roots, λ_1 and λ_2, are equal to zero, $\lambda_1 = 0$ and $\lambda_2 = 0$, it is seen that x(t) becomes undetermined. This can be shown by application of l'Hopital's Theorem. Such a system is said to be neutrally stable. Note that if only one root is zero, the system is still neutrally stable.

Figure 5.5 shows the various time–domain responses for the case of all–zero, all–negative and all–positive real characteristic equation roots.

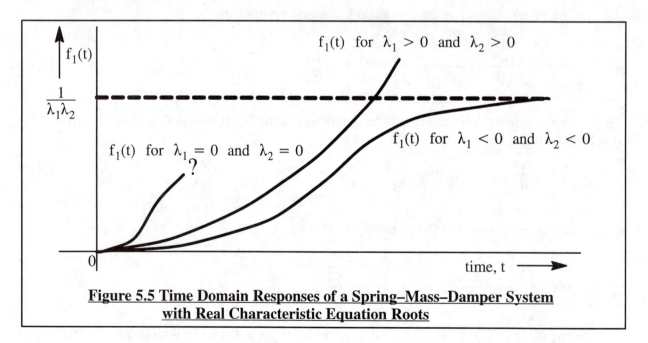

Figure 5.5 Time Domain Responses of a Spring–Mass–Damper System with Real Characteristic Equation Roots

Case 2: Both roots of Eqn (5.14) are complex

In this case, the complex roots must be each others conjugate:

$$\lambda_1 = n + j\omega \qquad\qquad \lambda_2 = n - j\omega \tag{5.20}$$

By substituting these forms of the roots into Eqn (5.19) it is found that:

$$x(t) = \frac{1}{n^2 + \omega^2} + \frac{e^{(n+j\omega)t}}{(n + j\omega)2j\omega} - \frac{e^{(n-j\omega)t}}{(n - j\omega)2j\omega} \tag{5.21}$$

With the help of De Moivre's Theorem (See Reference 5.5, page 467) this in turn can be written as follows:

$$x(t) = \frac{1}{n^2 + \omega^2}\left\{1 - e^{nt}\left(\cos\omega t - \frac{n}{\omega}\sin\omega t\right)\right\} \tag{5.22}$$

Clearly the system response in this case is oscillatory in nature. The actual character of the response depends on the real part, n, of the complex roots given by Eqns (5.20).

Again, three possibilities present themselves:

1) It is seen from Eqn (5.22) that as long as the real part of the complex roots, n<0, the oscillatory terms will subside and the system will reach a final position given by:

$$x(t \to \infty) = \frac{1}{n^2 + \omega^2} = \frac{1}{\lambda_1\lambda_2} \tag{5.23}$$

Such a system is called oscillatory convergent (oscillatory stable). Note the similarity of this result to that obtained for the case of all stable and real roots.

2) Similarly it is seen from Eqn (5.22) that when the real parts of the complex roots is positive, the amplitudes of the oscillations will tend to diverge. Such a system is called oscillatory divergent (oscillatory unstable).

3) If the real part of the complex roots is zero, the system will oscillate at a constant amplitude. Such a system is said to be neutrally stable.

Figure 5.6 shows examples of time–domain responses for the case of complex characteristic equation roots.

The following properties of the characteristic equation roots and their characteristics in the s–plane are to be noted. The reader is asked to refer to Figure 5.7.

First, the product of the characteristic equation roots is observed to be equal to the square of the undamped natural frequency as defined in Eqn (5.5):

$$\lambda_1\lambda_2 = n^2 + \omega^2 = \omega_n^2 \tag{5.24}$$

Notice that in the s–plane (see Figure 5.7) the undamped natural frequency is equal to the distance of each complex characteristic equation root (also called a pole) to the origin.

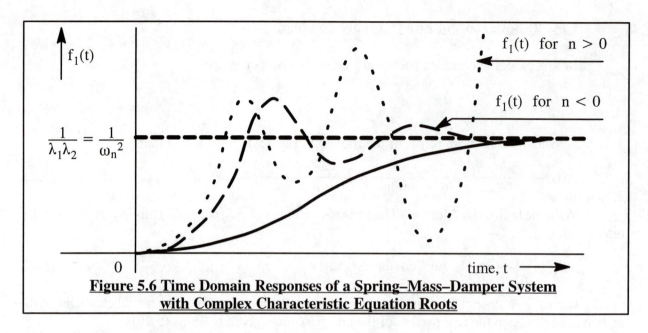

Figure 5.6 Time Domain Responses of a Spring–Mass–Damper System with Complex Characteristic Equation Roots

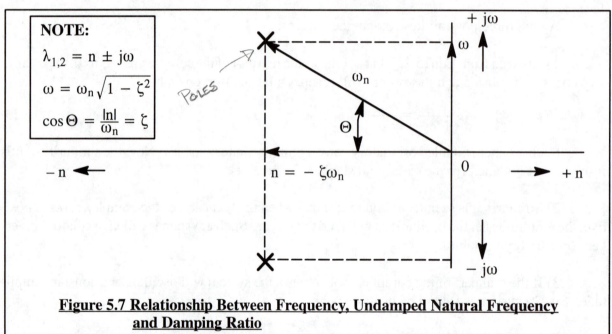

Figure 5.7 Relationship Between Frequency, Undamped Natural Frequency and Damping Ratio

Second, the sum of the characteristic equation roots is equal to twice the real part of each root, n. The real part, n of each root is also equal to the negative of the product of damping ratio {as defined by (Eqn 5.6)} and undamped natural frequency. This is seen by invoking Eqn (5.15):

$$\lambda_1 + \lambda_2 = 2n = -2\zeta\omega_n \qquad (5.25)$$

Note from Figure 5.7 that the damping ratio also equals the cosine of the angle between the pole–vector from the origin and the negative real axis.

By combining Eqns (5.24) and (5.25) it is seen that:

$$\omega = \omega_n \sqrt{1 - \zeta^2} \qquad (5.26)$$

From this result it can be observed that when the damping ratio becomes zero {this occurs when c=0 in Eqn (5.3)} the frequency of oscillation equals the undamped natural frequency:

$$\omega = \omega_n = \sqrt{\frac{k}{m}} \qquad \text{(for } c = 0) \qquad (5.27)$$

The spring–mass–damper system output, x(t), as expressed by Eqn (5.22), can be cast in a format which reflects the system damping ratio and undamped natural frequency. The reader is asked to show that the result of doing this is as follows:

$$x(t) = \frac{1}{\omega_n^2}\left\{1 - e^{-\zeta\omega_n t}\left[\cos(\omega_n\sqrt{1 - \zeta^2}t) + \frac{\zeta}{\sqrt{1 - \zeta^2}}\sin(\omega_n\sqrt{1 - \zeta^2}t)\right]\right\} =$$

$$= \frac{1}{\omega_n^2}\left\{1 - \frac{e^{-\zeta\omega_n t}}{\sqrt{1 - \zeta^2}}\sin\left((\omega_n\sqrt{1 - \zeta^2}t) + \psi\right)\right\} \quad \text{with}: \qquad (5.28)$$

$$\psi = \arcsin\sqrt{1 - \zeta^2}$$

The time–domain behavior of a spring–mass–damper system is clearly a function of two parameters: the damping ratio, ζ, and the undamped natural frequency, ω_n. The response of such a system for damping ratios ranging from 0.1 to 1.0 is shown in Figure 5.8. Note that the scales have been normalized. The reader would do well to keep the ten response plots of Figure 5.8 firmly in mind. This will help in visualizing dynamic stability and response characteristics of airplanes as are discussed in Sections 5.2 and 5.3.

From the presentations so far, it is evident that the stability character of the response of a system such as shown in Figure (5.3) is determined entirely by:

      a) the type of roots of the characteristic equation of that system

      b) the sign of the real part of the roots of the characteristic equation

It can be shown that this is also the case for any system which can be modelled by one or more linear differential equations with constant coefficients. The following stability criteria summarize the stability characteristics of any system with a characteristic equation similar to Eqn (5.14).

Dynamic Stability Criteria

1)   A linear system is stable if and only if the real parts of the roots of the characteristic equation of the system are negative.

2)   A linear system is convergent (stable) if the roots of the characteristic equation of the system are real and negative.

3)   A linear system is divergent (unstable) if the roots of the characteristic equation of the system are real and positive.

4)   A linear system is oscillatory convergent (stable) if the real parts of the roots of the characteristic equation of the system are negative.

5)   A linear system is oscillatory divergent (unstable) if the real parts of the roots of the characteristic equation of the system are positive.

6)   A linear system is neutrally stable if one of the roots of the characteristic equation of the system is zero or if the real parts of the roots of the characteristic equation of the system is zero.

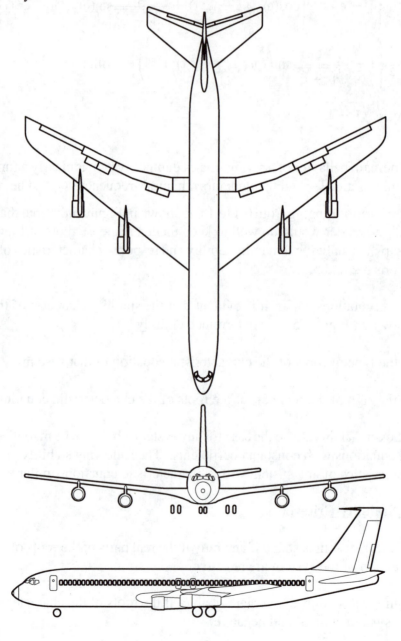

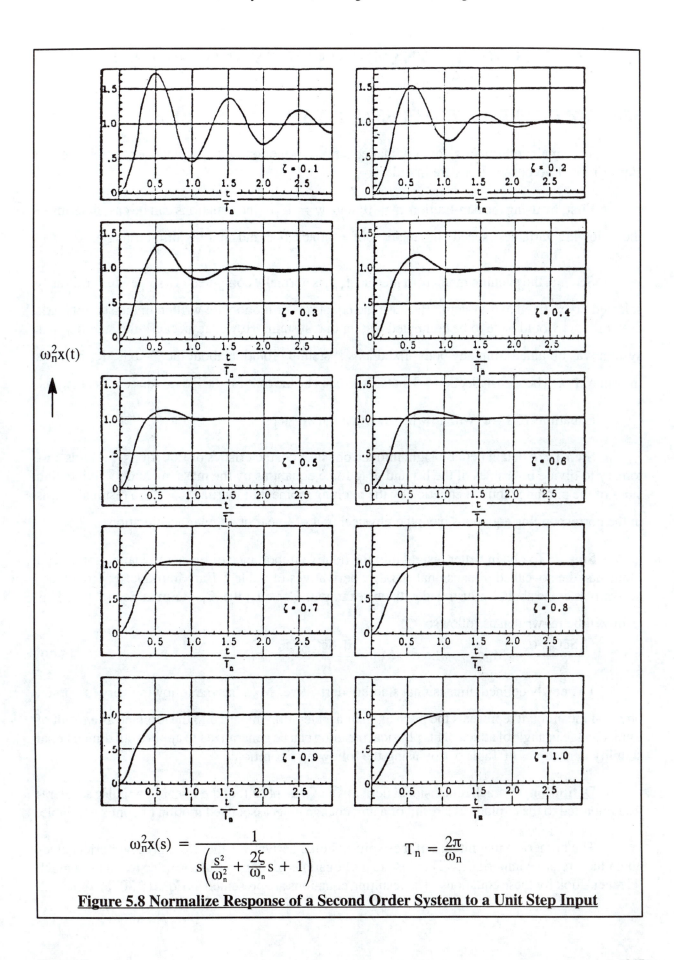

$$\omega_n^2 x(s) = \cfrac{1}{s\left(\cfrac{s^2}{\omega_n^2} + \cfrac{2\zeta}{\omega_n}s + 1\right)}$$

$$T_n = \frac{2\pi}{\omega_n}$$

Figure 5.8 Normalize Response of a Second Order System to a Unit Step Input

5.2 LONGITUDINAL, DYNAMIC STABILITY AND RESPONSE

5.2.1 LONGITUDINAL EQUATIONS AND TRANSFER FUNCTIONS

The small perturbation, longitudinal equations of motion of the airplane are represented by Eqns (5.1). Two observations are in order:

First, by using the substitution $q = \dot{\theta}$ and $w = U_1\dot{\alpha}$ the equations can be cast in terms of the following variables: speed, u, angle $-$ of $-$ attack α, and pitch $-$ attitude angle, θ.

Second, the pitching moment of inertia, I_{yy}, is normally computed in a somewhat arbitrarily selected body–fixed axis system. Because the equations of motion are written in the stability axis system, I_{yy}, would have to be computed also in that system. However, because the stability axis system was obtained from any body–fixed axis system by rotation about the Y–axis, I_{yy} remains the same. It will be seen in Section 5.3 that this will not be the case for the lateral–directional inertias.

Equations (5.1a–c) will now be rewritten in two steps:

Step 1: To obtain better insight into the physical characteristics of Equations (5.1) it is customary to divide both sides of the lift and drag force equations by the mass, m, and to divide both sides of the pitching moment equation by the pitching moment of inertia, I_{yy}. As a result all terms in the corresponding equations have the physical unit of linear or angular acceleration.

Step 2: To obtain better insight into the relative importance of the aerodynamic forces and moments, the so–called dimensional stability derivatives of Table 5.1 are introduced. How these derivatives come about is illustrated with one example. Consider the C_{m_α} term in Eqn (5.1c). This term will be re–written as follows:

$$\frac{\overline{q}_1 S \overline{c} C_{m_\alpha} \alpha}{I_{yy}} = M_\alpha \alpha \;, \quad \text{where}: \; M_\alpha = \frac{\overline{q}_1 S \overline{c} C_{m_\alpha}}{I_{yy}} \tag{5.29}$$

The newly defined dimensional stability derivative, M_α, has the following very important physical meaning: it represents the pitch angular acceleration imparted to the airplane as a result of a unit change in angle of attack. This physical meaning can be generalized to apply to all dimensional stability derivatives of Table 5.1 by using the following definition:

Definition: Each dimensional derivative represents either the linear or angular acceleration imparted to the airplane as a result of a unit change in its associated motion or control variable.

The numerical magnitudes of these dimensional derivatives therefore give numerical clues about their relative importance. Their use in the equations of motion (5.1a–c) also results in a much 'cleaner' look for these equations. The resulting equations are presented as Eqns (5.30) in Table 5.2.

Table 5.1 Definition of Longitudinal, Dimensional Stability Derivatives

$$X_u = \frac{-\bar{q}_1 S(C_{D_u} + 2C_{D_1})}{mU_1} \quad \frac{ft/sec^2}{ft/sec} \qquad M_u = \frac{\bar{q}_1 S\bar{c}(C_{m_u} + 2C_{m_1})}{I_{yy}U_1} \quad \frac{rad/sec^2}{ft/sec}$$

$$X_{T_u} = \frac{\bar{q}_1 S(C_{T_{x_u}} + 2C_{T_{x_1}})}{mU_1} \quad \frac{ft/sec^2}{ft/sec} \qquad M_{T_u} = \frac{\bar{q}_1 S\bar{c}(C_{m_{T_u}} + 2C_{m_{T_1}})}{I_{yy}U_1} \quad \frac{rad/sec^2}{ft/sec}$$

$$X_\alpha = \frac{-\bar{q}_1 S(C_{D_\alpha} - C_{L_1})}{m} \quad \frac{ft/sec^2}{rad} \qquad M_\alpha = \frac{\bar{q}_1 S\bar{c}C_{m_\alpha}}{I_{yy}} \quad \frac{rad/sec^2}{rad}$$

$$X_{\delta_e} = \frac{-\bar{q}_1 S C_{D_{\delta_e}}}{m} \quad \frac{ft/sec^2}{rad} \qquad M_{T_\alpha} = \frac{\bar{q}_1 S\bar{c}C_{m_{T_\alpha}}}{I_{yy}} \quad \frac{rad/sec^2}{rad/sec}$$

$$Z_u = \frac{-\bar{q}_1 S(C_{L_u} + 2C_{L_1})}{mU_1} \quad \frac{ft/sec^2}{ft/sec} \qquad M_{\dot{\alpha}} = \frac{\bar{q}_1 S\bar{c}^2 C_{m_{\dot{\alpha}}}}{2I_{yy}U_1} \quad \frac{rad/sec^2}{rad/sec}$$

$$Z_\alpha = \frac{-\bar{q}_1 S(C_{L_\alpha} + C_{D_1})}{m} \quad \frac{ft/sec^2}{rad} \qquad M_q = \frac{\bar{q}_1 S\bar{c}^2 C_{m_q}}{2I_{yy}U_1} \quad \frac{rad/sec^2}{rad/sec}$$

$$Z_{\dot{\alpha}} = \frac{-\bar{q}_1 S\bar{c}C_{L_{\dot{\alpha}}}}{2mU_1} \quad \frac{ft/sec^2}{rad/sec} \qquad M_{\delta_e} = \frac{\bar{q}_1 S\bar{c}C_{m_{\delta_e}}}{I_{yy}} \quad \frac{rad/sec^2}{rad}$$

$$Z_q = \frac{-\bar{q}_1 S\bar{c}C_{L_q}}{2mU_1} \quad \frac{ft/sec^2}{rad/sec}$$

$$Z_{\delta_e} = \frac{-\bar{q}_1 S C_{L_{\delta_e}}}{m} \quad \frac{ft/sec^2}{rad}$$

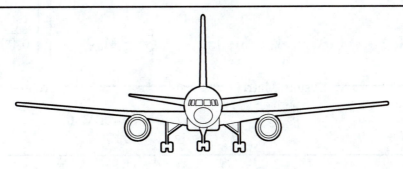

Table 5.2 Development of the Perturbed Longitudinal Equations of Motion with Dimensional Stability Derivatives in Matrix Format

$$\dot{u} = -g\theta\cos\theta_1 + X_u u + X_{T_u} u + X_\alpha \alpha + X_{\delta_e}\delta_e \tag{5.30a}$$

$$U_1\dot{\alpha} - U_1\dot{\theta} = -g\theta\sin\theta_1 + Z_u u + Z_\alpha \alpha + Z_{\dot{\alpha}}\dot{\alpha} + Z_q\dot{\theta} + Z_{\delta_e}\delta_e \tag{5.30b}$$

$$\ddot{\theta} = M_u u + M_{T_u} u + M_\alpha \alpha + M_{T_\alpha}\alpha + M_{\dot{\alpha}}\dot{\alpha} + M_q\dot{\theta} + M_{\delta_e}\delta_e \tag{5.30c}$$

Laplace transforming Eqns (5.30) for zero initial conditions:

$$(s - X_u - X_{T_u})u(s) \qquad -X_\alpha\alpha(s) \qquad g\cos\theta_1\theta(s) \qquad = X_{\delta_e}\delta_e(s) \tag{5.31a}$$

$$-Z_u u(s) \qquad \{s(U_1 - Z_{\dot{\alpha}}) - Z_\alpha\}\alpha(s) \qquad \{-(Z_q + U_1)s + g\sin\theta_1\}\theta(s) = Z_{\delta_e}\delta_e(s) \tag{5.31b}$$

$$-(M_u + M_{T_u})u(s) \qquad -\{M_{\dot{\alpha}}s + M_\alpha + M_{T_\alpha}\}\alpha(s) \qquad (s^2 - M_q s)\theta(s) \qquad = M_{\delta_e}\delta_e(s) \tag{5.31c}$$

Writing Eqns (5.31) in matrix and transfer function format:

Transfer Function Matrix ⟶

$$\begin{bmatrix} (s - X_u - X_{T_u}) & -X_\alpha & g\cos\theta_1 \\ \\ -Z_u & \{s(U_1 - Z_{\dot{\alpha}}) - Z_\alpha\} & \{-(Z_q + U_1)s + g\sin\theta_1\} \\ \\ -(M_u + M_{T_u}) & -\left(M_{\dot{\alpha}}s + M_\alpha + M_{T_\alpha}\right) & (s^2 - M_q s) \end{bmatrix} \begin{Bmatrix} \dfrac{u(s)}{\delta_e(s)} \\ \\ \dfrac{\alpha(s)}{\delta_e(s)} \\ \\ \dfrac{\theta(s)}{\delta_e(s)} \end{Bmatrix} = \begin{Bmatrix} X_{\delta_e} \\ \\ Z_{\delta_e} \\ \\ M_{\delta_e} \end{Bmatrix}$$

⟵ System Matrix ⟶

Control Power Matrix

$$\tag{5.32}$$

Equations (5.30) are Laplace transformed for zero initial conditions. The new variables are: $u(s)$, $\alpha(s)$ and $\theta(s)$ respectively, while $\delta_e(s)$ is the Laplace transformed elevator input. The result is Eqns (5.31). Next, equations (5.31a–c) are divided by $\delta_e(s)$. This gives rise to the so–called open–loop airplane transfer functions: $u(s)/\delta_e(s)$, $\alpha(s)/\delta_e(s)$ and $\theta(s)/\delta_e(s)$. The open–loop transfer functions can now be thought of as the new 'variables'. By casting the equations in a matrix format the result is Eqns (5.32) which are also shown in Table 5.2. The airplane open–loop transfer functions can be determined with matrix algebra. Each transfer function is then expressed as a ratio of two determinants. The resulting determinant ratios are shown in Table 5.3 as Equations (5.33), (5.36) and (5.38) respectively.

Note, that the speed–to–elevator transfer function, $u(s)/\delta_e(s)$, of Eqn (5.33) can be written as the following ratio of polynomials in the independent Laplace variable, s:

$$\frac{u(s)}{\delta_e(s)} = \frac{N_u}{D_1} = \frac{A_u s^3 + B_u s^2 + C_u s + D_u}{A_1 s^4 + B_1 s^3 + C_1 s^2 + D_1 s + E_1} \quad \text{— plant matrix, determinate as matrix} \tag{5.40}$$

Similarly, the angle–of–attack–to–elevator transfer function, $\alpha(s)/\delta_e(s)$, of Eqn (5.36) can be expressed as:

$$\frac{\alpha(s)}{\delta_e(s)} = \frac{N_\alpha}{D_1} = \frac{A_\alpha s^3 + B_\alpha s^2 + C_\alpha s + D_\alpha}{A_1 s^4 + B_1 s^3 + C_1 s^2 + D_1 s + E_1} \tag{5.41}$$

Finally, the pitch–attitude–to–elevator transfer function, $\theta(s)/\delta_e(s)$, of Eqn (5.38) can be written as:

$$\frac{\theta(s)}{\delta_e(s)} = \frac{N_\theta}{D_1} = \frac{A_\theta s^2 + B_\theta s + C_\theta}{A_1 s^4 + B_1 s^3 + C_1 s^2 + D_1 s + E_1} \tag{5.42}$$

It is seen that all transfer functions have the same denominator. When this denominator is set equal to zero the resulting equation is called the characteristics equation:

$$A_1 s^4 + B_1 s^3 + C_1 s^2 + D_1 s + E_1 = 0 \tag{5.43}$$

The roots of this characteristic equation determine the dynamic stability character of the airplane. These roots and how they are affected by flight condition, by airplane mass, by airplane mass distribution (c.g. location and inertias), by airplane geometry and by the airplane aerodynamic characteristics will be discussed in Sub–section 5.2.2 – 5.2.6.

It is also seen from Eqns (5.40)–(5.42) that the numerators are all different. The numerator polynomials affect the **magnitude of the response** of an airplane to a control surface input. However, ONLY the denominators affect the **dynamic stability character of the response** (i.e. the frequency or time–constant behavior).

Table 5.3 Longitudinal Airplane Transfer Functions

$$\frac{u(s)}{\delta_e(s)} = \frac{\begin{vmatrix} X_{\delta_e} & -X_\alpha & g\cos\theta_1 \\ Z_{\delta_e} & \{s(U_1 - Z_{\dot\alpha}) - Z_\alpha\} & \{-(Z_q + U_1)s + g\sin\theta_1\} \\ M_{\delta_e} & -\{M_{\dot\alpha}s + M_\alpha + M_{T_\alpha}\} & (s^2 - M_q s) \end{vmatrix}}{\begin{vmatrix} (s - X_u - X_{T_u}) & -X_\alpha & g\cos\theta_1 \\ -Z_u & \{s(U_1 - Z_{\dot\alpha}) - Z_\alpha\} & \{-(Z_q + U_1)s + g\sin\theta_1\} \\ -(M_u + M_{T_u}) & -\{M_{\dot\alpha}s + M_\alpha + M_{T_\alpha}\} & (s^2 - M_q s) \end{vmatrix}} = \frac{N_u}{\overline{D}_1}$$

$$(5.33)$$

$$\overline{D}_1 = A_1 s^4 + B_1 s^3 + C_1 s^2 + D_1 s + E_1 \quad , \quad \text{where:} \tag{5.34}$$

$$A_1 = U_1 - Z_{\dot\alpha}$$

$$B_1 = -(U_1 - Z_{\dot\alpha})(X_u + X_{T_u} + M_q) - Z_\alpha - M_{\dot\alpha}(U_1 + Z_q)$$

$$C_1 = (X_u + X_{T_u})\{M_q(U_1 - Z_{\dot\alpha} + Z_\alpha + M_{\dot\alpha}(U_1 + Z_q)\} + M_q Z_\alpha - Z_u X_\alpha + M_{\dot\alpha} g\sin\theta_1 +$$

$$\quad - (M_\alpha + M_{T_\alpha})(U_1 + Z_q)$$

$$D_1 = g\sin\theta_1\{M_\alpha + M_{T_\alpha} - M_{\dot\alpha}(X_u + X_{T_u})\} + g\cos\theta_1\{Z_u M_{\dot\alpha} + (M_u + M_{T_u})(U_1 - Z_{\dot\alpha})\} +$$

$$\quad + (M_u + M_{T_u})\{-X_\alpha(U_1 + Z_q)\} + Z_u X_\alpha M_q +$$

$$\quad + (X_u + X_{T_u})\{(M_\alpha + M_{T_\alpha})(U_1 + Z_q) - M_q Z_\alpha\}$$

$$E_1 = g\cos\theta_1\{(M_\alpha + M_{T_\alpha})Z_u - Z_\alpha(M_u + M_{T_u})\} +$$

$$\quad + g\sin\theta_1\{(M_u + M_{T_u})X_\alpha - (X_u + X_{T_u})(M_\alpha + M_{T_\alpha})\}$$

$$N_u = A_u s^3 + B_u s^2 + C_u s + D_u \quad , \quad \text{where:} \tag{5.35}$$

$$A_u = X_{\delta_e}(U_1 - Z_{\dot\alpha})$$

$$B_u = -X_{\delta_e}\{(U_1 - Z_{\dot\alpha})M_q + Z_\alpha + M_{\dot\alpha}(U_1 + Z_q) + Z_{\delta_e}X_\alpha\}$$

$$C_u = X_{\delta_e}\{M_q Z_\alpha + M_{\dot\alpha}g\sin\theta_1 - (M_\alpha + M_{T_\alpha})(U_1 + Z_q)\} +$$

$$\quad + Z_{\delta_e}\{-M_{\dot\alpha}g\cos\theta_q - X_\alpha M_q\} + M_{\delta_e}\{X_\alpha(U_1 + Z_q) - (U_1 - Z_{\dot\alpha})g\cos\theta_1\}$$

$$D_u = X_{\delta_e}(M_\alpha + M_{T_\alpha})g\sin\theta_1 - Z_{\delta_e}M_\alpha g\cos\theta_1 + M_{\delta_e}(Z_\alpha g\cos\theta_1 - X_\alpha g\sin\theta_1)$$

Table 5.3 (Continued) Longitudinal Airplane Transfer Functions

$$\frac{\alpha(s)}{\delta_e(s)} = \frac{\begin{vmatrix} (s - X_u - X_{T_u}) & X_{\delta_e} & g\cos\theta_1 \\ - Z_u & Z_{\delta_e} & \{-(Z_q + U_1)s + g\sin\theta_1\} \\ - (M_u + M_{T_u}) & M_{\delta_e} & (s^2 - M_q s) \end{vmatrix}}{\overline{D}_1} = \frac{N_\alpha}{\overline{D}_1}$$

(5.36)

$$N_\alpha = A_\alpha s^3 + B_\alpha s^2 + C_\alpha s + D_\alpha \quad , \quad \text{where:} \tag{5.37}$$

$$A_\alpha = Z_{\delta_e}$$

$$B_\alpha = X_{\delta_e} Z_u + Z_{\delta_e}\{- M_q - (X_u + X_{T_u})\} + M_{\delta_e}(U_1 + Z_q)$$

$$C_\alpha = X_{\delta_e}\{(U_1 + Z_q)(M_u + M_{T_u}) - M_q Z_u\} + Z_{\delta_e} M_q(X_u + X_{T_u}) +$$

$$+ M_{\delta_e}\{- g\sin\theta_1 - (U_1 + Z_q)(X_u + X_{T_u})\}$$

$$D_\alpha = - X_{\delta_e}(M_u + M_{T_u})g\sin\theta_1 + Z_{\delta_e}(M_u + M_{T_u})g\cos\theta_1 +$$

$$+ M_{\delta_e}\{(X_u + X_{T_u})g\sin\theta_1 - Z_u g\cos\theta_1\}$$

$$\frac{\theta(s)}{\delta_e(s)} = \frac{\begin{vmatrix} (s - X_u - X_{T_u}) & - X_\alpha & X_{\delta_e} \\ - Z_u & \{s(U_1 - Z_{\dot\alpha}) - Z_\alpha\} & Z_{\delta_e} \\ - (M_u + M_{T_u}) & - \{M_{\dot\alpha}s + M_\alpha + M_{T_\alpha}\} & M_{\delta_e} \end{vmatrix}}{\overline{D}_1} = \frac{N_\theta}{\overline{D}_1} \tag{5.38}$$

$$N_\theta = A_\theta s^2 + B_\theta s + C_\theta \quad , \quad \text{where:} \tag{5.39}$$

$$A_\theta = Z_{\delta_e} M_{\dot\alpha} + M_{\delta_e}(U_1 - Z_{\dot\alpha})$$

$$B_\theta = X_{\delta_e}\{Z_u M_{\dot\alpha} + (U_1 - Z_{\dot\alpha})(M_u + M_{T_u})\} + Z_{\delta_e}\{(M_\alpha + M_{T_\alpha}) - M_{\dot\alpha}(X_u + X_{T_u})\} +$$

$$+ M_{\delta_e}\{- Z_\alpha - (U_1 - Z_{\dot\alpha})(X_u + X_{T_u})\}$$

$$C_\theta = X_{\delta_e}\{(M_\alpha + M_{T_\alpha})Z_u - Z_\alpha(M_u + M_{T_u})\} +$$

$$+ Z_{\delta_e}\{- (M_\alpha + M_{T_\alpha})(X_u + X_{T_u}) + X_\alpha(M_u + M_{T_u})\} + M_{\delta_e}\{Z_\alpha(X_u + X_{T_u}) - X_\alpha Z_u\}$$

These statements about the way numerators and denominators affect airplane response, are true only for the so–called open–loop response of an airplane. In closed–loop situations (such as the case with auto–pilots and/or stability augmentation systems) the numerators **do affect** the closed loop stability of the airplane. This aspect of the significance of the numerator characteristic equations (i.e. numerator polynomials set equal to zero) will become clear in Chapters 9–11 where the behavior of automatic control systems is discussed.

Figure 5.9 shows how the open–loop transfer functions can be used to determine the response of an airplane to a given control input. The block diagram drawn in Figure 5.9 is used to help visualize the inter–relationship between input, transfer function and output.

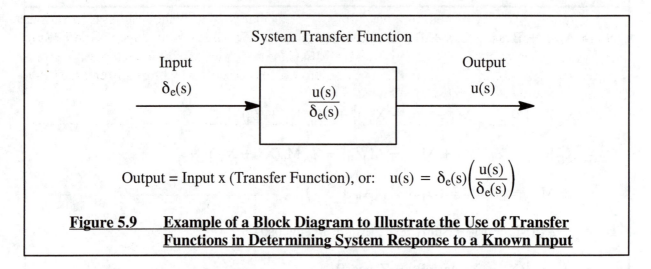

Output = Input x (Transfer Function), or: $u(s) = \delta_e(s)\left(\dfrac{u(s)}{\delta_e(s)}\right)$

Figure 5.9   Example of a Block Diagram to Illustrate the Use of Transfer Functions in Determining System Response to a Known Input

It turns out that the transfer functions as derived in Table 5.3 can be used not only to determine the response to elevator control surface inputs but also:

1) to determine the response to inputs from other types of controllers

and

2) to determine the response of the airplane to gust.

This will be discussed next.

1) Response of the airplane to control surface inputs other than the elevator:

If the response of an airplane to another control surface input is required, the only change that must be made is in the transfer function numerators, in particular in the control power terms. The following substitutions must be made in the numerators N_u, N_α and N_θ :

For response to a stabilizer input:

substitute X_{i_h}, Z_{i_h} and M_{i_h} for: X_{δ_e}, Z_{δ_e} and M_{δ_e} respectively.

For response to a canard input:

substitute X_c, Z_c and M_c for: X_{δ_e}, Z_{δ_e} and M_{δ_e} respectively.

For response to an incremental thrust input, ΔT (thrust–line along X):

substitute $(\Delta T)/m$, 0 and 0 for : X_{δ_e}, Z_{δ_e} and M_{δ_e} respectively.

For response to a step input gust angle of attack, $\Delta \alpha_g$:

The only change that must be made is again in the transfer function numerators, in particular in the control power terms. The following substitutions must be made in the numerators N_u, N_α and N_θ :

substitute X_α, Z_α and M_α for : X_{δ_e}, Z_{δ_e} and M_{δ_e} respectively.

Figure 5.10 may be helpful in visualizing the calculation of airplane responses to various types of control inputs. The reader should keep in mind, that responses to simultaneous inputs from various input sources can be determined by SUMMING the responses to individual inputs. The reason this procedure is correct is the fact that in a system which is described by linear differential equations, the principle of super–position holds!

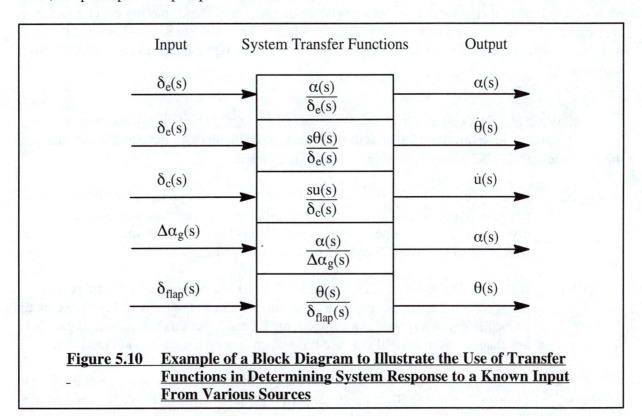

Figure 5.10   Example of a Block Diagram to Illustrate the Use of Transfer Functions in Determining System Response to a Known Input From Various Sources

5.2.2   LONGITUDINAL CHARACTERISTIC EQUATION ROOTS AND THEIR CONNECTION TO DYNAMIC STABILITY

Since the dynamic stability character of the airplane open loop transfer functions is determined by the roots of their characteristic equation, it is of interest to examine how these roots can break down from a mathematical viewpoint. Because the characteristic equation (5.43) has four roots, the following three possibilities arise:

I)   All roots are real

II)   Two roots are real and two are complex conjugates

III)   All roots are complex: two pairs of complex conjugates

Figure 5.11 illustrates all possible combinations of root locations (root break–downs) for a fourth order characteristic equation. Even though all these root break–downs can occur in the case of airplanes, the usual root breakdown by far (for airplanes designed with inherent stability) is the one labelled c1 in Figure 5.11. How other root break–downs arise will be discussed in Section 5.4.

Whether or not an airplane is dynamically, longitudinally stable is usually ascertained by in-specting computer print–outs of the roots of the characteristic Equation (5.43) in accordance with the stability criteria of pages 315–316. For stability, real roots must be negative and complex roots must have negative real parts.

Stability can also be predicted from the coefficients A_1 through E_1 in the characteristic Equation (5.43). This can be done by using the so–called Routh–Hurwitz stability criteria for the roots of a polynomial equation. For a more detailed discussion of these stability criteria and their applications the reader may wish to consult Refs 5.5 and 5.6. According to Routh–Hurwitz, the roots of a fourth order polynomial are stable if and only if the following inequalities are simultaneously satisfied:

$$A_1, \; B_1, \; C_1, \; D_1, \; E_1 \; > \; 0$$
$$D_1(B_1C_1 - A_1D_1) - B_1^2E_1 \; > \; 0 \qquad \text{(Routh's Discriminant)} \tag{5.44}$$

It is shown in Reference 5.7 that as the polynomial coefficients A_1 through D_1 are changed, the dynamic stability behavior changes in the following manner:

A)   If the 'free' coefficient E_1 is changed from > 0 to < 0, one real root changes from negative to positive. The time domain response will therefore contain a pure divergence as a component. In Figure 5.11 this behavior corresponds to a change from case a1) to case a2) or from case b1) to case b2).

B)   If Routh's Discriminant changes from >0 to <0, the real part of a complex root changes from negative to positive. The time domain response will therefore contain an oscillatory divergence as a component. Examples of this behavior in Figure 5.11 are changes from case b1) to case b3) and changes from case c1) to case c2).

The reader should recognize the fact, that changes in the coefficients A_1 through E_1 can come about by changes in airplane flight condition, airplane mass, airplane mass distribution (c.g. location and inertias), airplane geometry and airplane aerodynamic characteristics. By performing so–called sensitivity analyses, it is possible to gain insight into how the airplane designer can or can-not affect the dynamic stability and response behavior of an airplane. Sensitivity analyses are dis-cussed in Section 5.4.

With the widespread introduction of digital computers, the usefulness of the Routh–Hurwitz stability criteria (5.44) has declined. However, criterion A) still serves a useful purpose in that it enables an interesting connection between static and dynamic longitudinal stability. That is dis-cussed in Sub–section 5.2.3.

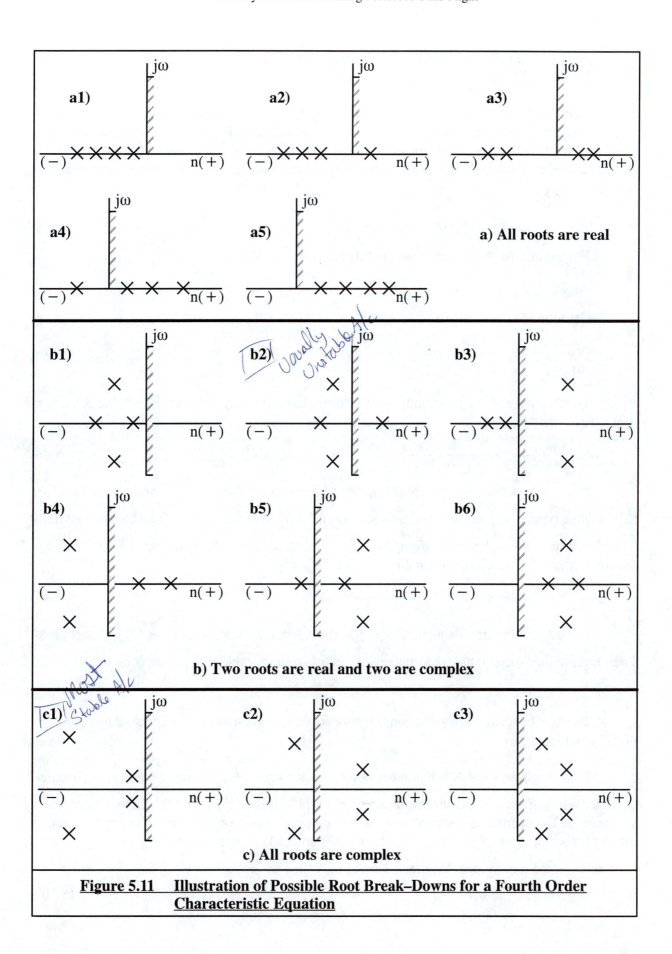

a) All roots are real

b) Two roots are real and two are complex

c) All roots are complex

Figure 5.11   Illustration of Possible Root Break–Downs for a Fourth Order Characteristic Equation

5.2.3 CONNECTION BETWEEN DYNAMIC AND STATIC LONGITUDINAL STABILITY

According to the stability criteria of inequality (5.44), one real root in the longitudinal characteristic equation changes from stable to unstable when the coefficient E_1 in Eqn (5.43) changes sign. An expression for this coefficient E_1 is shown in Table 5.3. Because the steady state pitch attitude angle, θ_1, is usually small enough to neglect the $\sin\theta_1$, term it follows that the stability condition can be approximated as follows:

$$(M_\alpha + M_{T_\alpha})Z_u - Z_\alpha(M_u + M_{T_u}) > 0 \qquad (5.45)$$

Neglecting the thrust contributions this becomes:

$$M_\alpha Z_u - Z_\alpha M_u > 0 \qquad (5.46)$$

Division by $Z_\alpha Z_u$ yields:

$$\frac{M_\alpha}{Z_\alpha} > \frac{M_u}{Z_u} \qquad (5.47)$$

With the help of the definitions for the dimensional stability derivatives in Table 5.1 this in turn may be written as:

$$\frac{C_{m_\alpha}}{C_{L_\alpha} + C_{D_1}} > \frac{C_{m_u}}{C_{L_u} + 2C_{L_1}} \qquad (5.48)$$

It is now observed that typical magnitudes for lift–curve–slope, C_{L_α}, range from 3 to 6 per radian while typical magnitudes for steady state drag coefficient, C_{D_1}, range from 0.0150 to 0.0500 (exceptions are very high drag configurations). As a consequence and by invoking Eqn (3.39) it is usually permissible to rewrite inequality (5.48) as follows:

$$\frac{C_{m_\alpha}}{C_{L_\alpha}} = (\overline{x}_{cg} - \overline{x}_{ac_A}) > \frac{C_{m_u}}{C_{L_u} + 2C_{L_1}} \qquad (5.49)$$

In the low subsonic Mach number range, the so–called 'tuck' derivative C_{m_u} is negligible. Therefore, in that speed range an airplane will not have an unstable real root as long as:

$$\overline{x}_{cg} < \overline{x}_{ac_A} \qquad (5.50a)$$

This will be recognized as the condition for airplane static stability as expressed by inequality (4.57) in Chapter 4.

In the high subsonic Mach number range, the derivative C_{m_u} cannot be neglected because of the tendency of the airplane aerodynamic center to shift aft {See Eqn (3.125)}. In the case of early subsonic jet transports when operating in an over–speed condition (above the normal operating Mach number) a value of $C_{m_u} = -0.10$ was not unusual. Assuming that $C_{L_u} + 2C_{L_1} \approx 1.0$, it is seen that the requirement for prevention of tuck then is:

$$\overline{x}_{cg} < \overline{x}_{ac_A} - 0.10 \qquad (5.50b)$$

How bad this type of divergence is depends on the rapidity with which the aerodynamic center shifts aft and on where the c.g. is located. Most older subsonic transports displayed a mild, but noticeable, divergence when operated at an over–speed condition. In modern transports, with improved aerodynamic wing design procedures and with the help of so–called Mach–trim systems (See Chapter 8), these tuck problems have largely disappeared.

5.2.4 EXAMPLES OF LONGITUDINAL TRANSFER FUNCTIONS

The following examples illustrate two types of transfer functions, one type associated with a typical business jet, the other type associated with a typical jet fighter. The former was designed as an inherently stable airplane, the latter as an inherently unstable airplane.

To determine the numerical values of the coefficients in the numerator and in the denominator polynomials of longitudinal transfer functions, the following steps are necessary:

Step 1: Determine the flight condition and corresponding airplane configuration

Step 2: Determine the airplane mass and mass distribution (pitching moment of inertia)

Step 3: Determine the dimensionless stability derivatives

Step 4: Determine the dimensional stability derivatives

Step 5: Determine the polynomial coefficients in the transfer function numerators and denominator

The Advanced Aircraft Analysis program (See Appendix A) was used to perform these steps. The results are summarized in Tables 5.4 and 5.5 for a business jet and for a jet fighter respectively. At the top of Tables 5.4 and 5.5 are the required input data; these data are determined as part of Steps 1–3. Below the input data are the output parameters in the form of dimensional stability derivatives and the transfer functions (Step 4). Note that the transfer functions (Step 5) are given in two formats: polynomial format and factored format. The significance of the results in Tables 5.4 and 5.5 will now be discussed.

By inspection of the denominator polynomials of the two airplanes in Tables 5.4 and 5.5, the following (rounded off) values are found for the denominator polynomial coefficients:

DENOMINATOR POLYNOMIAL COEFFICIENTS

For the Business Jet:

$A_1 = 676$
$B_1 = 1{,}359$
$C_1 = 5{,}440$
$D_1 = 57.4$
$E_1 = 45.9$

For the Jet Fighter:

$A_1 = 871$
$B_1 = 608$
$C_1 = -9{,}065$
$D_1 = -43.1$
$E_1 = -43.3$

(5.51)

Table 5.4 Longitudinal Transfer Functions for a Typical Business Jet in Cruise

WEIGHT SIZING	GEOMETRY	DRAG POLAR	WEIGHT & BALANCE	PERF. ANALYSIS	DYNAMICS	COST ANALYSIS	HELP / SETUP
PERFORM. SIZING	HIGH LIFT	STAB. & CONTROL	INSTALLED THRUST	S&C DERIVATIVES	CONTROL	DATA BASE	QUIT

OPEN LOOP DYNAMICS

LONGITUDINAL	LATERAL-DIRECT.	ROLL COUPLING	RETURN

LONGITUDINAL ANALYSIS

CALCULATE T.F.	SHOW T.F.	CHECK MODES	SENSITIVITY	RETURN

CALCULATE	THEORY	PRINT PARAMETERS	RETURN

COMPUTATION OF LONGITUDINAL TRANSFER FUNCTIONS : INPUT PARAMETERS

Altitude =	40000 ft	C_{m_1} =	0.0070	$C_{m\_T\_a}$ =	0.0000	C_{D_a} =	0.3000 1/rad
U_1 =	400.00 kts	C_{m_u} =	0.0500	C_{L_1} =	0.4183	C_{D_u} =	0.0000
W_current =	13000.0 lb	C_{m_a} =	-0.6400 1/rad	C_{L_u} =	0.4000	$C_{T\_X\_1}$ =	0.0330
S_w =	232.00 ft^2	$C_{m\_a.dot}$ =	-6.7000 1/rad	C_{L_a} =	5.8400 1/rad	$C_{T\_X\_u}$ =	-0.0660
Theta_1 =	0.00 deg	C_{m_q} =	-15.5000 1/rad	$C_{L\_a.dot}$ =	2.2000 1/rad	$C_{L\_d\_e}$ =	0.5560 1/rad
C_bar =	7.04 ft	$C_{m\_T\_1}$ =	-0.0070	C_{L_q} =	4.7000 1/rad	$C_{D\_d\_e}$ =	0.0000 1/rad
I_yy_B =	18800 slgft2	$C_{m\_T\_u}$ =	0.0034	C_{D_1} =	0.0330	$C_{m\_d\_e}$ =	-1.5200 1/rad

OUTPUT PARAMETERS

M_1 =	0.697	Z_a =	-445.7224 ft/s^2	M_q =	-0.9397 1/s	TC_long_2 =	989.234 s
n =	1.00 g	Z_a_dot =	-0.8705 ft/s	w_n_SP =	2.8324 rad/s	TC_long_3 =	? s
q_bar =	133.84 psf	Z_q =	-1.8598 ft/s	z_SP =	0.3535	TC_long_4 =	? s
(W/S)_TO =	56.03 psf	M_u =	0.0011 1/ft/s	w_n_P =	0.0920 rad/s	X_del_e =	0.0000 ft/s^2
X_u =	-0.0074 1/s	M_T_u =	-0.0002 1/ft/s	z_P =	0.0461	Z_del_e =	-42.1968 ft/s^2
X_T_u =	0.0000 1/s	M_a =	-7.4416 1/s^2	w_n_3 osc =	? rad/s	M_del_e =	-17.6737 1/s^2
X_a =	8.9782 ft/s^2	M_T_a =	0.0000 1/s^2	z_3rd osc =	?		
Z_u =	-0.1390 1/s	M_a_dot =	-0.4062 1/s	TC_long_1 =	1.999 s		

Design, Analysis and Research Corporation			/users/jan/aaafiles/Learjet-book	Nov 13, 1993	11:21

LONGITUDINAL TRANSFER FUNCTIONS

POLYNOMIAL SPEED TO ELEVATOR TRANSFER FUNCTION

$$\frac{-378.8510\ S^2 + 271887.5562\ S + 240328.1472}{+\ 675.9945\ S^4 + 1359.4138\ S^3 + 5440.2580\ S^2 + 57.4413\ S + 45.8947}$$

FACTORED SPEED TO ELEVATOR TRANSFER FUNCTION

$$\frac{-378.8510\ (S - 718.5464)(S + 0.8828)}{675.9945\ (S^2 + 2.0025\ S + 8.0223)(S^2 + 0.0085\ S + 0.0085)}$$

SPEED TO ELEVATOR TRANSFER FUNCTION K_gain = 5236.513881

POLYNOMIAL ANGLE OF ATTACK TO ELEVATOR TRANSFER FUNCTION

$$\frac{-42.1968\ S^3 - 11939.0234\ S^2 - 88.5773\ S - 79.2981}{+\ 675.9945\ S^4 + 1359.4138\ S^3 + 5440.2580\ S^2 + 57.4413\ S + 45.8947}$$

FACTORED ANGLE OF ATTACK TO ELEVATOR TRANSFER FUNCTION

$$\frac{-42.1968\ (S + 282.9295)(S^2 + 0.0074\ S + 0.0066)}{675.9945\ (S^2 + 2.0025\ S + 8.0223)(S^2 + 0.0085\ S + 0.0085)}$$

ANGLE OF ATTACK TO ELEVATOR TRANSFER FUNCTION K_gain = -1.727828

POLYNOMIAL PITCH ATTITUDE TO ELEVATOR TRANSFER FUNCTION

$$\frac{-11930.1746\ S^2 - 7652.0613\ S - 78.5229}{+\ 675.9945\ S^4 + 1359.4138\ S^3 + 5440.2580\ S^2 + 57.4413\ S + 45.8947}$$

FACTORED PITCH ATTITUDE TO ELEVATOR TRANSFER FUNCTION

$$\frac{-11930.1746\ (S + 0.6310)(S + 0.0104)}{675.9945\ (S^2 + 2.0025\ S + 8.0223)(S^2 + 0.0085\ S + 0.0085)}$$

PITCH ATTITUDE TO ELEVATOR TRANSFER FUNCTION K_gain = -1.710937

OK

Table 5.5 Longitudinal Transfer Functions for a Typical Jet Fighter in Cruise

WEIGHT SIZING	GEOMETRY	DRAG POLAR	WEIGHT & BALANCE	PERF. ANALYSIS	DYNAMICS	COST ANALYSIS	HELP / SETUP
PERFORM. SIZING	HIGH LIFT	STAB. & CONTROL	INSTALLED THRUST	S&C DERIVATIVES	CONTROL	DATA BASE	QUIT

OPEN LOOP DYNAMICS

LONGITUDINAL	LATERAL-DIRECT.	ROLL COUPLING	RETURN

LONGITUDINAL ANALYSIS

CALCULATE T.F.	SHOW T.F.	CHECK MODES	SENSITIVITY	RETURN

CALCULATE		THEORY		PRINT PARAMETERS	RETURN

COMPUTATION OF LONGITUDINAL TRANSFER FUNCTIONS : INPUT PARAMETERS

Altitude =	45000 ft	C_{m_1} =	0.0000	$C_{m_{T_a}}$ =	0.0000	C_{D_a} =	0.3621 1/rad		
U_1 =	516.00 kts	C_{m_u} =	-0.0219	C_{L_1} =	0.3022	C_{D_u} =	0.0630		
W_current =	16000.0 lb	C_{m_a} =	0.3478 1/rad	C_{L_u} =	0.2442	$C_{T_{X_1}}$ =	0.0500		
S_w =	302.00 ft^2	$C_{m_{a.dot}}$ =	-0.1150 1/rad	C_{L_a} =	3.5704 1/rad	$C_{T_{X_u}}$ =	0.0000		
Theta_1 =	0.00 deg	C_{m_q} =	-1.0050 1/rad	$C_{L_{a.dot}}$ =	0.1763 1/rad	$C_{L_{d_e}}$ =	0.3374 1/rad		
C_bar =	13.49 ft	$C_{m_{T_1}}$ =	0.0000	C_{L_q} =	2.8245 1/rad	$C_{D_{d_e}}$ =	0.0027 1/rad		
I_yy_B =	23575 slgft2	$C_{m_{T_u}}$ =	0.0000	C_{D_1} =	0.0267	$C_{m_{d_e}}$ =	0.2201 1/rad		

OUTPUT PARAMETERS

M_1 =	0.900	Z_a =	-377.6269 ft/s^2	M_q =	-0.2360 1/s	TC_long_2 =	-0.345 s
n =	1.00 g	Z_a_dot =	-0.1434 ft/s	w_n_SP =	? rad/s	TC_long_3 =	? s
q_bar =	175.32 psf	Z_q =	-2.2973 ft/s	z_SP =	?	TC_long_4 =	? s
(W/S)_TO =	52.98 psf	M_u =	-0.0008 1/ft/s	w_n_P =	? rad/s	X_del_e =	-0.2834 ft/s^2
X_u =	-0.0140 1/s	M_T_u =	0.0000 1/ft/s	z_P =	?	Z_del_e =	-35.4206 ft/s^2
X_T_u =	0.0121 1/s	M_a =	10.5394 1/s^2	w_n_3 osc =	0.0691 rad/s	M_del_e =	6.6706 1/s^2
X_a =	-6.2907 ft/s^2	M_T_a =	0.0000 1/s^2	z_3rd osc =	0.0367		
Z_u =	-0.1023 1/s	M_a_dot =	-0.0270 1/s	TC_long_1 =	0.278 s		

Design, Analysis and Research Corporation	gripen/45K/0.9	/users/jan/aaafiles/jas39	Nov 13, 1993	11:59

LONGITUDINAL TRANSFER FUNCTIONS

POLYNOMIAL SPEED TO ELEVATOR TRANSFER FUNCTION

$$\frac{- 246.8990\ S^3 + 50.8701\ S^2 - 218196.1871\ S - 68072.6109}{+ 871.0534\ S^4 + 608.3489\ S^3 - 9065.0155\ S^2 - 43.0913\ S - 43.3401}$$

FACTORED SPEED TO ELEVATOR TRANSFER FUNCTION

$$\frac{-246.8990\ (S + 0.3119)(S^2 + -0.5180\ S + 883.9084)}{871.0534\ (S - 2.8992)(S + 3.5925)(S^2 + 0.0051\ S + 0.0048)}$$

SPEED TO ELEVATOR TRANSFER FUNCTION K_gain = 1570.659768

POLYNOMIAL ANGLE OF ATTACK TO ELEVATOR TRANSFER FUNCTION

$$\frac{- 35.4206\ S^3 + 5785.7867\ S^2 + 11.5458\ S + 22.5053}{+ 871.0534\ S^4 + 608.3489\ S^3 - 9065.0155\ S^2 - 43.0913\ S - 43.3401}$$

FACTORED ANGLE OF ATTACK TO ELEVATOR TRANSFER FUNCTION

$$\frac{-35.4206\ (S - 163.3473)(S^2 + 0.0020\ S + 0.0039)}{871.0534\ (S - 2.8992)(S + 3.5925)(S^2 + 0.0051\ S + 0.0048)}$$

ANGLE OF ATTACK TO ELEVATOR TRANSFER FUNCTION K_gain = -0.519271

POLYNOMIAL PITCH ATTITUDE TO ELEVATOR TRANSFER FUNCTION

$$\frac{+ 5811.4238\ S^2 + 2157.2826\ S + 0.1343}{+ 871.0534\ S^4 + 608.3489\ S^3 - 9065.0155\ S^2 - 43.0913\ S - 43.3401}$$

FACTORED PITCH ATTITUDE TO ELEVATOR TRANSFER FUNCTION

$$\frac{5811.4238\ (S + 0.3712)(S + 0.0001)}{871.0534\ (S - 2.8992)(S + 3.5925)(S^2 + 0.0051\ S + 0.0048)}$$

PITCH ATTITUDE TO ELEVATOR TRANSFER FUNCTION K_gain = -0.003099

OK

It is clear by inspection that the jet fighter is unstable because its coefficients A_1–E_1 have differing signs. Note that the coefficients A_1–E_1 for the business jet all have the same sign. That is a necessary (but not sufficient) condition for stability according to criteria A and B on page 275.

The characteristic equation roots for the two airplanes are given in Eqns (5.52). They follow from the factored formats in Tables 5.4 and 5.5.

CHARACTERISTIC EQUATION ROOTS

For the Business Jet: **For the Jet Fighter:**

$$s_{1,2} = -1 \pm j(2.65) \qquad s_1 = +2.90 \qquad s_2 = -3.59$$
$$s_{3,4} = -0.0043 \pm j(0.092) \qquad s_{3,4} = -0.0026 \pm j(0.0693) \tag{5.52}$$

It is seen that the root break–down for the business jet is according to case c1) in Figure 5.11. There are two complex pairs of roots, one with a considerably greater frequency of oscillation than the other. The root with the highest frequency is referred to as the **short period mode**. The one with the lowest frequency is called the **phugoid mode**.

It is seen that the root break–down for the jet fighter is according to case b2) in Figure 5.11. The oscillatory root in this case is referred to as the **'third' oscillatory** mode for reasons which will become clear in Sub–section 5.4.1. The unstable real root would cause the airplane to diverge without action from the pilot.

It has been found useful to compare the dynamic behavior of airplanes with that of the spring–mass–damper system discussed in Section 5.1. Quadratic roots of characteristic equations are cast in a format similar to that of Eqn (5.11), that is by using undamped natural frequency and damping ratio as the parameters of choice. For a definition of undamped natural frequency and damping ratio the reader should consult Section 5.1.

Real roots of characteristic equations are cast in the form of so–called 'time–constants, T' as illustrated in Table C1 in Appendix C. Note that a time constant is defined as the negative inverse of the associated real root.

Introduction of these forms for the characteristic equation roots (using subscripts 'sp' for the short period mode and subscripts 'ph' for the phugoid mode) yields the following characteristics:

For the Business Jet:

$$s_{1,2} = \zeta_{1,2}\omega_{n_{1,2}} \pm j\omega_{n_{1,2}}\sqrt{1 - \zeta_{1,2}^2} \text{ or } s_{sp} = \zeta_{sp}\omega_{n_{sp}} \pm j\omega_{n_{sp}}\sqrt{1 - \zeta_{sp}^2} \tag{5.53}$$

with: $\zeta_{sp} = 0.35$ and $\omega_{n_{sp}} = 2.83$ rad/sec

and

$$s_{3,4} = \zeta_{3,4}\omega_{n_{3,4}} \pm j\omega_{n_{3,4}}\sqrt{1 - \zeta_{3,4}^2} \quad \text{or} \quad s_{ph} = \zeta_{ph}\omega_{n_{ph}} \pm j\omega_{n_{ph}}\sqrt{1 - \zeta_{ph}^2} \qquad (5.54)$$

$$\text{with:} \quad \zeta_{ph} = 0.05 \quad \text{and} \quad \omega_{n_{ph}} = 0.09 \quad \text{rad/sec}$$

Observe that the short period mode is much better damped than the phugoid mode. Also observe that the short period undamped natural frequency is more than an order of magnitude larger than that of the phugoid mode.

For the Jet Fighter:

$$s_1 = -\frac{1}{T_1} \quad \text{and} \quad s_2 = -\frac{1}{T_2} \qquad (5.55)$$

$$\text{with:} \quad T_1 = 0.28 \, \text{sec} \quad \text{and} \quad T_2 = -0.35 \, \text{sec}$$

and

$$s_{3,4} = \zeta_{3,4}\omega_{n_{3,4}} \pm j\omega_{n_{3,4}}\sqrt{1 - \zeta_{3,4}^2} \quad \text{or} \quad s_{3rd} = \zeta_{3rd}\omega_{n_{3rd}} \pm j\omega_{n_{3rd}}\sqrt{1 - \zeta_{3rd}^2} \qquad (5.56)$$

$$\text{with:} \quad \zeta_{3rd} = 0.04 \quad \text{and} \quad \omega_{n_{3rd}} = 0.07 \quad \text{rad/sec}$$

The unstable real root will cause this airplane to diverge without compensating action from either the pilot or from an automatic flight control system. As it turns out, in this instance an automatic flight control system is required.

As will be shown in Chapter 6, the magnitudes of undamped natural frequencies, damping ratios and time constant is intimately tied to acceptable or unacceptable flying quality behavior of airplanes. For that reason, it is important for airplane designers to understand which airplane design factors are the 'design drivers' which determine these dynamic stability parameters. The complete transfer functions of the airplane, as presented in Table 5.3, because of their algebraic complexity, do not afford such insight easily. It has been found that the short period and phugoid characteristics of inherently stable airplanes can be more easily predicted from an approximation to the equations of motion as listed in Table 5.2. These approximations and their applications will be discussed in Sub–sections 5.2.5 and 5.2.6 for the short period and for the phugoid characteristics respectively.

5.2.5   THE SHORT PERIOD APPROXIMATION

Whether or not any approximation to the airplane equations of motion can be considered a 'reasonable' one can be ascertained with the help of a so–called modal (or eigen–vector) analysis. An application of such an analysis to a business jet airplane will be discussed in Sub–section 5.2.9.

At this point the reader is asked to accept the fact that for inherently stable airplanes it is frequently acceptable to assume that the short period mode of motion takes place at approximately constant speed. If that is the case, the speed degree–of–freedom in Eqns (5.32) can be cast aside which reduces the perturbed, longitudinal equations to the following form:

$$\begin{bmatrix} \{s(U_1 - Z_{\dot{\alpha}}) - Z_\alpha\} & \{-(Z_q + U_1)s + g\sin\theta_1\} \\ -\{M_{\dot{\alpha}}s + M_\alpha + M_{T_\alpha}\} & (s^2 - M_q s) \end{bmatrix} \begin{Bmatrix} \dfrac{\alpha(s)}{\delta_e(s)} \\ \dfrac{\theta(s)}{\delta_e(s)} \end{Bmatrix} = \begin{Bmatrix} Z_{\delta_e} \\ M_{\delta_e} \end{Bmatrix} \qquad (5.57)$$

In most instances it has also been found acceptable to introduce the following additional approximations: $Z_{\dot{\alpha}} \ll U_1$, $Z_q \ll U_1$ and $\theta_1 \approx 0$. Furthermore, by considering the thrust contribution to static longitudinal stability as part of the total static longitudinal stability of the airplane and therefore by substituting $M_\alpha \mapsto M_\alpha + M_{T_\alpha}$, it is possible to write Eqn (5.57) as:

$$\begin{bmatrix} (sU_1 - Z_\alpha) & -U_1 s \\ -\{M_{\dot{\alpha}}s + M_\alpha\} & (s^2 - M_q s) \end{bmatrix} \begin{Bmatrix} \dfrac{\alpha(s)}{\delta_e(s)} \\ \dfrac{\theta(s)}{\delta_e(s)} \end{Bmatrix} = \begin{Bmatrix} Z_{\delta_e} \\ M_{\delta_e} \end{Bmatrix} \qquad (5.58)$$

The approximate angle–of–attack and pitch–attitude transfer functions can now be explicitly written as follows:

$$\frac{\alpha(s)}{\delta_e(s)} = \frac{\{Z_{\delta_e}s + (M_{\delta_e}U_1 - M_q Z_{\delta_e})\}}{U_1\left\{s^2 - \left(M_q + \dfrac{Z_\alpha}{U_1} + M_{\dot{\alpha}}\right)s + \left(\dfrac{Z_\alpha M_q}{U_1} - M_\alpha\right)\right\}} \qquad (5.59)$$

and

$$\frac{\theta(s)}{\delta_e(s)} = \frac{\{(U_1 M_{\delta_e} + Z_{\delta_e}M_{\dot{\alpha}})s + (M_\alpha Z_{\delta_e} - Z_\alpha M_{\delta_e})\}}{sU_1\left\{s^2 - \left(M_q + \dfrac{Z_\alpha}{U_1} + M_{\dot{\alpha}}\right)s + \left(\dfrac{Z_\alpha M_q}{U_1} - M_\alpha\right)\right\}} \qquad (5.60)$$

The free s in the denominator of the pitch–attitude–to–elevator transfer function is an indication of neutral stability with respect to changes in pitch attitude. This is expected because there are no restoring forces acting on an airplane as a result of changes in pitch attitude angle.

The denominator quadratic in Eqns (5.59) and (5.60) is in fact an approximation to the short period quadratic form: $(s^2 + 2\zeta_{sp}\omega_{n_{sp}}s + \omega_{n_{sp}}{}^2)$. It is now possible to write the following approximations for the short period undamped natural frequency and damping ratio:

$$\omega_{n_{sp}} \approx \sqrt{\frac{Z_\alpha M_q}{U_1} - M_\alpha} \qquad (5.61)$$

and

$$\zeta_{sp} \approx \frac{-(M_q + \frac{Z_\alpha}{U_1} + M_{\dot{\alpha}})}{2\omega_{n_{sp}}} \tag{5.62}$$

To see how accurate these approximations are, the appropriate data from Table 5.4 will be substituted into these two equations. It is found that:

$$\zeta_{sp} = 0.35 \quad \text{and} \quad \omega_{n_{sp}} = 2.84 \text{ rad/sec}$$

These results compare very well to those of Eqn (5.53). In calculating the approximate short period undamped natural frequency with Eqn (5.61), the reader will have noticed that $(Z_\alpha M_q)/U_1 \ll -M_\alpha$. This turns out to be generally correct as long as the c.g. is not too far aft. Therefore, an approximation to the approximation of the short period undamped natural frequency is:

$$\omega_{n_{sp}} \approx \approx \sqrt{-M_\alpha} = \sqrt{\frac{-C_{m_\alpha}\bar{q}_1 S\bar{c}}{I_{yy}}} \tag{5.63}$$

For the case at hand, this yields a frequency prediction of:

$$\omega_{n_{sp}} = 2.73 \text{ rad/sec}$$

Eqn (5.63) does provide the following information about three factors which normally 'drive' the magnitude of the short period undamped natural frequency of an airplane:

* Static longitudinal stability, $C_{m_\alpha} = C_{L_\alpha}(\bar{x}_{cg} - \bar{x}_{ac_A})$, and therefore the c.g.

 location relative to the airplane aerodynamic center. The frequency will be higher at forward c.g. than at aft c.g.

* Dynamic pressure in the steady state, $\bar{q}_1$. The frequency at any given altitude

 will be higher at high speed than at low speed.

* Pitching moment of inertia, I_{yy} . The frequency will be higher for airplanes with

 a low pitching moment of inertia. The airplane mass configuration therefore plays a role. All else being the same, an airplane with the engines mounted in the aft fuselage would tend to have a lower frequency than an airplane with the engines mounted under the wing.

It is instructive to compare the terms under the square root sign in Eqn (5.63) with the term (k/m) in Eqn (5.5). Evidently, the term $(C_{m_\alpha}\bar{q}_1 S\bar{c})$ can be thought of physically as a torsional spring, wrapped around the airplane Y–axis!

When examining Eqn (5.62), it is seen that for any given short period undamped natural frequency, the derivative terms M_q, Z_α/U_1 and $M_{\dot\alpha}$ determine the short period damping ratio. Of these, the pitch–damping derivative, M_q, turns out to be the most important one. A theoretical problem with the approximation of Eqn (5.62) is that the damping ratio is predicted to be always positive. Practical experience shows that this is in fact not correct.

It is also instructive to examine what happens if the term $\left(\dfrac{Z_\alpha M_q}{U_1} - M_\alpha\right)$ in the denominator of Eqn (5.60) becomes zero. Multiplying both sides of Eqn (5.60) by s, the following is obtained:

$$\frac{s\theta(s)}{\delta_e(s)} = \frac{\dot\theta(s)}{\delta_e(s)} = \frac{\left\{(U_1 M_{\delta_e} + Z_{\delta_e})s + (M_\alpha Z_{\delta_e} - Z_\alpha M_{\delta_e})\right\}}{U_1\left\{s^2 - \left(M_q + \dfrac{Z_\alpha}{U_1} + M_{\dot\alpha}\right)s\right\}} \tag{5.64}$$

This represents the pitch–rate–to–elevator transfer function of the airplane for the case that: $\left(\dfrac{Z_\alpha M_q}{U_1} - M_\alpha\right) = 0$. The roots of the characteristic equation are s=0 and $s = \left(M_q + \dfrac{Z_\alpha}{U_1} + M_{\dot\alpha}\right)$ respectively. Observe, that just because $\left(\dfrac{Z_\alpha M_q}{U_1} - M_\alpha\right) = 0$ is satisfied in some case, the term $\left(M_q + \dfrac{Z_\alpha}{U_1} + M_{\dot\alpha}\right)$ will, in general, not be zero! Therefore, one of the characteristic equation roots is a stable, real root (which leads to a convergence) and the other is a neutrally stable root which implies that the pitch rate response to elevator deflection will be constant! However, that in turn implies that the airplane is in a pull–up maneuver. Now examine in detail the condition which led to this result, namely that: $\left(\dfrac{Z_\alpha M_q}{U_1} - M_\alpha\right) = 0$.

By using the definitions for dimensional derivatives of Table 5.1 and by making the same approximations which were made in the derivation of Eqn (5.49) it is found that the constant pitch rate solution corresponds to the following center of gravity location:

$$\overline{x}_{cg} = \overline{x}_{ac_A} - \frac{C_{m_q}\varrho S\overline{c}}{4W} \tag{5.65}$$

This center of gravity location will be recognized as the airplane maneuver point (stick fixed), MP_{fix}, as defined in Eqn (4.121). This result establishes yet another connection between static and dynamic stability.

To help the reader visualize how an airplane responds to an elevator pulse according to the short period approximation, Figure 5.12 has been prepared. Note that the speed vector remains constant, while angle of attack and pitch attitude vary.

This ends the discussion of the short period approximation. Section 5.2.6 contains a similar discussion for the phugoid approximation.

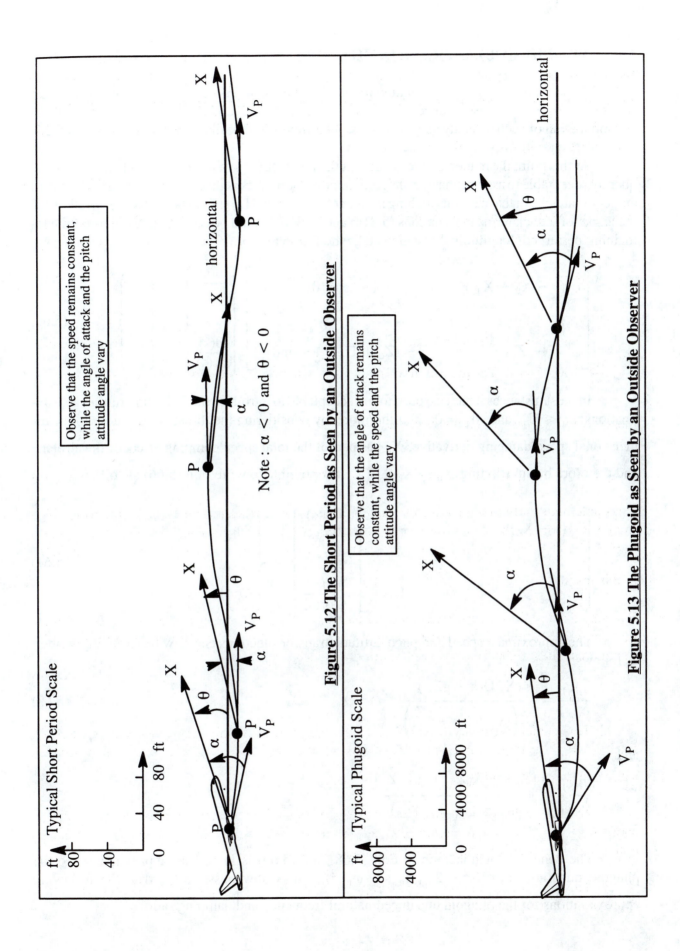

Typical Short Period Scale

Observe that the speed remains constant, while the angle of attack and the pitch attitude angle vary

Note : $\alpha < 0$ and $\theta < 0$

Figure 5.12 The Short Period as Seen by an Outside Observer

Typical Phugoid Scale

Observe that the angle of attack remains constant, while the speed and the pitch attitude angle vary

Figure 5.13 The Phugoid as Seen by an Outside Observer

5.2.6 THE PHUGOID APPROXIMATION

Whether or not any approximation to the airplane equations of motion can be considered a 'reasonable' one can be ascertained with the help of a so–called modal (or eigen–vector) analysis. An application of such an analysis to a business jet airplane will be discussed in Sub–section 5.2.9.

At this point the reader is asked to accept the fact that for inherently stable airplanes it is frequently acceptable to assume that the phugoid mode of motion takes place at approximately constant angle–of–attack. In that case the pitching moment equation (5.31c) should be cast aside. In addition, the angle–of–attack terms in Equations (5.31a) and (5.31b) should be discarded. As a result the remaining perturbed, longitudinal equations take the following form:

$$\begin{bmatrix} (s - X_u - X_{T_u}) & (+ g\cos\theta_1) \\ - Z_u & \{-(Z_q + U_1)s + g\sin\theta_1\} \end{bmatrix} \begin{Bmatrix} \dfrac{u(s)}{\delta_e(s)} \\ \dfrac{\theta(s)}{\delta_e(s)} \end{Bmatrix} = \begin{Bmatrix} X_{\delta_e} \\ Z_{\delta_e} \end{Bmatrix} \tag{5.66}$$

In most instances it has also been found acceptable to introduce the following further approximations $Z_q \ll U_1$ and $\theta_1 \approx 0$. Furthermore, by considering the thrust contribution to the dimensional speed damping derivative, X_u , as part of the total speed damping effect of the airplane and therefore by substituting $X_u \mapsto X_u + X_{T_u}$ it is possible to write Eqn (5.66) as follows:

$$\begin{bmatrix} (s - X_u) & + g \\ - Z_u & - U_1 s \end{bmatrix} \begin{Bmatrix} \dfrac{u(s)}{\delta_e(s)} \\ \dfrac{\theta(s)}{\delta_e(s)} \end{Bmatrix} = \begin{Bmatrix} X_{\delta_e} \\ Z_{\delta_e} \end{Bmatrix} \tag{5.67}$$

The approximate speed and pitch–attitude transfer functions can now be explicitly written as follows:

$$\frac{u(s)}{\delta_e(s)} = \frac{(X_{\delta_e} U_1 s + g Z_{\delta_e})}{U_1 \left(s^2 - X_u s - \dfrac{g Z_u}{U_1} \right)} \tag{5.68}$$

and

$$\frac{\theta(s)}{\delta_e(s)} = \frac{\left(Z_{\delta_e} s - X_u Z_{\delta_e} + g X_{\delta_e} Z_u \right)}{U_1 \left(s^2 - X_u s - \dfrac{g Z_u}{U_1} \right)} \tag{5.69}$$

The denominator quadratic in Eqn (5.68) and (5.69) is in fact an approximation to the phugoid quadratic form $(s^2 + 2\zeta_{ph}\omega_{n_{ph}}s + \omega_{n_{ph}}^2)$. It is now possible to write the following approximations for the phugoid undamped natural frequency and damping ratio:

$$\omega_{n_{ph}} \approx \sqrt{\frac{- gZ_u}{U_1}} \tag{5.70}$$

and

$$\zeta_{ph} \approx \frac{- X_u}{2\omega_{n_{ph}}} \tag{5.71}$$

To see how accurate these approximations are, the appropriate data from Table 5.4 will be substituted into these two equations. It is found that:

$$\zeta_{ph} = 0.05 \quad \text{and} \quad \omega_{n_{ph}} = 0.08 \ \text{rad/sec}$$

These results compare very well to those of Eqn (5.54).

To understand the design drivers in the case of phugoid undamped natural frequency and damping ratio, Eqns (5.70) and (5.71) will be analyzed in more detail. Substituting the definition for Z_u from Table 5.1 into Eqn (5.70) yields:

$$\omega_{n_{ph}} \approx \sqrt{\frac{\varrho g S}{2m}(C_{L_u} + 2C_{L_1})} \tag{5.72}$$

In the low subsonic speed range, the condition $C_{L_u} \ll C_{L_1}$ is satisfied. By recognizing that $C_{L_1} = W/\overline{q}S$ this can be further simplified to:

$$\omega_{n_{ph}} \approx \frac{g}{U_1}\sqrt{2} \tag{5.73}$$

Equation (5.73) implies that the undamped natural frequency of the phugoid motion is independent of the design of the airplane: it depends only on the steady state speed, U_1.

Next, substituting $X_u + X_{T_u} \mapsto X_u$ with the appropriate definitions from Table 5.1 into Eqn (5.71) yields:

$$\zeta_{ph} \approx \frac{- (X_u + X_{T_u})}{2\omega_{n_{ph}}} \approx \frac{\sqrt{2}(C_{D_u} - C_{T_{x_u}})}{4C_{L_1}} \tag{5.74}$$

The reader will recall from Sub–section 3.2.15 that the perturbed thrust–speed derivative, $C_{T_{x_u}}$, is dependent on the type of propulsive installation. Five different cases are discussed in Sub–section 3.2.15. For the case of a jet powered airplane in the low subsonic speed range, it can be shown that Eqn (5.74) further simplifies to:

$$\zeta_{ph} \approx \frac{\sqrt{2}}{2(C_{L_1}/C_{D_1})} \tag{5.75}$$

This result indicates that the phugoid damping ratio is inversely proportional to the airplane lift–to–drag ratio. Therefore, airplanes with high lift–to–drag ratios can be expected to have poor phugoid damping. Poor phugoid damping makes the control of speed difficult. On final approach this can be a problem. However, at low speed, with landing gear and flaps down, the lift–to–drag ratio is decreased significantly and therefore the phugoid damping ration is improved.

To help the reader visualize how an airplane responds to an elevator pulse according to the phugoid approximation, Figure 5.13 (see Page 337) has been prepared. Note that the angle of attack remains constant while speed and pitch attitude vary.

This ends the discussion of the phugoid approximation. Section 5.2.7 contains a discussion of airplane responses to a step elevator input.

5.2.7 RESPONSE TO AN ELEVATOR STEP INPUT

The response of the airplane to an arbitrary elevator input can be obtained by following the process suggested in Figure 5.9. To illustrate this process, consider the case of an elevator step input. The final value theorem (Eqn (C6) in Appendix C) will be used to find the magnitudes of the ultimate perturbation values of speed, u, angle–of–attack, α, and pitch–attitude–angle, θ. The reader should verify the following expressions by referring to Table 5.3.

$$\lim_{t \to \infty} u(t) = \lim_{s \to 0} \left\{ s \frac{\delta_e N_u}{s D_1} \right\} = \frac{\delta_e D_u}{E_1} \approx \frac{\delta_e(Z_{\delta_e} M_\alpha + M_{\delta_e} Z_\alpha)}{(M_\alpha Z_u - Z_\alpha M_u)} \tag{5.76}$$

$$\lim_{t \to \infty} \alpha(t) = \lim_{s \to 0} \left\{ s \frac{\delta_e N_\alpha}{s D_1} \right\} = \frac{\delta_e D_\alpha}{E_1} \approx \frac{\delta_e(Z_{\delta_e} M_u - M_{\delta_e} Z_u)}{(M_\alpha Z_u - Z_\alpha M_u)} \tag{5.77}$$

$$\lim_{t \to \infty} \theta(t) = \lim_{s \to 0} \left\{ s \frac{\delta_e N_\theta}{s D_1} \right\} = \frac{\delta_e D_\theta}{E_1} \approx$$
$$\approx \frac{\delta_e\{Z_{\delta_e}(- M_\alpha X_u + X_\alpha M_u) + M_{\delta_e}(Z_\alpha X_u - X_\alpha Z_u)\}}{(M_\alpha Z_u - Z_\alpha M_u)} \tag{5.78}$$

In obtaining Eqn (5.78) the additional assumption of negligible elevator drag ($X_{\delta_e} \approx 0$) was made. The quantities represented by Eqns (5.76)–(5.78), when added to their steady state counterparts, represent the new equilibrium (or trim) values for speed, angle–of–attack and pitch–attitude following a step input elevator command of δ_e radians. In the case of the airplane and flight condition of Table 5.4, the following numerical data are obtained for a step elevator input of +1 degree (1/57.3 rad):

$$\lim_{t \to \infty} u(t) \approx \frac{(1/57.3)\{(- (- 42.2)(- 7.44) + (- 17.7)(- 445.7)\}}{\{(- 7.44)(- 0.139) - (- 445.7)(0.0011)\}} \approx 94 \text{ fps} \tag{5.79}$$

$$\lim_{t\to\infty} \alpha(t) \approx \frac{(1/57.3)\{(-42.2)(0.0011)-(-17.7)(-0.139)\}}{\{(-7.44)(-0.139)-(-445.7)(0.0011)\}} \approx -0.5 \text{ deg} \qquad (5.80)$$

$$\lim_{t\to\infty} \theta(t) \approx \frac{(1/57.3)\left[-42.2\{-(-7.44)(-0.0074)+(8.98)(0.0011)\}\right]}{\{(-7.44)(-0.139)-(-445.7)(0.0011)\}} +$$

$$+ \frac{(1/57.3)\left[(-17.7)\{(-445.7)(-0.0074)-(8.98)(-0.139)\}\right]}{\{(-7.44)(-0.0139)-(-445.7)(0.0011)\}} \approx -0.9 \text{ deg} \qquad (5.81)$$

In the next Sub–section the reader is introduced to standard transfer function formats.

5.2.8 STANDARD FORMAT FOR THE LONGITUDINAL TRANSFER FUNCTIONS

For reasons which will become particularly clear in Chapter 8, it has been found useful to present airplane transfer functions in terms of their so–called 'standard formats'. In these standard formats the numerator and denominator polynomials of Table 5.3 are assumed to break down in a manner normally (but not always) found for any given (inherently stable) airplane. The standard format normally found for the open–loop transfer functions of inherently stable airplanes is given in Table 5.6, Eqns (5.82).

Note from Eqns (5.82) that for s=0 all components of the transfer function which depend on the Laplace variable s take on the value 1.0. Each transfer function at s=0 takes on a value given by the ratio of the free coefficient in the numerator to the free coefficient in the denominator. These values are referred to as the <u>zero–frequency gains</u> of the transfer functions. For the longitudinal transfer functions these zero–frequency gains (with the help of Table 5.3) are found as:

$$K_{u_{\delta_e}} = \frac{D_u}{E_1} \qquad\qquad K_{\alpha_{\delta_e}} = \frac{D_\alpha}{E_1} \qquad\qquad K_{\theta_{\delta_e}} = \frac{D_\theta}{E_1} \qquad (5.84)$$

For the business jet example of Table 5.4 the corresponding values as indicated in Table 5.6 are:

$$K_{u_{\delta_e}} = 5,236.5 \text{ ft/sec/rad} \qquad K_{\alpha_{\delta_e}} = -1.7278 \text{rad/rad} \qquad K_{\theta_{\delta_e}} = -1.7109 \text{rad/rad}$$

As will be shown in Chapter 8, with these transfer function forms, the construction and interpretation of airplane frequency response plots (also known as Bode plots) becomes easy.

5.2.9 THE LONGITUDINAL MODE SHAPES

In Sub–sections 5.2.5 and 5.2.6 the short period and phugoid approximations were introduced by assuming that speed and angle of attack respectively were unimportant motion variables in those approximations. This begs the question: is it possible to predict whether or not one or more motion variables can be neglected in the dynamic response of an airplane. Such a prediction can be made with the help of a modal analysis as shown next.

Table 5.6 Standard Format for the Longitudinal Transfer Functions

General Standard Format:

$$\frac{u(s)}{\delta_e(s)} = \frac{K_{u_{\delta_e}}(T_{u_1}s + 1)(T_{u_2}s + 1)}{\left(\dfrac{s^2}{\omega_{n_{sp}}^2} + \dfrac{2\zeta_{sp}s}{\omega_{n_{sp}}} + 1\right)\left(\dfrac{s^2}{\omega_{n_p}^2} + \dfrac{2\zeta_p s}{\omega_{n_{sp}}} + 1\right)} \tag{5.82a}$$

$$\frac{\alpha(s)}{\delta_e(s)} = \frac{K_{\alpha_{\delta_e}}(T_{\alpha_1}s + 1)\left(\dfrac{s^2}{\omega_{n_\alpha}^2} + \dfrac{2\zeta_\alpha}{\omega_{n_\alpha}} + 1\right)}{\left(\dfrac{s^2}{\omega_{n_{sp}}^2} + \dfrac{2\zeta_{sp}s}{\omega_{n_{sp}}} + 1\right)\left(\dfrac{s^2}{\omega_{n_p}^2} + \dfrac{2\zeta_p s}{\omega_{n_{sp}}} + 1\right)} \tag{5.82b}$$

$$\frac{\theta(s)}{\delta_e(s)} = \frac{K_{\theta_{\delta_e}}(T_{\theta_1}s + 1)(T_{\theta_2}s + 1)}{\left(\dfrac{s^2}{\omega_{n_{sp}}^2} + \dfrac{2\zeta_{sp}s}{\omega_{n_{sp}}} + 1\right)\left(\dfrac{s^2}{\omega_{n_p}^2} + \dfrac{2\zeta_p s}{\omega_{n_{sp}}} + 1\right)} \tag{5.82c}$$

Example Numerical Format for the Business Jet of Table 5.4:

$$\frac{u(s)}{\delta_e(s)} = \frac{5,236.5\left\{\left(\dfrac{1}{-718.5}\right)s + 1\right\}\left\{\left(\dfrac{1}{0.8828}\right)s + 1\right\}}{\left(\dfrac{s^2}{(2.8324)^2} + \dfrac{2(0.3535)s}{(2.8324)} + 1\right)\left(\dfrac{s^2}{(0.0920)^2} + \dfrac{2(0.0461)s}{(0.0920)} + 1\right)} \tag{5.83a}$$

$$\frac{\alpha(s)}{\delta_e(s)} = \frac{-1.7278\left\{\left(\dfrac{1}{282.9}\right)s + 1\right\}\left(\dfrac{s^2}{0.0812^2} + \dfrac{2(0.0456)s}{(0.0812)} + 1\right)}{\left(\dfrac{s^2}{(2.8324)^2} + \dfrac{2(0.3535)s}{(2.8324)} + 1\right)\left(\dfrac{s^2}{(0.0920)^2} + \dfrac{2(0.0461)s}{(0.0920)} + 1\right)} \tag{5.83b}$$

$$\frac{\theta(s)}{\delta_e(s)} = \frac{-1.7109\left\{\left(\dfrac{1}{0.6310}\right)s + 1\right\}\left\{\left(\dfrac{1}{0.0104}\right)s + 1\right\}}{\left(\dfrac{s^2}{(2.8324)^2} + \dfrac{2(0.3535)s}{(2.8324)} + 1\right)\left(\dfrac{s^2}{(0.0920)^2} + \dfrac{2(0.0461)s}{(0.0920)} + 1\right)} \tag{5.83c}$$

For a given elevator (or gust) input the response of an airplane can be thought of as consisting of the simultaneous oscillatory response of the variables speed, u(t), angle–of–attack, α(t), and pitch–attitude angle, θ(t). A longitudinal mode shape can be described by two quantities, one describes the relative magnitude of amplitudes in u, α and θ and the other describes the phase angles of these variables with respect to each other. The following analysis shows how such a mode shape can be determined and how such a mode shape can be used to decide whether or not an approximation (by discarding one or more motion variables) is acceptable.

Consider the perturbed equations of motion (5.31) in Table 5.2 and assume that the elevator terms are left out. This can happen by letting the elevator perturbation gradually approach the value of zero. The remaining equations describe the dynamics of the un–perturbed system. These equations are given as Eqns (5.85):

$$(s - X_u)u(s) \qquad - X_\alpha \alpha(s) \qquad\qquad g\cos\theta_1 \theta(s) \qquad\qquad = 0$$

$$- Z_u u(s) \qquad \{s(U_1 - Z_{\dot\alpha}) - Z_\alpha\}\alpha(s) \quad \{-(Z_q + U_1)s + g\sin\theta_1\}\theta(s) \quad = 0 \qquad (5.85)$$

$$- (M_u)u(s) \qquad - \{M_{\dot\alpha}s + M_\alpha\}\alpha(s) \qquad (s^2 - M_q s)\theta(s) \qquad\qquad = 0$$

To reduce the amount of algebra, the thrust derivatives in Eqn (5.85) have been assumed to be included in their aerodynamic counterparts.

One of the variables in Eqns (5.85) is now selected as the one against which the others are compared. The pitch attitude angle is arbitrarily selected to fulfill that role. Eqns (5.85) are now written in terms of the mode shapes u(s)/θ(s) and α(s)/θ(s) in the following manner:

$$(s - X_u)\frac{u(s)}{\theta(s)} \qquad - X_\alpha \frac{\alpha(s)}{\theta(s)} \qquad = \qquad - g\cos\theta_1$$

$$- Z_u \frac{u(s)}{\theta(s)} \qquad \{s(U_1 - Z_{\dot\alpha}) - Z_\alpha\}\frac{\alpha(s)}{\theta(s)} = -\{-(Z_q + U_1)s + g\sin\theta_1\} \qquad (5.86)$$

$$- (M_u)\frac{u(s)}{\theta(s)} \qquad - \{M_{\dot\alpha}s + M_\alpha\}\frac{\alpha(s)}{\theta(s)} \qquad = \qquad (s^2 - M_q s)$$

To solve for the mode shapes, any two of the three equations (5.86) can be used. Using the first and the third equation yields the following solutions:

$$\frac{u(s)}{\theta(s)} = \frac{\begin{vmatrix} - g\cos\theta_1 & - X_\alpha \\ - (s^2 - M_q s) & - \{M_{\dot\alpha}s + M_\alpha\} \end{vmatrix}}{\begin{vmatrix} (s - X_u) & - X_\alpha \\ - (M_u) & - (M_{\dot\alpha}s + M_\alpha) \end{vmatrix}} = \frac{a_1 s^2 + b_1 s + c_1}{a s^2 + b s + c} \qquad (5.87)$$

and:

$$\frac{\alpha(s)}{\theta(s)} = \frac{\begin{vmatrix} (s - X_u) & -g\sin\theta_1 \\ -M_u & -(s^2 - M_q s) \end{vmatrix}}{\begin{vmatrix} (s - X_u) & -X_\alpha \\ -(M_u) & -(M_{\dot{\alpha}}s + M_\alpha) \end{vmatrix}} = \frac{a_2 s^3 + b_2 s^2 + c_2 s + d_2}{a s^2 + b s + c} \qquad (5.88)$$

The polynomial coefficients in Eqns (5.87) and (5.88) are found by expansion of the determinants. The result is:

$$a = -M_{\dot{\alpha}} \qquad b = -M_\alpha + X_u M_{\dot{\alpha}} \qquad c = X_u M_\alpha - X_\alpha M_u$$

$$a_1 = -X_\alpha \qquad b_1 = M_{\dot{\alpha}} g\cos\theta_1 + X_\alpha M_q \qquad c_1 = M_\alpha g\cos\theta_1 \qquad (5.89)$$

$$a_2 = -1 \qquad b_2 = M_q + X_u \qquad c_2 = -X_u M_q \qquad d_2 = -M_u g\cos\theta_1$$

The solutions for the mode shapes are themselves ratios of s–domain polynomials. However, s itself, will (in general) also be a complex number. Therefore, each mode shape can be represented by the ratio of two complex numbers which in turn is a complex number. Any complex number, X can be written as:

$$X = X_0 e^{j\phi} \qquad (5.90)$$

where: X_0 is the absolute magnitude of the complex number and ϕ is its phase angle. By writing the mode shapes as a ratio of two complex numbers:

$$\frac{u(s)}{\theta(s)} \text{ or } \frac{\alpha(s)}{\theta(s)} = \frac{n_{num} + j\omega_{num}}{n_{den} + j\omega_{den}} \qquad (5.91)$$

where: the subscript 'num' signifies numerator and the subscript 'den' signifies denominator.

The magnitude of such a complex number can be found from:

$$\text{Magnitude} = \sqrt{\frac{n_{num}^2 + j\omega_{num}^2}{n_{den}^2 + j\omega_{den}^2}} \qquad (5.92)$$

The phase angle of such a complex number is determined from:

$$\text{Phase} \angle = \arctan\frac{\omega_{num}}{n_{num}} - \arctan\frac{\omega_{den}}{n_{den}} \qquad (5.93)$$

The mode shapes corresponding to the short period mode can now be obtained from Eqns (5.87) and (5.88) by substituting for s the short period root(s) of the characteristic equation as given by Eqn (5.53). Similarly, the mode shapes corresponding to the phugoid root are found also from Eqns (5.87) and (5.88) by substituting for s the phugoid root(s) of the characteristic equation as given by Eqn (5.54).

As a numerical example, such a substitution process has been carried out using the business jet data from Table 5.4 (See Input Parameters). The resulting complex numbers are depicted by phasors and phase angles in Figure 5.14a for the short period mode and in Figure 5.14b for the phugoid mode. It is clear from these figures that for this business jet example the assumptions of constant speed in the short period mode and constant angle of attack for the phugoid mode are justified.

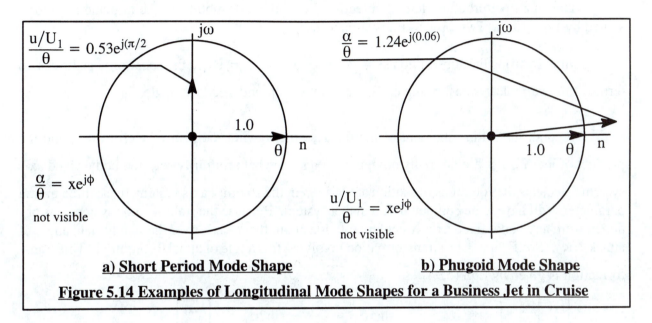

a) Short Period Mode Shape   b) Phugoid Mode Shape

Figure 5.14 Examples of Longitudinal Mode Shapes for a Business Jet in Cruise

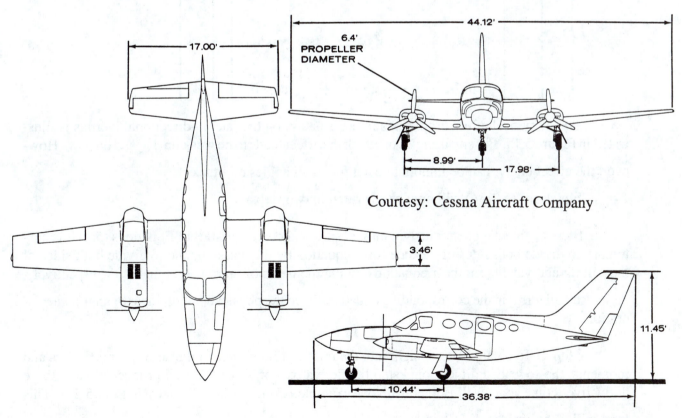

Courtesy: Cessna Aircraft Company

5.3   LATERAL–DIRECTIONAL, DYNAMIC STABILITY AND RESPONSE

5.3.1   LATERAL –DIRECTIONAL EQUATIONS AND TRANSFER FUNCTIONS

The small perturbation, lateral–directional equations of motion of the airplane are represented by Eqns (5.2). Two observations are in order:

First, by using the substitution $p = \dot{\phi}$, $r = \dot{\psi}$ and $v = U_1\beta$ the equations can be cast in terms of the variables: sideslip angle, β, bank angle, ϕ and heading angle, ψ

Second, the rolling moment of inertia, I_{xx}, the yawing moment of inertia, I_{zz}, and the product of inertia, I_{xz} are normally computed in a somewhat arbitrarily selected body–fixed axis system. Because the equations of motion are written in the stability axis system, these three inertia parameters will have to be computed also in that system. Because the stability axis system was obtained from any body–fixed axis system by rotation about the Y–axis over the steady state angle of attack, α_1, (See Figure 3.1) a transformation involving this angle of attack is required. This transformation is given by Eqn (5.94).

$$\begin{Bmatrix} I_{xx_s} \\ I_{zz_s} \\ I_{xz_s} \end{Bmatrix} = \begin{bmatrix} \cos^2\alpha_1 & \sin^2\alpha_1 & -\sin2\alpha_1 \\ \sin^2\alpha_1 & \cos^2\alpha_1 & \sin2\alpha_1 \\ \frac{1}{2}\sin2\alpha_1 & -\frac{1}{2}\sin2\alpha_1 & \cos^2\alpha_1 \end{bmatrix} \begin{Bmatrix} I_{xx_B} \\ I_{zz_B} \\ I_{xz_B} \end{Bmatrix} \qquad (5.94)$$

The numerical effect of this axis transformation on the lateral–directional inertias is illustrated in Figure 5.15. For small angles of attack the effect tends to be weak on I_{xx} and on I_{zz}. However, the effect on I_{xz} can be important even for small angles of attack.

Equations (5.2a–c) will now be rewritten in two steps:

Step 1: To obtain better insight into the physical characteristics of Equations (5.2) it is customary to divide both sides of the side force equation by the mass, m, and to divide both sides of the rolling and yawing moment equations by the moments of inertia, I_{xx}, and I_{zz}, respectively.

As a result all terms in the corresponding equations have the physical unit of linear or angular acceleration.

Step 2: To obtain better insight into the relative importance of the aerodynamic forces and moments, the so–called dimensional stability derivatives of Table 5.7 are introduced. How these derivatives come about is illustrated with one example. Consider the C_{n_β} term in Eqn (5.2c). This term will be re–written as follows:

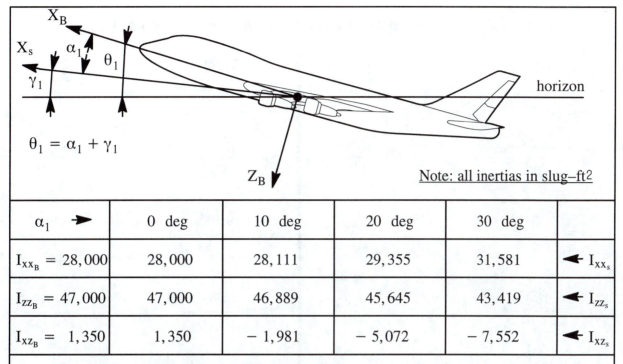

$$\theta_1 = \alpha_1 + \gamma_1$$

Note: all inertias in slug–ft2

α_1 →	0 deg	10 deg	20 deg	30 deg	
$I_{xx_B} = 28,000$	$28,000$	$28,111$	$29,355$	$31,581$	← I_{xx_s}
$I_{zz_B} = 47,000$	$47,000$	$46,889$	$45,645$	$43,419$	← I_{zz_s}
$I_{xz_B} = 1,350$	$1,350$	$-1,981$	$-5,072$	$-7,552$	← I_{xz_s}

Figure 5.15 Effect of Steady State Angle of Attack on the Lateral–Directional Inertias in Stability Axes

$$\frac{\overline{q}_1 S b C_{n_\beta} \beta}{I_{zz}} = N_\beta \beta \quad , \quad \text{where}: \ N_\beta = \frac{\overline{q}_1 S b C_{n_\beta}}{I_{zz}} \qquad (5.95)$$

The newly defined dimensional stability derivative, N_β, has the following very important physical meaning: it represents the yaw angular acceleration imparted to the airplane as a result of a unit change in angle of sideslip. This physical meaning can be generalized to apply to all dimensional stability derivatives of Table 5.7 by using the following definition:

Definition: Each dimensional derivative represents either the linear or angular acceleration imparted to the airplane as a result of a unit change in its associated motion or control variable.

The numerical magnitudes of these dimensional derivatives therefore give numerical clues about their relative importance. Their use in the equations of motion (5.2a–c) also results in a much 'cleaner' look for these equations. The resulting equations are presented as Eqns (5.96) in Table 5.8.

Equations (5.96) are Laplace transformed for zero initial conditions. The new variables are: $\beta(s)$, $\phi(s)$ and $\psi(s)$ respectively, while $\delta(s)$ is the Laplace transformed aileron or rudder input. The result is Eqns (5.97). Next, equations (5.97a–c) are divided by $\delta(s)$. This gives rise to the so–called open loop airplane transfer functions: $\beta(s)/\delta(s)$, $\phi(s)/\delta(s)$ and $\psi(s)/\delta(s)$. These open loop transfer functions can now be thought of as the new 'variables'. By casting the equations in a matrix format, the result is Eqns (5.98) which are also shown in Table 5.8. The airplane open loop transfer functions can be determined with matrix algebra. Each transfer function

Table 5.7 Definition of Lateral–Directional, Dimensional Stability Derivatives

$$Y_\beta = \frac{\bar{q}_1 S C_{y_\beta}}{m} \qquad \frac{ft/sec^2}{rad}$$

$$L_{\delta_r} = \frac{\bar{q}_1 S b C_{l_{\delta_r}}}{I_{xx}} \qquad \frac{rad/sec^2}{rad}$$

$$Y_p = \frac{\bar{q}_1 S b C_{y_p}}{2mU_1} \qquad \frac{ft/sec^2}{rad/sec}$$

$$N_\beta = \frac{\bar{q}_1 S b C_{n_\beta}}{I_{zz}} \qquad \frac{rad/sec^2}{rad}$$

$$Y_r = \frac{\bar{q}_1 S b C_{y_r}}{2mU_1} \qquad \frac{ft/sec^2}{rad/sec}$$

$$N_{T_\beta} = \frac{\bar{q}_1 S b C_{n_{T_\beta}}}{I_{zz}} \qquad \frac{rad/sec^2}{rad}$$

$$Y_{\delta_a} = \frac{\bar{q}_1 S C_{y_{\delta_a}}}{m} \qquad \frac{ft/sec^2}{rad}$$

$$N_p = \frac{\bar{q}_1 S b^2 C_{n_p}}{2I_{zz}U_1} \qquad \frac{rad/sec^2}{rad/sec}$$

$$Y_{\delta_r} = \frac{\bar{q}_1 S C_{y_{\delta_r}}}{m} \qquad \frac{ft/sec^2}{rad}$$

$$N_r = \frac{\bar{q}_1 S b^2 C_{n_r}}{2I_{zz}U_1} \qquad \frac{rad/sec^2}{rad/sec}$$

$$L_\beta = \frac{\bar{q}_1 S b C_{l_\beta}}{I_{xx}} \qquad \frac{rad/sec^2}{rad}$$

$$N_{\delta_a} = \frac{\bar{q}_1 S b C_{n_{\delta_a}}}{I_{zz}} \qquad \frac{rad/sec^2}{rad}$$

$$L_p = \frac{\bar{q}_1 S b^2 C_{l_p}}{2I_{xx}U_1} \qquad \frac{rad/sec^2}{rad/sec}$$

$$N_{\delta_r} = \frac{\bar{q}_1 S b C_{n_{\delta_r}}}{I_{zz}} \qquad \frac{rad/sec^2}{rad}$$

$$L_r = \frac{\bar{q}_1 S b^2 C_{l_r}}{2I_{xx}U_1} \qquad \frac{rad/sec^2}{rad/sec}$$

$$L_{\delta_a} = \frac{\bar{q}_1 S b C_{l_{\delta_a}}}{I_{xx}} \qquad \frac{rad/sec^2}{rad}$$

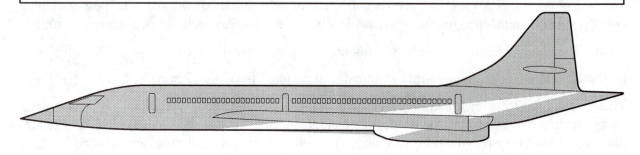

Table 5.8 Development of the Perturbed Lateral–Directional Equations of Motion with Dimensional Stability Derivatives in Matrix Format

$$U_1\dot{\beta} + U_1\dot{\psi} = g\phi\cos\theta_1 + Y_\beta\beta + Y_p\dot{\phi} + Y_r\dot{\psi} + Y_{\delta_a}\delta_a + Y_{\delta_r}\delta_r \quad \text{Lateral Accel} \tag{5.96a}$$

$$\ddot{\phi} - \overline{A}_1\ddot{\psi} = L_\beta\beta + L_p\dot{\phi} + L_r\dot{\psi} + L_{\delta_a}\delta_a + L_{\delta_r}\delta_r \quad \text{Roll Accel} \tag{5.96b}$$

$$\ddot{\psi} - \overline{B}_1\ddot{\phi} = N_\beta\beta + N_{T_\beta}\beta + N_p\dot{\phi} + N_r\dot{\psi} + N_{\delta_a}\delta_a + N_{\delta_r}\delta_r \quad \text{Yaw Accel} \tag{5.96c}$$

$$\text{NOTE}: \quad \overline{A}_1 = \frac{I_{xz}}{I_{xx}} \qquad \text{and} \qquad \overline{B}_1 = \frac{I_{xz}}{I_{zz}}$$

Laplace transforming Eqns (5.96) for zero initial conditions:

$$(sU_1 - Y_\beta)\beta(s) \qquad -(sY_p + g\cos\theta_1)\phi(s) \qquad s(U_1 - Y_r)\psi(s) = Y_\delta\delta(s) \tag{5.97a}$$

$$-L_\beta\beta(s) \qquad +(s^2 - L_ps)\phi(s) \qquad -(s^2\overline{A}_1 + sL_r)\psi(s) = L_\delta\delta(s) \tag{5.97b}$$

$$-(N_\beta + N_{T_\beta})\beta(s) \qquad -(s^2\overline{B}_1 + N_ps)\phi(s) \qquad (s^2 - sN_r)\psi(s) = N_\delta\delta(s) \tag{5.97c}$$

Writing Eqns (5.97) in matrix and transfer function format:

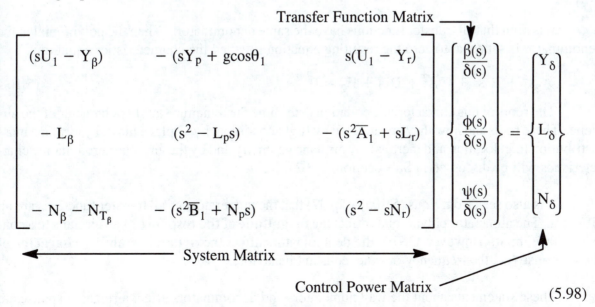

$$\begin{bmatrix} (sU_1 - Y_\beta) & -(sY_p + g\cos\theta_1) & s(U_1 - Y_r) \\ -L_\beta & (s^2 - L_ps) & -(s^2\overline{A}_1 + sL_r) \\ -N_\beta - N_{T_\beta} & -(s^2\overline{B}_1 + N_ps) & (s^2 - sN_r) \end{bmatrix} \begin{Bmatrix} \dfrac{\beta(s)}{\delta(s)} \\[2ex] \dfrac{\phi(s)}{\delta(s)} \\[2ex] \dfrac{\psi(s)}{\delta(s)} \end{Bmatrix} = \begin{Bmatrix} Y_\delta \\ L_\delta \\ N_\delta \end{Bmatrix} \tag{5.98}$$

Transfer Function Matrix

System Matrix

Control Power Matrix

is then expressed as a ratio of two determinants. The resulting determinant ratios are shown in Table 5.9 as Equations (5.99), (5.102) and (5.104) respectively.

Note, that the sideslip–to–aileron (or –rudder) transfer function, $\beta(s)/\delta(s)$, of Eqn (5.99) can be written as the following ratio of polynomials in the independent Laplace variable, s:

$$\frac{\beta(s)}{\delta(s)} = \frac{N_\beta}{\overline{D}_2} = \frac{s(A_\beta s^3 + B_\beta s^2 + C_\beta s + D_\beta)}{s(A_2 s^4 + B_2 s^3 + C_2 s^2 + D_2 s + E_2)} \tag{5.105}$$

Similarly, the bank–angle–to–aileron (or –rudder) transfer function, $\phi(s)/\delta_e(s)$, of Eqn (5.102) can be expressed as:

$$\frac{\phi(s)}{\delta(s)} = \frac{N_\phi}{\overline{D}_2} = \frac{s(A_\phi s^2 + B_\phi s + C_\phi)}{s(A_2 s^4 + B_2 s^3 + C_2 s^2 + D_2 s + E_2)} \tag{5.106}$$

Finally, the heading–to–aileron (or –rudder) transfer function, $\psi(s)/\delta(s)$, of Eqn (5.104) can be written as:

$$\frac{\psi(s)}{\delta(s)} = \frac{N_\psi}{\overline{D}_2} = \frac{A_\psi s^3 + B_\psi s^2 + C_\psi s + D_\psi}{s(A_2 s^4 + B_2 s^3 + C_2 s^2 + D_2 s + E_2)} \tag{5.107}$$

Note that in the sideslip and bank–angle transfer functions the free s in the numerator and denominator cancel each other. This cancellation does not occur in the heading transfer function. The physical significance of this is that the airplane is neutrally stable in heading because of the associated s=0 root in the characteristic equation.

It is seen that all transfer functions have the same denominator. When the polynomial in the denominator is set equal to zero the resulting equation is called the characteristics equation:

$$A_2 s^4 + B_2 s^3 + C_2 s^2 + D_2 s + E_2 = 0 \tag{5.108}$$

The roots of this characteristic equation determine the dynamic stability character of the airplane. These roots and how they are affected by flight condition, by airplane mass, by airplane mass distribution (c.g. location and inertias), by airplane geometry and by the airplane aerodynamic characteristics will be discussed in Sub–sections 5.3.2 – 5.3.7.

It is also seen from Eqns (5.105)–(5.107) that the numerators of all transfer functions are all different. The numerator polynomials affect the **magnitude of the response** of an airplane to a control surface input. However, ONLY the denominators affect the **dynamic stability character of the response** (i.e. the frequency or time–constant behavior).

These statements about the way numerators and denominators affect airplane response are true for the so–called open–loop response of an airplane. In closed loop situations (such as the case

Table 5.9 Lateral–Directional Airplane Transfer Functions

$$\frac{\beta(s)}{\delta(s)} = \frac{\begin{vmatrix} Y_\delta & -(sY_p + g\cos\theta_1) & s(U_1 - Y_r) \\ L_\delta & (s^2 - L_ps) & -(s^2\overline{A}_1 + sL_r) \\ N_\delta & -(s^2\overline{B}_1 + N_ps) & (s^2 - sN_r) \end{vmatrix}}{\begin{vmatrix} (sU_1 - Y_\beta) & -(sY_p + g\cos\theta_1) & s(U_1 - Y_r) \\ -L_\beta & (s^2 - L_ps) & -(s^2\overline{A}_1 + sL_r) \\ -(N_\beta + N_{T_\beta}) & -(s^2\overline{B}_1 + N_ps) & (s^2 - sN_r) \end{vmatrix}} = \frac{N_\beta}{D_2} \qquad (5.99)$$

$$\overline{D}_2 = s(A_2s^4 + B_2s^3 + C_2s^2 + D_2s + E_2) , \qquad \text{where :} \qquad (5.100)$$

$$A_2 = U_1(1 - \overline{A}_1\overline{B}_1)$$

$$B_2 = -Y_\beta(1 - \overline{A}_1\overline{B}_1) - U_1(L_p + N_r + \overline{A}_1N_p + \overline{B}_1L_r)$$

$$C_2 = U_1(L_pN_r - L_rN_p) + Y_\beta(N_r + L_p + \overline{A}_1N_p + \overline{B}_1L_r) - Y_p(L_\beta + N_\beta\overline{A}_1 + N_{T_\beta}\overline{A}_1) +$$
$$+ U_1(L_\beta\overline{B}_1 + N_\beta + N_{T_\beta}) - Y_r(L_\beta\overline{B}_1 + N_\beta + N_{T_\beta})$$

$$D_2 = -Y_\beta(L_pN_r - L_rN_p) + Y_p(L_\beta N_r - N_\beta L_r - N_{T_\beta}L_r) - g\cos\theta_1(L_\beta + N_\beta\overline{A}_1 + N_{T_\beta}\overline{A}_1) +$$
$$+ U_1(L_\beta N_p - N_\beta L_p - N_{T_\beta}L_p) - Y_r(L_\beta N_p - N_\beta L_p - N_{T_\beta}L_p)$$

$$E_2 = g\cos\theta_1(L_\beta N_r - N_\beta L_r - N_{T_\beta}L_r)$$

$$N_\beta = s(A_\beta s^3 + B_\beta s^2 + C_\beta s + D_\beta) , \qquad \text{where :} \qquad (5.101)$$

$$A_\beta = Y_\delta(1 - \overline{A}_1\overline{B}_1)$$

$$B_\beta = -Y_\delta(N_r + L_p + \overline{A}_1N_p + \overline{B}_1L_r) + Y_p(L_\delta + N_\delta\overline{A}_1) + Y_r(L_\delta\overline{B}_1 + N_\delta) +$$
$$- U_1(L_\delta\overline{B}_1 + N_\delta)$$

$$C_\beta = Y_\delta(L_pN_r - N_pL_r) + Y_p(N_\delta L_r - L_\delta N_r) + g\cos\theta_1(L_\delta + N_\delta\overline{A}_1) + Y_r(L_\delta N_p - N_\delta L_p) +$$
$$- U_1(L_\delta N_p - N_\delta L_p)$$

$$D_\beta = g\cos\theta_1(N_\delta L_r - L_\delta N_r)$$

Table 5.9 (Continued) Lateral–Directional Airplane Transfer Functions

$$\frac{\phi(s)}{\delta(s)} = \frac{\begin{vmatrix} (sU_1 - Y_\beta) & Y_\delta & s(U_1 - Y_r) \\ -L_\beta & L_\delta & -(s^2\overline{A}_1 + sL_r) \\ -(N_\beta + N_{T_\beta}) & N_\delta & (s^2 - sN_r) \end{vmatrix}}{\overline{D}_2} = \frac{N_\phi}{\overline{D}_2} \qquad (5.102)$$

$$N_\phi = s(A_\phi s^2 + B_\phi s + C_\phi) , \qquad where: \qquad (5.103)$$

$$A_\phi = U_1(L_\delta + N_\delta \overline{A}_1)$$

$$B_\phi = U_1(N_\delta L_r - L_\delta N_r) - Y_\beta(L_\delta + N_\delta \overline{A}_1) + Y_\delta(L_\beta + N_\beta \overline{A}_1 + N_{T_\beta}\overline{A}_1)$$

$$C_\phi = -Y_\beta(N_\delta L_r - L_\delta N_r) + Y_\delta(L_r N_\beta + L_r N_{T_\beta} - N_r L_\beta) +$$

$$+ (U_1 - Y_r)(N_\beta L_\delta + N_{T_\beta}L_\delta - L_\beta N_\delta)$$

$$\frac{\psi(s)}{\delta(s)} = \frac{\begin{vmatrix} (sU_1 - Y_\beta) & -(sY_p + g\cos\theta_1) & Y_\delta \\ -L_\beta & (s^2 - L_p s) & L_\delta \\ -(N_\beta + N_{T_\beta}) & -(s^2\overline{B}_1 + N_p s) & N_\delta \end{vmatrix}}{\overline{D}_2} = \frac{N_\psi}{\overline{D}_2} \qquad (5.104)$$

$$N_\psi = (A_\psi s^3 + B_\psi s^2 + C_\psi s + D_\psi) , \qquad where: \qquad (5.104)$$

$$A_\psi = U_1(N_\delta + L_\delta \overline{B}_1)$$

$$B_\psi = U_1(L_\delta N_p - N_\delta L_p) - Y_\beta(N_\delta + L_\delta \overline{B}_1) + Y_\delta(L_\beta \overline{B}_1 + N_\beta + N_{T_\beta})$$

$$C_\psi = -Y_\beta(L_\delta N_p - N_\delta L_p) + Y_p(N_\beta L_\delta + N_{T_\beta}L_\delta - L_\beta N_\delta) +$$

$$+ Y_\delta(L_\beta N_p - N_\beta L_p - N_{T_\beta}L_p)$$

$$D_\psi = g\cos\theta_1(N_\beta L_\delta + N_{T_\beta}L_\delta - L_\beta N_\delta)$$

with auto–pilots and/or stability augmentation systems) the numerators do affect the closed loop stability of the airplane. This aspect of the significance of the numerator characteristic equations (i.e. numerator polynomials set equal to zero) will become clear in Chapters 9, 10 and 11 where the behavior of automatic control systems are discussed.

Figure 5.16 shows how the open–loop transfer functions can be used to determine the response of an airplane to a control input. The block diagram drawn in Figure 5.16 is used to help visualize the inter–relationship between input, transfer function and output.

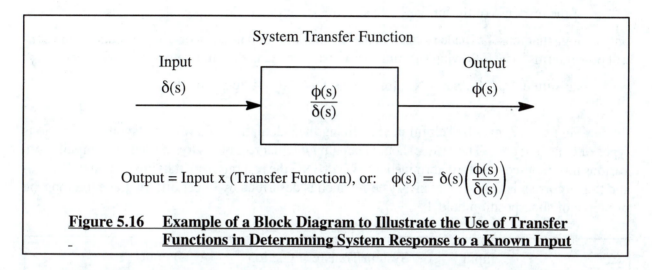

Figure 5.16   Example of a Block Diagram to Illustrate the Use of Transfer Functions in Determining System Response to a Known Input

It turns out that the transfer functions as derived in Table 5.9 can be used not only to determine the response to aileron (or rudder) control surface inputs but also:

> 1) to determine the response to inputs from other types of controllers

and

> 2) to determine the response of the airplane to gust.

This will be discussed next.

1) Response of the airplane to control surface inputs other than the aileron or rudder:

If the response of an airplane to another control surface input is required, the only change that must be made is in the transfer function numerators, in particular in the control power terms. The following substitutions must be made in the numerators N_β, N_ϕ and N_ψ :

For response to a vertical stabilizer input:

substitute Y_{i_v}, L_{i_v} and N_{i_v} for : Y_δ, L_δ and N_δ respectively.

For response to a vertical canard input:

substitute $Y_{i_{v_c}}$, $L_{i_{v_c}}$ and $N_{i_{v_c}}$ for : Y_δ, L_δ and N_δ respectively.

For response to an incremental, differential thrust input, with rolling moment, ΔL_T , and yawing moment, ΔN_T , consequences only:

substitute 0, ΔL_T and ΔN_T for : Y_δ, L_δ and N_δ respectively.

2) Response of the airplane to gust:

If the response of the airplane to a step input angle–of–sideslip gust, $\Delta \beta_g$, is required, the only change that must be made is again in the transfer function numerators, in particular in the control power terms. The following substitutions must be made in the numerators N_β, N_ϕ and N_ψ :

substitute Y_β, L_β and N_β for : Y_δ, L_δ and N_δ respectively.

Figure 5.17 may be helpful in visualizing the calculation of airplane responses to various types of control inputs. The reader should keep in mind that responses to simultaneous inputs from various input sources can be determined by SUMMING the responses to individual inputs. The reason this is correct is the fact that in a system which is described by linear differential equations the principle of superposition holds!

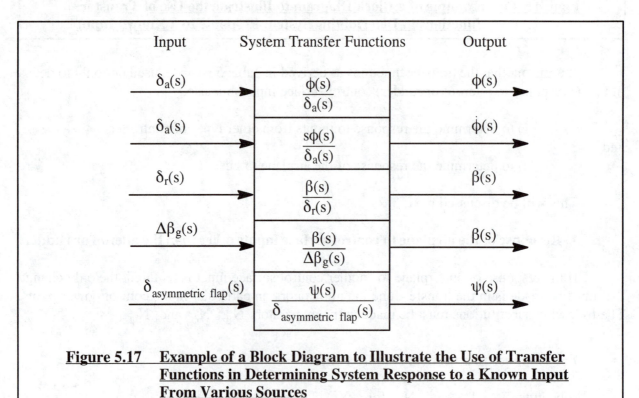

Figure 5.17   Example of a Block Diagram to Illustrate the Use of Transfer Functions in Determining System Response to a Known Input From Various Sources

5.3.2 LATERAL–DIRECTIONAL CHARACTERISTIC EQUATION ROOTS AND THEIR CONNECTION TO DYNAMIC STABILITY

Since the dynamic stability character of the airplane open loop transfer functions is determined by the roots of their characteristic equation, it is of interest to examine how these roots can break down from a mathematical viewpoint. Because the characteristic equation (5.108) has four roots, the following possibilities arise:

I)   All roots are real
II)   Two roots are real and two are complex conjugates
III)   All roots are complex: two pairs of complex conjugates

Figure 5.11 illustrates all possible combinations of root locations (root break–downs) for a fourth order characteristic equation. Even though all these root break–downs can occur in the case of airplanes, the usual root breakdown for the lateral–directional case is that represented by either Case B1 or Case B2 in Figure 5.11. How other root break–downs can arise will be discussed in Section 5.4.

Whether or not an airplane is dynamically, laterally–directionally stable is usually ascertained by inspecting computer print–outs of the roots of the characteristic equation (5.43) in accordance with the stability criteria of page 265. For stability, real roots must be negative and complex roots must have negative real parts.

Stability can also be predicted from the coefficients A_2 through E_2 in the characteristic equation (5.108). This can be done by using the so–called Routh–Hurwitz stability criteria for the roots of a polynomial equation. For a more detailed discussion of these stability criteria and their applications, the reader may wish to consult Refs 5.5 and 5.6. According to Routh–Hurwitz the roots of a fourth order polynomial are stable if and only if the following inequalities are simultaneously satisfied:

$$A_2, \ B_2, \ C_2, \ D_2, \ E_2 \ > \ 0$$

$$D_2(B_2C_2 - A_2D_2) - B_2^2E_2 \ > \ 0 \qquad \text{(Routh's Discriminant)}$$

(5.109)

It is shown in Reference 5.7 that as the polynomial coefficients A_2 through E_2 are changed, the dynamic stability behavior changes in the following manner:

A)   If the 'free' coefficient E_2 is changed from >0 to <0, one real root changes from negative to positive. The time domain response will therefore contain a pure divergence as a component. In Figure 5.11 this behavior corresponds to a change from case a1) to case a2) or from case b1) to case b2).

B)   If Routh's Discriminant changes from >0 to <0, the real part of a complex root changes from negative to positive. The time domain response will therefore contain an oscillatory divergence as a component. Examples of this behavior in Figure 5.11 are changes from case b1) to case b3) and changes from case c1) to case c2).

The reader should recognize the fact that changes in the coefficients A_2 through E_2 can come about by changes in airplane flight condition, airplane mass, airplane mass distribution (c.g. location and inertias), airplane geometry and airplane aerodynamic characteristics. By performing so–called sensitivity analyses it is possible to gain insight into how the airplane designer can or cannot affect the dynamic stability and response behavior of an airplane. Sensitivity analyses are discussed in Section 5.4.

With the widespread introduction of digital computers, the usefulness of the Routh–Hurwitz stability criteria (5.109) has declined. However, criterion A) still serves a useful purpose in that it enables an interesting connection between static and dynamic longitudinal stability. That is discussed in Sub–section 5.3.3.

5.3.3 CONNECTION BETWEEN DYNAMIC AND STATIC LATERAL–DIRECTIONAL STABILITY

According to the stability criteria of in equality (5.109), one real root in the lateral–directional characteristic equation changes from stable to unstable when the coefficient E_2 in Eqn (5.108) changes sign. An expression for this coefficient E_2 is shown in Table 5.9. Because the steady state pitch attitude angle, θ_1, and the acceleration of gravity, g, are both positive it follows that the requirement for stability is:

$$(L_\beta N_r - N_\beta L_r - N_{T_\beta} L_r) > 0 \tag{5.110}$$

Neglecting the thrust contribution, this can be written as:

$$(L_\beta N_r - N_\beta L_r) > 0 \quad \text{or}: \quad (C_{l_\beta} C_{n_r} - C_{n_\beta} C_{l_r}) > 0 \tag{5.111}$$

By referring to Chapter 4, the reader can verify that the derivatives C_{n_r}, C_{n_β} and C_{l_r} must normally satisfy the following sign conditions: $C_{n_r} < 0$, $C_{n_\beta} > 0$ and $C_{l_r} > 0$. As a consequence, to satisfy the dynamic stability criterion (5.111) it is necessary that the condition $C_{l_\beta} < 0$ be satisfied. The reader will recognize this as the requirement for lateral stability, as expressed by Eqn (4.41) discussed in Chapter 4. This establishes yet another connection between static and dynamic stability.

5.3.4 EXAMPLES OF LATERAL–DIRECTIONAL TRANSFER FUNCTIONS

The following examples illustrate two types of transfer functions: one type associated with a typical business jet, the other type associated with a typical jet fighter. The former was designed as an inherently stable airplane, the latter as an inherently unstable airplane.

To determine the numerical values of the coefficients in the numerator and in the denominator polynomials of lateral–directional transfer functions the following steps are necessary:

Step 1: Determine the flight condition and corresponding airplane configuration
Step 2: Determine the airplane mass and mass distribution (pitching moment of inertia)
Step 3: Determine the dimensionless stability derivatives
Step 4: Determine the dimensional stability derivatives
Step 5: Determine the polynomial coefficients in the transfer function numerators and denominator

The Advanced Aircraft Analysis program (See Appendix A) was used to perform these steps. The results are summarized in Tables 5.10 and 5.11 for a business jet and for a jet fighter respectively. At the top of Tables 5.10 and 5.11 are the required input data; these data are determined during Steps 1–3. Below the input data are the output parameters in the form of dimensional stability derivatives and the transfer functions (Step 4). Note that the transfer functions (Step 5) are given in two formats: polynomial format and factored format. The significance of the results in Tables 5.10 and 5.11 will now be discussed.

By inspection of the denominator polynomials of the two airplanes in Tables 5.10 and 5.11, the following (rounded off) values are found for the denominator polynomial coefficients:

DENOMINATOR POLYNOMIAL COEFFICIENTS

For the Business Jet:

$A_2 = 675$

$B_2 = 427$

$C_2 = 1,968$

$D_2 = 964$

$E_2 = 0.973$

For the Jet Fighter:

$A_2 = 861$

$B_2 = 830$

$C_2 = 1,574$　　　　　　(5.112)

$D_2 = 1,744$

$E_2 = 49.6$

It is clear by inspection of the factored denominators in Tables 5.10 and 5.11, that the business jet is dynamically stable while the fighter is dynamically unstable.

The characteristic equation roots for the two airplanes are given in Eqn (5.113). They follow from the factored formats in Tables 5.10 and 5.11.

CHARACTERISTIC EQUATION ROOTS

For the Business Jet:

$s_{1,2} = -0.0653 \pm j(1.69)$

$s_3 = -0.0010$

$s_4 = -0.5003$

For the Jet Fighter:

$s_{1,2} = +0.0502 \pm j(1.38)$

$s_3 = -0.0292$　　　　(5.113)

$s_4 = -1.0357$

It is seen that the root break–down for the business jet is according to case B1) in Figure 5.11. There is one complex pair of roots, and there are two real roots. The complex pair is referred to as the dutch roll mode, the real root closest to the origin (in the s–plane) is called the spiral root and the other real root is called the roll root.

Table 5.10 Lateral–Directional Transfer Functions for a Business Jet in Cruise

| WEIGHT SIZING | GEOMETRY | DRAG POLAR | WEIGHT & BALANCE | PERF. ANALYSIS | DYNAMICS | COST ANALYSIS | HELP / SETUP |
| PERFORM. SIZING | HIGH LIFT | STAB. & CONTROL | INSTALLED THRUST | S&C DERIVATIVES | CONTROL | DATA BASE | QUIT |

OPEN LOOP DYNAMICS

| LONGITUDINAL | LATERAL-DIRECT | ROLL COUPLING | RETURN |

LATERAL-DIRECTIONAL ANALYSIS

| CALCULATE T.F. | SHOW T.F. | CHECK MODES | SENSITIVITY | RETURN |

| CALCULATE | THEORY | PRINT PARAMETERS | RETURN |

COMPUTATION OF LATERAL-DIRECTIONAL TRANSFER FUNCTIONS : INPUT PARAMETERS

W_current =	13000.0 lb	I_xx_B =	28000 slgft2	C_n_T_B =	0.0000	C_l_d_r =	0.0172 1/rad
Altitude =	40000 ft	I_zz_B =	47000 slgft2	C_n_p =	0.0080 1/rad	C_n_d_a =	-0.0172 1/rad
S_w =	232.00 ft^2	I_xz_B =	1350 slgft2	C_n_r =	-0.2010 1/rad	C_n_d_r =	-0.0747 1/rad
U_1 =	400.00 kts	C_l_B =	-0.1100 1/rad	C_y_B =	-0.7300 1/rad	C_y_d_a =	0.0000 1/rad
Theta_1 =	0.00 deg	C_l_p =	-0.4530 1/rad	C_y_p =	0.0000 1/rad	C_y_d_r =	0.1380 1/rad
Alpha =	2.70 deg	C_l_r =	0.1630 1/rad	C_y_r =	0.4000 1/rad		
b_w =	34.20 ft	C_n_B =	0.1270 1/rad	C_l_d_a =	0.1780 1/rad		

OUTPUT PARAMETERS

(W/S)_TO =	56.03 psf	L_B =	-4.1845 1/s^2	z_D =	0.0387	TC_latd_4 =	? s
q_bar =	133.84 psf	L_p =	-0.4365 1/s	w_n_LatP =	? rad/s	Y_del_a =	0.0000 ft/s^2
I_xx_S =	27915 slgft2	L_r =	0.1571 1/s	z_LatP =	?	Y_del_r =	10.4733 ft/s^2
I_zz_S =	47085 slgft2	N_B =	2.8643 1/s^2	TC_SPIRAL =	989.234 s	L_del_a =	6.7714 1/s^2
I_xz_S =	450 slgft2	N_T_B =	0.0000 1/s^2	TC_ROLL =	1.999 s	L_del_r =	0.6543 1/s^2
Y_B =	-55.4022 ft/s^2	N_p =	0.0046 1/s	TC_latd_1 =	? s	N_del_a =	-0.3879 1/s^2
Y_p =	0.0000 ft/s	N_r =	-0.1148 1/s	TC_latd_2 =	? s	N_del_r =	-1.6847 1/s^2
Y_r =	0.7689 ft/s	w_n_D =	1.6882 rad/s	TC_latd_3 =	? s		

| Design, Analysis and Research Corporation | | /users/jan/aaafiles/Learjet-book | Nov 13, 1993 | 13:52 |

LATERAL TRANSFER FUNCTIONS

POLYNOMIAL ROLL TO AILERON TRANSFER FUNCTION

$$\frac{+ 4567.2805 \ S^3 + 858.5747 \ S^2 + 12024.2371 \ S}{+ 675.0200 \ S^5 + 426.5285 \ S^4 + 1968.3877 \ S^3 + 964.4216 \ S^2 + 0.9729 \ S}$$

FACTORED ROLL TO AILERON TRANSFER FUNCTION

$$\frac{4567.2805 \quad S(S^2 + 0.1880 \ S + 2.6327)}{675.0200 \quad S(S + 0.5003)(S + 0.0010)(S^2 + 0.1306 \ S + 2.8501)}$$

ROLL TO AILERON TRANSFER FUNCTION K_gain =12359.081577

POLYNOMIAL SIDESLIP TO AILERON TRANSFER FUNCTION

$$\frac{+ 217.9565 \ S^3 + 308.2716 \ S^2 + 22.7686 \ S}{+ 675.0200 \ S^5 + 426.5285 \ S^4 + 1968.3877 \ S^3 + 964.4216 \ S^2 + 0.9729 \ S}$$

FACTORED SIDESLIP TO AILERON TRANSFER FUNCTION

$$\frac{217.9565 \quad S(S + 1.3362)(S + 0.0782)}{675.0200 \quad S(S + 0.5003)(S + 0.0010)(S^2 + 0.1306 \ S + 2.8501)}$$

SIDESLIP TO AILERON TRANSFER FUNCTION K_gain =   23.402697

| CONTINUE | | CANCEL |

Table 5.10 (Continued) Lateral–Directional Transfer Functions for a Business Jet in Cruise

```
                     LATERAL TRANSFER FUNCTIONS

POLYNOMIAL HEADING TO AILERON TRANSFER FUNCTION

  - 218.2050 S^3 - 111.3266 S^2 - 7.6663 S + 564.6921
-----------------------------------------------------------------------------
  + 675.0200 S^5 + 426.5285 S^4 + 1968.3877 S^3 + 964.4216 S^2 + 0.9729 S

FACTORED HEADING TO AILERON TRANSFER FUNCTION

-218.2050   (S - 1.2147)(S^2 + 1.7249 S + 2.1304)
-----------------------------------------------------------------------------
675.0200    S(S + 0.5003)(S + 0.0010)(S^2 + 0.1306 S + 2.8501)

  HEADING TO AILERON TRANSFER FUNCTION K_gain =   580.417389

POLYNOMIAL ROLL TO RUDDER TRANSFER FUNCTION

  + 423.4061 S^3 - 136.5132 S^2 - 3501.1104 S
-----------------------------------------------------------------------------
  + 675.0200 S^5 + 426.5285 S^4 + 1968.3877 S^3 + 964.4216 S^2 + 0.9729 S

FACTORED ROLL TO RUDDER TRANSFER FUNCTION

423.4061    S(S - 3.0413)(S + 2.7189)
-----------------------------------------------------------------------------
675.0200    S(S + 0.5003)(S + 0.0010)(S^2 + 0.1306 S + 2.8501)

  ROLL TO RUDDER TRANSFER FUNCTION K_gain =-3598.607460

POLYNOMIAL SIDESLIP TO RUDDER TRANSFER FUNCTION

  + 10.4717 S^4 + 1137.6563 S^3 + 514.3222 S^2 - 6.0204 S
-----------------------------------------------------------------------------
  + 675.0200 S^5 + 426.5285 S^4 + 1968.3877 S^3 + 964.4216 S^2 + 0.9729 S

FACTORED SIDESLIP TO RUDDER TRANSFER FUNCTION

10.4717    S(S - 0.0114)(S + 108.1871)(S + 0.4655)
-----------------------------------------------------------------------------
675.0200    S(S + 0.5003)(S + 0.0010)(S^2 + 0.1306 S + 2.8501)

  SIDESLIP TO RUDDER TRANSFER FUNCTION K_gain =    -6.188006

POLYNOMIAL HEADING TO RUDDER TRANSFER FUNCTION

  - 1133.1894 S^3 - 557.8529 S^2 - 27.6814 S - 164.4570
-----------------------------------------------------------------------------
  + 675.0200 S^5 + 426.5285 S^4 + 1968.3877 S^3 + 964.4216 S^2 + 0.9729 S

FACTORED HEADING TO RUDDER TRANSFER FUNCTION

-1133.1894   (S + 0.7307)(S^2 + -0.2384 S + 0.1986)
-----------------------------------------------------------------------------
675.0200    S(S + 0.5003)(S + 0.0010)(S^2 + 0.1306 S + 2.8501)

  HEADING TO RUDDER TRANSFER FUNCTION K_gain = -169.036687

                           [  OK  ]
```

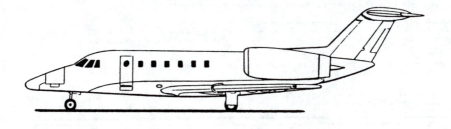

Table 5.11 Lateral–Directional Transfer Functions for a Jet Fighter in Cruise

| WEIGHT SIZING | GEOMETRY | DRAG POLAR | WEIGHT & BALANCE | PERF. ANALYSIS | DYNAMICS | COST ANALYSIS | HELP / SETUP |
| PERFORM. SIZING | HIGH LIFT | STAB. & CONTROL | INSTALLED THRUST | S&C DERIVATIVES | CONTROL | DATA BASE | QUIT |

OPEN LOOP DYNAMICS

| LONGITUDINAL | LATERAL-DIRECT | ROLL COUPLING | RETURN |

LATERAL-DIRECTIONAL ANALYSIS

| CALCULATE T.F. | SHOW T.F. | CHECK MODES | SENSITIVITY | RETURN |

| CALCULATE | THEORY | PRINT PARAMETERS | RETURN |

COMPUTATION OF LATERAL-DIRECTIONAL TRANSFER FUNCTIONS : INPUT PARAMETERS

W_current =	16000.0 lb	I_xx_B =	6127 slgft2	C_n_T_B =	0.0000	C_l_d_r =	0.0061 1/rad
Altitude =	45000 ft	I_zz_B =	33955 slgft2	C_n_p =	-0.0338 1/rad	C_n_d_a =	-0.0057 1/rad
S_w =	302.00 ft^2	I_xz_B =	0 slgft2	C_n_r =	-0.0897 1/rad	C_n_d_r =	-0.0146 1/rad
U_1 =	516.00 kts	C_l_B =	-0.1349 1/rad	C_y_B =	-0.4007 1/rad	C_y_d_a =	0.0000 1/rad
Theta_1 =	0.00 deg	C_l_p =	-0.2458 1/rad	C_y_p =	-0.0836 1/rad	C_y_d_r =	0.0469 1/rad
Alpha =	3.25 deg	C_l_r =	0.1260 1/rad	C_y_r =	0.2259 1/rad		
b_w =	26.36 ft	C_n_B =	0.0075 1/rad	C_l_d_a =	0.0830 1/rad		

OUTPUT PARAMETERS

(W/S)_TO =	52.98 psf	L_B =	-30.2744 1/s^2	z_D =	-0.0363	TC_latd_4 =	? s
q_bar =	175.32 psf	L_p =	-0.8350 1/s	w_n_LatP =	? rad/s	Y_del_a =	0.0000 ft/s^2
I_xx_S =	6216 slgft2	L_r =	0.4279 1/s	z_LatP =	?	Y_del_r =	4.9234 ft/s^2
I_zz_S =	33865 slgft2	N_B =	0.3072 1/s^2	TC_SPIRAL =	34.277 s	L_del_a =	18.6385 1/s^2
I_xz_S =	-1573 slgft2	N_T_B =	0.0000 1/s^2	TC_ROLL =	0.965 s	L_del_r =	1.3619 1/s^2
Y_B =	-42.0690 ft/s^2	N_p =	-0.0211 1/s	TC_latd_1 =	? s	N_del_a =	-0.2334 1/s^2
Y_p =	-0.1328 ft/s	N_r =	-0.0559 1/s	TC_latd_2 =	? s	N_del_r =	-0.6018 1/s^2
Y_r =	0.3588 ft/s	w_n_D =	1.3804 rad/s	TC_latd_3 =	? s		

| Design, Analysis and Research Corporation | gripen/45K/0.9 | /users/jan/aaafiles/jas39 | Nov 13, 1993 | 12:27 |

LATERAL TRANSFER FUNCTIONS

POLYNOMIAL ROLL TO AILERON TRANSFER FUNCTION

$$\frac{+ 16283.9016\ S^3 + 1607.6574\ S^2 - 1128.0173\ S}{+ 860.6745\ S^5 + 830.1730\ S^4 + 1574.1509\ S^3 + 1743.9844\ S^2 + 49.5590\ S}$$

FACTORED ROLL TO AILERON TRANSFER FUNCTION

$$\frac{16283.9016 \quad S(S - 0.2184)(S + 0.3171)}{860.6745 \quad S(S + 1.0357)(S + 0.0292)(S^2 + -0.1004\ S + 1.9056)}$$

ROLL TO AILERON TRANSFER FUNCTION K_gain = -22.761102

POLYNOMIAL SIDESLIP TO AILERON TRANSFER FUNCTION

$$\frac{+ 954.3628\ S^3 + 1104.8075\ S^2 + 29.9096\ S}{+ 860.6745\ S^5 + 830.1730\ S^4 + 1574.1509\ S^3 + 1743.9844\ S^2 + 49.5590\ S}$$

FACTORED SIDESLIP TO AILERON TRANSFER FUNCTION

$$\frac{954.3628 \quad S(S + 1.1299)(S + 0.0277)}{860.6745 \quad S(S + 1.0357)(S + 0.0292)(S^2 + -0.1004\ S + 1.9056)}$$

SIDESLIP TO AILERON TRANSFER FUNCTION K_gain = 0.603516

| CONTINUE | | CANCEL |

Table 5.11 (Continued) Lateral–Directional Transfer Functions for a Jet Fighter in Cruise

```
                        LATERAL TRANSFER FUNCTIONS

POLYNOMIAL HEADING TO AILERON TRANSFER FUNCTION

 - 957.2401 S^3 - 558.1981 S^2 - 24.5519 S - 42.5533
-----------------------------------------------------------------------------
 + 860.6745 S^5 + 830.1730 S^4 + 1574.1509 S^3 + 1743.9844 S^2 + 49.5590 S

FACTORED HEADING TO AILERON TRANSFER FUNCTION

-957.2401  (S + 0.6491)(S^2 + -0.0660 S + 0.0685)
-----------------------------------------------------------------------------
860.6745   S(S + 1.0357)(S + 0.0292)(S^2 + -0.1004 S + 1.9056)

 HEADING TO AILERON TRANSFER FUNCTION K_gain =   -0.858640

POLYNOMIAL ROLL TO RUDDER TRANSFER FUNCTION

 + 1318.7562 S^3 - 243.6487 S^2 - 15512.2427 S
-----------------------------------------------------------------------------
 + 860.6745 S^5 + 830.1730 S^4 + 1574.1509 S^3 + 1743.9844 S^2 + 49.5590 S

FACTORED ROLL TO RUDDER TRANSFER FUNCTION

1318.7562   S(S - 3.5233)(S + 3.3386)
-----------------------------------------------------------------------------
860.6745    S(S + 1.0357)(S + 0.0292)(S^2 + -0.1004 S + 1.9056)

 ROLL TO RUDDER TRANSFER FUNCTION K_gain = -313.005603

POLYNOMIAL SIDESLIP TO RUDDER TRANSFER FUNCTION

 + 4.8656 S^4 + 583.2384 S^3 + 510.8035 S^2 - 5.7525 S
-----------------------------------------------------------------------------
 + 860.6745 S^5 + 830.1730 S^4 + 1574.1509 S^3 + 1743.9844 S^2 + 49.5590 S

FACTORED SIDESLIP TO RUDDER TRANSFER FUNCTION

4.8656    S(S - 0.0111)(S + 118.9885)(S + 0.8935)
-----------------------------------------------------------------------------
860.6745    S(S + 1.0357)(S + 0.0292)(S^2 + -0.1004 S + 1.9056)

 SIDESLIP TO RUDDER TRANSFER FUNCTION K_gain =    -0.116073

POLYNOMIAL HEADING TO RUDDER TRANSFER FUNCTION

 - 579.2200 S^3 - 482.1999 S^2 - 15.5793 S - 564.7495
-----------------------------------------------------------------------------
 + 860.6745 S^5 + 830.1730 S^4 + 1574.1509 S^3 + 1743.9844 S^2 + 49.5590 S

FACTORED HEADING TO RUDDER TRANSFER FUNCTION

-579.2200   (S + 1.3486)(S^2 + -0.5161 S + 0.7230)
-----------------------------------------------------------------------------
860.6745    S(S + 1.0357)(S + 0.0292)(S^2 + -0.1004 S + 1.9056)

 HEADING TO RUDDER TRANSFER FUNCTION K_gain =   -11.395500

                             [      OK      ]
```

It is also seen that the root break–down for the jet fighter corresponds to the case labelled B3) in Figure 5.11. The unstable oscillatory root in this case is again referred to as the dutch–roll mode. The other real roots are called the spiral and roll roots respectively.

It has been found useful to compare the dynamic behavior of airplanes with that of the spring–mass–damper system discussed in Section 5.1. Quadratic roots of characteristic equations are cast in a format similar to that of Eqn (5.11), that is by using undamped natural frequency and damping ratio as the parameters of choice. For a definition of undamped natural frequency and damping ratio the reader should consult Section 5.1.

Real roots of characteristic equations are cast in the form of so–called 'time–constants, T' as illustrated in Table C1 in Appendix C. Note that a time constant is defined as the negative inverse of the associated real root.

Introduction of these forms for the characteristic equation roots (using subscripts 'd' for the dutch roll mode the subscript 'r' for the roll mode and the subscripts 's' for the spiral mode) yields the following characteristics:

For the Business Jet:

$$s_{1,2} = \zeta_{1,2}\omega_{n_{1,2}} \pm j\omega_{n_{1,2}}\sqrt{1 - \zeta_{1,2}^2} \quad \text{or} \quad s_d = \zeta_d\omega_{n_d} \pm j\omega_{n_d}\sqrt{1 - \zeta_d^2}$$

$$\text{(5.114a)}$$

with : $\zeta_d = 0.039$ and $\omega_{n_d} = 1.69$ rad/sec

and

$$s_3 = \frac{-1}{T_s} \quad \text{with}: \ s_3 = -0.0010 \ \text{sec}^{-1} \ \text{and} \ T_s = 989 \ \text{sec}$$

$$\text{(5.114b)}$$

$$s_4 = \frac{-1}{T_r} \quad \text{with}: \ s_4 = -0.5003 \ \text{sec}^{-1} \ \text{and} \ T_r = 2.0 \ \text{sec}$$

Observe that the dutch roll mode is very lightly damped. A yaw damper will be required to improve this. The dutch roll frequency is of the same order of magnitude as the short period {see Eqn (5.53)}. The spiral root is located almost at the origin while the roll root is located to the left of the origin.

For the Jet Fighter:

$$s_{1,2} = \zeta_{1,2}\omega_{n_{1,2}} \pm j\omega_{n_{1,2}}\sqrt{1 - \zeta_{1,2}^2} \quad \text{or} \quad s_d = \zeta_d\omega_{n_d} \pm j\omega_{n_d}\sqrt{1 - \zeta_d^2}$$

$$\text{(5.115a)}$$

with : $\zeta_d = -0.036$ and $\omega_{n_d} = 1.38$ rad/sec

and

$$s_3 = \frac{-1}{T_s} \quad \text{with}: \ s_3 = -0.0292 \ \text{sec}^{-1} \ \text{and} \ T_s = 34.3 \ \text{sec}$$

$$\text{(5.115b)}$$

$$s_4 = \frac{-1}{T_r} \quad \text{with}: \ s_4 = -1.0357 \ \text{sec}^{-1} \ \text{and} \ T_r = 0.97 \ \text{sec}$$

The unstable dutch roll root will cause this airplane to diverge in an oscillatory manner without compensating action from either the pilot or from an automatic flight control system. As it turns out, in this instance a yaw damper is required.

As will be shown in Chapter 6, the magnitudes of undamped natural frequencies, damping ratios and time constant are intimately tied to acceptable or unacceptable flying quality behavior of airplanes. For that reason it is important for airplane designers to understand which airplane design factors are the 'design drivers' which determine these dynamic stability parameters. The complete transfer functions of the airplane, as presented in Tables 5.10 and 5.11, because of their algebraic complexity, do not afford such insight easily. It has been found that the dutch–roll, spiral and roll characteristics of inherently stable airplanes can be more easily predicted from an approximation to the equations of motion as listed in Table 5.2. These approximations and their applications will be discussed in Sub–sections 5.3.5 through 5.3.7 for the dutch–roll, spiral and roll mode characteristics respectively.

5.3.5   THE DUTCH–ROLL APPROXIMATION

For airplanes with relatively small dihedral effect, the dutch–roll mode manifests itself as a motion which consists primarily of sideslipping and yawing. Even though rolling motions are also present in most dutch–rolls it has been found that a good approximation to the frequency of the dutch roll mode can be obtained by assuming negligible participation of the rolling degree of freedom. Eliminating the rolling degree of freedom from Eqns (5.98) in Table 5.8 yields the following approximate equations:

$$
\begin{bmatrix}
(sU_1 - Y_\beta) & s(U_1 - Y_r) \\
- N_\beta & (s^2 - sN_r)
\end{bmatrix}
\begin{Bmatrix}
\dfrac{\beta(s)}{\delta(s)} \\
\dfrac{\psi(s)}{\delta(s)}
\end{Bmatrix}
=
\begin{Bmatrix}
Y_\delta \\
N_\delta
\end{Bmatrix}
\tag{5.116}
$$

In these equations, the substitution $(N_\beta + N_{T_\beta}) \rightarrow N_\beta$ has also been made. The approximate sideslip and heading angle transfer functions can now be explicitly written as follows:

$$
\frac{\beta(s)}{\delta(s)} = \frac{\left\{ Y_\delta s + (N_\delta Y_r - N_\delta U_1 - Y_\delta N_r) \right\}}{\left[s^2 - s(N_r + \dfrac{Y_\beta}{U_1}) + \left\{ N_\beta + \dfrac{1}{U_1}(Y_\beta N_r - N_\beta Y_r) \right\} \right]}
\tag{5.117}
$$

and

$$
\frac{\psi(s)}{\delta(s)} = \frac{\left\{ N_\delta(sU_1 - Y_\beta) + N_\beta Y_\delta \right\}}{s\left[s^2 - s(N_r + \dfrac{Y_\beta}{U_1}) + \left\{ N_\beta + \dfrac{1}{U_1}(Y_\beta N_r - N_\beta Y_r) \right\} \right]}
\tag{5.118}
$$

The s=0 root in the denominator of the heading angle transfer function is again indicative of the fact that an airplane has neutral stability in heading. The quadratic in the denominator should be interpreted as an approximation to the dutch roll quadratic form $(s^2 + 2\zeta_d\omega_{n_d}s + \omega_{n_d}^2)$.

Therefore, it is possible to write the following approximations for the dutch roll undamped natural frequency and damping ratio:

$$\omega_{n_d} \approx \sqrt{\left\{N_\beta + \frac{1}{U_1}(Y_\beta N_r - N_\beta Y_r)\right\}} \qquad (5.119a)$$

and

$$\zeta_d \approx \frac{-(N_r + \frac{Y_\beta}{U_1})}{2\omega_{n_d}} \qquad (5.120b)$$

To see how accurate these approximations are, the appropriate data from Table 5.10 are substituted into these two equations. It is found that:

$$\omega_{n_d} = 1.69 \text{ rad/sec} \quad \text{and} \quad \zeta_d = 0.058 \qquad (5.120)$$

These results should be compared with those of Eqn (5.114a). The frequency compares very well but the damping ratio differs by about 50%. However, it is doubtful whether a pilot can tell the difference between a damping ratio of 0.039 and 0.058. From that viewpoint the dutch roll damping ratio prediction appears more reasonable. However, the reader will observe that Eqn (5.119) also predicts that as long as the derivatives N_r and Y_β are both negative, the dutch–roll damping ratio will always be positive. The reader should check with the jet fighter example that this is not correct! The reason is the fact that the elimination of the rolling degree of freedom in the dutch–roll approximation results in also neglecting the effect of L_β on dutch roll damping. As will be seen in Section 5.4 (sensitivity analyses section) the derivative L_β can have an important effect on the damping of the dutch roll mode.

While checking the dutch–roll frequency approximation of Eqn (5.118) the reader will have noticed the fact that $[(1/U_1)(Y_\beta N_r - N_\beta Y_r)] \ll N_\beta$. This turns out to be the case for most airplanes. Therefore, an approximation to the approximation for the dutch–roll undamped natural frequency is:

$$\omega_{n_d} \approx \approx \sqrt{N_\beta} = \sqrt{\frac{C_{n_\beta}\bar{q}_1 Sb}{I_{zz}}} \qquad (5.121)$$

For the case at hand, this yields a frequency prediction of:

$$\omega_{n_d} = 1.69 \text{ rad/sec}$$

Eqn (5.120) provides the following information about the three factors which usually 'drive' the magnitude of the dutch–roll undamped natural frequency:

* Static directional stability, C_{n_β} , and therefore the size, shape and moment arm of the vertical tail as well as the size and shape of the fuselage in its side projection are important. For a given fuselage shape and vertical tail shape and for a given vertical tail moment arm, the frequency will be higher for airplanes with a larger vertical tail.

* Dynamic pressure in the steady state, $\bar{q}_1$. The frequency at a given altitude will be higher at high speed than at low speed.

* Yawing moment of inertia, I_{zz} . The frequency will be higher for airplanes with a low yawing moment of inertia. The airplane mass configuration therefore plays a role. All else being the same, an airplane with the engines mounted in the aft fuselage would tend to have a lower frequency than an airplane with the engines mounted close to the center of gravity.

It is instructive to compare the terms under the square root sign in Eqn (5.120) with the term (k/m) in Eqn (5.5). Evidently, the term $(C_{n_\beta}\bar{q}_1 Sb)$ can be thought of as a torsional spring, wrapped around the airplane Z–axis!

Eqn (5.119) shows that for a given frequency, the damping ratio is determined by the derivatives N_r and Y_β . Both contribute to damping although the yaw–damping derivative, N_r , usually provides the most important contribution to dutch–roll damping.

Figure 5.18 shows what a dutch–roll mode looks like to an outside observer.

5.3.6 THE SPIRAL APPROXIMATION

In the spiral mode, all three lateral degrees of freedom, β, ϕ and ψ tend to participate although the sideslip angle participation is generally weakest. Despite this fact, the sideslip angle cannot be neglected because the aerodynamic moments which dominate the spiral mode are not caused by ϕ and ψ but by β, ϕ and ψ . Of the latter, the moments due to β and ψ are usually by far the most important. The spiral approximation is thus formed by neglecting the side force equation as well as by neglecting the roll rate terms in the remaining rolling and yawing moment equations. Carrying out these approximations in Eqns (5.98) in Table 5.8 yields:

$$
\begin{bmatrix}
-L_\beta & -s(s\bar{A}_1 + L_r) \\
-N_\beta & (s^2 - sN_r)
\end{bmatrix}
\begin{Bmatrix}
\dfrac{\beta(s)}{\delta(s)} \\[2ex]
\dfrac{\psi(s)}{\delta(s)}
\end{Bmatrix}
=
\begin{Bmatrix}
L_\delta \\
N_\delta
\end{Bmatrix}
\tag{5.122}
$$

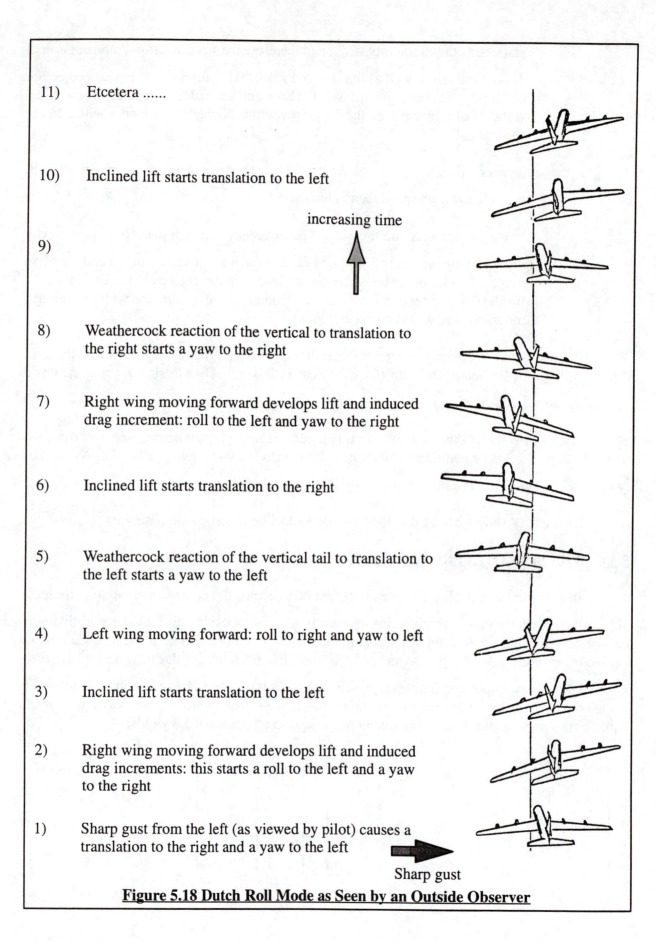

11)   Etcetera ......

10)   Inclined lift starts translation to the left

increasing time

9)

8)   Weathercock reaction of the vertical to translation to
      the right starts a yaw to the right

7)   Right wing moving forward develops lift and induced
      drag increment: roll to the left and yaw to the right

6)   Inclined lift starts translation to the right

5)   Weathercock reaction of the vertical tail to translation to
      the left starts a yaw to the left

4)   Left wing moving forward: roll to right and yaw to left

3)   Inclined lift starts translation to the left

2)   Right wing moving forward develops lift and induced
      drag increments: this starts a roll to the left and a yaw
      to the right

1)   Sharp gust from the left (as viewed by pilot) causes a
      translation to the right and a yaw to the left

Sharp gust

Figure 5.18 Dutch Roll Mode as Seen by an Outside Observer

Modern Flt Dynamics
by: Kolk

The approximate sideslip and heading angle transfer functions can now be written as:

$$\frac{\beta(s)}{\delta(s)} = \frac{s\{s(L_\delta - N_\delta \overline{A}_1) - (L_\delta N_r - N_\delta L_r)\}}{s\{-s(L_\beta + N_\beta \overline{A}_1) + (L_\beta N_r - N_\beta L_r)\}} \tag{5.123}$$

and

$$\frac{\psi(s)}{\delta(s)} = \frac{(-L_\beta N_\delta + L_\delta N_\beta)}{s\{-s(L_\beta + N_\beta \overline{A}_1) + (L_\beta N_r - N_\beta L_r)\}} \tag{5.124}$$

The free 's' terms in the sideslip transfer function cancel each other. The s=0 root in the heading transfer function again indicates neutral stability in heading. The approximate spiral root can be determined from the remaining first order term in the denominator as:

$$s_3 = s_{spiral} = \frac{(L_\beta N_r - N_\beta L_r)}{(L_\beta + N_\beta \overline{A}_1)} \tag{5.125}$$

To see how accurate this approximation is, the appropriate data from Table 5.10 are substituted into this equation. The result is:

$$s_3 = s_{spiral} \approx -0.0074 \text{ sec}^{-1} \text{ and } T_s \approx 135 \text{ sec} \tag{5.126}$$

Comparison with Eqn (5.114b) shows that the spiral approximation differs from the actual spiral root by a factor of 7. However, both methods predict the spiral root to be essentially at the origin. An interesting aspect of the spiral approximation of Eqn (5.125) is the following: assuming that the inertia ratio $\overline{A}_1$ is so small as to be negligible, the criterion for spiral root stability is that:

$$(L_\beta N_r - N_\beta L_r) > 0 \tag{5.127}$$

This stability criterion is seen to agree exactly with the stability criterion due to Routh as found in Eqn (5.111).

Figure 5.19 shows what a spiral mode (stable and unstable) looks like to an outside observer.

5.3.7 THE ROLL APPROXIMATION

In the roll approximation the assumption is made that the only important degree of freedom is the bank angle, ϕ. Eliminating all but the rolling equation of motion from Eqns (5.98) yields:

$$\frac{\phi(s)}{\delta_a(s)} = \frac{L_{\delta_a}}{(s^2 - sL_p)} \tag{5.128}$$

The characteristic equation of the rolling approximation contains two roots:

$$s_3 = 0 \text{ and } s_4 = s_{roll} \approx L_p \text{ and therefore : } T_r \approx -1/L_p \tag{5.129}$$

The s_3=0 root can be thought of as a degenerate spiral mode root. The other root is the roll–

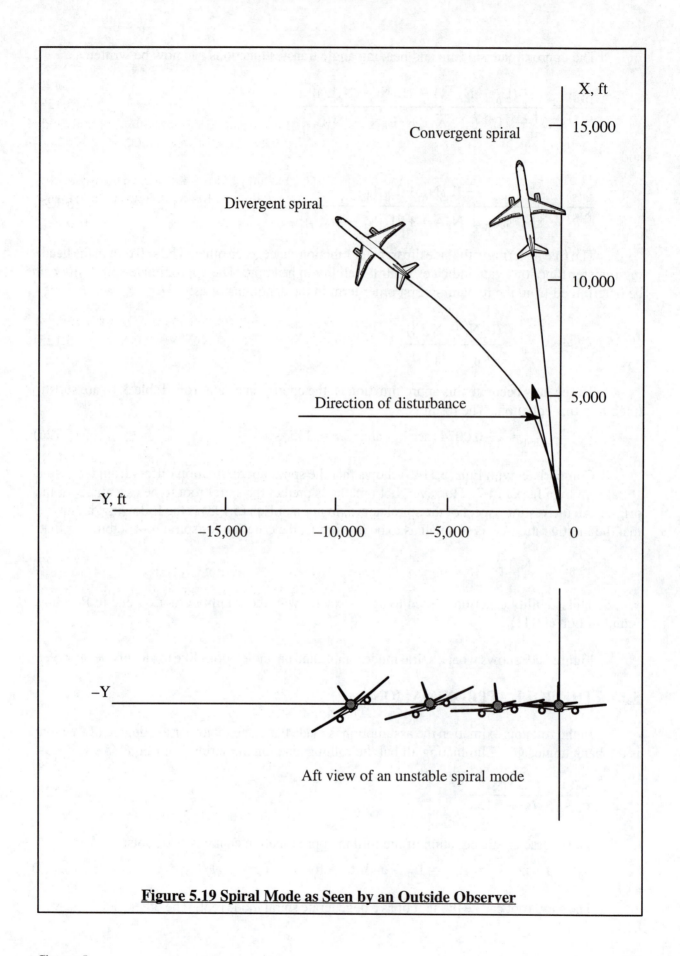

Figure 5.19 Spiral Mode as Seen by an Outside Observer

mode root. To see how accurate the latter is, the data of Table 5.10 yield:

$$s_{roll} \approx -0.4365 \text{ sec}^{-1} \text{ and } T_r \approx 2.29 \text{ sec} \tag{5.130}$$

According to Eqn (5.114b) the actual roll–mode time constant is 2.0 seconds. The roll mode approximation therefore gives a fair approximation in the case of the business jet.

The physical significance of the roll–mode time constant will become clear in the following. It is instructive to see how an airplane responds in roll to a step input aileron deflection. In that case Eqn (5.128) yields:

$$\frac{\phi(s)}{\delta_a(s)} = \frac{L_{\delta_a}}{(s^2 - sL_p)} \text{ and therefore}: \phi(s) = \frac{\delta_a}{s} \frac{L_{\delta_a}}{s(s - L_p)} \tag{5.131}$$

The reader is asked to show that by using Table C1 in Appendix C the time domain inverse for the bank angle response to a unit step input aileron deflection can be written as:

$$\phi(t) = -\left\{\frac{L_{\delta_a}\delta_a}{L_p}\right\}t + \left\{\frac{L_{\delta_a}\delta_a}{L_p^2}\right\}(e^{L_p t} - 1) \tag{5.132}$$

The predicted bank angle response is seen to consist of two parts: the first term is linear with time and the second term is exponential with time but will disappear for infinite time. Therefore, ultimately the bank angle will vary linearly with time. This, however, means that the airplane is in a constant roll rate maneuver. Figure 5.20 depicts how bank angle responds to a step aileron input and how roll rate responds to an aileron step input. Figure 5.21 shows what the roll mode looks like to an outside observer.

The roll rate is seen eventually to become constant. That eventual roll rate is called the maximum steady state roll rate for the particular magnitude of step aileron input. It is seen by differentiation of Eqn (5.132) that:

$$\dot{\phi}(t) = -\left\{\frac{L_{\delta_a}\delta_a}{L_p}\right\}(1 - e^{L_p t}) \tag{5.133}$$

From this equation it follows that the maximum steady state roll rate is given by:

$$\left\{\dot{\phi}(t)\right\}_{steady\ state} = \left\{\dot{\phi}\right\}_{ss} = -\left\{\frac{L_{\delta_a}\delta_a}{L_p}\right\} \tag{5.134}$$

Observe that when $t = T_r = \dfrac{-1}{L_p}$ is substituted into Eqn (5.133) the result is:

$$\dot{\phi}\left\{t = \frac{-1}{L_p}\right\} = -\left\{\frac{L_{\delta_a}\delta_a}{L_p}\right\}(1 - e^{-1}) = \dot{\phi}_{ss}(1 - \tfrac{1}{e}) = 0.63\dot{\phi}_{ss} \tag{5.135}$$

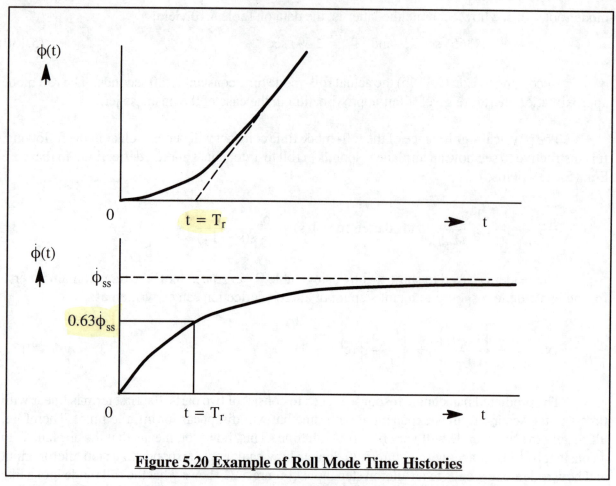

Figure 5.20 Example of Roll Mode Time Histories

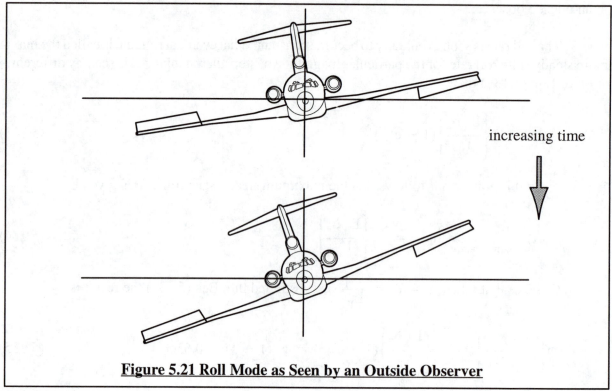

increasing time

Figure 5.21 Roll Mode as Seen by an Outside Observer

It is clear from Figure 5.20 that an airplane with a small roll–mode time constant, $T_r = \dfrac{-1}{L_p}$, will develop its commanded steady state roll rate quicker than an airplane with a large roll–mode time constant.

The bank angle response and roll rate response of airplanes is of prime concern to pilots. This is recognized by very strict minimum requirements for:

      *   bank angle reached in a given time as specified in civil flying quality regulations

and

      *   bank angle reached in a given time combined with a certain roll–mode time constant as specified in military flying quality regulations.

5.3.8   RESPONSE TO AILERON AND RUDDER STEP INPUTS

The response of the airplane to an arbitrary aileron or rudder input can be obtained by following the process suggested in Figure 5.17. To illustrate this process, consider the case of an aileron step input. The final value theorem (Eqn (C6) in Appendix C) will be used to find the magnitudes of the ultimate perturbation values of sideslip angle, β, bank angle, ϕ, and heading angle, ψ . The reader should verify the following expressions by referring to Table 5.9.

$$\lim_{t \to \infty} \beta(t) = \lim_{s \to 0} \left\{ s \frac{\delta_a N_\beta}{s \ D_2} \right\} = \frac{\delta_a D_\beta}{E_2} \approx \frac{\delta_a g(N_{\delta_a} L_r - L_{\delta_a} N_r)}{(L_\beta N_r - N_\beta L_r - N_{T_\beta} L_r)} \tag{5.136}$$

$$\lim_{t \to \infty} \phi(t) = \lim_{s \to 0} \left\{ s \frac{\delta_a N_\phi}{s \ D_2} \right\} = \frac{\delta_a C_\phi}{E_2} \approx$$

$$\approx \frac{\delta_a \left\{ - Y_\beta (N_{\delta_a} L_r - L_{\delta_a} N_r) + (U_1 - Y_r)(N_\beta L_{\delta_a} + N_{T_\beta} L_{\delta_a} - L_\beta N_{\delta_a}) \right\}}{g\cos\theta_1 (L_\beta N_r - N_\beta L_r - N_{T_\beta} L_r)} \tag{5.137}$$

$$\lim_{t \to \infty} \psi(t) = \lim_{s \to 0} \left\{ s \frac{\delta_a N_\psi}{s \ D_2} \right\} = \infty \tag{5.138}$$

To arrive at Eqn (5.136), the assumption $\theta_1 \approx 0$ was made. To arrive at Eqn (5.137), the assumption $Y_{\delta_a} \approx 0$ was made. The reason for the infinite heading angle is the fact that the free 's' in the denominator polynomial of the heading–to–aileron transfer function is not cancelled as is the case in the sideslip and bank angle transfer functions.

It is observed that for airplanes with exactly neutral spiral stability (i.e. $E_2 = 0$), the ultimate sideslip and bank angle response is infinite.

5.3.9   STANDARD FORMAT FOR THE LATERAL–DIRECTIONAL TRANSFER FUNCTIONS

For reasons which will become particularly clear in Chapter 8, it has been found useful to present airplane transfer functions in terms of their so–called 'standard formats'. In these standard formats the numerator and denominator polynomials of Table 5.9 are assumed to break down in a manner normally found for any given airplane. The standard format normally found for the lateral–directional transfer functions of inherently stable airplanes is given in Tables 5.12 and 5.13 in terms of Eqns (5.139) and (5.141) respectively.

It will be observed that the sideslip–to–aileron transfer function numerator breaks down into two first order terms. The sideslip–to–rudder transfer function numerator breaks down into three first order terms. The reason for the difference is that in the aileron case the assumption $Y_{\delta_a} \approx 0$ (i.e. no side–force due to aileron) was made. The consequence of this is to eliminate the coefficient A_β in the corresponding numerator polynomial. As a consequence the order of that numerator is reduced from three to two.

Numerical examples of these transfer functions for the case of the business jet are shown as Eqns (5.140) and (5.142) respectively. Note that for s=0 all components of the transfer function which depend on the Laplace variable s take on the value 1.0. Each transfer function, at s=0 takes on a value given by the ratio of the free coefficient in the numerator to the free coefficient in the denominator. These values are referred to as the zero–frequency gains of the transfer functions. For the lateral–directional transfer functions these zero–frequency gains (see Table 5.9) are found as:

$$K_{\beta_\delta} = \frac{D_\beta}{E_2} \qquad\qquad K_{\phi_\delta} = \frac{C_\phi}{E_2} \qquad\qquad K_{\psi_\delta} = \frac{D_\psi}{E_2} \qquad\qquad (5.143)$$

For the business jet example of Table 5.10 the corresponding values as indicated in Tables 5.12 and 5.13 are:

$$K_{\beta_{\delta_a}} = 23.4 \ \text{rad/rad} \qquad K_{\phi_{\delta_a}} = 12,359 \ \text{rad/rad} \qquad K_{\psi_{\delta_a}} = 580.4 \ \text{rad/rad}$$

and

$$K_{\beta_{\delta_r}} = -6.188 \ \text{rad/rad} \qquad K_{\phi_{\delta_r}} = -3,599 \ \text{rad/rad} \qquad K_{\psi_{\delta_r}} = -169.04 \ \text{rad/rad}$$

5.3.10 THE LATERAL–DIRECTIONAL MODE SHAPES

In Sub–sections 5.3.6 through 5.3.8 the spiral, roll and dutch roll approximations were introduced by assuming that various degrees of freedom were unimportant motion variables in those approximations. This begs the question: is it possible to predict whether or not one or more motion variables can be neglected in the dynamic response of an airplane. Such a prediction can be made with the help of a modal analysis.

For a given aileron, rudder or lateral gust input, the response of an airplane can be thought of as consisting of the simultaneous first and second order response of the variables sideslip angle, $\beta(t)$, bank angle, $\phi(t)$, and heading angle, $\psi(\tau)$. A lateral–directional mode shape can be described

Table 5.12 Standard Format for the Lateral–Directional Transfer Functions for Aileron Input

General Standard Format:

$$\frac{\beta(s)}{\delta_a(s)} = \frac{K_{\beta_{\delta_a}}(T_{\beta_{a_1}}s + 1)(T_{\beta_{a_2}}s + 1)}{(T_s s + 1)(T_r s + 1)\left(\frac{s^2}{\omega_{n_d}^2} + \frac{2\zeta_d s}{\omega_{n_d}} + 1\right)} \tag{5.139a}$$

$$\frac{\phi(s)}{\delta_a(s)} = \frac{K_{\phi_{\delta_a}}\left(\frac{s^2}{\omega_{n_{\phi a}}^2} + \frac{2\zeta_{\phi a} s}{\omega_{n_{\phi a}}} + 1\right)}{(T_s s + 1)(T_r s + 1)\left(\frac{s^2}{\omega_{n_d}^2} + \frac{2\zeta_d s}{\omega_{n_d}} + 1\right)} \tag{5.139b}$$

$$\frac{\psi(s)}{\delta_a(s)} = \frac{K_{\psi_{\delta_a}}(T_{\psi_a}s + 1)\left(\frac{s^2}{\omega_{n_{\psi a}}^2} + \frac{2\zeta_{\psi a} s}{\omega_{n_{\psi a}}} + 1\right)}{s(T_s s + 1)(T_r s + 1)\left(\frac{s^2}{\omega_{n_d}^2} + \frac{2\zeta_d s}{\omega_{n_d}} + 1\right)} \tag{5.139c}$$

Example Numerical Format for the Business Jet of Table 5.10:

$$\frac{\beta(s)}{\delta_a(s)} = \frac{23.4\left\{\left(\frac{1}{0.0782}\right)s + 1\right\}\left\{\left(\frac{1}{1.3362}\right)s + 1\right\}}{\left\{\left(\frac{1}{0.0010}\right)s + 1\right\}\left\{\left(\frac{1}{0.5003}\right)s + 1\right\}\left(\frac{s^2}{(1.6882)^2} + \frac{2(0.0387)s}{(1.6882)} + 1\right)} \tag{5.140a}$$

$$\frac{\phi(s)}{\delta_a(s)} = \frac{12,359\left(\frac{s^2}{1.6226^2} + \frac{2(0.0579)s}{(1.6226)} + 1\right)}{\left\{\left(\frac{1}{0.0010}\right)s + 1\right\}\left\{\left(\frac{1}{0.5003}\right)s + 1\right\}\left(\frac{s^2}{(1.6882)^2} + \frac{2(0.0387)s}{(1.6882)} + 1\right)} \tag{5.140b}$$

$$\frac{\psi(s)}{\delta_a(s)} = \frac{580.4\left\{\left(\frac{1}{-1.2147}\right)s + 1\right\}\left(\frac{s^2}{1.4596^2} + \frac{2(0.5909)s}{(1.6226)} + 1\right)}{s\left\{\left(\frac{1}{0.0010}\right)s + 1\right\}\left\{\left(\frac{1}{0.5003}\right)s + 1\right\}\left(\frac{s^2}{(1.6882)^2} + \frac{2(0.0387)s}{(1.6882)} + 1\right)} \tag{5.140c}$$

Table 5.13 Standard Format for the Lateral–Directional Transfer Functions for Rudder Input

General Standard Format:

$$\frac{\beta(s)}{\delta_r(s)} = \frac{K_{\beta_{\delta_r}}(T_{\beta_{r_1}}s + 1)(T_{\beta_{r_2}}s + 1)(T_{\beta_{r_3}}s + 1)}{(T_s s + 1)(T_r s + 1)\left(\dfrac{s^2}{\omega_{n_d}^2} + \dfrac{2\zeta_d s}{\omega_{n_d}} + 1\right)}$$

(5.141a)

$$\frac{\phi(s)}{\delta_r(s)} = \frac{K_{\phi_{\delta_r}}(T_{\phi_{r_1}}s + 1)(T_{\phi_{r_2}}s + 1)}{(T_s s + 1)(T_r s + 1)\left(\dfrac{s^2}{\omega_{n_d}^2} + \dfrac{2\zeta_d s}{\omega_{n_d}} + 1\right)}$$

(5.141b)

$$\frac{\psi(s)}{\delta_r(s)} = \frac{K_{\psi_{\delta_r}}(T_{\psi_r}s + 1)\left(\dfrac{s^2}{\omega_{n_{\psi r}}^2} + \dfrac{2\zeta_{\psi r}s}{\omega_{n_{\psi r}}} + 1\right)}{s(T_s s + 1)(T_r s + 1)\left(\dfrac{s^2}{\omega_{n_d}^2} + \dfrac{2\zeta_d s}{\omega_{n_d}} + 1\right)}$$

(5.141c)

Example Numerical Format for the Business Jet of Table 5.10:

$$\frac{\beta(s)}{\delta_r(s)} = \frac{-6.188\left\{\left(\dfrac{1}{-0.0114}\right)s + 1\right\}\left\{\left(\dfrac{1}{108.2}\right)s + 1\right\}\left\{\left(\dfrac{1}{0.4655}\right)s + 1\right\}}{\left\{\left(\dfrac{1}{0.0010}\right)s + 1\right\}\left\{\left(\dfrac{1}{0.5003}\right)s + 1\right\}\left(\dfrac{s^2}{(1.6882)^2} + \dfrac{2(0.0387)s}{(1.6882)} + 1\right)}$$

(5.142a)

$$\frac{\phi(s)}{\delta_r(s)} = \frac{-3,599\left\{\left(\dfrac{1}{-3.0413}\right)s + 1\right\}\left\{\left(\dfrac{1}{2.7189}\right)s + 1\right\}}{\left\{\left(\dfrac{1}{0.0010}\right)s + 1\right\}\left\{\left(\dfrac{1}{0.5003}\right)s + 1\right\}\left(\dfrac{s^2}{(1.6882)^2} + \dfrac{2(0.0387)s}{(1.6882)} + 1\right)}$$

(5.142b)

$$\frac{\psi(s)}{\delta_r(s)} = \frac{-169.04\left\{\left(\dfrac{1}{0.7307}\right)s + 1\right\}\left(\dfrac{s^2}{0.4456^2} + \dfrac{2(-0.2675)s}{(0.4456)} + 1\right)}{s\left\{\left(\dfrac{1}{0.0010}\right)s + 1\right\}\left\{\left(\dfrac{1}{0.5003}\right)s + 1\right\}\left(\dfrac{s^2}{(1.6882)^2} + \dfrac{2(0.0387)s}{(1.6882)} + 1\right)}$$

(5.142c)

by two quantities: one describes the relative magnitude of amplitudes in β, ϕ and ψ and the other describes the phase angles of these variables with respect to each other. The following analysis shows how such a mode shape can be determined and how such a mode shape can be used to decide whether or not an approximation (by discarding one or more motion variables) is acceptable.

Consider the perturbed equations of motion (5.96) in Table 5.8 and assume that the control power terms are left out. The remaining equations describe the dynamics of the unperturbed system. These equations are given as Eqns (5.144).

$$(sU_1 - Y_\beta)\beta(s) \qquad -(sY_p + g\cos\theta_1)\phi(s) \qquad s(U_1 - Y_r)\psi(s) = 0$$

$$-L_\beta\beta(s) \qquad +(s^2 - L_ps)\phi(s) \qquad -(s^2\overline{A}_1 + sL_r)\psi(s) = 0 \qquad (5.144)$$

$$-(N_\beta)\beta(s) \qquad -(s^2\overline{B}_1 + N_ps)\phi(s) \qquad (s^2 - sN_r)\psi(s) = 0$$

To reduce the amount of algebra, the thrust derivative, N_{T_β} , has been included in N_β .

One of the variables in Eqns (5.144) is now selected as the one against which the others are compared. The sideslip angle is arbitrarily selected to fulfill that role. Eqns (5.144) are now written in terms of the mode shapes $\phi(s)/\beta(s)$ and $\psi(s)/\beta(s)$ in the following manner:

$$-(sY_p + g\cos\theta_1)\frac{\phi(s)}{\beta(s)} \qquad s(U_1 - Y_r)\frac{\psi(s)}{\beta(s)} \qquad = \qquad (sU_1 - Y_\beta)$$

$$(s^2 - L_ps)\frac{\phi(s)}{\beta(s)} \qquad -(s^2\overline{A}_1 + sL_r)\frac{\psi(s)}{\beta(s)} \qquad = \qquad L_\beta \qquad (5.145)$$

$$-(s^2\overline{B}_1 + N_ps)\frac{\phi(s)}{\beta(s)} \qquad (s^2 - sN_r)\frac{\psi(s)}{\beta(s)} \qquad = \qquad N_\beta$$

To solve for the mode shapes, any two of the three equations (5.145) can be used. Using the second and third equations yields:

$$\frac{\phi(s)}{\beta(s)} = \frac{\begin{vmatrix} L_\beta & -(s^2\overline{A}_1 + sL_r) \\ N_\beta & (s^2 - sN_r) \end{vmatrix}}{\begin{vmatrix} (s^2 - L_ps) & -(s^2\overline{A}_1 + sL_r) \\ -(s^2\overline{B}_1 + N_ps) & (s^2 - sN_r) \end{vmatrix}} = \frac{a_1 s + b_1}{s(as^2 + bs + c)} \qquad (5.146)$$

and

$$\frac{\psi(s)}{\beta(s)} = \frac{\begin{vmatrix} (s^2 - L_p s) & L_\beta \\ - (s^2 \overline{B}_1 + N_p s) & N_\beta \end{vmatrix}}{\begin{vmatrix} (s^2 - L_p s) & - (s^2 \overline{A}_1 + s L_r) \\ - (s^2 \overline{B}_1 + N_p s) & (s^2 - s N_r) \end{vmatrix}} = \frac{a_2 s + b_2}{s(a s^2 + b s + c)} \qquad (5.147)$$

The polynomial coefficients in Eqns (5.146) and (5.147) are found by expansion of the determinants. The result is:

$$a = (1 - \overline{A}_1 \overline{B}_1) \qquad b = (- N_r - L_p - \overline{B}_1 L_r - N_p \overline{A}_1) \qquad c = (L_p N_r - L_r N_p)$$

$$a_1 = (L_\beta + \overline{A}_1 N_\beta) \qquad b_1 = (N_\beta L_r - L_\beta N_r) \qquad\qquad (5.148)$$

$$a_2 = N_\beta + \overline{B}_1 L_\beta) \qquad b_2 = L_\beta N_p - L_p N_\beta)$$

For the business jet example of Table 5.10 the following numerical values are found for these coefficients:

$$a = 0.9986 \qquad b = 0.5466 \qquad c = 0.0494$$

$$a_1 = - 4.0464 \qquad b_1 = - 0.0304 \qquad\qquad (5.149)$$

$$a_2 = 2.7441 \qquad b_2 = 1.2310$$

The mode shapes corresponding to the spiral, roll and dutch roll can now be computed by substituting the spiral, roll and dutch roll roots from Eqns (5.114) into Eqns (5.146) and (5.147). The following results are obtained:

$$\left(\frac{\phi(s)}{\beta(s)}\right)_{dutch\ roll} = 1.388 e^{j(-166.3/57.3)} \qquad \left(\frac{\psi(s)}{\beta(s)}\right)_{dutch\ roll} = 0.9823 e^{j(-1.1/57.3)}$$

$$\left(\frac{\phi(s)}{\beta(s)}\right)_{spiral} = + 541 \qquad\qquad \left(\frac{\psi(s)}{\beta(s)}\right)_{spiral} = - 25,170 \qquad (5.150)$$

$$\left(\frac{\phi(s)}{\beta(s)}\right)_{roll} = - 154 \qquad\qquad \left(\frac{\psi(s)}{\beta(s)}\right)_{roll} = + 11.0$$

These mode shapes are visualized in Figure 5.22 by using phasors and phase angles. The following conclusions are drawn relative to the actual mode shapes and the modal approximations discussed in Sub–sections 5.3.5 – 5.3.7:

1) For the dutch roll mode it is clear that none of the motion variables are negligible. The heading angle is seen to be of the same magnitude as the sideslip angle and lags 1 degree behind. It appears that the bank–angle lags 166.3 deg (about 180 deg.) behind the sideslip angle. The bank

angle magnitude is 1.4 times the magnitude of the sideslip angle. The latter ratio (known as the ϕ/β–ratio) plays an important role in airplane handling qualities. Dutch rolls are particularly objectionable if the ϕ/β–ratio is large!

2) For the spiral mode it is clear that the sideslip angle appears to be negligible. Bank angle is 180 degree out of phase with the heading angle. The spiral approximation therefore is reasonable.

3) For the roll mode, the sideslip angle participation is negligible. The heading angle participation is also small. The roll mode approximation is therefore reasonable.

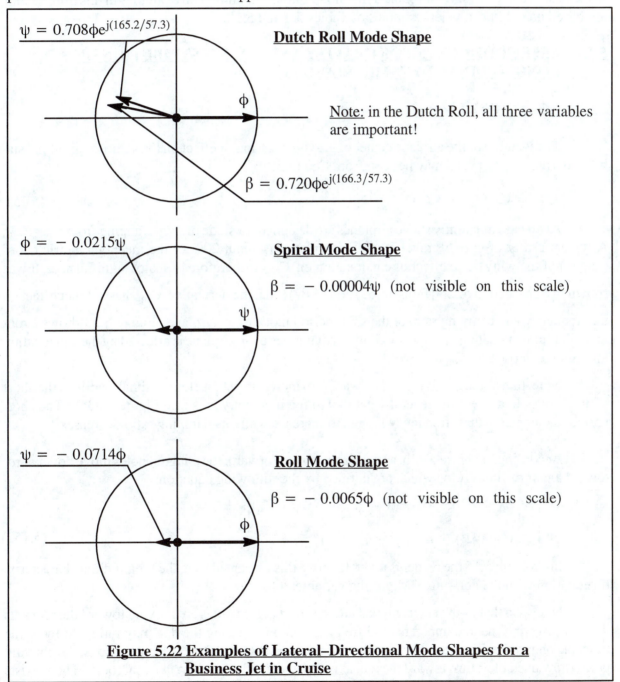

Figure 5.22 Examples of Lateral–Directional Mode Shapes for a Business Jet in Cruise

5.4 CENTER–OF–GRAVITY AND DERIVATIVE ROOT–LOCI AND THE ROLE OF SENSITIVITY ANALYSES

The purpose of this Section is to present and discuss the effect of varying the center–of–gravity location , the mass distribution and the stability derivatives on the dynamic stability characteristics of airplanes. A plot of frequency, damping ratio and/or inverse time constant versus any of these parameters is referred to as a sensitivity analysis. Such sensitivity analyses play an important role in the design and analysis of airplane dynamic stability. All numerical examples in this Sub–section are based on the business jet examples of Tables 5.4 and 5.10.

5.4.1 EFFECT OF CENTER OF GRAVITY AND MASS DISTRIBUTION ON LONGITUDINAL DYNAMIC STABILITY

Effect of C.G. Location

The location of the airplane center of gravity has a major effect on the static longitudinal stability derivative, C_{m_α} , as may be seen from Eqn (3.39):

$$C_{m_\alpha} = C_{L_\alpha}(\overline{x}_{cg} - \overline{x}_{ac_A}) \tag{5.151}$$

At aft c.g., inherently stable airplanes are designed for static margins ranging from 5%–10%. A typical center of gravity travel range for airplanes is about 20% of the mean geometric chord (m.g.c.) of the wing. The effect of c.g. location on C_{m_α} is therefore of major significance. It was shown in Sub–section 5.2.5 {Eqns (5.63) and (5.62)} that the derivative C_{m_α} has a direct effect on the frequency and damping ratio of the short period mode of an airplane. Figure 5.23 shows a root locus diagram indicating how the longitudinal dynamics of an airplane is affected by the c.g. location through the derivative C_{m_α}.

Note, that as the c.g. is moved forward (i.e. increasing static, longitudinal stability) the short period moves in a direction generally parallel to the imaginary axis (see Figure 5.23a). The short period undamped natural frequency is seen to increase while its damping ratio decreases.

According to Figure 5.23b, as the c.g. is moved forward, the phugoid poles move downward, toward a pair of finite zeros which are defined by the following equation:

$$(U_1 + Z_q)s^2 - \left\{ g\sin\theta_1 + (X_u + X_{T_u})(U_1 + Z_q) \right\}s +$$
$$+ \left\{ - gZ_u\cos\theta_1 + g(X_u + X_{T_U})\sin\theta_1 \right\} = 0 \tag{5.152}$$

In Problem 5.15 the reader is asked to prove this by considering the longitudinal characteristic equation with the derivative M_α as the variable.

Note also that as the c.g. is moved aft, the short period poles are moving toward the real axis thereby lowering the undamped natural frequency and increasing the damping ratio. At the same time, the phugoid poles move upward along the imaginary axis. After crossing this axis, the phugoid poles (now unstable!) turn toward the real axis and eventually split into two real roots. There exists a value for C_{m_α} for which the longitudinal characteristic equation has four real roots.

Stability and Control During Perturbed State Flight

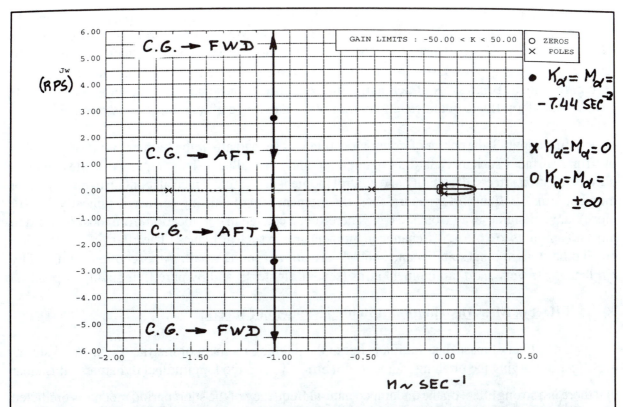

Figure 5.23a Effect of Center of Gravity Location on Longitudinal Characteristic Equation Roots (C.G. Root Locus: Short Period Resolution)

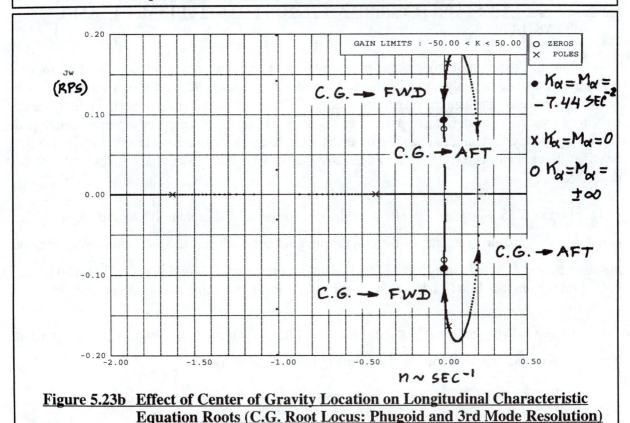

Figure 5.23b Effect of Center of Gravity Location on Longitudinal Characteristic Equation Roots (C.G. Root Locus: Phugoid and 3rd Mode Resolution)

By continuing to move the c.g. further aft, one real root moves toward positive infinity (divergence), one toward negative infinity (convergence) while the other two roots recombine into an oscillatory pair which is called the 'third oscillatory mode'. As the c.g. is moved aft toward infinity, these 3rd oscillatory poles move toward the same zero's given by Eqn (5.152). Most of this very aft c.g. root locus behavior **is of academic interest only** because airplanes develop unacceptable pilot–in–the–loop flying qualities long before such an extreme aft c.g. location is reached.

In Chapter 3, the center of gravity location was seen to affect the moment arms of a number of lifting surfaces such as canard, horizontal tail and vertical tail. This implies that the center of gravity location affects **all** stability and control moment derivatives since all contain expressions for moment arms. In transport type airplanes, the moment arm of a lifting surface is typically 3–5 (or more) m.g.c. lengths away from the c.g. Therefore, a change in c.g. location from most forward to most aft amounts to a 6% to 4% change in moment arm in such airplanes. The effect of c.g. location on all other longitudinal stability and control derivatives is quite small. An exception is formed by airplanes with very short tail moment arms (several fighters!) and by pure flying wing airplanes.

Effect of Mass Distribution: Pitching Moment of Inertia

The effect of mass distribution is felt in the pitching moment of inertia. Figure 5.24 shows the effect of varying the pitching moment of inertia, I_{yy}, on the longitudinal dynamics. It is clear that there is a strong effect on the undamped natural frequency of the short period mode {as predicted from Eqn (5.63)} but no appreciable effect on short period damping, nor on the phugoid dynamics.

5.4.2 EFFECT OF STABILITY DERIVATIVES ON LONGITUDINAL DYNAMIC STABILITY

During the preliminary design of new airplanes, in analyzing potential modifications for existing airplanes and in analyzing a competitor's airplane it is often desirable to understand which derivatives have a significant effect on airplane dynamics and which do not. The effect on dynamic stability of varying any derivative over a certain range can be represented by a plot of undamped natural frequency, damping ratio and/or inverse time constant as a function of variations in that derivative. Such a plot is referred to as a derivative sensitivity plot. Several examples will now be discussed.

Figure 5.25 illustrates the effect of the derivative, C_{L_α} (airplane lift–curve slope). It is noted that C_{L_α} has no appreciable effect on the phugoid nor on the undamped natural frequency of the short period. There is an appreciable effect on the short period damping ratio. This can be expected on the basis of Eqn (5.62) which contains C_{L_α} inside the dimensional derivative, Z_α.

Figure 5.26 depicts the effect of the derivative, C_{D_α} (induced drag derivative). It is seen that this derivative has an effect only on the damping ratio of the phugoid.

Figure 5.27 presents the effect of the derivative, C_{m_α} (static longitudinal stability derivative). It was already concluded that because of its dependence on the c.g. location, this derivative

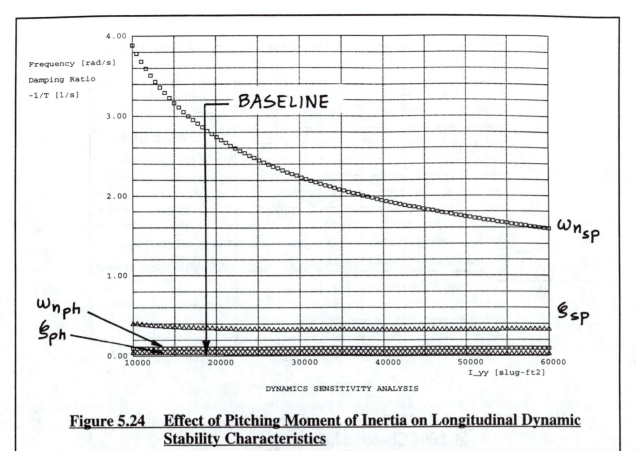

Figure 5.24   Effect of Pitching Moment of Inertia on Longitudinal Dynamic Stability Characteristics

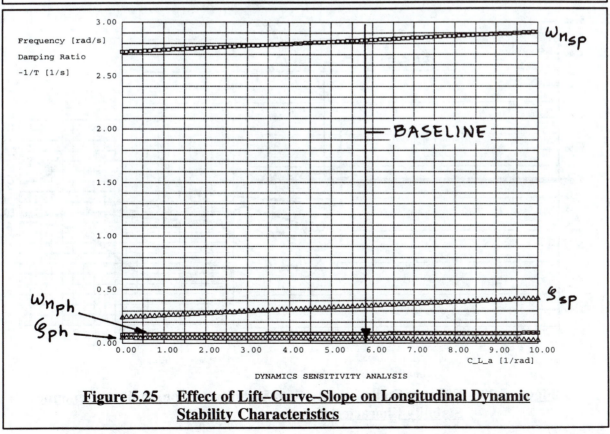

Figure 5.25   Effect of Lift–Curve–Slope on Longitudinal Dynamic Stability Characteristics

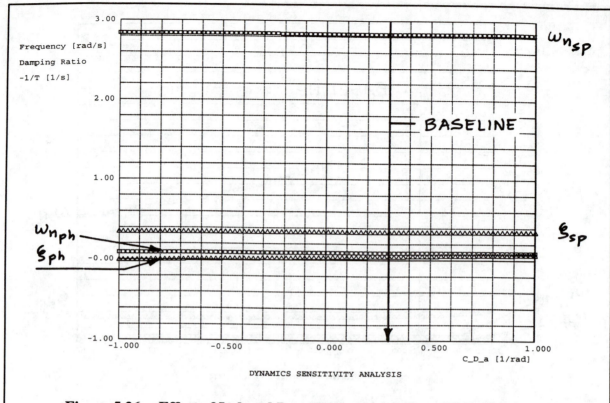

Figure 5.26   Effect of Induced Drag Derivative on Longitudinal Dynamic Stability Characteristics

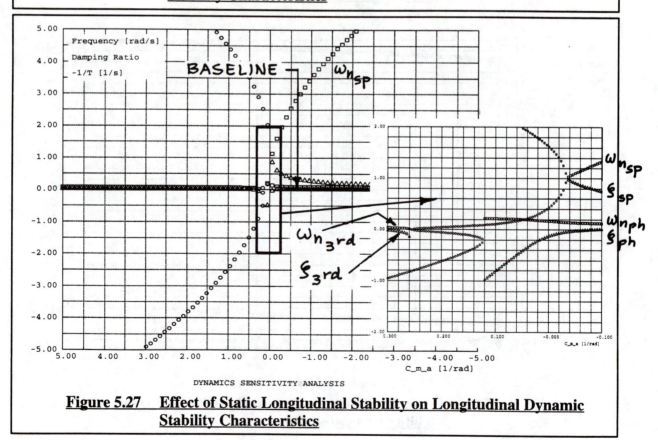

Figure 5.27   Effect of Static Longitudinal Stability on Longitudinal Dynamic Stability Characteristics

has an important effect on longitudinal dynamic stability. Figure 5.27 bears this out again. The reader is asked to show the connection between Figures 5.23 and 5.24!

Figure 5.28 illustrates the effect of the derivative C_{L_q}. Clearly, this derivative has no appreciable effect on any of the longitudinal modes. This information is useful in itself for two reasons:

1) spending much time and effort trying to estimate this derivative may not be worthwhile
2) feeding back pitch–rate to a control surface which affects lift only is not effective.

Figure 5.29 shows the powerful effect of the derivative C_{m_q} on the damping ratio of the short period mode. This effect is predicted by Eqn (5.62). Many high performance airplanes tend to develop poor short period damping which has a very negative effect on handling qualities. For that reason, pitch rate is often fed back to the elevator (or canard or stabilizer) to artificially enhance the damping. Such a system is called a pitch damper. Figure 5.29 clearly shows that if the sign of C_{m_q} reverses, the short period damping ratio becomes undamped. In actual pitch damper installations this can happen if either the gyro input or the pitch–damper–computer output are mis–wired. The synthesis of pitch dampers is discussed in Sub–section 5.5.1 and in detail in Chapter 11.

Figure 5.30 shows the effect of the tuck derivative, C_{m_u}, on longitudinal dynamics. Clearly, there is no effect on the short period dynamics but an important effect on the phugoid, both damping ratio and frequency. If an airplane develops transonic tuck (C_{m_u} becomes negative) it is seen that the phugoid splits into two real roots, one of which represents a divergence (the tuck mode !). Many high performance airplanes are equipped with a Mach–trim system to prevent such tuck.

small perturbation, lateral–directional equations of motion of the airplane are represented by Eqns (5.2). Two observations are in order:

5.4.3 EFFECT OF CENTER OF GRAVITY AND MASS DISTRIBUTION ON LATERAL–DIRECTIONAL DYNAMIC STABILITY

Effect of C.G. Location

The location of the airplane center of gravity has an effect on the vertical tail contribution to the static directional stability derivative, C_{n_β}, as may be seen from Eqn (3.85). In addition, the c.g. location does have an effect on the fuselage contribution to directional stability. The more aft the c.g. is the more unstable the fuselage contribution becomes.

At aft c.g., inherently stable airplanes are designed for static margins ranging from 5%–10%. A typical center of gravity travel range for airplanes is about 20% of the mean geometric chord (m.g.c.) of the wing. The effect of c.g. location on C_{n_β} is therefore not negligible. It was shown in Sub–section 5.3.5 {Eqns (5.119a) and (5.119b)} that the derivative C_{n_β} has a direct effect on the frequency and damping ratio of the dutch roll mode of an airplane. It was also shown in Sub–

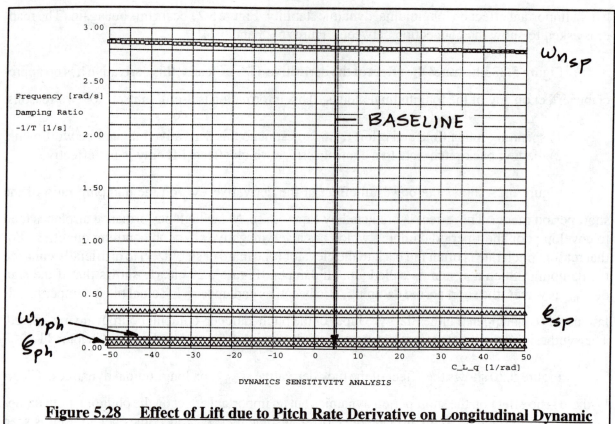

Figure 5.28   Effect of Lift due to Pitch Rate Derivative on Longitudinal Dynamic Stability Characteristics

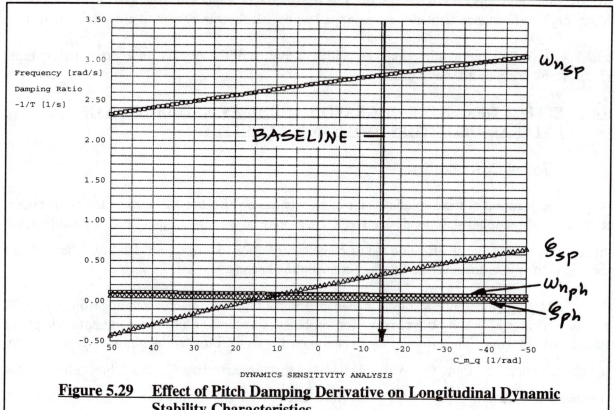

Figure 5.29   Effect of Pitch Damping Derivative on Longitudinal Dynamic Stability Characteristics

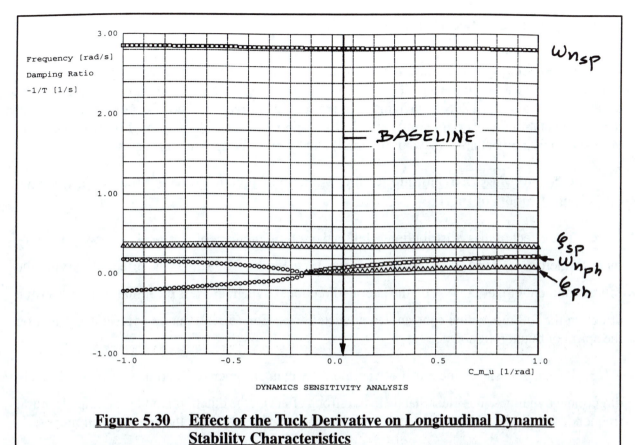

Figure 5.30   Effect of the Tuck Derivative on Longitudinal Dynamic Stability Characteristics

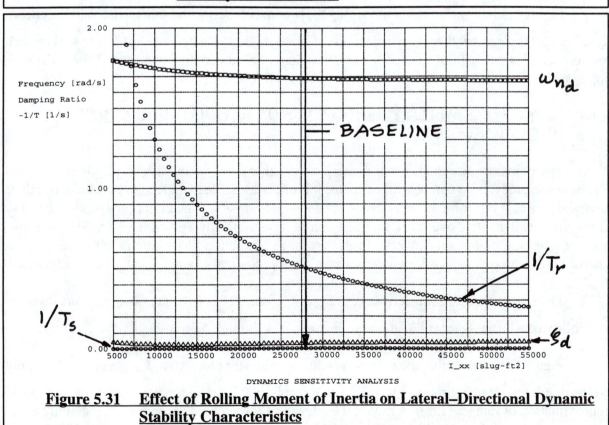

Figure 5.31   Effect of Rolling Moment of Inertia on Lateral–Directional Dynamic Stability Characteristics

section 5.3.6 that C_{n_β} affects the spiral mode directly.

In transport type airplanes, the moment arm of the vertical tail is typically 3–5 (or more) m.g.c. lengths away from the c.g. Therefore, a change in c.g. location from most forward to most aft amounts to a 6% to 4% change in moment arm in such airplanes. The effect of c.g. location on directional stability is therefore quite small. An important exception is formed by airplanes with very short tail moment arms (several fighters!) and by pure flying wing airplanes.

Effect of Mass Distribution: Rolling Moment of Inertia, Yawing Moment of Inertia and Product of Inertia

The effect of mass distribution is felt in the rolling moment of inertia, I_{xx}, the yawing moment of inertia, I_{zz}, and the product of inertia, I_{xz}. Figure 5.31 shows the effect of varying the rolling moment of inertia, I_{xx}, on the lateral–directional dynamics. It is clear that there is a strong effect on the roll mode time constant (as predicted from Eqn (5.129) but no appreciable effect on the spiral or dutch roll modes.

Figure 5.32 shows the effect of varying the yawing moment of inertia, I_{zz}, on the lateral–directional dynamics. It is clear that there is a strong effect on the dutch roll mode undamped natural frequency (as predicted from Eqn (5.121) but no appreciable effect on the spiral or roll modes.

Figure 5.33 shows the effect of varying the product of inertia, I_{xz}, on the lateral–directional dynamics. It is clear that there is no effect on the spiral mode and only a modest effect on the dutch roll mode undamped natural frequency as well as on the roll mode time constant. There is also an appreciable effect on the damping ratio of the dutch roll mode.

5.4.4 EFFECT OF STABILITY DERIVATIVES ON LATERAL–DIRECTIONAL DYNAMIC STABILITY

In preliminary design of new airplanes, in analyzing potential modifications for existing airplanes and in analyzing a competitor's airplane it is often desirable to understand which derivatives have a significant effect on airplane dynamics and which do not. The effect on dynamic stability of varying any derivative over a certain range can be represented by a plot of undamped natural frequency, damping ratio and/or inverse time constant as a function of variations in that derivative. Such a plot is referred to as a derivative sensitivity plot. Several examples will now be discussed.

The effect of the sideslip derivatives, C_{y_β}, C_{l_β} and C_{n_β} on the lateral–directional dynamic stability of a business jet is illustrated in Figures 5.34 through 5.36 respectively.

Figure 5.34 shows that the side–force–due–to–sideslip derivative, C_{y_β}, has an effect only on the dutch roll damping ratio. The reader will recall that this was predicted from the dutch roll approximation of Eqn (5.119b). A physical explanation for why the derivative C_{y_β} should be ex–

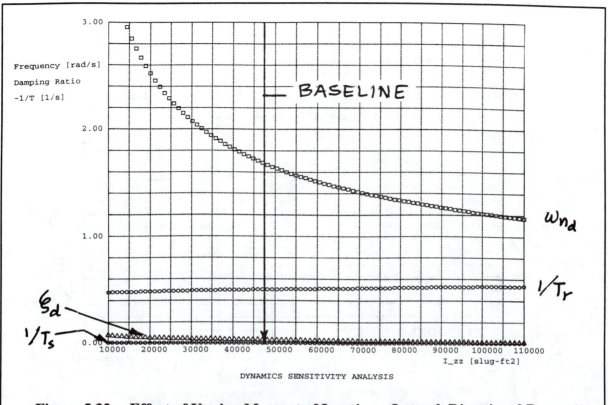

Figure 5.32   Effect of Yawing Moment of Inertia on Lateral–Directional Dynamic Stability Characteristics

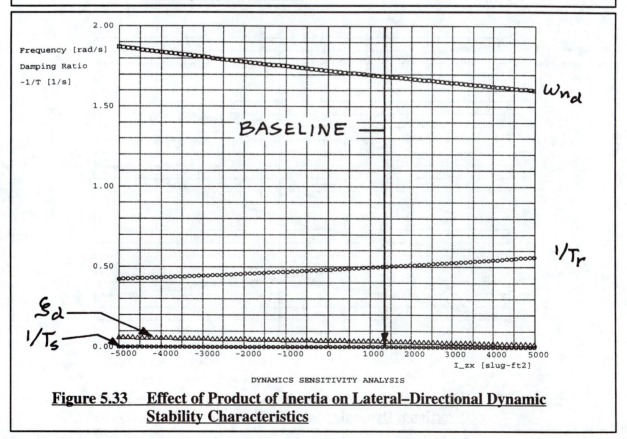

Figure 5.33   Effect of Product of Inertia on Lateral–Directional Dynamic Stability Characteristics

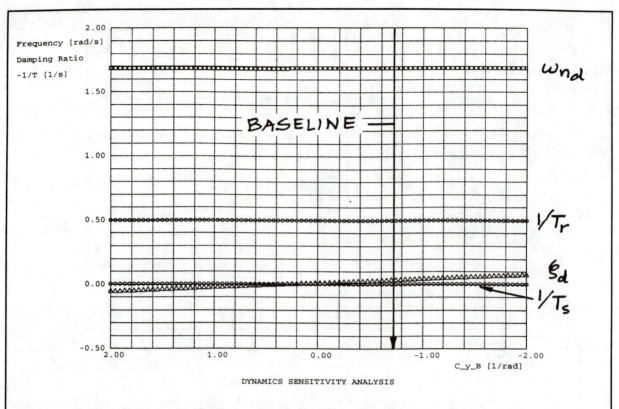

Figure 5.34   Effect of Side–force due to Sideslip Derivative on Lateral–Directional Dynamic Stability Characteristics

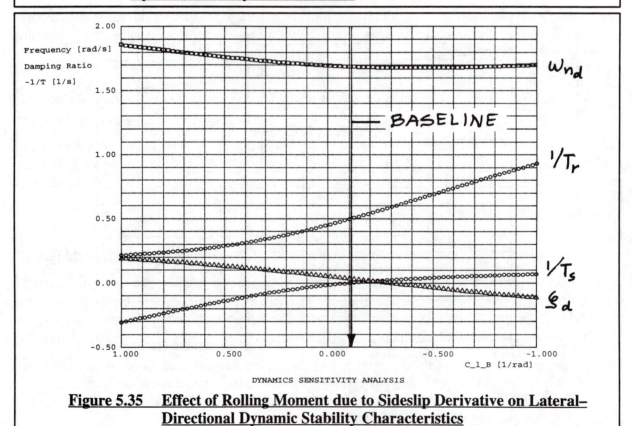

Figure 5.35   Effect of Rolling Moment due to Sideslip Derivative on Lateral–Directional Dynamic Stability Characteristics

pected to contribute to dutch roll damping follows from realizing that side–force due to sideslip can be thought of as a side–force which opposes the lateral velocity component $v = U_1\beta$. A force which opposes a velocity clearly qualifies as a damping force.

The effect of the airplane dihedral effect, C_{l_β}, on lateral–directional dynamic stability is shown in Figure 5.35. For the business jet example it is seen that increasing the dihedral effect (i.e. more negative C_{l_β}) has the following consequences:

1) Increased spiral stability

2) Decreased dutch roll damping ratio

3) Decreased roll time constant

Equation (5.127) shows that consequence 1) is predicted by the spiral mode approximation. Consequences 2) and 3) are not predicted by the dutch roll nor the roll approximation. The rolling moment due to sideslip term was neglected in both these approximations. This serves as a warning against assuming that modal approximations are acceptable for most airplane configurations!

The reader is reminded of the fact that the derivative C_{l_β} depends strongly on the geometric wing dihedral angle, Γ_w, and on the wing sweep angle, Λ_w. The wing sweep angle is usually determined by performance considerations (critical Mach number!). However, the wing dihedral angle can sometimes be used as a 'tailoring' device to achieve some desirable value of C_{l_β}, in turn to attain some balance between dutch–roll damping and spiral stability.

Figure 5.36 shows a derivative sensitivity plot indicating how the lateral–directional dynamics of an airplane is affected by the derivative C_{n_β}. This effect can be interpreted as a change in either c.g. location, as a change in vertical tail size or as a change in vertical tail lift–curve slope, through a change in the shape of the vertical tail (aspect ratio and sweep angle!). It is clear that C_{n_β} has a significant effect on the undamped natural frequency of the dutch roll. With the vertical tail gone (this makes C_{n_β} negative).

The effect of the directional stability derivative, C_{n_β}, on dynamic lateral–directional stability is depicted in Figure 5.36. It is clear that increased directional stability (i.e. increased vertical tail effectiveness) has a strong effect on the dutch roll undamped natural frequency as predicted by Eqn (5.119a) in the dutch roll approximation. For positive directional stability there is no effect on the other lateral–directional dynamic stability parameters. However, as C_{n_β} becomes negative, the dutch roll mode becomes negatively damped and then splits into two real roots: one is divergent, the other moves toward s=0. The spiral root becomes very stable while the roll mode time constant increases: the roll root moves toward the origin. This latter effect and the divergent root cause the flying quality behavior of the airplane to be unacceptable.

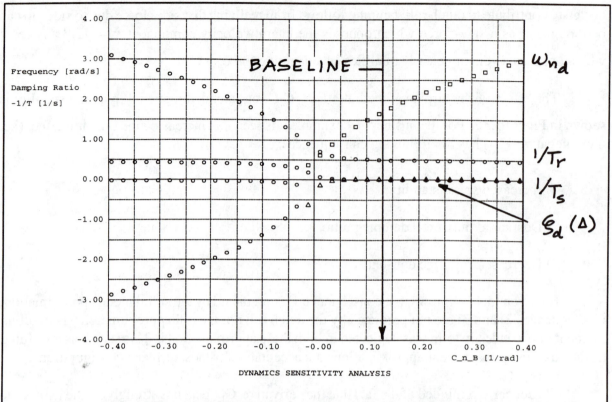

Figure 5.36   Effect of Yawing Moment due to Sideslip Derivative on Lateral-Directional Dynamic Stability Characteristics

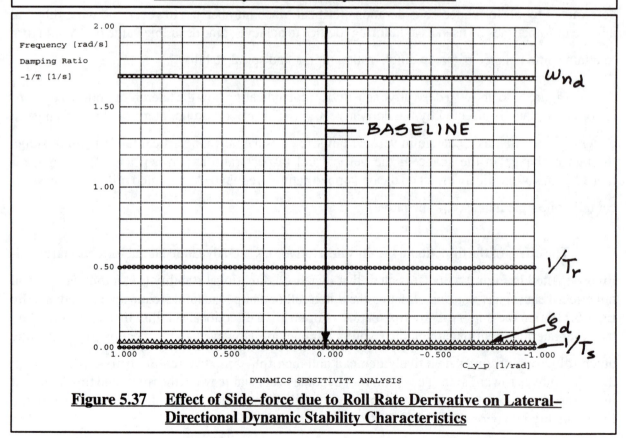

Figure 5.37   Effect of Side-force due to Roll Rate Derivative on Lateral-Directional Dynamic Stability Characteristics

The effect of the roll rate derivatives, C_{y_p}, C_{l_p} and C_{n_p} on the lateral–directional dynamic stability of a business jet is shown in Figures 5.37 through 5.39 respectively.

Figure 5.37 indicates that the side–force–due–to–roll–rate derivative, C_{y_p}, has no appreciable effect on dynamic stability. This derivative is also difficult to estimate accurately. This is not usually a problem because it is of very little consequence to dynamic stability.

The effect of the roll–damping derivative, C_{l_p}, on lateral–directional dynamic stability is shown in Figure 5.38a. Under attached flow conditions this derivative is always negative. It has a strong effect on the roll mode time constant as predicted from the roll mode approximation {see Eqn (5.129)}. Even under attached flow conditions, it is possible that the equivalent roll damping derivative, C_{l_p}, of an airplane can be artificially driven positive by a mis–wired roll damper. In that case, as seen in Figure 5.38b (which is an enlargement of the area around the origin in Figure 5.38a), the roll mode and the spiral combine into a so–called lateral phugoid which becomes undamped as C_{l_p} becomes more positive and which eventually splits back into two real roots, one of which gives rise to a pure divergence.

The effect of the yawing–moment–due–to–roll–rate derivative, C_{n_p}, on lateral–directional dynamic stability is illustrated in Figure 5.39. This derivative appears to have no effect on the spiral mode, no effect on the dutch roll undamped natural frequency and a weak effect on the dutch roll damping ratio and the roll mode time constant.

The effect of the yaw rate derivatives, C_{y_r}, C_{l_r} and C_{n_r} on the lateral–directional dynamic stability of a business jet is shown in Figures 5.40 through 5.42 respectively.

As seen in Figure 5.40 the side–force–due–to–yaw–rate derivative, C_{y_r}, has no appreciable effect on any of the lateral–directional modes.

Figure 5.41 indicates that the rolling–moment–due–to–yaw–rate derivative, C_{l_r}, has an appreciable effect only on the spiral mode. This is also predicted from the spiral mode approximation {see Eqn (5.127)}.

The yaw–damping (or yawing–moment–due–to–yaw–rate) derivative, C_{n_r}, according to Figure 5.42 has a significant effect on the dutch roll damping ratio as predicted from the dutch roll approximation, Eqn (5.119b). In fact, many high performance airplanes require yaw damping to improve the inherently poorly damped dutch roll mode. A yaw damper can be thought of as artificially augmenting the derivative C_{n_r} as will be seen in Sub–section 5.5.2.

Figure 5.42 also shows that the derivative C_{n_r} affects the spiral mode. This is predicted by the spiral mode approximation as seen from Eqn (5.127).

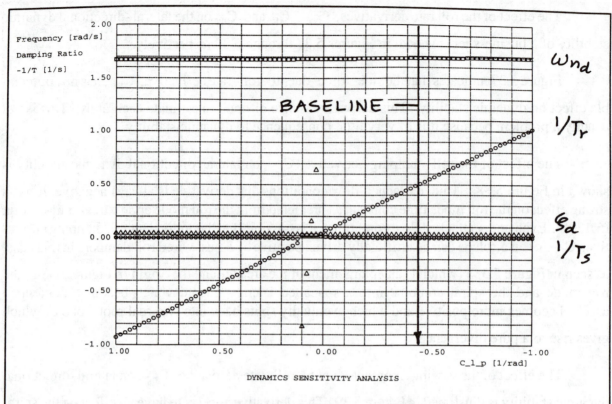

Figure 5.38a Effect of Rolling Moment due to Roll Rate Derivative on Lateral–Directional Dynamic Stability Characteristics

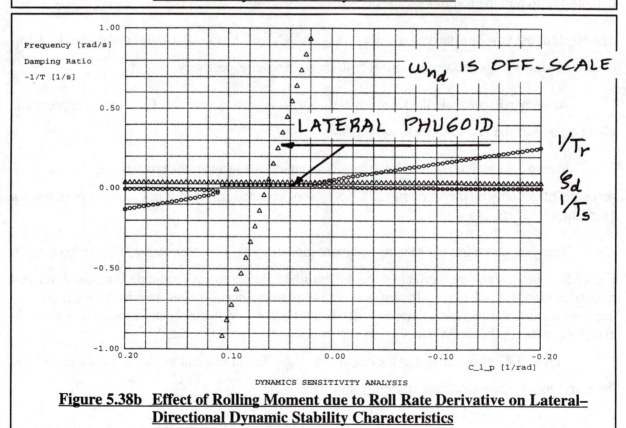

Figure 5.38b Effect of Rolling Moment due to Roll Rate Derivative on Lateral–Directional Dynamic Stability Characteristics

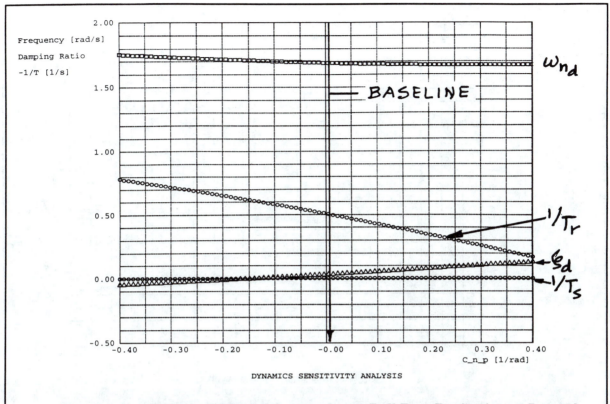

Figure 5.39   Effect of Yawing Moment due to Roll Rate Derivative on Lateral–Directional Dynamic Stability Characteristics

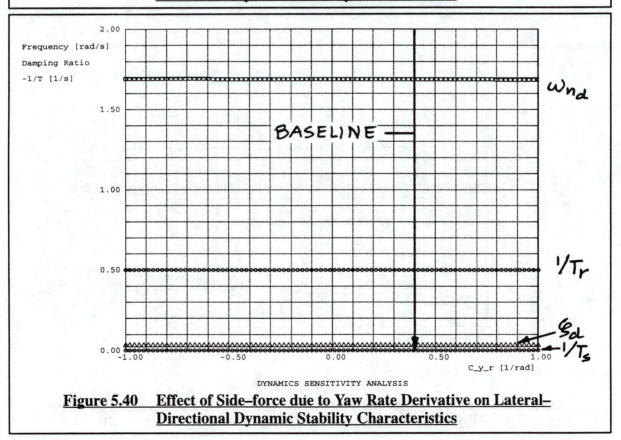

Figure 5.40   Effect of Side–force due to Yaw Rate Derivative on Lateral–Directional Dynamic Stability Characteristics

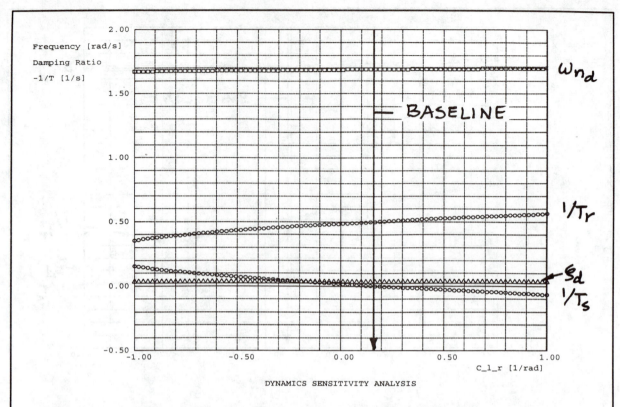

Figure 5.41 **Effect of Rolling Moment due to Yaw Rate Derivative on Lateral–Directional Dynamic Stability Characteristics**

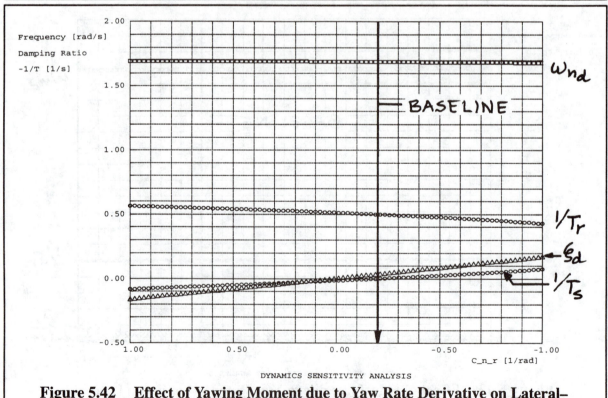

Figure 5.42 **Effect of Yawing Moment due to Yaw Rate Derivative on Lateral–Directional Dynamic Stability Characteristics**

5.5   EQUIVALENT STABILITY DERIVATIVES, STABILITY AUG–MENTATION AND DEPENDENCE ON CONTROL POWER

Many high performance airplanes (such as business jets, transport jets, fighters and bombers are found to be deficient in either static stability or dynamic stability. A fundamental reason for why this should be expected is to be found in the approximate equations for undamped natural frequencies, all of which tend toward zero for large inertias and low dynamic pressures. When the fundamental motion frequencies become too small, airplanes tend to become sluggish. In fact, as will be seen in Chapter 6, the handling quality requirements for military airplanes require that these motion frequencies not be less than some minimum value. Deficiencies in the damping ratio of the short period and the dutch roll as well as the roll–mode time constant occur at low dynamic pressures.

For a given motion frequency, the numerator damping terms in all approximations for damping ratio tend toward zero. As will also be shown in Chapter 6, the handling quality requirements for military airplanes require that these damping ratios not be less than some minimum value.

To 'fix' problems of inherent static or dynamic stability by changes in the configuration design is sometimes possible but often results in unacceptable increases in weight and drag and thereby in loss of performance. Nevertheless, in certain classes of airplane this approach can be taken and this is discussed also Chapter 6.

In high performance airplanes the 'fix' often is the installation of stability augmentation systems (SAS). These can take the form of pitch dampers, yaw dampers, roll dampers, angle–of–attack feedback and/or angle–of–sideslip feedback. The subject of analysis and synthesis of augmentation systems using classical control theory is taken up in Chapters 8 and 11. In this section, the idea of stability augmentation is discussed from a viewpoint of so–called 'equivalent stability derivatives'. Fundamental to this idea is the assumption that control surface actuators, feedback control computers and any required sensors are infinitely fast. This is called the no–lag assumption. In that case the action of the stability augmentation system can be thought of as a superposition of the inherent stability derivative of an airplane and the contribution to that derivative by the idealized stability augmentation system. The sum of these derivative contributions is called an 'equivalent stability derivative'.

Three examples will be discussed: pitch damping, yaw damping and angle–of–attack feedback. Requirements for pitch and yaw damping are commonly encountered by current high performance airplanes, even those with inherent stability. A requirement for angle of attack feedback does normally arise only with inherently unstable airplanes.

5.5.1   EQUIVALENT PITCH DAMPING DERIVATIVE

According to Table 5.4 the inherent damping ratio of the short period is $\zeta_{sp} = 0.35$. This magnitude of short period damping ratio is marginally acceptable. Assume that it is desired to improve this damping ratio to a target value of $\zeta_{sp} = 0.65$. Referring to the pitch damping derivative sensitivity plot of Figure 5.29, it is seen that this would require a change in the derivative C_{m_q} from its inherent airplane value of –15.5 to an equivalent derivative (augmented) value of –50.0. The difference is to be generated by a pitch damper which will be assumed to operate by moving the elevator in linear proportion to any pitch rate perturbation (such as induced by turbulence in the atmosphere) but such that any pitch rate perturbation is opposed. These statements can be cast in the following mathematical form:

$$C_{m_{q_{SAS-on}}} = C_{m_{q_{inherent}}} + \Delta C_{m_{q_{SAS}}} \tag{5.153}$$

The derivative $C_{m_{q_{SAS-on}}}$ is referred to as an equivalent stability derivative. The input due to the SAS, $\Delta C_{m_{q_{SAS}}}$, is determined from:

$$\Delta C_{m_{q_{SAS}}} \left(\frac{q\bar{c}}{2U_1} \right) = C_{m_{\delta_e}} \Delta \delta_{e_{SAS}} \tag{5.154}$$

so that:

$$\Delta \delta_{e_{SAS}} = K_q q \tag{5.155}$$

Eqn (5.155) should be thought of as the **idealized control law** for the pitch damper. A positive pitch rate perturbation will require a positive (i.e. trailing edge down) elevator deflection, to oppose the pitch rate because the control power derivative $C_{m_{\delta_e}}$ is itself negative {See Eqn (3.37)}.

The constant of proportionality, K_q, is called the pitch–rate–to–elevator feedback gain. This feedback gain can be determined from Eqns (5.153), (5.154) and (5.155) as:

$$K_q = \frac{\Delta C_{m_{q_{SAS}}} \bar{c}}{2U_1 C_{m_{\delta_e}}} = \frac{(C_{m_{q_{SAS-on}}} - C_{m_{q_{inherent}}})\bar{c}}{2U_1 C_{m_{\delta_e}}} \tag{5.156}$$

For the example business jet of Table 5.5 it is found that:

$$K_q = \frac{(-50.0 + 15.5)x7.04}{2x400x1.688x(-1.52)} = 0.12 \ \text{deg/deg/sec} \tag{5.157}$$

In this flight condition, a pitch rate of 3 deg/sec would already be considered a large pitch rate perturbation. The pitch damper would command 3x0.12=0.36 degrees of elevator deflection which is quite acceptable.

Eqn (5.157) represents a first order estimate of the pitch damper feedback gain required for the business jet example in the flight condition of Table 5.4. Note, that to arrive at this estimate of pitch damper feedback gain, knowledge of automatic control theory is not required! If the gain estimated from Eqn (5.157) were to come out very high, say 10 deg/deg/sec a pitch a 3 deg/sec pitch rate perturbation would require an elevator deflection of 30 degrees. That would be absurdly high and a signal to the designer that either the assumed pitch rate perturbation is too high or the airplane does not have adequate control power (i.e. the derivative $C_{m_{\delta_e}}$ is too small!).

In many instances it is necessary to limit the control deflection authority which is assigned to a damping device, such as a pitch damper. An example is shown in Figure 5.43. If the pitch damper authority over the elevator is limited to, say 5 degrees, the damper becomes saturated as soon as the 5 degree deflection is reached.

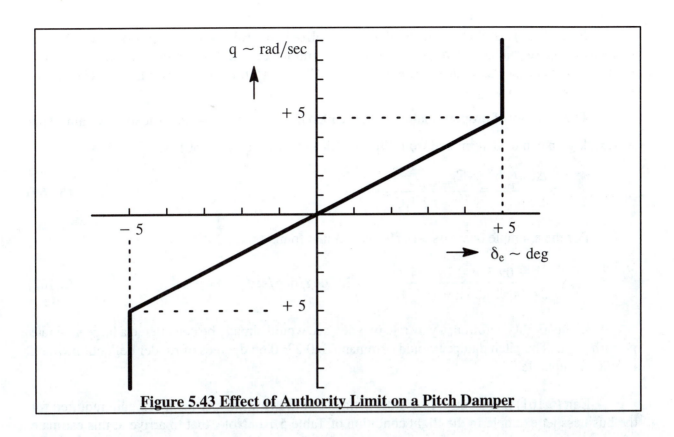

Figure 5.43 Effect of Authority Limit on a Pitch Damper

5.5.2   EQUIVALENT YAW DAMPING DERIVATIVE

According to Table 5.10 the inherent damping ratio of the dutch roll is $\zeta_d = 0.04$. This magnitude of dutch roll damping ratio is unacceptably low. Assume that it is desired to improve this damping ratio to a target value of $\zeta_{sp} = 0.15$. Referring to the yaw damping derivative sensitivity plot of Figure 5.42, it is seen that this would require a change in the derivative C_{n_r} from its inherent airplane value of –0.20 to an equivalent derivative (augmented) value of –0.85. The difference is to be generated by a yaw damper which will be assumed to operate by moving the rudder in linear proportion to any yaw rate perturbation (such as induced by turbulence in the atmosphere) but such that any yaw rate perturbation is opposed. These statements can be cast in the following mathematical form:

$$C_{n_{r_{SAS-on}}} = C_{n_{r_{inherent}}} + \Delta C_{n_{r_{SAS}}} \tag{5.158}$$

The derivative $C_{n_{r_{SAS-on}}}$ is referred to as an equivalent stability derivative. The input due to the SAS, $\Delta C_{n_{r_{SAS}}}$ is determined from:

$$\Delta C_{n_{r_{SAS}}} \left(\frac{rb}{2U_1} \right) = C_{n_{\delta_r}} \Delta \delta_{r_{SAS}} \tag{5.159}$$

so that:

$$\Delta \delta_{r_{SAS}} = K_r r \tag{5.160}$$

Eqn (5.160) should be thought of as the **idealized control law** for the yaw damper. A positive yaw rate perturbation will require a positive (i.e. trailing edge left) elevator deflection, to oppose the yaw rate because the control power derivative $C_{n_{\delta_r}}$ is itself negative {See Eqn (3.87)}.

The constant of proportionality, K_r, is called the yaw–rate–to–rudder feedback gain. This feedback gain can be determined from Eqns (5.158), (5.159) and (5.160) as:

$$K_r = \frac{\Delta C_{n_{r_{SAS}}} b}{2U_1 C_{n_{\delta_r}}} = \frac{(C_{n_{r_{SAS-on}}} - C_{n_{r_{inherent}}})\bar{c}}{2U_1 C_{n_{\delta_r}}} \tag{5.161}$$

For the example business jet of Table 5.5 it is found that:

$$K_r = \frac{(-0.85 + 0.20)\text{x}34.2}{2\text{x}400\text{x}1.688\text{x}(-0.0747)} = 0.22 \text{ deg/deg/sec} \tag{5.162}$$

In this flight condition, a yaw rate of 3 deg/sec would already be considered a large yaw rate perturbation. The pitch damper would command 3x0.22=0.66 degrees of rudder deflection which is quite acceptable.

Eqn (5.161) represents a first order estimate of the yaw damper feedback gain required for the business jet example in the flight condition of Table 5.10. Note, that to arrive at this estimate of yaw damper feedback gain, knowledge of automatic control theory is not required! If the gain estimated from Eqn (5.161) were to come out very high, say 10 deg/deg/sec a pitch a 3 deg/sec pitch rate perturbation would require an rudder deflection of 30 degrees. That would be absurdly high and a signal to the designer that either the assumed yaw rate perturbation is too high or the airplane does not have adequate control power (i.e. the derivative $C_{n_{\delta_r}}$ is too small!).

5.5.3   EQUIVALENT LONGITUDINAL STABILITY DERIVATIVE

According to Table 5.5 the jet fighter is inherently unstable with a static longitudinal stability derivative of $C_{m_\alpha} = +0.348$. This airplane was also seen to have an unconventional root break-down: an unstable real root (divergence), a stable real root and a third oscillatory mode. As will be seen in Chapter 6, a fighter must satisfy certain minimum requirements on the magnitude of its undamped natural frequency of the short period oscillation. For this example it will be assumed that $\omega_{n_{sp}} > 1.2$ rad/sec meets this frequency requirement. To achieve this level of undamped natural frequency, Eqn (5.63) is used to estimate the magnitude of the required equivalent longitudinal stability derivative:

$$C_{m_{\alpha_{SAS-on}}} = \frac{-(\omega_{n_{sp_{reqd}}})^2 I_{yy}}{\bar{q}_1 S\bar{c}} \tag{5.163}$$

For the example fighter this yields:

$$C_{m_{\alpha_{SAS-on}}} = \frac{-\left((1.2)^2 x 23,575\right)}{175.3 x 302 x 13.5} = -0.047 \quad 1/rad \tag{5.164}$$

The stability augmentation system in this case is required to generate the following:

$$\Delta C_{m_{\alpha_{SAS}}} = C_{m_{\alpha_{SAS-on}}} - C_{m_{\alpha_{inherent}}} \tag{5.165}$$

The derivative $C_{m_{\alpha_{SAS-on}}}$ is referred to as an equivalent stability derivative. The input due to the SAS, $\Delta C_{m_{\alpha_{SAS}}}$, is obtained by signalling the canard to move in such a manner as to oppose exactly any pitching moment coefficient generated by an angle of attack disturbance due to turbulence $\Delta\alpha_{turb.}$. Therefore:

$$\Delta C_{m_{\alpha_{SAS}}} \Delta\alpha_{turb.} = C_{m_{\delta_c}} \Delta\delta_{c_{SAS}} \tag{5.166}$$

The canard will be assumed to move in linear proportion to any angle–of–attack disturbance so that the following idealized control law applies:

$$\Delta\delta_{c_{SAS}} = K_\alpha \Delta\alpha_{turb.} \tag{5.167}$$

By combining Eqns (5.166) and (5.167) the required angle–of–attack–to–canard feedback gain, K_α , is found:

$$K_\alpha = \frac{\Delta C_{m_{\alpha_{SAS}}}}{C_{m_{\delta_c}}} \tag{5.168}$$

For the example fighter airplane of Table 5.10 it is found that:

$$K_\alpha = \frac{-0.047 - 0.348}{0.22} = -1.8 \quad deg/deg \tag{5.169}$$

In the cruise flight condition, if the airplane encounters a vertical gust of 22 ft/sec, the resulting induced angle of attack is 22/516x1.688 = 1.4 deg. This would give rise to a canard deflection command of –0.8 degrees which is acceptable.

The reader will by now realize that the magnitude of feedback gain required in any stability augmentation system depends strongly on the magnitude of available control power. During the preliminary design stage of an airplane it is therefore essential to determine whether or not any feedback gain requirements are reasonable from a physical viewpoint.

5.6   INERTIAL COUPLING DUE TO ROLL RATE AND PITCH RATE

All discussions of dynamic stability of airplanes up to this point have been based on motion perturbations relative to a steady state, straight line flight condition. For perturbed flight relative to a steady state, maneuvering flight condition (such as steady turns and steady pull–ups) the corresponding steady state angular rates P_1 , Q_1 and R_1 must be included in the perturbed equations of motion. That was the case with Eqns (1.75) and (1.76). In this Section the following cases will be considered:

* The effect of large steady state roll rate, P_1 , on dynamic stability, also referred to as inertial coupling due to roll rate is discussed in Sub–section 5.6.1

* The effect of large steady state pitch rate, Q_1 , on dynamic stability, also referred to as inertial coupling due to pitch rate is discussed in Sub–section 5.6.2

Examining Eqns (5.76) it is seen that the effect of non–zero steady state angular rates is to introduce additional moments into the three moment equations. These additional moments are all seen to be proportional to moments and/or products of inertia. That is why these effects are referred to as 'inertial–coupling effects'.

5.6.1   INERTIAL COUPLING DUE TO ROLL RATE

To analyze the dynamic stability of an airplane in the presence of large steady state roll rates, P_1 , the mathematical model of Ref. 5.9 will be used. In Ref. 5.9, H. Phillips assumes that the following assumptions can be made about the flight path of an airplane in a large steady state roll rate maneuver:

Assumption 1: the center of gravity of the airplane traverses a straight, horizontal line.

Assumption 2: any roll rate perturbations relative to the large steady state roll rate, P_1 , can be neglected.

Assumption 3: steady state pitch rate, Q_1 , and steady state yaw rate, R_1 , are both zero.

Assumption 4: the product of inertia, I_{xz} , is negligible.

The consequence of Assumption 1 is that the drag, lift and side force equations of motion can be dropped, since their solution is pre–supposed to be a straight line flight path.

The consequence of Assumption 2 is that the rolling moment equation can be dropped, since its solution is pre–supposed to be a constant roll rate.

Therefore, only the pitching and yawing equations of motion: (1.76b) and (1.76c) are required in the study of the dynamic stability of the fast rolling airplane. These equations, with introduction of Assumptions 3 and 4 included, can be written as follows:

$$I_{yy}\dot{q} + (I_{xx} - I_{zz})P_1 r = m_A + m_T \tag{5.170}$$

$$I_{zz}\dot{r} + (I_{yy} - I_{xx})P_1 q = n_A + n_T \tag{5.171}$$

To simplify the notation, the effect of the thrust moments will be assumed added to the aerodynamic moments. Next, Eqns (5.170) and (5.171) are divided by I_{yy} and I_{zz} respectively. By also introducing the appropriate dimensional stability derivatives from Tables 5.1 and 5.7 it is found that:

$$\dot{q} + \frac{(I_{xx} - I_{zz})}{I_{yy}}P_1 r = M_\alpha \alpha + M_{\dot{\alpha}}\dot{\alpha} + M_q q \tag{5.172}$$

$$\dot{r} + \frac{(I_{yy} - I_{xx})}{I_{zz}}P_1 q = N_\beta \beta + N_{\dot{\beta}}\dot{\beta} + N_r r \tag{5.173}$$

These two equations have four perturbation variables q, r, α and β. This number of variables must be reduced to two. That can be done by referring to Figure 5.44.

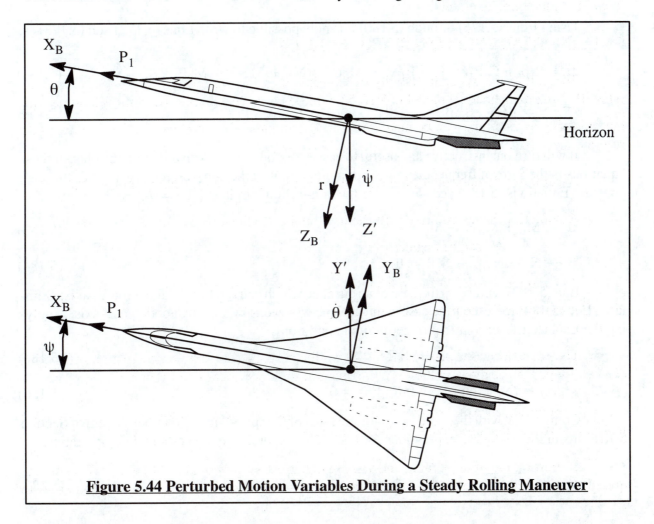

Figure 5.44 Perturbed Motion Variables During a Steady Rolling Maneuver

From Figure 5.44 using the assumption that all perturbed angles are small it is seen that:

$$\dot{\psi} = r\cos\theta - P_1\sin\theta \approx r - P_1\theta \tag{5.174}$$

$$\dot{\theta} = q\cos\psi + P_1\sin\psi \approx q + P_1\psi \tag{5.175}$$

After differentiation and re–arrangement this yields:

$$\dot{r} = \ddot{\psi} + P_1\dot{\theta} \tag{5.176}$$

$$\dot{q} = \ddot{\theta} - P_1\dot{\psi} \tag{5.177}$$

Because of Assumption 1 (straight line, horizontal flight path) it is further permissible to write:

$$\theta = \alpha \text{ and thus } \dot{\theta} = \dot{\alpha} \text{ and}: \ddot{\theta} = \ddot{\alpha} \tag{5.178}$$

$$\psi = -\beta \text{ and thus } \dot{\psi} = -\dot{\beta} \text{ and } \ddot{\psi} = -\ddot{\beta} \tag{5.179}$$

To simplify the notation, the following quantities are introduced:

$$C_1 = \frac{(I_{xx} - I_{zz})}{I_{yy}} \quad \text{and} \quad D_1 = \frac{(I_{yy} - I_{xx})}{I_{zz}} \tag{5.180}$$

Using Eqns (5.176) through (5.180) it is now possible to write Eqns (5.172) and (5.173) as:

$$\ddot{\alpha} + P_1\dot{\beta} + C_1P_1(-\dot{\beta} + P_1\alpha) = M_\alpha\alpha + (M_q + M_{\dot{\alpha}})\dot{\alpha} + M_qP_1\beta \tag{5.181}$$

$$-\ddot{\beta} + P_1\dot{\alpha} + D_1P_1(\dot{\alpha} + P_1\beta) = N_\beta\beta - (N_r - N_{\dot{\beta}})\dot{\beta} + N_rP_1\alpha \tag{5.182}$$

It will turn out instructive and useful to cast the aerodynamic derivatives on the r.h.s. of these equations in the form of frequencies and/or damping ratios of the non–rolling airplane. To this end, consider Equations (5.181) and (5.182) for the non–rolling airplane ($P_1 = 0$):

$$\ddot{\alpha} - (M_q + M_{\dot{\alpha}})\dot{\alpha} - M_\alpha\alpha = 0 \tag{5.183}$$

$$\ddot{\beta} - (N_r - N_{\dot{\beta}})\dot{\beta} + N_\beta\beta = 0 \tag{5.184}$$

Eqn (5.183) represents the case of an airplane which can rotate only about the Y–axis. Similarly, Eqn (5.184) represents the case of an airplane which can rotate only about the Z–axis. Applying the Laplace transformation for zero initial conditions:

$$s^2\alpha(s) - (M_q + M_{\dot{\alpha}})s\alpha(s) - M_\alpha\alpha(s) = 0 \tag{5.185}$$

$$s^2\beta(s) - (N_r - N_{\dot{\beta}})s\beta(s) + N_\beta\beta(s) = 0 \tag{5.186}$$

Comparison with the standard quadratic form of the spring–mass–damper system of Section 5.1 results in the following expressions for undamped natural frequencies and damping ratios:

$$\omega_{n_\alpha} = \sqrt{-M_\alpha} \quad \text{and} \quad \zeta_\alpha = \frac{-(M_q + M_{\dot{\alpha}})}{2\sqrt{-M_\alpha}} \tag{5.187}$$

$$\omega_{n_\beta} = \sqrt{N_\beta} \quad \text{and} \quad \zeta_\beta = \frac{-(N_r - N_{\dot\beta})}{2\sqrt{N_\beta}} \tag{5.188}$$

For any given airplane with a given mass distribution and in a given flight condition (Mach number and altitude), these undamped natural frequencies and damping ratios are characteristic of that airplane once the dimensional derivatives M_α, N_β, M_q, $M_{\dot\alpha}$, N_r and $N_{\dot\beta}$ are known.

The dimensional derivatives in Eqns (5.181) and (5.182) are now replaced by the undamped natural frequencies and damping ratios of Eqns (5.187) and (5.188). Next, the Laplace transformation for zero initial conditions is applied. The results of these manipulations are:

$$\left\{ s^2 + 2\zeta_\alpha\omega_{n_\alpha}s + (C_1P_1^2 + \omega_{n_\alpha}^2)\right\}\alpha(s) + \left\{ P_1(1 - C_1)s + 2\zeta_\alpha\omega_{n_\alpha}P_1\right\}\beta(s) = 0 \tag{5.189}$$

$$\left\{ -P_1(1 + D_1)s - 2\zeta_\beta\omega_{n_\beta}P_1\right\}\alpha(s) + \left\{ s^2 + 2\zeta_\beta\omega_{n_\beta}s + (\omega_{n_\beta}^2 - D_1P_1^2)\right\}\beta(s) = 0 \tag{5.190}$$

The roots of the characteristic determinant of this system of equations can be found by setting the system determinant equal to zero:

$$\begin{vmatrix} \left\{ s^2 + 2\zeta_\alpha\omega_{n_\alpha}s + (C_1P_1^2 + \omega_{n_\alpha}^2)\right\} & \left\{ P_1(1 - C_1)s + 2\zeta_\alpha\omega_{n_\alpha}P_1\right\} \\ \left\{ -P_1(1 + D_1)s - 2\zeta_\beta\omega_{n_\beta}P_1\right\} & \left\{ s^2 + 2\zeta_\beta\omega_{n_\beta}s + (\omega_{n_\beta}^2 - D_1P_1^2)\right\} \end{vmatrix} = 0 \tag{5.191}$$

Expansion of this equation yields a polynomial of the following type:

$$As^4 + Bs^3 + Cs^2 + Ds + E = 0 \tag{5.192}$$

To avoid divergence, Routh's stability criterion A) of page 275 will be invoked: E>0. For the case of Eqn (5.191) this yields the following stability criterion:

$$E = (C_1P_1^2 + \omega_{n_\alpha}^2)(\omega_{n_\beta}^2 - D_1P_1^2) + 4\zeta_\alpha\omega_{n_\alpha}\zeta_\beta\omega_{n_\beta}P_1^2 > 0 \tag{5.193}$$

By dividing by $(P_1)^2$ this can be written as:

$$\left\{ C_1 + \left(\frac{\omega_{n_\alpha}}{P_1}\right)^2\right\}\left\{ \left(\frac{\omega_{n_\beta}}{P_1}\right)^2 - D_1\right\} + 4\zeta_\alpha\left(\frac{\omega_{n_\alpha}}{P_1}\right)\zeta_\beta\left(\frac{\omega_{n_\beta}}{P_1}\right) > 0 \tag{5.194}$$

The quantities (ω_{n_α}/P_1) and (ω_{n_β}/P_1) can be thought of as variables X and Y respectively. The stability boundary corresponding to inequality (5.194) can then be written as:

$$(C_1 + X^2)(Y^2 - D_1) + 4\zeta_\alpha X \zeta_\beta Y = 0 \qquad (5.195)$$

Figure 5.45 shows a typical stability boundary resulting from computing $Y = \left(\omega_{n_\beta}/P_1\right)$ for a range of selected values for $X = \left(\omega_{n_\alpha}/P_1\right)$. The following observations are important:

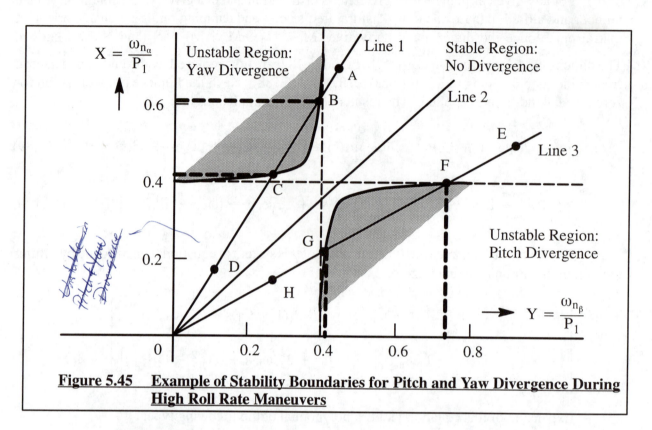

Figure 5.45   Example of Stability Boundaries for Pitch and Yaw Divergence During High Roll Rate Maneuvers

1) A straight line through the origin (such as either line 1, line 2 or line 3) has a slope equal to the ratio of undamped natural frequency in pitch to that in yaw. These undamped natural frequencies themselves are proportional to the corresponding longitudinal and directional static stability derivatives. Therefore, for a given airplane, in a given flight condition, the ratio of the dimensional static longitudinal to static directional stability derivatives determines the slope of a straight line through the origin.

If the slope is such that the line passes through the throat area in Figure 5.45 (Line 2) the airplane will not have an inertial coupling problem at any roll rate.

If the slope is that of line 1 in Figure 5.45 the airplane will encounter yaw inertial coupling for roll rates in between the following magnitudes:

$$\left(\omega_{n_\alpha}/X_C\right) \; < \; P_1 \; < \; \left(\omega_{n_\alpha}/X_B\right)$$

If the slope is that of line 3 in Figure 5.45 the airplane will encounter pitch inertial coupling for roll rates in between the following magnitudes:

$$\left(\omega_{n_\alpha}/X_G\right) \; < \; P_1 \; < \; \left(\omega_{n_\alpha}/X_F\right)$$

2) For any of the line 1, 2 or 3 a high value of roll rate corresponds to points along the line close to the origin. Similarly, a very low value or roll rate corresponds to points along the line toward infinity. The maximum steady state roll rate which an airplanes can achieve is given by Eqn (5.134). That maximum steady state roll rate gives rise to a given point on either line 1 or line 3.

If the maximum steady state roll rate of the airplane corresponds to a point such as A or E in Figure 5.45 the airplane cannot reach a critical value of roll rate. Inertial coupling will not occur.

If the maximum steady state roll rate of the airplane corresponds to a point such as D or H in Figure 5.45 the airplane can reach a super–critical value of roll rate. Inertial coupling will not occur for roll rates greater than those corresponding to points C and G in Figure 5.45.

When it is found that a given airplane design does have an inertial roll rate coupling problem three solutions suggest themselves:

A) By altering the ratio of static longitudinal stability to that of directional stability, the slope of the line in Figure 5.45 can be altered until it no longer intersects a stability boundary (i.e. until it passes through the throat area. Altering these stability ratios involves either a change in tail area or a change in angle–of–attack or angle–of–sideslip feedback gain.

B) By altering the damping ratios ζ_α or ζ_β, the width of the throat of the stability boundaries can be changed. Changes in ζ_α or ζ_β can be realized by changes in either pitch–rate or yaw–rate feedback gain. Note: changes in tail areas affect not only ζ_α and ζ_β, but also ω_{n_α} and ω_{n_β}.

C) By limiting lateral control deflection or lateral control power the maximum steady state roll rate can be kept below the critical value for inertial coupling. This is **NOT** an option in fighter aircraft where high maximum steady state roll rates are required.

Figure 5.46 shows an example of the roll–coupling characteristics of the jet fighter of Table 5.6. The airplane will diverge in pitch for roll rates in between those corresponding to points A and B. The airplane is capable of roll rates up to a value corresponding to point C. Figure 5.46 also shows the effect of increasing the directional stability of the airplane. Roll coupling is avoided, at least in this flight condition.

To illustrate the potentially violent nature of inertial coupling due to roll rate, Figure 5.46 has been included. The NACA X–3 was a high speed research airplane which experienced inertial coupling during a test flight in 1954. Similar problems were encountered by the F–100 Super Sabre fighter airplane of the same era. The solution in the case of the F–100 was a significantly enlarged vertical tail.

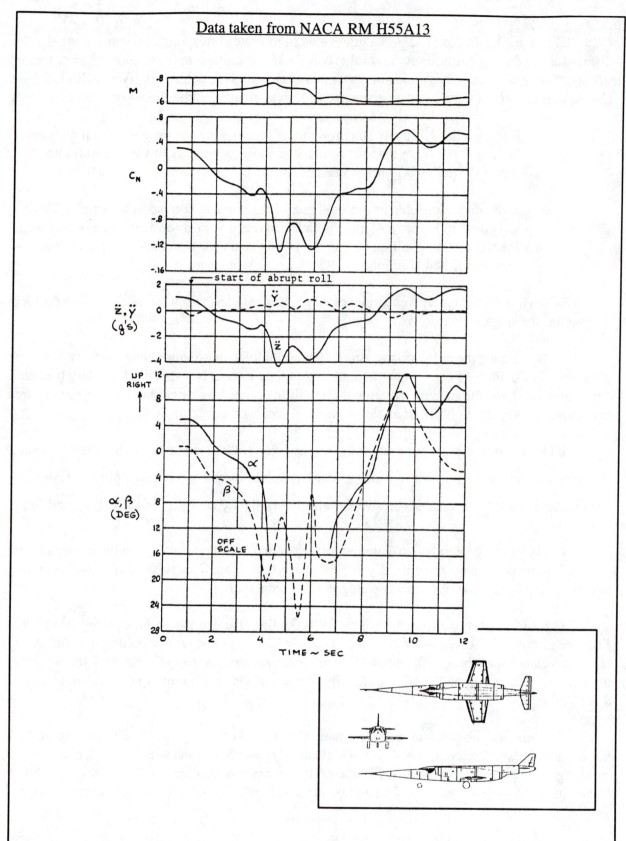

Figure 5.46   Time History of Motion Parameters Measured During an Abrupt Aileron Roll in the NACA X–3 at M=0.70 and h=30,000 ft

5.6.2 INERTIAL COUPLING DUE TO PITCH RATE

Fighter airplanes regularly must perform rapid pull–up or push–over maneuvers. A rapid pull–up maneuver gives rise to large positive (i.e. nose–up) pitch rates. A rapid push–over maneuver causes a large negative (i.e. nose down) pitch rate. Large pitch rates can cause the onset of another type of inertial coupling. This can be seen from Eqns (1.75b), (1.76a) and (1.76c) which are reproduced here for the case of $\Phi_1 = \Theta_1 = P_1 = R_1 = 0$:

$$m(\dot{v} + U_1 r) = mg\phi + f_{A_y} + f_{T_y} \tag{5.196}$$

$$I_{xx}\dot{p} - I_{xz}\dot{r} - I_{xz}Q_1 p + (I_{zz} - I_{yy})Q_1 r = l_A + l_T \tag{5.197}$$

$$I_{zz}\dot{r} + I_{xz}\dot{p} + I_{xz}Q_1 r + (I_{yy} - I_{xx})Q_1 p = n_A + n_T \tag{5.198}$$

The corresponding longitudinal equations of motion, (1.75a), (1.75c) and (1.76b) are assumed to be inherently satisfied and thus will not be considered in the discussion to follow.

The reader should be aware of the fact that in a pull–up or push–over maneuver, the pitch attitude angle of the airplane changes with time. Eqn (5.196) represents reality only for that small period of time during which θ can be considered to be small enough so that $\cos\theta = 0$ is a reasonable approximation. By introduction of the appropriate dimensional stability derivatives and inertial coefficients, it is possible to cast Eqns (196)–(198) in the following form:

$$\dot{v} + U_1 r = g\phi + Y_\beta\beta + Y_p p + Y_r r \tag{5.199}$$

$$\dot{p} - A_1\dot{r} - A_1 Q_1 p + C_1 Q_1 r = L_\beta\beta + L_p p + L_r r \tag{5.200}$$

$$\dot{r} - B_1\dot{p} + D_1 Q_1 p + B_1 Q_1 r = N_\beta\beta + N_p p + N_r r \tag{5.201}$$

The effect of steady state pitch rate can now be seen from Equations (5.200) and (5.201) by rewriting as follows:

$$\dot{p} - A_1\dot{r} = L_\beta\beta + (L_p + A_1 Q_1)p + (L_r - C_1 Q_1)r \tag{5.202}$$

$$\dot{r} - B_1\dot{p} = N_\beta\beta + (N_p - D_1 Q_1)p + (N_r - B_1 Q_1)r \tag{5.203}$$

Apparently, the significance of the effect of steady state pitch rate on the lateral–directional dynamic stability can be assessed by the following substitutions:

$$L_p \mapsto (L_p + A_1 Q_1) \qquad\qquad L_r \mapsto (L_r - C_1 Q_1) \tag{5.204}$$

$$N_p \mapsto (N_p - D_1 Q_1) \qquad\qquad N_r \mapsto (N_r - B_1 Q_1) \tag{5.205}$$

Figure 5.47 shows the effect of steady state pitch rate on these derivatives for the case of the example fighter of Table 5.11. Figure 5.48 indicates the effect this has on the lateral–directional dynamics of the airplane. It is seen that positive pitch rate tends to un–damp the dutch roll while moving the roll and spiral roots further apart. Negative pitch rate tends to damp the dutch roll while combining the spiral and roll roots to a so–called lateral phugoid oscillation.

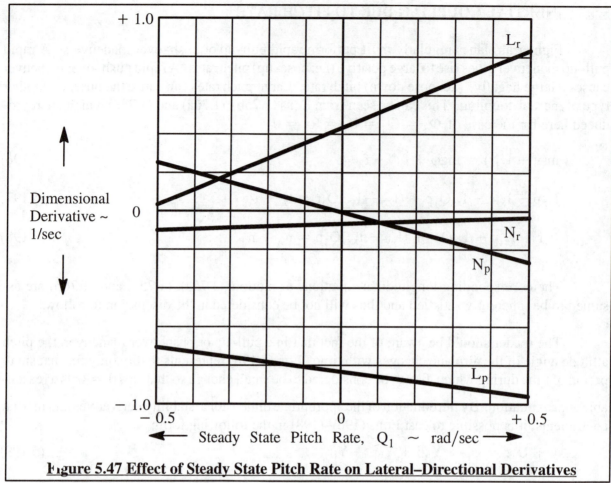

Figure 5.47 Effect of Steady State Pitch Rate on Lateral–Directional Derivatives

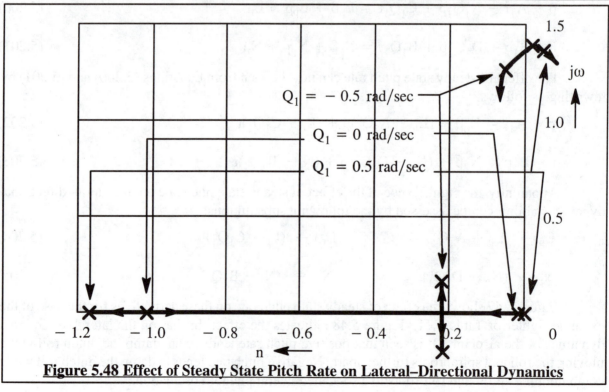

Figure 5.48 Effect of Steady State Pitch Rate on Lateral–Directional Dynamics

The reader should not read too much into these results. Large steady state pitch rates in pull–ups or push–overs cannot be maintained over long periods of time. Therefore, any change in the lateral–directional dynamics of the airplane may not be seen by the pilot in most practical situations.

5.7   SUMMARY FOR CHAPTER 5

After defining the meaning of the phrases 'dynamic stability', 'dynamic stability criteria' and 'response' an example is given of the dynamic stability and response characteristics of a simple, linear spring–mass–damper system. The application of Laplace transforms to the analysis of such a system as well as the idea of system open loop transfer functions are presented.

Next, the perturbed equations of motion of the airplane are written in terms of the dimensional stability derivatives. Following the Laplace transformation of these equations, the open loop transfer functions of the airplane are derived and their applications discussed. The connection between static and dynamic stability is indicated.

It is shown that by the introduction of certain approximations, the dynamic stability behavior of airplanes is determined by certain key dimensional derivatives which determine the make–up of the approximate transfer functions. The relationship of several of these key derivatives with the mass, spring and damping constant of the spring–mass–damper system is pointed out. The usefulness of the short period, phugoid, dutch roll, spiral and roll approximations are illustrated with numerical examples.

Complete airplane transfer functions are shown to break down into first order and quadratic components which are characterized by time–constants, undamped natural frequencies and damping ratios. The effect of variations of c.g. location, mass distribution and stability derivatives on the dynamic stability characteristics of airplanes is illustrated with sensitivity plots.

An introduction is given to idealized feedback systems and the relationship between feedback gain, control power and equivalent stability derivatives is pointed out.

Finally, it is shown that high roll and pitch rates give rise to inertial coupling phenomena. Preliminary methods for analysis of these phenomena are presented.

5.8   PROBLEMS FOR CHAPTER 5

5.1   Starting with Eqns (5.57) derive formulas for the short–period approximation to the angle–of–attack–to–pitch–rate–gust, $\alpha(s)/q_g(s)$, and pitch–attitude–angle–to–pitch–rate–gust, $\theta(s)/q_g(s)$, transfer functions.

5.2   Starting with Eqns (5.66) derive formulas for the short–period approximation to the speed–to–shear–gust, $u(s)/u_g(s)$, and pitch–attitude–angle–to–shear–gust, $\theta(s)/u_g(s)$, transfer functions.

5.3 Determine the required bank–angle–response–to–lateral–control–step–input for Airplanes D and H in Appendix B according to the military requirements of Table 6.16. Next, determine whether or not these airplanes have sufficient control power to meet these requirements. Use the roll mode approximation of Eqn (5.132).

5.4 Derive an expression for the bank–angle–versus–time response of an airplane, assuming that there is a time lag of τ seconds between the time of cockpit control application and aileron deflection.

5.5 Translate the derivative sensitivity plot of Figures 5.24, 5.29, 5.30, 5.31, 5.32, 5.35, 5.36 and 5.38 into root–loci where the derivative is a parameter along the loci.

5.6 A model is mounted in the wind–tunnel so that it can only rotate about its Y–axis. Show that the corresponding equation of motion is:

$$\ddot{\alpha} = M_\alpha \alpha + (M_{\dot{\alpha}}\dot{\alpha} + M_q)\dot{\alpha} + M_{\delta_e}\delta_e$$

Derive expressions for the undamped natural frequency and damping ratio and compare those with Eqns (5.61) and (5.62).

5.7 A model is mounted in the wind–tunnel so that it can only rotate about its Z–axis. Show that the corresponding equation of motion is:

$$\ddot{\psi} = -N_\beta \psi + (-N_{\dot{\beta}} + N_r)\dot{\psi} + N_{\delta_r}\delta_r$$

Derive expressions for the undamped natural frequency and damping ratio and compare those with Eqns (5.119a) and (5.119b).

5.8 A model is mounted in the wind–tunnel such that it can slide vertically (up and down) along its Z–axis and, at the same time, rotate about its Y–axis. Derive the small perturbation equations of motion for this model by starting with Eqns (5.30) in Table 5.2. If the model is equipped with an elevator, derive equations for the pitch–attitude and angle–of–attack to elevator transfer functions. Also, derive expressions for the undamped natural frequency and the damping ratio.

5.9 A model is mounted in the wind–tunnel such that it can slide horizontally (left and right) along its Y–axis and, at the same time, rotate about its Z–axis. Derive the small perturbation equations of motion for this model by starting with Eqns (5.96) in Table 5.8. If the model is equipped with a rudder, derive equations for the heading–angle and angle–of sideslip to rudder transfer functions. Also, derive expressions for the undamped natural frequency and the damping ratio.

5.10 Assume that the dutch roll undamped natural frequency and damping ratio of an airplane are predicted exactly from Eqns (5.121) and (5.119b) respectively. Assume further, that the derivatives C_{y_β}, C_{n_β} and C_{n_r} are made up solely of a vertical tail contribution. Discuss how frequency and damping ratio are affected by changes in the vertical tail area and the vertical tail moment arm.

5.11 Make a sketch of the time–domain response characteristics of a system which has the charac–
teristic root locations sketched in Figure 5.49: cases a) through f).

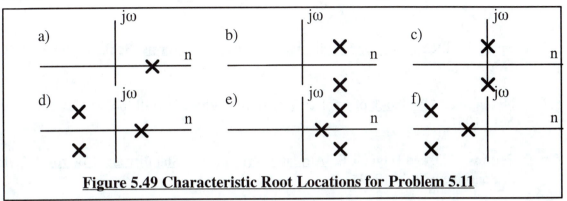

Figure 5.49 Characteristic Root Locations for Problem 5.11

5.12 For selected airplanes in Appendix B, determine the dynamic stability properties according
to the short period, phugoid, dutch roll, spiral and roll approximations. Compare the results
with those obtained from a complete three–degrees–of–freedom analysis.

5.13 For selected airplanes in Appendix B, determine and plot the mode shapes for the short peri–
od, phugoid, dutch roll, spiral and roll approximations. How well do these results with your
conclusions from problem 5.12?

5.14 For selected airplanes in Appendix B, perform and plot derivative and inertia sensitivity
analyses, study the results and summarize what can be learned from them. This problem is
most easily solved with the help of the AAA program of Appendix A.

5.15 Prove, that as the derivative M_α is varied toward a negative infinitely large magnitude, the

phugoid poles move toward a pair of finite zeros which are defined by:

$$(U_1 + Z_q)s^2 - \left\{ g\sin\theta_1 + (X_u + X_{T_u})(U_1 + Z_q) \right\} + s\left\{ -gZ_u\cos\theta_1 + g(X_u + X_{T_u})\sin\theta_1 \right\} = 0$$

5.16 The following differential equation describes a spring–mass–damper system:
$$\ddot{x} + 11\dot{x} + 30x = y$$
where: y is the input and x is the output of the system.

a) Determine the x(s)/y(s) transfer function of this system.

b) If $y = 10$ and the initial conditions are: $\ddot{x}(t = 0) = 20\text{fps}^2$ and

   $\dot{x}(t = 0) = 10\text{fps}$, find x(t)

c) State the final value theorem

d) Use the final value theorem to determine the value of x(t) at infinite t.

5.9   REFERENCES FOR CHAPTER 5

5.1   Anon.; MIL–F–8785–C, Military Specification, Flying Qualities of Piloted Airplanes; November, 1980.

5.2   Spiegel, M.R.; Theory and Problems of Laplace Transforms; Schaum Publishing Co., N.Y.; 1965.

5.3   Nixon, F.L.; Handbook of Laplace Transforms; Prentice Hall Inc, Englewoord Cliffs, N.J.; 1961.

5.4   Perkins, C.D. and Hage, R.E.; Airplane Performance, Stability and Control; J. Wiley & Sons, New York, 1949.

5.5   Kreyszig, E.; Advanced Engineering Mathematics; John Wiley & Sons, Inc., N.Y.; 1972.

5.6   Etkin, B.; Dynamics of Flight; John Wiley & Sons, Inc., N.Y.; 1959.

5.7   Hitchcock, F.L.; Improvement on the G.C.D. Method for Complex Roots; J.Math.Phys., Vol.23; p. 69–74; 1944.

5.8   Duncan, W.J.; The Principles of the Control and Stability of Aircraft; Cambridge University Press; England; 1952.

5.9   Phillips, W.H.; The Effect of Steady Rolling on Longitudinal and Directional Stability; NACA TN 1627, June 1948.

CHAPTER 6   FLYING QUALITIES, PILOT RATINGS, REGULATIONS AND APPLICATIONS

The purpose of this chapter is to present a brief discussion of how flying qualities are defined and regulated for civilian and military airplanes . The relationships between flying qualities, pilot ratings and the failure state of the flight controls are also pointed out. Finally, several approaches to the problem of how to design for good flying qualities are illustrated with examples.

6.1   FLYING QUALITIES AND PILOT RATINGS

In the case of airplanes which are flown by human pilots, the interaction between pilot cockpit control inputs and airplane response to the cockpit control inputs must be such that the pilot can achieve the mission objectives with reasonable physical and mental efforts. In other words, the airplane is required to have acceptable flying qualities (sometimes also called handling qualities) anywhere inside the operational flight envelope. For definitions of operational and other types of flight envelopes, the reader should consult References 6.1 through 6.4. Figure 6.1 shows typical examples of operational flight envelopes for a civilian and a military airplane.

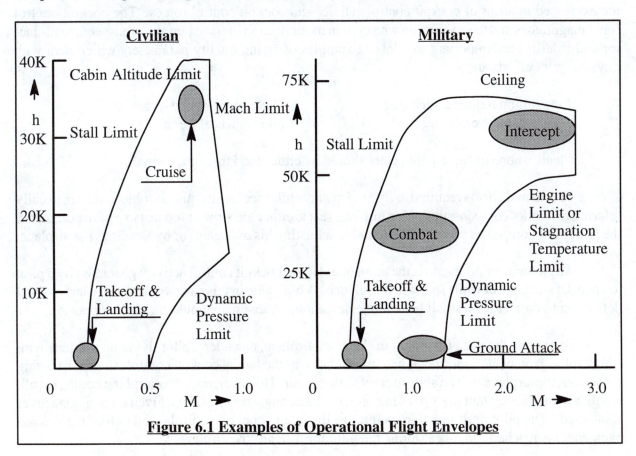

Figure 6.1 Examples of Operational Flight Envelopes

Fundamentally, the flying qualities of an airplane must be such that the following characteristics are present anywhere inside the operational flight envelope:

1) The airplane must have sufficient control power to maintain steady state, straight line flight as well as steady state maneuvering flight consistent with mission objectives.

2) The airplane must be maneuverable from one (steady state) flight condition to another.

3) The airplane must have sufficient control power to accomplish the following transitions:

* transition from ground operations to airborne operations (takeoff run, lift–off and initial steady state climb)
* transition form airborne operations to ground operations (steady state approach, touch–down and landing run)

These three characteristics must be present whether the engine(s) is (are) operating or not. That includes certain conditions of asymmetrical power which can be expected to occur. This is referred to as the minimum control speed condition. In the case of military airplanes, these three characteristics must be present with certain asymmetrical weapon and/or store loadings as well as under certain conditions of combat damage.

The physical pilot efforts required to fly an airplane, while meeting its mission objectives, are expressed in terms of cockpit control activity and cockpit control forces. The cockpit control force magnitudes and their variation with certain motion parameters (examples are: speed, load–factor and sideslip) are important to pilots. Examples of flying quality parameters which deal with physical pilot efforts are:

* maximum required stick force
* stick–force–per–'g'
* stick–force–speed–gradient
* aileron wheel force

Clearly, none of these parameters should be either too large or too small.

The mental efforts required to fly an airplane while meeting its mission objectives are usually referred to as pilot compensation. If an airplane reacts either too slow or too fast to a pilot command, the pilot must compensate for this behavior by 'adjusting his own gain' or by 'leading' the airplane.

An example of pilot gain is the amount of lateral cockpit control activity generated by a pilot to keep the wings level while flying in turbulence. A high gain in this case would mean a large wheel deflection to correct for a small bank angle deviation. A low gain would mean the opposite.

To explain the need for a pilot to 'lead' an airplane, consider a pilot flying an airplane with a high rolling moment of inertia. When the pilot moves the lateral cockpit controls to start a turning maneuver, the airplane will be slow to react to that input. However, once this airplane begins to roll, it will be equally reluctant to stop rolling once the bank angle required for a given turning maneuver is attained. The pilot must therefore neutralize the lateral cockpit controls well before the desired bank angle is reached. In other words, the pilot must 'lead' the airplane.

Clearly, a pilot should not have to excessively lead an airplane nor should he have to provide either too much or too little gain during any given mission segment.

To predict, whether or not an airplane has acceptable flying qualities, the following three ingredients are required:

1) A rating scale which pilots can use to rate the flying qualities of a given airplane in a given mission segment. To this end the Cooper–Harper pilot rating scale of Figure 6.2 has been developed. This scale is used by engineers and by engineering test pilots to evaluate and to predict airplane flying qualities.

2) Relationships between predictable airplane motion characteristics, cockpit control forces and cockpit control movements on the one side and flying qualities (as expressed by the Cooper–Harper scale of Figure 6.2) on the other side. Such relationships are defined in the military and civilian flying quality requirements. These requirements are referred to here as the regulations. References 6.1 through 6.4 contain these regulations.

3) A mathematical model of the airplane from which flying quality characteristics can be predicted. The material in Chapters 1–5 provides an introduction to such mathematical models.

4) A mathematical model of the human pilot operating in a closed loop with the airplane. Chapter 10 provides an introduction to this topic.

A summary of the most important regulatory requirements for flying qualities is contained in Sub–sections 6.2.2 and 6.2.3 for the longitudinal and lateral–directional cases respectively. For further details, the reader should consult the actual regulations in References 6.1 through 6.4.

6.2 MILITARY AND CIVILIAN FLYING QUALITY REQUIREMENTS: INTRODUCTION AND DEFINITIONS

The military requirements of References 6.1 and 6.2 contain numerical design guidelines which result in flying qualities which are adequate for the intended mission. Most, although not all, of the civilian requirements of References 6.3 and 6.4 are written in fairly general terms without providing numerically defined design guidelines. However, in the process of certifying civilian airplanes the civilian certifying authorities often follow the guidelines of References 6.1 and 6.2.

The intent of the regulations is to assure flying qualities which result in adequate mission performance and flight safety, regardless of the detail design implementation of the flight control system, for any type of airplane and in any mission flight phase.

The regulations , as written today, address airplanes equipped with cockpit controls which produce essentially pitching moments, rolling moments and yawing moments. If other types of cockpit control are contemplated the certifying authorities may impose additional or alternative requirements.

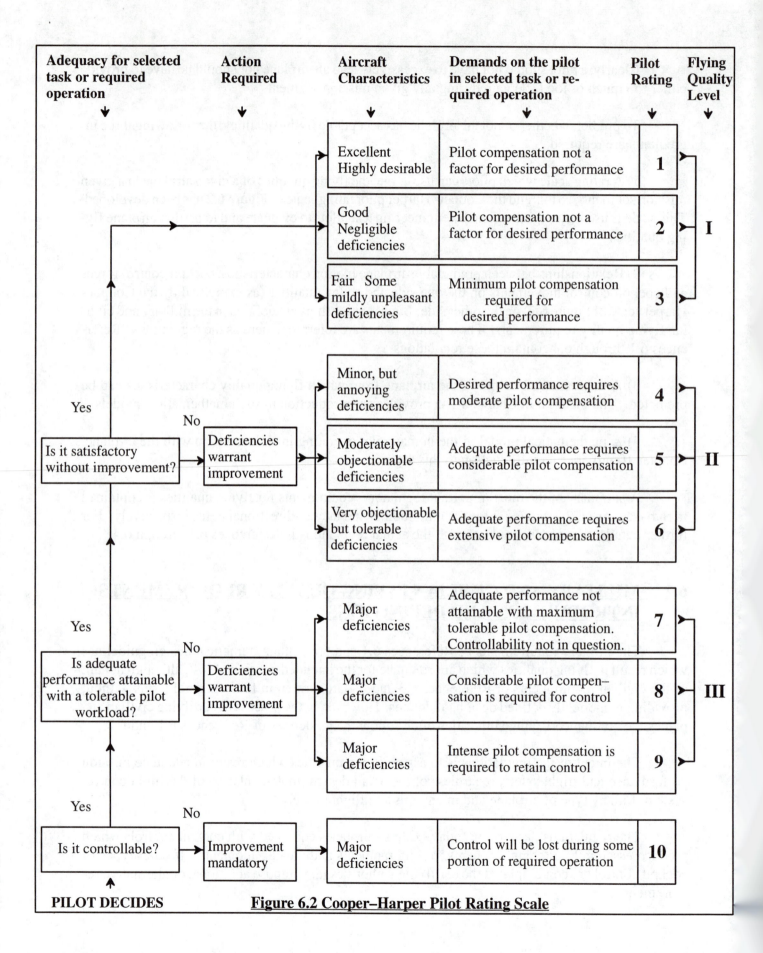

Figure 6.2 Cooper–Harper Pilot Rating Scale

As discussed in Chapter 4, many airplanes have irreversible flight control systems. In addition, as shown in Chapter 5, many airplanes require some form of stability augmentation to achieve good flying qualities. For such airplanes the failure state of the flight control system has a significant impact on the 'remaining' flying qualities. This leads to the necessity to incorporate in the regulations a relationship between acceptable levels of flying qualities and the probability of encountering certain types of failure.

Since airplanes vary widely in size, in mission and in performance capabilities, the military regulations specify flying quality requirements which are appropriate for each combination. The civilian requirements do not enter into that much detail. Instead, a division based on weight and mission application is used.

It is important to understand the definitions of airplane class, mission flight phase categories, flying quality levels and allowable probabilities of flight control system failure. These definitions are given in Sub–sections 6.2.1, 6.2.2 and 6.2.3 respectively.

6.2.1 DEFINITION OF AIRPLANE CLASSES

Table 6.1 shows a classification of airplanes according to MIL–F–8785C (Ref.6.1) with suggested applications to civilian airplanes. Several specific examples are given to help the reader in deciding where a given airplane might fit into Table 6.1.

When no airplane class is specified in a flying quality requirement, the intent is that such a requirement applies to all classes of airplanes. The letters 'L' and 'C' refer to land–based and carrier–based airplanes respectively.

6.2.2 DEFINITION OF MISSION FLIGHT PHASES

Each airplane mission can be broken down into a number of sequential flight phases. Because each flight phase requires different types of pilot actions and attention, it can be expected that flying quality requirements differ from one flight phase to another. Figure 6.3 shows two example mission profiles, one for a military and the other for a civilian airplane.

The flying qualities required of an airplane vary from one flight phase to another. In the military flying quality regulations all flight phases are grouped into three categories. Table 6.2 shows how these flight phase categories are defined. Table 6.2 also contains a suggested link between military flight phase categories and civilian flight phases.

6.2.3 DEFINITION OF FLYING QUALITY LEVELS AND ALLOWABLE FAILURE PROBABILITIES

The flying quality requirements of MIL–F–8785C (Reference 6.1) and MIL–STD–1797A (Reference 6.2) are presented for three levels of flying qualities. These three flying quality levels, in decreasing order of desirability, are defined as follows:

Table 6.1 Definition of Airplane Classes

MIL-F-8785C	Examples	Civilian Equivalent	Examples
Class I Small, light airplanes such as: * Light utility * Primary trainer * Light observation	* Cessna T-41 * Beech T-34C * Rockwell OV-10A	Very Light Aircraft (VLA) and FAR 23 category airplanes	* Cessna 210 * Piper Tomahawk * Edgeley Optica
Class II Medium weight, low-to-medium maneuverability airplanes such as: * Heavy utility / search and rescue * Light or medium transport / cargo / tanker * Early warning / electronic counter-measures / airborne command, control or communications relay * Anti-submarine * Assault transport * Reconnaissance * Tactical Bomber * Heavy Attack * Trainer for Class II	* Fairchild C-26A/B * Fairchild C-123 * Grumman E-2C * Boeing E-3A * Lockheed S-3A * Lockheed C-130 * Fairchild OA-10 * Douglas B-60 * Grumman A-6 * Beech T-1A	FAR 25 category airplanes	* Boeing 737, * Airbus A 320, * McDD MD-80
Class III Large, heavy, low-to-medium maneuverability airplanes such as: * Heavy transport / cargo / tanker * Heavy bomber * Patrol / early warning / electronic counter-measures / airborne command, control or communications relay * Trainer for Class III	* McDD C-17 * Boeing B-52H * Lockheed P-3 * Boeing E-3D * Boeing TC-135	FAR 25 category airplanes	* Boeing 747, * Airbus 340, * McDD MD-11
Class IV High maneuverability airplanes such as: * Fighter / interceptor * Attack * Tactical reconnaissance * Observation * Trainer for Class IV	* Lockheed F-22 * McDD F-15E * McDD RF-4 * Lockheed SR-71 * Northrop T-38	FAR 23 aerobatic category airplanes	* Pitts Special, * Sukhoi Su-26M

Mission Profile: Attack Airplane

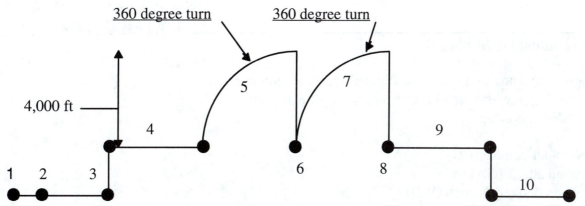

1) Engine start and warm–up
2) Taxi
3) Takeoff and accelerate to 350 kts at sea–level
4) Dash 200 nm at 350 kts
5) 360 degree, sustained, 4.5g turn, including a 4,000 ft altitude gain

6) Release 2 bombs and fire 50% ammo
7) 360 degree, sustained, 4.5g turn, including a 4,000 ft altitude gain
8) Release 2 bombs and fire 50% ammo
9) Dash 200 nm at 350 kts
10) Landing, taxi, shutdown (no res.)

Mission Profile: Passenger Transport

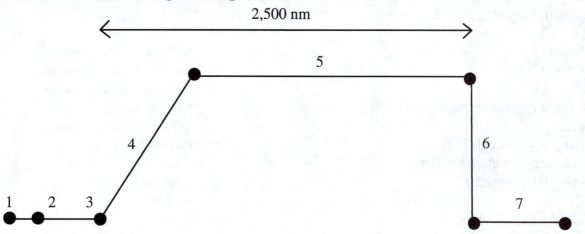

1) Engine start and warm–up
2) Taxi
3) Takeoff
4) Climb to 45,000 ft

5) Cruise
6) Descent
7) Landing, taxi, shutdown

Figure 6.3   Examples of Mission Profiles and Flight Phases for a Military and a Civilian Airplane

Table 6.2 Definition of Flight Phase Categories

MIL–F–8785C	Suggested Civilian Equivalent: VLA, FAR 23 and FAR 25

Non–terminal Flight Phases

Category A: Those non–terminal flight phases that require rapid maneuvering, precision tracking or precise flight path control. Included in this category are:

a) Air–to–air combat (CO)	None
b) Ground attack (GA)	None
c) Weapon delivery/launch (WD)	None
d) Aerial recovery (AR)	None
e) Reconnaissance (RC)	Observation, Pipeline spotting and monitoring
f) In–flight refuelling (receiver) (RR)	None as yet
g) Terrain following (TF)	None
h) Anti–submarine search (AS)	Fish spotting
i) Close formation flying (FF)	Air–show demonstrations

Category B: Those non–terminal flight phases that are normally accomplished using gradual maneuvers and without precision tracking, although accurate flight–path control may be required. Included in this category are:

a) Climb (CL)	Various climb segments
b) Cruise (CR)	Various cruise segments
c) Loiter (LO)	Flight in holding pattern
d) In–flight refuelling (tanker) (RT)	None as yet
e) Descent	Various descent segments
f) Emergency descent (ED)	Emergency descent
g) Emergency deceleration (DE)	None
h) Aerial delivery (AD)	Parachute drop

Terminal Flight Phases

Category C: Terminal flight phases are normally accomplished using gradual maneuvers and usually require accurate flight path control. Included in this category are:

a) Takeoff (TO)	Various takeoff segments
b) Catapult takeoff (CT)	None
c) Approach (PA)	Various approach segments
d) Wave–off / go–around (WO)	Aborted approach
e) Landing (L)	Various landing segments

Level 1: (I) Flying qualities clearly adequate for the mission Flight Phase

Level 2: (II) Flying qualities adequate to accomplish the mission Flight Phase, but some increase in pilot workload or degradation in mission effectiveness, or both, exists.

Level 3: (III) Flying qualities such that the airplane can be controlled safely, but pilot workload is excessive or mission effectiveness is inadequate, or both. Category A Flight Phases can be terminated safely, and Category B and C Flight Phases can be completed.

The relationship between these three flying quality levels and pilot ratings on the Cooper–Harper scale is indicated in Figure 6.2. **Airplanes must be designed to satisfy the Level 1 flying quality requirements with all systems in their normal operating state.** The probability of encountering a degradation in flying qualities to Level 2 or to Level 3 is related to the probability of failure of those systems deemed crucial for safe flight at Level 1 flying qualities. Table 6.3 shows how the three flying quality levels are related to failure probabilities. The numbers for civilian equivalence are based on an interpretation (by the author) of the civil airworthiness code shown in Figure 6.4.

The term operational flight envelope as used in Table 6.3 indicates the boundaries of speed, altitude and load factor within which the airplane must be capable of operating to accomplish its mission. Examples of operational flight envelopes were given in Figure 6.1.

The term "service flight envelope" refers to those boundaries of speed, altitude and load factor which correspond to airplane limits. The boundaries of the service flight envelope may coincide with those of the operational flight envelope. Under no circumstances may the boundaries of the service flight envelope fall within the boundaries of the operational envelope. For a detailed definition of flight envelopes the reader should consult references 6.1 through 6.4.

A summary of the most important longitudinal and lateral–directional flying quality requirements for military and civilian airplanes is given in Sections 6.3 and 6.4 respectively. As will be seen, these requirements differ from one Level to the next.

Table 6.3 Flying Quality Levels Related to Airplane Failure State			
Probability of Encountering	Within Operational Flight Envelope MIL–F–8785C	Within Service Flight Envelope MIL–F–8785C	Civilian Equivalent within Operational Flight Envelope
Level 2 after failure:	$< 10^{-2}$ per flight		$< 10^{-4}$ per flight
Level 3 after failure:	$< 10^{-4}$ per flight	$< 10^{-2}$ per flight	$< 10^{-6}$ per flight

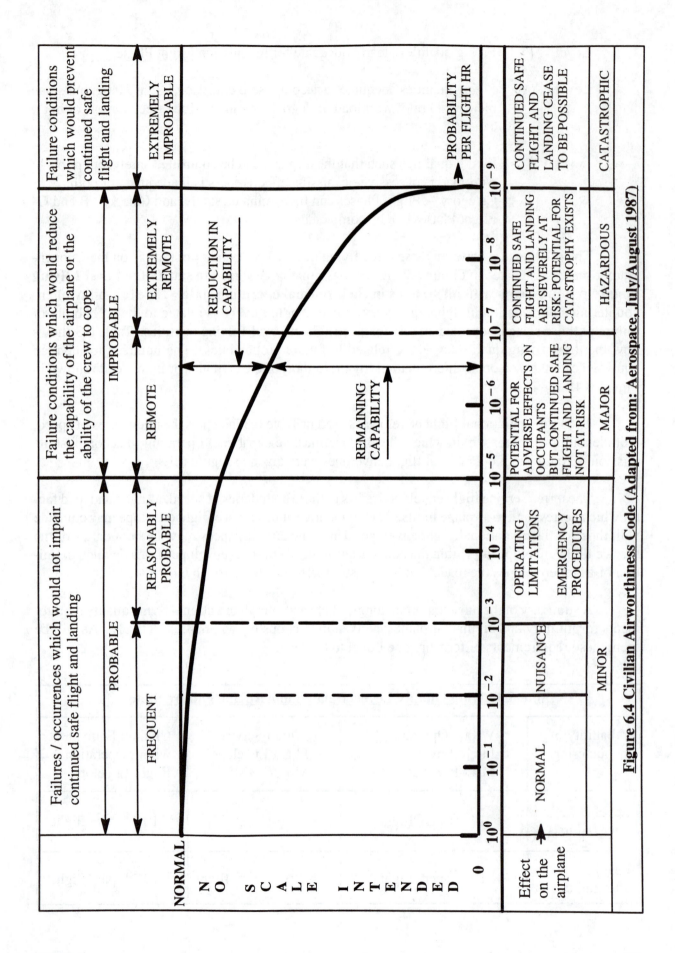

Figure 6.4 Civilian Airworthiness Code (Adapted from: Aerospace, July/August 1987)

6.3   LONGITUDINAL FLYING QUALITY REQUIREMENTS

The longitudinal flying quality requirements of References 6.1 through 6.3 are included verbatim as Appendices A and B in Part VII of Reference 6.6. This section contains a summary only of those requirements which should be addressed during the early stages of design analysis of new airplanes. The reader should consult the actual regulations before considering a flying quality assessment to be completed. In several instances, when the FAR/VLA regulations do not contain specific requirements, the author has included a statement of 'Civilian Equivalent'. The author suggests these civilian equivalents requirements as sound design practice only.

6.3.1   LONGITUDINAL CONTROL FORCES

The longitudinal control force requirements, which are summarized here, apply to airplanes equipped with conventional stick– or wheel–type cockpit controllers. The regulations deal with the following situations:

* 6.3.1.1 Control forces in maneuvering flight   * 6.3.1.2 Control forces in steady state flight

* 6.3.1.3 Control forces in takeoff and landing   * 6.3.1.4 Control forces in dives

6.3.1.1 Control Forces in Maneuvering Flight

The control–force–versus–load–factor gradients (stick–force per 'g' of Chapter 4) must fall within the limits specified in Table 6.4. In addition, there must be no significant non–linearities in the control–force–versus–load–factor–gradients.

6.3.1.2 Control Forces in Steady State Flight

When a pilot changes the configuration of an airplane, the accompanying changes in longitudinal control forces must be within certain limits. Examples of typical configuration changes are:

* Lowering the landing gear   * Lowering the flaps

* Deploying a speed brake   * Changing engine power or thrust

* Sudden failure of a critical engine   * Sudden failure of a second critical engine

It is the responsibility of the designer to identify other configuration changes which are peculiar to a new design.

When a pilot maneuvers the airplane from one steady state flight condition to another, the required changes in longitudinal control forces must not exceed the force levels of Table 6.5.

In addition, the slope of stick– or wheel–force with speed (the so–called stick–force–speed–gradient, $\partial F_s/\partial V_P$) must be stable. Relative to any given trim speed in the operational flight envelope, a push–force on the cockpit controller (stick or wheel) must be required to increase speed while

Table 6.4 Longitudinal Control Force Limits in Maneuvering Flight

MIL–F–8785C: Level	Minimum Allowable Gradient $\partial F_s / \partial n \sim$ lbs/g	Maximum Allowable Gradient $\partial F_s / \partial n \sim$ lbs/g
Center Stick Controllers		
Level 1	the higher of : $\dfrac{21}{(n_{limit} - 1)}$ and 3.0	$\dfrac{240}{(n/\alpha)}$ but not more than 28.0 nor less than $\dfrac{56}{(n_{limit} - 1)}$ *
Level 2	the higher of : $\dfrac{18}{(n_{limit} - 1)}$ and 3.0	$\dfrac{360}{(n/\alpha)}$ but not more than 42.5 nor less than $\dfrac{85}{(n_{limit} - 1)}$
Level 3	the higher of : $\dfrac{12}{(n_{limit} - 1)}$ and 2.0	56.0

* For $n_{limit} < 3.0$, $\partial F_s / \partial n = 28.0$ for Level 1, and $\partial F_s / \partial n = 42.5$ for Level 2.

Wheel Controllers		
Level 1	the higher of : $\dfrac{35}{(n_{limit} - 1)}$ and 6.0	$\dfrac{500.0}{(n/\alpha)}$ but not more than 120.0 nor less than $\dfrac{120.0}{(n_{limit} - 1)}$
Level 2	the higher of : $\dfrac{30}{(n_{limit} - 1)}$ and 6.0	$\dfrac{775.0}{(n/\alpha)}$ but not more than 182.0 nor less than $\dfrac{182.0}{(n_{limit} - 1)}$
Level 3	5.0	240.0

Civilian Requirements:		
VLA	**FAR–23**	**FAR–25**
$\partial F_s / \partial n > \dfrac{15.7}{n_{limit}}$	For wheel controllers : $\dfrac{\partial F_s}{\partial n} > \dfrac{(W_{TO}/140)}{n_{limit}}$ and $\dfrac{15.0}{n_{limit}}$ but not more than : $\dfrac{35.0}{n_{limit}}$ For stick controllers : $\dfrac{\partial F_s}{\partial n} > \dfrac{W}{140}$	no requirement : It is suggested to use MIL–F–8785C

Table 6.5 Maximum Allowable Longitudinal Control Forces (lbs)			
	VLA	**FAR 23**	**FAR 25**
a) For **temporary** force application:			
Center Stick Controller	45.0	60.0	no requirement
Wheel Controller (Applied to rim)	56.2	75.0	75.0
b) For **prolonged** application:			
Any Type Controller	4.5	10.0	10.0
MIL–F–8785C: No requirement			

a pull–force must be required to decrease speed. In addition, the slope, $\partial F_s/\partial V_P$, must meet the following requirements:

For VLA: the slope, $\partial F_s/\partial V_P$, must be perceptible

For FAR 23: the slope, $\partial F_s/\partial V_P$, must be perceptible

For FAR 25: the slope, $\partial F_s/\partial V_P$, must be stable and not less than 1 lbs per 6 kts

For MIL–F–8785C the slope, $\partial F_s/\partial V_P$, must be stable

A stable stick–force–speed gradient, coupled with a low control system break–out force, guarantees inherent static longitudinal stability as perceived by a pilot. This desirable characteristic exhibits itself in the so–called return–to–trim–speed behavior of the airplane as discussed in Sub–section 4.5.1 (see also Figure 4.31).

The flying quality requirements of References 6.1 through 6.4 all require some form of re–turn–to–trim–speed behavior, normally expressed as a percentage of the trim–speed. Typical re–quirements are:

For VLA: air–speed must return to within +/– 10 % of the original trim speed after application of a 40 lbs longitudinal control force.

For FAR 23: air–speed must return to within +/– 10 % of the original trim speed after application of a 40 lbs longitudinal control force. For commuter type airplanes the air–speed must return to within +/– 7.5% of the original trim speed after application of a 40 lbs longitudinal control force in cruise only.

For FAR 25: air–speed must return to within +/– 10 % of the original trim speed after application of a longitudinal control force which has the effect of changing speed by +/– 15 % of the trimspeed. This requirement applies in climb, approach and landing.

air–speed must return to within +/– 7.5 % of the original trim speed after application of a longitudinal control force which has the effect of changing speed by +/– 15 % of the trimspeed. This requirement applies in cruise.

For MIL–F–8785C: air–speed must not diverge from the trim–speed with controls–free and with controls–fixed for Levels 1 and 2. For Level 3 the time–to–double the a–periodic speed divergence must not be less than 6 sec.

6.3.1.3 Control Forces in Takeoff and Landing

With the trim controls fixed at a setting defined by the manufacturer, the longitudinal control forces in takeoff and landing must not exceed the values listed in Table 6.6.

Table 6.6 Maximum Allowable Longitudinal Control Forces (lbs) In Takeoff and Landing				
MIL–F–8785C: **Airplane Class:**	**Takeoff**		**Airplane Class:**	**Landing**
	Pull	Push		Pull only
Nose–wheel and bicycle–gear airplanes			All gear con–figurations	
Classes I, IV–C	20.0	10.0	Classes I, II–C	35.0
Classes II–C, IV–L	30.0	10.0	Classes II–L	50.0
Classes II–L, III	50.0	20.0		
Tail–wheel airplanes			**VLA / FAR 23 / FAR 25:** See Table 6.5 for implied requirements and Paragraph .175 for details.	
Classes I, II–C, IV	20.0	10.0		
Classes II–L, III	35.0	15.0		

6.3.1.4 Control Forces in Dives

According to Ref. 6.1, control forces in dives to all attainable airspeeds shall not exceed the following values:

For center–stick controllers: 50 lbs of push   or 10 lbs of pull

For wheel controllers: 75 lbs of push   or 15 lbs of pull

This requirement applies to all airplanes, when trimmed in level flight within the service flight envelope. There is no similar requirement in the civilian regulations.

6.3.2 PHUGOID DAMPING

The long–period air–speed oscillations (phugoid) which occur when an airplane seeks a stabilized air–speed following a disturbance must meet the requirements of Table 6.7

<table>
<tr><td colspan="3" align="center">Table 6.7 Phugoid Damping Requirements</td></tr>
<tr><td>MIL–F–8785C</td><td></td><td>VLA, FAR 23 and FAR 25</td></tr>
<tr><td>Level I:</td><td>$\zeta_{ph} \geq 0.04$</td><td>No requirement</td></tr>
<tr><td>Level II:</td><td>$\zeta_{ph} \geq 0$</td><td>No requirement</td></tr>
<tr><td>Level III:</td><td>$T_{2_{ph}} \geq 55 \, sec$</td><td>No requirement</td></tr>
</table>

Phugoid damping characteristics can be predicted with the general or with the approximate method of Section 5.2. The time–to–double the phugoid amplitude, $T_{2_{ph}}$, may be computed from the following considerations. Since the phugoid is an oscillatory phenomenon, its amplitude can be written as the following function of time: $A_{ph}e^{(-\zeta_{ph}\omega_{n_{ph}}t)}\sin(\omega_{n_{ph}}t + \phi_{ph})$. The time to double the amplitude, $T_{2_{ph}}$, follows from the following equation:

$$A_{ph}e^{-\zeta_{ph}\omega_{n_{ph}}(t_1 + T_{2_{ph}})} = 2A_{ph}e^{-\zeta_{ph}\omega_{n_{ph}}(t_1)} \tag{6.1}$$

By taking the natural logarithm at both sides it is found that:

$$T_{2_{ph}} = \frac{\ln 2}{-\zeta_{ph}\omega_{n_{ph}}} \tag{6.2}$$

If the phugoid damping ratio is negative, the time–to–double the phugoid amplitude will be positive. If the phugoid damping ratio is positive, the time–to–double the phugoid amplitude will be negative. The physical meaning is that in that case Eqn (6.2) reflects the time–to–halve the phugoid amplitude, $T_{1/2_{ph}}$. Eqn (6.2) can be applied generically to any oscillatory motion.

6.3.3 FLIGHT PATH STABILITY

Flight path stability, $d\gamma/dV_P$ is defined in terms of the change in flight–path–angle, γ, with speed, as caused by a change in pitch control only (no change in throttle setting). For the landing approach flight phase (Flight Phase Category C, Approach), the curve of flight–path–angle, γ, versus true air–speed, U_1, shall have a local slope at $V_{0_{min}}$ which is either negative or less positive than the numbers given in Table 6.8. In addition, the slope, $d\gamma/dV_P$, at $V_{0_{min}} - 5$ kts must not be more positive than 0.05 deg/knot compared to the slope at $V_{0_{min}}$. This is illustrated in Figure 6.5.

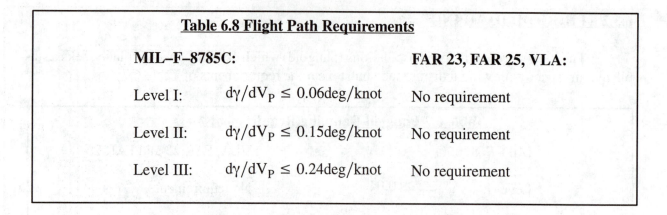

Table 6.8 Flight Path Requirements

	MIL–F–8785C:	FAR 23, FAR 25, VLA:
Level I:	$d\gamma/dV_P \leq 0.06 \text{deg/knot}$	No requirement
Level II:	$d\gamma/dV_P \leq 0.15 \text{deg/knot}$	No requirement
Level III:	$d\gamma/dV_P \leq 0.24 \text{deg/knot}$	No requirement

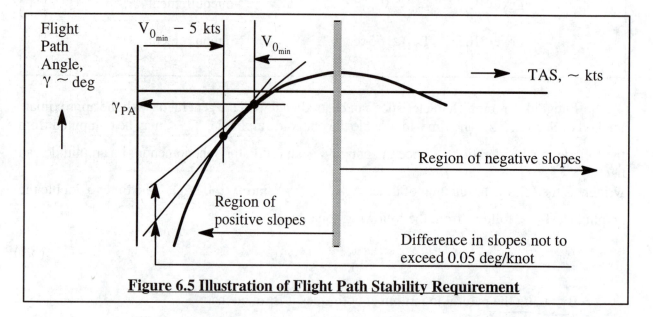

Figure 6.5 Illustration of Flight Path Stability Requirement

The speed, $V_{0_{min}}$ is defined as the minimum operating speed of the airplane during final approach. For military aircraft that speed is typically $1.15 V_{s_{PA}}$ for carrier–based aircraft and $1.20 V_{s_{PA}}$ for land–based aircraft. For civilian aircraft that speed is typically $1.30 V_{s_{PA}}$.

Flight path stability may be predicted with the generalized trim analysis method presented in Section 4.6. The slope $d\gamma/dV_P$ is a component of the r.h.s. matrix in Eqn (4.232).

6.3.4   SHORT PERIOD FREQUENCY AND DAMPING

MIL–F–8785C requires the (**equivalent**) short period undamped natural frequency, $\omega_{n_{sp}}$, of the short period mode to be within the limits shown in Figure 6.6 for three Flight Phase Categories. Although the FAR/VLA requirements do not set specific limits on $\omega_{n_{sp}}$, common design practice is to adopt the military requirements. Reference 6.2 is a recent replacement specification for MIL–F–8785C of Reference 6.1. In MIl–STD–1797A, there appears a requirement for a so–called Control Anticipation Parameter (CAP). This parameter and its relationship to airplane maneuver margin is discussed in Sub–section 6.3.5.

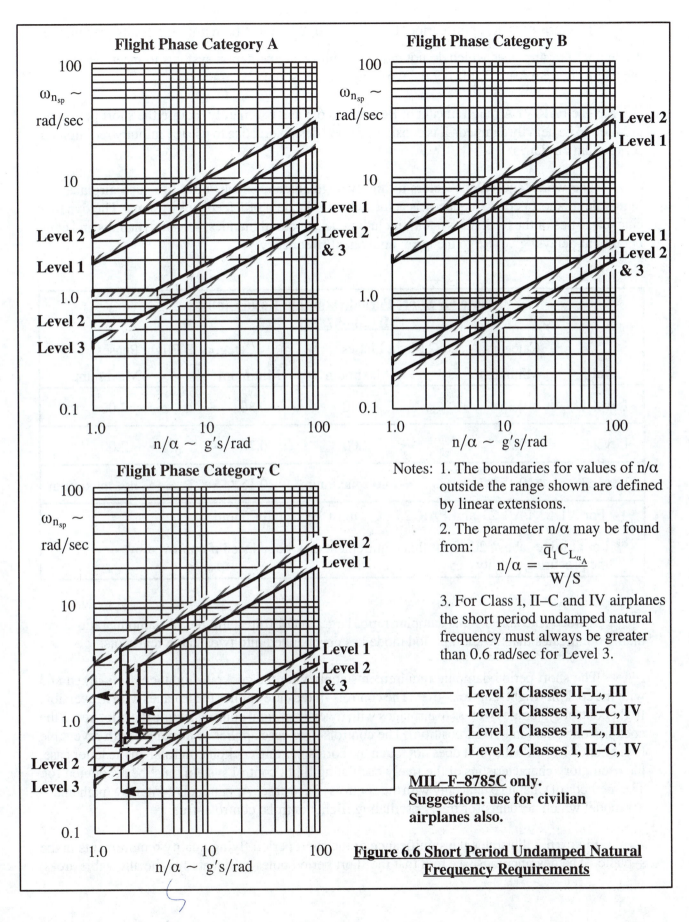

Notes: 1. The boundaries for values of n/α outside the range shown are defined by linear extensions.

2. The parameter n/α may be found from:

$$n/\alpha = \frac{\overline{q}_1 C_{L_{\alpha_A}}}{W/S}$$

3. For Class I, II–C and IV airplanes the short period undamped natural frequency must always be greater than 0.6 rad/sec for Level 3.

Level 2 Classes II–L, III
Level 1 Classes I, II–C, IV
Level 1 Classes II–L, III
Level 2 Classes I, II–C, IV

MIL–F–8785C only.
Suggestion: use for civilian airplanes also.

Figure 6.6 Short Period Undamped Natural Frequency Requirements

The (**equivalent**) short period damping ratio, ζ_{sp}, must be within the limits presented in Table 6.9. For airplanes which do not require stability augmentation systems to meet the requirements of Figure 6.6 and Table 6.9 the word **equivalent** should be omitted.

The FAR/VLA requirements of References 6.3 and 6.4 merely require the short period oscillation to be heavily damped. It is considered good design practice to use the military requirement for civilian airplanes.

The word 'equivalent' refers to highly augmented airplanes **only**. In such airplanes, an 'equivalent' short period frequency is achieved with the help of a feedback system. The dynamic characteristics of the feedback system (including its actuator dynamics, sensor dynamics and computational delays) give rise to the term 'equivalent' frequency.

<u>**Table 6.9 Short Period Damping Ratio Limits**</u>
MIL–F–8785C

Level	Category A and C Flight Phases		Category B Flight Phases	
	Minimum	Maximum	Minimum	Maximum
Level 1*	0.35 $\;\leftarrow \zeta_{sp} \rightarrow\;$ 1.30		0.30 $\;\leftarrow \zeta_{sp} \rightarrow\;$ 2.00	
Level 2	0.25 $\;\leftarrow \zeta_{sp} \rightarrow\;$ 2.00		0.20 $\;\leftarrow \zeta_{sp} \rightarrow\;$ 2.00	
Level 3	0.15 ** $\;\leftarrow \zeta_{sp} \rightarrow\;$ no maximum		0.15 * $\;\leftarrow \zeta_{sp} \rightarrow\;$ no maximum	

* For VLA, FAR 23 and FAR 25: ζ_{sp} must be heavily damped

** For altitudes above 20,000 ft this requirement may be reduced if approved by the procuring activity

It is seen in Table 6.9 that damping ratios larger than 1.0 are admitted. A damping ratio larger than 1.0 indicates that the short period mode has degenerated into two, stable real roots.

The short period damping requirements apply with the cockpit–flight–controls–fixed and with the cockpit–flight–controls–free. The controls–fixed case applies to airplanes with irreversible flight control systems as well as to airplanes with reversible flight controls, while the pilot keeps the cockpit controllers in a fixed position. The controls–free case applies to airplanes with reversible flight controls, while the pilot does not touch the corresponding cockpit controls. In the latter case, the oscillatory characteristics of the freely oscillating flight control system must be accounted for. The methods of Chapter 5 deal only with the controls–fixed case. Appendix D contains a mathematical model which accounts for freely oscillating flight controls: controls–free.

Figure 6.7 illustrates the significance of the short period flying quality requirements in the s–plane. The designer must see to it that the short period poles are located in the allowable areas.

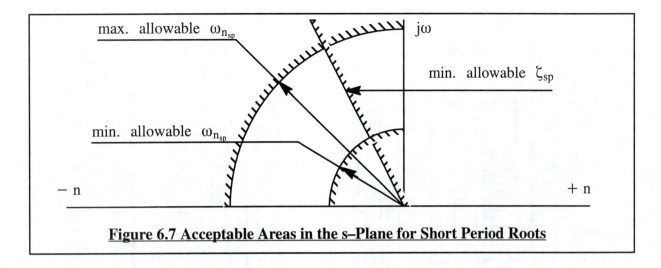

Figure 6.7 Acceptable Areas in the s–Plane for Short Period Roots

6.3.5   CONTROL ANTICIPATION PARAMETER

MIL–STD–1797A (Reference 6.2) contains a requirement that airplanes must stay within a minimum and maximum range of values of the so–called Control Anticipation Parameter (CAP) over a range of allowable short period damping ratios. For <u>highly augmented</u> airplanes, this require-ment has in fact replaced the short period undamped natural frequency and damping ratio require-ments of Figure 6.6 and Table 6.9. For <u>non–augmented</u> airplanes the author recommends continued use of Figure 6.6 and Table 6.9.

In preliminary design it is acceptable to use the following equation to estimate the control anticipation parameter (CAP):

$$CAP = \frac{\omega_{n_{sp}}^2}{n_\alpha} \tag{6.3}$$

where: $\omega_{n_{sp}}$ is the undamped natural frequency of the short period mode

$n_\alpha = \partial n / \partial \alpha$ which is also referred to as the gust– or load–factor–sensitivity of an airplane.

Figure 6.8 shows how allowable CAP–values are related to the short period damping ratio for various categories of Flight Phases and to handling quality Levels. It is shown next, that the CAP is mathematically related to the following quantities:

* maneuver margin (See: Section 4.3)   * wing m.g.c.

* overall airplane length   * dimensionless radius of gyration about the Y–axis.

According to Eqn (5.61), the following approximation holds for $\omega_{n_{sp}}^2$:

$$\omega_{n_{sp}}^2 = \frac{Z_\alpha M_q}{U_1} - M_\alpha \tag{6.4}$$

By partially differentiating Eqn (4.91) with respect to angle–of–attack it is found that:

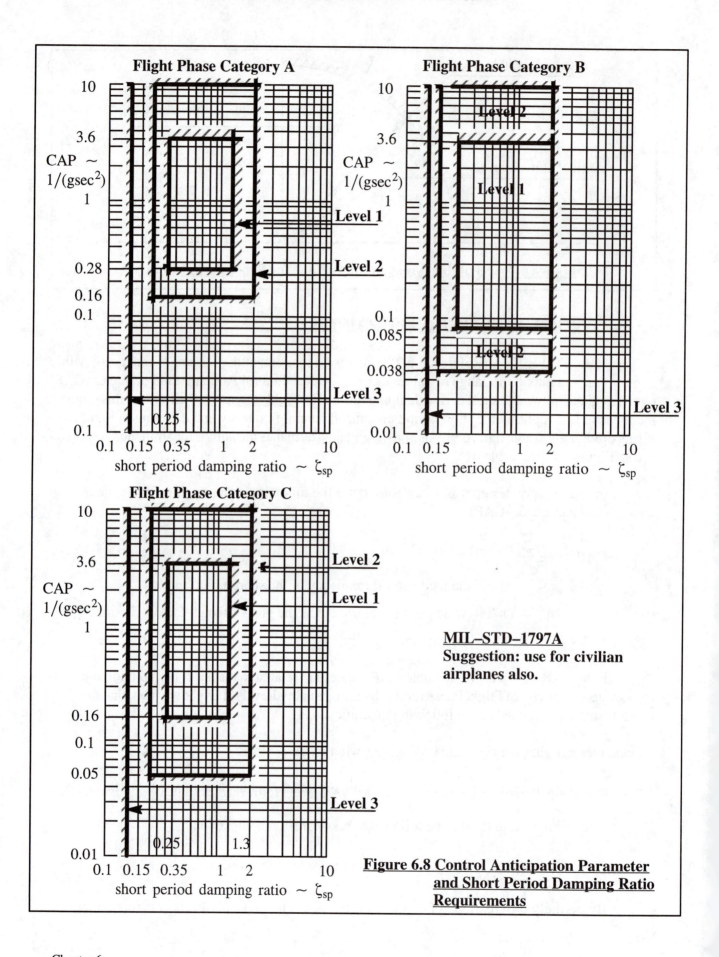

Figure 6.8 Control Anticipation Parameter and Short Period Damping Ratio Requirements

$$n_\alpha \approx \frac{\overline{q}_1 C_{L_\alpha}}{(W/S)} \qquad (6.5)$$

The dimensional derivatives in Eqn (6.4) are defined in Table 5.1 as:

$$Z_\alpha \approx \frac{-\overline{q}_1 S C_{L_\alpha}}{m} \qquad (6.6)$$

$$M_q = \frac{\overline{q}_1 S \overline{c}^2 C_{m_q}}{2 I_{yy} U_1} \qquad (6.7)$$

$$M_\alpha \approx \frac{\overline{q}_1 S \overline{c} C_{m_\alpha}}{I_{yy}} \qquad (6.8)$$

It should be recalled from Eqn (3.39) that the dimensionless derivatives C_{m_α} and C_{L_α} are related to the non–dimensional distance between airplane c.g. and a.c. in the following manner:

$$C_{m_\alpha} = C_{L_\alpha}(\overline{x}_{cg} - \overline{x}_{ac_A}) \qquad (6.9)$$

By substituting Eqns (6.4) through (6.9) in Eqn (6.3) and by rearranging, the reader is asked to show that:

$$CAP = \frac{W\overline{c}}{I_{yy}}(-\overline{x}_{cg} + \overline{x}_{ac_A} - \frac{g\rho S \overline{c} C_{m_q}}{4W}) \qquad (6.10)$$

From Chapter 4, Eqn (4.121) it is recognized that the maneuver point of an airplane can be written as follows:

$$\overline{x}_{MP} = \overline{x}_{ac_A} - \frac{g\rho S \overline{c} C_{m_q}}{4W} \qquad (6.11)$$

Therefore, Eqn (6.10) can be cast in the following form:

$$CAP = \frac{W\overline{c}}{I_{yy}}(\overline{x}_{MP} - \overline{x}_{cg}) = \frac{W\overline{c}}{I_{yy}} MM \qquad (6.12)$$

where: MM is the so–called maneuver margin of an airplane.

The pitching moment of inertia, I_{yy} , is related to the following airplane design parameters:

* weight, W   * non–dimensional radius of gyration, $\overline{R}_y$

* overall length,   * mean geometric chord, $\overline{c}$

in accordance with:

$$I_{yy} = (\frac{L^2 W \overline{R}_y^2}{4g})$$

(6.13)

By combining Eqns (6.12) and (6.13) it is found that:

$$CAP = \frac{4\overline{c}gMM}{L^2\overline{R}_y^2}$$

(6.14)

The minimum and maximum allowable CAP values from MIL–STD–1797A can therefore be translated into a minimum and maximum allowable maneuver margin for any airplane, as long as airplane geometric size (as expressed by $\overline{c}$ and L) and its longitudinal mass distribution (as expressed by $\overline{R}_y$) are known. Equation (6.12) suggests that for very large airplanes the minimum acceptable maneuver margin will increase relative to that required for smaller airplanes to maintain some minimum acceptable CAP value.

6.4 LATERAL–DIRECTIONAL FLYING QUALITY REQUIREMENTS

The lateral–directional flying quality requirements of References 6.1 through 6.3 have been copied and included verbatim as Appendices A and B in Part VII of Reference 6.5. This section contains a summary of only those requirements which should be addressed during the early stages of design analysis of new airplanes. The reader should consult the actual regulations before considering a flying quality assessment to be completed. In several instances, when the FAR/VLA regulations do not contain specific requirements a statement of 'Civilian Equivalent' is included. The author suggests these civilian equivalents requirements as sound design practice only.

6.4.1 LATERAL–DIRECTIONAL CONTROL FORCES

The lateral–directional control force requirements, which are summarized here, apply to airplanes equipped with conventional stick– or wheel–type cockpit controllers. The regulations deal with many specific situations which are summarized as follows:

* 6.4.1.1 Roll control forces
* 6.4.1.2 Directional control forces with asymmetric loadings
* 6.4.1.3 Directional and roll control forces with one engine inoperative

6.4.1.1 Roll Control Forces

The stick or wheel control forces required to obtain the roll performance of Sub–section 6.4.6 may not be greater than those listed in Table 6.10, nor may these forces be less than the control system break–out forces plus:

for Level 1:   1/4 the values of Table 6.10
for Level 2:   1/8 the values listed in Table 6.10
for Level 3:   zero.

Table 6.10 Maximum Allowable Roll Control Forces (lbs)				
MIL–F–8785C:		Flight Phase Category	Maximum Allowable Stick Force	Maximum Allowable Wheel Force
Level	Airplane Class			
Level 1	I, II–C, IV	A, B	20.0	40.0
		C	20.0	20.0
	II–L, III	A, B	25.0	50.0
		C	25.0	25.0
Level 2	I, II–C, IV	A, B	30.0	60.0
		C	20.0	20.0
	II–L, III	A, B	30.0	60.0
		C	30.0	30.0
Level 3	All	All	35.0	70.0

In VLA, FAR 23 and FAR 25: No requirements, except that the maximum forces of Table 6.11 may not be exceeded.

6.4.1.2 Directional Control Forces with Asymmetric Loadings

When initially trimmed for a symmetrical loading, it must be possible to maintain a straight line flight path, following any required asymmetrical loading with:

* rudder pedal forces less than 100 lbs for Levels 1 and 2

and

* rudder pedal forces less than 180 lbs for Level 3.

This is a MIL–F–8785C requirement. There is no corresponding civilian requirement.

6.4.1.3 Directional and Roll Control Forces with One Engine Inoperative

With the trim controls fixed, the maximum allowable directional and roll control forces with an engine inoperative may not exceed the values listed in Table 6.11.

Table 6.11 Maximum Allowable Directional and Roll Control Forces (lbs)

	VLA	FAR 23	FAR 25
a) For **temporary** force application:			
Wheel Controller (Applied to rim)	45.0	60.0	60.0
Rudder Pedal	90.0	150.0	150.0
b) For **prolonged** application:			
Wheel Controller (Applied to rim)	3.4	5.0	5.0
Rudder Pedal	22.5	20.0	20.0

MIL–F–8785C: No requirement, except that the pedal force required in one engine–out at takeoff may not exceed 180 lbs.

6.4.2 DUTCH ROLL FREQUENCY AND DAMPING

The dutch roll undamped natural frequency, ω_{n_d}, and damping ratio, ζ_d, should meet the requirements of Table 6.12. For military airplanes, additional damping requirements are imposed if the ratio of bank–angle to sideslip–angle in the dutch roll mode exceeds the following value:

$$\left|\frac{\phi}{\beta}\right| > \frac{20}{\omega_{n_d}^2} \tag{6.15}$$

where: ω_{n_d} is in rad/sec.

These additional damping requirements are as follows:

$$\text{Level 1}: \Delta\zeta_d\omega_{n_d} = 0.014\left\{(\omega_{n_d}^2)\left|\frac{\phi}{\beta}\right| - 20\right\} \tag{6.16a}$$

$$\text{Level 2}: \Delta\zeta_d\omega_{n_d} = 0.009\left\{(\omega_{n_d}^2)\left|\frac{\phi}{\beta}\right| - 20\right\} \tag{6.16b}$$

$$\text{Level 3}: \Delta\zeta_d\omega_{n_d} = 0.005\left\{(\omega_{n_d}^2)\left|\frac{\phi}{\beta}\right| - 20\right\} \tag{6.16c}$$

It is seen that the civilian requirements in Table 6.12 are less specific than the military requirements. Whenever there is is doubt about which dutch roll requirements should be used, good design practice is to use the military requirements. Methods for predicting numerical magnitudes for the dutch roll undamped natural frequency, ω_{n_d}, and damping ratio, ζ_d, are found in Sub–sections 5.3.4 and 5.3.5.

Table 6.12 Minimum Dutch Roll Undamped Natural Frequency and Damping Ratio Requirements

Mil–F–8785C

Level	Flight Phase Category	Airplane Class	Min. ζ_d *	Min. $\zeta_d \omega_{n_d}$ * rad/sec	Min. ω_{n_d} rad/sec
Level 1	A (Combat and Ground Attack)	IV	0.4	–	1.0
	A (Other)	I and IV	0.19	0.35	1.0
		II and III	0.19	0.35	0.4**
	B	All	0.08	0.15	0.4**
	C	I, II–C and IV	0.08	0.15	1.0
		II–L and III	0.08	0.10	0.4**
Level 2	All	All	0.02	0.05	0.4**
Level 3	All	All	0	–	0.4**

* The governing requirement is that which yields the largest value of ζ_d.
   Note : For Class III ζ_d = 0.7 is the maximum vale required.
** Class III airplanes may be excepted from these requirements, subject specific approval.

Civilian Requirements:

FAR 23 and VLA: ζ_d > 0.052 with controls − free and controls − fixed

FAR 25: ζ_d > 0 with controls − free and must be controllable
              without exceptional pilot skills

6.4.3 SPIRAL STABILITY

There are no specific requirements for spiral stability in any airplane. However, the military requirements place limits on the allowable divergence of the spiral mode. These limits are presented in Table 6.13 and must be met with the cockpit controls free. The author suggests, that these limits also be used for civilian airplanes.

6.4.4 COUPLED ROLL–SPIRAL (= LATERAL PHUGOID) STABILITY

When a pilot commands a roll, it is normally not permitted that an airplane exhibit coupled roll–spiral response in those flight conditions which require other than gentle maneuvering. For example in Combat and Ground–Attack flight conditions (Flight Phase Category A) such coupled roll–spiral (called lateral–phugoid in Chapter 5) is not allowed.

Table 6.13 Minimum Time to Double the Amplitude in the Spiral Mode
MIL–F–8785C

Flight Phase Category	Level 1	Level 2	Level 3
A and C	$T_{2_s} > 12$ sec	$T_{2_s} > 8$ sec	$T_{2_s} > 4$ sec
B	$T_{2_s} > 20$ sec	$T_{2_s} > 8$ sec	$T_{2_s} > 4$ sec
Civilian Requirements:	None		

In Flight Phase Categories B and C a coupled roll–spiral response will be permitted provided the product of undamped natural frequency, $\omega_{n_{rs}}$, and damping ratio, ζ_{rs}, does not exceed the following values:

Level 1 : $\quad \zeta_{rs}\omega_{n_{rs}} > 0.5$ $\qquad$ (6.17a)

Level 2 : $\quad \zeta_{rs}\omega_{n_{rs}} > 0.3$ $\qquad$ (6.17b)

Level 3 : $\quad \zeta_{rs}\omega_{n_{rs}} > 0.15$ $\qquad$ (6.17c)

There are no similar requirements for civil airplanes. The author suggests to use the military guidelines in this case.

6.4.5 ROLL MODE TIME CONSTANT

The airplane roll mode time constant, T_r, is a measure of the rapidity of roll response. A small roll time constant signifies a rapid build–up of roll rate following a lateral control input by the pilot. To visualize this, see Figure 5.20. Table 6.14 shows the military requirements placed on the roll mode time constant, T_r. For civilian airplanes, the author suggests to use the military requirements as a guideline.

Table 6.14 Maximum Allowable Roll Mode Time Constant
MIL–F–8785C

Flight Phase Category	Airplane Class	Level 1	Level 2	Level 3
A	I and IV	$T_r < 1.0$ sec	$T_r < 1.4$ sec	$T_r < 10.0$ sec *
A	II and III	$T_r < 1.4$ sec	$T_r < 3.0$ sec	–
B	All	$T_r < 1.4$ sec	$T_r < 3.0$ sec	$T_r < 10.0$ sec
C	I, II–C and IV	$T_r < 1.0$ sec	$T_r < 1.4$ sec	$T_r < 10.0$ sec *
C	II–L and III	$T_r < 1.4$ sec	$T_r < 3.0$ sec	–
Civilian Requirements:	None		* **Applies to MIL–STD–1797A, Class IV only!**	

6.4.6 ROLL CONTROL EFFECTIVENESS

Following a full deflection of the lateral cockpit controls, airplanes must exhibit a minimum bank angle response within a certain specified time. The elapsed time, t, is counted from the time of cockpit control force application. Therefore, any flight control system lag and any aeroelastic compliance within the flight control system must be accounted for.

Military Airplanes:

The roll control effectiveness requirements are summarized in Table 6.15 for Class I, II and III airplanes.

The notation, $t_{\phi=0\,deg}^{\phi=60\,deg}$ in Table 6.15 indicates the time it takes from a bank angle of 0 degrees to reach a bank angle of 60 degrees following full deflection of the lateral cockpit controls.

In preliminary design it is acceptable to use Eqn (5.132) to determine the roll control effectiveness of an airplane.

For Class IV airplanes the roll effectiveness requirements are summarized in Table 6.16. These requirements may not be sufficient for combat and ground attack flight phases. References 6.1 and 6.2 should be consulted for the requirements in those cases.

Civilian Airplanes:

For civilian airplanes the roll effectiveness requirements are summarized in Table 6.17. Comparison with the military requirements will show that the civilian requirements are less demanding. The times indicated in Table 6.17 must not be exceeded.

Since roll control effectiveness at low speed and at low altitudes is frequently a matter of safety, the author suggests using the appropriate military requirements whenever possible.

6.4.7 YAWING MOMENTS IN STEADY SIDESLIPS

The following requirement must be met, according to all civilian and military flying quality regulations (References 6.1–6.4):

A right rudder pedal force must produce a negative sideslip angle while a left rudder pedal force must produce a positive sideslip angle.

In general, this requirement can be met only if the airplane is directionally stable, $C_{n_\beta} > 0$, and as long as the rudder hingemoment derivatives are reasonably linear.

Table 6.15 Roll Effectiveness Requirements

MIL–F–8785C:　　　　　　　　　　　　　　　　**NOTE: All times, t in seconds**

Airplane Class	Level	Flight Phase Category					
		A		B		C	
		$\phi=60$ deg t $\phi=0$ deg	$\phi=45$ deg t $\phi=0$ deg	$\phi=60$ deg t $\phi=0$ deg	$\phi=45$ deg t $\phi=0$ deg	$\phi=30$ deg t $\phi=0$ deg	$\phi=25$ deg t $\phi=0$ deg
I	1	1.3	–	1.7	–	1.3	–
I	2	1.7	–	2.5	–	1.8	–
I	3	2.6	–	3.4	–	2.6	–
II–L	1	–	1.4	–	1.9	1.8	–
II–L	2	–	1.9	–	2.8	2.5	–
II–L	3	–	2.8	–	3.8	3.6	–
II–C	1	–	1.4	–	1.9	–	1.0
II–C	2	–	1.9	–	2.8	–	1.5
II–C	3	–	2.8	–	3.8	–	2.0

Class III		Flight Phase Category		
		A	B	C
Level	Speed Range *	$\phi=30$ deg t $\phi=0$ deg	$\phi=30$ deg t $\phi=0$ deg	$\phi=30$ deg t $\phi=0$ deg
1	Low	1.8	2.3	2.5
1	Medium	1.5	2.0	2.5
1	High	2.0	2.3	2.5
2	Low	2.4	3.9	4.0
2	Medium	2.0	3.3	4.0
2	High	2.5	3.9	4.0
3	All	3.0	5.0	6.0

* For complete definition of speed ranges, see Reference 6.1. For preliminary design purposes use the following definitions:

　　Low speed range represents takeoff and approach speeds
　　Medium speed range represents speeds up to 70% of maximum level speed
　　High speed range represents speeds from 70% to 100% of maximum level speed

		Flight Phase Category				
		A			B	C
Level	Speed Range *	$\phi=30\,deg$ t $\phi=0\,deg$	$\phi=50\,deg$ t $\phi=0\,deg$	$\phi=90\,deg$ t $\phi=0\,deg$	$\phi=90\,deg$ t $\phi=0\,deg$	$\phi=30\,deg$ t $\phi=0\,deg$
1	Very Low	1.1	–	–	2.0	1.1
	Low	1.1	–	–	1.7	1.1
	Medium	–	–	1.3	1.7	1.1
	High	–	1.1	–	1.7	1.1
2	Very Low	1.6	–	–	2.8	1.3
	Low	1.5	–	–	2.5	1.3
	Medium	–	–	1.7	2.5	1.3
	High	–	1.3	–	2.5	1.3
3	Very Low	2.6	–	–	3.7	2.0
	Low	2.0	–	–	3.4	2.0
	Medium	–	–	2.6	3.4	2.0
	High	–	2.6	–	3.4	2.0

Table 6.16 Roll Effectiveness Requirements for Class IV Airplanes
MIL–F–8785C: NOTE: All times, t in seconds

* For complete definition of speed ranges, see Reference 6.1. For preliminary design purposes use the following definitions:
 Very low speed range represents speeds close to stall in all configurations
 Low speed range represents takeoff and approach speeds
 Medium speed range represents speeds up to 70% of maximum level speed
 High speed range represents speeds from 70% to 100% of maximum level speed

Note: All times, t in seconds			VLA	FAR 23	FAR 25
Flight Phase	Speed	Weight (lbs)	$\phi = +30\deg$ t $\phi = -30\deg$	$\phi = +30\deg$ t $\phi = -30\deg$	
Takeoff	$1.2V_{S_{TO}}$	$W \leq 6,000$	5	5	No requirement
		$W > 6,000$	Not applicable	$t = \dfrac{W + 500}{1,300}$	No requirement
Landing	$1.3V_{S_{PA}}$	$W \leq 6,000$	4	4	No requirement
		$W > 6,000$	Not applicable	$t = \dfrac{W + 2,800}{2,200}$	No requirement

Table 6.17 Roll Effectiveness Requirements for Civilian Airplanes

Note: For FAR 25 it is suggested to use the Class II or Class III military requirements

6.4.8 SIDE FORCES IN STEADY SIDESLIPS

The following requirement must be met, according to all civilian and military flying quality regulations(References 6.1–6.4):

> For the sideslips produced under Sub–section 6.4.7 an increase in right (positive) bank angle shall accompany an increase in right (positive) sideslip angle while an increase in left (negative) bank angle shall accompany an increase in left (negative) sideslip angle.

In general, this requirement can be met only if the side–force–due–to–sideslip derivative is negative, $C_{y_\beta} < 0$.

6.4.9 ROLLING MOMENTS IN STEADY SIDESLIPS

The following requirement must be met, according to all civilian and military flying quality regulations (References 6.1–6.4):

> For the sideslips produced under Sub–section 6.4.7, left (negative) roll–control deflection and force shall accompany left (negative) sideslips while right (positive) roll–control deflection and force shall accompany right (positive) sideslips.

In general, this requirement can be met only if the net rolling–moment–due–to–sideslip derivative is negative, $C_{l_\beta} < 0$.

6.5   CHARACTERISTICS OF THE FLIGHT CONTROL SYSTEM

The flying quality requirements discussed in Sections 6.3 and 6.4 deal primarily with the reaction of the airplane to pilot inputs. These pilot inputs are transmitted to the flight control surfaces or to flight control surface actuators via cables, push–rods and wire bundles (electrical or optical). In most high performance airplanes, the pilot inputs are digitized and operated upon by one or more software packages before being forwarded to signal paths which lead to the actuators. This control signalling process can cause delays and distortions.

In many instances, the pilot decides on a control input based on some flight crucial quantity (such as attitude) which is displayed on the instrument panel. Many of these displays are driven by sensor outputs which in turn are operated upon by a computer before being sent to the display(s). This display signalling process also can cause delays and distortions.

As a result, the following three factors can have a detrimental effect on the perception of airplane flying qualities:

1) Detailed design execution of the signal paths from the cockpit controllers to the flight control surfaces. Important design aspects which require attention are:

* lags in mechanical signal paths to the control surfaces or to the control surface actuators

* mechanical signal path compliance (deflection under load!)

* actuator blow–down under load

* electrical or fly–by–wire signal distortions

2) Lags in actuator response to signal inputs

3) Lags in displays

Many of these factors are the subject of rather detailed regulations. Because of rapid changes in technology, these types of regulations change frequently. Regulatory requirements placed on the detailed design of flight control systems and displays are beyond the scope of this text.

For an introduction to the detailed design of flight control systems and their associated mechanical and hydraulic systems, the reader should consult Part IV of Reference 6.6.

Of major importance to the pilot's perception of flying qualities are the so–called control system break–out forces. These break–out forces are of concern to designers of all airplanes equipped with reversible flight control systems. Break–out forces are also of concern to designers of airplanes with irreversible flight control systems as long as the signal paths from cockpit to actuators are mechanical.

Table 6.18 lists the maximum allowable control system break–out forces. Large break–out forces have a negative effect on the apparent longitudinal stability (as exhibited to the pilot through the return–to–trim–speed behavior) of Sub–section 6.3.1.

Control Mode	Controller Type	Airplane Classes			
		Classes I, II–C and IV		Classes II–L and III	
		Minimum	Maximum	Minimum	Maximum
Pitch	Stick	0.5	3.0	0.5	5.0
	Wheel	0.5	4.0	0.5	7.0
Roll	Stick	0.5	2.0	0.5	4.0
	Wheel	0.5	3.0	0.5	6.0
Yaw	Pedal	1.0	7.0	1.0	14.0

Table 6.18 Allowable Control System Break–out Forces (lbs)

Another item of concern to the pilot's perception of flying qualities are phase lags between control surface deflections and cockpit control inputs. Table 6.19 shows the maximum allowable control surface lags at frequencies also specified in Table 6.19. These lags apply to all amplitudes of the cockpit control inputs.

Table 6.19 Allowable Phase Lags Between Cockpit Controller and Flight Control Surface (Degrees)

Level	Flight Phase Categories A and C	Flight Phase Category B
Level 1	15	30
Level 2	30	45
Level 3	60	60

Control Mode	Upper Frequency at which Maximum Phase Lag is Allowed
Pitch	the larger of $\omega_{n_{sp}}$ and 2.0 rad/sec
Roll and Yaw	the larger of ω_{n_d}, $\frac{1}{T_r}$ and 2.0 rad/sec

6.6   RELATION BETWEEN FLYING QUALITY REQUIREMENTS AND DESIGN

To assure that a new airplane design has acceptable flying qualities it is necessary to analyze (determine) the stability, control and response characteristics of a the new design. The predicted behavior is then compared with flying quality requirements. If needed, appropriate deign changes are made, where–upon an analysis is again carried out. In this section, the following examples of this process are discussed:

6.6.1 Design for Roll Control Effectiveness

6.6.2 Design for Inherent Spiral and Dutch Roll Stability

6.6.3 Design for Augmented Static and Dynamic Stability in Pitch

6.6.1   DESIGN FOR ROLL CONTROL EFFECTIVENESS

The example considered here concerns a jet trainer airplane (Land–based, L) which is intended as a trainer for Class IV type airplanes. Therefore, this airplane is to be considered also a Class IV airplane. The general characteristics of this airplane pertinent to roll control effectiveness are given in Table 6.20. These characteristics were determined with the help of a three–view of the airplane (to get the geometric data) and with the AAA program of Appendix A. Note the significant effect of flight speed on the dimensional derivatives.

The roll control effectiveness of this airplane will be checked for Flight Phase Category C at two speeds: $U_1 = 1.2V_{s_{PA}}$ (low) and $U_1 = 1.05V_{s_{PA}}$ (very low). According to Table 6.16, to meet the Level 1 roll control effectiveness requirements, the airplane must be able to reach a bank angle of 30 degrees (from zero bank) after 1.1 seconds: $\phi(t = 1.1) > 30^0$. In addition, according to Table 6.14 its roll mode time constant should be less than 1.4 seconds: $T_r < 1.4\,\text{sec}$.

The roll time constant, T_r, can be estimated from Eqn (5.129) while the bank angle after 1.1 seconds can be estimated from Eqn (5.132). It is seen from the data in Table 6.20 that the example airplane easily meets the requirements.

Whether or not an airplane meets the required bank angle, $\phi(t)$, often depends on the magnitude of the dimensional roll control power derivative, L_{δ_a}. This derivative, in turn, depends mostly on the dimensionless roll control power derivative, $C_{l_{\delta_a}}$. Finally, the latter depends on the chord-wise and spanwise size of the ailerons. In the design of most airplanes, a conflict arises between required flap space and required aileron space. Such conflicts are normally resolved by trade studies involving variations in chord–wise and spanwise sizing of flaps and ailerons. Sometimes other roll control devices (such as spoilers and/or differential stabilizers) have to be used to solve the problem.

Table 6.20 Roll Effectiveness Data for a Small Jet Trainer

W = 5,511 lbs   S = 136 ft^2 b = 26.3 ft   Altitude : sealevel, standard

I_{xx_B} = 877 slugft^2 I_{zz_B} = 6,126 slugft^2 I_{xz_B} = 200 slugft^2

$C_{l_{\delta_a}}$ = 0.148 1/rad C_{l_p} = − 0.35 1/rad $\delta_{a_{max}}$ = 25 deg = 0.44 rad

	$1.2V_{s_{PA}}$ = 149 fps	$1.05V_{s_{PA}}$ = 130 fps
Speed, U_1 (fps)		
Dynamic pressure, $\bar{q}_1$ (psf)	26.31	20.07
Angle of attack, α (deg)	2	5
I_{xx_s} (slugft^2)	870	883
$L_p = \dfrac{\bar{q}_1 S b^2 C_{l_p}}{2 I_{xx_s} U_1}$ (1/sec)	−3.35	−2.88
$L_{\delta_a} = \dfrac{\bar{q}_1 S b C_{l_{\delta_a}}}{I_{xx_s}}$ (1/sec^2)	16.0	12.0
Roll time constant, $T_r \approx \dfrac{-1}{L_p}$ (sec)	0.30	0.35
Requirement : T_r < 1.0 sec	requirement met	requirement met
Bank angle in 1.1 sec, ϕ(t = 1.1 sec)	134	80
Requirement : ϕ(t = 1.1 sec) > 30 deg	requirement met	requirement met

6.6.2   DESIGN FOR INHERENT SPIRAL AND DUTCH ROLL STABILITY

The example considered here concerns a single engine, propeller driven light airplane. Many airplanes in this category have a slightly unstable spiral mode and relatively poor dutch roll damping. Figure 6.9 shows a three–view of this airplane as well as the pertinent lateral–directional baseline data for conducting a lateral–directional dynamic stability analysis.

For the flight condition of Figure 6.9 the airplane has the following characteristics:

$$\frac{1}{T_s} = -0.006 \qquad \zeta_d = 0.065$$

The airplane meets the current FAR 23 requirements for the spiral and for the dutch roll damping. See Tables 6.13 and 6.12 respectively. Nevertheless, the following question is asked at a design review meeting, "What are the consequences of designing to a more stringent requirement, such as a slightly stable spiral and a slightly better dutch–roll damping ratio?"

After some debate at this design review meeting, it is decided to translate the question into:

"How should the configuration be changed to achieve the following characteristics:

$$\frac{1}{T_s} = + 0.020 \qquad\qquad \zeta_d = 0.100 \qquad ?"$$

It is known from inequality (5.127) that the dimensional rolling–moment–due–to–sideslip derivative, L_β , and therefore the dimensionless rolling–moment–due–to–sideslip derivative, C_{l_β} , has a major influence on the spiral root location. Figure 6.10 shows how the spiral behavior varies with the derivative C_{l_β} . According to Figure 6.10, to meet the spiral design objective it is necessary to change the derivative C_{l_β} from a value of –0.122 1/rad to –0.170 1/rad. Such a change in C_{l_β} is most easily achieved by a change in wing geometric dihedral angle. See Chapter 4, page 96.

Figure 6.11 indicates how the derivative C_{l_β} for the airplane of Figure 6.9 is affected by the geometric dihedral angle of the wing, Γ_w . To arrive at the data in Figure 6.11, the methods of Reference 6.6, Part VI were used. It is seen from Figure 6.11 that to change the derivative C_{l_β} from a value of –0.122 to one of –0.170 requires an increase in the wing geometric dihedral angle from the actual 3 degrees to approximately 7 degrees.

A problem which confronts designers in nearly all airplanes is that if C_{l_β} is used to 'tailor' the spiral behavior of the airplane in the stable direction, the corresponding more negative value of C_{l_β} leads to a lower dutch roll damping ratio. To improve the latter (without the use of a yaw damper) requires an increase in the size of the vertical tail. Figure 6.12 shows the effect of the derivative C_{l_β} on the dutch roll damping ratio for a range of vertical tail areas (maintaining the tail moment arm and the tail planform shape). It is seen that for the original vertical tail area of 18 ft2 the increased negative magnitude of C_{l_β} does indeed lower the dutch roll damping. To bring the dutch roll damping ratio up to the desired value of 0.100 it is necessary to increase the vertical tail area to about 30 ft2 . However, changing the vertical tail area, will in turn increase the negative magnitude of C_{l_β} . Figure 6.13 shows this effect. It is concluded that this change is sufficiently small as to be negligible. The design objectives for the stable spiral and improved dutch roll damping ratio are therefore achievable by making the following configuration design changes:

increase S_v from $\rightarrow S_v = 18$ ft^2 to $\rightarrow S_v = 30$ ft^2 AND SIMULTANEOUSLY

increase Γ_w from $\rightarrow \Gamma_w = 3$ degrees to $\rightarrow \Gamma_w = 7$ degrees

Two questions now arise: 1) does the resulting airplane still 'look' all right?
2) what do the changes do to the airplane performance?

The answer to the first question is largely a matter of taste and perceived marketability. The answer to the second question requires a drag polar and weight and balance analysis. Since the

$W = 2,600$ lbs	$U_1 = 107$ fps	Altitude : sealevel	$S_w = 180$ ft^2
$b_w = 36.9$ ft	$A_w = 7.5$	$\Gamma_w = 3.0$ deg	$\lambda_w = -.7$
$S_h = 41.4$ ft^2	$b_h = 11.7$ ft	$S_v = 18.0$ ft^2	$l_f = 26.2$ ft
$d_f = 4.9$ ft	$C_{y_\beta} = -0.303$	$C_{y_p} = -0.213$	$C_{y_r} = +0.201$
Note: all derivatives are in 1/rad	$C_{l_\beta} = -0.122$	$C_{l_p} = -0.494$	$C_{l_r} = +0.204$
	$C_{n_\beta} = +0.070$	$C_{n_p} = -0.096$	$C_{n_r} = -0.115$

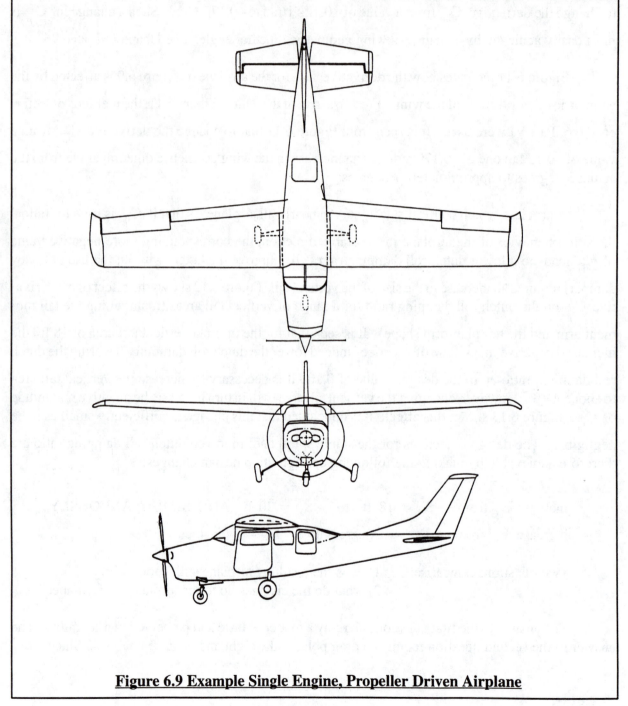

Figure 6.9 Example Single Engine, Propeller Driven Airplane

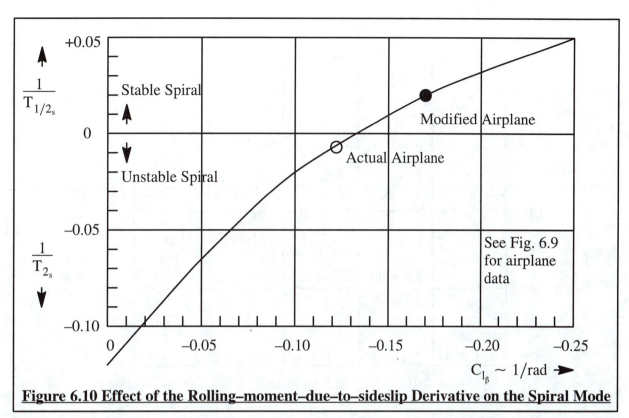

Figure 6.10 Effect of the Rolling–moment–due–to–sideslip Derivative on the Spiral Mode

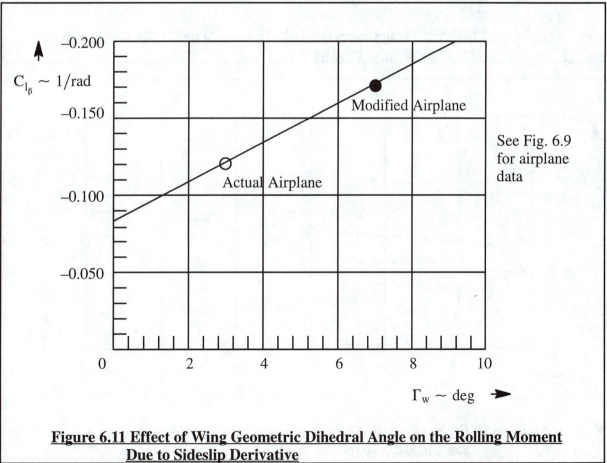

Figure 6.11 Effect of Wing Geometric Dihedral Angle on the Rolling Moment Due to Sideslip Derivative

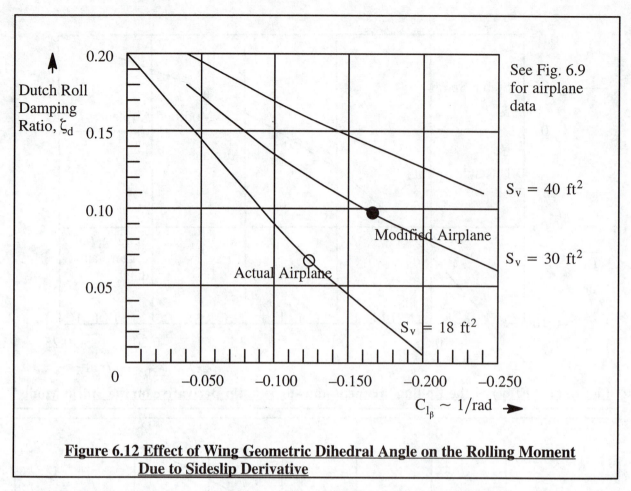

Figure 6.12 Effect of Wing Geometric Dihedral Angle on the Rolling Moment Due to Sideslip Derivative

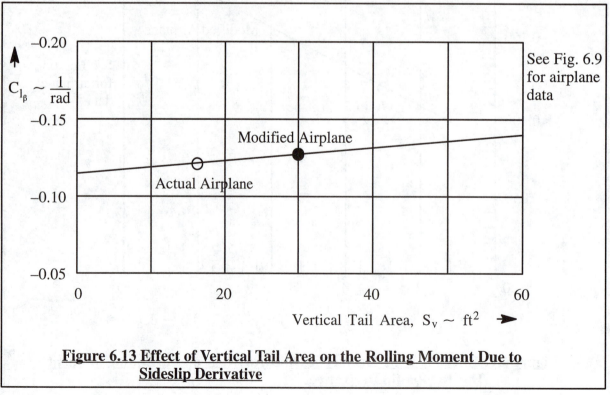

Figure 6.13 Effect of Vertical Tail Area on the Rolling Moment Due to Sideslip Derivative

wetted vertical tail area is increased, the zero–lift drag of the airplane will increase. The resulting decrease in cruise speed for this airplane was calculated to be 3.5 mph (from 194.5 to 191.0 mph). The increase in vertical tail area also shifts the aft center of gravity aft (due to increased tail weight). The effect of this on the allowable c.g. range of the airplane should also be determined.

Designing for good inherent dynamic stability nearly always results in some performance, weight and balance penalties. The designer must find the appropriate balance between the various conflicting factors to arrive at an acceptable design.

6.6.3 DESIGN FOR AUGMENTED STATIC AND DYNAMIC STABILITY IN PITCH

Rather significant improvements in airplane payload–range performance are possible by reducing tail areas and by relaxing the requirement for inherent static and dynamic stability. As an example, in a typical small business jet, the cruise lift–to–drag ratio, $L/D_{cruise} = 10.0$, and the zero–lift drag coefficient is $\overline{C}_{D_{0_{cruise}}} = 0.0336$. The total horizontal and vertical tail contribution to zero–lift drag is 0.0027. Therefore, if it were possible to completely eliminate the tail surfaces (which it is not!), the theoretically attainable cruise lift–to–drag ratio would be:

$$L/D_{cruise_{no-tails}} = \frac{0.336}{0.0336 - 0.0027} = 10.8$$

This represents a considerable improvement. In addition, there would be the synergistic benefit of reduced empty weight and reduced manufacturing cost. However, complete elimination of the tails is impossible, because the **sum of the following control power requirements** must be met by the tail:

* Control power to trim at forward and aft c.g.
* Control power to maneuver
* Control power for stability augmentation

The following design considerations are presented to illustrate typical limitations to horizontal tail size reduction which confront the designer:

6.6.3.1 Effect of Horizontal Tail Size on Longitudinal Stability and Control Derivatives
6.6.3.2 Stability Augmentation by Angle–of–attack and Pitch–rate Feedback
6.6.3.3 Effect of Horizontal Tail Area on Controllability in Gust and on Maneuvering
6.6.3.4 Effect of Horizontal Tail Area on Trim

6.6.3.1 Effect of Horizontal Tail Size on Longitudinal Stability and Control Derivatives

The baseline characteristics for a small business jet airplane are listed in Table 6.21. To determine the effect of horizontal tail size on various stability and control derivatives, the following approximate equations (6.18a through 6.18e):

Table 6.21 Baseline Geometry and Derivative Data for a Small Business Jet

$W = 13,009$ lbs	$m = 404$ slugs	$S = 232$ ft^2	$\bar{c} = 7.0$ ft
$I_{yy} = 18,800$ slugft^2	$h = 40,000$ ft	$M_1 = 0.70$	$U_1 = 675$ fps
$\bar{q}_1 = 134$ psf	$\bar{x}_{cg} = 0.315$	$S_h = 54$ ft^2 $\quad l_h = (\bar{x}_{ac_h} - \bar{x}_{cg})\bar{c} = 22$ ft	

$C_{L_\alpha} = 5.84$ rad^{-1}	$C_{L_{\alpha_{wf}}} = 5.29$ rad^{-1}	$C_{L_{\alpha_h}} = 3.4$ rad^{-1}	$\dfrac{d\varepsilon}{d\alpha} = 0.30$
$C_{m_\alpha} = -0.64$ rad^{-1}	$\dfrac{dC_m}{dC_L} = -0.11$	$\bar{x}_{ac} = 0.425$	$\bar{x}_{ac_{wf}} = 0.107$
$C_{m_{\dot\alpha}} = -6.8$ rad^{-1}	$C_{m_q} = -15.5$ rad^{-1}	$\tau_e = 0.5$	

$$C_{L_\alpha} \approx C_{L_{\alpha_{wf}}} + C_{L_{\alpha_h}}\frac{S_h}{S_w}\left(1 - \frac{d\varepsilon}{d\alpha}\right) \tag{6.18a}$$

$$C_{m_\alpha} \approx C_{L_{\alpha_{wf}}}(\bar{x}_{cg} - \bar{x}_{ac_{wf}}) - C_{L_{\alpha_h}}\frac{S_h}{S_w}(\bar{x}_{ac_h} - \bar{x}_{cg})\left(1 - \frac{d\varepsilon}{d\alpha}\right) \tag{6.18b}$$

$$C_{m_{\delta_e}} \approx C_{L_{\alpha_h}}\frac{S_h}{S_w}\frac{l_h}{\bar{c}}\tau_e \tag{6.18c}$$

$$C_{m_q} \approx -2.0C_{L_{\alpha_h}}\frac{S_h}{S_w}\left(\frac{l_h}{\bar{c}}\right)^2 \tag{6.18d}$$

$$C_{m_{\dot\alpha}} \approx 0.433C_{m_q} \tag{6.18e}$$

Using the baseline data of Table 6.21 these derivatives are expressed as numerical functions of the horizontal tail area in Eqns 6.19a through 6.19e:

$$C_{L_\alpha} = 5.29 + 0.0102S_h \tag{6.19a}$$

$$C_{m_\alpha} = 1.10 - 0.0322S_h \tag{6.19b}$$

$$C_{m_{\delta_e}} = -0.023S_h \tag{6.19c}$$

$$C_{m_q} = -0.29S_h \tag{6.19d}$$

$$C_{m_{\dot\alpha}} = -0.13S_h \tag{6.19e}$$

Figure 6.14 shows plots corresponding to Eqns (6.19). Note the strong effect of horizontal tail area on most of these derivatives. Table 6.22 shows how these changes in horizontal tail area affect the short period characteristics of the airplane. These data were determined with Eqns (5.61) and (5.62). Figure 6.15 indicates that the airplane gradually becomes sluggish. The short period frequency crosses the Level 1 and then the Level 2 flying quality boundaries. Even though the damping ratio improves, the flying qualities become unacceptable due to this sluggishness. Figure 6.16 shows a root–locus with horizontal tail area as the parameter along the root–locus.

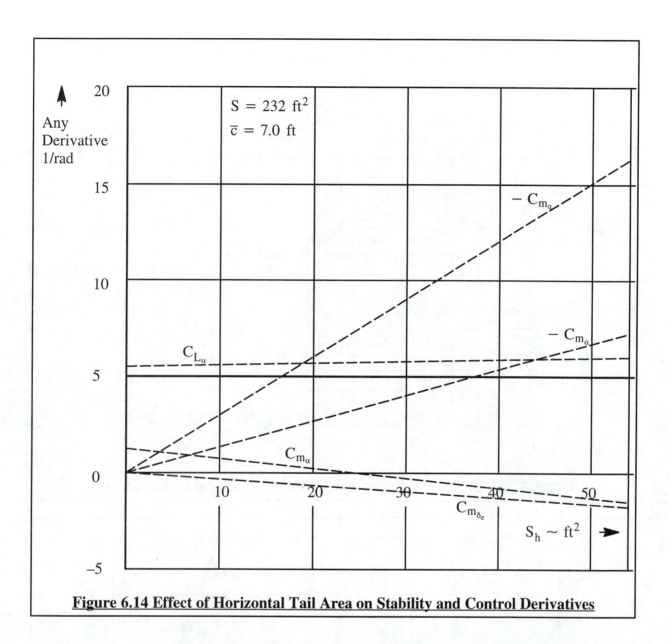

Figure 6.14 Effect of Horizontal Tail Area on Stability and Control Derivatives

$S_h \sim ft^2$	$\omega_{n_{sp}} \sim rad/sec$	ζ_{sp}	$\zeta_{sp}\omega_{n_{sp}} \sim rad/sec$	Number on Root Locus of Figure 6.15
54	2.84	0.37	1.05	1
50	2.56	0.39	0.99	2
45	2.15	0.43	0.92	3
40	1.64	0.52	0.85	4
35	0.87	0.91	0.79	5

Table 6.22 Effect of Horizontal Tail Area on Short Period Characteristics

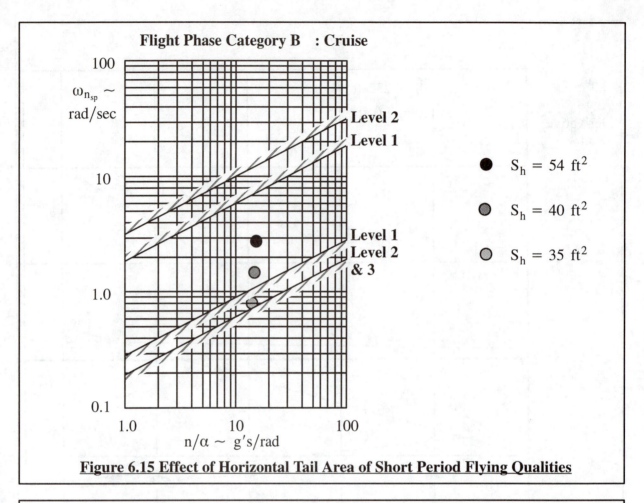

Figure 6.15 Effect of Horizontal Tail Area of Short Period Flying Qualities

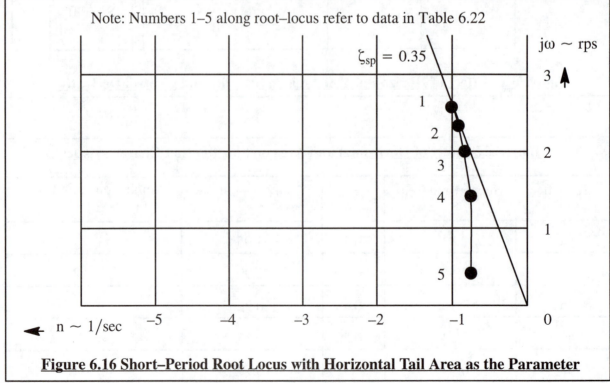

Figure 6.16 Short–Period Root Locus with Horizontal Tail Area as the Parameter

6.6.3.2 Stability Augmentation by Angle–of–attack and Pitch–rate Feedback

To 'restore' the airplane flying qualities to the level prevailing with the original horizontal tail area of 54 ft^2 requires stability augmentation. For purposes of illustration of the principles involved it will be assumed that the airplane should be restored to its original (but now equivalent) values of the derivatives C_{m_α} and C_{m_q}. Figure 6.17 shows a block–diagram of the required stability augmentation system.

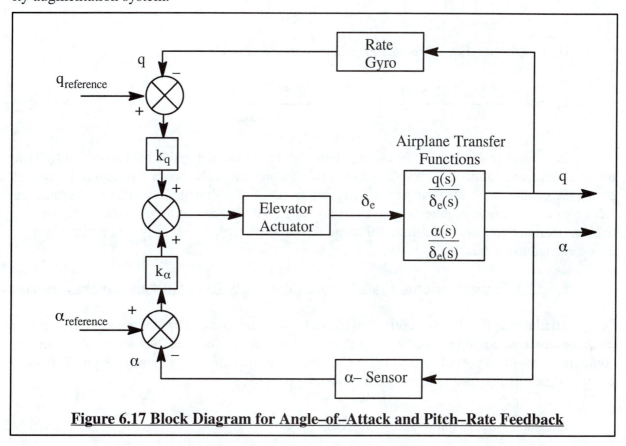

Figure 6.17 Block Diagram for Angle–of–Attack and Pitch–Rate Feedback

Exact methods of analyzing such feedback systems is discussed in Chapters 8 and 11. At this point, the equivalent derivative concept of Section 5.5 will be used to estimate the required feedback gains in the stability augmentation system. It should be recalled that in the equivalent derivative concept the effect of sensor and servo dynamics is neglected.

To relate the horizontal tail area to the feedback gain required, the following relations, which follow from the equivalent derivative concept, are used:

For angle–of–attack feedback:

$$k_\alpha = \frac{\Delta C_{m_{\alpha_{required}}}}{C_{m_{\delta_{e_{available}}}}} = \frac{C_{m_{\alpha_{desired}}} - C_{m_{\alpha_{available}}}}{C_{m_{\delta_{e_{available}}}}} \qquad (6.20)$$

By substituting Equations (6.19b) and (6.19c) it follows that:

$$k_\alpha = \frac{-0.64 - (1.10 - 0.0322S_h)}{-0.023S_h} = \frac{-1.74 + 0.0322S_h}{-0.023S_h} \qquad (6.21)$$

For pitch–rate feedback:

$$k_q = \frac{\Delta C_{m_{q_{required}}}}{C_{m_{\delta_{e_{available}}}}} \left(\frac{\overline{c}}{2U_1}\right) = \frac{C_{m_{q_{desired}}} - C_{m_{q_{available}}}}{C_{m_{\delta_{e_{available}}}}} \left(\frac{\overline{c}}{2U_1}\right) \qquad (6.22)$$

By substituting Equations (6.19d) and (6.19c) it follows that:

$$k_q = \frac{(-15.5 + 0.29S_h)}{-0.023S_h}\left(\frac{7}{2 \times 675}\right) = \frac{-15.5 + 0.29S_h}{-4.44S_h} \qquad (6.23)$$

Equations (6.21) and (6.23) clearly show that both feedback gains tend toward infinity as the tail area tends to zero. Figure 6.18 shows this graphically. The larger the required feedback gains, the greater the control surface activity due to stability augmentation will be in turbulence. Because control power requirements for stability augmentation are additive to those required for trim and maneuvering, there is a limit to the amount of control surface authority which can be reasonably assigned to the feedback system.

6.6.3.3 Effect of Horizontal Tail Area on Controllability in Gust and on Maneuvering

To illustrate the effect of horizontal tail size on the amount of elevator required to arrest the pitching moment caused by a step input gust, consider the following case. Assume the airplane encounters a step–input gust of 21 ft/sec while 'skirting' the anvil cloud of a thunderstorm. This step–input gust results in a gust induced angle of attack given by:

$$\Delta\alpha_{gust} = \frac{21}{675} = 0.031 \text{ rad} = 1.8 \text{ deg} \qquad (6.24)$$

This gust induced angle of attack causes a pitching moment coefficient which has to be arrested by a change in elevator angle given by:

$$C_{m_\alpha}\Delta\alpha_{gust} = C_{m_{\delta_e}}\Delta\delta_{e_{gust}} \qquad (6.25)$$

With Eqns (6.19b) and (6.19c) this yields the following incremental elevator deflection:

$$\Delta\delta_{e_{gust}} = \frac{(1.10 - 0.0322S_h)}{-0.023S_h} \qquad (6.26)$$

This amount of elevator deflection is also plotted as a function of horizontal tail area in Figure 6.18. It is seen again that control power becomes a severely limiting factor when tail sizes are reduced too much.

It is left to the reader to determine the amount of elevator required to maneuver the airplane. This would follow from the product of the maneuvering load factor required and the elevator–versus–load–factor gradient as given by Eqns (4.108) and (4.120).

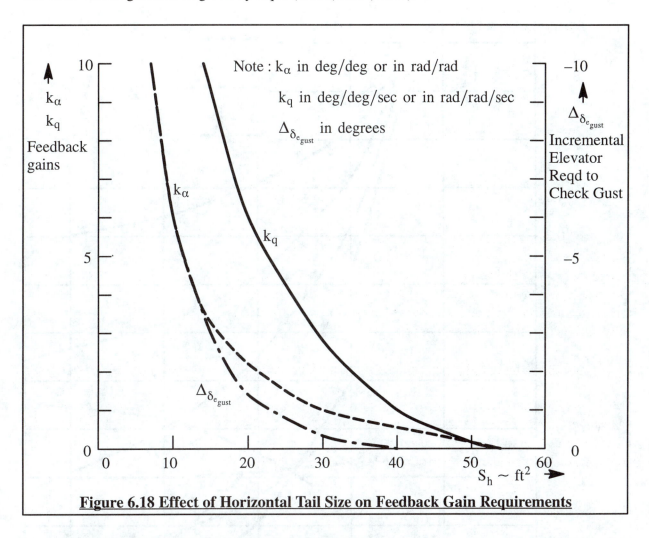

Figure 6.18 Effect of Horizontal Tail Size on Feedback Gain Requirements

6.6.3.4 Effect of Horizontal Tail Area on Trim

The amount of elevator angle required to (moment) trim an airplane can be determined with Eqn (4.47). This amount of elevator required to trim is seen to be a function of c.g. location and (through the various derivatives) of horizontal tail area. Figure 6.19 shows a typical plot of elevator required to trim versus horizontal tail area, for various c.g. locations and steady state lift coefficients. The reader must keep in mind that the total amount of control power required in a given flight condition is the sum of:

* control power required to trim (at the most adverse c.g.) for a given flight condition
* control power required to maneuver for a given flight condition
* control power required to provide stability augmentation

The sum of these control power requirements should not cause the longitudinal control surface to be deflected beyond surface stall.

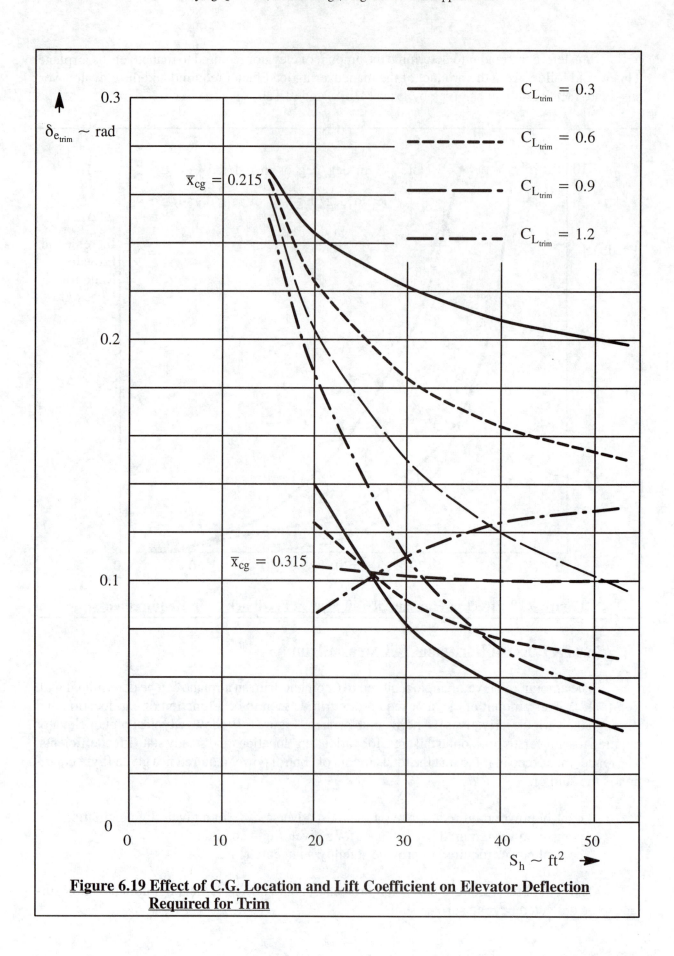

Figure 6.19 Effect of C.G. Location and Lift Coefficient on Elevator Deflection Required for Trim

6.7 SUMMARY FOR CHAPTER 6

In this chapter, a summary has been presented of the numerical relationship between civilian and military requirements (regulations) for flying qualities and certain airplane design parameters. With the help of these relationships it is possible for the designer to predict the flying qualities of a given design. By making changes to certain design aspects of an airplane (such as tail placement, tail size and tail planform shape) it is possible to determine how a design which has certain deficiencies in flying qualities must be changed to assure good flying qualities.

Airplane design and manufacturing technology is undergoing significant evolutionary developments. One result of this is that any 'regulations' should be viewed as temporary. Development and introduction of highly automated flight control and navigation systems requires that regulations be continually adjusted to be consistent with the new technology. In the case of the Boeing 777 for example, special conditions have been evolved by the FAA, by the manufacturer and by the operators to assure that the new technology flight control system offers good flying qualities and adequate safety. These new special conditions also address the question of what flight and ground tests are required to assure compliance with the new special conditions. The flying quality requirements as presented in this chapter should therefore be viewed in this light.

6.8 PROBLEMS FOR CHAPTER 6

6.1 For the airplane of Table 6.20, determine the magnitude of rolling moment of inertia for which that airplane meets the roll effectiveness requirements exactly. If wing–tip–mounted stores are contemplated for this airplane, what is the maximum store weight which can be allowed from a roll effectiveness viewpoint?

6.2 For Airplane J in Appendix B, determine how much of the vertical tail could be lost due to gust damage before the dutch roll mode would deteriorate to Level III flying qualities?

6.3 For airplane H in Appendix B, determine the short period undamped natural frequency and damping ratio if the left stabilizer is lost due to combat damage. What flying quality level does this correspond to?

6.4 A business jet airplane has the following characteristics in the landing configuration:

$I_{xx} = 30,000$ slugft^2 with full tiptanks $C_{l_{\delta_a}} = 0.00261/$deg $S = 232$ ft^2

$I_{xx} = 11,000$ slugft^2 with empty tiptanks $C_{l_p} = -0.385$ 1/rad $b = 34.2$ ft

Assume that in the landing configuration the airplane must meet the Level 1 requirements for Class II–L airplanes of Tables 6.14 and 6.15. Calculate and plot the roll time constant and the bank angle in 1.8 seconds as a function of speed at sea–level. If the normal approach speed of the airplane is 180 fps, does the airplane meet the Level 1 requirements?

6.5   For airplane D in Appendix B, perform a study of the effect on the short period undamped natural frequency and damping ratio of varying the horizontal tail area. Use the method out–lined in Sub–section 6.6.3.

6.6   For airplane F in Appendix B, perform a study similar to the one of Sub–section 6.6.2. Assume 'target values' for the spiral time constant and for the dutch roll damping ratio which are appropriate for that airplane.

6.9   REFERENCES FOR CHAPTER 6

6.1   Anon.; MIL–F–8785C, Military Specification Flying Qualities of Piloted Airplanes; November 5, 1980; Air Force Flight Dynamics Laboratory, WPAFB, Dayton, Ohio.

6.2   Anon.; MIL–STD–1797A, Flying Qualities of Piloted Aircraft; January 30, 1990; Air Force Flight Dynamics Laboratory, WPAFB, Dayton, Ohio.

6.3   Anon.; Code of Federal Regulations (CFR), Title 14, Parts 1 to 59, January 1, 1992; US Government Printing Office, Superintendent of Documents, Mail Stop SSOP, Washington DC. (Note: FAR 35 and FAR 25 are components of CFR, Title 14)

6.4   Anon.; Joint Aviation Requirements, JAR–VLA Very Light Aeroplanes; Civil Aviation Authority, January 1, 1992; Printing and Publication Services, Greville House, 37 Gratton Road, Cheltenham, Glos. GL50 2BN, United Kingdom.

6.5   Anon.; MIL–F–9490D, Military Specification Flight Control Systems–General Specifi-cation for Installation and Test of Piloted Aircraft; June 6, 1975; Air Force Flight Dynamics Laboratory, WPAFB, Dayton, Ohio.

6.6   Roskam, J.; Airplane Design, Parts I – VIII; Roskam Aviation and Engineering Corporation, 2550 Riley Road, Ottawa, Kansas, 66067.

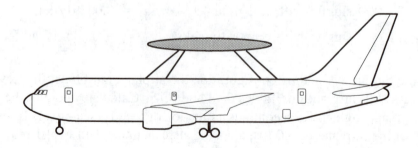

APPENDIX A: DESCRIPTION OF THE ADVANCED AIRCRAFT ANALYSIS (AAA) PROGRAM

A1:   GENERAL CAPABILITIES OF THE AAA PROGRAM

The Advanced Aircraft Analysis (AAA) program described in this appendix was developed to reduce the time and cost required to design and analyze new and existing, fixed wing airplane configurations. In the process of designing a new airplane or analyzing an already existing airplane, engineers must determine the following characteristics of that airplane:

* drag	* installed thrust (or power)	* performance
* weight	* weight breakdown	* inertias
* stability	* control (open and closed loop)	* cost

The AAA program was developed to allow engineers to do this very rapidly and in a truly user–friendly manner. The AAA program is arranged in a modular fashion. Each module addresses a specific phase of design and/or analysis of the preliminary design decision making process. The various modules of the program are briefly described in Section A2.

Since this textbook deals with airplane stability and control, only the stability and control aspects of the AAA program are described in some detail in Section A3.

The AAA program is based on material presented in References A1, A2 and A3.

The AAA Program is available on a variety of platforms under several licensing options. The AAA program as well as References A1–A3 are marketed by:

Design, Analysis and Research Corporation

120 East Ninth Street, Suite 2

Lawrence, Kansas 66044, USA

Tel. 913–832–0434   Fax: 913–832–0524

A2:   BRIEF DESCRIPTION OF AAA PROGRAM MODULES

The AAA program consists of 15 independent modules. Each module is designed to perform tasks which need to be completed in the evaluation of a given airplane at each stage of its preliminary design development. New capabilities are constantly added to the program. The description given here applies to Version 1.5 which was released in December of 1993.

The program applies to civil as well as to military fixed–wing airplanes. **Conventional, pure canard and three–surface airplanes** with jet, turboprop or piston–prop propulsive installations can be handled by the program. At any stage of the design process, a report quality screen–dump and/or parameter print–out can be commanded.

The user can, at any time, ask for a definition of a particular design parameter. Where needed, a graphical or tabular definition is also available. In many instances the program suggests ranges of values for certain parameters.

A2.1 Weight Sizing Module

This module allows determination of mission segment fuel fractions as well as estimates of take–off weight, empty weight and fuel weight for an arbitrary mission specification. For military airplanes, the effect of dropping weapons or stores can be accounted for.

Sensitivity of take–off weight with respect to various mission, aerodynamic and propulsion parameters can be determined.

A2.2 Performance Sizing Module

With this module, the user can determine the relation between take–off thrust–to–weight ratio (or weight–to–power ratio) and take–off wing–loading for any airplane, based on mission and airworthiness performance requirements. All pertinent civil and military airworthiness regulations of FAR 23, FAR 25, MIL–C–005011B (USAF) and AS–5263 (USNAVY) can be considered. Plots of $(W/S)_{TO}$ versus $(T/W)_{TO}$ {or versus $(W/P)_{TO}$} can be generated on any scale.

A2.3 Geometry Module

In this module, the planform geometry of a straight tapered and cranked lifting surface can be determined. All estimated geometry parameters (such as area, mean geometric chord, aspect ratio, taper ratio and sweep angle) can be displayed as 2–D drawings. This module can be used for wings, canards, horizontal tails, vertical tails and fuselages.

A2.4 High Lift Module

This module allows the user to calculate the maximum lift coefficients of wings with and without trailing edge flaps. The effect of airfoil type and Reynolds number are accounted for. The program will calculate and display the flap size needed to achieve a given maximum lift coefficient.

A2.5 Drag Polar Module

Two methods for estimating airplane drag polars are available in this module: a simplified (Class I) method and a detailed (Class II) method. In the Class I method, the program can calculate drag polars based on statistical relations between airplane type, take–off weight and wetted area. Plots of C_L versus C_D, C_L versus C_L/C_D and C_L versus $(C_L)^3/(C_D)^2$ can be generated on any scale desired by the user. In the Class II method, the program determines the drag polar of all individual components of an airplane. Plots of component drag polar contributions and total drag polar can be generated. Corrections for laminar flow can be included at the option of the user. Drag can also be plotted as a function of Mach number and flap angle. The Class II method applies to subsonic, transonic and supersonic flight.

A2.6   Stability and Control Module

This module can be used for sizing of horizontal and vertical tail surfaces to given stability or volume coefficient requirements. Longitudinal trim diagrams, which account for the effect of control surface stall, can be generated. The effect of stick, wheel and/or rudder pedal forces on longitudinal and lateral–directional trim can be determined. The program also calculates all required gradients, such as: $\frac{\partial F_s}{\partial n}, \frac{\partial F_s}{\partial V}$, etc. Neutral points, stick–free and stick–fixed can be determined. Effects of bob–weight and down–spring can be included at the option of the user.

A2.7   Weight and Balance Module

Two methods for estimating airplane weight breakdown are available in this module: a simplified (Class I) method and a detailed (Class II) method. In the Class I method, the program can calculate the component weight breakdown of an airplane as well as its inertias, based on statistical data. In the Class II method, the program estimates the weight of airplanes with the help of various formulas which relate component weight to significant design parameters. Plots of center of gravity versus weight can be generated for arbitrary load and un–load scenarios. V–n diagrams for FAR 23, FAR 25 and MIL–A–8861(ASG) specifications can be determined.

A2.8   Installed Thrust Module

With this module the installed thrust (or power) as well as specific fuel consumption can be estimated from given engine manufacturers data for piston, turboprop, prop–fan and turbojet/fan engines. Installed data can be plotted versus altitude and Mach number for a range of engine ratings. Propeller characteristics can be estimated from manufacturer's data. The user can also estimate effects of power extractions (mechanical, electrical and hydraulic). Inlets and nozzles can be sized.

A2.9   Performance Analysis Module

In this module the field length, stall, climb, range, endurance, dive, glide and maneuvering characteristics of an airplane can be evaluated. Payload–weight diagrams can be generated. This module uses more sophisticated methods than the Performance Sizing Module of A2.2.

A2.10 Stability and Control Derivatives Module

In this module the subsonic stability and control derivatives of conventional, canard and three–surface configurations can be analyzed. In addition, elevator control surface hinge–moment derivatives for various nose shapes and horn configurations can be estimated.

A2.11 Dynamics Module

With this module the open–loop airplane transfer functions can be determined, including the standard flying quality parameters of the short period, phugoid, roll, spiral and dutch–roll modes. The sensitivity of airplane undamped natural frequency, damping ratio and time–constant to arbitrary changes in stability derivatives and inertial characteristics can be plotted to any scale desired by the user. The program can determine whether the airplane meets the Level I, II or III flying quality requirements of MIL–F–8785C. Roll coupling stability diagrams can be generated. The open–loop airplane transfer functions are automatically transferred to the Control Module.

A2.12 Control Module

In this module, Root–Locus plots and Bode plots can be generated for open–loop and closed–loop control systems. The transfer functions of sensors, actuators and other loop components can be entered at the option of the user. The effect of tilt angles on yaw damper and roll damper performance can be evaluated.

A2.13 Cost Analysis Module

Estimates for airplane RDTE (Research, Development, Technology and Evaluation), manufacturing, prototype, direct and indirect operating cost and life cycle cost can be made for military as well as for civil airplanes. Quick estimates of airplane and engine prices can be made.

A2.14 Database Module

This module manages the data for all AAA modules. Design information can be stored or retrieved and parameters in the data–base can be viewed, edited or printed. This module also allows the user to determine atmospheric characteristics for standard and off–standard conditions.

A2.15 Help/Setup Module

This module displays help in using the AAA program. Setup allows the user to select between S.I. and British units. Project and company information can be entered here.

A3: STABILITY AND CONTROL CAPABILITIES OF THE AAA PROGRAM

A significant part of design and analysis efforts is spent in assuring that the stability and control characteristics of an airplane are acceptable from a flying qualities viewpoint so that the airplane can be certified according to civilian and/or military airworthiness regulations. In addition to a wide variety of preliminary design capabilities, the AAA program allows the designer to determine the following stability and control properties:

1) Calculation of stability, control and hinge–moment derivatives. Figure A1 shows an example of a lateral–directional stability derivative calculation (of C_{n_β}) for a twin turboprop commuter airplane.

2) Calculation of airplane trim characteristics. This is done with the help of a longitudinal trim diagram. Figure A2 shows an example trim diagram.

3) Stick–force and control surface deflections required to trim. Neutral point stick–fixed and stick–free.

4) Stick–force–versus–speed, stick–force versus–load–factor and flight–path–versus–speed gradients. Figure A3 gives an example output for items 3) and 4).

5) Lateral–directional engine–inoperative calculations for:

    * Aileron and rudder deflection required
    * Aileron wheel force and rudder pedal force required

    Figure A4 shows results for an engine–out lateral–directional trim solution.

6) Calculation of moments of inertia. Figure A5 shows an example.

7) Calculation of open loop transfer functions and corresponding frequency, damping ratio and time–constant characteristics such as:

    * Short period, phugoid and/or third oscillatory mode
    * Dutch roll, spiral, roll and/or lateral phugoid

    Figure A6 and A7 provide example outputs for the dynamic modes of a twin turbo–prop commuter airplane. Examples of AAA outputs of airplane transfer functions are given in Appendix C.

8) Determining the flying quality level according to Mil–F–8785C and showing graphically where the airplane is relative to the minimum requirements. Figure A8 contains an example for the case of dutch roll.

9) Performing and plotting sensitivity studies which show how various dynamic stability parameters vary as a function of any stability derivative or moment of inertia. Figure A9 depicts an example of how the longitudinal modes vary with the static longitudinal stability derivative, C_{m_α}.

10) Plotting open and closed loop root–locus and Bode diagrams. The program allows the user to study such closed loop characteristics as:

    * stability augmentation systems   * auto–pilot loops
    * pilot–in–the–loop controllability

    Figure A10 shows an example of a Bode plot of the bank–angle–to–aileron transfer function of a twin turboprop commuter airplane. Figure A11 gives a root–locus diagram for a yaw–damper in the same airplane.

11) All stability and control coefficients and derivatives are based on the reference geometry of the wing. Figure A12 shows an example of the reference geometry for a so–called 'equivalent straight tapered' wing. Any cranked wing planform can be transformed into a straight tapered planform which is then used in the calculation of derivatives and coefficients.

The AAA program has been found to be very useful in an instructional environment: students can rapidly discover which design parameters have the greatest effect on items 1–10. Students can also be given real world homework assignments. AAA takes away the need for hours of tedious preparation of input data.

The program provides on–line written and graphical definitions for input parameters. This is done by selecting INFO or HELP on the calculator pad. The calculator pad pops onto the screen any time an input variable or output variable is selected by the user. Selection is done with a mouse/cursor combination. By selecting THEORY the program also identifies the theoretical models and assumptions made in various modules. This helps the user understand the underlying theories and equations.

A4: REFERENCES FOR APPENDIX A

A1 Roskam, J.; Airplane Flight Dynamics and Automatic Flight Controls, Parts I and II; 1994 and 1995 respectively.
(Part I contains approximately 570 pages and Part II contains approximately 500 pages)

A2 Lan, C. E. and Roskam, J.; Airplane Aerodynamics and Performance; 1988.
(This text contains 546 pages)

A3 Roskam, J.; Airplane Design, Parts I – VIII; 1989.
(This eight–volume text contains 202, 310, 454, 416, 209, 550, 351 and 368 pages respectively)

Publisher for A1–A3:

Roskam Aviation and Engineering Corporation, 120 East Ninth Street, Suite 2, Lawrence, Kansas, 66044, USA.

Sales and Marketing for A1–A3:

Design, Analysis and Research Corporation, 120 East Ninth Street, Suite 2, Lawrence, Kansas, 66044, USA.
Tel. 913–832–0434   Fax: 913–832–0524

ADVANCED AIRCRAFT ANALYSIS

| WEIGHT SIZING | GEOMETRY | DRAG POLAR | WEIGHT & BALANCE | PERF. ANALYSIS | DYNAMICS | COST ANALYSIS | HELP / SETUP |
| PERFORM. SIZING | HIGH LIFT | STAB. & CONTROL | INSTALLED THRUST | S&C DERIVATIVES | CONTROL | DATA BASE | QUIT |

STABILITY & CONTROL DERIVATIVES

| LONG. STABILITY | LAT-DIR STABILITY | LONG. CONTROL | LAT-DIR CONTROL | RETURN |

TYPE OF CONFIGURATION

| TAIL AFT | CANARD | THREE SURFACE | RETURN |

TYPE OF VERTICAL TAIL

| SINGLE VT. TAIL | TWIN VT. TAIL | RETURN |

LATERAL-DIRECTIONAL STABILITY DERIVATIVES

| SIDESLIP | SIDESLIP RATE | ROLL RATE | YAW RATE | RETURN |

SIDESLIP RELATED DERIVATIVES

| C_yB | C_lB | C_n_B | RETURN |

| THEORY | CALCULATE | PRINT PARAMETERS | RETURN |

SIDESLIP RELATED DERIVATIVES : INPUT PARAMETERS

Altitude =	1000 ft	S_h =	75.00 ft^2	clav)M=0 =	6.0420 1/rad	Z_{cg} = 4.50 ft
U_1 =	125.00 kts	Z_h =	-3.625 ft	X_{ac_v} =	66.00 ft	S_{B_s} = 260.500 ft^2
Alpha =	6.45 deg	X/C_v =	0.1597	Z_{ac_v} =	10.74 ft	h_1 = 5.500 ft
S_w =	300.00 ft^2	S_v =	50.00 ft^2	L_{fus} =	57.29 ft	h_2 = 5.500 ft
AR_w =	11.00	AR_v =	1.77	Z_f =	6.00 ft	h_{max} = 5.500 ft
^C/4_w =	0.000 deg	TR_v =	0.35	2r1 =	2.83 ft	B_{width} = 5.50 ft
Z_w =	3.00 ft	^C/4_v =	34.200 deg	X_{cg} =	38.50 deg	X_{apex_f} = 10.000 ft

OUTPUT PARAMETERS

M_1 =	0.190	AR_{v_eff} = 1.63	$C_{n\_B\_v}$ = 0.2185 1/rad
RN_f =	75.0374 x 10^6	$C_{n\_B\_f}$ = -0.0829 1/rad	C_{n_B} = 0.1357 1/rad

Figure A1   Calculation of the Directional Stability Derivative, C_{n_β}

| Design, Analysis and Research Corporation | Cruise, Power On | jr's_commuter | Oct 4, 1993 | 11:46 |

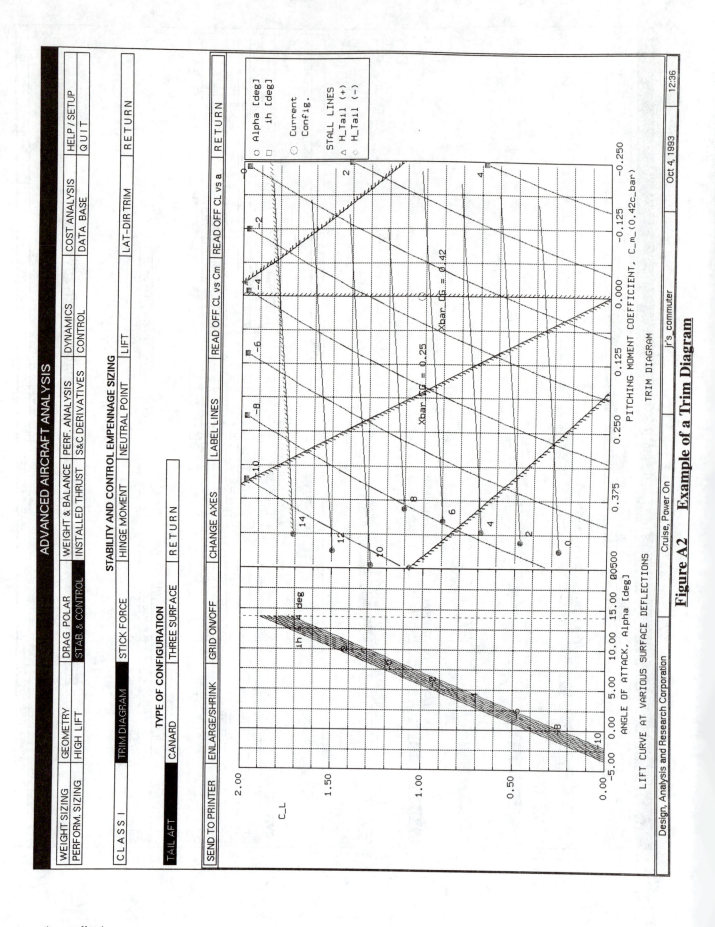

Figure A2   Example of a Trim Diagram

ADVANCED AIRCRAFT ANALYSIS

| WEIGHT SIZING | GEOMETRY | DRAG POLAR | WEIGHT & BALANCE | PERF. ANALYSIS | DYNAMICS | COST ANALYSIS | HELP / SETUP |
| PERFORM. SIZING | HIGH LIFT | STAB. & CONTROL | INSTALLED THRUST | S&C DERIVATIVES | CONTROL | DATA BASE | QUIT |

STABILITY AND CONTROL EMPENNAGE SIZING

| CLASS 1 | TRIM DIAGRAM | STICK FORCE | HINGE MOMENT | NEUTRAL POINT | LIFT | LAT-DIR TRIM | RETURN |

LONGITUDINAL TRIM

| PULL-UP | LEVEL TURN | RETURN |

SELECT FIRST CONTROL VARIABLE

| ANGLE OF ATTACK | FLIGHT PATH ANGLE | ELEVATOR ANGLE | TAB ANGLE | TAIL INCIDENCE | STICK FORCE | RETURN |

SELECT SECOND CONTROL VARIABLE

| ANGLE OF ATTACK | FLIGHT PATH ANGLE | ELEVATOR ANGLE | TAIL INCIDENCE | STICK FORCE | RETURN |

| CALCULATE | PRINT PARAMETERS | RETURN |

LONGITUDINAL TRIM : INPUT PARAMETERS

$delta\_t$	=	7.79 deg	X_ac_wf	=	35.90 ft	K_2 = 10.00 lbft	$C\_L\_i\_h$ = 0.7000 1/rad
l_h	=	-1.400 deg	S_h	=	75.00 ft^2	K_3 = -10.00 lbft/rad	$C\_m\_i\_h$ = -3.4000 1/rad
$Altitude$	=	1000 ft	$C\_L\_a\_h$	=	3.2432 1/rad	K_4 = -15.00 lbft/rad2	$C\_L\_d\_e$ = 0.3500 1/rad
U_1	=	125.00 kts	n_h	=	1.050	K_5 = 0.00 lbft/rad	$C\_m\_d\_e$ = -1.7000 1/rad
$W\_current$	=	16000.0 lb	$de/da\ Jh$	=	0.2539	PHI_t = 0.00 deg	C_h_d = -0.4000 1/rad
I_xz_S	=	-1681 slgft2	e_o_h	=	3.00 deg	dT = 3.00 ft	$C\_L\_d\_t$ = 0.0010 1/rad
n	=	1.00 g	X_ac_h	=	62.19 ft	T_set = 2000 lb	$C\_m\_d\_t$ = -0.1000 1/rad
S_w	=	300.00 ft^2	X_cg	=	38.00 ft	C_h_a = -0.1200 1/rad	$C\_h\_d\_t$ = -0.0500 1/rad
AR_w	=	11.00	S_e	=	20.00 ft^2	C_L_o = 0.3500	C_L_q = 6.9060 1/rad
TR_w	=	0.30	C_bar_e	=	1.30 ft	$C\_D\_o\_cln$ = 0.1200	C_m_q = -29.9054 1/rad
$\hat{C}/4\_w$	=	0.000 deg	G_e	=	0.75 rad/ft	B_DP_cln = 0.0400	
X_apex_w	=	35.000 ft	K_1	=	0.50	C_m_o = 0.0925	
$C\_L\_a\_wf$	=	5.4578 1/rad	W_bob	=	8.0 lb	C_h_o = 0.0000 1/rad	

CONTROL VARIABLES : OUTPUT

$Alpha$	=	6.47 deg	$dele$ = 0.456 deg	C_L_1 = 1.0236	$Xbar\_cg$ = 0.4231
da/dV	=	-0.1566 deg/kts	dd_e/dV = 0.1023 deg/kts	M_1 = 0.190	$Xbar\_ac$ = 0.5401
da/dn	=	9.9894 deg/g	dd_e/dn = -6.2737 deg/g	q_bar = 51.37 psf	$S.M.$ = 11.70 %
$gamma$	=	-1.86 deg	F_s = -0.0 lb	C_bar = 5.73 ft	NP_free = 0.4868
$dGamma/dV$	=	-0.0661 deg/kts	dF_s/dV = -0.6906 lb/kts	C_L_a = 6.0930 1/rad	SM_free = 6.37 %
$dGamma/dn$	=	-3.1951 deg/g	dF_s/dn = 32.2725 lb/g	C_m_a = -0.7127 1/rad	

Figure A3   Calculation of Stick Force, Control Deflection, Stick-force Gradients, Neutral Point Stick-fixed and Stick-free

| Design, Analysis and Research Corporation | Cruise, Power On | jr's commuter | Oct 4, 1993 | 11:59 |

ADVANCED AIRCRAFT ANALYSIS

WEIGHT SIZING	GEOMETRY	DRAG POLAR	WEIGHT & BALANCE	PERF. ANALYSIS	DYNAMICS	COST ANALYSIS	HELP / SETUP
PERFORM. SIZING	HIGH LIFT	STAB. & CONTROL	INSTALLED THRUST	S&C DERIVATIVES	CONTROL	DATA BASE	QUIT

STABILITY AND CONTROL EMPENNAGE SIZING

CLASS I	TRIM DIAGRAM	STICK FORCE	HINGE MOMENT	NEUTRAL POINT	LIFT	LAT-DIR TRIM	RETURN

LONGITUDINAL TRIM

STRAIGHT FLIGHT	TURNING FLIGHT	RETURN

SELECT FIRST CONTROL VARIABLE

BANK ANGLE	SIDESLIP	AILERON ANGLE	RUDDER ANGLE	AILERON TAB	RUDDER TAB	RETURN

SELECT SECOND CONTROL VARIABLE

BANK ANGLE	SIDESLIP	AILERON ANGLE	RUDDER ANGLE	AILERON TAB	AILERON TAB	RETURN

SELECT THIRD CONTROL VARIABLE

BANK ANGLE	SIDESLIP	AILERON ANGLE	RUDDER ANGLE	AILERON FORCE	RUDDER FORCE	RETURN

CALCULATE	PRINT PARAMETERS	RETURN

LATERAL-DIRECTIONAL TRIM : INPUT PARAMETERS

Phi	=	-1.93 deg	Z_w	=	3.00 ft
d_a_t	=	0.00 deg	Z_f	=	6.00 ft
d_r_t	=	0.00 deg	S_v	=	50.00 ft^2
Altitude	=	1000 ft	n_v	=	1.000
U_1	=	125.00 kts	X_ac_v	=	66.00 ft
W_current	=	16000.0 lb	X_cg	=	38.00 ft
Alpha	=	6.47 deg	S_a	=	20.00 ft^2
I_xx_B	=	19000 slgft2	C_bar_a	=	1.10 ft
I_yy_B	=	43000 slgft2	G_a	=	0.40 rad/ft
I_zz_B	=	60000 slgft2	S_r	=	20.00 ft^2
I_xz_B	=	3000 slgft2	C_bar_r	=	1.30 ft
S_w	=	300.00 ft^2	G_r	=	1.50 rad/ft
AR_w	=	11.00	PHI_t	=	0.00 deg
^C/4_w	=	0.000 deg	psi_T	=	0.00 deg

Y_t	=	6.00 ft	C_y_d_r	=	0.2000 1/rad
T_set	=	2000 lb	C_l_d_r	=	0.0200 1/rad
F_OEI	=	1.15	C_n_d_r	=	-0.0900 1/rad
C_h_B_r	=	0.0500 1/rad	C_h_d_r	=	-0.3000 1/rad
C_y_r	=	0.4371 1/rad	C_y_d_a_t	=	1.0000 1/rad
C_l_r	=	0.3224 1/rad	C_l_d_a_t	=	1.0000 1/rad
C_n_r	=	-0.2241 1/rad	C_n_d_a_t	=	1.0000 1/rad
C_y_B	=	-0.6826 1/rad	C_h_d_a_t	=	1.0000 1/rad
C_l_B	=	-0.0589 1/rad	C_y_d_r_t	=	1.0000 1/rad
C_n_B	=	0.1357 1/rad	C_l_d_r_t	=	1.0000 1/rad
C_y_d_a	=	0.0000 1/rad	C_n_d_r_t	=	1.0000 1/rad
C_l_d_a	=	0.1800 1/rad	C_h_d_r_t	=	1.0000 1/rad
C_n_d_a	=	-0.0100 1/rad	K_6	=	0.00 lbft/rad
C_h_d_a	=	-0.4000 1/rad	K_7	=	0.00 lbft/rad

q_bar	=	51.37 psf
I_zz_S	=	60151 slgft2
I_xz_S	=	-1665 slgft2

CONTROL VARIABLES : OUTPUT

F_a	=	-10.1 lb	Beta	=	0.00 deg
F_r	=	-105.3 lb	del_a	=	-1.601 deg
M_1	=	0.190	del_r	=	10.04 deg

Design, Analysis and Research Corporation	Cruise, Power On	jr's commuter	Oct 4, 1993	12:41

Figure A4   Lateral-directional Trim Solution: Aileron and Rudder Deflections and Aileron–wheel and Rudder–pedal Control Forces

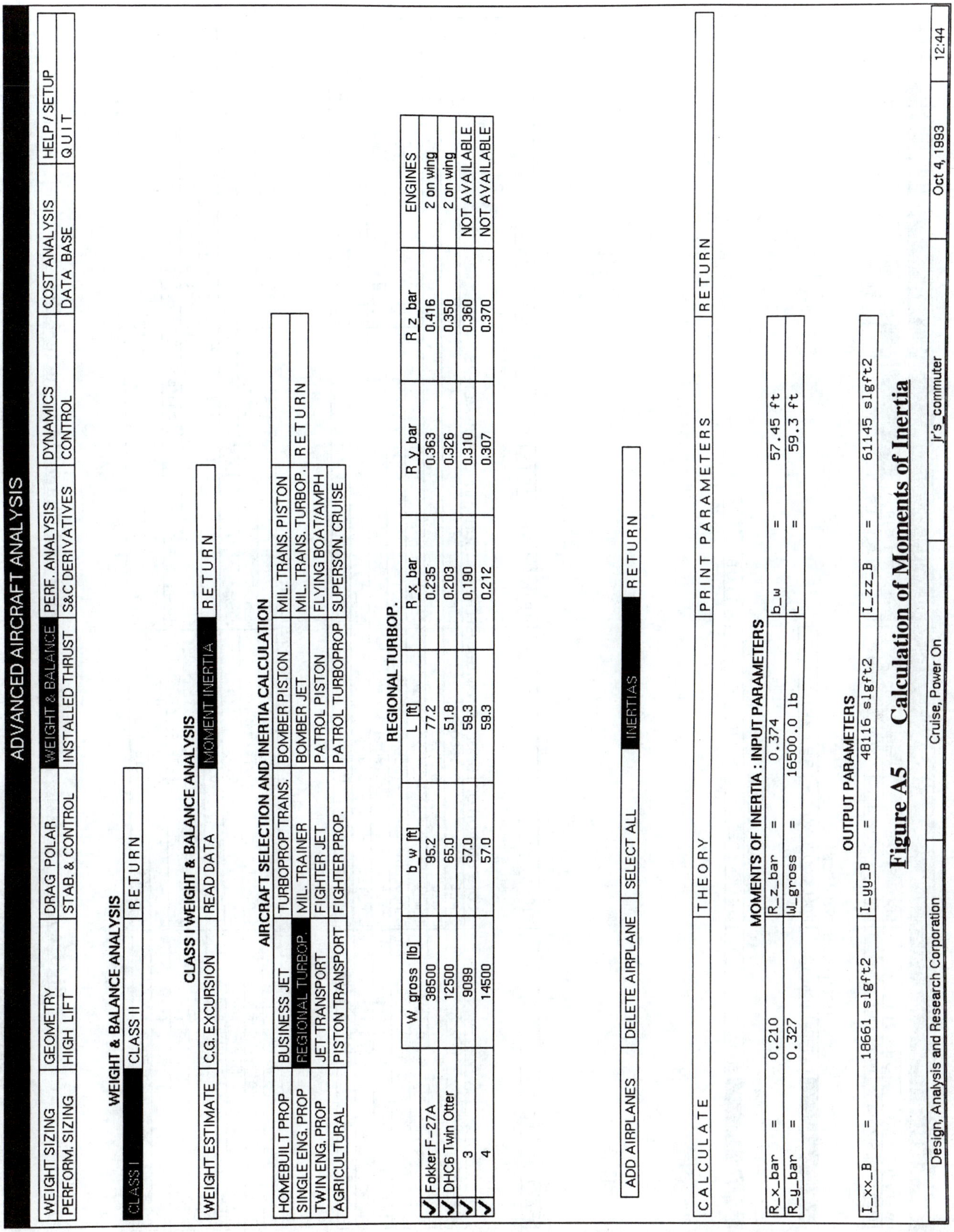

ADVANCED AIRCRAFT ANALYSIS

WEIGHT SIZING	GEOMETRY	DRAG POLAR	WEIGHT & BALANCE	PERF. ANALYSIS	DYNAMICS	COST ANALYSIS	HELP / SETUP
PERFORM. SIZING	HIGH LIFT	STAB. & CONTROL	INSTALLED THRUST	S&C DERIVATIVES	CONTROL	DATA BASE	QUIT

WEIGHT & BALANCE ANALYSIS

CLASS I	CLASS II	RETURN

CLASS I WEIGHT & BALANCE ANALYSIS

WEIGHT ESTIMATE	C.G. EXCURSION	READ DATA	MOMENT INERTIA	RETURN

AIRCRAFT SELECTION AND INERTIA CALCULATION

HOMEBUILT PROP	BUSINESS JET	TURBOPROP TRANS.	BOMBER PISTON	MIL. TRANS. PISTON	
SINGLE ENG. PROP	REGIONAL TURBOP.	MIL. TRAINER	BOMBER JET	MIL. TRANS. TURBOP.	RETURN
TWIN ENG. PROP	JET TRANSPORT	FIGHTER JET	PATROL PISTON	FLYING BOAT/AMPH	
AGRICULTURAL	PISTON TRANSPORT	FIGHTER PROP.	PATROL TURBOPROP	SUPERSON. CRUISE	

REGIONAL TURBOP.

	W_gross [lb]	b_w [ft]	L [ft]	R_x bar	R_y bar	R_z bar	ENGINES
Fokker F-27A	38500	95.2	77.2	0.235	0.363	0.416	2 on wing
DHC6 Twin Otter	12500	65.0	51.8	0.203	0.326	0.350	2 on wing
3	9099	57.0	59.3	0.190	0.310	0.360	NOT AVAILABLE
4	14500	57.0	59.3	0.212	0.307	0.370	NOT AVAILABLE

ADD AIRPLANES	DELETE AIRPLANE	SELECT ALL	INERTIAS	RETURN

CALCULATE	THEORY	PRINT PARAMETERS	RETURN

MOMENTS OF INERTIA : INPUT PARAMETERS

R_x_bar =	0.210	R_z_bar =	0.374	b_w =	57.45 ft
R_y_bar =	0.327	W_gross =	16500.0 lb	L =	59.3 ft

OUTPUT PARAMETERS

I_xx_B =	18661 slgft2	I_yy_B =	48116 slgft2	I_zz_B =	61145 slgft2

Figure A5   Calculation of Moments of Inertia

Design, Analysis and Research Corporation	Cruise, Power On	Jr's commuter	Oct 4, 1993	12:44

ADVANCED AIRCRAFT ANALYSIS

| WEIGHT SIZING | GEOMETRY | DRAG POLAR | WEIGHT & BALANCE | PERF. ANALYSIS | DYNAMICS | COST ANALYSIS | HELP / SETUP |
| PERFORM. SIZING | HIGH LIFT | STAB. & CONTROL | INSTALLED THRUST | S&C DERIVATIVES | CONTROL | DATA BASE | QUIT |

OPEN LOOP DYNAMICS

| LONGITUDINAL | LATERAL–DIRECT. | ROLL COUPLING | RETURN |

LONGITUDINAL ANALYSIS

| CALCULATE T.F. | SHOW T.F. | CHECK MODES | SENSITIVITY | RETURN |

| CALCULATE | THEORY | PRINT PARAMETERS | RETURN |

COMPUTATION OF LONGITUDINAL TRANSFER FUNCTIONS : INPUT PARAMETERS

Altitude =	1000 ft	C_{m_1} =	0.0000	$C_{m_{T_a}}$ =	0.0000	C_{D_a} = 0.4575 1/rad
U_1 =	125.00 kts	C_{m_u} =	0.0593	C_{L_1} =	1.0236	C_{D_u} = 0.0000
$W_{current}$ =	16000.0 lb	C_{m_a} =	-0.7127 1/rad	C_{L_u} =	0.0387	$C_{T_{X_1}}$ = 0.0338
S_w =	300.00 ft^2	$C_{m_a.dot}$ =	-7.3968 1/rad	C_{L_a} =	6.0930 1/rad	$C_{T_{X_u}}$ = 0.0000
$Theta_1$ =	0.00 deg	C_{m_q} =	-29.9054 1/rad	$C_{L_a.dot}$ =	1.7881 1/rad	$C_{L_{d_e}}$ = 0.3500 1/rad
C_{bar} =	5.73 ft	$C_{m_{T_1}}$ =	0.0000	C_{L_q} =	6.9060 1/rad	$C_{D_{d_e}}$ = 0.0000 1/rad
I_{yy_B} =	48116 slgft2	$C_{m_{T_u}}$ =	0.0000	C_{D_1} =	0.1557	$C_{m_{d_e}}$ = -1.7000 1/rad

OUTPUT PARAMETERS

M_1 =	0.190	Z_a =	-193.5754 ft/s^2	M_q =	-0.7445 1/s	TC_2 = ? s
n =	0.99 g	$Z_{a.dot}$ =	-0.7518 ft/s	$w_{n_{SP}}$ =	1.4093 rad/s	TC_3 = ? s
q_{bar} =	51.37 psf	Z_q =	-2.9037 ft/s	z_{SP} =	0.6593	TC_4 = ? s
$(W/S)_{TO}$ =	53.33 psf	M_u =	0.0005 1/ft/s	w_{n_P} =	0.1956 rad/s	X_{del_e} = 0.0000 ft/s^2
X_u =	-0.0457 1/s	M_{T_u} =	0.0000 1/ft/s	z_P =	0.0443	Z_{del_e} = -10.8425 ft/s^2
X_{T_u} =	0.0099 1/s	M_a =	-1.3073 1/s^2	w_{n_3} osc =	? rad/s	M_{del_e} = -3.1182 1/s^2
X_a =	17.5383 ft/s^2	M_{T_a} =	0.0000 1/s^2	z_{3rd} osc =	?	
Z_u =	-0.3063 1/s	$M_{a.dot}$ =	-0.1841 1/s	TC_1 =	? s	

| Design, Analysis and Research Corporation | Cruise, Power On | jr's_commuter | Oct 4, 1993 | 12:48 |

Figure A6   Calculation of Short Period and Phugoid Characteristics

ADVANCED AIRCRAFT ANALYSIS

WEIGHT SIZING	GEOMETRY	DRAG POLAR	WEIGHT & BALANCE	PERF. ANALYSIS	DYNAMICS	COST ANALYSIS	HELP / SETUP
PERFORM. SIZING	HIGH LIFT	STAB. & CONTROL	INSTALLED THRUST	S&C DERIVATIVES	CONTROL	DATA BASE	QUIT

OPEN LOOP DYNAMICS

LONGITUDINAL	LATERAL-DIRECT.	ROLL COUPLING	RETURN

LATERAL-DIRECTIONAL ANALYSIS

CALCULATE T.F.	SHOW T.F.	CHECK MODES	SENSITIVITY	RETURN

CALCULATE	THEORY	PRINT PARAMETERS	RETURN

COMPUTATION OF LATERAL-DIRECTIONAL TRANSFER FUNCTIONS : INPUT PARAMETERS

$W\_current$ = 16000.0 lb	I_xx_B = 18661 slgft2	$C\_n\_T\_B$ = 0.0000	$C\_l\_d\_r$ = 0.0200 1/rad
Altitude = 1000 ft	I_zz_B = 61145 slgft2	C_n_p = -0.1529 1/rad	$C\_n\_d\_a$ = -0.0100 1/rad
S_w = 300.00 ft^2	I_xz_B = 3000 slgft2	C_n_r = -0.2241 1/rad	$C\_n\_d\_r$ = -0.0900 1/rad
U_1 = 125.00 kts	C_l_B = -0.0589 1/rad	C_y_B = -0.6826 1/rad	$C\_y\_d\_a$ = 0.0000 1/rad
$Theta\_1$ = 0.00 deg	C_l_p = -0.5678 1/rad	C_y_p = -0.0485 1/rad	$C\_y\_d\_r$ = 0.2000 1/rad
Alpha = 6.47 deg	C_l_r = 0.3224 1/rad	C_y_r = 0.4371 1/rad	
b_w = 57.45 ft	C_n_B = 0.1357 1/rad	$C\_l\_d\_a$ = 0.1800 1/rad	

OUTPUT PARAMETERS

$(W/S)\_TO$ = 53.33 psf	L_B = -2.8155 1/s^2	z_D = 0.2158	TC_4 = ? s
q_bar = 51.37 psf	L_p = -3.6932 1/s	w_n_LatP = ? rad/s	Y_del_a = 0.0000 ft/s^2
I_xx_S = 18528 slgft2	L_r = 2.0970 1/s	z_LatP = ?	Y_del_r = 6.1957 ft/s^2
I_zz_S = 61277 slgft2	N_B = 1.9597 1/s^2	TC_SPIRAL = -20.449 s	L_del_a = 8.6003 1/s^2
I_xz_S = -1831 slgft2	N_T_B = 0.0000 1/s^2	TC_ROLL = 0.274 s	L_del_r = 0.9556 1/s^2
Y_B = -21.1447 ft/s^2	N_p = -0.3007 1/s	TC_1 = 0.274 s	N_del_a = -0.1445 1/s^2
Y_p = -0.2047 ft/s	N_r = -0.4409 1/s	TC_2 = -20.449 s	N_del_r = -1.3002 1/s^2
Y_r = 1.8433 ft/s	w_n_D = 1.5670 rad/s	TC_3 = ? s	

Design, Analysis and Research Corporation	Cruise, Power On	jr's_commuter	Oct 4, 1993	12:52

Figure A7   Calculation of Dutch Roll, Spiral and Roll Characteristics

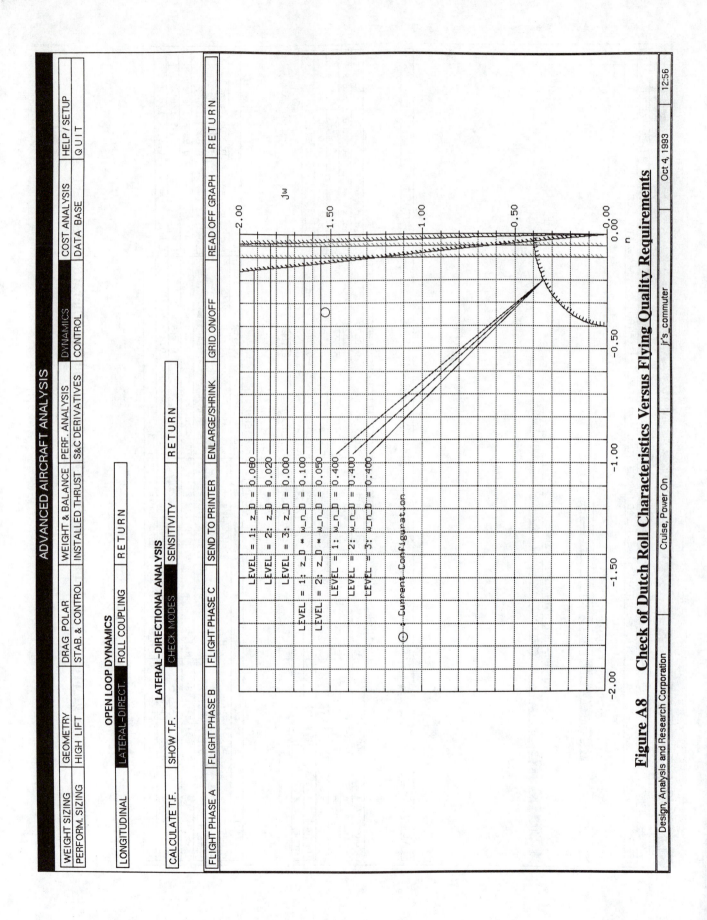

Figure A8   Check of Dutch Roll Characteristics Versus Flying Quality Requirements

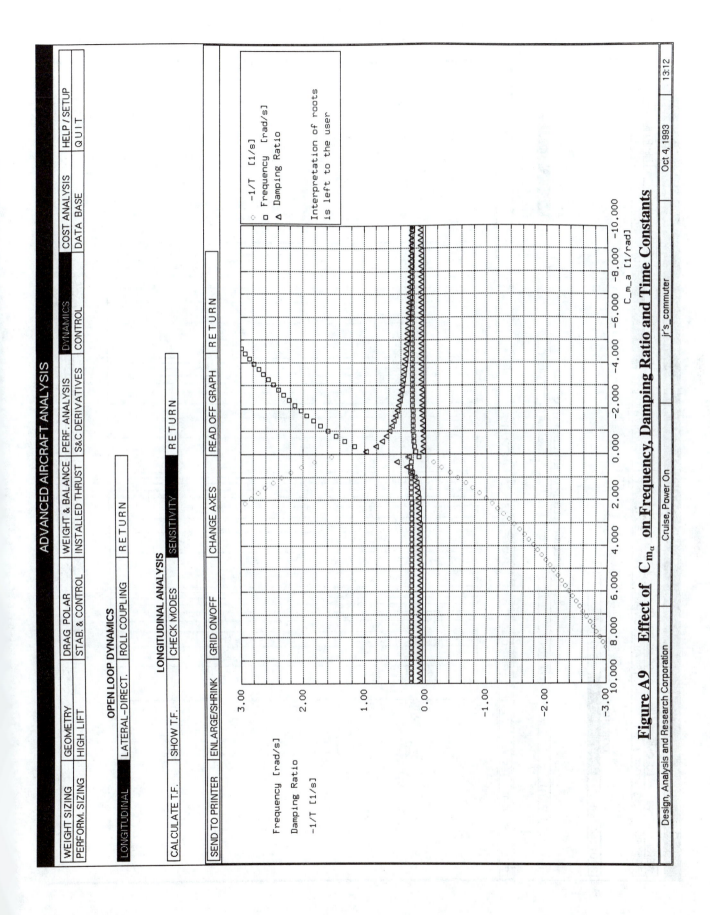

Figure A9   Effect of C_{m_α} on Frequency, Damping Ratio and Time Constants

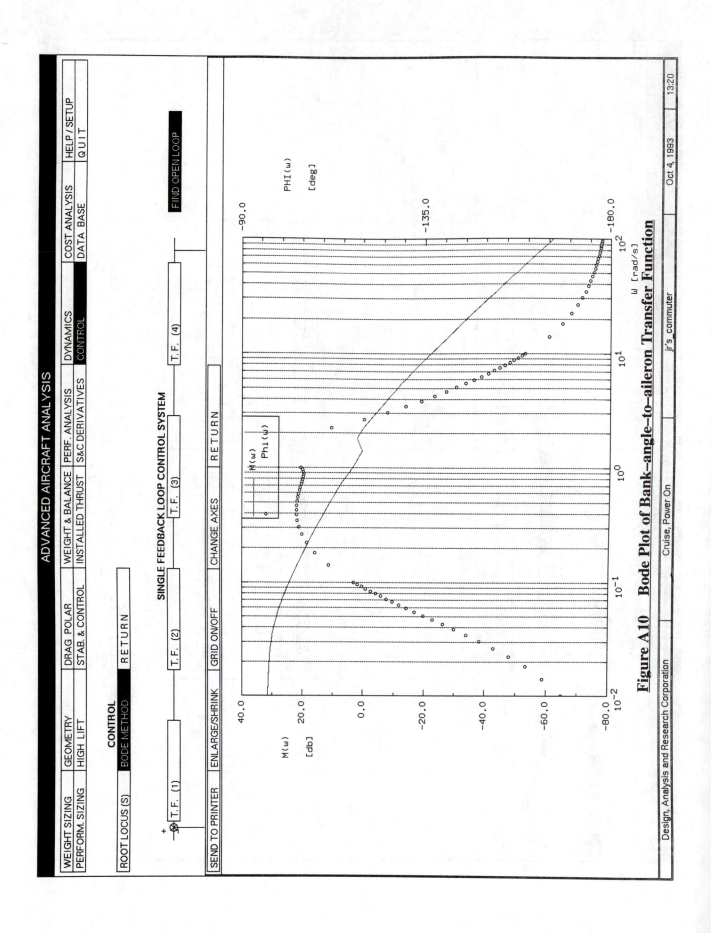

Figure A10   Bode Plot of Bank–angle–to–aileron Transfer Function

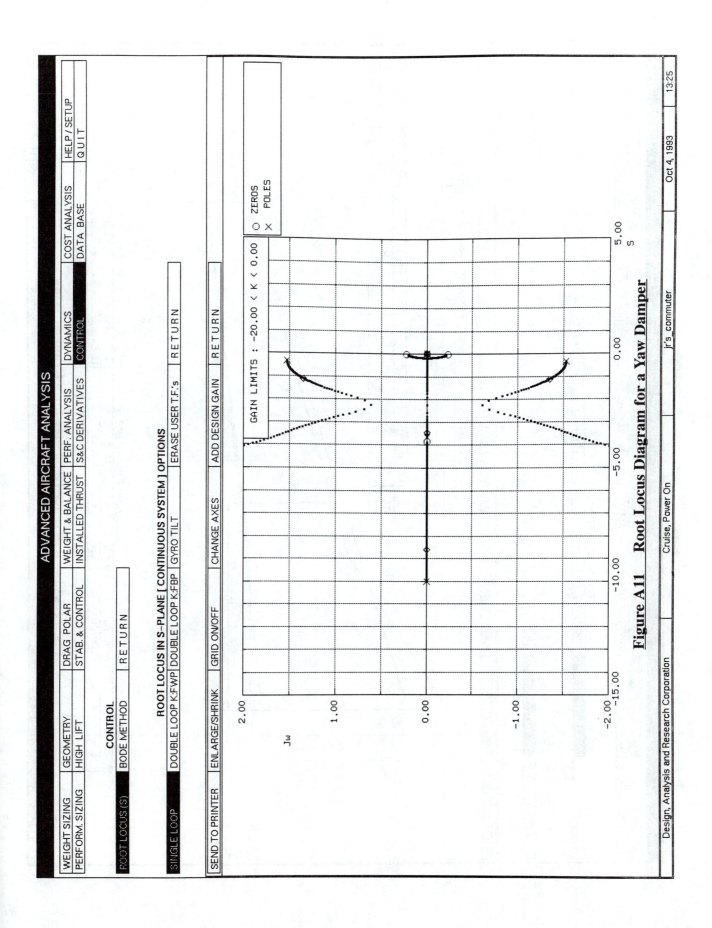

Figure A11   Root Locus Diagram for a Yaw Damper

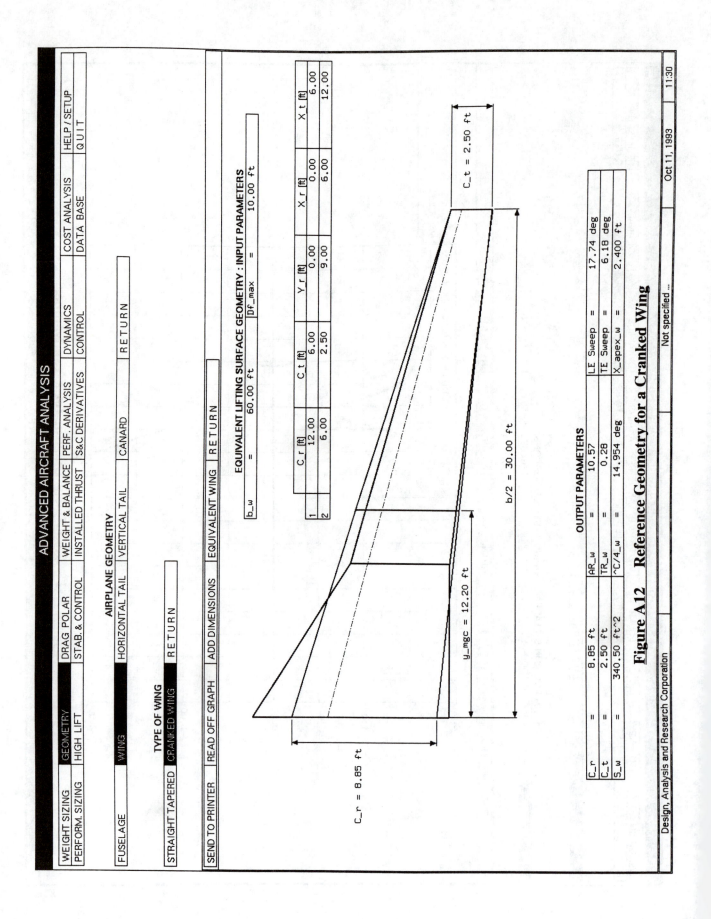

Figure A12   Reference Geometry for a Cranked Wing

APPENDIX B: AIRPLANE DATA

The purpose of this appendix is to present geometric, mass, inertial, stability, control and (where available) hingemoment data for a range of airplanes and flight conditions. The airplanes are identified as Airplanes A through J:

Airplane A   is representative of a small, single piston–engine general aviation airplane such as the Cessna 182 (See Table B1: Pages 480–486)

Airplane B   is representative of a small, twin piston–engine general aviation airplane such as the Cessna 310 (See Table B2: Pages 487–493)

Airplane C   is representative of a small, single jet–engine, military training airplane such as the SIAI–Marchetti S–211 (See Table B3: Pages 494–500)

Airplane D   is representative of a small, twin jet–engine, military training airplane such as the Cessna T–37A (See Table B4: Pages 501–507)

Airplane E   is representative of a small, regional, twin–turboprop commuter airplane such as the Beech 99 (See Table B5: Pages 508–514)

Airplane F   is representative of a corporate four piston–engine airplane such as the Cessna 620 (See Table B6: Pages 515–521)

Airplane G   is representative of a corporate twin jet–engine airplane such as the Learjet 24 (See Table B7: Pages 522–528)

Airplane H   is representaive of a single jet–engine interceptor fighter airplane such as the Lockheed F–104 (See Table B8: Pages 529–535)

Airplane I   is representative of a twin jet–engine fighter/attack airplane such as the McDonnell F–4 (See Table B9: Pages 536–542)

Airplane J   is representative of a large four jet–engine commercial transport airplane such as the Boeing 747–200 (See Table B10: Pages 543–549)

Tables B1–B10 also include examples of the open loop, longitudinal and lateral–directional, modes and transfer functions of these airplanes.

Table B1   Stability and Control Derivatives for Airplane A (Pages 480–486)

Three–view

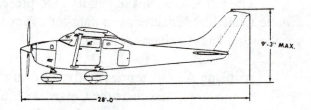

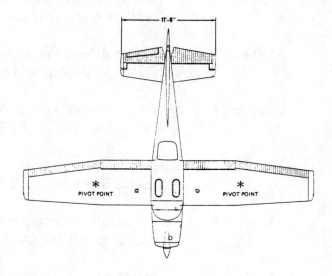

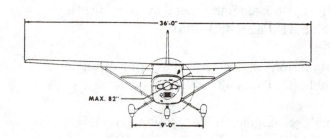

Reference Geometry

S (ft²)	174
$\bar{c}$ (ft)	4.9
b (ft)	36.0

Flight Condition Data	Climb	Cruise	Approach
Altitude, h (ft)	0	5,000	0
Mach Number, M	0.120	0.201	0.096
TAS, U_1 (ft/sec)	133.5	220.1	107.1
Dynamic pressure, $\bar{q}$ (lbs/ft²)	21.2	49.6	13.6
C.G. location, fraction $\bar{c}$	26.4	26.4	26.4
Angle of attack, α_1 (deg)	5.4	0	4

Mass Data

	Climb	Cruise	Approach
W (lbs)	2,650	2,650	2,650
I_{xx_B} (slugft²)	948	948	948
I_{yy_B} (slugft²)	1,346	1,346	1,346
I_{zz_B} (slugft²)	1,967	1,967	1,967
I_{xz_B} (slugft²)	0	0	0

Table B1 (Continued)   Stability and Control Derivatives for Airplane A (Pages 480–486)

Flight Condition	Climb	Cruise	Approach
Steady State Coefficients			
C_{L_1}	0.719	0.307	1.120
C_{D_1}	0.057	0.032	0.132
$C_{T_{x_1}}$	0.057	0.032	0.132
C_{m_1}	0	0	0
$C_{m_{T_1}}$	0	0	0

Longitudinal Coefficients and Stability Derivatives (Stability Axes, Dimensionless)

	Climb	Cruise	Approach
C_{D_0}	0.0270	0.0270	0.0605
C_{D_u}	0	0	0
C_{D_α}	0.380	0.121	0.547
$C_{T_{x_u}}$	−0.171	−0.096	−0.396
C_{L_0}	0.307	0.307	0.807
C_{L_u}	0	0	0
C_{L_α}	4.41	4.41	4.41
$C_{L_{\dot{\alpha}}}$	1.7	1.7	1.7
C_{L_q}	3.9	3.9	3.9
C_{m_0}	0.04	0.04	0.09
C_{m_u}	0	0	0
C_{m_α}	−0.650	−0.613	−0.611
$C_{m_{\dot{\alpha}}}$	−5.57	−7.27	−5.40
C_{m_q}	−15.2	−12.4	−11.4
$C_{m_{T_u}}$	0	0	0
$C_{m_{T_\alpha}}$	0	0	0

Longitudinal Control and Hinge Moment Derivatives (Stability Axes, 1/rad)

	Climb	Cruise	Approach
$C_{D_{\delta_e}}$	0	0	0
$C_{L_{\delta_e}}$	0.43	0.43	0.43
$C_{m_{\delta_e}}$	−1.369	−1.122	−1.029
$C_{D_{i_h}}$	not applicable		
$C_{L_{i_h}}$	not applicable		
$C_{m_{i_h}}$	not applicable		

Table B1 (Continued)   **Stability and Control Derivatives for Airplane A (Pages 480–486)**

Flight Condition	Climb	Cruise	Approach

Longitudinal Control and Hinge Moment Derivatives: Cont'd (Stability Axes, 1/rad)

	Climb	Cruise	Approach
C_{h_α}	–0.0545	–0.0584	–0.0549
$C_{h_{\delta_e}}$	–0.594	–0.585	–0.594

Lateral–Directional Stability Derivatives (Stability Axes, Dimensionless)

	Climb	Cruise	Approach
C_{l_β}	–0.0895	–0.0923	–0.969
C_{l_p}	–0.487	–0.484	–0.494
C_{l_r}	0.1869	0.0798	0.2039
C_{y_β}	–0.404	–0.393	–0.303
C_{y_p}	–0.145	–0.075	–0.213
C_{y_r}	0.267	0.214	0.201
C_{n_β}	0.0907	0.0587	0.0701
$C_{n_{T_\beta}}$	0	0	0
C_{n_p}	–0.0649	–0.0278	–0.0960
C_{n_r}	–0.1199	–0.0937	–0.1151

Lateral–Directional Control and Hinge Moment Derivatives (Stability Axes, Dimensionless)

	Climb	Cruise	Approach
$C_{l_{\delta_a}}$	0.229	0.229	0.229
$C_{l_{\delta_r}}$	0.0147	0.0147	0.0147
$C_{y_{\delta_a}}$	0	0	0
$C_{y_{\delta_r}}$	0.187	0.187	0.187
$C_{n_{\delta_a}}$	–0.0504	–0.0216	–0.0786
$C_{n_{\delta_r}}$	–0.0805	–0.0645	–0.0604
$C_{h_{\alpha_a}}$	???	???	???
$C_{h_{\delta_a}}$	–0.369	–0.363	–0.369
$C_{h_{\beta_r}}$	0.0819	0.0819	0.0819
$C_{h_{\delta_r}}$	–0.579	–0.567	–0.579

Table B1 (Continued)   Stability and Control Derivatives for Airplane A (Pages 480–486)

Longitudinal Transfer Function Data

Altitude	=	5000 ft	M_1	=	0.201
U_1	=	130.39 kts	n	=	1.00 g
$W_{current}$	=	2650.0 lb	q_{bar}	=	49.60 psf
S_w	=	174.00 ft^2	$(W/S)\_TO$	=	15.23 psf
$Theta_1$	=	0.00 deg	X_u	=	-0.0304 1/s
C_{bar}	=	4.90 ft	X_T_u	=	-0.0152 1/s
I_yy_B	=	1346 slgft2	X_a	=	19.4588 ft/s^2
C_m_1	=	0.0000	Z_u	=	-0.2919 1/s
C_m_u	=	0.0000	Z_a	=	-464.7095 ft/s^2
C_m_a	=	-0.6130 1/rad	Z_a_dot	=	-1.9799 ft/s
$C\_m\_a.dot$	=	-7.2700 1/rad	Z_q	=	-4.5422 ft/s
C_m_q	=	-12.4000 1/rad	M_u	=	0.0000 1/ft/s
$C\_m\_T_1$	=	0.0000	M_T_u	=	0.0000 1/ft/s
$C\_m\_T_u$	=	0.0000	M_a	=	-19.2591 1/s^2
$C\_m\_T_a$	=	0.0000	M_T_a	=	0.0000 1/s^2
C_L_1	=	0.3070	M_a_dot	=	-2.5428 1/s
C_L_u	=	0.0000	M_q	=	-4.3370 1/s
C_L_a	=	4.4100 1/rad			
$C\_L\_a.dot$	=	1.7000 1/rad			
C_L_q	=	3.9000 1/rad			
C_D_1	=	0.0320			
C_D_a	=	0.1210 1/rad	w_n_SP	=	5.2707 rad/s
C_D_u	=	0.0000	z_SP	=	0.8442
$C\_T\_X_1$	=	0.0320	w_n_P	=	0.1711 rad/s
$C\_T\_X_u$	=	-0.0960	z_P	=	0.1289
$C\_L\_d_e$	=	0.4300 1/rad	X_del_e	=	0.0000 ft/s^2
$C\_D\_d_e$	=	0.0000 1/rad	Z_del_e	=	-44.9854 ft/s^2
$C\_m\_d_e$	=	-1.1220 1/rad	M_del_e	=	-35.2508 1/s^2

POLYNOMIAL ANGLE OF ATTACK TO ELEVATOR TRANSFER FUNCTION

```
  - 44.9854 S^3 - 7794.8686 S^2 - 355.6293 S - 330.5164
-------------------------------------------------------------------------------
  + 222.0551 S^4 + 1985.9525 S^3 + 6262.2861 S^2 + 329.8825 S + 180.5762
```

FACTORED ANGLE OF ATTACK TO ELEVATOR TRANSFER FUNCTION

```
-44.9854  (S + 173.2302)(S^2 + 0.0454 S + 0.0424)
-------------------------------------------------------------------------------
222.0551  (S^2 + 8.8994 S + 27.7798)(S^2 + 0.0441 S + 0.0293)
```

ANGLE OF ATTACK TO ELEVATOR TRANSFER FUNCTION K_gain =   -1.830343

POLYNOMIAL SPEED TO ELEVATOR TRANSFER FUNCTION

```
  - 875.3615 S^2 + 96137.8071 S + 498397.2852
-------------------------------------------------------------------------------
  + 222.0551 S^4 + 1985.9525 S^3 + 6262.2861 S^2 + 329.8825 S + 180.5762
```

Table B1 (Continued) Stability and Control Derivatives for Airplane A (Pages 480–486)

```
FACTORED SPEED TO ELEVATOR TRANSFER FUNCTION

-875.3615  (S - 114.7866)(S + 4.9602)
--------------------------------------------------------------------------
222.0551  (S^2 + 8.8994 S + 27.7798)(S^2 + 0.0441 S + 0.0293)



SPEED TO ELEVATOR TRANSFER FUNCTION K_gain = 2760.037863


POLYNOMIAL PITCH ATTITUDE TO ELEVATOR TRANSFER FUNCTION

 - 7713.2340 S^2 - 15867.0001 S - 908.2451
--------------------------------------------------------------------------
 + 222.0551 S^4 + 1985.9525 S^3 + 6262.2861 S^2 + 329.8825 S + 180.5762



FACTORED PITCH ATTITUDE TO ELEVATOR TRANSFER FUNCTION

-7713.2340  (S + 1.9982)(S + 0.0589)
--------------------------------------------------------------------------
222.0551  (S^2 + 8.8994 S + 27.7798)(S^2 + 0.0441 S + 0.0293)


PITCH ATTITUDE TO ELEVATOR TRANSFER FUNCTION K_gain =  -5.029704
```

Lateral–Directional Transfer Function Data

W_current	=	2650.0 lb		(W/S)_TO	=	15.23 psf
Altitude	=	5000 ft		q_bar	=	49.60 psf
S_w	=	174.00 ft^2		I_xx_S	=	948 slgft2
U_1	=	130.39 kts		I_zz_S	=	1967 slgft2
Theta_1	=	0.00 deg		I_xz_S	=	0 slgft2
Alpha	=	0.00 deg		Y_B	=	-41.1146 ft/s^2
b_w	=	36.00 ft		Y_p	=	-0.6417 ft/s
I_xx_B	=	948 slgft2		Y_r	=	1.8311 ft/s
I_zz_B	=	1967 slgft2		L_B	=	-30.2497 1/s^2
I_xz_B	=	0 slgft2		L_p	=	-12.9738 1/s
C_l_B	=	-0.0923 1/rad		L_r	=	2.1391 1/s
C_l_p	=	-0.4840 1/rad		N_B	=	9.2717 1/s^2
C_l_r	=	0.0798 1/rad		N_T_B	=	0.0000 1/s^2
C_n_B	=	0.0587 1/rad		N_p	=	-0.3591 1/s
C_n_T_B	=	0.0000		N_r	=	-1.2105 1/s
C_n_p	=	-0.0278 1/rad		w_n_D	=	3.2448 rad/s
C_n_r	=	-0.0937 1/rad		z_D	=	0.2066
C_y_B	=	-0.3930 1/rad		TC_SPIRAL	=	55.922 s
C_y_p	=	-0.0750 1/rad		TC_ROLL	=	0.077 s
C_y_r	=	0.2140 1/rad		TC_1	=	0.077 s
C_l_d_a	=	0.2290 1/rad		TC_2	=	55.922 s
C_l_d_r	=	0.0147 1/rad		Y_del_a	=	0.0000 ft/s^2
C_n_d_a	=	-0.0216 1/rad		Y_del_r	=	19.5634 ft/s^2
C_n_d_r	=	-0.0645 1/rad		L_del_a	=	75.0507 1/s^2
C_y_d_a	=	0.0000 1/rad		L_del_r	=	4.8177 1/s^2
C_y_d_r	=	0.1870 1/rad		N_del_a	=	-3.4117 1/s^2
				N_del_r	=	-10.1879 1/s^2

Table B1 (Continued)   Stability and Control Derivatives for Airplane A (Pages 480–486)

POLYNOMIAL SIDESLIP TO AILERON TRANSFER FUNCTION

+ 696.4302 S^3 + 17900.0258 S^2 + 2683.9498 S

+ 220.0752 S^5 + 3162.7190 S^4 + 6212.5579 S^3 + 30261.6885 S^2 + 539.1737 S

FACTORED SIDESLIP TO AILERON TRANSFER FUNCTION

696.4302   S(S + 25.5517)(S + 0.1508)

220.0752   S(S + 13.0127)(S + 0.0179)(S^2 + 1.3405 S + 10.5287)

SIDESLIP TO AILERON TRANSFER FUNCTION K_gain =   4.977895

POLYNOMIAL SIDESLIP TO RUDDER TRANSFER FUNCTION

+ 19.5634 S^4 + 2497.8410 S^3 + 29711.2702 S^2 - 512.7145 S

+ 220.0752 S^5 + 3162.7190 S^4 + 6212.5579 S^3 + 30261.6885 S^2 + 539.1737 S

FACTORED SIDESLIP TO RUDDER TRANSFER FUNCTION

19.5634   S(S - 0.0172)(S + 114.4019)(S + 13.2945)

220.0752   S(S + 13.0127)(S + 0.0179)(S^2 + 1.3405 S + 10.5287)

SIDESLIP TO RUDDER TRANSFER FUNCTION K_gain =   -0.950926

POLYNOMIAL ROLL TO AILERON TRANSFER FUNCTION

+ 16516.7989 S^3 + 21473.1354 S^2 + 132776.7201 S

+ 220.0752 S^5 + 3162.7190 S^4 + 6212.5579 S^3 + 30261.6885 S^2 + 539.1737 S

FACTORED ROLL TO AILERON TRANSFER FUNCTION

16516.7989   S(S^2 + 1.3001 S + 8.0389)

220.0752   S(S + 13.0127)(S + 0.0179)(S^2 + 1.3405 S + 10.5287)

ROLL TO AILERON TRANSFER FUNCTION K_gain =   246.259658

Table B1 (Continued)   Stability and Control Derivatives for Airplane A (Pages 480–486)

POLYNOMIAL ROLL TO RUDDER TRANSFER FUNCTION

```
 + 1060.2487 S^3 - 3906.2643 S^2 - 58494.3958 S
---------------------------------------------------------------------------
 + 220.0752 S^5 + 3162.7190 S^4 + 6212.5579 S^3 + 30261.6885 S^2 + 539.1737 S
```

FACTORED ROLL TO RUDDER TRANSFER FUNCTION

```
1060.2487   S(S - 9.4949)(S + 5.8106)
---------------------------------------------------------------------------
220.0752    S(S + 13.0127)(S + 0.0179)(S^2 + 1.3405 S + 10.5287)
```

ROLL TO RUDDER TRANSFER FUNCTION K_gain = -108.488972

POLYNOMIAL HEADING TO AILERON TRANSFER FUNCTION

```
 - 750.8413 S^3 - 15813.4284 S^2 - 3308.3966 S + 19037.9166
---------------------------------------------------------------------------
 + 220.0752 S^5 + 3162.7190 S^4 + 6212.5579 S^3 + 30261.6885 S^2 + 539.1737 S
```

FACTORED HEADING TO AILERON TRANSFER FUNCTION

```
-750.8413   (S - 0.9773)(S + 20.7903)(S + 1.2479)
---------------------------------------------------------------------------
220.0752    S(S + 13.0127)(S + 0.0179)(S^2 + 1.3405 S + 10.5287)
```

HEADING TO AILERON TRANSFER FUNCTION K_gain =   35.309434

POLYNOMIAL HEADING TO RUDDER TRANSFER FUNCTION

```
 - 2242.0954 S^3 - 29706.6792 S^2 - 2770.5323 S - 8464.9288
---------------------------------------------------------------------------
 + 220.0752 S^5 + 3162.7190 S^4 + 6212.5579 S^3 + 30261.6885 S^2 + 539.1737 S
```

FACTORED HEADING TO RUDDER TRANSFER FUNCTION

```
-2242.0954  (S + 13.1775)(S^2 + 0.0720 S + 0.2865)
---------------------------------------------------------------------------
220.0752    S(S + 13.0127)(S + 0.0179)(S^2 + 1.3405 S + 10.5287)
```

HEADING TO RUDDER TRANSFER FUNCTION K_gain = -15.699819

Table B2   Stability and Control Derivatives for Airplane B (Pages 487–493)

Three–view

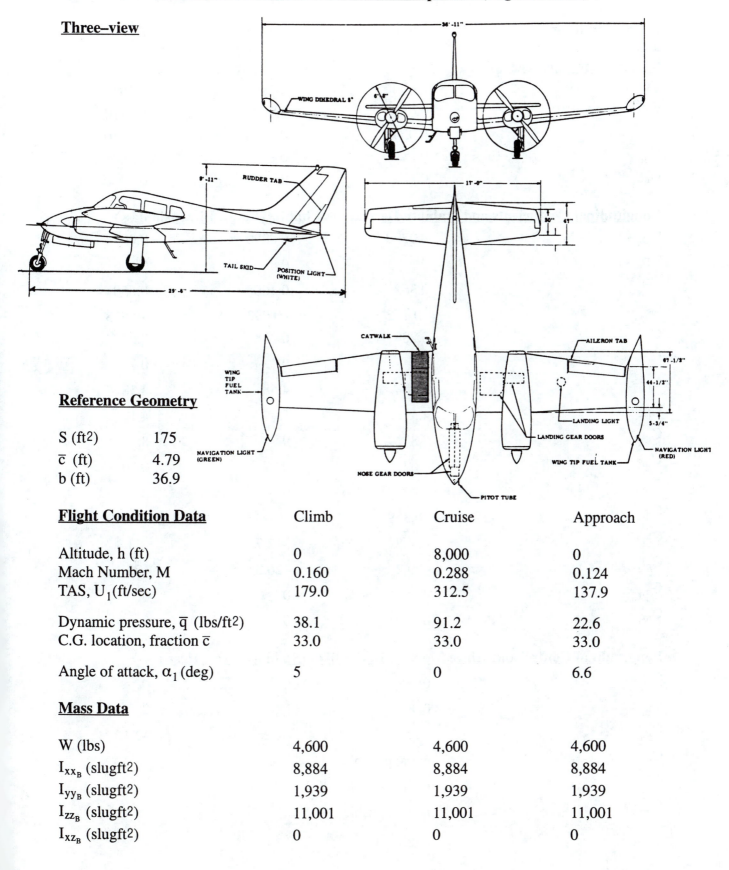

Reference Geometry

S (ft2)	175
$\bar{c}$ (ft)	4.79
b (ft)	36.9

Flight Condition Data

	Climb	Cruise	Approach
Altitude, h (ft)	0	8,000	0
Mach Number, M	0.160	0.288	0.124
TAS, U_1 (ft/sec)	179.0	312.5	137.9
Dynamic pressure, $\bar{q}$ (lbs/ft2)	38.1	91.2	22.6
C.G. location, fraction $\bar{c}$	33.0	33.0	33.0
Angle of attack, α_1 (deg)	5	0	6.6

Mass Data

	Climb	Cruise	Approach
W (lbs)	4,600	4,600	4,600
I_{xx_B} (slugft2)	8,884	8,884	8,884
I_{yy_B} (slugft2)	1,939	1,939	1,939
I_{zz_B} (slugft2)	11,001	11,001	11,001
I_{xz_B} (slugft2)	0	0	0

Table B2 (Continued)   Stability and Control Derivatives for Airplane B (Pages 487–493)

Flight Condition	Climb	Cruise	Approach

Steady State Coefficients

	Climb	Cruise	Approach
C_{L_1}	0.690	0.288	1.163
C_{D_1}	0.0540	0.0310	0.1710
$C_{T_{x_1}}$	0.0540	0.0310	0.1710
C_{m_1}	0	0	0
$C_{m_{T_1}}$	0	0	0

Longitudinal Coefficients and Stability Derivatives (Stability Axes, Dimensionless)

	Climb	Cruise	Approach
C_{D_0}	0.0290	0.0290	0.0974
C_{D_u}	0	0	0
C_{D_α}	0.362	0.160	0.650
$C_{T_{x_u}}$	−0.162	−0.093	−0.513
C_{L_0}	0.288	0.288	0.640
C_{L_u}	0	0	0
C_{L_α}	4.58	4.58	4.58
$C_{L_{\dot\alpha}}$	4.5	5.3	4.1
C_{L_q}	8.8	9.7	8.4
C_{m_0}	0.07	0.07	0.10
C_{m_u}	0	0	0
C_{m_α}	−0.339	−0.137	−0.619
$C_{m_{\dot\alpha}}$	−14.8	−12.7	−11.4
C_{m_q}	−29.2	−26.3	−25.1
$C_{m_{T_u}}$	0	0	0
$C_{m_{T_\alpha}}$	0	0	0

Longitudinal Control and Hinge Moment Derivatives (Stability Axes, 1/rad)

	Climb	Cruise	Approach
$C_{D_{\delta_e}}$	0	0	0
$C_{L_{\delta_e}}$	0.90	0.81	0.77
$C_{m_{\delta_e}}$	−2.53	−2.26	−2.16
$C_{D_{i_h}}$	not applicable		
$C_{L_{i_h}}$	not applicable		
$C_{m_{i_h}}$	not applicable		

<u>**Table B2 (Continued)**</u>   <u>**Stability and Control Derivatives for Airplane B (Pages 487–493)**</u>

<u>**Flight Condition**</u>	Climb	Cruise	Approach
<u>**Longitudinal Control and Hinge Moment Derivatives: Cont'd (Stability Axes, 1/rad)**</u>			
C_{h_α}	–0.0826	–0.0863	–0.0925
$C_{h_{\delta_e}}$	–0.742	–0.742	–0.742
<u>**Lateral–Directional Stability Derivatives (Stability Axes, Dimensionless)**</u>			
C_{l_β}	–0.0923	–0.1096	–0.0965
C_{l_p}	–0.552	–0.551	–0.566
C_{l_r}	0.1746	0.0729	0.2433
C_{y_β}	–0.610	–0.698	–0.577
C_{y_p}	–0.2093	–0.1410	–0.2897
C_{y_r}	0.356	0.355	0.355
C_{n_β}	0.1552	0.1444	0.1683
$C_{n_{T_\beta}}$	0	0	0
C_{n_p}	–0.0615	–0.0257	–0.1021
C_{n_r}	–0.1561	–0.1495	–0.1947
<u>**Lateral–Directional Control and Hinge Moment Derivatives (Stability Axes, Dimensionless)**</u>			
$C_{l_{\delta_a}}$	0.1720	0.1720	0.1720
$C_{l_{\delta_r}}$	0.0192	0.0192	0.0192
$C_{y_{\delta_a}}$	0	0	0
$C_{y_{\delta_r}}$	0.230	0.230	0.230
$C_{n_{\delta_a}}$	–0.0402	–0.0168	–0.0676
$C_{n_{\delta_r}}$	–0.1152	–0.1152	–0.1152
$C_{h_{\alpha_a}}$	???	???	???
$C_{h_{\delta_a}}$	–0.481	–0.453	–0.481
$C_{h_{\beta_r}}$	0.0722	0.0722	0.0722
$C_{h_{\delta_r}}$	–0.602	–0.590	–0.602

Table B2 (Continued)   Stability and Control Derivatives for Airplane B (Pages 487–493)

Longitudinal Transfer Function Data

Altitude	=	0 ft		M_1	=	0.160
U_1	=	106.04 kts		n	=	1.00 g
W_current	=	4600.0 lb		q_bar	=	38.07 psf
S_w	=	175.00 ft^2		(W/S)_TO	=	26.29 psf
Theta_1	=	5.00 deg		X_u	=	-0.0281 1/s
C_bar	=	4.79 ft		X_T_u	=	-0.0141 1/s
I_yy_B	=	1939 slgft2		X_a	=	15.2843 ft/s^2
C_m_1	=	0.0000		Z_u	=	-0.3593 1/s
C_m_u	=	0.0000		Z_a	=	-215.9370 ft/s^2
C_m_a	=	-0.3390 1/rad		Z_a_dot	=	-2.8060 ft/s
C_m_a.dot	=	-14.8000 1/rad		Z_q	=	-5.4873 ft/s
C_m_q	=	-29.2000 1/rad		M_u	=	0.0000 1/ft/s
C_m_T_1	=	0.0000		M_T_u	=	0.0000 1/ft/s
C_m_T_u	=	0.0000		M_a	=	-5.5793 1/s^2
C_m_T_a	=	0.0000		M_T_a	=	0.0000 1/s^2
C_L_1	=	0.6900		M_a_dot	=	-3.2595 1/s
C_L_u	=	0.0000		M_q	=	-6.4308 1/s
C_L_a	=	4.5800 1/rad				
C_L_a.dot	=	4.5000 1/rad		w_n_3 osc	=	0.1647 rad/s
C_L_q	=	8.8000 1/rad		z_3rd osc	=	0.1338
C_D_1	=	0.0540		TC_1	=	0.107 s
C_D_a	=	0.3620 1/rad		TC_2	=	0.725 s
C_D_u	=	0.0000		X_del_e	=	0.0000 ft/s^2
C_T_X_1	=	0.0540		Z_del_e	=	-41.9386 ft/s^2
C_T_X_u	=	-0.1620		M_del_e	=	-41.6392 1/s^2
C_L_d_e	=	0.9000 1/rad				
C_D_d_e	=	0.0000 1/rad				
C_m_d_e	=	-2.5300 1/rad				

POLYNOMIAL ANGLE OF ATTACK TO ELEVATOR TRANSFER FUNCTION

```
- 41.9386 S^3 - 7495.5567 S^2 - 199.3076 S - 474.5850
---------------------------------------------------------------------------
+ 181.7858 S^4 + 1958.1258 S^3 + 2435.2386 S^2 + 156.2160 S + 63.5906
```

FACTORED ANGLE OF ATTACK TO ELEVATOR TRANSFER FUNCTION

```
-41.9386  (S + 178.7008)(S^2 + 0.0262 S + 0.0633)
---------------------------------------------------------------------------
181.7858  (S + 9.3480)(S + 1.3796)(S^2 + 0.0441 S + 0.0271)
```

ANGLE OF ATTACK TO ELEVATOR TRANSFER FUNCTION K_gain =   -7.463127

POLYNOMIAL SPEED TO ELEVATOR TRANSFER FUNCTION

```
- 641.0008 S^2 + 123693.0423 S + 282474.6952
---------------------------------------------------------------------------
+ 181.7858 S^4 + 1958.1258 S^3 + 2435.2386 S^2 + 156.2160 S + 63.5906
```

Table B2 (Continued)   Stability and Control Derivatives for Airplane B (Pages 487–493)

FACTORED SPEED TO ELEVATOR TRANSFER FUNCTION

```
-641.0008   (S - 195.2259)(S + 2.2573)
-------------------------------------------------------------------------------
181.7858   (S + 9.3480)(S + 1.3796)(S^2 + 0.0441 S + 0.0271)
```

SPEED TO ELEVATOR TRANSFER FUNCTION K_gain = 4442.079652

POLYNOMIAL PITCH ATTITUDE TO ELEVATOR TRANSFER FUNCTION

```
 - 7432.7155 S^2 - 9070.9460 S - 598.0300
-------------------------------------------------------------------------------
 + 181.7858 S^4 + 1958.1258 S^3 + 2435.2386 S^2 + 156.2160 S + 63.5906
```

FACTORED PITCH ATTITUDE TO ELEVATOR TRANSFER FUNCTION

```
-7432.7155   (S + 1.1505)(S + 0.0699)
-------------------------------------------------------------------------------
181.7858   (S + 9.3480)(S + 1.3796)(S^2 + 0.0441 S + 0.0271)
```

PITCH ATTITUDE TO ELEVATOR TRANSFER FUNCTION K_gain =   -9.404371

Lateral–Directional Transfer Function Data

W_current	=	4600.0 lb		(W/S)_TO	=	26.29 psf
Altitude	=	0 ft		q_bar	=	38.07 psf
S_w	=	175.00 ft^2		I_xx_S	=	8900 slgft2
U_1	=	106.04 kts		I_zz_S	=	10985 slgft2
Theta_1	=	5.00 deg		I_xz_S	=	-184 slgft2
Alpha	=	5.00 deg		Y_B	=	-28.4250 ft/s^2
b_w	=	36.90 ft		Y_p	=	-1.0054 ft/s
I_xx_B	=	8884 slgft2		Y_r	=	1.7101 ft/s
I_zz_B	=	11001 slgft2		L_B	=	-2.5495 1/s^2
I_xz_B	=	0 slgft2		L_p	=	-1.5718 1/s
C_l_B	=	-0.0923 1/rad		L_r	=	0.4972 1/s
C_l_p	=	-0.5520 1/rad		N_B	=	3.4733 1/s^2
C_l_r	=	0.1746 1/rad		N_T_B	=	0.0000 1/s^2
C_n_B	=	0.1552 1/rad		N_p	=	-0.1419 1/s
C_n_T_B	=	0.0000		N_r	=	-0.3601 1/s
C_n_p	=	-0.0615 1/rad		w_n_D	=	1.9400 rad/s
C_n_r	=	-0.1561 1/rad		z_D	=	0.1050
C_y_B	=	-0.6100 1/rad		TC_SPIRAL	=	-44.476 s
C_y_p	=	-0.2093 1/rad		TC_ROLL	=	0.584 s
C_y_r	=	0.3560 1/rad		TC_1	=	0.584 s
C_l_d_a	=	0.1720 1/rad		TC_2	=	-44.476 s
C_l_d_r	=	0.0192 1/rad		Y_del_a	=	0.0000 ft/s^2
C_n_d_a	=	-0.0402 1/rad		Y_del_r	=	10.7176 ft/s^2
C_n_d_r	=	-0.1152 1/rad		L_del_a	=	4.7510 1/s^2
C_y_d_a	=	0.0000 1/rad		L_del_r	=	0.5303 1/s^2
C_y_d_r	=	0.2300 1/rad		N_del_a	=	-0.8997 1/s^2
				N_del_r	=	-2.5781 1/s^2

Table B2 (Continued)   Stability and Control Derivatives for Airplane B (Pages 487–493)

```
POLYNOMIAL SIDESLIP TO AILERON TRANSFER FUNCTION

 + 168.7800 S^3 + 521.7640 S^2 + 40.5023 S
------------------------------------------------------------------------------
 + 178.9180 S^5 + 375.1483 S^4 + 789.6410 S^3 + 1134.8049 S^2 - 25.9185 S


FACTORED SIDESLIP TO AILERON TRANSFER FUNCTION

168.7800    S(S + 3.0117)(S + 0.0797)
------------------------------------------------------------------------------
178.9180    S(S - 0.0225)(S + 1.7119)(S^2 + 0.4074 S + 3.7637)


  SIDESLIP TO AILERON TRANSFER FUNCTION K_gain =    -1.562683


POLYNOMIAL SIDESLIP TO RUDDER TRANSFER FUNCTION

 + 10.7139 S^4 + 478.7750 S^3 + 758.2996 S^2 - 34.9602 S
------------------------------------------------------------------------------
 + 178.9180 S^5 + 375.1483 S^4 + 789.6410 S^3 + 1134.8049 S^2 - 25.9185 S


FACTORED SIDESLIP TO RUDDER TRANSFER FUNCTION

10.7139    S(S - 0.0448)(S + 43.0410)(S + 1.6910)
------------------------------------------------------------------------------
178.9180    S(S - 0.0225)(S + 1.7119)(S^2 + 0.4074 S + 3.7637)


  SIDESLIP TO RUDDER TRANSFER FUNCTION K_gain =    1.348853


POLYNOMIAL ROLL TO AILERON TRANSFER FUNCTION

 + 853.6582 S^3 + 361.7453 S^2 + 2554.5759 S
------------------------------------------------------------------------------
 + 178.9180 S^5 + 375.1483 S^4 + 789.6410 S^3 + 1134.8049 S^2 - 25.9185 S


FACTORED ROLL TO AILERON TRANSFER FUNCTION

853.6582    S(S^2 + 0.4238 S + 2.9925)
------------------------------------------------------------------------------
178.9180    S(S - 0.0225)(S + 1.7119)(S^2 + 0.4074 S + 3.7637)


  ROLL TO AILERON TRANSFER FUNCTION K_gain =    -98.562052
```

Table B2 (Continued)   Stability and Control Derivatives for Airplane B (Pages 487–493)

```
POLYNOMIAL ROLL TO RUDDER TRANSFER FUNCTION

 + 104.4505 S^3 - 206.7270 S^2 - 860.9920 S
------------------------------------------------------------------------------
 + 178.9180 S^5 + 375.1483 S^4 + 789.6410 S^3 + 1134.8049 S^2 - 25.9185 S


FACTORED ROLL TO RUDDER TRANSFER FUNCTION

104.4505    S(S - 4.0264)(S + 2.0472)
------------------------------------------------------------------------------
178.9180    S(S - 0.0225)(S + 1.7119)(S^2 + 0.4074 S + 3.7637)


  ROLL TO RUDDER TRANSFER FUNCTION K_gain =    33.219266


POLYNOMIAL HEADING TO AILERON TRANSFER FUNCTION

 - 175.2497 S^3 - 401.5655 S^2 - 73.6397 S + 455.3900
------------------------------------------------------------------------------
 + 178.9180 S^5 + 375.1483 S^4 + 789.6410 S^3 + 1134.8049 S^2 - 25.9185 S


FACTORED HEADING TO AILERON TRANSFER FUNCTION

-175.2497   (S - 0.8456)(S^2 + 3.1370 S + 3.0729)
------------------------------------------------------------------------------
178.9180    S(S - 0.0225)(S + 1.7119)(S^2 + 0.4074 S + 3.7637)


  HEADING TO AILERON TRANSFER FUNCTION K_gain =   -17.570107


POLYNOMIAL HEADING TO RUDDER TRANSFER FUNCTION

 - 463.0227 S^3 - 774.5867 S^2 - 50.1800 S - 151.6343
------------------------------------------------------------------------------
 + 178.9180 S^5 + 375.1483 S^4 + 789.6410 S^3 + 1134.8049 S^2 - 25.9185 S


FACTORED HEADING TO RUDDER TRANSFER FUNCTION

-463.0227   (S + 1.7205)(S^2 + -0.0476 S + 0.1903)
------------------------------------------------------------------------------
178.9180    S(S - 0.0225)(S + 1.7119)(S^2 + 0.4074 S + 3.7637)


  HEADING TO RUDDER TRANSFER FUNCTION K_gain =    5.850439
```

Table B3   Stability and Control Derivatives for Airplane C (Pages 494–500)

Three–view

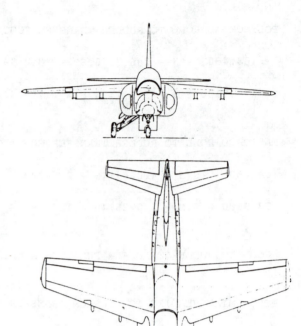

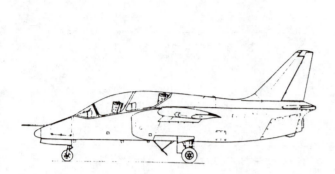

Reference Geometry

S (ft^2)	136
$\bar{c}$ (ft)	5.4
b (ft)	26.3

Flight Condition Data	Approach	Cruise 1	Cruise 2
Altitude, h (ft)	0	25,000	35,000
Mach Number, M	0.111	0.600	0.600
TAS, U_1 (ft/sec)	124	610	584
Dynamic pressure, $\bar{q}$ (lbs/ft^2)	18.2	198.0	125.7
C.G. location, fraction $\bar{c}$	0.25	0.25	0.25
Angle of attack, α_1 (deg)	8	0	0.9

Mass Data

	Approach	Cruise 1	Cruise 2
W (lbs)	3,500	4,000	4,000
I_{xx_B} (slugft^2)	750	800	800
I_{yy_B} (slugft^2)	4,600	4,800	4,800
I_{zz_B} (slugft^2)	5,000	5,200	5,200
I_{xz_B} (slugft^2)	200	200	200

Table B3 (Continued)   Stability and Control Derivatives for Airplane C (Pages 494–500)

Flight Condition	Approach	Cruise 1	Cruise 2
Steady State Coefficients			
C_{L_1}	1.414	0.149	0.234
C_{D_1}	0.2100	0.0220	0.0250
$C_{T_{x_1}}$	0.2100	0.0220	0.0250
C_{m_1}	0	0	0
$C_{m_{T_1}}$	0	0	0

Longitudinal Coefficients and Stability Derivatives (Stability Axes, Dimensionless)

	Approach	Cruise 1	Cruise 2
C_{D_0}	0.0900	0.0205	0.0205
C_{D_u}	0	0.05	0.05
C_{D_α}	1.14	0.12	0.17
$C_{T_{x_u}}$	−0.45	−0.05	−0.055
C_{L_0}	0.65	0.149	0.149
C_{L_u}	0.071	0.084	0.132
C_{L_α}	5.0	5.5	5.5
$C_{L_{\dot\alpha}}$	3.0	4.2	4.2
C_{L_q}	9.0	10.0	10.0
C_{m_0}	−0.07	−0.08	−0.08
C_{m_u}	0	0	0
C_{m_α}	−0.60	−0.24	−0.24
$C_{m_{\dot\alpha}}$	−7.0	−9.6	−9.6
C_{m_q}	−15.7	−17.7	−17.7
$C_{m_{T_u}}$	0	0	0
$C_{m_{T_\alpha}}$	0	0	0

Longitudinal Control and Hinge Moment Derivatives (Stability Axes, 1/rad)

	Approach	Cruise 1	Cruise 2
$C_{D_{\delta_e}}$	0	0	0
$C_{L_{\delta_e}}$	0.39	0.38	0.35
$C_{m_{\delta_e}}$	−0.90	−0.88	−0.82
$C_{D_{i_h}}$	0	0	0
$C_{L_{i_h}}$	1.0	0.99	0.99
$C_{m_{i_h}}$	−2.3	−2.3	−2.3

Table B3 (Continued)   Stability and Control Derivatives for Airplane C (Pages 494–500)

Flight Condition	Approach	Cruise 1	Cruise 2

Longitudinal Control and Hinge Moment Derivatives: Cont'd (Stability Axes, 1/rad)

	Approach	Cruise 1	Cruise 2
C_{h_α}	−0.22	−0.22	−0.22
$C_{h_{\delta_e}}$	−0.504	−0.504	−0.504

Lateral–Directional Stability Derivatives (Stability Axes, Dimensionless)

	Approach	Cruise 1	Cruise 2
C_{l_β}	−0.140	−0.110	−0.110
C_{l_p}	−0.350	−0.390	−0.390
C_{l_r}	0.560	0.280	0.310
C_{y_β}	−0.94	−1.00	−1.00
C_{y_p}	−0.010	−0.140	−0.120
C_{y_r}	0.590	0.610	0.620
C_{n_β}	0.160	0.170	0.170
$C_{n_{T_\beta}}$	0	0	0
C_{n_p}	−0.030	0.090	0.080
C_{n_r}	−0.310	−0.260	−0.260

Lateral–Directional Control and Hinge Moment Derivatives (Stability Axes, Dimensionless)

	Approach	Cruise 1	Cruise 2
$C_{l_{\delta_a}}$	0.110	0.100	0.100
$C_{l_{\delta_r}}$	0.030	0.050	0.050
$C_{y_{\delta_a}}$	0	0	0
$C_{y_{\delta_r}}$	0.260	0.0280	0.0280
$C_{n_{\delta_a}}$	−0.030	−0.003	−0.005
$C_{n_{\delta_r}}$	−0.110	−0.120	−0.120
$C_{h_{\alpha_a}}$	−0.143	−0.143	−0.143
$C_{h_{\delta_a}}$	−0.500	−0.500	−0.500
$C_{h_{\beta_r}}$	0.25	0.25	0.25
$C_{h_{\delta_r}}$	−0.380	−0.380	−0.380

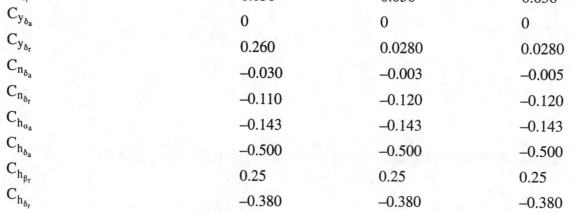

Table B3 (Continued)   Stability and Control Derivatives for Airplane C (Pages 494–500)

Longitudinal Transfer Function Data

Altitude	=	0 ft		M_1	=	0.111
U_1	=	73.46 kts		n	=	1.00 g
W_current	=	3500.0 lb		q_bar	=	18.27 psf
S_w	=	136.00 ft^2		(W/S)_TO	=	25.74 psf
Theta_1	=	8.00 deg		X_u	=	-0.0774 1/s
C_bar	=	5.40 ft		X_T_u	=	-0.0055 1/s
I_yy_B	=	4600 slgft2		X_a	=	6.2582 ft/s^2
C_m_1	=	0.0000		Z_u	=	-0.5340 1/s
C_m_u	=	0.0000		Z_a	=	-118.9972 ft/s^2
C_m_a	=	-0.6000 1/rad		Z_a_dot	=	-1.4921 ft/s
C_m_a.dot	=	-7.0000 1/rad		Z_q	=	-4.4764 ft/s
C_m_q	=	-15.7000 1/rad		M_u	=	0.0000 1/ft/s
C_m_T_1	=	0.0000		M_T_u	=	0.0000 1/ft/s
C_m_T_u	=	0.0000		M_a	=	-1.7500 1/s^2
C_m_T_a	=	0.0000		M_T_a	=	0.0000 1/s^2
C_L_1	=	1.4140		M_a_dot	=	-0.4446 1/s
C_L_u	=	0.0710		M_q	=	-0.9972 1/s
C_L_a	=	5.0000 1/rad				
C_L_a.dot	=	3.0000 1/rad		w_n_SP	=	1.6452 rad/s
C_L_q	=	9.0000 1/rad		z_SP	=	0.7418
C_D_1	=	0.2100		w_n_P	=	0.2929 rad/s
C_D_a	=	1.1400 1/rad		z_P	=	0.0191
C_D_u	=	0.0000		X_del_e	=	0.0000 ft/s^2
C_T_X_1	=	0.2100		Z_del_e	=	-8.9077 ft/s^2
C_T_X_u	=	-0.4500		M_del_e	=	-2.6251 1/s^2
C_L_d_e	=	0.3900 1/rad				
C_D_d_e	=	0.0000 1/rad				
C_m_d_e	=	-0.9000 1/rad				

POLYNOMIAL ANGLE OF ATTACK TO ELEVATOR TRANSFER FUNCTION

$$\frac{- 8.9077 \ S^3 - 323.3421 \ S^2 - 14.9885 \ S - 43.6912}{+ 125.4782 \ S^4 + 307.6638 \ S^3 + 353.8063 \ S^2 + 30.0714 \ S + 29.1274}$$

FACTORED ANGLE OF ATTACK TO ELEVATOR TRANSFER FUNCTION

$$\frac{-8.9077 \quad (S + 36.2566)(S^2 + 0.0427 \ S + 0.1353)}{125.4782 \quad (S^2 + 2.4407 \ S + 2.7066)(S^2 + 0.0112 \ S + 0.0858)}$$

ANGLE OF ATTACK TO ELEVATOR TRANSFER FUNCTION K_gain =   -1.500000

POLYNOMIAL SPEED TO ELEVATOR TRANSFER FUNCTION

$$\frac{- 55.7460 \ S^2 + 8349.5123 \ S + 9529.4560}{+ 125.4782 \ S^4 + 307.6638 \ S^3 + 353.8063 \ S^2 + 30.0714 \ S + 29.1274}$$

Table B3 (Continued)   Stability and Control Derivatives for Airplane C (Pages 494–500)

FACTORED SPEED TO ELEVATOR TRANSFER FUNCTION

```
-55.7460  (S - 150.9107)(S + 1.1328)
------------------------------------------------------------------------------
125.4782  (S^2 + 2.4407 S + 2.7066)(S^2 + 0.0112 S + 0.0858)
```

SPEED TO ELEVATOR TRANSFER FUNCTION K_gain = 327.164213

POLYNOMIAL PITCH ATTITUDE TO ELEVATOR TRANSFER FUNCTION

```
 - 325.4282 S^2 - 323.7640 S - 33.3761
------------------------------------------------------------------------------
 + 125.4782 S^4 + 307.6638 S^3 + 353.8063 S^2 + 30.0714 S + 29.1274
```

FACTORED PITCH ATTITUDE TO ELEVATOR TRANSFER FUNCTION

```
-325.4282  (S + 0.8781)(S + 0.1168)
------------------------------------------------------------------------------
125.4782  (S^2 + 2.4407 S + 2.7066)(S^2 + 0.0112 S + 0.0858)
```

PITCH ATTITUDE TO ELEVATOR TRANSFER FUNCTION K_gain =   -1.145864

Lateral–Directional Transfer Function Data

W_current =	3500.0 lb		(W/S)_TO =	25.74 psf
Altitude =	0 ft		q_bar =	18.27 psf
S_w =	136.00 ft^2		I_xx_S =	777 slgft2
U_1 =	73.46 kts		I_zz_S =	4973 slgft2
Theta_1 =	8.00 deg		I_xz_S =	-393 slgft2
Alpha =	8.00 deg		Y_B =	-21.4697 ft/s^2
b_w =	26.30 ft		Y_p =	-0.0242 ft/s
I_xx_B =	750 slgft2		Y_r =	1.4292 ft/s
I_zz_B =	5000 slgft2		L_B =	-11.7711 1/s^2
I_xz_B =	200 slgft2		L_p =	-3.1211 1/s
C_l_B =	-0.1400 1/rad		L_r =	4.9938 1/s
C_l_p =	-0.3500 1/rad		N_B =	2.1025 1/s^2
C_l_r =	0.5600 1/rad		N_T_B =	0.0000 1/s^2
C_n_B =	0.1600 1/rad		N_p =	-0.0418 1/s
C_n_T_B =	0.0000		N_r =	-0.4320 1/s
C_n_p =	-0.0300 1/rad		w_n_D =	1.7980 rad/s
C_n_r =	-0.3100 1/rad		z_D =	0.2118
C_y_B =	-0.9400 1/rad		TC_SPIRAL =	-8.089 s
C_y_p =	-0.0100 1/rad		TC_ROLL =	0.276 s
C_y_r =	0.5900 1/rad		TC_1 =	0.276 s
C_l_d_a =	0.1100 1/rad		TC_2 =	-8.089 s
C_l_d_r =	0.0300 1/rad		Y_del_a =	0.0000 ft/s^2
C_n_d_a =	-0.0300 1/rad		Y_del_r =	5.9384 ft/s^2
C_n_d_r =	-0.1100 1/rad		L_del_a =	9.2487 1/s^2
C_y_d_a =	0.0000 1/rad		L_del_r =	2.5224 1/s^2
C_y_d_r =	0.2600 1/rad		N_del_a =	-0.3942 1/s^2
			N_del_r =	-1.4455 1/s^2

Table B3 (Continued)   Stability and Control Derivatives for Airplane C (Pages 494–500)

POLYNOMIAL SIDESLIP TO AILERON TRANSFER FUNCTION

```
 + 137.7740 S^3 + 499.1699 S^2 + 64.5896 S
--------------------------------------------------------------------------
 + 119.0192 S^5 + 507.5201 S^4 + 648.9080 S^3 + 1307.0734 S^2 - 172.4879 S
```

FACTORED SIDESLIP TO AILERON TRANSFER FUNCTION

```
137.7740    S(S + 3.4887)(S + 0.1344)
--------------------------------------------------------------------------
119.0192    S(S - 0.1236)(S + 3.6262)(S^2 + 0.7616 S + 3.2329)
```

SIDESLIP TO AILERON TRANSFER FUNCTION K_gain =   -0.374459

POLYNOMIAL SIDESLIP TO RUDDER TRANSFER FUNCTION

```
 + 5.7005 S^4 + 224.8549 S^3 + 678.9163 S^2 - 195.2623 S
--------------------------------------------------------------------------
 + 119.0192 S^5 + 507.5201 S^4 + 648.9080 S^3 + 1307.0734 S^2 - 172.4879 S
```

FACTORED SIDESLIP TO RUDDER TRANSFER FUNCTION

```
5.7005    S(S - 0.2643)(S + 36.1210)(S + 3.5877)
--------------------------------------------------------------------------
119.0192    S(S - 0.1236)(S + 3.6262)(S^2 + 0.7616 S + 3.2329)
```

SIDESLIP TO RUDDER TRANSFER FUNCTION K_gain =   1.132035

POLYNOMIAL ROLL TO AILERON TRANSFER FUNCTION

```
 + 1171.4603 S^3 + 454.2025 S^2 + 1857.9873 S
--------------------------------------------------------------------------
 + 119.0192 S^5 + 507.5201 S^4 + 648.9080 S^3 + 1307.0734 S^2 - 172.4879 S
```

FACTORED ROLL TO AILERON TRANSFER FUNCTION

```
1171.4603    S(S^2 + 0.3877 S + 1.5860)
--------------------------------------------------------------------------
119.0192    S(S - 0.1236)(S + 3.6262)(S^2 + 0.7616 S + 3.2329)
```

ROLL TO AILERON TRANSFER FUNCTION K_gain =   -10.771696

Table B3 (Continued)   Stability and Control Derivatives for Airplane C (Pages 494–500)

```
POLYNOMIAL ROLL TO RUDDER TRANSFER FUNCTION

  + 403.4749 S^3 - 766.2161 S^2 - 1534.7513 S
------------------------------------------------------------------------------
  + 119.0192 S^5 + 507.5201 S^4 + 648.9080 S^3 + 1307.0734 S^2 - 172.4879 S


FACTORED ROLL TO RUDDER TRANSFER FUNCTION

403.4749    S(S - 3.1187)(S + 1.2197)
------------------------------------------------------------------------------
119.0192    S(S - 0.1236)(S + 3.6262)(S^2 + 0.7616 S + 3.2329)


 ROLL TO RUDDER TRANSFER FUNCTION K_gain =     8.897733


POLYNOMIAL HEADING TO AILERON TRANSFER FUNCTION

  - 139.6122 S^3 - 224.6739 S^2 - 35.0775 S + 471.7029
------------------------------------------------------------------------------
  + 119.0192 S^5 + 507.5201 S^4 + 648.9080 S^3 + 1307.0734 S^2 - 172.4879 S


FACTORED HEADING TO AILERON TRANSFER FUNCTION

-139.6122   (S - 1.0759)(S^2 + 2.6852 S + 3.1403)
------------------------------------------------------------------------------
119.0192    S(S - 0.1236)(S + 3.6262)(S^2 + 0.7616 S + 3.2329)


 HEADING TO AILERON TRANSFER FUNCTION K_gain =    -2.734701


POLYNOMIAL HEADING TO RUDDER TRANSFER FUNCTION

  - 203.9638 S^3 - 589.7395 S^2 - 56.9493 S - 373.1381
------------------------------------------------------------------------------
  + 119.0192 S^5 + 507.5201 S^4 + 648.9080 S^3 + 1307.0734 S^2 - 172.4879 S


FACTORED HEADING TO RUDDER TRANSFER FUNCTION

-203.9638   (S + 3.0014)(S^2 + -0.1100 S + 0.6095)
------------------------------------------------------------------------------
119.0192    S(S - 0.1236)(S + 3.6262)(S^2 + 0.7616 S + 3.2329)


 HEADING TO RUDDER TRANSFER FUNCTION K_gain =     2.163271
```

Table B4   Stability and Control Derivatives for Airplane D (Pages 501–507)

Three–view

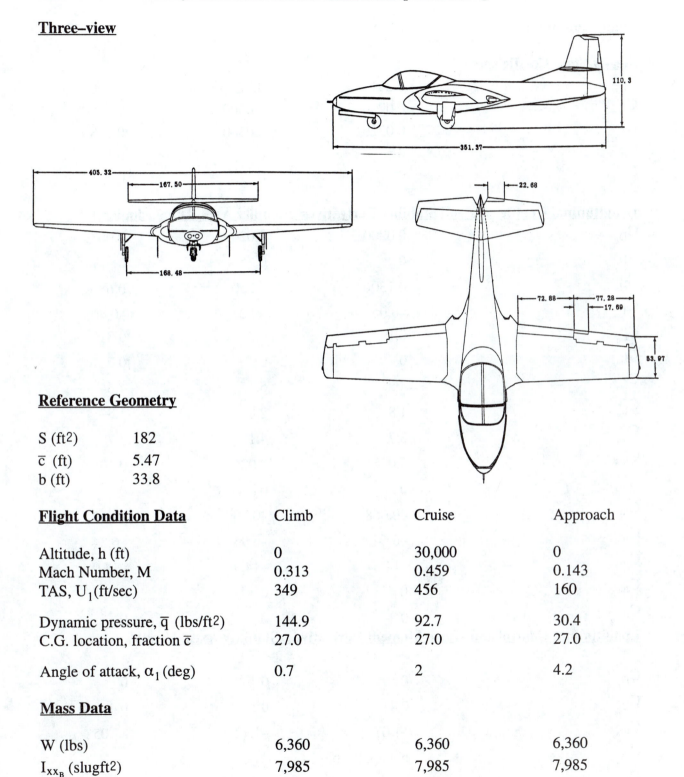

Reference Geometry

S (ft²)	182
$\bar{c}$ (ft)	5.47
b (ft)	33.8

Flight Condition Data	Climb	Cruise	Approach
Altitude, h (ft)	0	30,000	0
Mach Number, M	0.313	0.459	0.143
TAS, U_1 (ft/sec)	349	456	160
Dynamic pressure, $\bar{q}$ (lbs/ft²)	144.9	92.7	30.4
C.G. location, fraction $\bar{c}$	27.0	27.0	27.0
Angle of attack, α_1 (deg)	0.7	2	4.2

Mass Data

	Climb	Cruise	Approach
W (lbs)	6,360	6,360	6,360
I_{xx_B} (slugft²)	7,985	7,985	7,985
I_{yy_B} (slugft²)	3,326	3,326	3,326
I_{zz_B} (slugft²)	11,183	11,183	11,183
I_{xz_B} (slugft²)	0	0	0

Table B4 (Continued)   Stability and Control Derivatives for Airplane D (Pages 501–507)

Flight Condition	Climb	Cruise	Approach
Steady State Coefficients			
C_{L_1}	0.241	0.378	1.150
C_{D_1}	0.0220	0.0300	0.1580
$C_{T_{x_1}}$	0.0220	0.0300	0.1580
C_{m_1}	0	0	0
$C_{m_{T_1}}$	0	0	0
Longitudinal Coefficients and Stability Derivatives (Stability Axes, Dimensionless)			
C_{D_0}	0.0200	0.0200	0.0689
C_{D_u}	0	0	0
C_{D_α}	0.130	0.250	0.682
$C_{T_{x_u}}$	−0.05	−0.07	−0.40
C_{L_0}	0.19	0.20	0.81
C_{L_u}	0	0	0
C_{L_α}	4.81	5.15	4.64
$C_{L_{\dot\alpha}}$	1.8	2.0	1.8
C_{L_q}	3.7	4.1	3.7
C_{m_0}	0.025	0.025	0.10
C_{m_u}	0	0	0
C_{m_α}	−0.668	−0.700	−0.631
$C_{m_{\dot\alpha}}$	−6.64	−6.95	−6.84
C_{m_q}	−14.3	−14.9	−14.0
$C_{m_{T_u}}$	0	0	0
$C_{m_{T_\alpha}}$	0	0	0
Longitudinal Control and Hinge Moment Derivatives (Stability Axes, 1/rad)			
$C_{D_{\delta_e}}$	0	0	0
$C_{L_{\delta_e}}$	0.4	0.5	0.4
$C_{m_{\delta_e}}$	−1.07	−1.12	−1.05
$C_{D_{i_h}}$	not applicable		
$C_{L_{i_h}}$	not applicable		
$C_{m_{i_h}}$	not applicable		

Table B4 (Continued)   Stability and Control Derivatives for Airplane D (Pages 501–507)

Flight Condition	Climb	Cruise	Approach

Longitudinal Control and Hinge Moment Derivatives: Cont'd (Stability Axes, 1/rad)

	Climb	Cruise	Approach
C_{h_α}	–0.00784	–0.00775	–0.00739
$C_{h_{\delta_e}}$	–0.347	–0.497	–0.347

Lateral–Directional Stability Derivatives (Stability Axes, Dimensionless)

	Climb	Cruise	Approach
C_{l_β}	–0.0851	–0.0944	–0.0822
C_{l_p}	–0.440	–0.442	–0.458
C_{l_r}	0.0590	0.0926	0.2540
C_{y_β}	–0.361	–0.346	–0.303
C_{y_p}	–0.0635	–0.0827	–0.1908
C_{y_r}	0.314	0.300	0.263
C_{n_β}	0.1052	0.1106	0.1095
$C_{n_{T_\beta}}$	0	0	0
C_{n_p}	–0.0154	–0.0243	–0.0768
C_{n_r}	–0.1433	–0.1390	–0.1613

Lateral–Directional Control and Hinge Moment Derivatives (Stability Axes, Dimensionless)

	Climb	Cruise	Approach
$C_{l_{\delta_a}}$	0.1788	0.1810	0.1788
$C_{l_{\delta_r}}$	0.015	0.015	0.015
$C_{y_{\delta_a}}$	0	0	0
$C_{y_{\delta_r}}$	0.2	0.2	0.2
$C_{n_{\delta_a}}$	–0.0160	–0.0254	–0.0760
$C_{n_{\delta_r}}$	–0.0365	–0.0365	–0.0365
$C_{h_{\alpha_a}}$	???	???	???
$C_{h_{\delta_a}}$	–0.226	–0.226	–0.226
$C_{h_{\beta_r}}$	0.1146	0.1146	0.1146
$C_{h_{\delta_r}}$	–0.372	–0.372	–0.372

Table B4 (Continued)   Stability and Control Derivatives for Airplane D (Pages 501–507)

Longitudinal Transfer Function Data

Altitude	=	30000 ft	
U_1	=	270.14 kts	
W_current	=	6360.0 lb	
S_w	=	182.00 ft^2	
Theta_1	=	2.00 deg	
C_bar	=	5.47 ft	
I_yy_B	=	3326 slgft2	
C_m_1	=	0.0000	
C_m_u	=	0.0000	
C_m_a	=	-0.7000 1/rad	
C_m_a.dot	=	-6.9500 1/rad	
C_m_q	=	-14.9000 1/rad	
C_m_T_1	=	0.0000	
C_m_T_u	=	0.0000	
C_m_T_a	=	0.0000	
C_L_1	=	0.3780	
C_L_u	=	0.0000	
C_L_a	=	5.1500 1/rad	
C_L_a.dot	=	2.0000 1/rad	
C_L_q	=	4.1000 1/rad	
C_D_1	=	0.0300	
C_D_a	=	0.2500 1/rad	
C_D_u	=	0.0000	
C_T_X_1	=	0.0300	
C_T_X_u	=	-0.0700	
C_L_d_e	=	0.5000 1/rad	
C_D_d_e	=	0.0000 1/rad	
C_m_d_e	=	-1.1200 1/rad	

M_1	=	0.458	
n	=	1.00 g	
q_bar	=	92.58 psf	
(W/S)_TO	=	34.95 psf	
X_u	=	-0.0111 1/s	
X_T_u	=	-0.0019 1/s	
X_a	=	10.8087 ft/s^2	
Z_u	=	-0.1400 1/s	
Z_a	=	-437.4153 ft/s^2	
Z_a_dot	=	-1.0131 ft/s	
Z_q	=	-2.0768 ft/s	
M_u	=	0.0000 1/ft/s	
M_T_u	=	0.0000 1/ft/s	
M_a	=	-19.3979 1/s^2	
M_T_a	=	0.0000 1/s^2	
M_a_dot	=	-1.1553 1/s	
M_q	=	-2.4768 1/s	
w_n_SP	=	4.6523 rad/s	
z_SP	=	0.4927	
w_n_P	=	0.0934 rad/s	
z_P	=	0.0526	
X_del_e	=	0.0000 ft/s^2	
Z_del_e	=	-42.2216 ft/s^2	
M_del_e	=	-31.0366 1/s^2	

POLYNOMIAL ANGLE OF ATTACK TO ELEVATOR TRANSFER FUNCTION

```
 - 42.2216 S^3 - 14191.7548 S^2 - 149.4537 S - 137.9759
-----------------------------------------------------------------------
 + 456.9617 S^4 + 2099.4660 S^3 + 9914.8881 S^2 + 115.4904 S + 86.2350
```

FACTORED ANGLE OF ATTACK TO ELEVATOR TRANSFER FUNCTION

```
-42.2216   (S + 336.1153)(S^2 + 0.0105 S + 0.0097)
-----------------------------------------------------------------------
456.9617   (S^2 + 4.5846 S + 21.6436)(S^2 + 0.0098 S + 0.0087)
```

ANGLE OF ATTACK TO ELEVATOR TRANSFER FUNCTION K_gain =   -1.600000

POLYNOMIAL SPEED TO ELEVATOR TRANSFER FUNCTION

```
 - 456.3609 S^2 + 296829.8192 S + 406732.2497
-----------------------------------------------------------------------
 + 456.9617 S^4 + 2099.4660 S^3 + 9914.8881 S^2 + 115.4904 S + 86.2350
```

Table B4 (Continued)   Stability and Control Derivatives for Airplane D (Pages 501–507)

FACTORED SPEED TO ELEVATOR TRANSFER FUNCTION

```
-456.3609   (S - 651.7952)(S + 1.3674)
-------------------------------------------------------------------------
456.9617   (S^2 + 4.5846 S + 21.6436)(S^2 + 0.0098 S + 0.0087)
```

SPEED TO ELEVATOR TRANSFER FUNCTION K_gain = 4716.558886

POLYNOMIAL PITCH ATTITUDE TO ELEVATOR TRANSFER FUNCTION

```
 - 14133.7557 S^2 - 12940.1035 S - 212.3526
-------------------------------------------------------------------------
 + 456.9617 S^4 + 2099.4660 S^3 + 9914.8881 S^2 + 115.4904 S + 86.2350
```

FACTORED PITCH ATTITUDE TO ELEVATOR TRANSFER FUNCTION

```
-14133.7557   (S + 0.8988)(S + 0.0167)
-------------------------------------------------------------------------
456.9617   (S^2 + 4.5846 S + 21.6436)(S^2 + 0.0098 S + 0.0087)
```

PITCH ATTITUDE TO ELEVATOR TRANSFER FUNCTION K_gain =   -2.462488

Lateral–Directional Transfer Function Data

W_current =	6360.0 lb		(W/S)_TO =	34.95 psf	
Altitude =	30000 ft		q_bar =	92.58 psf	
S_w =	182.00 ft^2		I_xx_S =	7989 slgft2	
U_1 =	270.14 kts		I_zz_S =	11179 slgft2	
Theta_1 =	2.00 deg		I_xz_S =	-112 slgft2	
Alpha =	2.00 deg		Y_B =	-29.2173 ft/s^2	
b_w =	33.80 ft		Y_p =	-0.2588 ft/s	
I_xx_B =	7985 slgft2		Y_r =	0.9390 ft/s	
I_zz_B =	11183 slgft2		L_B =	-6.7297 1/s^2	
I_xz_B =	0 slgft2		L_p =	-1.1679 1/s	
C_l_B =	-0.0944 1/rad		L_r =	0.2447 1/s	
C_l_p =	-0.4420 1/rad		N_B =	5.6345 1/s^2	
C_l_r =	0.0926 1/rad		N_T_B =	0.0000 1/s^2	
C_n_B =	0.1106 1/rad		N_p =	-0.0459 1/s	
C_n_T_B =	0.0000		N_r =	-0.2625 1/s	
C_n_p =	-0.0243 1/rad		w_n_D =	2.4092 rad/s	
C_n_r =	-0.1390 1/rad		z_D =	0.0470	
C_y_B =	-0.3460 1/rad		TC_SPIRAL =	271.310 s	
C_y_p =	-0.0827 1/rad		TC_ROLL =	0.790 s	
C_y_r =	0.3000 1/rad		TC_1 =	0.790 s	
C_l_d_a =	0.1810 1/rad		TC_2 =	271.310 s	
C_l_d_r =	0.0150 1/rad		Y_del_a =	0.0000 ft/s^2	
C_n_d_a =	-0.0254 1/rad		Y_del_r =	16.8886 ft/s^2	
C_n_d_r =	-0.0365 1/rad		L_del_a =	12.9033 1/s^2	
C_y_d_a =	0.0000 1/rad		L_del_r =	1.0693 1/s^2	
C_y_d_r =	0.2000 1/rad		N_del_a =	-1.2940 1/s^2	
			N_del_r =	-1.8595 1/s^2	

Table B4 (Continued)   Stability and Control Derivatives for Airplane D (Pages 501–507)

POLYNOMIAL SIDESLIP TO AILERON TRANSFER FUNCTION

+ 644.0174 S^3 + 1367.8551 S^2 + 97.7970 S

+ 455.8852 S^5 + 682.2214 S^4 + 2779.2781 S^3 + 3360.8268 S^2 + 12.3497 S

FACTORED SIDESLIP TO AILERON TRANSFER FUNCTION

644.0174   S(S + 2.0499)(S + 0.0741)

455.8852   S(S + 1.2663)(S + 0.0037)(S^2 + 0.2265 S + 5.8041)

SIDESLIP TO AILERON TRANSFER FUNCTION K_gain =   7.918973

POLYNOMIAL SIDESLIP TO RUDDER TRANSFER FUNCTION

+ 16.8863 S^4 + 874.8441 S^3 + 1050.7889 S^2 - 5.5526 S

+ 455.8852 S^5 + 682.2214 S^4 + 2779.2781 S^3 + 3360.8268 S^2 + 12.3497 S

FACTORED SIDESLIP TO RUDDER TRANSFER FUNCTION

16.8863   S(S - 0.0053)(S + 50.5775)(S + 1.2357)

455.8852   S(S + 1.2663)(S + 0.0037)(S^2 + 0.2265 S + 5.8041)

SIDESLIP TO RUDDER TRANSFER FUNCTION K_gain =   -0.449612

POLYNOMIAL ROLL TO AILERON TRANSFER FUNCTION

+ 5891.4614 S^3 + 1777.3570 S^2 + 29208.1767 S

+ 455.8852 S^5 + 682.2214 S^4 + 2779.2781 S^3 + 3360.8268 S^2 + 12.3497 S

FACTORED ROLL TO AILERON TRANSFER FUNCTION

5891.4614   S(S^2 + 0.3017 S + 4.9577)

455.8852   S(S + 1.2663)(S + 0.0037)(S^2 + 0.2265 S + 5.8041)

ROLL TO AILERON TRANSFER FUNCTION K_gain = 2365.091648

Table B4 (Continued)   Stability and Control Derivatives for Airplane D (Pages 501–507)

```
POLYNOMIAL ROLL TO RUDDER TRANSFER FUNCTION

 + 499.3974 S^3 - 162.4592 S^2 - 2964.0008 S
------------------------------------------------------------------------
 + 455.8852 S^5 + 682.2214 S^4 + 2779.2781 S^3 + 3360.8268 S^2 + 12.3497 S


FACTORED ROLL TO RUDDER TRANSFER FUNCTION

499.3974   S(S - 2.6043)(S + 2.2790)
------------------------------------------------------------------------
455.8852   S(S + 1.2663)(S + 0.0037)(S^2 + 0.2265 S + 5.8041)


 ROLL TO RUDDER TRANSFER FUNCTION K_gain = -240.005862


POLYNOMIAL HEADING TO AILERON TRANSFER FUNCTION

 - 648.6980 S^3 - 1000.5959 S^2 - 78.0196 S + 2038.5145
------------------------------------------------------------------------
 + 455.8852 S^5 + 682.2214 S^4 + 2779.2781 S^3 + 3360.8268 S^2 + 12.3497 S


FACTORED HEADING TO AILERON TRANSFER FUNCTION

-648.6980   (S - 1.0733)(S^2 + 2.6158 S + 2.9278)
------------------------------------------------------------------------
455.8852   S(S + 1.2663)(S + 0.0037)(S^2 + 0.2265 S + 5.8041)


 HEADING TO AILERON TRANSFER FUNCTION K_gain =  165.065891


POLYNOMIAL HEADING TO RUDDER TRANSFER FUNCTION

 - 852.6958 S^3 - 970.9207 S^2 + 53.1470 S - 206.6877
------------------------------------------------------------------------
 + 455.8852 S^5 + 682.2214 S^4 + 2779.2781 S^3 + 3360.8268 S^2 + 12.3497 S


FACTORED HEADING TO RUDDER TRANSFER FUNCTION

-852.6958   (S + 1.3240)(S^2 + -0.1854 S + 0.1831)
------------------------------------------------------------------------
455.8852   S(S + 1.2663)(S + 0.0037)(S^2 + 0.2265 S + 5.8041)


 HEADING TO RUDDER TRANSFER FUNCTION K_gain =  -16.736246
```

Table B5   Stability and Control Derivatives for Airplane E (Pages 508–514)

Three–view

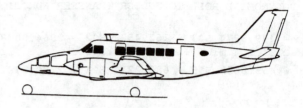

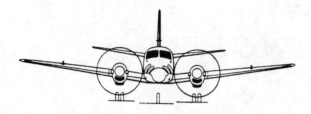

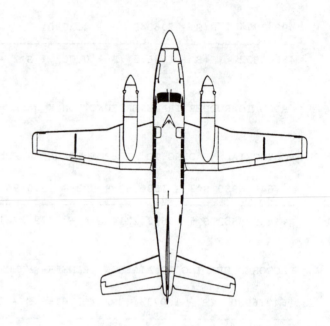

Reference Geometry

S (ft²)	280
$\bar{c}$ (ft)	6.5
b (ft)	46

Flight Condition Data	Approach	Cruise (low)	Cruise (high)
Altitude, h (ft)	0	5,000	20,000
Mach Number, M	0.152	0.310	0.434
TAS, U_1 (ft/sec)	170	340	450
Dynamic pressure, $\bar{q}$ (lbs/ft²)	34.2	118.3	128.2
C.G. location, fraction $\bar{c}$	0.16	0.16	0.16
Angle of attack, α_1 (deg)	3.5	0	1.1

Mass Data

	Approach	Cruise (low)	Cruise (high)
W (lbs)	11,000	7,000	11,000
I_{xx_B} (slugft²)	15,189	10,085	15,189
I_{yy_B} (slugft²)	20,250	15,148	20,250
I_{zz_B} (slugft²)	34,141	23,046	34,141
I_{xz_B} (slugft²)	4,371	1,600	4,371

Table B5 (Continued)   **Stability and Control Derivatives for Airplane E (Pages 508–514)**

Flight Condition	Approach	Cruise (low)	Cruise (high)
Steady State Coefficients			
C_{L_1}	1.15	0.211	0.306
C_{D_1}	0.162	0.0298	0.0298
$C_{T_{x_1}}$	0.162	0.0298	0.0298
C_{m_1}	0	0	0
$C_{m_{T_1}}$	0	0	0
Longitudinal Coefficients and Stability Derivatives (Stability Axes, Dimensionless)			
C_{D_0}	0.0969	0.0270	0.0270
C_{D_u}	0	0	0
C_{D_α}	0.933	0.131	0.131
$C_{T_{x_u}}$	−0.324	−0.0596	−0.0596
C_{L_0}	0.760	0.201	0.201
C_{L_u}	0.027	0.020	0.020
C_{L_α}	6.24	5.48	5.48
$C_{L_{\dot{\alpha}}}$	2.7	2.5	2.5
C_{L_q}	8.1	8.1	8.1
C_{m_0}	0.10	0.05	0.05
C_{m_u}	0	0	0
C_{m_α}	−2.08	−1.89	−1.89
$C_{m_{\dot{\alpha}}}$	−9.1	−9.1	−9.1
C_{m_q}	−34.0	−34.0	−34.0
$C_{m_{T_u}}$	0	0	0
$C_{m_{T_\alpha}}$	0	0	0
Longitudinal Control and Hinge Moment Derivatives (Stability Axes, 1/rad)			
$C_{D_{\delta_e}}$	0	0	0
$C_{L_{\delta_e}}$	0.58	0.60	0.60
$C_{m_{\delta_e}}$	−1.9	−2.0	−2.0
$C_{D_{i_h}}$	0	0	0
$C_{L_{i_h}}$	1.3	1.35	1.35
$C_{m_{i_h}}$	−3.9	−4.1	−4.1

Table B5 (Continued)   **Stability and Control Derivatives for Airplane E (Pages 508–514)**

Flight Condition	Approach	Cruise (low)	Cruise (high)

Longitudinal Control and Hinge Moment Derivatives: Cont'd (Stability Axes, 1/rad)

	Approach	Cruise (low)	Cruise (high)
C_{h_α}	???	???	???
$C_{h_{\delta_e}}$	???	???	???

Lateral–Directional Stability Derivatives (Stability Axes, Dimensionless)

	Approach	Cruise (low)	Cruise (high)
C_{l_β}	–0.13	–0.13	–0.13
C_{l_p}	–0.50	–0.50	–0.50
C_{l_r}	0.06	0.14	0.14
C_{y_β}	–0.59	–0.59	–0.59
C_{y_p}	–0.21	–0.19	–0.19
C_{y_r}	0.39	0.39	0.39
C_{n_β}	0.120	0.080	0.080
$C_{n_{T_\beta}}$	0	0	0
C_{n_p}	–0.005	0.019	0.019
C_{n_r}	–0.204	–0.197	–0.197

Lateral–Directional Control and Hinge Moment Derivatives (Stability Axes, Dimensionless)

	Approach	Cruise (low)	Cruise (high)
$C_{l_{\delta_a}}$	0.156	0.156	0.156
$C_{l_{\delta_r}}$	0.0087	0.0109	0.0106
$C_{y_{\delta_a}}$	0	0	0
$C_{y_{\delta_r}}$	0.144	0.148	0.144
$C_{n_{\delta_a}}$	–0.0012	–0.0012	–0.0012
$C_{n_{\delta_r}}$	–0.0763	–0.0772	–0.0758
$C_{h_{\alpha_a}}$	???	???	???
$C_{h_{\delta_a}}$	???	???	???
$C_{h_{\beta_r}}$	???	???	???
$C_{h_{\delta_r}}$	???	???	???

Table B5 (Continued)　　　Stability and Control Derivatives for Airplane E (Pages 508–514)

Longitudinal Transfer Function Data

Altitude	=	20000 ft			M_1	=	0.434	
U_1	=	266.59 kts			n	=	1.00 g	
$W\_current$	=	11000.0 lb			q_bar	=	128.28 psf	
S_w	=	280.00 ft^2			$(W/S)\_TO$	=	39.29 psf	
$Theta_1$	=	1.10 deg			X_u	=	-0.0138 1/s	
C_bar	=	6.50 ft			X_T_u	=	0.0000 1/s	
I_yy_B	=	20250 slgft2			X_a	=	18.2703 ft/s^2	
C_m_1	=	0.0000			Z_u	=	-0.1466 1/s	
C_m_u	=	0.0000			Z_a	=	-575.2323 ft/s^2	
C_m_a	=	-1.8900 1/rad			Z_a_dot	=	-1.8852 ft/s	
$C\_m\_a.dot$	=	-9.1000 1/rad			Z_q	=	-6.1082 ft/s	
C_m_q	=	-34.0000 1/rad			M_u	=	0.0000 1/ft/s	
$C\_m\_T\_1$	=	0.0000			M_T_u	=	0.0000 1/ft/s	
$C\_m\_T\_u$	=	0.0000			M_a	=	-21.7904 1/s^2	
$C\_m\_T\_a$	=	0.0000			M_T_a	=	0.0000 1/s^2	
C_L_1	=	0.3060			M_a_dot	=	-0.7578 1/s	
C_L_u	=	0.0200			M_q	=	-2.8314 1/s	
C_L_a	=	5.4800 1/rad						
$C\_L\_a.dot$	=	2.5000 1/rad			w_n_SP	=	5.0015 rad/s	
C_L_q	=	8.1000 1/rad			z_SP	=	0.4849	
C_D_1	=	0.0298			w_n_P	=	0.0950 rad/s	
C_D_a	=	0.1310 1/rad			z_P	=	0.0625	
C_D_u	=	0.0000			X_del_e	=	0.0000 ft/s^2	
$C\_T\_X\_1$	=	0.0298			Z_del_e	=	-62.6410 ft/s^2	
$C\_T\_X\_u$	=	-0.0596			M_del_e	=	-23.0586 1/s^2	
$C\_L\_d\_e$	=	0.6000 1/rad						
$C\_D\_d\_e$	=	0.0000 1/rad						
$C\_m\_d\_e$	=	-2.0000 1/rad						

POLYNOMIAL ANGLE OF ATTACK TO ELEVATOR TRANSFER FUNCTION

```
 - 62.6410 S^3 - 10412.5899 S^2 - 129.8301 S - 107.8977
-------------------------------------------------------------------------------
 + 451.8346 S^4 + 2197.1573 S^3 + 11332.6989 S^2 + 154.0270 S + 101.9633
```

FACTORED ANGLE OF ATTACK TO ELEVATOR TRANSFER FUNCTION

```
-62.6410  (S + 166.2140)(S^2 + 0.0124 S + 0.0104)
-------------------------------------------------------------------------------
451.8346  (S^2 + 4.8509 S + 25.0149)(S^2 + 0.0119 S + 0.0090)
```

ANGLE OF ATTACK TO ELEVATOR TRANSFER FUNCTION K_gain =   -1.058201

POLYNOMIAL SPEED TO ELEVATOR TRANSFER FUNCTION

```
 - 1144.4693 S^2 + 141313.7394 S + 380639.6108
-------------------------------------------------------------------------------
 + 451.8346 S^4 + 2197.1573 S^3 + 11332.6989 S^2 + 154.0270 S + 101.9633
```

Table B5 (Continued)   Stability and Control Derivatives for Airplane E (Pages 508–514)

```
FACTORED SPEED TO ELEVATOR TRANSFER FUNCTION

-1144.4693   (S - 126.1126)(S + 2.6373)
------------------------------------------------------------------------------
451.8346   (S^2 + 4.8509 S + 25.0149)(S^2 + 0.0119 S + 0.0090)


SPEED TO ELEVATOR TRANSFER FUNCTION K_gain = 3733.103383


POLYNOMIAL PITCH ATTITUDE TO ELEVATOR TRANSFER FUNCTION

 - 10371.2086 S^2 - 12042.5102 S - 226.3310
------------------------------------------------------------------------------
 + 451.8346 S^4 + 2197.1573 S^3 + 11332.6989 S^2 + 154.0270 S + 101.9633


FACTORED PITCH ATTITUDE TO ELEVATOR TRANSFER FUNCTION

-10371.2086   (S + 1.1420)(S + 0.0191)
------------------------------------------------------------------------------
451.8346   (S^2 + 4.8509 S + 25.0149)(S^2 + 0.0119 S + 0.0090)


PITCH ATTITUDE TO ELEVATOR TRANSFER FUNCTION K_gain =   -2.219730
```

Lateral–Directional Transfer Function Data

W_current	=	11000.0 lb	(W/S)_TO	=	39.29 psf
Altitude	=	20000 ft	q_bar	=	128.28 psf
S_w	=	280.00 ft^2	I_xx_S	=	15028 slgft2
U_1	=	266.59 kts	I_zz_S	=	34302 slgft2
Theta_1	=	1.10 deg	I_xz_S	=	4004 slgft2
Alpha	=	1.10 deg	Y_B	=	-61.5970 ft/s^2
b_w	=	46.00 ft	Y_p	=	-1.0140 ft/s
I_xx_B	=	15189 slgft2	Y_r	=	2.0813 ft/s
I_zz_B	=	34141 slgft2	L_B	=	-14.2925 1/s^2
I_xz_B	=	4371 slgft2	L_p	=	-2.8100 1/s
C_l_B	=	-0.1300 1/rad	L_r	=	0.7868 1/s
C_l_p	=	-0.5000 1/rad	N_B	=	3.8534 1/s^2
C_l_r	=	0.1400 1/rad	N_T_B	=	0.0000 1/s^2
C_n_B	=	0.0800 1/rad	N_p	=	0.0468 1/s
C_n_T_B	=	0.0000	N_r	=	-0.4850 1/s
C_n_p	=	0.0190 1/rad	w_n_D	=	1.8740 rad/s
C_n_r	=	-0.1970 1/rad	z_D	=	0.0356
C_y_B	=	-0.5900 1/rad	TC_SPIRAL	=	40.169 s
C_y_p	=	-0.1900 1/rad	TC_ROLL	=	0.306 s
C_y_r	=	0.3900 1/rad	TC_1	=	0.306 s
C_l_d_a	=	0.1560 1/rad	TC_2	=	40.169 s
C_l_d_r	=	0.0106 1/rad	Y_del_a	=	0.0000 ft/s^2
C_n_d_a	=	-0.0012 1/rad	Y_del_r	=	15.0338 ft/s^2
C_n_d_r	=	-0.0758 1/rad	L_del_a	=	17.1510 1/s^2
C_y_d_a	=	0.0000 1/rad	L_del_r	=	1.1654 1/s^2
C_y_d_r	=	0.1440 1/rad	N_del_a	=	-0.0578 1/s^2
			N_del_r	=	-3.6511 1/s^2

Table B5 (Continued)   Stability and Control Derivatives for Airplane E (Pages 508–514)

POLYNOMIAL SIDESLIP TO AILERON TRANSFER FUNCTION

$$- 888.1303 \ S^3 + 252.7854 \ S^2 + 264.4851 \ S$$

$$+ 435.9557 \ S^5 + 1495.3368 \ S^4 + 1758.4115 \ S^3 + 5051.8377 \ S^2 + 124.6967 \ S$$

FACTORED SIDESLIP TO AILERON TRANSFER FUNCTION

$$-888.1303 \quad S(S - 0.7063)(S + 0.4216)$$

$$435.9557 \quad S(S + 3.2716)(S + 0.0249)(S^2 + 0.1335 \ S + 3.5119)$$

SIDESLIP TO AILERON TRANSFER FUNCTION K_gain =   2.121027

POLYNOMIAL SIDESLIP TO RUDDER TRANSFER FUNCTION

$$+ 14.5663 \ S^4 + 1622.0629 \ S^3 + 4598.9072 \ S^2 - 73.7606 \ S$$

$$+ 435.9557 \ S^5 + 1495.3368 \ S^4 + 1758.4115 \ S^3 + 5051.8377 \ S^2 + 124.6967 \ S$$

FACTORED SIDESLIP TO RUDDER TRANSFER FUNCTION

$$14.5663 \quad S(S - 0.0159)(S + 108.4456)(S + 2.9277)$$

$$435.9557 \quad S(S + 3.2716)(S + 0.0249)(S^2 + 0.1335 \ S + 3.5119)$$

SIDESLIP TO RUDDER TRANSFER FUNCTION K_gain =   -0.591520

POLYNOMIAL ROLL TO AILERON TRANSFER FUNCTION

$$+ 7710.1719 \ S^3 + 4778.2179 \ S^2 + 29739.2664 \ S$$

$$+ 435.9557 \ S^5 + 1495.3368 \ S^4 + 1758.4115 \ S^3 + 5051.8377 \ S^2 + 124.6967 \ S$$

FACTORED ROLL TO AILERON TRANSFER FUNCTION

$$7710.1719 \quad S(S^2 + 0.6197 \ S + 3.8571)$$

$$435.9557 \quad S(S + 3.2716)(S + 0.0249)(S^2 + 0.1335 \ S + 3.5119)$$

ROLL TO AILERON TRANSFER FUNCTION K_gain = 238.492770

Table B5 (Continued)   Stability and Control Derivatives for Airplane E (Pages 508–514)

POLYNOMIAL ROLL TO RUDDER TRANSFER FUNCTION

$$\frac{+\ 86.6662\ S^3\ -\ 1225.7765\ S^2\ -\ 21560.8896\ S}{+\ 435.9557\ S^5\ +\ 1495.3368\ S^4\ +\ 1758.4115\ S^3\ +\ 5051.8377\ S^2\ +\ 124.6967\ S}$$

FACTORED ROLL TO RUDDER TRANSFER FUNCTION

$$\frac{86.6662\quad S(S\ -\ 24.3574)(S\ +\ 10.2138)}{435.9557\quad S(S\ +\ 3.2716)(S\ +\ 0.0249)(S^2\ +\ 0.1335\ S\ +\ 3.5119)}$$

ROLL TO RUDDER TRANSFER FUNCTION K_gain = -172.906628

POLYNOMIAL HEADING TO AILERON TRANSFER FUNCTION

$$\frac{+\ 874.8018\ S^3\ +\ 407.6949\ S^2\ -\ 26.7579\ S\ +\ 2086.3085}{+\ 435.9557\ S^5\ +\ 1495.3368\ S^4\ +\ 1758.4115\ S^3\ +\ 5051.8377\ S^2\ +\ 124.6967\ S}$$

FACTORED HEADING TO AILERON TRANSFER FUNCTION

$$\frac{874.8018\quad (S\ +\ 1.5193)(S^2\ +\ -1.0533\ S\ +\ 1.5697)}{435.9557\quad S(S\ +\ 3.2716)(S\ +\ 0.0249)(S^2\ +\ 0.1335\ S\ +\ 3.5119)}$$

HEADING TO AILERON TRANSFER FUNCTION K_gain =   16.731062

POLYNOMIAL HEADING TO RUDDER TRANSFER FUNCTION

$$\frac{-\ 1581.6056\ S^3\ -\ 4775.3808\ S^2\ -\ 427.5017\ S\ -\ 1524.6101}{+\ 435.9557\ S^5\ +\ 1495.3368\ S^4\ +\ 1758.4115\ S^3\ +\ 5051.8377\ S^2\ +\ 124.6967\ S}$$

FACTORED HEADING TO RUDDER TRANSFER FUNCTION

$$\frac{-1581.6056\quad (S\ +\ 3.0349)(S^2\ +\ -0.0156\ S\ +\ 0.3176)}{435.9557\quad S(S\ +\ 3.2716)(S\ +\ 0.0249)(S^2\ +\ 0.1335\ S\ +\ 3.5119)}$$

HEADING TO RUDDER TRANSFER FUNCTION K_gain =   -12.226545

Table B6   Stability and Control Derivatives for Airplane F (Pages 515–521)

Three–view

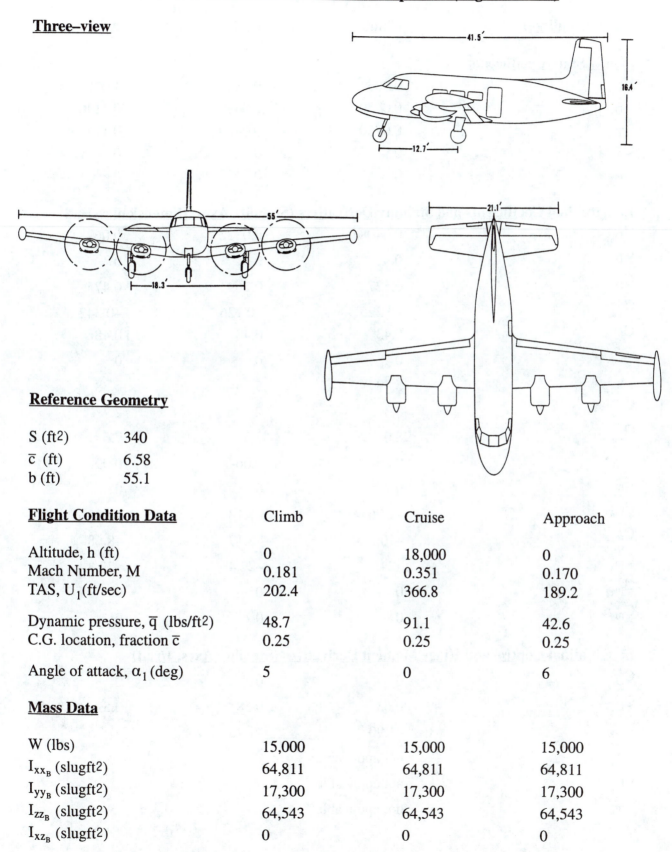

Reference Geometry

S (ft^2)	340
$\bar{c}$ (ft)	6.58
b (ft)	55.1

Flight Condition Data

	Climb	Cruise	Approach
Altitude, h (ft)	0	18,000	0
Mach Number, M	0.181	0.351	0.170
TAS, U_1 (ft/sec)	202.4	366.8	189.2
Dynamic pressure, $\bar{q}$ (lbs/ft^2)	48.7	91.1	42.6
C.G. location, fraction $\bar{c}$	0.25	0.25	0.25
Angle of attack, α_1 (deg)	5	0	6

Mass Data

W (lbs)	15,000	15,000	15,000
I_{xx_B} (slugft^2)	64,811	64,811	64,811
I_{yy_B} (slugft^2)	17,300	17,300	17,300
I_{zz_B} (slugft^2)	64,543	64,543	64,543
I_{xz_B} (slugft^2)	0	0	0

Table B6 (Continued)   Stability and Control Derivatives for Airplane F (Pages 515–521)

Flight Condition	Climb	Cruise	Approach
Steady State Coefficients			
C_{L_1}	0.903	0.484	1.038
C_{D_1}	0.0750	0.0420	0.1140
$C_{T_{x_1}}$	0.0750	0.0420	0.1140
C_{m_1}	0	0	0
$C_{m_{T_1}}$	0	0	0
Longitudinal Coefficients and Stability Derivatives (Stability Axes, Dimensionless)			
C_{D_0}	0.0408	0.0322	0.0628
C_{D_u}	0	0	0
C_{D_α}	0.527	0.269	0.475
$C_{T_{x_u}}$	−0.225	−0.126	−0.342
C_{L_0}	0.43	0.48	0.48
C_{L_u}	0	0	0
C_{L_α}	5.38	5.55	5.38
$C_{L_{\dot\alpha}}$	3.3	2.7	2.7
C_{L_q}	8.0	7.5	7.6
C_{m_0}	0.06	0.06	0.09
C_{m_u}	0	0	0
C_{m_α}	−1.06	−1.18	−1.00
$C_{m_{\dot\alpha}}$	−10.3	−8.17	−8.68
C_{m_q}	−24.7	−22.4	−22.8
$C_{m_{T_u}}$	0	0	0
$C_{m_{T_\alpha}}$	0	0	0
Longitudinal Control and Hinge Moment Derivatives (Stability Axes, 1/rad)			
$C_{D_{\delta_e}}$	0	0	0
$C_{L_{\delta_e}}$	0.63	0.58	0.59
$C_{m_{\delta_e}}$	−1.90	−1.73	−1.75
$C_{D_{i_h}}$	not applicable		
$C_{L_{i_h}}$	not applicable		
$C_{m_{i_h}}$	not applicable		

Table B6 (Continued)   Stability and Control Derivatives for Airplane F (Pages 515–521)

Flight Condition	Climb	Cruise	Approach

Longitudinal Control and Hinge Moment Derivatives: Cont'd (Stability Axes, 1/rad)

	Climb	Cruise	Approach
C_{h_α}	0	0	0
$C_{h_{\delta_e}}$	−0.178	−0.212	−0.212

Lateral–Directional Stability Derivatives (Stability Axes, Dimensionless)

	Climb	Cruise	Approach
C_{l_β}	−0.1080	−0.1381	−0.1172
C_{l_p}	−0.570	−0.566	−0.576
C_{l_r}	0.2176	0.1166	0.2307
C_{y_β}	−0.886	−0.883	−0.907
C_{y_p}	−0.315	−0.227	−0.343
C_{y_r}	0.448	0.448	0.447
C_{n_β}	0.1848	0.1739	0.1871
$C_{n_{T_\beta}}$	0	0	0
C_{n_p}	−0.0924	−0.0501	−0.1026
C_{n_r}	−0.208	−0.200	−0.224

Lateral–Directional Control and Hinge Moment Derivatives (Stability Axes, Dimensionless)

	Climb	Cruise	Approach
$C_{l_{\delta_a}}$	0.1776	0.1776	0.1776
$C_{l_{\delta_r}}$	0.0200	0.0200	0.0200
$C_{y_{\delta_a}}$	0	0	0
$C_{y_{\delta_r}}$	0.20	0.20	0.20
$C_{n_{\delta_a}}$	−0.0367	−0.0194	−0.0417
$C_{n_{\delta_r}}$	−0.1054	−0.1054	−0.1054
$C_{h_{\alpha_a}}$	???	???	???
$C_{h_{\delta_a}}$	−0.462	−0.376	−0.462
$C_{h_{\beta_r}}$	0.0602	0.0602	0.0602
$C_{h_{\delta_r}}$	−0.588	−0.537	−0.588

Table B6 (Continued)   Stability and Control Derivatives for Airplane F (Pages 515–521)

Longitudinal Transfer Function Data

Altitude	=	0 ft		M_1	=	0.169	
U_1	=	112.09 kts		n	=	1.00 g	
$W_{current}$	=	15000.0 lb		$\bar{q}$	=	42.53 psf	
S_w	=	340.00 ft^2		$(W/S)\_TO$	=	44.12 psf	
$Theta_1$	=	6.00 deg		X_u	=	-0.0374 1/s	
C_bar	=	6.58 ft		X_T_u	=	-0.0187 1/s	
I_yy_B	=	17300 slgft2		X_a	=	17.4632 ft/s^2	
C_m_1	=	0.0000		Z_u	=	-0.3404 1/s	
C_m_u	=	0.0000		Z_a	=	-170.4133 ft/s^2	
C_m_a	=	-1.0000 1/rad		Z_a_dot	=	-1.4565 ft/s	
$C\_m\_a.dot$	=	-8.6800 1/rad		Z_q	=	-4.0997 ft/s	
C_m_q	=	-22.8000 1/rad		M_u	=	0.0000 1/ft/s	
$C\_m\_T_1$	=	0.0000		M_T_u	=	0.0000 1/ft/s	
$C\_m\_T_u$	=	0.0000		M_a	=	-5.5002 1/s^2	
$C\_m\_T_a$	=	0.0000		M_T_a	=	0.0000 1/s^2	
C_L_1	=	1.0380		M_a_dot	=	-0.8303 1/s	
C_L_u	=	0.0000		M_q	=	-2.1809 1/s	
C_L_a	=	5.3800 1/rad					
$C\_L\_a.dot$	=	2.7000 1/rad		w_n_SP	=	2.7097 rad/s	
C_L_q	=	7.6000 1/rad		z_SP	=	0.7199	
C_D_1	=	0.1140		w_n_P	=	0.2051 rad/s	
C_D_a	=	0.4750 1/rad		z_P	=	0.0871	
C_D_u	=	0.0000		X_del_e	=	0.0000 ft/s^2	
$C\_T\_X_1$	=	0.1140		Z_del_e	=	-18.3007 ft/s^2	
$C\_T\_X_u$	=	-0.3420		M_del_e	=	-9.6254 1/s^2	
$C\_L\_d\_e$	=	0.5900 1/rad					
$C\_D\_d\_e$	=	0.0000 1/rad					
$C\_m\_d\_e$	=	-1.7500 1/rad					

POLYNOMIAL ANGLE OF ATTACK TO ELEVATOR TRANSFER FUNCTION

```
 - 18.3007 S^3 - 1822.3980 S^2 - 69.7621 S - 103.0202
-----------------------------------------------------------------------------
 + 190.6352 S^4 + 750.5300 S^3 + 1434.2726 S^2 + 81.2760 S + 58.8687
```

FACTORED ANGLE OF ATTACK TO ELEVATOR TRANSFER FUNCTION

```
-18.3007   (S + 99.5433)(S^2 + 0.0377 S + 0.0566)
-----------------------------------------------------------------------------
190.6352   (S^2 + 3.9013 S + 7.3422)(S^2 + 0.0357 S + 0.0421)
```

ANGLE OF ATTACK TO ELEVATOR TRANSFER FUNCTION K_gain =   -1.750000

POLYNOMIAL SPEED TO ELEVATOR TRANSFER FUNCTION

```
 - 319.5876 S^2 + 26420.8184 S + 49830.2577
-----------------------------------------------------------------------------
 + 190.6352 S^4 + 750.5300 S^3 + 1434.2726 S^2 + 81.2760 S + 58.8687
```

Table B6 (Continued)   Stability and Control Derivatives for Airplane F (Pages 515–521)

FACTORED SPEED TO ELEVATOR TRANSFER FUNCTION

$$\frac{-319.5876 \quad (S - 84.5164)(S + 1.8449)}{190.6352 \quad (S^2 + 3.9013\ S + 7.3422)(S^2 + 0.0357\ S + 0.0421)}$$

SPEED TO ELEVATOR TRANSFER FUNCTION K_gain = 846.464416

POLYNOMIAL PITCH ATTITUDE TO ELEVATOR TRANSFER FUNCTION

$$\frac{- 1819.7453\ S^2 - 1641.6803\ S - 143.5503}{+ 190.6352\ S^4 + 750.5300\ S^3 + 1434.2726\ S^2 + 81.2760\ S + 58.8687}$$

FACTORED PITCH ATTITUDE TO ELEVATOR TRANSFER FUNCTION

$$\frac{-1819.7453 \quad (S + 0.8040)(S + 0.0981)}{190.6352 \quad (S^2 + 3.9013\ S + 7.3422)(S^2 + 0.0357\ S + 0.0421)}$$

PITCH ATTITUDE TO ELEVATOR TRANSFER FUNCTION K_gain =   -2.438483

Lateral–Directional Transfer Function Data

W_current	=	15000.0 lb		(W/S)_TO	=	44.12 psf
Altitude	=	0 ft		q_bar	=	42.53 psf
S_w	=	340.00 ft^2		I_xx_S	=	64808 slgft2
U_1	=	112.09 kts		I_zz_S	=	64546 slgft2
Theta_1	=	6.00 deg		I_xz_S	=	28 slgft2
Alpha	=	6.00 deg		Y_B	=	-28.1334 ft/s^2
b_w	=	55.10 ft		Y_p	=	-1.5494 ft/s
I_xx_B	=	64811 slgft2		Y_r	=	2.0192 ft/s
I_zz_B	=	64543 slgft2		L_B	=	-1.4410 1/s^2
I_xz_B	=	0 slgft2		L_p	=	-1.0313 1/s
C_l_B	=	-0.1172 1/rad		L_r	=	0.4131 1/s
C_l_p	=	-0.5760 1/rad		N_B	=	2.3097 1/s^2
C_l_r	=	0.2307 1/rad		N_T_B	=	0.0000 1/s^2
C_n_B	=	0.1871 1/rad		N_p	=	-0.1845 1/s
C_n_T_B	=	0.0000		N_r	=	-0.4027 1/s
C_n_p	=	-0.1026 1/rad		w_n_D	=	1.5875 rad/s
C_n_r	=	-0.2240 1/rad		z_D	=	0.1298
C_y_B	=	-0.9070 1/rad		TC_SPIRAL	=	-47.494 s
C_y_p	=	-0.3430 1/rad		TC_ROLL	=	0.839 s
C_y_r	=	0.4470 1/rad				
C_l_d_a	=	0.1776 1/rad		TC_1	=	0.839 s
C_l_d_r	=	0.0200 1/rad		TC_2	=	-47.494 s
C_n_d_a	=	-0.0417 1/rad		Y_del_a	=	0.0000 ft/s^2
C_n_d_r	=	-0.1054 1/rad		Y_del_r	=	6.2036 ft/s^2
C_y_d_a	=	0.0000 1/rad		L_del_a	=	2.1836 1/s^2
C_y_d_r	=	0.2000 1/rad		L_del_r	=	0.2459 1/s^2
				N_del_a	=	-0.5148 1/s^2
				N_del_r	=	-1.3011 1/s^2

Table B6 (Continued)   Stability and Control Derivatives for Airplane F (Pages 515–521)

POLYNOMIAL SIDESLIP TO AILERON TRANSFER FUNCTION

```
 + 92.7863 S^3 + 243.5732 S^2 + 21.3324 S
----------------------------------------------------------------------------
 + 189.1787 S^5 + 299.4014 S^4 + 563.2602 S^3 + 556.0521 S^2 - 11.9605 S
```

FACTORED SIDESLIP TO AILERON TRANSFER FUNCTION

```
92.7863   S(S + 2.5344)(S + 0.0907)
----------------------------------------------------------------------------
189.1787   S(S - 0.0211)(S + 1.1915)(S^2 + 0.4122 S + 2.5201)
```

SIDESLIP TO AILERON TRANSFER FUNCTION K_gain =   -1.783567

POLYNOMIAL SIDESLIP TO RUDDER TRANSFER FUNCTION

```
 + 6.2036 S^4 + 252.0165 S^3 + 271.2165 S^2 - 14.0290 S
----------------------------------------------------------------------------
 + 189.1787 S^5 + 299.4014 S^4 + 563.2602 S^3 + 556.0521 S^2 - 11.9605 S
```

FACTORED SIDESLIP TO RUDDER TRANSFER FUNCTION

```
6.2036   S(S - 0.0495)(S + 39.5163)(S + 1.1573)
----------------------------------------------------------------------------
189.1787   S(S - 0.0211)(S + 1.1915)(S^2 + 0.4122 S + 2.5201)
```

SIDESLIP TO RUDDER TRANSFER FUNCTION K_gain =   1.172940

POLYNOMIAL ROLL TO AILERON TRANSFER FUNCTION

```
 + 413.0424 S^3 + 187.5472 S^2 + 823.8478 S
----------------------------------------------------------------------------
 + 189.1787 S^5 + 299.4014 S^4 + 563.2602 S^3 + 556.0521 S^2 - 11.9605 S
```

FACTORED ROLL TO AILERON TRANSFER FUNCTION

```
413.0424   S(S^2 + 0.4541 S + 1.9946)
----------------------------------------------------------------------------
189.1787   S(S - 0.0211)(S + 1.1915)(S^2 + 0.4122 S + 2.5201)
```

ROLL TO AILERON TRANSFER FUNCTION K_gain = -68.880671

Table B6 (Continued)   Stability and Control Derivatives for Airplane F (Pages 515–521)

POLYNOMIAL ROLL TO RUDDER TRANSFER FUNCTION

+ 46.4127 S^3 - 84.9735 S^2 - 254.6216 S

+ 189.1787 S^5 + 299.4014 S^4 + 563.2602 S^3 + 556.0521 S^2 - 11.9605 S

FACTORED ROLL TO RUDDER TRANSFER FUNCTION

46.4127   S(S - 3.4302)(S + 1.5993)

189.1787   S(S - 0.0211)(S + 1.1915)(S^2 + 0.4122 S + 2.5201)

ROLL TO RUDDER TRANSFER FUNCTION K_gain = 21.288527

POLYNOMIAL HEADING TO AILERON TRANSFER FUNCTION

- 97.2067 S^3 - 191.0852 S^2 - 32.9320 S + 137.6426

+ 189.1787 S^5 + 299.4014 S^4 + 563.2602 S^3 + 556.0521 S^2 - 11.9605 S

FACTORED HEADING TO AILERON TRANSFER FUNCTION

-97.2067 (S - 0.6713)(S^2 + 2.6371 S + 2.1092)

189.1787   S(S - 0.0211)(S + 1.1915)(S^2 + 0.4122 S + 2.5201)

HEADING TO AILERON TRANSFER FUNCTION K_gain = -11.508088

POLYNOMIAL HEADING TO RUDDER TRANSFER FUNCTION

- 246.1281 S^3 - 284.7168 S^2 - 20.5770 S - 41.8190

+ 189.1787 S^5 + 299.4014 S^4 + 563.2602 S^3 + 556.0521 S^2 - 11.9605 S

FACTORED HEADING TO RUDDER TRANSFER FUNCTION

-246.1281 (S + 1.2045)(S^2 + -0.0477 S + 0.1411)

189.1787   S(S - 0.0211)(S + 1.1915)(S^2 + 0.4122 S + 2.5201)

HEADING TO RUDDER TRANSFER FUNCTION K_gain = 3.496427

Table B7   Stability and Control Derivatives for Airplane G (Pages 522–528)

Three–view

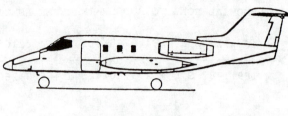

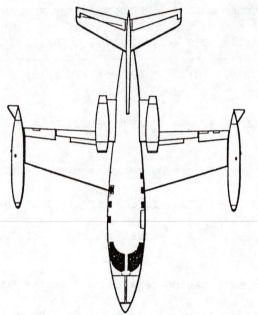

Reference Geometry

S (ft²)	230
$\bar{c}$ (ft)	7.0
b (ft)	34.0

Flight Condition Data	Approach	Cruise (Max Wht)	Cruise(Low Wht)
Altitude, h (ft)	0	40,000	40,000
Mach Number, M	0.152	0.7	0.7
TAS, U_1 (ft/sec)	170	677	677
Dynamic pressure, $\bar{q}$ (lbs/ft²)	34.3	134.6	134.6
C.G. location, fraction $\bar{c}$	0.32	0.32	0.32
Angle of attack, α_1 (deg)	5.0	2.7	1.5

Mass Data

	Approach	Cruise (Max Wht)	Cruise (Low Wht)
W (lbs)	13,000	13,000	9,000
I_{xx_B} (slugft²)	28,000	28,000	6,000
I_{yy_B} (slugft²)	18,800	18,800	17,800
I_{zz_B} (slugft²)	47,000	47,000	25,000
I_{xz_B} (slugft²)	1,300	1,300	1,400

Table B7 (Continued)   **Stability and Control Derivatives for Airplane G (Pages 522–528)**

Flight Condition	Approach	Cruise (Max Wht)	Cruise(Low Wht)
Steady State Coefficients			
C_{L_1}	1.64	0.41	0.28
C_{D_1}	0.2560	0.0335	0.0279
$C_{T_{x_1}}$	0.2560	0.0335	0.0279
C_{m_1}	0	0	0
$C_{m_{T_1}}$	0	0	0

Longitudinal Coefficients and Stability Derivatives (Stability Axes, Dimensionless)

	Approach	Cruise (Max Wht)	Cruise(Low Wht)
C_{D_0}	0.0431	0.0216	0.0216
C_{D_u}	0	0.104	0.104
C_{D_α}	1.06	0.30	0.22
$C_{T_{x_u}}$	−0.60	−0.07	−0.07
C_{L_0}	1.2	0.13	0.13
C_{L_u}	0.04	0.40	0.28
C_{L_α}	5.04	5.84	5.84
$C_{L_{\dot\alpha}}$	1.6	2.2	2.2
C_{L_q}	4.1	4.7	4.7
C_{m_0}	0.047	0.050	0.050
C_{m_u}	−0.01	0.050	0.070
C_{m_α}	−0.66	−0.64	−0.64
$C_{m_{\dot\alpha}}$	−5.0	−6.7	−6.7
C_{m_q}	−13.5	−15.5	−15.5
$C_{m_{T_u}}$	0.006	−0.003	−0.003
$C_{m_{T_\alpha}}$	0	0	0

Longitudinal Control and Hinge Moment Derivatives (Stability Axes, 1/rad)

	Approach	Cruise (Max Wht)	Cruise(Low Wht)
$C_{D_{\delta_e}}$	0	0	0
$C_{L_{\delta_e}}$	0.40	0.46	0.46
$C_{m_{\delta_e}}$	−0.98	−1.24	−1.24
$C_{D_{i_h}}$	0	0	0
$C_{L_{i_h}}$	0.85	0.94	0.94
$C_{m_{i_h}}$	−2.1	−2.5	−2.5

Table B7 (Continued)   **Stability and Control Derivatives for Airplane G (Pages 522–528)**

Flight Condition	Approach	Cruise (Max Wht)	Cruise(Low Wht)

Longitudinal Control and Hinge Moment Derivatives: Cont'd (Stability Axes, 1/rad)

	Approach	Cruise (Max Wht)	Cruise (Low Wht)
C_{h_α}	–0.105	–0.132	–0.132
$C_{h_{\delta_e}}$	–0.378	–0.476	–0.476

Lateral–Directional Stability Derivatives (Stability Axes, Dimensionless)

	Approach	Cruise (Max Wht)	Cruise (Low Wht)
C_{l_β}	–0.173	–0.110	–0.100
C_{l_p}	–0.390	–0.450	–0.450
C_{l_r}	0.450	0.160	0.140
C_{y_β}	–0.730	–0.730	–0.730
C_{y_p}	0	0	0
C_{y_r}	0.400	0.400	0.400
C_{n_β}	0.150	0.127	0.124
$C_{n_{T_\beta}}$	0	0	0
C_{n_p}	–0.130	–0.008	–0.022
C_{n_r}	–0.260	–0.200	–0.200

Lateral–Directional Control and Hinge Moment Derivatives (Stability Axes, Dimensionless)

	Approach	Cruise (Max Wht)	Cruise (Low Wht)
$C_{l_{\delta_a}}$	0.149	0.178	0.178
$C_{l_{\delta_r}}$	0.014	0.019	0.021
$C_{y_{\delta_a}}$	0	0	0
$C_{y_{\delta_r}}$	0.140	0.140	0.140
$C_{n_{\delta_a}}$	–0.050	–0.020	–0.020
$C_{n_{\delta_r}}$	–0.074	–0.074	–0.074
$C_{h_{\alpha_a}}$	???	???	???
$C_{h_{\delta_a}}$	???	???	???
$C_{h_{\beta_r}}$	???	???	???
$C_{h_{\delta_r}}$	???	???	???

Table B7 (Continued)   Stability and Control Derivatives for Airplane G (Pages 522–528)

Longitudinal Transfer Function Data

Altitude	=	0 ft		M_1	=	0.152	
U_1	=	100.71 kts		n	=	1.00 g	
W_current	=	13000.0 lb		q_bar	=	34.34 psf	
S_w	=	230.00 ft^2		(W/S)_TO	=	56.52 psf	
Theta_1	=	5.00 deg		X_u	=	-0.0589 1/s	
C_bar	=	7.00 ft		X_T_u	=	-0.0101 1/s	
I_yy_B	=	18800 slgft2		X_a	=	11.3367 ft/s^2	
C_m_1	=	0.0000		Z_u	=	-0.3818 1/s	
C_m_u	=	-0.0100		Z_a	=	-103.5160 ft/s^2	
C_m_a	=	-0.6600 1/rad		Z_a_dot	=	-0.6439 ft/s	
C_m_a.dot	=	-5.0000 1/rad		Z_q	=	-1.6501 ft/s	
C_m_q	=	-13.5000 1/rad		M_u	=	-0.0002 1/ft/s	
C_m_T_1	=	0.0000		M_T_u	=	0.0001 1/ft/s	
C_m_T_u	=	0.0060		M_a	=	-1.9408 1/s^2	
C_m_T_a	=	0.0000		M_T_a	=	0.0000 1/s^2	
C_L_1	=	1.6400		M_a_dot	=	-0.3027 1/s	
C_L_u	=	0.0400		M_q	=	-0.8174 1/s	
C_L_a	=	5.0400 1/rad					
C_L_a.dot	=	1.6000 1/rad		w_n_SP	=	1.5616 rad/s	
C_L_q	=	4.1000 1/rad		z_SP	=	0.5636	
C_D_1	=	0.2560		w_n_P	=	0.2358 rad/s	
C_D_a	=	1.0600 1/rad		z_P	=	0.0671	
C_D_u	=	0.0000		X_del_e	=	0.0000 ft/s^2	
C_T_X_1	=	0.2560		Z_del_e	=	-7.8184 ft/s^2	
C_T_X_u	=	-0.6000		M_del_e	=	-2.8818 1/s^2	
C_L_d_e	=	0.4000 1/rad					
C_D_d_e	=	0.0000 1/rad					
C_m_d_e	=	-0.9800 1/rad					

POLYNOMIAL ANGLE OF ATTACK TO ELEVATOR TRANSFER FUNCTION

$$\frac{- 7.8184\ S^3 - 492.0217\ S^2 - 25.8286\ S - 34.6877}{+ 170.6233\ S^4 + 305.7196\ S^3 + 435.0697\ S^2 + 29.8732\ S + 23.1410}$$

FACTORED ANGLE OF ATTACK TO ELEVATOR TRANSFER FUNCTION

$$\frac{-7.8184\ \ (S + 62.8796)(S^2 + 0.0514\ S + 0.0706)}{170.6233\ \ (S^2 + 1.7601\ S + 2.4386)(S^2 + 0.0317\ S + 0.0556)}$$

ANGLE OF ATTACK TO ELEVATOR TRANSFER FUNCTION K_gain = -1.498972

POLYNOMIAL SPEED TO ELEVATOR TRANSFER FUNCTION

$$\frac{- 88.6353\ S^2 + 10112.1693\ S + 9166.6414}{+ 170.6233\ S^4 + 305.7196\ S^3 + 435.0697\ S^2 + 29.8732\ S + 23.1410}$$

Table B7 (Continued)   Stability and Control Derivatives for Airplane G (Pages 522–528)

FACTORED SPEED TO ELEVATOR TRANSFER FUNCTION

```
-88.6353   (S - 114.9868)(S + 0.8994)
-----------------------------------------------------------------------
170.6233   (S^2 + 1.7601 S + 2.4386)(S^2 + 0.0317 S + 0.0556)
```

SPEED TO ELEVATOR TRANSFER FUNCTION K_gain =   396.120995

POLYNOMIAL PITCH ATTITUDE TO ELEVATOR TRANSFER FUNCTION

```
 - 489.3354 S^2 - 316.8998 S - 32.0013
-----------------------------------------------------------------------
 + 170.6233 S^4 + 305.7196 S^3 + 435.0697 S^2 + 29.8732 S + 23.1410
```

FACTORED PITCH ATTITUDE TO ELEVATOR TRANSFER FUNCTION

```
-489.3354   (S + 0.5224)(S + 0.1252)
-----------------------------------------------------------------------
170.6233   (S^2 + 1.7601 S + 2.4386)(S^2 + 0.0317 S + 0.0556)
```

PITCH ATTITUDE TO ELEVATOR TRANSFER FUNCTION K_gain =   -1.382884

Lateral–Directional Transfer Function Data

W_current	=	13000.0 lb	(W/S)_TO	=	56.52 psf
Altitude	=	0 ft	q_bar	=	34.34 psf
S_w	=	230.00 ft^2	I_xx_S	=	27919 slgft2
U_1	=	100.71 kts	I_zz_S	=	47081 slgft2
Theta_1	=	5.00 deg	I_xz_S	=	-369 slgft2
Alpha	=	5.00 deg	Y_B	=	-14.2686 ft/s^2
b_w	=	34.00 ft	Y_p	=	0.0000 ft/s
I_xx_B	=	28000 slgft2	Y_r	=	0.7819 ft/s
I_zz_B	=	47000 slgft2	L_B	=	-1.6639 1/s^2
I_xz_B	=	1300 slgft2	L_p	=	-0.3751 1/s
C_l_B	=	-0.1730 1/rad	L_r	=	0.4329 1/s
C_l_p	=	-0.3900 1/rad	N_B	=	0.8555 1/s^2
C_l_r	=	0.4500 1/rad	N_T_B	=	0.0000 1/s^2
C_n_B	=	0.1500 1/rad	N_p	=	-0.0742 1/s
C_n_T_B	=	0.0000	N_r	=	-0.1483 1/s
C_n_p	=	-0.1300 1/rad	w_n_D	=	1.0413 rad/s
C_n_r	=	-0.2600 1/rad	z_D	=	-0.0453
C_y_B	=	-0.7300 1/rad	TC_SPIRAL	=	-34.137 s
C_y_p	=	0.0000 1/rad	TC_ROLL	=	1.363 s
C_y_r	=	0.4000 1/rad			
C_l_d_a	=	0.1490 1/rad	Y_del_a	=	0.0000 ft/s^2
C_l_d_r	=	0.0140 1/rad	Y_del_r	=	2.7364 ft/s^2
C_n_d_a	=	-0.0500 1/rad	L_del_a	=	1.4331 1/s^2
C_n_d_r	=	-0.0740 1/rad	L_del_r	=	0.1347 1/s^2
C_y_d_a	=	0.0000 1/rad	N_del_a	=	-0.2852 1/s^2
C_y_d_r	=	0.1400 1/rad	N_del_r	=	-0.4220 1/s^2

Table B7 (Continued)   Stability and Control Derivatives for Airplane G (Pages 522–528)

POLYNOMIAL SIDESLIP TO AILERON TRANSFER FUNCTION

```
 + 50.1518 S^3 + 82.1337 S^2 + 2.8556 S
-------------------------------------------------------------------------------
 + 169.9617 S^5 + 103.6534 S^4 + 169.3730 S^3 + 130.1231 S^2 - 3.9599 S
```

FACTORED SIDESLIP TO AILERON TRANSFER FUNCTION

```
50.1518   S(S + 1.6022)(S + 0.0355)
-------------------------------------------------------------------------------
169.9617   S(S - 0.0293)(S + 0.7334)(S^2 + -0.0943 S + 1.0844)
```

SIDESLIP TO AILERON TRANSFER FUNCTION K_gain =   -0.721137

POLYNOMIAL SIDESLIP TO RUDDER TRANSFER FUNCTION

```
 + 2.7362 S^4 + 73.0267 S^3 + 33.2130 S^2 - 5.2154 S
-------------------------------------------------------------------------------
 + 169.9617 S^5 + 103.6534 S^4 + 169.3730 S^3 + 130.1231 S^2 - 3.9599 S
```

FACTORED SIDESLIP TO RUDDER TRANSFER FUNCTION

```
2.7362   S(S - 0.1234)(S + 26.2238)(S + 0.5890)
-------------------------------------------------------------------------------
169.9617   S(S - 0.0293)(S + 0.7334)(S^2 + -0.0943 S + 1.0844)
```

SIDESLIP TO RUDDER TRANSFER FUNCTION K_gain =   1.317052

POLYNOMIAL BANK ANGLE TO AILERON TRANSFER FUNCTION

```
 + 244.2348 S^3 + 35.6460 S^2 + 128.4237 S
-------------------------------------------------------------------------------
 + 169.9617 S^5 + 103.6534 S^4 + 169.3730 S^3 + 130.1231 S^2 - 3.9599 S
```

FACTORED BANK ANGLE TO AILERON TRANSFER FUNCTION

```
244.2348   S(S^2 + 0.1459 S + 0.5258)
-------------------------------------------------------------------------------
169.9617   S(S - 0.0293)(S + 0.7334)(S^2 + -0.0943 S + 1.0844)
```

BANK ANGLE TO AILERON TRANSFER FUNCTION K_gain = -32.431294

Table B7 (Continued)   Stability and Control Derivatives for Airplane G (Pages 522–528)

POLYNOMIAL BANK ANGLE TO RUDDER TRANSFER FUNCTION

+ 23.8372 S^3 - 30.2418 S^2 - 101.3111 S

+ 169.9617 S^5 + 103.6534 S^4 + 169.3730 S^3 + 130.1231 S^2 - 3.9599 S

FACTORED BANK ANGLE TO RUDDER TRANSFER FUNCTION

23.8372   S(S - 2.7913)(S + 1.5226)

169.9617   S(S - 0.0293)(S + 0.7334)(S^2 + -0.0943 S + 1.0844)

BANK ANGLE TO RUDDER TRANSFER FUNCTION K_gain =   25.584449

POLYNOMIAL HEADING TO AILERON TRANSFER FUNCTION

- 50.3835 S^3 - 40.4765 S^2 - 3.0427 S + 24.0869

+ 169.9617 S^5 + 103.6534 S^4 + 169.3730 S^3 + 130.1231 S^2 - 3.9599 S

FACTORED HEADING TO AILERON TRANSFER FUNCTION

-50.3835   (S - 0.5687)(S^2 + 1.3721 S + 0.8407)

169.9617   S(S - 0.0293)(S + 0.7334)(S^2 + -0.0943 S + 1.0844)

HEADING TO AILERON TRANSFER FUNCTION K_gain =   -6.082742

POLYNOMIAL HEADING TO RUDDER TRANSFER FUNCTION

- 71.9185 S^3 - 32.2701 S^2 - 1.1857 S - 18.8159

+ 169.9617 S^5 + 103.6534 S^4 + 169.3730 S^3 + 130.1231 S^2 - 3.9599 S

FACTORED HEADING TO RUDDER TRANSFER FUNCTION

-71.9185   (S + 0.8188)(S^2 + -0.3701 S + 0.3195)

169.9617   S(S - 0.0293)(S + 0.7334)(S^2 + -0.0943 S + 1.0844)

HEADING TO RUDDER TRANSFER FUNCTION K_gain =   4.751643

Table B8   Stability and Control Derivatives for Airplane H (Pages 529–535)

Three–view

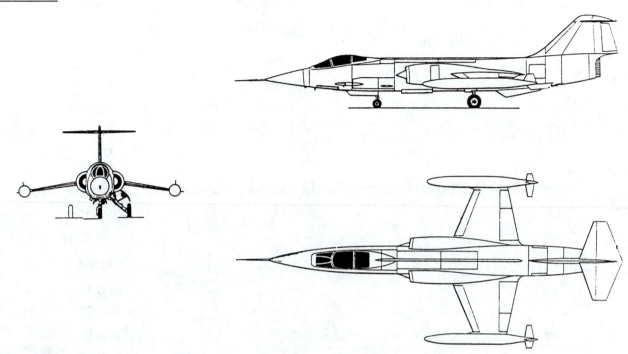

Reference Geometry

S (ft²)	196
$\bar{c}$ (ft)	9.6
b (ft)	21.9

Flight Condition Data

	Approach	Cruise
Altitude, h (ft)	0	55,000
Mach Number, M	0.257	1.800
TAS, U_1 (ft/sec)	287	1,742
Dynamic pressure, $\bar{q}$ (lbs/ft²)	97.8	434.5
C.G. location, fraction $\bar{c}$	0.07	0.07
Angle of attack, α_1 (deg)	10	2

Mass Data

W (lbs)	16,300	16,300
I_{xx_B} (slugft²)	3,600	3,600
I_{yy_B} (slugft²)	59,000	59,000
I_{zz_B} (slugft²)	60,000	60,000
I_{xz_B} (slugft²)	0	0

Table B8 (Continued)   **Stability and Control Derivatives for Airplane H (Pages 529–535)**

Flight Condition	Approach	Cruise

Steady State Coefficients

	Approach	Cruise
C_{L_1}	0.850	0.191
C_{D_1}	0.2634	0.0553
$C_{T_{x_1}}$	0.2634	0.0553
C_{m_1}	0	0
$C_{m_{T_1}}$	0	0

Longitudinal Coefficients and Stability Derivatives (Stability Axes, Dimensionless)

	Approach	Cruise
C_{D_0}	0.1189	0.0480
C_{D_u}	0	−0.060
C_{D_α}	0.455	0.384
$C_{T_{x_u}}$	−0.50	−0.13
C_{L_0}	0.240	0.122
C_{L_u}	0	−0.20
C_{L_α}	3.440	2.005
$C_{L_{\dot\alpha}}$	0.66	0.82
C_{L_q}	2.30	1.90
C_{m_0}	0.03	−0.028
C_{m_u}	0	0
C_{m_α}	−0.644	−1.308
$C_{m_{\dot\alpha}}$	−1.640	−2.050
C_{m_q}	−5.84	−4.83
$C_{m_{T_u}}$	0	0
$C_{m_{T_\alpha}}$	0	0

Longitudinal Control and Hinge Moment Derivatives (Stability Axes, 1/rad)

	Approach	Cruise
$C_{D_{\delta_e}}$	not applicable	
$C_{L_{\delta_e}}$	not applicable	
$C_{m_{\delta_e}}$	not applicable	
$C_{D_{i_h}}$	0	0
$C_{L_{i_h}}$	0.684	0.523
$C_{m_{i_h}}$	−1.60	−1.31

Table B8 (Continued)   **Stability and Control Derivatives for Airplane H (Pages 529–535)**

Flight Condition

	Approach	Cruise

Longitudinal Control and Hinge Moment Derivatives: Cont'd (Stability Axes, 1/rad)

	Approach	Cruise
C_{h_α}	not applicable	
$C_{h_{\delta_e}}$	not applicable	

Lateral–Directional Stability Derivatives (Stability Axes, Dimensionless)

	Approach	Cruise
C_{l_β}	−0.175	−0.093
C_{l_p}	−0.285	−0.272
C_{l_r}	0.265	0.154
C_{y_β}	−1.180	−1.045
C_{y_p}	0	0
C_{y_r}	0	0
C_{n_β}	0.507	0.242
$C_{n_{T_\beta}}$	0	0
C_{n_p}	−0.144	−0.093
C_{n_r}	−0.753	−0.649

Lateral–Directional Control and Hinge Moment Derivatives (Stability Axes, Dimensionless)

	Approach	Cruise
$C_{l_{\delta_a}}$	0.0392	0.0173
$C_{l_{\delta_r}}$	0.0448	0.0079
$C_{y_{\delta_a}}$	0	0
$C_{y_{\delta_r}}$	0.329	0.087
$C_{n_{\delta_a}}$	0.0042	0.0025
$C_{n_{\delta_r}}$	−0.1645	−0.0435
$C_{h_{\alpha_a}}$	???	???
$C_{h_{\delta_a}}$	???	???
$C_{h_{\beta_r}}$	???	???
$C_{h_{\delta_r}}$	???	???

Table B8 (Continued)   Stability and Control Derivatives for Airplane H (Pages 529–535)

Longitudinal Transfer Function Data

Altitude	=	0 ft		M_1	=	0.257	
U_1	=	170.02 kts		n	=	1.00 g	
$W_{current}$	=	16300.0 lb		q_{bar}	=	97.87 psf	
S_w	=	196.00 ft^2		$(W/S)\_TO$	=	83.16 psf	
$Theta_1$	=	10.00 deg		X_u	=	-0.0695 1/s	
C_{bar}	=	9.60 ft		X_{T_u}	=	0.0035 1/s	
I_{yy_B}	=	59000 slgft2		X_a	=	14.9560 ft/s^2	
C_{m_1}	=	0.0000		Z_u	=	-0.2243 1/s	
C_{m_u}	=	0.0000		Z_a	=	-140.2225 ft/s^2	
C_{m_a}	=	-0.6440 1/rad		Z_{a_dot}	=	-0.4180 ft/s	
$C_{m_a.dot}$	=	-1.6400 1/rad		Z_q	=	-1.4566 ft/s	
C_{m_q}	=	-5.8400 1/rad		M_u	=	0.0000 1/ft/s	
$C_{m_T_1}$	=	0.0000		M_{T_u}	=	0.0000 1/ft/s	
$C_{m_T_u}$	=	0.0000		M_a	=	-2.0100 1/s^2	
$C_{m_T_a}$	=	0.0000		M_{T_a}	=	0.0000 1/s^2	
C_{L_1}	=	0.8500		M_{a_dot}	=	-0.0856 1/s	
C_{L_u}	=	0.0000		M_q	=	-0.3049 1/s	
C_{L_a}	=	3.4400 1/rad					
$C_{L_a.dot}$	=	0.6600 1/rad		w_{n_SP}	=	1.4679 rad/s	
C_{L_q}	=	2.3000 1/rad		z_{SP}	=	0.3075	
C_{D_1}	=	0.2634		w_{n_P}	=	0.1479 rad/s	
C_{D_a}	=	0.4550 1/rad		z_P	=	0.1385	
C_{D_u}	=	0.0000		X_{del_e}	=	0.0000 ft/s^2	
$C_{T_X_1}$	=	0.2634		Z_{del_e}	=	-25.8984 ft/s^2	
$C_{T_X_u}$	=	-0.5000		M_{del_e}	=	-4.9939 1/s^2	
$C_{L_d_e}$	=	0.6840 1/rad					
$C_{D_d_e}$	=	0.0000 1/rad					
$C_{m_d_e}$	=	-1.6000 1/rad					

POLYNOMIAL ANGLE OF ATTACK TO ELEVATOR TRANSFER FUNCTION

$$\frac{- 25.8984\ S^3 - 1435.4151\ S^2 - 66.6826\ S - 33.6512}{+ 287.3857\ S^4 + 271.2473\ S^3 + 636.1609\ S^2 + 31.0502\ S + 13.5446}$$

FACTORED ANGLE OF ATTACK TO ELEVATOR TRANSFER FUNCTION

$$\frac{-25.8984\ (S + 55.3788)(S^2 + 0.0461\ S + 0.0235)}{287.3857\ (S^2 + 0.9029\ S + 2.1547)(S^2 + 0.0410\ S + 0.0219)}$$

ANGLE OF ATTACK TO ELEVATOR TRANSFER FUNCTION K_gain = -2.484472

POLYNOMIAL SPEED TO ELEVATOR TRANSFER FUNCTION

$$\frac{- 387.3356\ S^2 + 23961.0113\ S + 20955.5903}{+ 287.3857\ S^4 + 271.2473\ S^3 + 636.1609\ S^2 + 31.0502\ S + 13.5446}$$

Table B8 (Continued)   Stability and Control Derivatives for Airplane H (Pages 529–535)

FACTORED SPEED TO ELEVATOR TRANSFER FUNCTION

$$\frac{-387.3356 \quad (S - 62.7237)(S + 0.8625)}{287.3857 \quad (S^2 + 0.9029\ S + 2.1547)(S^2 + 0.0410\ S + 0.0219)}$$

SPEED TO ELEVATOR TRANSFER FUNCTION K_gain = 1547.154040

POLYNOMIAL PITCH ATTITUDE TO ELEVATOR TRANSFER FUNCTION

$$\frac{- 1432.9547\ S^2 - 742.7324\ S - 59.5152}{+ 287.3857\ S^4 + 271.2473\ S^3 + 636.1609\ S^2 + 31.0502\ S + 13.5446}$$

FACTORED PITCH ATTITUDE TO ELEVATOR TRANSFER FUNCTION

$$\frac{-1432.9547 \quad (S + 0.4193)(S + 0.0991)}{287.3857 \quad (S^2 + 0.9029\ S + 2.1547)(S^2 + 0.0410\ S + 0.0219)}$$

PITCH ATTITUDE TO ELEVATOR TRANSFER FUNCTION K_gain =   -4.394013

Lateral–Directional Transfer Function Data

W_current	=	16300.0 lb	(W/S)_TO	=	83.16 psf
Altitude	=	0 ft	q_bar	=	97.87 psf
S_w	=	196.00 ft^2	I_xx_S	=	5301 slgft2
U_1	=	170.02 kts	I_zz_S	=	58299 slgft2
Theta_1	=	10.00 deg	I_xz_S	=	-9645 slgft2
Alpha	=	10.00 deg	Y_B	=	-44.6786 ft/s^2
b_w	=	21.90 ft	Y_p	=	0.0000 ft/s
I_xx_B	=	3600 slgft2	Y_r	=	0.0000 ft/s
I_zz_B	=	60000 slgft2	L_B	=	-13.8692 1/s^2
I_xz_B	=	0 slgft2	L_p	=	-0.8619 1/s
C_l_B	=	-0.1750 1/rad	L_r	=	0.8014 1/s
C_l_p	=	-0.2850 1/rad	N_B	=	3.6533 1/s^2
C_l_r	=	0.2650 1/rad	N_T_B	=	0.0000 1/s^2
C_n_B	=	0.5070 1/rad	N_p	=	-0.0396 1/s
C_n_T_B	=	0.0000	N_r	=	-0.2070 1/s
C_n_p	=	-0.1440 1/rad	w_n_D	=	2.8810 rad/s
C_n_r	=	-0.7530 1/rad	z_D	=	0.1281
C_y_B	=	-1.1800 1/rad	TC_SPIRAL	=	-966.957 s
C_y_p	=	0.0000 1/rad	TC_ROLL	=	0.967 s
C_y_r	=	0.0000 1/rad	TC_1	=	0.967 s
C_l_d_a	=	0.0392 1/rad	TC_2	=	-966.957 s
C_l_d_r	=	0.0448 1/rad	Y_del_a	=	0.0000 ft/s^2
C_n_d_a	=	0.0042 1/rad	Y_del_r	=	12.4570 ft/s^2
C_n_d_r	=	-0.1645 1/rad	L_del_a	=	3.1067 1/s^2
C_y_d_a	=	0.0000 1/rad	L_del_r	=	3.5505 1/s^2
C_y_d_r	=	0.3290 1/rad	N_del_a	=	0.0303 1/s^2
			N_del_r	=	-1.1853 1/s^2

Table B8 (Continued) Stability and Control Derivatives for Airplane H (Pages 529–535)

POLYNOMIAL SIDESLIP TO AILERON TRANSFER FUNCTION

+ 138.8075 S^3 + 124.5049 S^2 + 21.1488 S

+ 200.5823 S^5 + 355.3425 S^4 + 1817.6079 S^3 + 1720.6151 S^2 - 1.7814 S

FACTORED SIDESLIP TO AILERON TRANSFER FUNCTION

138.8075   S(S + 0.6693)(S + 0.2276)

200.5823   S(S - 0.0010)(S + 1.0346)(S^2 + 0.7380 S + 8.3000)

  SIDESLIP TO AILERON TRANSFER FUNCTION K_gain = -11.872326

POLYNOMIAL SIDESLIP TO RUDDER TRANSFER FUNCTION

+ 8.7071 S^4 + 522.7889 S^3 + 516.9667 S^2 - 6.8065 S

+ 200.5823 S^5 + 355.3425 S^4 + 1817.6079 S^3 + 1720.6151 S^2 - 1.7814 S

FACTORED SIDESLIP TO RUDDER TRANSFER FUNCTION

8.7071   S(S - 0.0130)(S + 59.0359)(S + 1.0189)

200.5823   S(S - 0.0010)(S + 1.0346)(S^2 + 0.7380 S + 8.3000)

  SIDESLIP TO RUDDER TRANSFER FUNCTION K_gain =   3.820969

POLYNOMIAL ROLL TO AILERON TRANSFER FUNCTION

+ 875.7196 S^3 + 327.8840 S^2 + 3407.2931 S

+ 200.5823 S^5 + 355.3425 S^4 + 1817.6079 S^3 + 1720.6151 S^2 - 1.7814 S

FACTORED ROLL TO AILERON TRANSFER FUNCTION

875.7196   S(S^2 + 0.3744 S + 3.8908)

200.5823   S(S - 0.0010)(S + 1.0346)(S^2 + 0.7380 S + 8.3000)

  ROLL TO AILERON TRANSFER FUNCTION K_gain =-1912.752646

Table B8 (Continued)   Stability and Control Derivatives for Airplane H (Pages 529–535)

POLYNOMIAL ROLL TO RUDDER TRANSFER FUNCTION

```
 + 1637.8237 S^3 - 62.2256 S^2 - 1004.2890 S
-----------------------------------------------------------------------
 + 200.5823 S^5 + 355.3425 S^4 + 1817.6079 S^3 + 1720.6151 S^2 - 1.7814 S
```

FACTORED ROLL TO RUDDER TRANSFER FUNCTION

```
1637.8237    S(S - 0.8023)(S + 0.7643)
-----------------------------------------------------------------------
200.5823    S(S - 0.0010)(S + 1.0346)(S^2 + 0.7380 S + 8.3000)
```

ROLL TO RUDDER TRANSFER FUNCTION K_gain = 563.777878

POLYNOMIAL HEADING TO AILERON TRANSFER FUNCTION

```
 - 138.8075 S^3 - 49.4245 S^2 - 4.3303 S + 372.9196
-----------------------------------------------------------------------
 + 200.5823 S^5 + 355.3425 S^4 + 1817.6079 S^3 + 1720.6151 S^2 - 1.7814 S
```

FACTORED HEADING TO AILERON TRANSFER FUNCTION

```
-138.8075   (S - 1.2742)(S^2 + 1.6303 S + 2.1085)
-----------------------------------------------------------------------
200.5823    S(S - 0.0010)(S + 1.0346)(S^2 + 0.7380 S + 8.3000)
```

HEADING TO AILERON TRANSFER FUNCTION K_gain = -209.345936

POLYNOMIAL HEADING TO RUDDER TRANSFER FUNCTION

```
 - 508.7194 S^3 - 338.6218 S^2 - 5.8614 S - 109.9050
-----------------------------------------------------------------------
 + 200.5823 S^5 + 355.3425 S^4 + 1817.6079 S^3 + 1720.6151 S^2 - 1.7814 S
```

FACTORED HEADING TO RUDDER TRANSFER FUNCTION

```
-508.7194   (S + 0.9125)(S^2 + -0.2468 S + 0.2368)
-----------------------------------------------------------------------
200.5823    S(S - 0.0010)(S + 1.0346)(S^2 + 0.7380 S + 8.3000)
```

HEADING TO RUDDER TRANSFER FUNCTION K_gain = 61.697394

Table B9   Stability and Control Derivatives for Airplane I (Pages 536–542)

Three–view

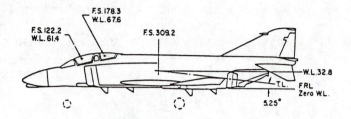

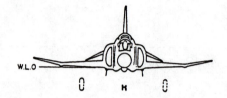

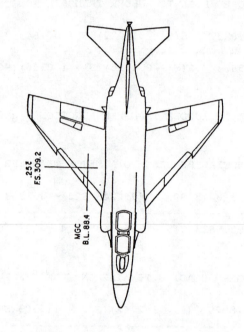

Reference Geometry

S (ft²)	530
$\bar{c}$ (ft)	16.0
b (ft)	38.7

Flight Condition Data

	Approach	Cruise (M<1)	Cruise (M>1)
Altitude, h (ft)	0	35,000	55,000
Mach Number, M	0.206	0.900	1.800
TAS, U_1(ft/sec)	230	876	1,742
Dynamic pressure, $\bar{q}$ (lbs/ft²)	62.9	283.2	434.5
C.G. location, fraction $\bar{c}$	0.29	0.29	0.29
Angle of attack, α_1 (deg)	11.7	2.6	3.3

Mass Data

W (lbs)	33,200	39,000	39,000
I_{xx_B} (slugft²)	23,700	25,000	25,000
I_{yy_B} (slugft²)	117,500	122,200	122,200
I_{zz_B} (slugft²)	133,700	139,800	139,800
I_{xz_B} (slugft²)	1,600	2,200	2,200

Table B9 (Continued)   Stability and Control Derivatives for Airplane I (Pages 536–542)

Flight Condition	Approach	Cruise (M<1)	Cruise (M>1)
Steady State Coefficients			
C_{L_1}	1.0	0.26	0.17
C_{D_1}	0.2000	0.0300	0.0480
$C_{T_{x_1}}$	0.2000	0.0300	0.0480
C_{m_1}	0	0	0
$C_{m_{T_1}}$	0	0	0

Longitudinal Coefficients and Stability Derivatives (Stability Axes, Dimensionless)

	Approach	Cruise (M<1)	Cruise (M>1)
C_{D_0}	0.0269	0.0205	0.0439
C_{D_u}	0	0.027	−0.054
C_{D_α}	0.555	0.300	0.400
$C_{T_{x_u}}$	−0.4500	−0.064	−0.1000
C_{L_0}	0.430	0.100	0.010
C_{L_u}	0	0.270	−0.180
C_{L_α}	2.80	3.75	2.80
$C_{L_{\dot{\alpha}}}$	0.63	0.86	0.17
C_{L_q}	1.33	1.80	1.30
C_{m_0}	+0.020	+0.025	−0.025
C_{m_u}	0	−0.117	+0.054
C_{m_α}	−0.098	−0.400	−0.780
$C_{m_{\dot{\alpha}}}$	−0.950	−1.300	−0.250
C_{m_q}	−2.00	−2.70	−2.00
$C_{m_{T_u}}$	0	0	0
$C_{m_{T_\alpha}}$	0	0	0

Longitudinal Control and Hinge Moment Derivatives (Stability Axes, 1/rad)

	Approach	Cruise (M<1)	Cruise (M>1)
$C_{D_{\delta_e}}$	not applicable		
$C_{L_{\delta_e}}$	not applicable		
$C_{m_{\delta_e}}$	not applicable		
$C_{D_{i_h}}$	−0.14	−0.10	−0.15
$C_{L_{i_h}}$	0.24	0.40	0.25
$C_{m_{i_h}}$	−0.322	−0.580	−0.380

Table B9 (Continued)   Stability and Control Derivatives for Airplane I (Pages 536–542)

Flight Condition	Approach	Cruise (M<1)	Cruise (M>1)

Longitudinal Control and Hinge Moment Derivatives: Cont'd (Stability Axes, 1/rad)

	Approach	Cruise (M<1)	Cruise (M>1)
C_{h_α}	not applicable		
$C_{h_{\delta_e}}$	not applicable		

Lateral–Directional Stability Derivatives (Stability Axes, Dimensionless)

	Approach	Cruise (M<1)	Cruise (M>1)
C_{l_β}	−0.156	−0.080	−0.025
C_{l_p}	−0.272	−0.240	−0.200
C_{l_r}	0.205	0.070	0.040
C_{y_β}	−0.655	−0.680	−0.700
C_{y_p}	0	0	0
C_{y_r}	0	0	0
C_{n_β}	0.199	0.125	0.090
$C_{n_{T_\beta}}$	0	0	0
C_{n_p}	0.013	−0.036	0
C_{n_r}	−0.320	−0.270	−0.260

Lateral–Directional Control and Hinge Moment Derivatives (Stability Axes, Dimensionless)

	Approach	Cruise (M<1)	Cruise (M>1)
$C_{l_{\delta_a}}$	0.0570	0.0420	0.0150
$C_{l_{\delta_r}}$	0.0009	0.0060	0.0030
$C_{y_{\delta_a}}$	−0.0355	−0.0160	−0.010
$C_{y_{\delta_r}}$	0.124	0.095	0.050
$C_{n_{\delta_a}}$	0.0041	−0.0010	−0.0009
$C_{n_{\delta_r}}$	−0.072	−0.066	−0.025
$C_{h_{\alpha_a}}$	???	???	???
$C_{h_{\delta_a}}$	???	???	???
$C_{h_{\beta_r}}$	???	???	???
$C_{h_{\delta_r}}$	???	???	???

Table B9 (Continued)   Stability and Control Derivatives for Airplane I (Pages 536–542)

Longitudinal Transfer Function Data

Altitude	=	35000 ft	
U_1	=	518.96 kts	
W_current	=	39000.0 lb	
S_w	=	530.00 ft^2	
Theta_1	=	2.60 deg	
C_bar	=	16.00 ft	
I_yy_B	=	122200 slgft2	
C_m_1	=	0.0000	
C_m_u	=	-0.1170	
C_m_a	=	-0.4000 1/rad	
C_m_a.dot	=	-1.3000 1/rad	
C_m_q	=	-2.7000 1/rad	
C_m_T_1	=	0.0000	
C_m_T_u	=	0.0000	
C_m_T_a	=	0.0000	
C_L_1	=	0.2600	
C_L_u	=	0.2700	
C_L_a	=	3.7500 1/rad	
C_L_a.dot	=	0.8600 1/rad	
C_L_q	=	1.8000 1/rad	
C_D_1	=	0.0300	
C_D_a	=	0.3000 1/rad	
C_D_u	=	0.0270	
C_T_X_1	=	0.0300	
C_T_X_u	=	-0.0640	
C_L_d_e	=	0.4000 1/rad	
C_D_d_e	=	-0.1000 1/rad	
C_m_d_e	=	-0.5800 1/rad	

M_1	=	0.900
n	=	1.00 g
q_bar	=	283.17 psf
(W/S)_TO	=	73.58 psf
X_u	=	-0.0122 1/s
X_T_u	=	-0.0006 1/s
X_a	=	-4.8986 ft/s^2
Z_u	=	-0.1105 1/s
Z_a	=	-462.9218 ft/s^2
Z_a_dot	=	-0.9619 ft/s
Z_q	=	-2.0134 ft/s
M_u	=	-0.0026 1/ft/s
M_T_u	=	0.0000 1/ft/s
M_a	=	-7.8602 1/s^2
M_T_a	=	0.0000 1/s^2
M_a_dot	=	-0.2333 1/s
M_q	=	-0.4846 1/s
w_n_3 osc	=	2.8472 rad/s
z_3rd osc	=	0.2210
TC_1	=	25.389 s
TC_2	=	-25.100 s
X_del_e	=	12.2466 ft/s^2
Z_del_e	=	-48.9864 ft/s^2
M_del_e	=	-11.3973 1/s^2

POLYNOMIAL ANGLE OF ATTACK TO ELEVATOR TRANSFER FUNCTION

$$\frac{- 48.9864\ S^3 - 9985.6978\ S^2 - 139.3202\ S - 35.6784}{+ 876.8633\ S^4 + 1102.8926\ S^3 + 7106.2935\ S^2 - 4.9526\ S - 11.1541}$$

FACTORED ANGLE OF ATTACK TO ELEVATOR TRANSFER FUNCTION

$$\frac{-48.9864\ (S + 203.8323)(S^2 + 0.0139\ S + 0.0036)}{876.8633\ (S - 0.0398)(S + 0.0394)(S^2 + 1.2582\ S + 8.1064)}$$

ANGLE OF ATTACK TO ELEVATOR TRANSFER FUNCTION K_gain = 3.198674

POLYNOMIAL SPEED TO ELEVATOR TRANSFER FUNCTION

$$\frac{+ 10738.6016\ S^3 + 13610.0294\ S^2 + 453125.8259\ S + 155272.0233}{+ 876.8633\ S^4 + 1102.8926\ S^3 + 7106.2935\ S^2 - 4.9526\ S - 11.1541}$$

Table B9 (Continued)   Stability and Control Derivatives for Airplane I (Pages 536–542)

FACTORED SPEED TO ELEVATOR TRANSFER FUNCTION

```
10738.6016   (S + 0.3453)(S^2 + 0.9221 S + 41.8776)
-----------------------------------------------------------------------
876.8633   (S - 0.0398)(S + 0.0394)(S^2 + 1.2582 S + 8.1064)
```

SPEED TO ELEVATOR TRANSFER FUNCTION K_gain =-13920.616547

POLYNOMIAL PITCH ATTITUDE TO ELEVATOR TRANSFER FUNCTION

```
 - 9982.4646 S^2 - 5045.9068 S - 60.9416
-----------------------------------------------------------------------
 + 876.8633 S^4 + 1102.8926 S^3 + 7106.2935 S^2 - 4.9526 S - 11.1541
```

FACTORED PITCH ATTITUDE TO ELEVATOR TRANSFER FUNCTION

```
-9982.4646   (S + 0.4931)(S + 0.0124)
-----------------------------------------------------------------------
876.8633   (S - 0.0398)(S + 0.0394)(S^2 + 1.2582 S + 8.1064)
```

PITCH ATTITUDE TO ELEVATOR TRANSFER FUNCTION K_gain =   5.463602

Lateral–Directional Transfer Function Data

W_current	=	39000.0 lb	(W/S)_TO	=	73.58	psf
Altitude	=	35000 ft	q_bar	=	283.17	psf
S_w	=	530.00 ft^2	I_xx_S	=	25037	slgft2
U_1	=	518.96 kts	I_zz_S	=	139763	slgft2
Theta_1	=	2.60 deg	I_xz_S	=	-3011	slgft2
Alpha	=	2.60 deg	Y_B	=	-83.2769	ft/s^2
b_w	=	38.70 ft	Y_p	=	0.0000	ft/s
I_xx_B	=	25000 slgft2	Y_r	=	0.0000	ft/s
I_zz_B	=	139800 slgft2	L_B	=	-18.5587	1/s^2
I_xz_B	=	2200 slgft2	L_p	=	-1.2300	1/s
C_l_B	=	-0.0800 1/rad	L_r	=	0.3587	1/s
C_l_p	=	-0.2400 1/rad	N_B	=	5.1946	1/s^2
C_l_r	=	0.0700 1/rad	N_T_B	=	0.0000	1/s^2
C_n_B	=	0.1250 1/rad	N_p	=	-0.0331	1/s
C_n_T_B	=	0.0000	N_r	=	-0.2479	1/s
C_n_p	=	-0.0360 1/rad	w_n_D	=	2.3956	rad/s
C_n_r	=	-0.2700 1/rad	z_D	=	0.0482	
C_y_B	=	-0.6800 1/rad	TC_SPIRAL	=	77.022	s
C_y_p	=	0.0000 1/rad	TC_ROLL	=	0.748	s
C_y_r	=	0.0000 1/rad				
C_l_d_a	=	0.0420 1/rad	TC_1	=	0.748	s
C_l_d_r	=	0.0060 1/rad	TC_2	=	77.022	s
C_n_d_a	=	-0.0010 1/rad	Y_del_a	=	-1.9595	ft/s^2
C_n_d_r	=	-0.0660 1/rad	Y_del_r	=	11.6343	ft/s^2
C_y_d_a	=	-0.0160 1/rad	L_del_a	=	9.7433	1/s^2
C_y_d_r	=	0.0950 1/rad	L_del_r	=	1.3919	1/s^2
			N_del_a	=	-0.0416	1/s^2
			N_del_r	=	-2.7428	1/s^2

Table B9 (Continued)   **Stability and Control Derivatives for Airplane I (Pages 536–542)**

POLYNOMIAL SIDESLIP TO AILERON TRANSFER FUNCTION

$$\frac{- 1.9544\ S^4 + 217.3759\ S^3 + 636.1162\ S^2 + 76.3060\ S}{+ 873.6315\ S^5 + 1380.7964\ S^4 + 5301.0394\ S^3 + 6769.8305\ S^2 + 87.0037\ S}$$

FACTORED SIDESLIP TO AILERON TRANSFER FUNCTION

$$\frac{-1.9544 \quad S(S - 114.0811)(S + 2.7307)(S + 0.1253)}{873.6315 \quad S(S + 1.3366)(S + 0.0130)(S^2 + 0.2309\ S + 5.7388)}$$

SIDESLIP TO AILERON TRANSFER FUNCTION K_gain = 0.877043

POLYNOMIAL SIDESLIP TO RUDDER TRANSFER FUNCTION

$$\frac{+ 11.6041\ S^4 + 2445.8956\ S^3 + 3053.5834\ S^2 - 20.3121\ S}{+ 873.6315\ S^5 + 1380.7964\ S^4 + 5301.0394\ S^3 + 6769.8305\ S^2 + 87.0037\ S}$$

FACTORED SIDESLIP TO RUDDER TRANSFER FUNCTION

$$\frac{11.6041 \quad S(S - 0.0066)(S + 209.5221)(S + 1.2626)}{873.6315 \quad S(S + 1.3366)(S + 0.0130)(S^2 + 0.2309\ S + 5.7388)}$$

SIDESLIP TO RUDDER TRANSFER FUNCTION K_gain = -0.233463

POLYNOMIAL ROLL TO AILERON TRANSFER FUNCTION

$$\frac{+ 8538.5611\ S^3 + 2951.7568\ S^2 + 43861.6068\ S}{+ 873.6315\ S^5 + 1380.7964\ S^4 + 5301.0394\ S^3 + 6769.8305\ S^2 + 87.0037\ S}$$

FACTORED ROLL TO AILERON TRANSFER FUNCTION

$$\frac{8538.5611 \quad S(S^2 + 0.3457\ S + 5.1369)}{873.6315 \quad S(S + 1.3366)(S + 0.0130)(S^2 + 0.2309\ S + 5.7388)}$$

ROLL TO AILERON TRANSFER FUNCTION K_gain = 504.134977

Table B9 (Continued)   Stability and Control Derivatives for Airplane I (Pages 536–542)

POLYNOMIAL ROLL TO RUDDER TRANSFER FUNCTION

+ 1508.1220 S^3 - 639.4342 S^2 - 38337.1395 S

+ 873.6315 S^5 + 1380.7964 S^4 + 5301.0394 S^3 + 6769.8305 S^2 + 87.0037 S

FACTORED ROLL TO RUDDER TRANSFER FUNCTION

1508.1220   S(S - 5.2583)(S + 4.8343)

873.6315   S(S + 1.3366)(S + 0.0130)(S^2 + 0.2309 S + 5.7388)

ROLL TO RUDDER TRANSFER FUNCTION K_gain = -440.638051

POLYNOMIAL HEADING TO AILERON TRANSFER FUNCTION

- 220.2790 S^3 - 358.7315 S^2 - 44.7945 S + 1584.5260

+ 873.6315 S^5 + 1380.7964 S^4 + 5301.0394 S^3 + 6769.8305 S^2 + 87.0037 S

FACTORED HEADING TO AILERON TRANSFER FUNCTION

-220.2790   (S - 1.4872)(S^2 + 3.1157 S + 4.8369)

873.6315   S(S + 1.3366)(S + 0.0130)(S^2 + 0.2309 S + 5.7388)

HEADING TO AILERON TRANSFER FUNCTION K_gain =   18.212169

POLYNOMIAL HEADING TO RUDDER TRANSFER FUNCTION

- 2428.6583 S^3 - 3160.9790 S^2 - 203.2968 S - 1388.3758

+ 873.6315 S^5 + 1380.7964 S^4 + 5301.0394 S^3 + 6769.8305 S^2 + 87.0037 S

FACTORED HEADING TO RUDDER TRANSFER FUNCTION

-2428.6583   (S + 1.4998)(S^2 + -0.1983 S + 0.3811)

873.6315   S(S + 1.3366)(S + 0.0130)(S^2 + 0.2309 S + 5.7388)

HEADING TO RUDDER TRANSFER FUNCTION K_gain = -15.957664

Table B10   Stability and Control Derivatives for Airplane J (Pages 543–549)

Three–view

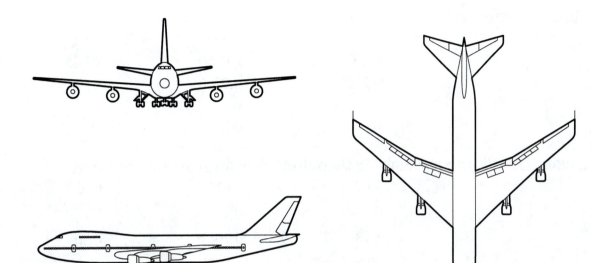

Reference Geometry

S (ft^2)   5,500
$\bar{c}$ (ft)   27.3
b (ft)   196

Flight Condition Data	Approach	Cruise (low)	Cruise (high)
Altitude, h (ft)	0	20,000	40,000
Mach Number, M	0.198	0.650	0.900
TAS, U_1 (ft/sec)	221	673	871
Dynamic pressure, $\bar{q}$ (lbs/ft^2)	58.0	287.2	222.8
C.G. location, fraction $\bar{c}$	0.25	0.25	0.25
Angle of attack, α_1 (deg)	8.5	2.5	2.4

Mass Data

W (lbs)	564,000	636,636	636,636
I_{xx_B} (slugft^2)	13,700,000	18,200,000	18,200,000
I_{yy_B} (slugft^2)	30,500,000	33,100,000	33,100,000
I_{zz_B} (slugft^2)	43,100,000	49,700,000	49,700,000
I_{xz_B} (slugft^2)	830,000	970,000	970,000

Table B10 (Continued)   Stability and Control Derivatives for Airplane J (Pages 543–549)

Flight Condition	Approach	Cruise (low)	Cruise (high)
Steady State Coefficients			
C_{L_1}	1.76	0.40	0.52
C_{D_1}	0.2630	0.0250	0.0450
$C_{T_{x_1}}$	0.2630	0.0250	0.0450
C_{m_1}	0	0	0
$C_{m_{T_1}}$	0	0	0

Longitudinal Coefficients and Stability Derivatives (Stability Axes, Dimensionless)

	Approach	Cruise (low)	Cruise (high)
C_{D_0}	0.0751	0.0164	0.0305
C_{D_u}	0	0	0.22
C_{D_α}	1.13	0.20	0.50
$C_{T_{x_u}}$	−0.5523	−0.055	−0.950
C_{L_0}	0.92	0.21	0.29
C_{L_u}	−0.22	0.13	−0.23
C_{L_α}	5.67	4.4	5.5
$C_{L_{\dot\alpha}}$	6.7	7.0	8.0
C_{L_q}	5.65	6.6	7.8
C_{m_0}	0	0	0
C_{m_u}	0.071	0.013	−0.09
C_{m_α}	−1.45	−1.00	−1.60
$C_{m_{\dot\alpha}}$	−3.3	−4.0	−9.0
C_{m_q}	−21.4	−20.5	−25.5
$C_{m_{T_u}}$	0	0	0
$C_{m_{T_\alpha}}$	0	0	0

Longitudinal Control and Hinge Moment Derivatives (Stability Axes, 1/rad)

	Approach	Cruise (low)	Cruise (high)
$C_{D_{\delta_e}}$	0	0	0
$C_{L_{\delta_e}}$	0.36	0.32	0.30
$C_{m_{\delta_e}}$	−1.40	−1.30	−1.20
$C_{D_{i_h}}$	0	0	0
$C_{L_{i_h}}$	0.75	0.70	0.65
$C_{m_{i_h}}$	−3.0	−2.7	−2.5

Table B10 (Continued)   Stability and Control Derivatives for Airplane J (Pages 543–549)

Flight Condition	Approach	Cruise (low)	Cruise (high)
Longitudinal Control and Hinge Moment Derivatives: Cont'd (Stability Axes, 1/rad)			
C_{h_α}	???	???	???
$C_{h_{\delta_e}}$	???	???	???
Lateral–Directional Stability Derivatives (Stability Axes, Dimensionless)			
C_{l_β}	–0.281	–0.160	–0.095
C_{l_p}	–0.502	–0.340	–0.320
C_{l_r}	0.195	0.130	0.200
C_{y_β}	–1.08	–0.90	–0.90
C_{y_p}	0	0	0
C_{y_r}	0	0	0
C_{n_β}	0.184	0.160	0.210
$C_{n_{T_\beta}}$	0	0	0
C_{n_p}	–0.222	–0.026	0.020
C_{n_r}	–0.360	–0.280	–0.330
Lateral–Directional Control and Hinge Moment Derivatives (Stability Axes, Dimensionless)			
$C_{l_{\delta_a}}$	0.053	0.013	0.014
$C_{l_{\delta_r}}$	0	0.008	0.005
$C_{y_{\delta_a}}$	0	0	0
$C_{y_{\delta_r}}$	0.179	0.120	0.060
$C_{n_{\delta_a}}$	0.0083	0.0018	–0.0028
$C_{n_{\delta_r}}$	–0.113	–0.100	–0.095
$C_{h_{\alpha_a}}$	???	???	???
$C_{h_{\delta_a}}$	???	???	???
$C_{h_{\beta_r}}$	???	???	???
$C_{h_{\delta_r}}$	???	???	???

Table B10 (Continued)   Stability and Control Derivatives for Airplane J (Pages 543–549)

Longitudinal Transfer Function Data

Altitude	=	40000 ft	M_1	=	0.900
U_1	=	516.00 kts	n	=	1.00 g
$W\_current$	=	636636.0 lb	q_bar	=	222.72 psf
S_w	=	5500.00 ft^2	$(W/S)\_TO$	=	115.75 psf
$Theta\_1$	=	2.40 deg	X_u	=	-0.0218 1/s
C_bar	=	27.30 ft	X_T_u	=	-0.0604 1/s
I_yy_B	=	33100000 slgft2	X_a	=	1.2227 ft/s^2
C_m_1	=	0.0000	Z_u	=	-0.0569 1/s
C_m_u	=	-0.0900	Z_a	=	-339.0036 ft/s^2
C_m_a	=	-1.6000 1/rad	Z_a_dot	=	-7.6658 ft/s
$C\_m\_a.dot$	=	-9.0000 1/rad	Z_q	=	-7.4741 ft/s
C_m_q	=	-25.5000 1/rad	M_u	=	-0.0001 1/ft/s
$C\_m\_T\_1$	=	0.0000	M_T_u	=	0.0000 1/ft/s
$C\_m\_T\_u$	=	0.0000	M_a	=	-1.6165 1/s^2
$C\_m\_T\_a$	=	0.0000	M_T_a	=	0.0000 1/s^2
C_L_1	=	0.5200	M_a_dot	=	-0.1425 1/s
C_L_u	=	-0.2300	M_q	=	-0.4038 1/s
C_L_a	=	5.5000 1/rad			
$C\_L\_a.dot$	=	8.0000 1/rad	w_n_SP	=	1.3215 rad/s
C_L_q	=	7.8000 1/rad	z_SP	=	0.3532
C_D_1	=	0.0450	TC_1	=	16.340 s
C_D_a	=	0.5000 1/rad	TC_2	=	58.050 s
C_D_u	=	0.2200	X_del_e	=	0.0000 ft/s^2
$C\_T\_X\_1$	=	0.0450	Z_del_e	=	-18.3410 ft/s^2
$C\_T\_X\_u$	=	-0.9500	M_del_e	=	-1.2124 1/s^2
$C\_L\_d\_e$	=	0.3000 1/rad			
$C\_D\_d\_e$	=	0.0000 1/rad			
$C\_m\_d\_e$	=	-1.2000 1/rad			

POLYNOMIAL ANGLE OF ATTACK TO ELEVATOR TRANSFER FUNCTION

```
 - 18.3410 S^3 - 1055.6956 S^2 - 84.9709 S - 1.9952
-----------------------------------------------------------------------------
 + 878.5677 S^4 + 888.9681 S^3 + 1599.5636 S^2 + 121.1943 S + 1.6175
```

FACTORED ANGLE OF ATTACK TO ELEVATOR TRANSFER FUNCTION

```
-18.3410  (S + 57.4786)(S^2 + 0.0806 S + 0.0019)
-----------------------------------------------------------------------------
878.5677  (S + 0.0612)(S + 0.0172)(S^2 + 0.9334 S + 1.7464)
```

ANGLE OF ATTACK TO ELEVATOR TRANSFER FUNCTION K_gain =   -1.233487

POLYNOMIAL SPEED TO ELEVATOR TRANSFER FUNCTION

```
 - 22.4263 S^2 + 32442.6029 S + 12108.4240
-----------------------------------------------------------------------------
 + 878.5677 S^4 + 888.9681 S^3 + 1599.5636 S^2 + 121.1943 S + 1.6175
```

Table B10 (Continued)   Stability and Control Derivatives for Airplane J (Pages 543–549)

FACTORED SPEED TO ELEVATOR TRANSFER FUNCTION

$$\frac{-22.4263 \quad (S - 1447.0080)(S + 0.3731)}{878.5677 \quad (S + 0.0612)(S + 0.0172)(S^2 + 0.9334\ S + 1.7464)}$$

SPEED TO ELEVATOR TRANSFER FUNCTION K_gain = 7485.685023

POLYNOMIAL PITCH ATTITUDE TO ELEVATOR TRANSFER FUNCTION

$$\frac{- 1062.5244\ S^2 - 468.6144\ S - 31.4031}{+ 878.5677\ S^4 + 888.9681\ S^3 + 1599.5636\ S^2 + 121.1943\ S + 1.6175}$$

FACTORED PITCH ATTITUDE TO ELEVATOR TRANSFER FUNCTION

$$\frac{-1062.5244 \quad (S + 0.3586)(S + 0.0824)}{878.5677 \quad (S + 0.0612)(S + 0.0172)(S^2 + 0.9334\ S + 1.7464)}$$

PITCH ATTITUDE TO ELEVATOR TRANSFER FUNCTION K_gain = -19.414087

Lateral–Directional Transfer Function Data

W_current	=	636636.0 lb	(W/S)_TO	=	115.75 psf
Altitude	=	40000 ft	q_bar	=	222.72 psf
S_w	=	5500.00 ft^2	I_xx_S	=	18174070 slgft2
U_1	=	516.00 kts	I_zz_S	=	49725930 slgft2
Theta_1	=	2.40 deg	I_xz_S	=	-351328 slgft2
Alpha	=	2.40 deg	Y_B	=	-55.0231 ft/s^2
b_w	=	196.00 ft	Y_p	=	0.0000 ft/s
I_xx_B	=	18200000 slgft2	Y_r	=	0.0000 ft/s
I_zz_B	=	49700000 slgft2	L_B	=	-2.1137 1/s^2
I_xz_B	=	970000 slgft2	L_p	=	-0.5054 1/s
C_l_B	=	-0.1600 1/rad	L_r	=	0.1932 1/s
C_l_p	=	-0.3400 1/rad	N_B	=	0.7725 1/s^2
C_l_r	=	0.1300 1/rad	N_T_B	=	0.0000 1/s^2
C_n_B	=	0.1600 1/rad	N_p	=	-0.0141 1/s
C_n_T_B	=	0.0000	N_r	=	-0.1521 1/s
C_n_p	=	-0.0260 1/rad	w_n_D	=	0.9112 rad/s
C_n_r	=	-0.2800 1/rad	z_D	=	0.0643
C_y_B	=	-0.9000 1/rad	TC_SPIRAL	=	78.264 s
C_y_p	=	0.0000 1/rad	TC_ROLL	=	1.689 s
C_y_r	=	0.0000 1/rad	TC_1	=	1.689 s
C_l_d_a	=	0.0130 1/rad	TC_2	=	78.264 s
C_l_d_r	=	0.0080 1/rad	Y_del_a	=	0.0000 ft/s^2
C_n_d_a	=	0.0018 1/rad	Y_del_r	=	7.3364 ft/s^2
C_n_d_r	=	-0.1000 1/rad	L_del_a	=	0.1717 1/s^2
C_y_d_a	=	0.0000 1/rad	L_del_r	=	0.1057 1/s^2
C_y_d_r	=	0.1200 1/rad	N_del_a	=	0.0087 1/s^2
			N_del_r	=	-0.4828 1/s^2

Table B10 (Continued)   Stability and Control Derivatives for Airplane J (Pages 543–549)

```
POLYNOMIAL SIDESLIP TO AILERON TRANSFER FUNCTION

 - 6.5121 S^3 + 3.7340 S^2 + 0.8827 S
-----------------------------------------------------------------------
 + 870.7830 S^5 + 628.6269 S^4 + 791.3719 S^3 + 438.0016 S^2 + 5.4686 S


FACTORED SIDESLIP TO AILERON TRANSFER FUNCTION

-6.5121    S(S - 0.7533)(S + 0.1799)
-----------------------------------------------------------------------
870.7830   S(S + 0.5919)(S + 0.0128)(S^2 + 0.1172 S + 0.8304)


 SIDESLIP TO AILERON TRANSFER FUNCTION K_gain =    0.161417


POLYNOMIAL SIDESLIP TO RUDDER TRANSFER FUNCTION

 + 7.3354 S^4 + 425.9739 S^3 + 218.0615 S^2 - 2.4517 S
-----------------------------------------------------------------------
 + 870.7830 S^5 + 628.6269 S^4 + 791.3719 S^3 + 438.0016 S^2 + 5.4686 S


FACTORED SIDESLIP TO RUDDER TRANSFER FUNCTION

7.3354    S(S - 0.0110)(S + 57.5543)(S + 0.5276)
-----------------------------------------------------------------------
870.7830   S(S + 0.5919)(S + 0.0128)(S^2 + 0.1172 S + 0.8304)


 SIDESLIP TO RUDDER TRANSFER FUNCTION K_gain =    -0.448333


POLYNOMIAL ROLL TO AILERON TRANSFER FUNCTION

 + 149.4192 S^3 + 33.6557 S^2 + 133.0699 S
-----------------------------------------------------------------------
 + 870.7830 S^5 + 628.6269 S^4 + 791.3719 S^3 + 438.0016 S^2 + 5.4686 S


FACTORED ROLL TO AILERON TRANSFER FUNCTION

149.4192   S(S^2 + 0.2252 S + 0.8906)
-----------------------------------------------------------------------
870.7830   S(S + 0.5919)(S + 0.0128)(S^2 + 0.1172 S + 0.8304)


 ROLL TO AILERON TRANSFER FUNCTION K_gain =    24.333635
```

Table B10 (Continued)   Stability and Control Derivatives for Airplane J (Pages 543–549)

```
POLYNOMIAL ROLL TO RUDDER TRANSFER FUNCTION

 + 100.1689 S^3 - 76.5459 S^2 - 823.1939 S
---------------------------------------------------------------------------
 + 870.7830 S^5 + 628.6269 S^4 + 791.3719 S^3 + 438.0016 S^2 + 5.4686 S


FACTORED ROLL TO RUDDER TRANSFER FUNCTION

100.1689   S(S - 3.2742)(S + 2.5100)
---------------------------------------------------------------------------
870.7830   S(S + 0.5919)(S + 0.0128)(S^2 + 0.1172 S + 0.8304)


 ROLL TO RUDDER TRANSFER FUNCTION K_gain = -150.532188


POLYNOMIAL HEADING TO AILERON TRANSFER FUNCTION

 + 6.5121 S^3 + 2.1241 S^2 + 0.1082 S + 4.7950
---------------------------------------------------------------------------
 + 870.7830 S^5 + 628.6269 S^4 + 791.3719 S^3 + 438.0016 S^2 + 5.4686 S


FACTORED HEADING TO AILERON TRANSFER FUNCTION

6.5121   (S + 1.0190)(S^2 + -0.6928 S + 0.7226)
---------------------------------------------------------------------------
870.7830   S(S + 0.5919)(S + 0.0128)(S^2 + 0.1172 S + 0.8304)


 HEADING TO AILERON TRANSFER FUNCTION K_gain =    0.876826


POLYNOMIAL HEADING TO RUDDER TRANSFER FUNCTION

 - 421.1418 S^3 - 234.6564 S^2 - 10.4259 S - 29.8066
---------------------------------------------------------------------------
 + 870.7830 S^5 + 628.6269 S^4 + 791.3719 S^3 + 438.0016 S^2 + 5.4686 S


FACTORED HEADING TO RUDDER TRANSFER FUNCTION

-421.1418   (S + 0.6756)(S^2 + -0.1184 S + 0.1048)
---------------------------------------------------------------------------
870.7830    S(S + 0.5919)(S + 0.0128)(S^2 + 0.1172 S + 0.8304)


 HEADING TO RUDDER TRANSFER FUNCTION K_gain =    -5.450543
```

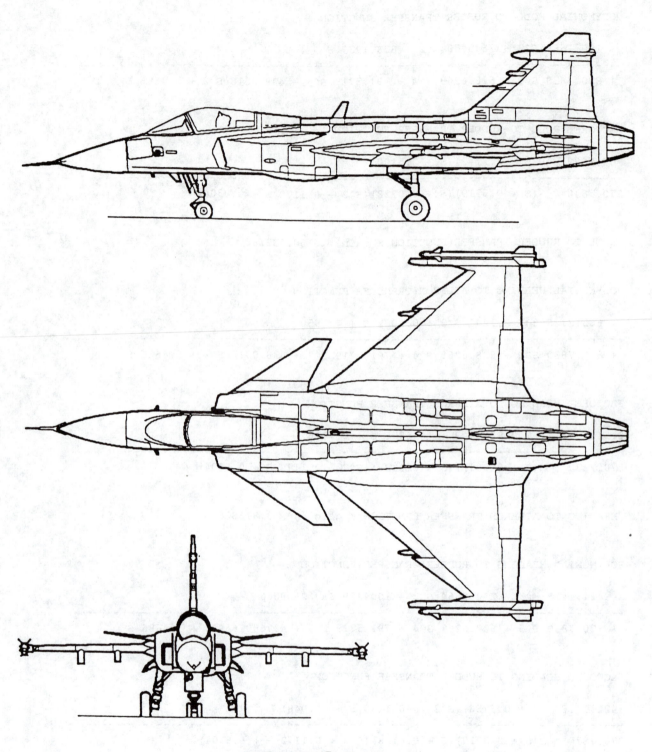

JAS 39 Gripen

APPENDIX C: SUMMARY OF LAPLACE TRANSFORM PROPERTIES

The purpose of this appendix is to summarize the those properties of Laplace transforms which are essential in the understanding of the material in Chapter 5. For more detailed study of the subject the reader is referred to References C1 and C2.

Definition of Laplace Transform

In the development of the airplane transfer functions in Chapter 5, use is made of the so–called one–sided Laplace transformation. The one–sided Laplace transform of a function f(t) is defined as:

$$\mathcal{L}\{f(t)\} = f(s) = \int_0^\infty e^{-st}f(t)dt \tag{C1}$$

Warning: the notations f(t) and f(s) do NOT imply the same functional dependences!

Note that the Laplace variable, s, has the unit of 1/sec. For that reason it is referred to as a frequency.

By applying this definition to those functions in the time domain which occur frequently in airplane dynamic stability problems the transforms of Table C1 are obtained.

Linearity property

The Laplace transform can be thought of as a linear operator. Therefore, the following computational rule applies:

$$\mathcal{L}\{c_1 f_1(t) + c_2 f_2(t)\} = c_1\mathcal{L}\{f_1(t)\} + c_2\mathcal{L}\{f_2(t)\} = c_1 f_1(s) + c_2 f_2(s) \tag{C2}$$

Transforms of derivatives

If $\mathcal{L}\{f(t)\} = f(s)$, the following holds for the derivatives of f(t):

For the first derivative: $\mathcal{L}\{f'(t)\} = sf(s) - f(0)$ (C3)

For the second derivative: $\mathcal{L}\{f''(t)\} = s^2f(s) - sf(0) - f'(0)$ (C4)

For the third derivative: $\mathcal{L}\{f'''(t)\} = s^3f(s) - s^2f(0) - sf'(0) - f''(0)$ (C5)

The quantities f(0), f'(0) and f''(0) are referred to as the initial conditions. They represent the values of f(t), f'(t) and f''(t) at t=0 respectively.

The operator s can therefore be thought of as a differentiator. This property is the key reason for the utility of Laplace transforms in dynamics problems. Through the use of this property, differential equations with time, t, as independent variable are changed into algebraic equations, with s, frequency as the independent variable.

Transform of an integral

If $\mathcal{L}\{f(t)\} = f(s)$, the following property holds:

$$\mathcal{L}\int_0^t f(t)dt = \frac{f(s)}{s} \tag{C1}$$

The operator 1/s can therefore be thought of as an integrator.

Final value theorem

If $\mathcal{L}\{f(t)\} = f(s)$ and if f(s) has only stable poles (i.e. stable roots of its characteristic equation) the following holds:

$$\lim_{t \to \infty}\{f(t)\} = \lim_{s \to 0}\{sf(s)\} \tag{C6}$$

This property allows the calculation of a time–domain property from an s–domain function. A corollary theorem is the initial value theorem.

Initial value theorem

If $\mathcal{L}\{f(t)\} = f(s)$, then:

$$\lim_{t \to 0}\{f(t)\} = \lim_{s \to \infty}\{sf(s)\} \tag{C7}$$

REFERENCES

C1   Spiegel, M.R.; Theory and Problems of Laplace Transforms; Schaum Publishing Co., N.Y.; 1965.

C2   Nixon, F.L.; Handbook of Laplace Transforms; Prentice Hall Inc, Englewoord Cliffs, N.J.; 1961.

Summary of Laplace Transform Properties

Table C1 Table of Laplace Transforms

	Root Factor Format $f(s)$	Root Factor Format $f(t)$	Time–constant / Frequency / Damping–ratio Format $f(s)$	Time–constant / Frequency / Damping–ratio Format $f(t)$
1	$\frac{1}{s}$	1		
2	$\frac{1}{s^2}$	t		
3	$\frac{1}{s^n}$ $(n=1,2,3...)$	$\frac{t^{n-1}}{(n-1)!}$ $(0!=1)$		
4	1	unit impulse at $t=0$		
5	$\frac{1}{s-a}$	e^{at}	$\frac{1}{1+Ts}$	$\frac{1}{T}e^{-\frac{t}{T}}$
6	$\frac{1}{(s-a)^n}$ $(n=1,2,3....)$	$\frac{t^{n-1}e^{at}}{(n-1)!}$ $(0!=1)$	$\frac{1}{(1+Ts)^n}$	$\frac{1}{T^n(n-1)!}t^{n-1}e^{-\frac{t}{T}}$
7	$\frac{1}{s^2+a^2}$	$\frac{\sin at}{a}$	$\frac{\omega_n^2}{s^2+\omega_n^2}$	$\omega_n\sin\omega_n t$
8	$\frac{s}{s^2+a^2}$	$\cos at$	$\frac{\omega_n^2 s}{s^2+\omega_n^2}$	$\omega_n^2\cos\omega_n t$
9	$\frac{1}{(s-b)^2+a^2}$	$\frac{e^{bt}\sin at}{a}$	$\frac{\omega_n^2}{s^2+2\zeta\omega_n s+\omega_n^2}$	$\frac{\omega_n}{\sqrt{1-\zeta^2}}e^{-\zeta\omega_n t}\sin(\omega_n\sqrt{1-\zeta^2})t$
10	$\frac{s-b}{(s-b)^2+a^2}$	$e^{bt}\cos at$	$\frac{\omega_n^2(1+Ts)}{(s^2+2\zeta\omega_n s+\omega_n^2)}$	$\omega_n\sqrt{\left[\dfrac{1-2T\zeta\omega_n+T^2\omega_n^2}{1-\zeta^2}\right]}e^{-\zeta\omega_n t}\sin\left((\omega_n\sqrt{1-\zeta^2})t+\psi\right)$ where: $\psi=\arctan\left\{\dfrac{T\omega_n\sqrt{1-\zeta^2}}{1-T\zeta\omega_n}\right\}$

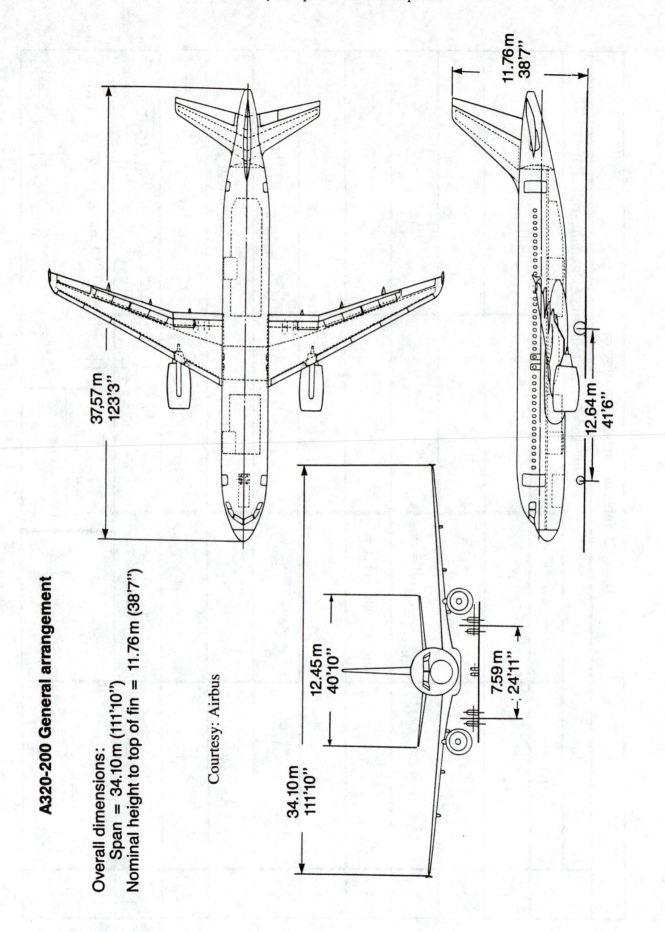

A320-200 General arrangement

Overall dimensions:
Span = 34.10 m (111'10")
Nominal height to top of fin = 11.76 m (38'7")

Courtesy: Airbus

37,57 m
123'3"

11.76 m
38'7"

12.64 m
41'6"

12.45 m
40'10"

7.59 m
24'11"

34.10 m
111'10"

APPENDIX D: ON THE EFFECT OF FREE, REVERSIBLE FLIGHT CONTROLS ON AIRPLANE DYNAMIC STABILITY

In the discussions of perturbed airplane dynamics (longitudinal and lateral–directional) in Chapter 5, it was tacitly assumed that the flight controls surfaces are kept fixed in some reference (trim) position. This is referred to as a 'controls–fixed' assumption.

This assumption is inherently satisfied in the case of airplanes with irreversible flight controls, as long as there is no significant blow–down of the control surfaces under aerodynamic loading. This assumption is also satisfied in the case of airplanes with reversible flight controls, as long as the pilot keeps the control surfaces fixed and as long as there is no significant elastic compliance in the control system.

For airplanes with reversible flight controls, when operated with the 'controls–free', the mathematical models of perturbed airplane dynamics in Chapter 5 are not sufficient. When the flight controls are allowed to oscillate, additional equations are required, which account for:

a) oscillation of the flight controls,

and

b) the coupling of the flight control oscillations into the airplane equations of motion.

In this appendix, a mathematical model is provided which allows freely oscillating flight controls to be accounted for in the perturbed equations of motion of an airplane. Two cases will be considered:

* A typical longitudinal case

* A typical lateral–directional case

D 1 A TYPICAL LONGITUDINAL CASE

Only the case of a freely oscillating elevator will be considered. It is left up to the reader to apply the methodology to cases involving the oscillation of other types of longitudinal flight control surfaces. The following assumptions are made:

1) The elevator is mass–balanced. This means that the center of gravity of the flight control surface itself is located on the control surface hingeline. Chapter 4 in Part IV of Reference D1 contains examples of how flight control surfaces are mass–balanced.

Except for very low performance (i.e. slow) airplanes, the flight control surfaces in an airplane with a reversible flight control system are nearly always mass–balanced.

2) Friction in the flight control system is negligible. Design guides for designing flight control systems with low friction are given in Chapter 4 of Part IV of Reference D1.

3) The elevator and its associated mechanical actuation system have a 'combined' moment of inertia, I_e , about the elevator hinge–line

4) The following elevator hingemoment derivatives about the elevator hinge–line must be accounted for: C_{h_u}, C_{h_α}, C_{h_q}, $C_{h_{\delta_e}}$ and $C_{h_{\dot\delta_e}}$.

On basis of these assumptions, the small perturbation equation of motion of the elevator–plus–controls system is:

$$\left\{ C_{h_u}\frac{u}{U_1} + C_{h_\alpha}\alpha_h + C_{h_q}\left(\frac{q\bar{c}}{2U_1}\right) + C_{h_{\delta_e}}\delta_e + C_{h_{\dot\delta_e}}\left(\frac{\dot\delta_e \bar{c}_e}{2U_1}\right) \right\}\bar{q}_h S_e \bar{c}_e = I_e(\ddot\theta + \ddot\delta_e) \qquad (D1)$$

where: α_h in this equation, is the **perturbed** horizontal tail angle of attack.

The hingemoment derivatives in this equation are defined as follows:

$$C_{h_u} = \frac{\partial C_h}{\partial(u/U_1)} = U_1 \frac{\partial C_h}{\partial u} = M_1 \frac{\partial C_h}{\partial M} \qquad (D2)$$

Since: $\alpha_h = \alpha - \varepsilon = (1 - \frac{d\varepsilon}{d\alpha})\alpha$ it follows that:

$$C_{h_\alpha} = \frac{\partial C_h}{\partial \alpha_h} = C_{h_\alpha}(1 - \frac{d\varepsilon}{d\alpha})\alpha \qquad (D3)$$

$$C_{h_q} = \frac{\partial C_h}{\partial(\frac{q\bar{c}}{2U_1})} = \frac{2U_1}{\bar{c}}\frac{\partial C_h}{\partial q} \qquad (D4)$$

Because the perturbed pitch rate about the airplane c.g., q, translates into a change in angle of attack of the horizontal tail, $\alpha_h = \dfrac{q(x_{ac_h} - x_{cg})}{U_1}$, it is possible to write:

$$C_{h_{\text{due pitch rate}}} = C_{h_q}(\frac{q\bar{c}}{2U_1}) = C_{h_\alpha}\frac{q(x_{ac_h} - x_{cg})}{U_1} \qquad (D5)$$

and, therefore:

$$C_{h_q} = 2C_{h_\alpha}(\bar{x}_{ac_h} - \bar{x}_{cg}) \qquad (D6)$$

$$C_{h_{\delta_e}} = \frac{\partial C_h}{\partial \delta_e} \qquad (D7)$$

$$C_{h_{\dot\delta_e}} = \frac{\partial C_h}{\partial(\frac{\dot\delta_e \bar{c}_e}{2U_1})} = -\frac{\bar{c}_h}{\bar{c}_e}(C + DC_{L_{\alpha_h}}) \qquad (D8)$$

where: the elevator rate coefficients C and D may be determined from Figure D1.

The elevator rate, $\dot{\delta}_e$, in effect causes a change in lift over the elevator and therefore over the horizontal tail. Therefore, there will also be a pitching moment due to elevator rate which should be accounted for in the airplane equations of motion. This leads to a new pitching moment derivative, $C_{m_{\dot{\delta}_e}}$ which (as shown in Reference D2) may be determined from:

$$C_{m_{\dot{\delta}_e}} = \frac{\partial C_m}{\partial(\frac{\dot{\delta}_e \bar{c}_e}{2U_1})} = -\frac{\bar{c}_h}{\bar{c}_e}(A + BC_{L_{\alpha_h}}) \tag{D9}$$

where: the coefficients A and B may be determined form Figure D2.

This pitching moment derivative due to elevator rate must be included in the perturbed pitching moment equation (5.30c) in Table 5.2.

It will be left as an exercise to the reader, to adjoin Eqn (D1) to the perturbed longitudinal equations (5.30) in Table 5.2. As part of this exercise, new dimensional stability derivatives must be defined. That too is left as an exercise to the reader.

As it turns out, the freely oscillating longitudinal controls tend to couple first with the short period motion of an airplane. This leads to a so–called porpoising motion which shows itself to the pilot mostly as an oscillatory motion of the cockpit controls (stick or wheel) coupled with a variation in normal acceleration. According to Reference D2 it is often acceptable to assume that the oscillations take place at constant speed so that the phugoid dynamics may be ignored.

D 2   A TYPICAL LATERAL–DIRECTIONAL CASE

It will be assumed in the lateral–directional case that the ailerons are mass–balanced and that the control system friction level in the aileron control circuit is low. In that case, Reference D2 (page 470) concludes that the dynamics of freely oscillating ailerons on the overall lateral dynamics of an airplane can be neglected. However, the effect of freely oscillating rudder–plus–controls cannot always be neglected. The following assumptions are made:

1) The rudder is mass–balanced. This means that the center of gravity of the flight control surface itself is located on the control surface hingeline. Chapter 4 in Part IV of Reference D1 contains examples of how flight control surfaces are mass–balanced.

Except for very low performance (i.e. slow) airplanes, the flight control surfaces in an airplane with a reversible flight control system are nearly always mass–balanced.

2) Friction in the flight control system is negligible. Design guides for designing flight control systems with low friction are given in Chapter 4 of Part IV of Reference D1.

3) The rudder and its associated mechanical actuation system have a 'combined' moment of inertia, I_r, about the rudder hinge–line

4) The following rudder hingemoment derivatives about the rudder hinge–line must be accounted for: $C_{h_{r_\beta}}$, $C_{h_{r_r}}$, $C_{h_{\delta_r}}$, and $C_{h_{\dot\delta_r}}$.

A freely oscillating rudder, even with proper mass balancing, can couple into the dutch roll mode of an airplane and cause dynamic stability problems. Therefore, the following equation must be adjoined to Eqns (5.96) of Table 5.8:

$$\left\{ C_{h_{r_\beta}}\beta + C_{h_{r_r}}\left(\frac{rb}{2U_1}\right) + C_{h_{\delta_r}}\delta_r + C_{h_{\dot\delta_r}}\left(\frac{\dot\delta_r\bar c_r}{2U_1}\right) \right\}\bar q_v S_r \bar c_r = I_r(\ddot\psi + \ddot\delta_r) \qquad (D10)$$

where the hingemoment derivatives have the following definition:

$$C_{h_{r_\beta}} = \frac{\partial C_{h_r}}{\partial\beta} \qquad (D11)$$

$$C_{h_{r_r}} = \frac{2\partial C_{h_{r_\beta}}(x_{ac_v} - x_{cg})}{b} \qquad (D12)$$

$$C_{h_{\delta_e}} = \frac{\partial C_h}{\partial\delta_e} \qquad (D13)$$

$$C_{h_{\dot\delta_r}} = \frac{\partial C_{h_r}}{\partial\left(\dfrac{\dot\delta_r\bar c_r}{2U_1}\right)} = -\frac{\bar c_v}{\bar c_r}(C + DC_{L_{\alpha_v}}) \qquad (D14)$$

The rudder rate, $\dot\delta_r$, in effect causes a change in side force over the rudder and therefore over the vertical tail. Therefore, there will also be a yawing moment due to rudder rate which should be accounted for in the airplane equations of motion. This leads to a new yawing moment derivative, $C_{h_{r_{\dot\delta_r}}}$, which must be accounted for in the perturbed yawing moment equation:

$$C_{n_{\dot\delta_r}} = \frac{\partial C_n}{\partial\left(\dfrac{\dot\delta_r b}{2U_1}\right)} = -\frac{\bar c_v}{b}(A + BC_{L_{\alpha_v}}) \qquad (D9)$$

This yawing moment due to rudder rate derivative must be included in the perturbed yawing moment equation (5.96c) in Table 5.8.

It will be left as an exercise to the reader to adjoin Eqn (D10) to the perturbed lateral–directional equations (5.96) in Table 5.8. As part of this exercise, new dimensional stability derivatives must be defined. That too is left as an exercise to the reader.

As it turns out, the freely oscillating directional controls tend to couple first with the dutch roll motion of an airplane. This leads to a so–called snaking motion which can be very annoying. For more details the reader should consult Reference D2.

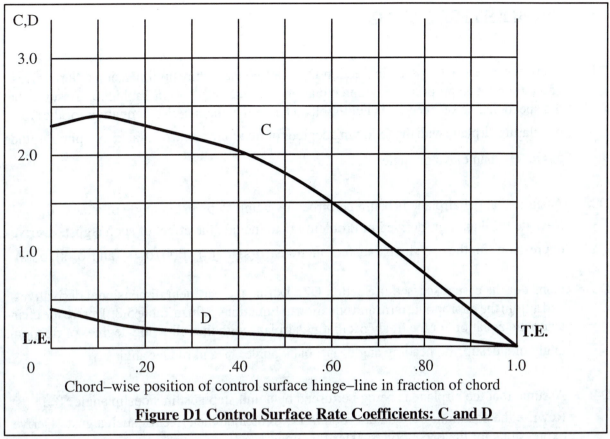

Chord–wise position of control surface hinge–line in fraction of chord

Figure D1 Control Surface Rate Coefficients: C and D

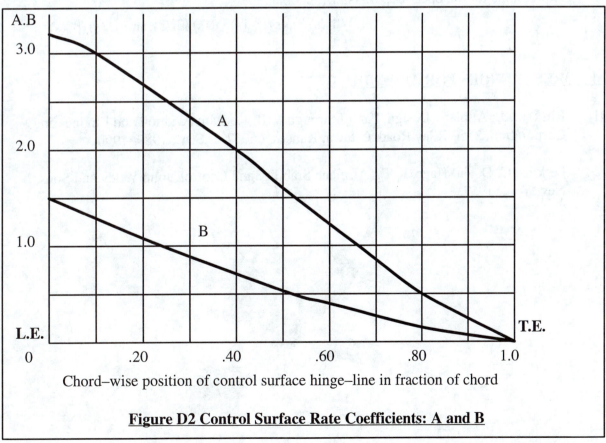

Chord–wise position of control surface hinge–line in fraction of chord

Figure D2 Control Surface Rate Coefficients: A and B

D3   PROBLEMS FOR APPENDIX D

D1.   Consider the case discussed in Section D1. Define the pertinent dimensional derivatives and adjoin the appropriate term and equation to Equations 5.30 in Table 5.2. Assume that the speed degree of freedom is negligible. Derive the characteristic equation for the freely oscillating airplane with the following degrees of freedom: angle of attack, α, pitch attitude angle, θ, and elevator angle, δ_e.

D2.   Assume that the airplane is being perturbed by a unit step gust in angle of attack, α_g. Rewrite the equations derived in Problem D1 to include the effect of such a gust. Derive expressions for the open loop transfer functions: $\alpha(s)/\alpha_g(s)$, $\theta(s)/\alpha_g(s)$ and $\delta_e(s)/\alpha_g(s)$.

D3.   Consider the case discussed in Section D2. Define the pertinent dimensional derivatives and adjoin the appropriate term and equation to Equations 5.96 in Table 5.8. Derive the characteristic equation for the freely oscillating airplane with the following degrees of freedom: angle of sideslip, β, heading angle, ψ, bank angle, ϕ and rudder angle, δ_r.

D4.   Assume that the airplane is being perturbed by a unit step gust in sideslip angle, β_g. Rewrite the equations derived in Problem D3 to include the effect of such a gust. Derive expressions for the open loop transfer functions:

$$\beta(s)/\beta_g(s), \quad \psi(s)/\beta_g(s), \quad \phi(s)/\beta_g(s) \text{ and } \delta_r(s)/\beta_g(s) \quad .$$

D4   REFERENCES FOR APPENDIX D

D1   Roskam, J.; Airplane Design, Parts I through VIII; Roskam Aviation and Engineering Corporation, 2550 Riley Road, Ottawa, Kansas, 66067, U.S.A.; 1989–1990.

D2   Perkins, C. D. and Hage, R. E.; Airplane Stability and Control; John Wiley and Sons, New York, 1957.

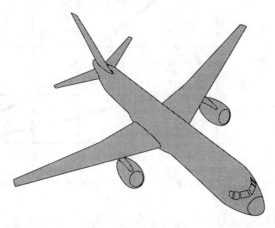

INDEX TO PART I

Courtesy: Scaled Composites

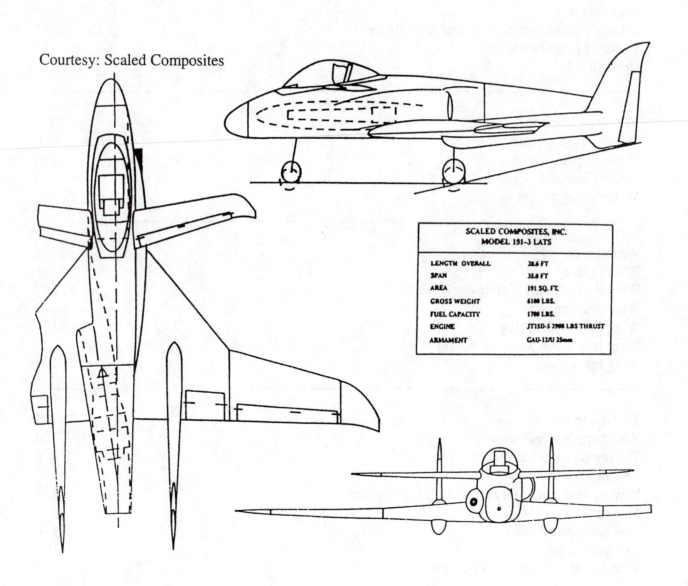

SCALED COMPOSITES, INC.	
MODEL 151–3 LATS	
LENGTH OVERALL	28.6 FT
SPAN	35.0 FT
AREA	191 SQ. FT.
GROSS WEIGHT	6100 LBS.
FUEL CAPACITY	1700 LBS.
ENGINE	JT15D-5 2900 LBS THRUST
ARMAMENT	GAU-12/U 25mm

Notes

Notes

Notes

Notes

Notes

Notes

Notes

Notes

Notes

Airplane Flight Dynamics and Automatic Flight Controls, Parts I and II

Dr. Jan Roskam

Broaden Your Knowledge and Deepen Your Understanding About Airplane Flight Dynamics
Core Resources for Aeronautical Engineers and Academic Institutions

Dr. Roskam brings together his extensive experience in industry and in academia to explain theory, methods, tools and tricks of airplane design and analysis

Part I • 576 pages • softcover • 8$\frac{1}{2}$" x 11" ISBN 1-884885-17-9 *New Edition*

Exhaustive coverage is provided of the methods for analysis and synthesis of the steady and perturbed state stability and control of fixed wing airplanes. This widely used book has been updated with modern flying quality criteria.

general steady and perturbed state equations of motion for a rigid airplane • concepts and use of stability & control derivatives • physical and mathematical explanations of stability & control derivatives • solutions and applications of the steady state equations of motion from a viewpoint of airplane analysis and design • emphasis on airplane trim, take-off rotation and engine-out control • open loop transfer functions • analysis of fundamental dynamic modes: phugoid, short period, roll, spiral and dutch roll • equivalent stability derivatives and the relation to automatic control of unstable airplanes • flying qualities and the Cooper-Harper scale: civil and military regulations • extensive numerical data on stability, control and hingemoment derivatives

Part II • 381 pages • softcover • 8$\frac{1}{2}$" x 11" ISBN 1-884885-18-7 *New Edition*

Exhaustive coverage is provided of the methods for analysis and synthesis of automatic flight control systems using classical control theory. This widely used book has been updated with the latest software methods.

elastic airplane stability and control coefficients and derivatives • method for determining the equilibrium and manufacturing shape of an elastic airplane • subsonic and supersonic numerical examples of aeroelasticity effects on stability & control derivatives • bode and root-locus plots with open and closed loop airplane applications, and coverage of inverse applications • stability augmentation systems: pitch dampers, yaw dampers and roll dampers • synthesis concepts of automatic flight control modes: control-stick steering, auto-pilot hold, speed control, navigation and automatic landing • digital control systems using classical control theory applications with Z-transforms • applications of classical control theory • human pilot transfer functions

DARcorporation, 120 East Ninth Street, Suite 2, Lawrence, Kansas 66044, USA
Telephone: (913) 832-0434   Fax: (913) 832-0524

1-800-327-7144

Airplane Design, Parts I - VIII
Dr. Jan Roskam

Broaden Your Knowledge and Deepen Your Understanding About Airplane Design
Core Resources for Aeronautical Engineers and Academic Institutions

Dr. Roskam brings together his extensive experience in industry and in academia to explain theory, methods, tools and tricks of airplane design and analysis

Internationally acknowledged as a practical reference that covers the art and science of the entire airplane design and development process. Many educators and industry practitioners rely on this compilation as both a textbook and a key reference.

▶ Part I
• 202 pages   • hardcover   • $8\frac{1}{2}$" x 11"   ISBN 1-884885-04-7

estimating take-off gross weight, empty weight and mission fuel weight • sensitivity studies and growth factors • estimating wing area • take-off thrust and maximum clean, take-off and landing lift • sizing to stall speed, take-off distance, landing distance, climb, maneuvering and cruise speed requirements • matching of all performance requirements via performance matching diagrams

▶ Part II
• 310 pages   • hardcover   • $8\frac{1}{2}$" x 11"   ISBN 1-884885-05-5

selection of the overall configuration • design of cockpit and fuselage layouts • selection and integration of the propulsion system • Class I method for wing planform design • Class I method for verifying clean airplane maximum lift coefficient and for sizing high lift devices • Class I method for empennage sizing and disposition, control surface sizing and disposition, landing gear sizing and disposition, weight and balance analysis, stability and control analysis and drag polar determination

▶ Part III
• 454 pages   • hardcover   • $8\frac{1}{2}$" x 11"   ISBN 1-884885-06-3

cockpit (or flight deck) layout design • aerodynamic design considerations for the fuselage layout • interior layout design of the fuselage • fuselage structural design considerations • wing aerodynamic and operational design considerations • wing structural design considerations • empennage aerodynamic and operational design considerations • empennage structural and integration design consideration • integration of propulsion system • preliminary structural arrangement, material selection and manufacturing breakdown

▶ Part IV
• 416 pages   • hardcover   • $8\frac{1}{2}$" x 11"   ISBN 1-884885-07-1

landing gear layout design • weapons integration and weapons data • flight control system layout data • fuel system layout design • hydraulic system design • electrical system layout design • environmental control system layout design • cockpit instrumentation, flight management and avionics system layout design • de-icing and anti-icing system layout design • escape system layout design • water and waste systems layout design • safety and survivability considerations

---

DARcorporation, 120 East Ninth Street, Suite 2, Lawrence, Kansas 66044, USA
Telephone: (913) 832-0434   Fax: (913) 832-0524

1-800-327-7144

Airplane Design, Parts I - VIII
Dr. Jan Roskam

Part V • 209 pages • hardcover • $8\frac{1}{2}$" x 11" ISBN 1-884885-08-X

Class I methods for estimating airplane component weights and airplane inertias • Class II methods for estimating airplane component weights, structure weight, powerplant weight, fixed equipment weight and airplane inertias • methods for constructing v-n diagrams • Class II weight and balance analysis • locating component centers of gravity

Part VI • 550 pages • hardcover • $8\frac{1}{2}$" x 11" ISBN 1-884885-09-8

summary of drag causes and drag modeling • Class II drag polar prediction methods •airplane drag data • installed power and thrust prediction methods • installed power and thrust data • lift and pitching moment prediction methods • airplane high lift data • methods for estimating stability, control and hingemoment derivatives • stability and control derivative data

Part VII • 351 pages • hardcover • $8\frac{1}{2}$" x 11" ISBN 1-884885-10-1

controllability, maneuverability and trim • static and dynamic stability • ride and comfort characteristics • performance prediction methods • civil and military airworthiness regulations for airplane performance and stability and control • the airworthiness code and the relationship between failure states, levels of performance and levels of flying qualities

Part VIII • 368 pages • hardcover • $8\frac{1}{2}$" x 11" ISBN 1-884885-11-X

cost definitions and concepts • method for estimating research, development, test and evaluation cost • method for estimating prototyping cost • method for estimating manufacturing and acquisition cost • method for estimating operating cost • example of life cycle cost calculation for a military airplane • airplane design optimization and design-to-cost considerations • factors in airplane program decision making

Airplane Aerodynamics and Performance
Dr. C. T. Lan & Dr. Jan Roskam

Nearly all aerospace engineering curricula include as required material a course on airplane aerodynamics and airplane performance. This textbook delivers a comprehensive account of airplane aerodynamics and performance.

• 547 pages • hardcover • $8\frac{1}{2}$" x 11" ISBN 1-884885-00-4

the atmosphere • basic aerodynamic principles and applications • airfoil theory • wing theory • airplane drag • airplane propulsion systems • propeller theory • fundamentals of flight mechanics for steady symmetrical flight • climb performance and speed • take-off and landing performance • range and endurance • maneuvers and flight envelope

DARcorporation, 120 East Ninth Street, Suite 2, Lawrence, Kansas 66044, USA
Telephone: (913) 832-0434   Fax: (913) 832-0524

1-800-327-7144

G.A.-CAD

Looking for an Automated Airplane Design System that Integrates Analysis and Drafting into a Stand-alone Framework ?

G.A.-CAD Is Definitely Worth Looking At
No More Spreadsheet Hassles or Data Incompatibility !

COMING SOON !

*D*escription

G.A.-CAD, General Aviation Computer Aided Design, is a user-friendly personal computer based preliminary design system for General Aviation aircraft. The program provides a powerful framework to support the non-unique process of aircraft preliminary design. The system will allow design engineers to rapidly evolve an aircraft configuration from weight sizing through detailed performance calculations and cost estimations and it incorporates a full featured drafting tool. The program is intended to reduce preliminary design cost and to bring advanced methods to businesses which normally do not have the computational and/or modern design/analysis capabilities.

- Reduced design time: computer aided design methods can reduce design and development time by 50% and replace tedious hand calculations. Current design cycle times cover 2-4 years. This can be reduced to 1-2 years.
- Better product through improved design: more alternative designs can be evaluated in the same time span, which can lead to improved quality.
- Reduced design cost: due to less training and less calculation errors substantial savings in design time and related cost can be realized.
- Reduced certification time and cost: the performance, stability and control and structural analysis and design aspect of G.A.-CAD will be of significant benefit to those manufacturers with little experience in getting General Aviation airplanes certified.

*F*eatures

G.A.-CAD is a completely new design, incorporating the lessons learned in the development of the Advanced Aircraft Analysis (AAA) software on UNIX platforms and taking full advantage of the unique experience of DARcorporation personnel in developing airplane design systems.

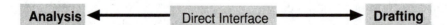

Analysis ← Direct Interface → **Drafting**

Weight • Performance • Geometry • Aerodynamics • Thrust/Power • Stability and Control • Dynamics • Loads • Structures • Cost

Obscuration and vision plots • Area/CG curves • Airfoil manager • Geometry tools (wetted area, volumes, CGs) • Object oriented aircraft components (fuselage, wing, tail, canard, inlets, canopy, landing gear, structural arrangements)

DARcorporation, 120 East Ninth Street, Suite 2, Lawrence, Kansas 66044, USA
Telephone: (913) 832-0434   Fax: (913) 832-0524